MW01063454

Distinguished Service
The Life of Wisconsin Governor Walter J. Kohler, Jr.

Distinguished Service
The Life of Wisconsin Governor Walter J. Kohler, Jr.

Thomas C. Reeves

MARQUETTE
UNIVERSITY

PRESS

Library of Congress Cataloging-in-Publication Data

Reeves, Thomas C., 1936-
Distinguished service : the life of Wisconsin governor Walter J. Kohler, Jr. /
Thomas C. Reeves.
   p. cm.
Includes bibliographical references and index.
ISBN-13: 978-0-87462-017-7 (hardcover : alk. paper)
ISBN-10: 0-87462-017-1 (hardcover : alk. paper)
1. Kohler, Walter J. (Walter Jodok), 1904-1976. 2. Governors—Wisconsin—
Biography. 3. Wisconsin—Politics and government—1951- I. Title.
F586.42.K64R44 2006
977.5'043092—dc22

                                              2006005187

Cover photo: Walter J, Kohler, Jr., campaign photograph, 1950.
Leslie Kohler Hawley collection.

⊛The paper used in this publication meets the minimum requirements of the
American National Standard for Information Sciences—
Permanence of Paper for Printed Library Materials, ANSI Z39.48-1992.

Association of American
University Presses

MARQUETTE UNIVERSITY PRESS
MILWAUKEE

The Association of Jesuit University Presses

Table of Contents

Also by Thomas C. Reeves

Freedom and the Foundation: The Fund for the Republic in the Era of McCarthyism

(ed.) Foundations Under Fire

(ed.) McCarthyism

Gentleman Boss: The Life of Chester Alan Arthur

The Life and Times of Joe McCarthy: A Biography

(ed.) John F. Kennedy: The Man, the Politician, the President

A Question of Character: A Life of John F. Kennedy

(ed.) James Lloyd Breck, Apostle of the Wilderness

The Empty Church: The Suicide of Liberal Christianity

Twentieth-Century America: A Brief History

America's Bishop: The Life and Times of Fulton J. Sheen

In memorium
Prof. Walter C. Schackenberg (1917-73)

A Brief Kohler Genealogy

John Michael Kohler (1805-74). In 1838, he married Maria Anna Moosbrugger (1816-53). The couple had seven children (two died in infancy), including John Michael Kohler II (see below). In 1853, he married Maria Theresia Natter (1828-1913). The couple had ten children.

John Michael Kohler II (or Jr.) (1844-1900). In 1871, he married Lillie Vollrath (1848-1883). The couple had six children: Evangeline A. E. (1872-1954), Robert John (1873-1905), Walter Jodok Kohler (see below), Marie Christine (1876-1943), Lillie Babette (1878-1965), and Carl Jacob (1880-1904). In 1887, he married Lillie's sister, Wilhelmina (Minnie) Vollrath (1852-1929). The couple had one child, Herbert Vollrath Kohler (see below).

Walter Jodok Kohler (1875-1940). In 1900, he married Charlotte Henrietta "Lottie" Schroeder (1869-1947). The couple had four sons:

> *John Michael Kohler III* (1902-68). In 1933, he married Julilly House (1908-76). The couple had four children: John Michael, Jr. [IV] (Michael) (1934—), William Collins (1937—), Julilly Waller (1942—), and Marie House (1951—).

> *Walter Jodok Kohler, Jr.* (1904-76). In 1932, he married Marie Celeste McVoy (1900-1974). She had a daughter, Jacquelin Holden (Jackie) (1924-81) from a previous marriage (1922-32) to Canadian banker's son Edward W. J. (Jack) Holden. Walter and Celeste had two children: Terry Jodok (1934—) and Charlotte Nicolette (Niki) (1936—). The couple was divorced in 1946. Celeste then married Robin MacFadden (1900-75). In 1948, Walter married Charlotte McAleer (1912-95).

> *Carl James (Jim)* (1905-60). In 1925, he married Dorothy Loraine Dings (1904-89). The couple had four boys: Carl James, Jr. (1926-81), Conrad Dings (1929-80), Walter Jodok III (1932-98), and Peter Galt (1934—).

Robert Eugene (1908-90). In 1933, he married Margaret Brewster Taylor (Peggy) (1908-87). The couple had three children: Robert Eugene Jr. (1937—), Victoria Greenwood (Vickie) (1940—), and Gillian Brewster (Jill) (1942—). In 1989, Robert married Martha Thorkelson Riddell (1909-92). She had three children from a previous marriage to Robert D. Riddell (1905-1973): Mary (1937—), Robert D. Jr. (1939—), and Ann S. (1943-1999).

Herbert Vollrath Kohler (1891-1968). In 1937, he married Ruth Miriam De Young (1906-1953). The couple had three children: Herbert Vollrath, Jr. (1939—), Ruth De Young II (1941—), and Frederic Cornell (1943-1998).

A Brief Vollrath Genealogy

Jacob Johann Vollrath (1824-1898). In 1847, he married Elisabetha M. Fuchs (1821-1906). The couple had six children:

Lillie (1848-1883). In 1871, she married John Michael Kohler. The couple had six children (see the Kohler genealogy).

Andrew Jackson (1850-1913). In 1879, he married Anna M. Liebl (1859-1927). The couple had seven children.

Wilhemina (Minnie) (1852-1929). In 1887, she married John Michael Kohler. The couple had one child (see the Kohler genealogy).

Mary (1856-1937). In 1880, she married John R. Reiss (1852-1906). The first of their two children was Minneline (1881-1952). In 1912, she married John M. Detling (1880-1948).

Carl August Wolfgang (C.A.W.) (1859-1932). In 1890, he married Laura Imig (1865-1947). The couple had five children. Their second child was Ruth (1892-1969). In 1917, she married Hugh Ross (1880-1957). The couple had two children. The third child born to C.A.W. and his wife was Jean C. (1894-1976). In 1921, he married Laura Pantzer (1895-1976). The couple had five children. The fifth child born to C.A.W. and his wife was Robert P. (1906-1962). He married Erna Eckhardt (1909-1969). The couple had two children.

Nahyda Deborah (Hyddie) (1861-1938). In 1894, she married Rudolph Weimer (1865-1942). The first of their two children was Margaret (1895-1966). In 1929, she married Sidney Heywood (1897-1962). The second child born to Nahyda and her husband was Elizabeth (1897-1966). In 1922, she married Eugene E. Panzer II (1900-1946). The second of their two children was Mary E. Pantzer (1927-1980), who did not marry.

Introduction

Wisconsin Senator Joe McCarthy died on May 2, 1957. Only a few years earlier the most feared and famous politician in America, he had been reduced by shock and self-pity into a pathetic creature who deliberately drank himself to death. The nationally televised Army-McCarthy hearings in 1954 had revealed him to be a pitiless bully who smeared the reputations of anyone who challenged him. His evidence of Communist treason in high places, to most reasonable people, seemed shaky when not outrageously false.

Later that year, McCarthy was censured by the United States Senate. He was shunned by President Eisenhower, by many Republican Party leaders, and by his old friend J. Edgar Hoover, Director of the FBI. Reporters deliberately ignored him. Major media editorialists and cartoonists mocked McCarthy and his "ism" without mercy. The senator was not present at the Republican national convention of 1956, and his name was rarely mentioned. One journalist referred to him as a "ghost."[1]

Essentially a simple and unsophisticated man, Joe was overwhelmed by the scorn and rejection, choosing death as an alternative to the pain. Frantic efforts by a loving wife and an assortment of friends to boost his morale and restore his health got nowhere. The senator was only 48.[2]

There were two leading candidates to fill McCarthy's Senate seat. The favorite in the eyes of many in Wisconsin and elsewhere was former Governor Walter J. Kohler, Jr. A good-looking Yale graduate, wealthy industrialist, and GOP moderate, Kohler had won election as governor each time he ran, in 1950, 1952, and 1954. The record of his three administrations was, by most accounts, highly admirable. In late 1956, the *Milwaukee Journal* declared, "his six year reign has surely been the most productive of major and lasting achievement since the great Progressive decade that came to its climax in 1911…Walter Kohler, Jr. has been one of Wisconsin's ablest governors—sincere, conscientious, intelligent, accomplishful [sic]. The many fine fruits of his administration will do him lasting honor."[3] The *Wisconsin State Journal*, in an editorial called "Farewell to a Great Governor," stated that "in the six years of Walter J. Kohler's service to his state, this commonwealth has been in safe, responsible, strong, and scrupulously honest hands."[4]

Good character was highly important to Kohler. He declared in 1956, "I am proud to say that there has not been the slightest whisper against my honor or integrity."[5] Syndicated political commentator John Wyngaard described Kohler as "a thoroughly earnest public officer and a gentleman" whose "principal assets are dignity, a strong feeling for personal propriety, a natural integrity of outlook and spirit, and a keen intelligence."[6] Republican State Senator Warren Knowles once said of Kohler, "he has become to the citizens of Wisconsin the very symbol of honesty, character and integrity in public office."[7]

President Eisenhower had often expressed admiration for the 53-year-old Wisconsin Governor, saying that he was the type of man Republicans should be developing as presidential timber.[8] In 1957 Ike publicly endorsed Kohler for the vacant senate seat, noting that he was one his "great admirers,"[9] but it was widely known that the long dominant Republican Party in Wisconsin was badly split between McCarthyites and Eisenhower moderates. Many of the late Senator's followers harbored intense animosity toward both Kohler and the president for allegedly failing to remain loyal to their hero after the election of 1952, a race in which McCarthy helped and supported both candidates. McCarthy followers quickly decided to field candidates in the primary contest of 1957, throwing Kohler's political future into doubt.[10] Seven Republicans eventually entered the primary contest, including the lieutenant governor and two congressmen.

The hope for the Democrats was William Proxmire, a leader in the revival of the long moribund Democratic Party in Wisconsin.[11] The tall, slim, balding, 41-year-old politician was liked throughout the state if only because people could not help but admire his indefatigable persistence. Since entering Wisconsin in 1949 from his native Illinois, Proxmire had been running for political office. After winning a seat in the state Assembly in 1950, he ran for Governor three times, losing twice to Kohler and in 1956 to Vernon Thompson. Personally wealthy (he was a physician's son who married a Rockefeller), he largely devoted his incredible energy to seven-day-a-week campaigning, year in and year out.

McCarthy was a major issue in the 1957 race. Proxmire and such Democratic allies as Gaylord Nelson, Patrick Lucey, Henry S. Reuss, James E. Doyle, and *Madison Capital Times* publisher William T. Evjue, had often harshly criticized Walter Kohler and the moderate Republicans for aiding and abetting the Senator's rampages. They charged that Republicans had made the most of McCarthy's popularity to win votes and only later, after the senator's star had fallen, did they have the decency to distance themselves from him. How could Kohler, they asked, talk about integrity when he had appeased a demagogue for years to strengthen his own political power?

Indeed, it was widely known that Governor Kohler was the man who persuaded candidate Eisenhower in 1952 to placate McCarthy by excising a passage in a Milwaukee campaign speech praising General George C. Marshall. Earlier, McCarthy had recklessly labeled Marshall, a highly distinguished soldier and secretary of state, as part of "a conspiracy on a scale so immense as to dwarf any previous such venture in the history of man. A conspiracy of infamy so black that, when it is finally exposed, its principals shall be forever deserving of the maledictions of all honest men."[12]

Democrat James E. Doyle declared, "In 1952, when he thought to profit by it, Governor Kohler expressly and pointedly and repeatedly endorsed McCarthy. But in 1954, with McCarthy at last consigned to the trash heap by men of sterner stuff than Kohler, the governor, glassy of eye and saggy of jaw, mumbles, 'What was that name again?'"[13]

Moreover, in the course of his two campaigns against Kohler, Proxmire had contended repeatedly that his opponent was guilty of lying, insensitivity, and bad judgment. He and his fellow Democrats had also made much of Kohler's wealth and privilege, contending that he could not possibly represent the common people of Wisconsin.

In fact, Proxmire and his allies knew little about Kohler's wealth beyond data obtained from public tax records. Many Wisconsinites thought, inaccurately, that Walter was part of the hard-nosed management that was resisting a prolonged and bitter strike at the Kohler Company, in Kohler, Wisconsin, 56 miles north of Milwaukee.

Indeed, surprisingly few people knew much of anything about the three-time governor who sought to be a senator. Walter Kohler seldom talked about himself and almost never discussed his family. His second wife, Charlotte, said even less in public. Walter's education was described sketchily in the press, reporters often failed to explore the complete record of his distinguished service in World War II, and the details of his departure from his family's corporation and his takeover of the Vollrath Company, a Sheboygan business, in 1947 were known only to a handful of insiders.

Part of the failure to explore Walter Kohler's past was due in large part to the reluctance of the press during this time to examine and make public the personal lives of politicians. This is how the many private escapades of John F. Kennedy and Lyndon Johnson escaped public attention. But Kohler's personal dignity and reserve, his consistent cordiality, his impressive record of achievements in office, and his persistent attention to the issue of integrity in public office also put him above suspicion and largely out of the range of journalistic fire.

❖→❖→❖→◉←❖←❖←❖

As a student of politics in the 1950s, I long wondered who Kohler really was. Was he another Richard Nixon, a largely duplicitous and mendacious politician looking out at all times for himself? Was he a crusader like Fighting Bob La Follette, Wisconsin's premier political figure? Was he a glib political actor and manipulator like Senator Everett Dirksen of Illinois? Was he a domineering and inflexible businessman like his uncle, Herbert V. Kohler, Sr., who ran the Kohler Company? I didn't know, and there was very little scholarship to guide me. Historians had been so intent on celebrating the Progressives and their liberal successors that they had largely ignored their conservative opponents.

Nor did I understand the relationship between the first Governor Walter Kohler, who served in Madison from 1929-31, and the second of his four sons, Walter, Jr. The senior Kohler, who had also virtually escaped the attention of scholars, was highly admired throughout Wisconsin during his lifetime, both as a successful and visionary businessman and as a government administrator.

I was also curious about Walter Kohler, Jr.'s two wives and two children, and other members of his family. Why had the Kohlers been so successful? What made them tick? I gasped at the complexity of the first complete Kohler genealogy I encountered.

Despite the fact that Walter was the boss's son and worked for the Kohler Company for more than two decades, an authorized Company history published in 2003 said very little about him. He is practically ignored in the Company's historical exhibit at the Design Center (more than 160,000 visitors a year), across the street from the main factory in Kohler. I thought this quite odd.

Moreover, I wanted to test the Democratic Party thesis that Kohler and the Eisenhower wing of the G.O.P. in Wisconsin had played a double game, using McCarthy when it was helpful and abandoning him when it wasn't. That sort of political strategy could not be thought ethical, even if it worked. Or could it?

I could find no published account of Kohler's stunning loss to Proxmire in 1957 that seemed persuasive. The upset surely did not occur merely because of the Democrat's high-voltage campaigning, for that had failed three consecutive times to produce victory. Proxmire himself, when I interviewed him about twenty years later for my biography of Joe McCarthy, chose to be smug rather than helpful.

In the course of interviewing people for this book, I learned that some insiders were convinced that severe health problems had prevented the former Governor from campaigning actively. But that rumor was denied by Walter's son, Terry.[14]

Moreover, I could not understand why the defeat of 1957 should have mattered so greatly to Walter. Even his son could not explain his father's decision to call a halt to what was widely predicted to be a brilliant political career.

So, the challenges for the historian were formidable. The research proved rewarding. What I discovered in the course of my work was a fascinating story that shed light on political, social, and business history in Wisconsin and elsewhere. The man I encountered in the public and private documents, family photos, and personal interviews with scores of relatives, friends, foes, and observers, proved to be more interesting than even his best friends and loudest critics knew. Much of what I uncovered appears here for the first time.

Being no fan of hagiography, I have approached this initial full-scale biography of Kohler with the historian's properly critical eye. I have long held the currently unfashionable belief that historians should make every effort to be objective, following the evidence no matter where it leads and using the powers of analysis, to the best of one's ability, without regard for ideology.

An understanding of the life and times of Walter J. Kohler, Jr., I am convinced, is long overdue and should prove valuable for a wide variety of readers, from casual students of Wisconsin history to scholars who want better to understand politics, business, and labor in the state and to delve further into the Second Red Scare. Many, I hope, will find this unusual and intriguing story simply enjoyable as an end in itself.

Notes

[1] Paul Ringler, "McCarthy, to GOP, Is Forgotten Ghost," *Milwaukee Journal*, August 22, 1956.

[2] See Thomas C. Reeves, *The Life and Times of Joe McCarthy: A Biography* (New York: Stein and Day, 1982), *passim*.

[3] Editorial, *Milwaukee Journal*, December 20, 1956.

[4] Editorial, *Wisconsin State Journal*, January 7, 1957.

[5] "'Models of Integrity Party Goal'—Kohler," *Milwaukee Journal*, May 25, 1956.

[6] John Wyngaard, "Gov. Kohler: Assets And Liabilities," *LaCrosse Tribune*, May 12, 1954.

[7] State Convention nominating speech of 1952, in Republican Party Papers.

[8] William R. Bechtel, "Kohler Lauds Speech by Ike as 'Magnificent,'" *Milwaukee Journal*, August 24, 1956.

[9] See "Smith Denies Davis Claim," *ibid.*, July 26, 1957, and "Ike Backs Kohler," *ibid.*, August 7, 1957.

[10] See, for example, Edwin R. Bayley, "GOP Leaders in State Set to Dump McCarthy," *ibid.*, November 25, 1956, and Bayley's "President Special Election to Pick His Successor," *ibid.*, May 3, 1957.

[11] See Jay G. Sykes, *Proxmire* (Washington: Robert B. Luce, Inc., 1972), 1-41.

[12] Reeves, *The Life and Times of Joe McCarthy*, pp. 372-74, 437-440.

[13] "Doyle Makes Senator Issue," *Milwaukee Journal*, October 13, 1954.

[14] Interviews with Walter Vollrath, Jr. and Terry Kohler, November 4, 2004.

Chapter One

The Kohlers and the Vollraths

A biography, of course, is the story of a single person. But in this case the object of our study is part of a large and extraordinary family that for over a century has played an important role in Wisconsin history and today is known throughout the world. The Kohlers have been successful in business, philanthropy, community building, recreation, the art world, and, at times, in politics. To know who Walter J. Kohler, Jr. was, one is required to know more than a little about the remarkable family from which he came.

And there is a second family to be considered. The Vollraths were linked with the Kohlers in many ways, beginning with marriages that took place in the late 19th century. Kohlers were associated with the Vollrath Company throughout almost all of its history, and Walter J. Kohler, Jr. spent nearly 30 years as head of the corporation. His son Terry soon assumed leadership after his father's death and remains at the helm of the now widespread Vollrath complex of businesses.

Both the Kohlers and the Vollraths had similar Germanic origins, traditions, and goals. To know about the one family, on any but the most superficial level, requires knowledge of the other. The values and visions that have guided virtually all of the members of both families, and the trials and tribulations of those who have attempted to live by them, are inevitably part of the biography of any one of its members.

The Kohler story on this continent begins with a relative, Johan Kaspar Mossbrugger. Kaspar, as he was known, was born in 1819 in the village of Schoppernau, in the beautiful Alpine valley of the Bregenzerwald on the western border of Austria. A journeyman plaster finisher, he emigrated to Montreal in 1849 to help remodel the Cathedral of Notre Dame. While there, he married Elmire Vezina, a lovely young woman educated in a convent. In 1852, the couple and their two children emigrated to Illinois in search of cheap land. They soon moved to Minnesota and established an 80 acre farm about five miles north of St. Paul in an area known as Little Canada, which had been opened to settlers by a Frenchman in 1844.

Kaspar had a sister, Maria Anna, who lived in Schnepfau, Austria, another Alpine village near his birthplace. She was married to Johann Michael Kohler. By 1853 the Kohlers had had seven children, two dying in childbirth. In 1854, longing to have his sister and her family living nearby, Kaspar persuaded his brother-in-law to join him in Minnesota, promising a partnership in a dairy business. He purchased a 160 acre farm which he promised to split with Kohler, and he may have sent passenger fare. What he didn't know, because Kohler didn't tell him, was that his sister had died at the time the offer was made and accepted. Indeed, Kohler had already remarried, scandalizing some of his strict Catholic neighbors. Moreover, his wife, former family housekeeper Maria Theresia Natter, 23 years his junior, was pregnant.[1] One can imagine the shock on Kaspar's face when he greeted the steam boat in St. Paul to discover Kohler, his young wife and newborn baby, and five children from the first marriage. It was then that he learned that his beloved sister had died at age 36.

Johann Michael Kohler was born in 1805 in Schnepfau. His ancestors have been traced in Austria to 1632. Johann Michael came from a poor family of dairy farmers and cheese makers. Through diligence and drive, he purchased an inn and also owned a fairly large farm. Hard times and the offer from Minnesota prompted him to sell everything and head for America. An obituary in an Austrian newspaper said later that "He was probably the first person from the Bregenzerwald who, filled with such a pure enthusiasm that it bordered on reverie, decided to disregard all external circumstances and emigrate as a 50 year-old man."[2]

Johann and his family sailed from LeHavre in June, 1854. The voyage to New York lasted 54 days, and the family traveled in steerage, the least expensive and most uncomfortable form of ship travel. The Kohlers soon made their way to Galena, Illinois, where a daughter was born. They then took a steamboat to St. Paul and met Kaspar. The rolling land and numerous lakes no doubt reminded the Kohlers of their native land, although they surely missed the mountains.

Clearing a farm near the Musbruggers, the Kohlers lived at first in a log cabin. In time, they built a three story home and numerous outbuildings. Both families made a success of their dairy business. The Kohlers sold cheese, butter, cord wood, and hay for income. (Four generations of Kohlers would farm the 160 acre spread until 1989, when it was sold to developers.) Johann and Theresia would have ten children between 1854 and 1870.[3]

Johann anglicized his name to John when he applied for citizenship in September, 1854. Six years later, John Michael Kohler became a United States citizen. Intelligent and reportedly well-read, he had no doubt mastered English by this time.[4] A photo of John shows a dark and perhaps handsome face, barely discernible through a thick beard, and eyes that suggest determination and might even be thought sinister.

According to family tradition, John had a dreadful temper and a generally nasty personality.[5] There was apparently an incident aboard ship on the way to America that illustrated his disagreeable attitude: he clashed with the Captain while flatly refusing to help the crew during a storm.[6] An official history of the Kohlers described John as "an independent thinker, even to the point of obstinacy."[7] In Minnesota, according to one account, he broke with the Roman Catholic Church when a priest publicly reprimanded him for something he had said or done. He and his family marched out of the parish, an act that permanently ended the Kohler family's ancient connection with the Church and contributed to an indifference toward organized religion that has characterized many Kohlers since that time.[8]

John Michael's fourth child with his first wife was John Michael II, born in 1844. At ten, he was the fourth oldest of the five children who sailed for America with their father and stepmother. (The oldest was Jodok, born in 1838. The name can be traced to the 17th century in the Moosbrugger family and remains to this day within the Kohler family as a middle name, a link to the family's Austrian roots.)

The younger John Michael was raised on the family farm. A son would say later that when the Kohlers lived in the log cabin in the mid-1850s, John Michael II "knew something of the want that accompanied the pioneer period."[9] One can imagine the hard work and bitter weather that the young man endured. Even worse, according to another descendant, was the continued wrath of his father. Young John left home when he was ten or twelve and went to live with a female in-law. He was on his own and would never return to the farm.[10]

At 18, John Michael drove a delivery truck in St. Paul. He was then employed as a clerk. In 1865, he moved to Chicago, where he worked as a salesman for three years. While working days, he supplemented his meager education with some night classes at Dyhrenfurth Commercial College. He then took a job as a traveling salesman for a wholesale grocery house, and a year later served in the same capacity for a furniture company.[11] John Michael's travels regularly took him to Sheboygan, Wisconsin, a city of more than 5,000 on the shores of Lake Michigan, 56 miles north of Milwaukee. There the handsome 27-year-old fell in love with a schoolteacher, Lillie Vollrath, 24, the oldest child of local industrialist Jacob J. Vollrath. Kohler moved to Sheboygan in 1871, and he and Lillie were married on July 5 at fashionable Grace Episcopal Church.

Lillie's father obviously saw great promise in Kohler. Prior to the wedding, to insure his daughter's prosperity, he required his young son-in-law to go to work for him at the Union Steel and Iron Foundry. He wanted to train John Michael to take over the business as soon as he mastered the essentials.[12] Kohler had to learn them largely by working in the factory itself, a grueling task that he accepted with zeal. Foundry work required hard labor in an often hellish environment, twelve hours a day, six days a week. Kohler's father-in-law had endured such work most of his life.

Jacob Johann Vollrath was born in 1824 in the rural village of Dorrebach, in Rhenish Prussia. His family had been in Dorrebach since at least the mid-18th century. His father, who died in Jacob's infancy, was a successful small businessman until the Napoleonic Wars destroyed his textile mill. The Vollraths, like the Kohlers, had long been rural, agricultural people. Unlike the Catholic Kohlers, they were Lutheran in background.[13]

Having an innate talent for things mechanical, Jacob, at 19, completed his apprenticeship as an iron moulder. Fleeing conscription into the Prussian Army, he somehow raised the $80 to $100 necessary to sail to the United States and, following a 56 day journey from Antwerp, landed in New York in 1844. It must have jolted the young man from tiny Dorrebach to find himself in a city of 600,000. It is possible that here, in the paperwork required of immigrants, that Jacob Johann became Jacob John.

Jacob worked in New York, traveled to Albany, and, according to a plan created while in Germany, awaited the arrival of his mother, step-father, and their children. When united, the family traveled the 364 miles to Buffalo, and then sailed across the Great Lakes to Milwaukee. They were headed for a relative's home in the village of Rockfield, 20 miles northwest of Milwaukee, where they planned to buy land and create a farm. The federal government was selling land for $1.25 an acre, with a minimum purchase of 80 acres.

Lacking agricultural skills, Jacob soon returned to Milwaukee to find work in a foundry. In Milwaukee, he met Elisabetha Margaretha Fuchs, three and a half years his senior, who had immigrated to America with her widowed father in 1843 from a German village about ten miles from Jacob's family home. Jacob and Elisabetha were married in 1847. Six years later, with three children, the couple moved to Sheboygan, then a crude (dirt roads, stray hogs in the public square) village of about 2,700 which was about to receive its charter as a city. Sheboygan soon became a booming port city; the county would grow from 133 in 1840 to 26,875 in 1860.

After years of slaving for others (in the census of 1850 Jacob described himself as a "laborer"), Vollrath was eager to create his own business in Sheboygan. After a shaky beginning with weak and untrustworthy partners, he started a company that produced agricultural implements and cast-iron cooking utensils. He prospered as his family grew larger; four more children were born to the Vollraths through 1861. By the time John Michael Kohler wed Lillie, in 1871, Jacob was a partner in the Union Steel and Iron Foundry, manufacturer of plows, railroad frogs (the device that enables a train to move from one set of tracks to cross intersecting tracks) and an assortment of castings used by local furniture manufacturers. A few months later, he owned the company.[14]

In 1873, three months after the country was plunged into a severe financial depression, Vollrath either gave or sold the company at a low price to Kohler and a partner.[15] He then went out on his own to found another company that would eventually bear his surname. A photo exists of the large frame shack that housed the company when Kohler became a leader. Some 22 workers posed for the picture, including a pair of boys who may well have been employees.[16]

In 1878, Kohler's partner sold his interest to Herman Hayssen and John Stehn, fellow German immigrants who were machinists at the plant. The factory burned down in 1880, and the company moved to larger quarters in Sheboygan. The firm of Kohler, Hayssen and Stehn was soon producing such articles as ornamental hitching posts, iron fences, road scrapers, and cast columns for buildings. By 1881, the firm had a good-sized factory, employed 30 men, many of them German speaking immigrants, and did an annual business in the $30,000 to $40,000 range.

In the new factory, the company added an enamel shop designed to produce tea kettles and other enamelware. In 1883, the company entered the plumbing products business when John Michael put ornamental feet on a cast-iron water trough, transforming it into a bathtub. Within four years, plumbing products and enamelware accounted for more than two-thirds of the company's business.[17]

A photo of John Michael at this time shows a dark, handsome face, featuring a mustache and goatee, bright eyes, and a pleasant expression. In a later photo, he is heavier, but his general appearance has changed little and the expression remained agreeable.[18] By all accounts, John Michael was extraordinarily hard working, aggressive, personable, and considerate of others. An employee once described him as "gentle and kind," noting that he "sympathized with suffering, and his sympathy was expressed in practical ways."[19] Now a successful manufacturer, Kohler was widely recognized as one of Sheboygan's leading citizens.[20]

John Michael and Lillie were quickly blessed with a large family. Evangeline was born in 1872, Robert in 1873, Walter Jodok in 1875, Marie Christine in 1876, Lillie in 1878, and Carl Jacob in 1880. Of these six, only Walter was to have children and carry on the Kohler family name.

In 1882, Kohler began construction of an elaborate new home on the corner of New York Avenue and Sixth Street, the heart of fashionable Sheboygan. (Walter had been born in a simple wooden cottage in Sheboygan.) It was completed in early 1883. The style, developed in England and popular in America between 1840 and 1880, has been called "Italian Villa." The large, brick, two story home, with a complete basement and attic, featured arched windows and door openings, ornate porches and gable brackets, low-pitched roof lines, and a three-sided bay on the East side. Sculptured keystones above the windows and ornamental iron cresting above the porches were probably made at the Kohler foundry. There were four outside entrances, an expansive lawn, a large oak tree, a fountain, and an iron gazebo. A two-story brick carriage house included living quarters for the family servants.

While the Kohler home was being erected, John Michael and two associates remodeled a building they owned near the construction site, turning it into the Sheboygan Opera House, where plays and musical performances were performed in German and English. A local reporter noted, "Ceiling and walls were gracefully frescoed, inclined floors were placed in the auditorium and gallery, opera chairs were installed—creating a House superior to anything ever before had in this city." Kohler managed the opera house, brought in major touring actors, and even acted himself in several of the theater's productions.

The Opera House and the Kohler home well reflected the city's prosperity and eagerness to become sophisticated. A few years earlier, Kohler had helped fund a new Turner Hall, which served as the cultural center of the city. The gala inauguration featured a Grand Ball with a full orchestra.[21]

Tragedy struck the Kohler family on March 2, 1883, a few weeks after the family moved into their new home. Lillie Kohler died at age 35. Relatives flocked to assist her grieving husband and six children. Lillie's sister Mary, who was Mrs. John Reiss, moved in with her husband and infant daughter. (Like Kohler, Reiss had been taken into the family firm by Jacob Vollrath.) Another sister, Wilhelmina, "Minnie" Vollrath, was often present to help out.

Sheboygan society approved fully, four years later, when John Michael wed Minnie. The new Mrs. Kohler was a vivacious 35-year-old, interested in music and drama. The couple had only one child, Herbert, born on October 21, 1891.[22] He would marry and have children who would also perpetuate the Kohler name.

Life in the Kohler home was both cheerful and stimulating. Minnie, loved by all, engaged the children in music lessons and amateur theatrics. The family piano was in constant use. Marie was trained as a singer. Walter played the cornet, fife, and drums. The youngsters were active in a variety of sports. Marie played basketball and tennis, was a good skater, and enjoyed swimming. The family kept horses, and Walter and Marie, imitating their father, became accomplished riders.

Hospitality was a way of life with the Kohlers. Family parties were frequent, and neighbors, relatives, acquaintances, and business associates poured into the family home throughout the year. The children were taught early in life how to entertain with taste and good manners and to be tolerant and charitable. At Thanksgiving, baskets were taken to the sick and unfortunate before the family sat down to dinner. A similar practice occurred at Christmas, which the Kohlers celebrated lavishly

Although organized Christianity played little part in the lives of family members (the Kohlers made small and fashionably proper contributions of money and time to the local Episcopal Church), a strong sense of ethics, focusing on the ancient verities such as integrity, self-discipline, hard work, learning, and service to others, was deeply ingrained in the mind of each Kohler child. If he had been asked about the source of his moral thought, John Michael might have said that it was based on "right reason," admitting as well the influence of classical literature, Germanic tradition, and Christian teaching. Kohler, like Jacob Vollrath and his son Andrew, was an active member of the Masonic Lodge.

To John Michael, honesty and integrity were indispensable. In personal relationships, as in business, one must be thoroughly respectable and above reproach. Consideration for others was linked to this belief. In the Kohler home gossip and tale-bearing were strictly forbidden. On the family mantel, Evangeline etched the words, "Around this hearth let no evil word be spoken."

Walter, who no doubt learned it at home, would always have on his desk the Ruskin quotation, "Life without labor is guilt, labor without art is brutality." Marie thought that religion carried the imperative, "Do Something." The girls were trained intensively in the household arts, learning that there was to be no waste or neglect. The boys, as we shall see, were put to work in the foundry in their teens, that they might learn hard work and the technical and interpersonal skills necessary for effective company leadership.

John Michael believed that good books were a vital ingredient in the home, and his children were strongly encouraged to read and study. As one account put it, "Books were an adornment; but above all they were for use, and at the impressionable age there was formed the life-long habit of reading the best." Marie was the first in the history of her family to graduate from college.[23] Walter would always surround himself with books and read deeply and widely.

John Michael, then, was both the founder of the family business that would lead the Kohlers into great wealth and international fame, he was also the creator of the family code of ethics. That code would be broken by family members in the future, but its existence, and John Michael's example, were not forgotten.

In Sheboygan, the family patriarch put the Kohler ethic into action by founding the local Humane Society and the Home for the Friendless. He continued to be a leader of the arts. He had many friends in the Odd Fellows, to which he belonged, as well as the Masons.

For all of his family and cultural interests, good deeds, and friends, most of John Michael's time and energy were devoted to his business. And the investment proved profitable. In 1888, Kohler, Hayssen & Stehn was incorporated with a capital stock of $75,000, and the company employed 125 men. Kohler was the company president.

John Michael's wealth, prominence, and popularity almost inevitably led him into civic duties of a political nature. In 1880 and 1882, he served as a member of the County Board of Supervisors. In 1890 and 1891, he served as a member of the City Council. In this capacity, he discovered and stopped a scheme about a bridge that would have swindled the city out of between $5,000 and $6,000. In 1892, at 48, he was elected Mayor. A Republican, Kohler's popularity was such that he overcame the Democratic majority that dominated local politics.[24] (The Vollraths were also staunch Republicans.)[25] Citizens of Sheboygan referred to Minnie as "Madame" as a sign of their respect.[26]

In 1899, John Michael spent $1,400 to purchase 21 acres of farmland its owner had named Riverside, four miles west of Sheboygan. He intended to move his entire company there on high ground just north of the Sheboygan River. It was an expensive and risky plan; one newspaper called it "Kohler's folly." But John Michael had big plans for the future. Business was booming, and he wanted the new plant to concentrate solely on cast-iron enamelware and other plumbing supplies.[27]

The new foundry was completed in October, 1900. It employed 250 men. Then, on November 5, John Michael suddenly died. For about a week, he had been receiving medical treatment for "pulmonary congestion," probably congestive heart failure. He felt well enough to attend his son Walter's wedding at Kenosha. Two days later, at home, John Michael collapsed and died. He was only 56. The Kohler home was plunged into grief. The three Kohler daughters, remaining single, would live in the family home for the rest of their long lives, frequently dressed in black.[28]

The entire Sheboygan area expressed deep sadness and sorrow. The business manager of the *Sheboygan County News* wrote to Robert Kohler, "Your father was held in the highest regard by all who knew him, for his many sterling qualities, business capacity, enterprise, sociability and his sincere and earnest effort in behalf of the unfortunate and needy, which seemed to be ever uppermost in his mind."[29] A close friend of John Michael's told Robert, "Your dear father's unselfish, unfailing interest in and devotion to my early welfare I cannot hope to repay in kind…"[30] Another friend wrote, "Truly during the 33 years of our acquaintance there was no one held in higher esteem by me than he—whose memory I shall always cherish."[31] The *Sheboygan Herald* declared editorially:

"The deceased ranked as one of the most enterprising and progressive business men in our city."[32]

Some 200 employees of Kohler, Haysen & Stehn headed the funeral procession which started from the Kohler home. Scores of Masons and Odd Fellows came next, followed by 76 carriages filled with mourners. The service was held at Grace Episcopal Church. At the grave, one of the speakers was a company worker who addressed the crowd in German, "with much impressiveness," said a local newspaper.[33]

Compounding the grief felt by the Kohlers and all the citizens of Sheboygan, in February, 1901, the entire Kohler factory was destroyed by fire. The estimated $66,000 loss, however, was largely covered by insurance. As Kohler sons Robert, Walter, and Carl scrambled to find ways of keeping the business going in Sheboygan while the rebuilding got underway, John Michael's partners, Hayssen and Stehn, decided to sell out, leery of reconstructing a plant in rural Riverside. The company, already pressed for funds, paid $27,000 for the stock. Following this transaction, the company was entirely owned by the Kohler family and was renamed J. M. Kohler Sons Co. (In 1912, this would be changed to the Kohler Company, the same year voters in the area chose to name the area around the plant the village of Kohler.)[34]

While the new factory was being rebuilt, and even after its completion, a year after the fire, the company faced increasingly severe financial problems. The Kohler brothers had borrowed $50,000 to help construct and operate the new plant.[35] The plant payroll, according to Walter J. Kohler, Sr., was $40,000 a year.[36] A story circulated that the postman, on nearing the Kohler plant, would place his buggy whip in a vertical position when there were enough checks in the mail to keep the men employed. When the whip lay flat, there would be layoffs.[37]

As the financial woes of the company deepened in the summer of 1904, Carl, 24, the youngest son of John Michael and Assistant Superintendent of the Riverside plant, grew increasingly desperate. According to family tradition, he committed suicide in order to enable the company to collect on his life insurance. The explanation given to the press was that Carl accidentally drank carbolic acid while searching for medicine in a bedroom cabinet.[38]

At the time of his death, Carl was living in the Kohler family home with his three sisters and brother Robert, John Michael's successor as company president. Both men were unmarried. One day after the first anniversary of Carl's death, Robert, 36, died of a stroke in his room.

The official report said the cause of death was "cerebral hemorrhage and melancholia"[39]

In 1905, the future of the Kohler company now lay with 30-year-old Walter. The other surviving male in the family, Herbert V. Kohler, Minnie's son, was only fourteen years old. Walter and his wife Charlotte, at the time of Robert's death, already had three sons of their own. The second of the three, Walter Jr., the focus of this biography, was born four months before his uncle's suicide.

✦✦✦◉✦✦✦

In 1905, Walter Kohler found himself not only President of the J. M. Kohler Sons Company, but also had a major role to play in a prospering Sheboygan business run by relatives, the Jacob J. Vollrath Manufacturing Company.

When Jacob J. Vollrath went out on his own in 1873, leaving his foundry business largely to his son-in-law, he sought to develop the process of porcelain enameling of cast iron. To do this, he sent his oldest son, Andrew, 23, to Germany to secure a job in a factory that had mastered the process. Andrew, who spoke German fluently, was to disguise his connection to his American firm and steal the secret formulas. He had to make a second trip before he had all the necessary data. (In a biographical sketch produced in Sheboygan in 1894, Jacob was hailed as the "inventor" of porcelain enameling.)[40]

Following Andrew's successful journeys in international industrial espionage, Vollrath changed the name of his company to the Sheboygan Cast Steel Company, which became one of the nation's largest suppliers of enameled steel sheet ware. By 1881, Jacob employed 40 men and grossed $50,000 a year. In 1884, the name was changed again to the Jacob J. Vollrath Manufacturing Company. Two years later, its plant covered an entire block.[41]

The Vollraths celebrated their prosperity by building a large home on thirty acres of land north of the city and overlooking Lake Michigan. The first important social event to take place in the home was the wedding, on November 3, 1887, of John Michael Kohler and Minnie Vollrath.[42] That same year Sheboygan had a population of 11,500 and could boast of 25 manufacturing plants.

Jacob J. died in 1898 at 73, leaving all of his estate to his wife Elisabetha. Upon her death, said the will, the estate was to be divided into six equal parts: one share was to go to Lillie's children, and one to each of the five remaining Vollrath children.[43] John Michael Kohler, by his marriages to both Lillie and Minnie, would become the major Vollrath heir, controlling the stock of his wife and children. (It was understood at the time that men made the decisions about financial matters, which meant that female stockholders usually permitted husbands and, if single, close male relatives to control their assets.) Elisabetha died in 1906, six years after John Michael's death. Walter Kohler, settling in as President of his family company, now assumed the authority his father would have had in the Jacob J. Vollrath Manufacturing Company, controlling a third of the company's stock.

The new company president was Andrew "Jake" Vollrath, Jacob J.'s oldest son. Born in 1850, he had followed his father's vocation, learning the moulder's trade and the enameling business in his father's foundries. He was the son, it will be recalled, who had gone to Germany on the clandestine mission.

In the early twentieth century, Andrew was imposing to behold: at 5'9", he sported 300 pounds and had a 60 inch waist. He, his wife Annie, and their seven children lived in an appropriately lavish neo-Victorian home on a twelve acre piece of land. For all of his success, Andrew had a serious problem: his personality. The Vollrath family historian has observed, "In contrast to accounts of Jacob J., Andrew had developed a definite personality trait of harshness that included a tendency to overexcitability and a temper that in its full fury has been described, by those who should know, as something absolutely terrifying."[44]

Andrew had often voiced resentment about the authority of the Kohlers in the company's operations (He had fought with John Michael years earlier when the two of them worked in the foundry). He didn't care for the authority John Reiss held in the company or in the will; Jacob J. had made his son-in-law a personal adviser and company insider. And Andrew often quarreled bitterly with his brothers and sisters about a lot of things. Soon after Elizabeth's death, the other Vollrath children, Minnie, Mary, Carl A.W., and Nahyda, exercised a clause in their father's will and bought out their temperamental brother.

In an act of sheer spite, Andrew used the funds, with additional money, to create his own company, which competed directly with the family firm. He even named it the Vollrath Company and called himself "America's Pioneer Enameler." He changed his company's name to the Porcelain Enameling Association of America after his brother, Carl

A.W., new President of the Jacob J. Vollrath Company, filed a lawsuit against him.

Andrew died in 1913. The Vollrath family historian wrote, "It is said that he died from an attack of apoplexy brought on by a fit of temper as he was attempting to physically oust an offensive salesman from the premises of his factory." Andrew left behind a serious breach in the family that took several decades to heal. (In 1923, Andrew's sons would change their company's name to Polar Ware, which made stainless steel. Both Polarware and the Vollrath Company continue operations to this day in Sheboygan.)[45]

The prosperity of the Kohlers and the Vollraths, then, was as closely intertwined as their bloodlines. This was especially true of the Vollraths who had bought off Andrew and committed themselves to their father's business. While Walter Kohler struggled to restore the good fortunes of the company he headed, he also served as an important officer and Board member of the Vollrath Company, as it was now called from its incorporation in 1908.[46] At the time, he was only 33 years old, but his many talents belied his youth and limited experience. Walter was to contribute greatly to the prosperity of both companies, his community, and the State of Wisconsin. Indeed, like his father, he was a truly remarkable man.

Notes

[1] Copy, notes of a 1979 conversation between Walter J. Kohler III and Lillie A. Felder in Schoppernau, Austria, Terry Kohler papers.

[2] The 1874 account from the *Bregenzerwalder Blatt* was translated and provided to me by Michael Kohler, and is in his file.

[3] See Gordon C. Moosbrugger to Julia Kohler, May 17, 1989, Terry Kohler Papers; http://genforum.genealogy.com/cgi-bin/print.cgi?kohler::446.html; Gareth D. Hiebert (ed.), Little Canada, A Voyageur's Vision (Stillwater, Minnesota: The Croixside Press, 1989), vii, 13-14, 290-1; Julilly Kohler interview, October 7, 2003; Mark Nicklawske, "Kohler Farm falls to development," North Suburban Press [White Bear Lake, Minnesota], May 9, l989. Kohler genealogies are in the Michael Kohler papers. The family genealogist was Walter J. Kohler III, and his work has been carried on by a daughter, Ann Fichtner, of West Bend, Wisconsin. Ann Fichtner interview.

[4] A copy of the citizenship document is in the Mary Kohler Ahern papers, as is a photograph of the family home in Minnesota.

[5] Julilly Kohler interview, October 7, 2003; copy, notes of a 1979 conversation between Walter J. Kohler III and Lillie A. Felder, Terry Kohler papers.

[6] See copy Michael Kohler's "Spectator club Paper, April 16, 2002, 'The Origins of Kohler Company,'" Michael Kohler file.

[7] Richard Blodgett, *A Sense of Higher Design: The Kohlers of Kohler* (Lyme, Connecticut: Greenwich Publishing Group, 2003), 34.

[8] Robert E. Kohler, Jr., interview. The official Kohler history, citing "family lore," has John Michael II breaking with the Church after being denied a request to visit a dying nun. Blodgett, *A Sense of Higher Design*, p. 43.

[9] Clipping from the *Milwaukee Journal*, May 13, 1930, in the Walter Kohler, Sr. file.

[10] Julilly Kohler interview, October 7, 2003.

[11] "Death of J. M. Kohler," *Sheboygan Herald*, November 10, 1900.

[12] Terry Kohler interview, June 12, 2003.

[13] Jacob J. Vollrath III, *Vollrath: 'Das Alte Geschlecht,' Dorrebach-Sheboygan* (Sheboygan, Wisconsin: unpublished, 1980), 1-20, 55, 65-66. Copies are in the Mary Kohler Ahern papers and the Walter J. Vollrath, Jr. papers. The Ahern copy has valuable additions and corrections inserted by Robert Kohler, one of Walter's sons, who was interested in family history. Jacob J. Vollrath III (1923-2000) also created a family genealogy found in the Ahern and Phillip Vollrath papers.

[14] Vollrath, *ibid.*, 20-54, 58.

[15] See Blodgett, *A Sense of Higher Design*, 36, where the sale figure $5,000 appears. Cf. Vollrath, *Vollrath: 'Das Alte Geschlecht,'*, 59-60.

16 See the 1930 campaign flyer "From Laborer's Job to Governor's Chair" in the Sheboygan County Historical Society.

17 See Blodgett, *A Sense of Higher Design*, 37-41.

18 See *ibid.*, 42; "Marie Christine Kohler," *Kohler of Kohler News*, November, 1943, 3.

19 Blodgett, *A Sense of Higher Design*, 41.

20 For more on the Kohlers and Vollraths, see Janice Hildebrand, *Sheboygan County: 150 Years of Progress, an Illustrated History* (Northridge, California: Windsor Publications, 1988), 55-58; "Kohlers, Vollraths Left Mark," *Sheboygan Press*, August 1, 1978; "Kohler: A Midget 100 Years Ago, A Giant Today," *ibid.*, December 3, 1973. For population data, see United States Department of the Interior, *Statistics of the Population of the United States at the Tenth Census June 1, 1880* (Washington, D.C.: Government Printing Office, 1883), 85.

21 Blodgett, *A Sense of Higher Design*, 42-43; Sheboygan County Landmarks, Ltd., *Landmarks: J. M. Kohler Home* (Sheboygan, Wisconsin: Sheboygan Press, n.d.), *passim*. This booklet, which lacks page numbers, is available at the Sheboygan County Historical Society.

22 *Ibid.* On Reiss, see Vollrath, *Vollrath: 'Das Alte Geschlecht,'* 76. Nahyda married a school teacher, Rudolph Weimer, and he too was taken into the Vollrath company. *Ibid.*, 77-78.

23 "Marie Christine Kohler," *Kohler of Kohler News*, November, 1943, *passim*; "Miss Evangeline Kohler Is Laid To Rest After Rites," an undated clipping of August, 1954 found in the "Kohler Family, Evangeline, Marie, Lillie, General Information File," at the Sheboygan County Historical Society. On Walter's musical talents, see the 1930 campaign flyer, "From Laborer's Job to Governor's Chair," Terry Kohler papers.

24 "Death of J. M. Kohler," *Sheboygan Herald*, November 10, 1900; undated clippings, "For Mayor" and "J. M. Kohler Gets There," in the John Michael Kohler II file.

25 *Portrait and Biographical Record of Sheboygan County, Wis....*(Chicago: Excelsior Publishing Co., 1894), 250, 613.

26 *Landmarks: J. M. Kohler Home.*

27 Blodgett, *A Sense of Higher Design*, 43-45; Vollrath, *Vollrath: 'Das Alte Geschlecht,'* 62.

28 "Death of J. M. Kohler," *Sheboygan Herald*, November 10, 1900. Family legend has it that the girls remained unmarried during John Michael's lifetime because no suitors seemed sufficiently worthy to the father. Walter Vollrath, Jr. interview.

29 W. C. Thomas to Robert J. Kohler, November, 1900, Kohler Family Papers

30 Alfred Marschner to Robert J. Kohler, n.d., *ibid.*

[31] William T. Lamback to Robert J. Kohler, November 7, 1900, ibid.

[32] "Death of J. M. Kohler," *Sheboygan Herald*, November 7, 1900.

[33] In 1931, Marie Kohler had German architect Kaspar Albrecht design and direct the construction of the Waelderhaus, a monument to her late father. Located just south of the main Kohler plant, the Waelderhaus was built in the style of a house barn, and is a replica of the architecture prominent in the Bregenzerwald area, where John Michael was born.

[34] Blodgett, *A Sense of Higher Design*, pp. 45, 67, 96.

[35] Ibid., 47.

[36] Clipping from the *Milwaukee Journal*, May 13, 1930, Walter J. Kohler Sr. file.

[37] Walter Vollrath, Jr. interview.

[38] Ibid; Julilly Kohler interview, October 7, 2003; "Carbolic Acid Kills Carl Kohler," *Sheboygan Daily Journal*, August 6, 1904. Carl was an Army veteran who had served in Puerto Rico. Vollrath, *Vollrath: 'Das Alte Geschlecht'*, 63.

[39] "Find Robert Kohler Dead At His Home," *Sheboygan Daily Journal*, August 4, 1905; Vollrath, *Vollrath: 'Das Alte Geschlecht,'* 79. One Kohler family historian, Julilly Kohler, thinks that her family has a genetic flaw that may have surfaced in the first John Michael Kohler and could help explain the deaths of Carl and Robert. It is a strain of mental illness, she claims, often expressed in depression and sometimes reaching mental retardation and schizophrenia, that has struck repeatedly among family members, down to the present. Julilly Kohler interview, October 7, 2003. Clear evidence for this hypothesis, however, may be found only in a single grandchild of John Michael II, and two great-grandchildren. Given the large family tree, these cases may be statistically insignificant.

[40] *Portrait and Biographical Record of Sheboygan County*, 612. See Vollath, *Vollrath: 'Das Alte Geschlecht,'* 67-70; Walter Vollrath, Jr. interview.

[41] See the company booklet *Vollrath Celebrates 125 Years in Business* (Sheboygan, 1998), 1; Vollrath, *Vollrath: 'Das Alte Geschlecht,',* 73.

[42] Ibid., 74-75.

[43] See ibid., 91-92.

[44] Ibid., 80.

[45] Ibid., 94-99; Hildebrand, *Sheboygan County*, 59-62; Walter Vollrath, Jr. interview.

[46] Vollrath Company Minutes, April 13, 1908.

Chapter Two

Educated Gentlemen

Walter Jodok Kohler was born in Sheboygan on March 3, 1875. His mother, Lillie, died the day before his eighth birthday. The youngster's reaction to his step-mother, Minnie, was by all accounts positive. As an adult, he displayed a photograph of her on his desk for the rest of his life. Indeed, all of the Kohler children seem to have loved Minnie.

John Michael Kohler, however, was clearly the most formative force in Walter's life. Walter adored his father and thoroughly absorbed the moral and ethical precepts that were part of life in the Kohler home during the Gilded Age. In later life, Walter would be well-known for his staunch commitment to personal integrity, industry, and humanitarianism. He loved to read and to engage in sports, especially horseback riding, baseball, and bowling. Even as a youngster, his magnetic personality, good manners, and attractive physical features made him popular in the community.

At an early age, Walter was baptized at Grace Episcopal Church in Sheboygan, where he would remain a nominal member for the rest of his life. Like his father, he would never be wholeheartedly attached to any church or denomination. His high principles of personal conduct were grounded in the same, largely secular and personal sources that guided his father. Later in life, again like his father and others in the Kohler and Vollrath families, he would join the Masonic Lodge.[1]

Walter was educated in the local public schools until he was 15, having completed the eighth grade. He then persuaded his father to take him on full time at the company. He was 5' 7" inches tall, about the same height as his father, trim and strong. A long-time Kohler employee later said of Walter, "He was a good worker, I want to tell you, as hard as anybody."[2] Walter's first job was in the enameling department, one of the toughest assignments in the plant. Laboring at hot furnaces 12 hours a day, six days a week, he and his fellow workers broke pig iron by hand. At one point, he worked sixty consecutive hours. The salary was $1.25 a day. That pay level, Walter said years later, was considered "pretty fair for those days." Young Kohler obviously neither sought nor received special favor as the boss's son.

Walter spent three years in the enameling department and in the foundry. On his 18th birthday, he was made foreman, and his salary increased to $12 a week. He later transferred to the warehouse and then moved to the office, where he learned the financial side of the business.[3] By the time his father died, Walter had toiled for a decade at the plant. He was a veteran of 15 years (half his life) at the company when he became its president. He knew the business and the people who worked there.

On November 3, 1900, Walter married Charlotte Henrietta Schroeder, a 31 year old art teacher in Sheboygan. "Lottie" had been born in Kenosha in 1869, one of eight children of August Henry and Dorothea Jones Schroeder. The Schroeders were German immigrants who came to the United States in 1854 and settled in Southport, later renamed Kenosha. August served in the Civil War and was wounded at the battle of Kennesaw Mountain. In Kenosha, August was a partner in a successful harness making firm. He died in 1889. His wife and seven of their children were still alive at the turn of the century. The Schroeders were middle class Lutherans. One son, Frederick C. Schroeder, was a prominent Kenosha photographer.[4]

Following graduation from the local high school, Charlotte took special courses at the University of Wisconsin summer schools, had private instruction in Chicago, studied art at Kemper Hall in Kenosha, and completed courses at the Milwaukee Art Institute and the Pratt Institute in Brooklyn, New York. She was not, however, a college graduate. Few teachers at the time, mostly low paid women, were able to enjoy four years of higher education.[5]

In 1897 Charlotte began to teach art in Sheboygan. As an art supervisor in the public schools, she inaugurated the use of color drawing. (It had all been done in black and white.) She was a painter herself and was no doubt a popular teacher and administrator, as she was later known for being exceptionally gracious and pleasing. A grandson remembers her "gentle, artistic personality."[6]

Photographs reveal Charlotte's considerable beauty. A Kenosha newspaper reporter observed at her wedding, "Miss Lottie Schroeder has long been considered one of Kenosha's most beautiful and cultured ladies, and many people will regret that she will go to another city to make her home." This raises the question why she remained single for so long in an age when a woman began to worry about spinsterhood at 25. Perhaps she was extraordinarily selective. Few could deny that she found a good match in the good looking factory foreman, six years her junior, with a bright future in his father's company.

The couple was married in Kenosha on November 3, 1900 in the lavishly decorated south parlor of the bride's home (complete with orchestra), surrounded by relatives on both sides of the family. Several Kohlers and Vollraths were on hand, including Evangeline, the maid of honor. The wedding service was read by a Congregationalist minister, using the rite of the Episcopal Church.[7] Two days later, the shocking news of John Michael Kohler's death interrupted the honeymoon.[8]

Walter and Charlotte first lived in Riverside, not far from the Kohler plant. In 1903, they moved into the former Clarenbach house, just north of the Kohler family home.[9] After the deaths of Carl and Robert, Walter's brothers, the couple, now with two children, moved into the family home. There they would live for nearly two decades, sharing the house's ample space with Minnie, Walter's three unmarried sisters, and young Herbert.

Minnie was the senior female authority in the house, and she expected deference. But Charlotte soon learned, to her consternation, that the three Kohler sisters also outranked her in family decision-making, even though she was older than the trio. Lillie, who was the most outspoken, according to a neighbor, devoted much of her time to gardening and travel. Marie was a community activist and became Walter's closest family member when he later entered politics. Evangeline, the oldest, was more like Charlotte: quiet, artistic, much given to reading and painting china. All three, wealthy and independent, and always together, were accustomed to having their way in all things. Walter very often deferred to their wishes, whether his wife agreed or not. When, for example, they refused to redecorate the house, it remained as it was in their childhood.

As the years passed, Charlotte increasingly retreated into her world of art, flowers, gardening, astronomy, and local education, becoming sometimes passive and moody, leaving the boisterous matters of current events to her husband, his business and political associates, and his domineering sisters. A relative recalls that the four boys born to Walter and Charlotte strongly sensed the differences between their dynamic, magnetic, outgoing father and their increasingly withdrawn mother, even though the couple remained devoted to one another, and by all outward appearances were happily married. They vied for their father's attention, and the winner in that subtle struggle was almost always Walter J. Kohler, Jr.[10]

❦ ❦ ❦ ❦ ❦ ❦ ❦

The first child born to Walter and Charlotte, in 1902, was named John Michael Kohler III. The second son, Walter Jodok, Jr. (hereafter referred to as Walter, while his father will be Walter Sr.), was born in Sheboygan on the fourth day of the fourth month of the fourth year of the twentieth century.[11] Two sons would follow: Carl James (hereafter called Jim, the name he and all others used) in 1905, and Robert Eugene in 1908.

From birth, Walter was a healthy, attractive child; a particularly striking photo of 1904 shows him being held by his proud mother. Apparently because of his parents' indifference toward religion, he was not baptized until he reached the age of four. A Congregational minister conducted the service in the family home.[12]

The relationship between the Kohlers and the Congregational church remains obscure. A photograph shows 12-year-old Walter attending a Congregationalist picnic. In any case, Walter never thought of himself as a Congregationalist. At different times in his life, reflecting family membership at Grace Episcopal Church in Sheboygan, he would describe himself as an Episcopalian. The doctrinal and ecclesiastical differences between these Protestant denominations would never interest him.

In his youth, Walter absorbed the German language from older family members, who still used it on occasion. He studied the piano, and played from time to time throughout his life. He was sent to public school, which he attended from 1908 to 1917, and told to take his studies seriously. Walter's high intelligence (his son thought his I.Q. in the 140s), and his family-inspired work ethic, enabled him to handle the demands of the classroom with ease.[13]

His older brother, John, had above-average intelligence, but he could not match Walter's grades. Then too, Walter quickly grew taller and better looking than John; he was more athletic, and more outspoken and personable. He seemed better able to emulate and please his father. There was a mild but perceptible tension between the two oldest Kohler boys in their early youth that was soon to grow and remain permanent.[14]

From their earliest days, the four Kohler sons knew themselves to be in the upper socio-economic ranks of society. Their home was one of the finest in Sheboygan, nannies attended to their every wish, and servants were living in the home at least by 1910.[15] Moreover, their father trained them, in the family tradition, to be outstanding citizens: personal integrity, good manners, good taste, hard work, and positive relations with others were paramount. The Kohler ethic, hammered out by Walter's grandfather, was a powerful force in the youth of all four Kohler boys.

The boys also learned a lot about fun. They started riding horses as toddlers. Golf, tennis, skiing, and ice hockey were on their schedules before long. Walter enjoyed boxing with his father, an admirer of Teddy Roosevelt, advocate of the strenuous life.[16] Family parties and civic entertainments were frequent.

One of the highlights of each year, for Walter and all of the Kohlers, was the family Christmas Eve party. Some 30 or more people would arrive at the Kohler home for the annual festivity, which included lavish food, a huge Christmas tree, and presents galore, distributed by a Santa Claus dressed in a red corduroy suit with white fur. Red-caped Girl Scouts sang songs, and Walter Sr. often jumped to his feet to lead all in favorite carols, frequently in German. If the entire celebration was more of a German tradition than a religious exercise, it was nonetheless a time for the Kohlers and their friends to enjoy each other's company and to give thanks, in some general way, for the many blessings they enjoyed. On Christmas Eve, Walter's three sisters traveled to the factory and distributed baskets of food to all employees.[17]

In the early twentieth century, under the inspired and determined leadership of Walter Sr., the Kohler Company blossomed. Profits soared as the company embraced new production techniques and introduced new products. In 1911, the Company introduced the one-piece built-in bathtub. Soon came the industry's first one-piece bathroom lavatory and the one-piece kitchen sink. By 1914, the company was employing 950 people and had sales offices in San Francisco, Chicago, New York, Boston, and London. During The First World War, the Company shifted production to mine anchors, projectiles, and shells, and the plant expanded almost annually to keep up with business opportunities. After the war, the Company added the manufacturing of electrical generators to their ever-expanding line of plumbing supplies. In the

1920s, the Kohler Company was one of the Big Three in the nation's plumbing industry.

Walter Sr., having worked with the men who toiled for the Company's prosperity, rewarded his employees to an extent that few employers anywhere in the country could match. As superintendent, while his father was alive, he was able to reduce the work week in the enameling furnaces to the eight hour day, six day week. That policy now spread throughout the plant, salaries were hiked, and safety features such as goggles were introduced. In 1909, Walter Sr. introduced a workmen's compensation program.

In 1913, Walter Sr. and Charlotte traveled to Europe with Milwaukee architect Richard Philipp, part of a plan to build homes in Kohler for the Company's employees and their families. The first houses in Kohler Village began to appear in 1917. That same year, Walter Sr. supplied employees with group life and health insurance. In 1918, the Company opened the American Club, a handsome, Tudor-style living and recreational facility across from the main plant building for some 250 newly arrived immigrants who could not afford to own their own homes. Free classes in language, civics, and history encouraged immigrants to join the mainstream of American life.

A company newspaper, *Kohler of Kohler News*, kept employees informed and amused. Walter Sr. saw to it that his workers enjoyed a free goose for the Christmas table, and rewarded retirees with a handsome watch. The boss could be seen regularly at the bowling alley, enjoying himself with his workers, whom he called "members of our organization."

Every day, wearing a blue clerk's jacket and an old felt hat, Walter Sr. visited the plant floor. He knew almost all of the men by name and understood the details of their jobs. He heard complaints and sometimes made suggestions. Employees liked and respected the company president for his hands-on leadership and for the fact that he cared for their personal welfare as well as corporate profits.[18] He would later tell a Milwaukee audience, "We are not employers and employees up there—we are fellow workers."[19]

In 1924, Walter Sr. began the Quarter-Century Club, one of the first of its kind in American industry. (By 2003, more than 5,000 employees had belonged to the Club, and of that group 68 had served a half century or more. Walter Sr. was the first 50-year employee.) Club members eagerly anticipated their annual dinner, sponsored by the company.[20]

✦✦✦◉✦✦✦

Walter Sr.'s soaring personal income enabled him to elevate his aspirations for his sons and half-brother Herbert. He wanted each of the five young men to attend a first-rate, exclusive, and expensive boarding school in the East, and then graduate from a college or university of the same rank. He began this process with Herbert, who was sent to Phillips Academy and then to Yale, setting a pattern that would be followed for generations of Kohler males. Walter Sr. was determined to provide his heirs with the finest formal education possible, an advantage in life that he had been denied. Moreover, he knew well the additional value of elite diplomas. In America, they were (and are) similar to patents of nobility, almost always yielding respect and admiration, and often opening doors to high society and positions of rank in the corporate and political world. The Kohler boys of Sheboygan were to become the Kohler gentlemen of the nation and the world.[21]

Phillips Academy was located in Andover, Massachusetts, 21 miles north of Boston. Better known as Andover, the all-male high school was founded in 1778. Paul Revere designed the school's seal, John Hancock signed its Act of Incorporation, and President George Washington once addressed the student body. The academic curriculum at the Academy was highly demanding, and most graduates were almost automatically guaranteed entrance into Ivy League colleges and universities. Beyond academic preparation, the institution provided its students with the manners and demeanor necessary to become gentlemen. This was the most obvious impact of all the best preparatory schools.

For some reason, perhaps academic, John was kept behind one year, and Wally, as family intimates called Walter, was advanced a year, enabling the two boys to travel East together in the fall of 1917 to enroll in Andover.[22] Walter was only 13 when he and his older brother said farewell to family members at the railroad depot to begin their formal instruction in becoming educated gentlemen. The third Kohler son, Jim, would travel to Andover in 1920, when he reached the age of 15. Robert, who preferred to be known as Bob, would enter in 1923 when he too was 15.

In those years, Andover had 33 faculty members and some 500 students. There were two divisions of study; Scientific and Classical. Walter chose Scientific and John selected Classical.

Grades for the class of 1921 were lost years later in a fire, but it seems certain that Walter excelled academically. We lack a record of the courses he took, but Latin was part of his schedule, and he probably studied French.[23] We know that Walter purchased a copy of Sir Walter Scott's novel *Quentin Durward* in his first year, and it was perhaps then that he encountered the book he said later thrilled him the most: Robert Lewis Stevenson's *Treasure Island*.[24] Walter no doubt deeply absorbed the chivalry and rectitude taught in these books.

Outside the classroom, Walter belonged to a fraternity and was highly active in inter-mural sports, being on wrestling, football, and baseball teams. In addition to sports, Walter sang second tenor in the Glee Club and Choir and belonged to the Yale Club, signifying his choice for college work. In sharp contrast, John's only membership was in the Mandolin Club, where he played second mandolin.[25]

One of John's daughters later recalled that the prep school experience completely destroyed what remained of the relationship between Walter and John. Walter was a good-looking, self-confident, thoughtful achiever who excelled at everything he attempted. John was in his brother's large shadow at Andover and did not appreciate it.[26] To avoid further competition, John decided that after graduation he would attend the University of Wisconsin rather than Yale. He majored in economics, earning a B- grade point average.[27]

Jim was another exception to the Kohler tradition of Andover and Yale. After Andover, he graduated from the Massachusetts Institute of Technology with a degree in engineering. He had the best scientific mind in the family.[28]

Bob, the youngest Kohler boy, tried to follow the family tradition but faced an early hurdle. The best looking and least serious of the Kohler boys, Bob was expelled from Andover for having an empty beer bottle in his room. He had been drinking off campus, in the tradition of millions who ignored prohibition, and long resented what he considered an unjust punishment. One can imagine the stern language employed by his no-nonsense father on learning of the disgrace. Bob soon transferred to a similar prep school and eventually entered Yale, where he struggled academically but graduated with a major in English.[29]

The Kohler Family papers contain full records of each of the boys' personal expenses during their years in prep school and college, and even beyond, when their father continued to give them an allowance to boost their Kohler Company salaries. At school, Walter and his brothers were required to submit budgets and note every expenditure. Walter Sr., while generous, was teaching his sons frugality and fiscal responsibility. Walter learned his lesson extraordinarily well, and would be highly attentive to financial details for the rest of his life.

Through the fall of 1917 and the first month of the next year, for example, Walter deposited $280 in his bank account, spent $158.90, and had four dollars in his wallet. That left him "$125.10 capital." His expenses in September included $8.00 for a football uniform, $10.00 for a swimming ticket, $3.10 for school books, and 25 cents for chapel. The following month he spent 25 cents for a haircut, $2.00 for a football helmet, 50 cents for a Latin book, $1.00 for pictures to decorate his room, $2.00 for a Liberty bond, and 20 cents for thumb tacks. Every penny, in accordance with the strict rules laid down by his father, was accounted for.

In a letter to his sons of January 6, 1920, Walter Sr. wrote, "The cost of living is so high that each and every one of us must live on a rational basis. See how you can beat the budget this year, and if you save anything you will be allowed to bank it in the local savings bank to your personal credit." Still, Walter Sr. was not Scrooge. "While I do not expect you to go into any extraordinary expenditures or to get into trouble, if developments should be such that you need help remember that you should always come to me with a plain exposition of all the facts and I will be of what help I can."[30] The Kohler brothers knew that in any circumstance they could depend upon the full support of their father. He wanted, indeed required, them to succeed in the business of becoming educated, responsible gentlemen.

The cost for Walter's first year at Andover was $910.40. That figure escalated to $2,134.17 in the senior year. Walter's Andover education in 2005 dollars would cost $63,8249.57. The total cost of prep school for the boys, in 2005 dollars, would be $331,526.06.[31]

One might predict that the sons of so wealthy a man would devote their summers to travel and recreation. But it was not so for the Kohler boys. Walter Sr. was determined that their education would include the same introduction to labor that he endured. He made it clear to his sons from the beginning that they were to devote their lives to the Kohler Company after college, and he knew of no better way to introduce them to the reality of this world than through hard work, beginning at the lowest level. Honest sweat was part of the Kohler ethic.

Walter began his factory chores in the summer of 1918, after his first year of Andover. At 14, along with his brother John, he was sent to work in the "core room," which he later called "the dirtiest job I ever had." The core room was a dreaded place where rye-flour paste, kerosene, and lampblack were mixed in the construction of cores for World War I sea mines. Workers spat tobacco on Walter's shoes to welcome him to the Company.

During the next three summers, Walter worked in packaging, became an "electric helper," and then went to the general assembly unit. By this time he had reached his full height of 5′ 9½″. He was trim and fit; in 1925, he weighed 158.[32] (He would never top 169.) All through Yale, Walter continued his labors at the plant. His final summer was spent in the "Enamel-Powder" area, another dirty and physically demanding area where his father had worked as a lad.

Throughout his years as a summer employee, Walter scored almost uniformly enthusiastic performance evaluations by supervisors. His willingness to work hard, along with his quiet and pleasing manner, earned him the respect of his fellow laborers. He would always be popular at the Kohler Company. Walter's brothers held the same and similar positions through their prep school and college summers.[33]

Walter entered Yale in 1921. This was a particularly interesting time in the 221 year history of the College. Yale University, of which the College was a part, had enjoyed remarkable growth under the presidency of Arthur Twining Hadley, who retired in 1920. His successor, James Rowland Angell, was to be even more dynamic, rebuilding Yale in the course of his 16 years in office. Scholars of the first rank flocked to New Haven during the 1920s, leading many to conclude that an intellectual renaissance had occurred on campus after the First World War. The popular English Department was especially outstanding in the years Walter attended Yale.[34]

Walter was one of 849 freshmen to enter the all-male College, the largest class ever. Total enrollment had jumped from 2,000 in 1900 to 3,000 in 1920, and in 1923 Yale officials would begin to limit admissions for the first time. There was a student housing problem, and many feared that Yale was losing its atmosphere of collegiality. Walter said later that his social contacts, in accord with campus policy, were limited largely to members of his class.[35]

Judging from the published history of the Class of 1925, students were mostly upper and upper middle class whites of Anglo-Saxon origin who had attended exclusive prep schools. Their general background is illustrated in the several accounts of swank parties in New York during the school year and summers spent sailing in Connecticut, racing on the Seine, cruising in the Caribbean, golfing at Newport, traveling in the Balkans, and dallying in Venice. An opinion survey of class members revealed a high socio-economic level quite typical of the Ivy League institutions at the time. The leading religious denomination of the students, for example, was Episcopalian, and Congregationalist placed second. The G.O.P. was the overwhelming favorite among political parties.[36]

Beyond their studies, the Yale students in Walter's class were intensely interested, as young males of all descriptions are, in athletics, carousing, smoking, and drinking. A class history article observed that "it was a novelty, after the more or less cloistered life and restricted privileges of prep school, to be allowed to come and go as we saw fit, to stay out as late at night as we wished, or to go to the movies or the theatre at the slightest provocation." The stereotypes of flaming youth in the Roaring Twenties—wild youth, raccoon coats, fast cars, the Whiffenpoofs at Mory's, football fever, and madness for movies—are all found in the class history.[37]

Yale was at the center of much of the decade's cultural uproar. The Yale athletic complex, including the $750,000 football stadium that opened in 1914, celebrated big-time college sports. Boat races on the Housatonic River at Derby, Connecticut attracted throngs of students dressed in costumes, eager to party. Yale became a dominant force in rowing, representing the United States at the 1925 Olympics in Paris, and winning the gold medal. The songs of Cole Porter, Class of 1913, were big on campus. Playwright and novelist Thornton Wilder had graduated in 1920. Rudy Vallee entered the University in 1922 and became a national singing star four years later.

As was the new fashion, a great many Yale students smoked. (Cigarette production in the United States more than doubled between 1918 and 1928. Cigarettes were 10 cents a pack in the 1920s.) And perhaps an even larger number drank alcoholic beverages. Campus polls showed that 64 percent of students drank between 1916 to 1920. Once prohibition outlawed alcoholic beverages, in the words of the current Yale archivist, "…most Yale undergraduates considered drinking to be no longer a matter of choice but an obligation. Hip flasks of bootlegged Scotch and gin carried in the pockets of raccoon coats and tuxedos became common, along with campus riots, sprees, and 'bottle nights,' when empty vessels projected out of dorm windows splintered on the College walks."[38] Walter Kohler may well have seemed prudish and rustic to many of his more sophisticated classmates, when he was noticed at all

"Kinky," as Walter became known because of his curly hair, quickly became involved in student life. He turned out for freshman baseball, football, and wrestling, and worked for the *Yale Daily News*. He soon learned, however, that his athletic ability could not compete with those making varsity squads, and he discontinued active involvement in sports after his first year.[39]

Walter's financial accounts kept during the Yale years reveal that his father provided him with almost all of the necessities and luxuries that other students enjoyed. He was well-dressed ($100 for a tuxedo at a time when a new wool suit could be purchased for $15.85), traveled a bit, purchased golf clubs, took piano lessons, and had plenty of cash in his pocket at all times. He did not have a car, however, as many classmates did.[40]

Walter began to smoke cigarettes while at Yale, and he no doubt enjoyed at least a small part in the playboy world of many his classmates. Dues paid to the Mory's Association, duly listed on his expense account, may indicate at least a measure of drinking and partying. Walter's roommate for three years, Guido Rahr of Manitowoc, later told his son a few stories about life at Yale, emphasizing the good times during prohibition.[41] (Walter never discussed his years at Yale with his son.) But Walter was not a leader in extracurricular activities. Indeed, the class history, which includes a biography of each student, reveals a student who fit in perfectly and was not exceptional in any way. One who was such a leader, Benjamin Spock, later became the Class's most famous graduate, known throughout the world as a baby doctor, author, and political activist.[42]

The class history barely mentioned study. Anti-intellectualism was rife throughout the leading colleges and universities in the 1920s. The student newspaper editor at Cornell asserted, "A man is somehow ashamed to admit that he is in college to get an education, and that he values his education more than athletic insignia or election to an honorary society. If he does admit it, he suffers in popular esteem; and few men have the courage of their convictions." Most students, he reported, "learn the precise amount of preparation necessary to fool their old foolish professors." At Ohio State, it was not considered "collegiate" to participate in classroom discussion. At Princeton, said the campus newspaper editor, overly enthusiastic study was thought to be "bad form," adding that "Too constant attendance at the Library is likely to lead to derogatory classification." A majority of the members of the Yale class of 1922 admitted preferring to win an athletic letter than earning a Phi Beta Kappa key. Fraternities and sororities were increasingly powerful in the 1920s; usually about 40% of students belonged to them. Frolic and fads were almost always of supreme importance to these organizations, and they contributed greatly to the peer group conformity that denigrated serious learning.

Cheating on examinations and term papers was common everywhere and was, in the words of an historian, "a well-sanctioned group experience." Professors were often held in contempt and suspicion, characterized by such descriptions as "bone-dry" lecturer and "dry-as-dust pedant." A Dean at Ohio State lamented, "whoever believes that the teacher exerts any considerable influence, outside his role as subject-matter instructor, simply does not know the situation."[43]

Still, the academic hurdles at Yale were formidable and had to be taken seriously at least part of the time, even by those trained in the best of prep schools. The first year was devoted to required courses such as mathematics, English, and a foreign language. Sophomores seeking a Bachelor of Philosophy degree could then choose one of three programs to pursue for the remainder of their three years: History and Politics, Social and Political Science, or Mathematics, Physics, and Chemistry. Walter chose Social and Political Science.

The academic records of the Class of 1925 have been lost, but Walter stated years later that he took thirty hours in each of three fields: economics, history, and English. The program also required courses in psychology, general biology, and anthropology. From his expense accounts, we learn that he took chemistry and zoology.[44]

There was also a daily chapel requirement at Yale, as there had been at Andover. Yale had been originally a Congregationalist establishment, but by 1921 the institution had become, in the words of historian George W. Pierson, "generally Protestant and undenominational." Walter later told his son that after eight years of mandatory church services, he had "caught up," meaning that he endured enough of that for a lifetime. Thereafter, his church attendance would be limited almost exclusively to weddings and funerals.[45]

While Walter did not make the elite circle of academic achievers in his class, there is every reason to believe that he was a solid student. Two of his class papers have survived. One, on Plato's *Republic*, was written for a Classics course. The other, on Leonardo da Vinci, was a term paper written when he was a senior. Both reveal considerable effort and thought.[46]

Walter believed he had profited greatly from his years at Andover and Yale. Years later, when Governor, he would write to a schoolgirl, "I believe the attainment of a good education was the most important event in my life, since I feel that knowledge is not only important but essential to advancement and success in one's chosen business or profession and also to the enjoyment of a broad life."[47] He wrote to a young Wisconsin woman, "In my opinion a person's education is second in importance only to his health." He continued, "My education helped me to learn to think things out and begin to understand why things are as they are. It also taught me that there is so much on earth about which we know so little; that there is so much of interest in life to learn that we should never—even after we are out of school—stop trying to learn and to understand."[48] At a public gathering, Walter endorsed an education that was "positive and dynamic," one "which is permeated with creative imagination, which is as high as the sky and as wide as the horizon, and which will put across its message of 'good will to men' in a variety of ways…." He considered it "the most important tool" in developing mutual understanding and fair play.[49]

One assumes that Walter's deep appreciation of the value of education came later, for immediately after graduation, he briefly considered becoming a professional song writer. One can imagine his desire not to return to the Kohler Company; he'd been slaving away in the bowels of the plant since he was 14, and even if he didn't have to return to the core room, the 21-year-old must have dreamed of a more romantic life, away from the fumes, sweat, and noise of the plant and beyond the sight of a demanding, albeit loving, father. The fantasy lasted only a very short time. He later told a magazine writer that he abandoned the idea when he realized that he was simply too poor a piano player.[50] Unspoken was the fact that Walter Sr. wanted his boys at work for the family company. And his wish was a command.

The cost of Walter Jr.'s Yale education would amount to $137,611.89 in 2005 dollars. In return, Walter Sr. expected loyalty, gratitude, and service. In July, 1925, Walter was back in the Kohler family home and employed as a "time-study" man at the plant. This involved the attempt to put into practice Frederick Taylor's principles of "scientific factory management."[51] For the first time, Walter was a white collar worker at the company.

After they graduated from college, both John and Bob Kohler also had aspirations for careers outside the family business. They wanted to be architects. But their father vetoed their plans. After leaving the University of Wisconsin in the same year Walter graduated from Yale, John joined his younger brother at the plant in "time-study." Only Jim, with his scientific education, returned happily to the Kohler Company.[52]

❖~❖~❖~◆~❖~❖~❖

By now it was clear that the four Kohler boys, who were never very close, could be divided into two groups. John and Jim were like Charlotte, their mother: quiet, introspective, somewhat awkward, not always sure of themselves. Walter and Bob more closely resembled their father, being self-confident, socially adept, always handsomely dressed, and well-spoken. Julilly Kohler, recalling what her mother told her and what she later saw for herself, likened Walter to actor Cary Grant and Bob to actor-dancer Fred Astaire, describing both Kohlers as dashing young man of the Roaring Twenties. Walter was the son most like his father, only more reserved and less extroverted. "Uncle Wally was charming and totally at ease with himself," Julilly stated. Bob greatly admired Walter, she said, and tried throughout his life to emulate him in every way.[53]

Walter's son Terry would later describe his father in language similar to Julilly's, noting that Walter was scrupulously honest, hard working, "laid back," "subtle," "driven," and "focused." Terry thought his father neither introverted nor extroverted, and considered him at all times moderate and open-minded. He was not egocentric, Terry recalled, and was consistently reluctant to talk about his life and times. He was "at ease with himself."[54]

By 1925 that self-confidence stemmed in large part, of course, from the fact that Walter had much in life that most others lacked: loving and supportive parents, wealth, good-looks, high intelligence, top educational credentials, and a future in the corporate world that appeared exceedingly bright. Walter also believed he had a firm grasp of what was right and wrong, and he fully accepted the family code of ethics that challenged him to move from sympathy to charity, from good will to good works.

In the tradition of his grandfather and father, Walter believed that truth and proper conduct could be discerned from an innate moral sense, no doubt given by the Creator and nurtured by environment, both in childhood and in the development of intellect through education. This was in general harmony with the teachings of several major Greek and Roman thinkers, as well as leaders of the 18th century Enlightenment. Indeed, the deistic faith of George Washington and Thomas Jefferson was close to the more-or-less secular religion almost all of the Kohlers would embrace throughout Walter's life and beyond.

Commenting on why he began the first inaugural address with a prayer, America's first President declared, "It would be peculiarly improper to omit in this first official act my fervent supplications to that Almighty Being who rules over the Universe." If this faith was not explicitly Christian, it contained Christian virtues, especially personal integrity and concern for one's neighbor. Its emphasis on tolerance also helped it to exist harmoniously within the intellectual and religious environment of the United States at all socio-economic levels.[55]

If the Kohler ethic was more practical, convenient, and earth-bound than a fervid religious faith or a water-tight ideological system, it nevertheless had its positive uses, and many found it appealing. If it could be said to be superficial, self-serving, and too close to the ethics of Babbitt, one can argue that worse rules for human happiness and prosperity are easily found. Many ideologues over the centuries could have spared the world considerable misery by absorbing the simple and timeless rules of living that almost all the Kohlers absorbed from the cradle and tried to live by.

The eternal consequences of such an approach to human existence, from an orthodox Christian standpoint, are another question, one that few Kohlers sought to explore. The demands of making money and the delights offered by wealth occupied a great deal of their time and energy. Washington's Almighty Being, after all, was an impersonal Creator who did not require worship, sacrifice, or theological study.

Theology, church history, and contemporary religious activity were topics just not on Walter's map. When he first applied for work at the Kohler Company, in 1918, he merely drew a horizontal line in the box asking for religious preference.[56] Walter was not, however, anti-religious; he would always respect the beliefs or practices of others, speak positively about God and religion in general, and he celebrated the religious holidays observed by the great majority of Americans. That was the Kohler way.[57]

Walter rarely talked about his inner convictions, and when he did he preferred to stick to generalities about integrity in government service. But while serving as Governor he would write several personal letters to inquiring youngsters that provide us with rare insights into his mind and heart. To a boy in Granton, Wisconsin, he wrote, "You are absolutely right in realizing that success in later life depends primarily on the formation of good habits and attitudes during your youth." Walter defined success as personal happiness. But happiness was more than mere pleasure, he advised. "It would be a pleasure to have a bicycle, but if you took a bicycle that belonged to someone else, you could never be happy with it. If you earned the money to buy that bicycle, you have a feeling of happiness about it—and then you would be successful." Walter recommended one especially good habit to the boy: "Be honest with other people, but equally important, be honest with yourself."[58]

Walter told a young woman in Evansville, Wisconsin, that he could summarize his personal code of conduct in a very few words: "I don't tell untruths or bluff or bully anyone, and I try very hard to understand the other person's point of view."[59]

To a young man in Madison, he wrote, "My own idea is that the good citizen is one who does his best to conduct himself in both his public and his private life according to the Golden Rule. He who respects his fellow men and behaves toward them as he would have them behave toward him cannot fail to be a good individual and a good citizen."[60]

Walter wrote to a West Allis girl, "If I were to advise you, I would say merely that your own judgment and common sense will tell you what is right and what is wrong. If you are ever in doubt about any action or activity which you may be considering, ask yourself how your parents would feel if they were aware of your actions, and refrain from doing anything which would displease them or endanger your own reputation." Such conduct may deprive one of momentary pleasure, "but that is a small sacrifice to make if it preserves for you the respect of your fellowman during the long life which lies before you."[61]

When a young woman from La Rue, Ohio asked for Walter's favorite quotation, he replied, "Some day you will read Shakespeare's plays. In Hamlet, Act 1 Scene 3, you will discover Polonius' advice to his son and therein my favorite quotation: 'This above all; to thine own self be true, and it must follow as the night the day, thou can'st not then be false to any man.'"[62]

❧ ❧ ❧ ❀ ❦ ❦ ❦

Back in Wisconsin, Walter moved in with his parents and brother John in the family's new estate in Kohler called Riverbend Farm. Located on a bend of the Sheboygan River, amid natural woodland beauty, a mile to the south and west of the factory, the 56-room 23,265 square foot English Tudor home was begun in 1921 and completed in 1923. (A 21-room coach house, maintenance building, cloister walkway, and a greenhouse added up to a total square footage of 34,432.)[63] Its basic design was based on observations and studies made by Walter Sr. and Milwaukee architect Richard Philipp, who had traveled together in Europe primarily to study industrial villages.

The finest craftsmen, using the most lavish materials, were employed in creating at Riverbend what appeared to many to be a baronial mansion. The huge house featured smooth stucco combined with rustic brick, a slate roof, leaded window casements, timbered ceilings, stone and tile floors, carved fireplaces, a massive stone staircase, and mullioned windows with leaded casements and stained glass inserts. Rooms, including a library, drawing room, and billiard and game room, were decorated with ornamental plaster ceilings, tile walls, grotesqueries, bas relief, and medallions. Dark furniture, often Jacobean oak and William and Mary walnut, was placed throughout. A rare Queen Anne bureau-bookcase, made in about 1719, in burl-walnut veneer, and a Chippendale bachelor chest of 1780 attracted attention, as did displays of antique glass, English porcelain, and Italian pottery. A large 16th century Flemish tapestry was featured prominently. A bas-relief ceramic sculpture in the library over the fireplace by Charlotte Kohler reminded many of her artistic credentials and the small role she played in planning the house and gardens.[64]

The 40-acres surrounding the home were designed by the Olmstead Brothers of Boston, landscape architects for New York's Central Park, the Boston Public Garden, the Harvard University campus, and the grounds of the nation's Capitol. There were rustic stone walls, rock gardens, sunken lawns, formal beds, a bowling green, a lily pond, a picnic pavilion and well, a man-made stream, a polo field, and an "ambulatory," a long covered walk, that united the main house with the greenhouse, tool area, and garage. A German gardener who worked there in 1930 told a newspaper reporter that the Riverbend gardens were more beautiful than that of his last place of employment—the gardens of Prince Heinrich in Bavaria.[65]

The family, however, and many others in the Kohler and Sheboygan area, thought of Riverbend primarily as a home rather than a showplace. A *Sheboygan Press* article would later state that at Riverbend, "good taste rather than lavishness reigns."[66] Julilly Kohler, who was raised there in a later generation, observed that when one enters Riverbend, there is no grand hall or huge staircase that makes a statement about wealth. "It's a home immediately."[67] However that may be, Riverbend was described in the 1930s as one of the 40 most beautiful mansions in the United States.[68] In 1969, it was included in a book called *Great Houses of America*, one of thirty distinguished buildings constructed between the last years of the seventeenth century and the late 1920's. There the Kohler home is compared favorably with Thomas Jefferson's Monticello and the garish William Randolph Hearst palace in San Simeon, California.[69]

Walter Sr. would never tell anyone about the cost of Riverbend Farm, but estimates from the late 1920s placed its value at between one million and one and half million dollars.[70]

Strolling through Kohler, after his return home from Yale, Walter might well have been surprised by the rapid development of Kohler Village. While Walter Sr. had been generous toward himself and his family in Riverbend, he was also intent on channeling his prosperity toward his employees in an extraordinary way. Kohler Village was another product of the Kohler ethic, a humanitarian response to the needs of those who worked hard for the company and therefore, in Walter Sr.'s eyes, deserved to live a good life.

The Kohler Company president had no intention of creating another "company town," with cookie cutter houses jammed together in narrow streets and run by a paternalistic boss who owned the homes and charged high rent. In his mind, home ownership in a clean, beautiful, and rationally designed community was vital to his employees' happiness.

Walter Sr.'s dream was based on the "garden city" movement popular among nineteenth century European social reformers. It featured individually designed, attractive, and privately owned single and two-family homes, placed west and south of the manufacturing complex, largely out of the sight and smell of the twenty-five acre factory. In 1917, the Olmsted Brothers completed a 50-year master plan for Kohler Village,

a design that included broad avenues, parks, and trees. Architect Philipp
was employed to design houses.

Walter Sr. deeded large tracts of land to the Kohler Improvement
Company, which constructed the houses and sold them to employees at
cost. The builders were Kohler Company employees, and every house
was carefully supervised to maintain high quality. Low-cost mortgage
financing was arranged by the Kohler Building and Loan Association,
owned by the employees themselves. In the 1920s, homes ranged in
price from $5,000 to $12,000. Workers were required to come up with
a down payment of 10 to 20 percent of the total purchase price before
they could qualify for Association assistance. (In 1928, fewer than a third
of the Kohler work force lived in the Village. Most lived in Sheboygan,
many taking a trolley to work each day.)

In the West II development, constructed in the late 1920s, workers
had a broad choice of homes. As two scholars later put it, "prospective
buyers could choose from English, American colonial, and traditional
bungalow designs built of brick, stucco, or wood." It would be in this
lovely area, across the street from Ravine Park, that Walter and Bob
Kohler would move after their marriages.

The company constructed a demonstration house every year, to inspire
employees to create something of the sort for themselves. Walter Sr.
saw to it that each such home came equipped with built-in bookshelves,
to encourage homeowners to read, and a piano, rather than a radio, to
encourage musical participation.

The Village soon had an excellent school system, and in 1927, Marie
Kohler joined with her brothers and sisters in creating the Kohler Family
Scholarships, to assist local students attending the University of Wisconsin. Kohler also had a crack fire department, and a recreation hall
capable of accommodating 1,000 people. The Nature Theatre in Ravine
Park was an outdoor civic center where citizens came together to hear
music, watch plays, and listen to speeches. (In 1919, John Philip Sousa
and his world-famous band performed at the dedication of the Theatre
and paid a return visit in 1925.) They could also enjoy an outdoor sports
complex. The Kohler band and an assortment of prize-winning athletic
teams quickly became famous throughout the state.[71]

Kohler residents enjoyed the annual Festival and Field Day, which
featured vaudeville performers, a horseshoe tournament, and a baseball
throwing contest. There was a Village Fair, which offered prizes in more

than 100 categories, including flowers and baked goods. Village children could take piano lessons at the Kohler Music Studio.[72]

Not surprisingly, morale among the Kohler Village inhabitants was extraordinarily high. The company employees were proud of what had been achieved and were determined to maintain the high standards of their community. A visitor in 1932, during the dark days of the Great Depression, wrote, "In vain during my two days here have I sought evidences of slipshod municipal housekeeping. Not a street marker has gone tipsy. Nowhere has refuse accumulated. Not a seedy looking person have I encountered....The intense self-respect of the people, their thrift and their deep pride in their homes keep Kohler what it was—a spotless town of 2,000 inhabitants where one policeman in the daytime and two at night are more than enough for directing traffic and controlling such passers-by who might violate the proprieties of conduct which are the code of this village."[73]

✦✦✦◉✦✦✦

During the balance of the decade, each Kohler son received an allowance on top of his company salary. This was to insure that the young men lived in a style that was appropriate to their rank. They were no longer to be tested in the fires of the foundry; they were gentlemen, the boss's sons, who were expected, in time, to take over the company.

In 1927, the earliest data extant, Walter's salary was $125 a month. His allowance was $250 a month. Moreover, Walter Sr. also covered his son's expenses at Riverbend and other items such as membership in the Sheboygan Country Club and new clothes. In 1928, Walter's salary went up to $225, and in May of that year, the allowance dropped to $150 a month and remained there through 1931, the last figures we have. Walter's salary in 1929 and 1930 was $350 a month, and with his allowance that meant $500. (In 1930, the average Kohler Company worker received 70 cents an hour, or $134.40 a month.) Walter's annual salary of $6,000 in 1930, in 2004 dollars, would be $68,011.98. Unmarried, only 25, and living in a luxurious home attended by servants, Walter enjoyed a privileged existence at the very top of the socio-economic scale. Moreover, Walter Sr. paid the entire cost of a European excursion by his second son.[74]

The 1925 trip, Walter's first overseas, was a graduation present. John would be given a similar treat a year later. Travel was a vital ingredient in the making of a gentleman. Aside from its many pleasures, travel had long been thought vital to the educated and sophisticated for its historical perspective. Travel was also, like speaking French and having a butler, another sign of belonging to the "proper" class of people. Cocktail and dinner parties could be enlivened by the hour with tales of where in the world one had been recently. A large number of Walter's classmates at Yale had been abroad by the time they graduated; two had been overseas nine times, and one had gone ten times.[75]

Walter left the United States in October, 1925 and traveled across Europe alone for several months, going as far as North Africa. Regrettably, he left no specific account of his excursion, but we know that it cost his father $2,254.[76]

Walter's career in the Company began slowly but soon improved. In October, 1926 he moved from "Time Study" to what was described on his employment record as "Mill Room Misc." Walter later told an interviewer that the job involved ceramic research. In January, 1927 he was transferred to the Sales Department. Walter was no doubt pleased by his new job, as he would now have ample opportunity to travel and employ his considerable powers of persuasion for the good of the company. His older brother John was also moving into sales and would soon be elevated to manager of the Company's Chicago branch office. In July, 1928, Jim became a full-time research engineer in the family firm.[77]

In the late 1920s, the Kohler Company was booming. An employee, Anton Brotz, invented the modern gasoline-powered generator, and Walter Sr., seeing the possibilities, went into the business. The Kohler Automatic Power & Light, as the product was called, was snapped up by customers all over the globe. The federal government used the generators to power revolving lights that guided pilots engaged in the nation's first overnight airmail service in 1925.

Walter Sr. expanded the company's manufacture of plumbing supplies as well, entering the china and brassware business and constructing the world's largest pottery plant to manufacture toilets and sinks. In 1926 the Kohler electric sink made its debut, one of the world's first motor-powered dishwashers. The following year Kohler introduced an all metal faucet, including the handle. In 1928 came the introduction of the Kohler Electric Clothes washer. Cast-iron furnaces and radiators began to be produced. Company ads for complete bathrooms, in several colors, set industry standards, and in 1929 the Metropolitan Museum of Art in New York featured Kohler products in a landmark exhibition on industrial design.[78]

Company profits rose from $853,000 in 1918 to $3,366,771 in 1925, and were continuing to grow during the balance of the decade.[79]

The Vollrath Company, in which Walter Sr. was deeply involved, was also prospering. At the turn of the century, the company had dropped the manufacture of plumbing goods and devoted itself exclusively to the production of cooking utensils. In 1907 the company catalogue listed 484 items, including kettles, pitchers, tea kettles, coffee pots, and cooking pots, available in several colors. By 1912 the company moved into a large new plant in Sheboygan and had 325 employees. Steam table panels and equipment entered the catalog in 1919, and cast iron restaurant stools, counter guards, and coat hooks soon appeared. By 1928, Vollrath sold more than 800 separate items and had branches in New York and San Francisco.[80]

By this time, the Kohlers were among the wealthiest citizens of Wisconsin. And there was more good news for family members: in 1928, Walter Sr. decided to run for Governor. His second son may well have wondered about the extent to which the Kohler campaign would enlist his services, for at Yale he had studied enough government and history to know quite a bit about politics. But, at 24, Walter was not yet interested in engaging directly in political campaigning. He was still being trained in the Kohler Company, and was living at home. His father thought of him largely still as a boy, to be ordered about rather than consulted.

The principal excitement in Walter's life in 1928 was flying. He began his pilot training at a local airfield, scheduling his lessons at 6;00 a.m., "before father was up." Walter said later, "I had learned to fly before he knew about it. He didn't object—after all, he had his own plane—but he never approved, either."[81] He received his pilot's license from the Department of Commerce in November, 1928.[82]

Still, Walter was to become involved in Walter Sr.'s gubernatorial campaign in 1928 and catch his first glimpse of what campaigning in Wisconsin was truly like. He learned along with his father.

Notes

[1] The entire issue of *Kohler of Kohler News*, May, 1940 is devoted to the life and times of Walter J. Kohler, Sr. Pages 3-4 discuss the early years. See also

Richard S. Davis, "Kohler Village Workers Mourn Toiler Who Left Indelible Mark in Community," *Milwaukee Journal*, April 23, 1940.

[2] *Ibid*. On Walter's height, see Julilly Kohler interview, October 7, 1903. This is consistent with photographs.

[3] "Life Without Labor Is Guilt...," *Milwaukee Sentinel*. April 22, 1940; Fred C. Sheasby, "Heckler Fails to Jar Kohler," *Milwaukee Journal*, September 9, 1930; "Community And State Mourn Death Of Walter J. Kohler," *ibid*., April 22, 1940.

[4] See *Commemorative Biographical Record of Prominent and Representative Men of Racine and Kenosha Counties* (Chicago: J. H. Beers, 1906), 610-611; "Mrs. Walter J. Kohler Is Summoned Sunday, *Sheboygan Press*, February 3, 1947; Nancy Greenwood Williams, *First Ladies of Wisconsin: The Governors' Wives* (Kalamazoo, Michigan: —ana Publishing, 1991), 151. The "middle class" determination was based on observations by Dr. Steve Hutchens, Kenosha librarian and scholar, of the Schroeder home at 260 Lake Avenue, which in 1927 became 4717 5th Avenue and is still inhabited. E-mail, S. M. Hutchens to the author, December 16, 2004, Charlotte Schroeder Kohler file.

[5] Wisconsin closed the last of its two year teacher training institutions in the 1970s.

[6] E-mail, Michael Kohler to the author, December 3, 2004, Charlotte Schroeder Kohler file.

[7] "Palms and Roses," *Kenosha Evening News*, November 3, 1900.

[8] In 1906, Charlotte's mother was living in Sheboygan, no doubt with Charlotte's sister, Minnie Krez. Another sister, Louisa Berriman, later moved from New York to Sheboygan. Charlotte's grandson, Michael Kohler, remembers visiting Louisa in his youth. "Aunt Lou," he recalls, "was somewhat of a character—and was considerably more assertive than Charlotte." Michael also knew Minnie Krez's son, without knowing the family connection. E-mail, Michael Kohler to the author, December 4, 2004, Charlotte Schroeder Kohler file. The Schroeders faded from the Kohler-Vollrath story early in the twentieth century, perhaps because of their relatively modest incomes and social position.

[9] "Mrs. Walter J. Kohler Is Summoned Sunday," *Sheboygan Press*, February 3, 1947; *Landmarks: J. M. Kohler Home*. When Walter, Jr. was born in April, 1904, the family lived at 717 No. 7th Street in Sheboygan. Walter J. Kohler, Jr.'s Certificate of Birth, Terry Kohler papers.

[10] *Landmarks: J. M. Kohler Home*; Julilly Kohler interview, October 7, 2003; Walter J. Vollrath, Jr. interview. Vollrath, who lived across the street from the Kohler home for many years, called the sisters "the essence of the word eccentric." See Blodgett, *A Sense of Higher Design*, 112-114. Recollections

of this sort by Julilly Kohler came originally from her mother, Julilly House Kohler, and her father, John M. Kohler, Charlotte's son.

11 Wisconsin birth records, as reported by Ancestry.com, list Saint Croix County as the birthplace of John, Jim, Walter, and Herbert V. Kohler. In fact, all were born in Sheboygan. Saint Croix County is in the far western part of the state.

12 The baptismal certificate, dated June 28, 1908, is in the Terry Kohler papers. Minnie and Evangeline Kohler were the witnesses.

13 Terry Kohler interview of June 12, 2003.

14 Julilly Kohler interview, October 7, 2003; Marie Kohler interview.

15 The 1910 federal census is available on Ancestry.com.

16 Richard S. Davis, "Governorship Is First Kohler Political Job," *Milwaukee Journal*, November 9, 1950; Walter J. Kohler to his parents, January 5, 1918, Kohler Family papers; Walter J. Kohler, Sr. to his sons, January 6, 1920, *ibid*; Alfred Steinberg, "Is This the Man to Beat McCarthy?," *Colliers*, November 24, 1951, 77.

17 *Landmarks: J. M. Kohler Home*; Marylin Bender, *At The Top*, (Garden City, New York: Doubleday, 1975), 253.

18 See Blodgett, *A Sense of Higher Design*, pp. 50-53, 61-63, 66-67, 76-77, 98-103.

19 Fred C. Sheasby, "Peppy Kohler Rally Jammed," *Milwaukee Journal*, August 30, 1928.

20 Blodgett, *A Sense of Higher Design*, 107.

21 Terry Kohler interview, August 13, 2003; Peter and Nancy Kohler interview, August 11, 2003.

22 Julilly Kohler interview, October 7, 2003.

23 When reporting later for military duty, Walter stated that he knew German and French. An expense account (see below) notes the purchase of a Latin book. Terry Kohler recalled that his father studied Latin at Andover and may have continued it at Yale. E-mail, Terry Kohler to the author, January 23, 2004, Yale file.

24 Copy, Walter J. Kohler, Jr. to Hal Stevens, November 24, 1953, Walter J. Kohler, Jr. Papers.

25 The Kohler Family Papers contain a copy of *Pot Pourri*, the Academy yearbook for 1921, from which this information is taken. See especially pages 33, 55, 88, 90. On Walter's fraternity membership (Phi Beta Chi), see the undated copy of a typed statement written by Walter to a Yale publication, Miscellaneous File, Terry Kohler papers.

26 Julilly Kohler interview, October 7, 2003.

27 Michael Kohler to the author, January 9, 2005, and copies of his father's transcripts, are in the John Michael Kohler III file.

28 Peter and Nancy Kohler interview, August 11, 2003.

[29] Vicki and Jill Kohler interview; Robert E. Kohler, Jr., interview.

[30] Walter J. Kohler, Sr. to his sons, January 6, 1920, Kohler Family papers.

[31] John, $5,249.40; Walter $5,817.92; Jim, $7,083.74; Robert, $12,003.16.

[32] The height and weight of young Walter is noted on his 1918 Kohler Company application form, amended in 1925. Personnel file.

[33] The employment records of the Kohler boys are in the Kohler Company archives. I have placed copies in the files of John and Jim, and Walter's is in the Personnel file in my collection. I was unable to secure an employment record for Bob. See Walter's comments in Richard S. Davis, "Governorship Is First Kohler Political Job," *Milwaukee Journal*, November 9, 1950. The description of the core room is in Steinberg, "Is This the Man to Beat McCarthy?," 77. On Walter's popularity at the plant, see Terry Kohler interview of June 12, 2003.

[34] Brooks Mathers Kelley, *Yale, A History* (New Haven and London: Yale University Press, 1974), 314, 366-392; George W. Pierson, *Yale: A Short History* (New Haven, Connecticut: Yale University, 1976), 27, 30.

[35] Copy, undated, typed statement written by Walter J. Kohler, Jr. to a Yale publication, Miscellaneous file, Terry Kohler papers. While the College was limited to males, Yale had welcomed women in other branches of its institution since 1869. By 1900, Yale had granted more doctorates to women than any other university. The first black graduated from the College in 1874. Pierson, *Yale: A Short History*, pp. 53-54.

[36] Walter Grey Preston, Jr. (ed.), *History of the Class of 1925 Yale College* (New Haven, Connecticut: Class Secretaries Bureau, 1925), 20, 32, 45, 48, 59, 385-387.

[37] *Ibid.*, pp. 16-21, 51-55, 64-67, 387.

[38] Judith Ann Schiff, "Old Yale: A Toast to 'Legal Inebriation,'" published in the *Yale Alumni Magazine* in December, 1968 and available at *www.yalealumnimagazine.com/issues/98_12/old_yale.html*. Drinking was common in many major colleges and universities at the time. See Paul S. Fass, *The Damned and the Beautiful: American Youth in the 1920's* (New York: Oxford University Press, 1979 paperback edition), 311-324.

[39] A photo exists in the in the Leslie Kohler Hawley collection of Walter and the football team.

[40] Records in the Kohler Family papers.

[41] Guide R. Rahr, Jr. interview. See Preston, *History of the Class of 1925*, 259. On Mory's and the Whiffenpoofs, see www.morys1849.org.

[42] Preston, *History of the Class of 1925*, 201. For Spock, see *ibid.*, 56, 59, 61, 65, 70, 297.

[43] Fass, *The Damned and the Beautiful*, 142-157, 172-182.

[44] *The Course Of Study In Yale College For The Year 1921-22*, 19-21, courtesy of the Yale University archives; Officer Qualifications Questionnaire, undated, Terry Kohler papers; records in the Kohler Family papers.

[45] Terry Kohler interview, June 12, 2003. Mandatory chapel attendance was abolished in 1926, having become extremely unpopular with students. Kelley, *Yale, A History*, 387; Pierson, *Yale: A Short History*, 18. Grace Episcopal Church in Sheboygan, with which the Kohlers were often formally associated, has no records of any kind on Walter. E-mails, Betty Potter to the author, February 26, 2004, Religion file.

[46] Both are in the Terry Kohler papers.

[47] Copy, Walter J. Kohler, Jr. to Rosalie Knight, October 16, 1951, Box 35, Walter J. Kohler, Jr. papers.

[48] Copy, Walter J. Kohler, Jr. to Jo Ann Cupery, May 24, 1955, *ibid.*

[49] "B'nai B'rith Honors Trio," *Milwaukee Journal*, November 12, 1953.

[50] Steinberg, "Is This The Man to Beat McCarthy?," 77; Terry Kohler interview, June 12, 2003.

[51] Walter's employment record, Personnel file. The job description is found in *Decennial Record of the Class Of 1925 Yale College*," 32, a 1935 publication in the Yale University archives.

[52] Robert E. Kohler, Jr., interview; Michael Kohler interview; John's employment record in his personal file. By 1926, Walter Sr. had spent a total of $50,602.38 on college educations for his sons. We have no record of Herbert Kohler's educational expenses, which were undoubtedly also paid by Walter, Sr.

[53] Julilly Kohler interview, October 7, 2003. See also the interview with Vicki and Jill Kohler, December 19, 2003.

[54] Terry Kohler interview, June 12, 2003.

[55] Marie was the most Christian of the Kohlers. She helped the Episcopal Church financially throughout the area and was active in her local parish, Grace Church, Sheboygan. See "Servant of God," *Kohler of Kohler News*, November, 1943, 25. For brief and interesting commentary on the Founding Fathers, see Vincent Phillip Munoz, "He Can't Believe It," *Wall Street Journal*, January 14, 2005.

[56] The application, from the Kohler Company files, is in the Personnel file.

[57] The photograph is in the Mary Kohler Ahern papers. Terry Kohler, Walter's son, would be baptized and confirmed an Episcopalian. See Terry Kohler interviews of June 12, 2003 and August 4, 2004.

[58] Copy, Walter J. Kohler, Jr. to Bobby Rosandich, September 30, 1952, box 35, Walter J. Kohler, Jr. papers.

[59] Copy, Walter J. Kohler, Jr. to Carol Ann Holm, April 5, 1955, *ibid.*

[60] Copy, Walter J. Kohler, Jr. to Randi Richter, March 19, 1954, *ibid.*

[61] Copy, Walter J. Kohler, Jr. to Lucille Barth, November 17, 1953, *ibid.*

[62] Copy, Walter J. Kohler, Jr. to Suzanna Rose Lovett, May 19, 1952, *ibid.*

[63] E-mail, Michael Kohler to the author, February 8, 2005, Riverbend file. This data came from the Kohler Company's architectural department, and I am indebted to Mike Kohler for acquiring it.

[64] Dawn Jax Belleau, "Beauty, Order And Restraint," *Sheboygan Press*, February 10, 1981. See "Recollections of Riverbend," a 1985 publication of the John Michael Kohler Arts Center, Riverbend file; Richard W. E. Perrin, *The Architecture of Wisconsin* (Madison, Wisconsin, State Historical Society of Wisconsin, 1967), 109-11. On Charlotte's role in the home and gardens, see Williams, *First Ladies of Wisconsin*, 153.

[65] "Community And State Mourn Death Of Walter J. Kohler," *Sheboygan Press*, April 22, 1940.

[66] *Ibid.*

[67] Julilly Kohler interview, October 7, 2003.

[68] Blodgett, *A Sense of Higher Design*, 242.

[69] Henry Lionel Williams and Ottalie K. Williams, *Great Houses of America* (New York: G.P. Putnam's Sons, 1969), 258-266.

[70] Walter J. Pfister, "Wisconsin Rivals Seek Office By Air," *New York World*, August 26, 1928.

[71] See Blodgett, *A Sense of Higher Design*, 92-99, 106-107; Norman W. Gregg, "Wisconsin's Most Beautiful Village," *The Wisconsin Magazine*, April, 1928, 77-79; James C. Young, "A Model Town That Grew On A Prairie," *New York Times Magazine*, October 11, 1931, 11; James O'Donnell Bennett, "In Good Times And Bad Kohler Is Happy Town," *Chicago Daily Tribune*, July 18, 1932; Arnold R. Alanen and Thomas J. Peltin, "Kohler, Wisconsin: Planning and Paternalism in a Model Industrial Village," *Journal of the American Institute of Planners*, April, 1976, 145-158. This last piece, from which the West II quotation was taken (p. 151), is valuable but marred by a leftist bent. On the Kohler Family Scholarships, see "Student and Teacher," *Kohler of Kohler News*, November, 1943, 10.

[72] Blodgett, *A Sense of Higher Design*, 107.

[73] Bennett, "In Good Times and Bad Kohler Is Happy Town," *Chicago Daily Tribune*, July 18, 1932.

[74] Walter's expense sheets are from the Kohler Family papers, and copies are in the Personnel file. Salary figures are from the Kohler Company, and a copy of this data is in the Kohler Company Archives file. The 70 cent an hour average is found in "Kohler on the Stand," *Milwaukee Journal*, May 13, 1930.

[75] Preston, *History of the Class of 1925*, 387; Davis, "Governorship Is First Kohler Political Job," *Milwaukee Journal*, November 9, 1950.

[76] Walter's passport is in the Terry Kohler papers. The cost of the first trip is on Walter's expense sheet in the Kohler Family papers. Information about

the trip appears in a 1944 handwritten Officer Qualifications Questionnaire, Terry Kohler papers.

[77] See Walter's employment records in the Personnel file, and the personnel
records of John and Jim in their files. The reference to ceramic research is
in *Decennial Record of the Class of 1925, Yale College*.

[78] Blodgett, *A Sense of Higher Design*, 62-76.

[79] Walter H. Uphoff, *Kohler on Strike, Thirty Years of Conflict* (Boston: Beacon
Press, 1966), 10.

[80] *Vollrath Celebrates 125 Years in Business*, 1-11.

[81] Davis, "Governorship Is First Kohler Political Job," *Milwaukee Journal*, November 9, 1950.

[82] Walter's student pilot's permit, dated September 16, 1928, and his private
pilot's license, dated November 16, 1928 are in the Terry Kohler papers.
The permit reveals that Walter was trained by Lt. Werner O. Bunge, Walter Sr.'s pilot.

Chapter Three

The First Governor Kohler

The Republican Party dominated Wisconsin politics in the late 1920s. It had been founded in Wisconsin before the Civil War, and between 1865 and turn of the century, Republicans had won the governorship in all but three elections. As historian Richard C. Haney put it, "Lumber, dairy, and railroad interests all saw the GOP as the party which best represented them." In 1900, charismatic reformer Robert M. Lafollette won the governorship, and he dominated state politics for the next quarter century, as governor and United States Senator. Democrats and Socialists made inroads, especially along Lake Michigan and in Milwaukee, and many in rural areas were attracted to the Greenbackers and Populists. But the major activities of state politics took place largely within the tent of the Republican party.

In 1904, just four years after La Follette captured party machinery in the state, the GOP was at war with itself and had split into two factions: Progressives and Stalwarts. The former were loyal to the Progressive Movement, the tradition made famous by La Follette that used the power of government to spread democracy, clean up government, and redistribute income. The Stalwarts were largely conservatives who sought low taxes, favors for business, and smaller and more efficient government. Both factions saw themselves as advocates of freedom and morality. Much of the animosity between the two factions was also personal.

Democrats looked on, lacking popularity and authority, and plagued by weak leadership. As Haney put it, "Democrats fell back upon a conservative, laissez-faire traditionalism, leaving the most important political battles to the stalwarts and progressives within the GOP." In 1922, Democrats failed to win enough primary votes to qualify for a separate ballot in the November elections. Winning the GOP nomination to an office was tantamount to election.

In 1924, La Follette formally broke with the GOP and ran a presidential campaign on his own. State Republican leaders, outraged that La Follette was campaigning against Republican Calvin Coolidge, formed

the Republican Voluntary Committee (RVC), a statewide confedera-
tion of Stalwart Republicans. When La Follette died in 1925, Robert
La Follette, Jr. won the special election, leaving stalwarts fuming.

During the 1926 GOP convention, fighting broke out among the
Stalwarts, the division being largely between a moderate, business-
oriented faction and a more conservative, ideological faction. Walter
Sr., new to these battles, joined several other industrial leaders in the
moderate/business faction. When all the ballots were counted, the RVC
controlled the State Senate, La Follette Progressives controlled the State
Assembly, and maverick Secretary of State, Fred Zimmerman, with
the backing of Kohler and his allies, held the governorship. By 1928,
Stalwarts were eager to heal party wounds and come together behind
winning candidates. But there was still much anger among Republican
activists. Whoever won the gubernatorial nomination and election
would be faced with two years of bitter partisan struggle.[1]

By this time, Walter Sr. was attracting considerable attention from
Republicans. In 1916 he had been named a presidential elector. Two years
later he was elected to the University of Wisconsin Board of Regents.
From 1921 to 1924, Kohler served as president of the Board, stirring
students and alumni to complete the Memorial Union.[2] Wherever he
went, people responded positively to his sunny disposition, high intelligence, commitment to hard work, and his obvious integrity. Generous
financial contributions no doubt also helped Kohler win friends within
the GOP. To many in the Party, Walter Sr. embodied the spirit of the
enlightened businessman, highly popular in the late 1920s. Moreover,
it became clear by 1928 that the wealthy industrialist had political
ambitions.

In 1928, Kohler received an impressive number of votes to be a
Delegate at Large to the national convention at Kansas City. The other
three Delegates were La Follette Progressives. Many "regulars," as the
Stalwarts called themselves, thought Kohler just the man to unite their
wing of the party and defeat Governor Zimmerman, who had grown
unpopular due to a state income tax hike. (Wisconsin now had the
highest income tax in the nation.)

In June, Walter Sr. agreed to be "drafted" by Republicans in the
gubernatorial contest.[3] At a convention in Green Bay, Stalwarts gave
him their support. The *Milwaukee Journal* highly approved, comparing
Kohler with GOP presidential candidate Herbert Hoover, and noting

that he "is an agreeable gentleman with the habit of talking directly and frankly of what is in his mind."[4]

Progressives ran a candidate of their own, Congressman Joseph D. Beck. He enjoyed the support of Senators La Follette and John J. Blaine. (Blaine had been the progressive Governor from 1921 to 1927.) Herbert Hoover, though no doubt favoring Kohler privately, chose not to take sides in the gubernatorial race.[5]

During the course of the summer, Walter Sr. carefully organized his campaign and stumped energetically across the state, declaring himself in favor of low taxes, aid to farmers, conservation, better highways, the St. Lawrence Seaway, and clean, efficient, and responsive government. "I am a liberal and have tried to live a life of constructive progress," he said in Green Bay.[6] A favorite campaign theme was his success in business. "I am charged by the opposition with not being a politician, and I am heartily in accord with the statement."[7] He told a group of reporters in July, "In my opinion the state government is really a large business and should be run with the same regard for system and method that one would run a private business."[8] If elected, Kohler said, he would ignore the spoils system and retain and hire the best people no matter what their political affiliation.[9]

Walter Sr. also made it clear as well that he was a sensitive and generous employer. He said in Milwaukee, "The first essential that every man is interested in is good wages. Nothing can take the place of that. Hours should be reasonable and permit of adequate time for healthful relaxation and entertainment. Continuity of employment is a factor of outstanding importance in the lives of people who work. I believe in these things—good wages and continuity of employment. Nothing more tragic can happen to a family than to have the head of the family lose his job."[10]

The candidate might have cited other proofs of his concern for those in his employ. The company had one of the best ventilating systems in the country to protect workers in their often dirty and difficult work, and it contained its own medical and dental departments. Moreover, Walter Sr. provided workers with a recreation club and facilities for baseball, tennis, and horseshoes. Workers enjoyed a smoking and reading room during lunch hours. And every Monday afternoon, there was a band concert.[11]

In every speech, Walter Sr. invited his listeners to Kohler. Visitors were regularly fed at the American Club, entertained by the 100-piece

Kohler band, given guided tours through the factory and Kohler Village, and welcomed at a reception at Riverbend.[12] In early August, for example, 500 Milwaukeeans, members of the Kohler for Governor club, drove to Kohler. Walter Sr. himself led visitors through the factory and delivered a ten minute speech during a huge luncheon. "We have tried in Kohler to do things in a constructive way," he said. "We are humbly proud of the things you see here." A contingent of Milwaukee factory workers trekked to Kohler later in the same week and were treated similarly.[13] The stream of visitors continued throughout the summer and much of the fall. In late August, Marie Kohler, Walter Sr.'s sister, invited women to visit Kohler.[14]

One veteran Progressive publicly endorsed Kohler as a result of what he saw in the candidate's home town. "I firmly believe that if it were possible for all the people of Wisconsin to visit the Kohler plant and the model industrial village at Kohler, 90 percent of them would vote for Mr. Kohler."[15]

Walter Sr. was the first political candidate in Wisconsin to campaign extensively by airplane. He had his own plane, employed a professional pilot, and flew out of an airstrip he constructed in Kohler. The $10,000 aircraft was a Ryan brougham monoplane, an almost exact replica of Charles A Lindbergh's "Spirit of St. Louis," which had made history a year earlier. The silver plane measured 28 feet in length with a wingspan of 42 feet. It could contain four passengers, who sat in leather upholstered seats behind the pilot.

The airplane, which had a top speed of 90 miles per hour, permitted Kohler to visit many places in a single day. Here is the schedule for August 2: Verona, 8:30 a.m.; Belleville, 9:30 a.m.; New Glarus, 10:15 a.m.; Monticello, 10:45 a.m.; Monroe, 11:30 a.m.; Argyle, 1:15 p.m.; Burlington, 2:00 p.m.; Mineral Point, 3:30 p.m.; Platteville, 6:00 p.m.; Lancaster, 8:30 p.m.[16] From July 15 to August 30 Walter Sr. and his pilot made 104 flights, covering 7,280 miles.[17] The name "Village of Kohler" appeared on the pilot-side door, and the word "KOHLER" in large letters on the underside of the wing let observers on the ground know who was overhead.

While such travel saved time, it could also be dangerous. Kohler and his pilot once faced a terrible storm and had to turn back. On another occasion, they landed in a hay field near Pittsville in order to attend a large Indian powwow. (The candidate accepted a pipe but refused to wear a Winnebago bonnet, fearing that it would be looked on as a publicity stunt.)[18] The plane once dropped one of its wheels with the candidate and Walter aboard, forcing the pilot to make a delicate landing on one wheel.[19]

Walter Sr. also traveled furiously by automobile throughout the state, accompanied by a Kohler Company employee, George L. Geiger, who served as his secretary. Kohler's task was to reach the 1.5 million voters (out of a population of about 3 million), in 1,281 towns, 151 cities, 366 villages, and 71 counties. Wisconsin has an area of 54,450 square miles; it was 474 miles by automobile from Kenosha, in the far southeastern corner of the state, to Superior in the northwest corner; 271 miles from Marinette in the northeast to Platteville in the southwest. And efforts had to be made to reach the some 450 newspapers in the state whose endorsements were sought. The Kohler devotion to hard work was amply tested throughout this campaign.

While not an accomplished public speaker, Kohler was persuasive and likeable. A *Milwaukee Journal* reporter commended him for the brevity of a speech he delivered in Fond du Lac in only 26 minutes, and observed, "He read his speech earnestly and clearly, although a bit hurriedly. He made a good impression. He is not crowd shy. The audience was keenly attentive and demonstrative."[20] By early August, Walter Sr. was delivering speeches without notes and appearing at ease on the stump.[21] He often attracted large audiences. At a water carnival in Fremont, he addressed a crowd of about 8,000.[22] He drew 5,000 in Waukesha and 3,000 in Oconomowoc.[23] In Beloit, a Zimmerman stronghold, he addressed 2,500 people.[24] More than 1,500 attended a rally in Appleton, more than had turned out for Senator La Follette a month earlier.[25] Walter Sr. spoke at scores of small gatherings as well, once appearing at a picnic held by the fire department of tiny Slinger.[26]

Progressives and their allies began criticizing Kohler almost as soon as he began campaigning. Henry Olh, Jr., president of the State Federation of Labor, condemned what he called Walter Sr.'s "anti-union shop policy," and charged that the working people of Kohler, whose labors had made their employer wealthy, should not be "elevating him politically so that he may further industrial policies lacking every vestige of rights and freedom."[27]

In a stinging reply, Walter Sr. stated that he employed both union and non-union workers, that Kohler Company wages were 28.9 percent higher than the average for Wisconsin factory workers, and that 92 percent of all married men in Kohler owned their own lots and homes, while 75 percent of them owned automobiles. He also called attention to the many benefits, such as life and disability insurance, and workmen's compensation, that workers enjoyed, and touted the company policy of building up supplies of products during business slumps in order to avoid layoffs.[28] Leaders of the Plumbers and Steamfitters' Local 401, of Sheboygan, backed Kohler in the dispute, arguing that the Kohler Company had never been hostile to union workers and stood for "high wages, short hours, safe conditions, continuous employment and a friendly attitude toward workmen."[29]

In campaign speeches, Walter Sr. often noted his own years of hard labor at the company plant and the low wages and long hours he endured. A favorite campaign photograph showed the young Kohler in factory clothes, sporting a handsome smile.

With two weeks to go before the primary, Progressives, led by the blatantly partisan *Madison Capital Times*, attacked Kohler for being wealthy and allegedly having access to a "slush fund" to defeat opponents. They denied that a business man was by definition qualified to run a state.[30] Walter Sr. replied, in a Milwaukee speech, that the Progressives were "a little willful group," adding, "I have no desire to be a professional politician or to use their methods." His desire in running for Governor was solely to serve the people of Wisconsin. To those who ask what is the matter with Wisconsin, he declared, "Nothing is the matter with Wisconsin except its politics."[31]

Just days before the primary, Governor Zimmerman asked and received permission to address Kohler Company employees. In a campaign speech in Sheboygan, the Governor claimed that, based on income tax records (then open to public scrutiny), Walter Sr. was making $3 million a year. (The figure was not disputed. In 2004 dollars, that would amount to an annual income of $33,210,526.) He also attacked conditions in Kohler Village and in the Kohler plant. Zimmerman drew cheers from a crowd of some 500 when he referred to Kohler factory workers as "slaves." No man who worked for Kohler, he said, "could call his soul his own."[32] The impending vote in the primary would soon gauge the strength of anti-Kohler sentiment in the area.

In the week before the election, Walter Sr. advocated a stronger state children's code. These were laws about state aid to dependent children, child adoption, boarding homes and institutions, and the like. This was a cause dear to the heart of his socially active sister Marie, who gave

a short speech on the candidate's behalf at an Oconomowoc rally.[33]
Progressives then began calling Kohler a war profiteer.[34]

Walter Sr. won the September 4 primary handily, collecting 20,000
more votes than his Progressive opponent. He carried the industrial
areas of Milwaukee and Racine, and even the Socialist Tenth Ward in
Milwaukee. The *Milwaukee Journal* reporter who followed the Kohler
campaign observed that workers ignored labor leaders who opposed
Kohler. "One reason is that thousands of workers in their visits to the
village of Kohler liked what they saw there. Another reason is that workers believed Mr. Kohler's recital of progressive labor measures which
have been installed by the Kohler company."[35] In a telling vote, Walter
Sr. won 741 of the 785 votes cast in Kohler Village.[36]

The election won national attention. The *New York Herald-Tribune*
thought that the victory furnished "solid ground for expecting a Hoover
victory in Wisconsin in November." Locally, the *Racine Times-Call* declared, "It was a political upheaval of the first magnitude and reached
into every county in the state. If Mr. Kohler is elected in November,
Wisconsin will enter a new political era....He is a safe, sane, careful yet
forceful character." The Progressive *Madison Capital Times*, on the other
hand, claimed that the election contest had been corrupted with illegal
campaign expenses, and that Kohler should be prevented from taking
office.[37] Leading Democrats took this same approach.

The candidate's son Walter spent part of election night at the Kohler
recreation hall, which was filled with workers listening to the returns on
a radio. "Was there much excitement?," he said to a reporter. "Well, when
it came through that Whitefish Bay [a Milwaukee suburb] had gone
for my father six to one you should have heard them yell. They nearly
lifted the roof. And there for a while when it was close you could have
heard a pin drop." A newspaper photograph showed Walter standing
next to his mother at Riverbend, seated before the radio, as they both
listened to news reports.

The following day, Walter Sr. flew to Chicago to visit a sick friend.
On his return to Kohler, he was greeted by Walter and a pack of reporters. Walter wore a Kohler button on his lapel and a broad grin on
his face.

That evening, the 100-piece Kohler band and 3,000 residents of the
area paraded a mile through an avenue of red flares to Riverbend, assembling on the lawn and cheering for their home town victor. Walter
Sr. told reporters he had flown 7,000 miles, given 200 speeches, and

had eaten far too many of his beloved bratwurst sandwiches during the exhausting campaign. He said he looked forward to spending some time in his garden, which he had barely seen in a month.[38]

Charlotte Kohler had made only a single appearance during the primary campaign. Marie had twice spoken publicly for her brother, and she and her sisters assisted visitors to Kohler. Walter and his brothers played no public role in the campaign other than helping to welcome the legions of visitors to Riverbend all summer. But Walter surely learned much from his father's successful candidacy, political lessons about issues and handling opponents, and practical lessons about organizing and financing a campaign, public speaking, transportation, and working crowds. He would soon learn much more.

After the primary race of 1928, the press discovered Walter for the first time. Of all the Kohlers, he most closely resembled his father, in every way. And Walter Sr. was now one of the most popular political figures in Wisconsin.

At the Republican platform convention in Madison, Stalwarts and Progressives continued their often bitter struggle for party supremacy. At one point, an all-night meeting was on the verge of riot. Stalwarts won by a narrow margin. The platform promised a businesslike administration, incorporating the positions taken by Kohler during the primary race, and endorsing the national Hoover-Curtis ticket. Stalwarts also beat back an effort by Progressives to investigate Kohler's campaign expenditures, pushing through a motion to probe several recent elections, including the presidential race by Robert M. La Follette. During the battles, Kohler stayed aloof, leaving the fighting to lieutenants and preserving his reputation as a dignified gentleman.[39]

Progressives charged that Kohler had violated the Corrupt Practices Act, and a John Doe investigation in Dane County of Walter Sr.'s campaign expenditures soon began. Kohler welcomed the probe, saying he had nothing to hide. But at the same time, he labeled the investigation partisan, which it clearly was. Socialist Mayor Daniel Hoan of Milwaukee claimed that Kohler's campaign expenditures were in the neighborhood of $250,000. Walter Sr. dismissed this allegation and told an audience in Superior that he had spent within 30 percent of the legal amount permitted office seekers. "My opponents," he said, "are on my trail like a pack of wolves....They oppose me because they regard me as a menace to the political oligarchy which has been in control of the state for the last 30 years."[40] He told a Milwaukee audience, "Personally, I have one code of ethics which I have followed in business and private life and I have lived up to that code in this campaign."[41]

The facts of the campaign expenditure issue were complicated. The Wisconsin Corrupt Practices Act placed a limit of $4,000 on the governor's race, that amount being expended by a candidate personally or on his behalf. Moneys raised by assisting committees were not included in the $4,000 limit, the assumption being that a candidate would not control such funds and might well even be unaware of them.

In his campaign report, Walter Sr. said that he spent $2,194.47 in the primary contest. (Beck reported spending $1,665.68, and La Follete said he spent $2,212.67 on his Senate contest.) Big money, however, was spent by others on behalf of Kohler. The report listed 270 contributors. The Republican State Committee spent $41,993.89 and still owed $4,860.46. Funds pouring in to the State Committee and local committees were not charged to Walter Sr.'s $4,000 limit, and GOP officials and the candidate's attorneys thought they had complied fully with the law. Progressives and Democrats, however, claimed that Kohler campaigners did not live up to the spirit and intent of the law. They argued loudly that "fat cats" had bought the election.[42] The contention was designed to defeat Kohler in the November election.

In early October, Progressives filed a petition in the Wisconsin Supreme Court alleging violations of the Corrupt Practices Act and asking that certification of Kohler's nomination be canceled. Specific allegations, appearing for the first time, included the failure by Walter Sr. to list the cost of meals provided for Kohler visitors and the cost of bus expense for the Kohler Band.[43] The next day, Walter Sr. received a subpoena requiring him to testify in the John Doe investigation. The Secretary of the Republican State Committee was also summoned.

By this time, Stalwarts had amassed evidence of what they considered excessive campaign expenditures by Progressives. George L. Gilkey, manager of Kohler's primary campaign, went public immediately with allegations of financial irregularities. Two letters sent to each voter in the state, he said, would alone cost about $80,000. (Privately, Walter Sr., and no doubt others in his camp, received full reports of the tax returns and debts of major Progressives.)[44] Stalwarts filed three counteractions against Progressives, including Senator La Follette, prompting a second John Doe investigation.[45] This was full scale, intra-GOP warfare.

On October 9, the Supreme Court ruled in Kohler's favor, denying the petition to keep his name off the ballot. Expressing vindication,

Walter Sr. told an audience in Sheboygan that he agreed fully with the Corrupt Practices Act but believed it should be made "simpler and more stringent."[46] His attorney, in an argument before the Supreme Court, had said, "Mr. Kohler feels that the conservative Republican state committee spent entirely too much money."[47] Later that month, a *Milwaukee Journal* report revealed that, according to official records, total expenditures in the Kohler primary campaign amounted to $104,874.92. Beyond Walter Sr.'s modest personal expense, Kohler family members had chipped in $4,763, and some 26 local organizations, mostly Kohler clubs, had raised and spent the balance.[48]

Left unsettled, among other matters, was the money spent on meals and entertainment for the thousands of visitors to Kohler. Didn't the candidate have control over such funds? If he did, Progressives argued, he surely spent more than his $4,000 limit. Socialist Mayor Hoan of Milwaukee saw the expenditures as "the beginning of the building of a corrupt political machine....Men do not spend this much money for their health, but expect adequate returns."[49] The Mayor of Madison, running against Kohler on the Democratic Party ticket, declared that the Stalwart aim was to lower income taxes on corporations.[50] The judge in the John Doe investigation requested and received all relevant Kohler Company ledgers and files.[51]

Walter Sr. told a Bay View audience that the money over and beyond his personal expenditure of under $2,800 was money raised and spent by others and that he had nothing to do with it. He called for a strengthening of the Corrupt Practices Act to make sure that federal office holders no longer used franking privileges to flood the state with campaign literature and that state office holders did not campaign for others while on the job. Both were obvious shots at La Follette. "It has been charged that I know little about politics, and while this is undeniably true, I have learned during the last few months a great deal about how some professional politicians conduct campaigns. I have learned that anyone, no matter how frantically partisan or how without reputation he may be, can make wild and unsubstantiated charges against a candidate for public office."[52] The entire reputation of the Kohler family was at stake, and Walter Sr. knew it.

As the election neared, Kohler continued to campaign tirelessly. Two sons made an appearance with the candidate: Walter and his brother John attended the opening of an airport in Wisconsin Rapids. Walter Sr. would tell a reporter proudly, "My son, Walter, is a licensed pilot."[53]

Keeping quiet about prohibition, Walter Sr. was no doubt delighted to be given the support of both the Anti-Saloon League and the Association Opposed to Prohibition, the first time a candidate for Governor had been backed by both wets and drys in the same campaign.[54] It was increasingly clear that most people had a favorable impression of Kohler and were not taking Progressive charges seriously.

In the November election, Kohler handily defeated Madison Mayor Albert Schmedeman, collecting 58 percent of the votes. The vote in Kohler was 764 to 29 in favor of the home town candidate.[55] Herbert Hoover won 54 percent of the votes cast for President. The State Senate was predicted to be solidly behind Kohler.[56]

At the same time, Senate candidate Robert La Follette, Jr. carried every county in the state, while refusing to back Hoover, whom he thought too favorable to big business. (Bob's brother Phil and Senator Blaine endorsed Democratic presidential candidate Al Smith.) The Progressives were still a powerful force in Wisconsin politics, and they were determined to regain the governorship.[57] Walter Sr. knew that the attacks upon him and his administration would be relentless. A political reporter at the *Milwaukee Journal* commented, "So far as it is possible, the La Follette-Blaine forces will annoy, embarrass and block Gov. Elect Kohler in a deliberate attempt to make him sick and tired of politics and drive him home at the end of two years."[58]

On January 6, 1929, a special train took almost the entire Kohler family from Milwaukee to Madison for the inauguration ceremonies. Charlotte, whose handsome and tasteful apparel drew the detailed attention of a reporter, said, "I'm not in the least nervous. It's just a particularly nice part of life." The thrill, she said, was "way down deep." She fussed a bit about Walter and Bob, who stood on the platform in Milwaukee without coats in the zero degree weather. Mrs. Kohler was making arrangements for the move into the Executive Mansion in a few days.

The temperature was 8 degrees below zero when the family joined the parade from the railway station in Madison to the capitol building. Members of the Kohler band, resplendent in their blue uniforms, and the Plymouth and Sheboygan Falls drum corps could not play their instruments, but drummers tried to keep marchers in step. The Plymouth band carried several banners, including one that read "Wisconsin keeps clean with Kohler." The crowd was large and enthusiastic.

The service itself, broadcast for the first time on the radio all across the state, was held indoors at the Capitol building. The Kohler band played the "Stars and Stripes," the Madison Mozart Club performed Handel's "Hallelujah Chorus," and the Civic Orchestra string quartet played. Charlotte sat on the platform between her sons Bob and Jim, holding their hands. Walter Sr., dressed formally in cutaway coat and gray and black trousers, with a white carnation in his lapel, took the oath from Chief Justice Marvin B. Rosenberry. Everyone sang "America," and the Kohler band proceeded to play "On Wisconsin."[59] An admirer soon sent a kitchen broom to the executive office, encouraging the new governor to begin sweeping removals and a general cleanup.[60]

Walter was present, along with his mother and other family members, when the new Governor gave his first message to both houses of the state legislature. Among other things, Kohler called for the reorganization of state government on an efficient business basis, construction of 5,000 miles of all-weather roads, more state parks, a new children's code, and general tax relief. The 8,000 word, 55 minute address was interrupted only once by applause: Stalwarts clapped loudly when Walter, Sr. endorsed an investigation into campaign expenditures in 1924, 1926, and 1928. Everyone knew that this included the La Follette presidential race and the Blaine senatorial campaign.[61]

In the months that followed, Kohler worked extraordinarily hard to put his campaign promises into action. He revealed himself to be a political independent who rejected the spoils system (the appointment of political pals to government positions without regard to qualifications), a bureaucratic reformer, a conservationist, something of a feminist (he was solidly in favor of women in business), a champion of children, a defender of the University of Wisconsin, and a reluctant opponent of prohibition.[62]

In May, 1929, Wisconsin repealed the state prohibition enforcement law. Pressure had been applied on Kohler by President Hoover and others to veto efforts to weaken the 18th Amendment, but Walter Sr. bowed before what was obviously the will of the legislature and the public in general. Still, he urged Wisconsin citizens to obey the federal law. Long a moderate drinker himself, he vowed that as Governor he would stick strictly to ginger ale.[63]

Walter Sr. also kept his hand directly in the operations of the Kohler Company. He spent week days in Madison and weekends in Kohler Village.[64] In August, Walter Sr. announced improvements in the Kohler factories costing a million dollars. He declared proudly that with six pottery kilns, for the manufacture of clay plumbing fixtures, the company would be able to hire 600 to 700 more men. "Yes, I have faith in the future of Wisconsin," he told a reporter, "I do not believe any business man who examines the matter carefully can come to any other conclusion than the one I have."[65] At his own expense, Kohler had his company's plumbing fixtures installed throughout the historic executive mansion, and added a bathroom. He wanted only the best for Madison.[66]

Walter did not move to the state capital. He and Bob continued to live at Riverbend. John, working in Chicago, came up for weekends. Jim, married since 1925, was living in an apartment in Sheboygan. Walter Sr. made it clear to his sons that their primary obligation was to the company.[67] They visited Madison on occasion, however, and joined their parents elsewhere. In February, for example, Walter and John were with their parents in Wausau, at the home of a wealthy supporter, all engaging in winter sports. The Governor skied for three hours, often tumbling into the snow, and Walter got into a brief snowball fight with his mother. The whole family went skating at a local rink.[68]

In January, Charlotte granted an interview to a reporter, describing her plans for redecorating the executive mansion and her work on a bookplate for Walter which would use symbols of the Kohler family. (On a trip to Austria, she and her husband had traced the family's genealogy 300 years.) She also told of her initial interest in politics, the previous spring, when a friend asked her to organize a district. Walter, she said, had told her that he would like to do something of the same. "It's your duty," Charlotte told her son.[69] This appears to have been the first glimmer of interest by Walter in Wisconsin politics. Pursuing his duty, Walter attended the GOP State Convention in 1929. He would not miss another until 1942, when he went off to war.[70]

In March, 1929, the Governor took Walter and John with him to Washington to participate in the inauguration of Herbert Hoover. They were part of a 300 man delegation of "manufacturers, bankers, and politicians," eager to prove that the state was business-friendly. Delegates wore "Wisconsin" red and white ribbons, and buttons with a picture of the school in Ripon, where the GOP was founded. One hundred cadets from St. John's Military Academy in Delafield were also on hand. A Republican State Senator from Superior who was present called the inauguration "the happiest day of my life."

Walter later remembered riding in a car with his brother on a cold, rainy day during the parade that preceded the swearing-in ceremony. He attended a reception given by President Calvin Coolidge, recalling that "Silent Cal" stood next to the dining room table eating handfuls of salted nuts and responding to the conversation of guests in monosyllables. At the inaugural ball, Walter met a woman who had been married seven times. (Not something one encountered routinely in the Sheboygan area.) He also remembered being with his father when he chatted for five minutes with Hoover after the inaugural ceremony. According to a newspaper report, the new President told Kohler that his election meant the end of the La Follette-Blaine dynasty in Wisconsin. The prediction about the fate of the Progressives would prove overly optimistic.[71]

During 1929, Walter was sent to work in the Kohler Company's Trenton, New Jersey plant. For six months, he lived in Philadelphia, traveling along the eastern seaboard selling his company's products.[72] He no doubt marveled at the stock market crash in late October.

In 1929, 5 percent of the population received 26.1 percent of the nation's income. The Kohlers were in that privileged five percent; they did not, however, speculate in the stock market or suffer immediately from the crash. As economic conditions worsened in November, the golden age of the businessman, the era of endless prosperity touted by Coolidge, Hoover and Walter Sr., seemed headed for disaster. At the height of the good times, an article in the *Ladies Home Journal* by millionaire John J. Raskob had contended that "Everybody Ought to Be Rich," and some 7 or 8 percent of the population got in on the "Hoover bull market." At the close of 1929, the article produced sarcasm and anger rather than optimism.

In the presidential election of 1928, urban voters, largely immigrant and Catholic, first began to be attracted to the Democratic Party. Al Smith, a New Yorker, the grandchild of Irish immigrants, and a foe of prohibition, attracted more votes than any Democrat ever had. He carried the nation's twelve largest cities. Liberal intellectuals were moving to the Democratic Party, and so were many economically frustrated Midwestern farmers. The South was only put off by Smith's Catholicism, and might well be recruited. A major party realignment appeared to be underway even before the stock market crash. Hard times greatly increased the chances of Democrats to overturn the Republican dominance of the 1920s. What would happen in Wisconsin, where Democrats were historically weak, remained anyone's guess, but it was certain that Progressives would make every effort to blame the Governor and his cigar smoking, country club friends for the state's economic woes.

In December, Walter was in Wisconsin, in time to help his family in a medical emergency. Walter Sr. had a kidney stone operation at the Mayo Clinic, in Rochester, Minnesota. He was soon back in Madison, hard at work. On a journey to the northern part of the state, he gave seven speeches and shook thousands of hands in one day, followed by a train delay that kept him up and active into the early hours of the morning.[73] In mid-month, he was forced to return to Mayo, suffering from pain and exhaustion. After a telephone conversation with hospital officials, Walter assured reporters that his father's condition was satisfactory. The Governor spent Christmas at the hospital, and remained there through the first week of January.[74]

On the advice of physicians, Walter Sr. decided to recuperate for a time in Florida, a trendy vacation spot. Walter was told that he was to come along. He was planning another European trip, but as always he acceded to his father's wishes. The Kohlers traveled to an island resort where there was fishing, sailing, swimming, golf, and tennis. Walter said later that the trip intensified his interest in sports. It also was the beginning of his life-long attraction to the Sunshine State.[75]

In late March, 1930, the Governor, feeling fully recovered, announced his candidacy for reelection. His Progressive opponent, it was already clear, would be 33-year-old Phil La Follette, Senator La Follette's brother.[76] A major obstacle in Kohler's reelection bid was a formal charge filed in July, 1929 by Phil La Follette and William T. Evjue of the *Madison Capitol Times* requesting the courts to remove Kohler from office for violating the Corrupt Practices Act in the 1928 election.

The charge had been made earlier: Walter Sr., it was alleged, spent far more money to win the governor's race during the primary than the law allowed. The specifics involved expenses surrounding the guests who had poured into Kohler during the race, company funds used to pay for such items as the Kohler band, and the creation of the Wisconsin State Republican Committee to raise funds, a group not recognized, according to the Progressives, as a GOP committee. The $4,000 limit set by law had clearly been violated, the Progressives argued, and the violations were made with the knowledge and consent of the current Governor of Wisconsin.

Walter Sr.'s secret John Doe testimony had not gone well. The candidate revealed considerable confusion about the exact sources of campaign funds, and seemed to have relied too heavily upon advice given by his company's legal and accounting experts.[77] Still, no action was taken against the Governor. When the July charges were filed, Kohler attorneys decided to attack the constitutionality of the Corrupt Practices Act. A judge in Sheboygan agreed with this argument and struck down the law. The Wisconsin State Supreme Court, however, reversed that decision in early 1930, and the Governor found himself again, in a civil suit, facing the Progressive charge that he was a liar and a cheat and must, by the provisions of the Act, be removed from office.[78] In a press release, the Governor outlined the history of what he said was nothing but persecution by political opponents, and he welcomed a trial.[79]

The case went to trial on April 22, 1930 in the circuit court at the Sheboygan Court House. The arguments lasted three and a half weeks. Walter and other members of the family were present during much of the proceedings to hear the Governor tell the story of his life, describe his concern for his employees over the years, give details about every aspect of his election campaign, and to declare his absolute commitment to integrity, both in business and in politics. The Kohler trial was followed carefully all across the state and even attracted national attention.

The courtroom was packed with spectators and newspaper reporters, many of them sympathetic toward the home town boy who became the region's first Governor and largest employer (more than 4,000 workers with an annual payroll of $6 million a year). The jury deliberated an hour and thirty-four minutes before delivering its unanimous verdict: the defendant was innocent of all charges. Pandemonium broke out in the courtroom. The Governor's three sisters embraced him, as did Walter. Walter Sr. shook the hand of each juror, calling all twelve men by name. Once the cheering died down, Kohler calmly but firmly stated that the entire proceeding was an obnoxious attempt by Progressives to destroy him. (A counteroffensive, launched by Stalwarts at about the same time, attempted to remove three state officers who were Progressives, alleging a number of election law violations. Nothing came of it, either.)[80]

In retrospect, the verdict was justified. A few of Walter Sr.'s explanations about his relationship to campaign activities by family members and employees seem a bit shaky, but it is clear that the candidate, new to politics, had not deliberately violated the law, and that was the premier issue in the case. Moreover, he had no nefarious intent, as Progressives claimed, for seeking the office of Governor. Throughout its two years, the Kohler Administration would be without a trace of scandal.

With his character vindicated, and his popularity high, Walter Sr. quickly resumed his reelection campaign. On May 27, the Governor,

Charlotte, and Walter entered a large banquet room in Sheboygan where a crowd of 600 greeted them with prolonged applause and cheers, while the local high school band played "On Wisconsin." Walter Sr. made a few general remarks about his delight in being present. He did not talk about politics or the recent trial, and he didn't have to. The people of Sheboygan were clearly in his camp. Charlotte invited the ladies to Riverbend on Tuesday to see the grounds and flower gardens.[81]

The Kohler airplane was soon in the air, carrying the Governor throughout the state. In a single day in June, Walter Sr. traveled 400 miles to give three speeches within five hours.[82] The charm, intelligence, energy, and wealth of the Kohlers were again running at full steam.

On August 8, the entire Kohler family was present in a box at the Milwaukee Auditorium to hear the Governor deliver a keynote speech, officially launching his campaign. A capacity crowd of 2,500 people was on hand, and the speech was broadcast on the radio throughout the state. Walter Sr. wore a dark blue suit with his trademark white carnation in his lapel. When he first strode to the flag-draped platform, he acknowledged the thundering applause with a bow and a wave of his straw hat. Being extraordinarily proud of his father, Walter no doubt cheered as loudly as anyone.

In his speech, the Governor drew much attention by calling for the legality of beer and favoring a national referendum on the entire question of prohibition. (In April, 1929, a statewide referendum opposed prohibition two-to-one, and Kohler signed a bill repealing state enforcement of the ban on alcoholic beverages.) While opposing the return of the saloon, often a source of crime and individual tragedy, he declared, "There is no menace to health or morals in the drinking of beer of moderate alcoholic content, and this product in wholesome quality should be available to the farmer, the factory worker and all citizens, its manufacture and sale carried on under positive control." The Governor was especially concerned about the spread of organized crime that was engulfing America and entering Wisconsin because of the 18th amendment.

Walter Sr. described numerous achievements under his administration and rejected the Progressive charge that he was responsible for the depression, calling the allegation "cheap demagoguery." He also denied Progressive reports that he was conspiring with a cartel of banks that would crush independent and local financial institutions.

The Kohler political philosophy, he said, was middle-of-the-road: "There are two menaces to constructive progress, the reactionary who regards the present structure as a finished thing rather than a foundation for future growth, and the radical who would destroy the foundation rather than build upon it."[83] Both Milwaukee newspapers wrote glowing reports of the speech and supported Kohler's reelection.[84]

The Kohler family was slightly more active in the reelection campaign than it had been two years earlier. Walter played an important role in his father's campaign for the first time, handling press releases and working on speeches.[85] He was also present with his father in Racine, where the world-champion Philadelphia Athletics played the Racine All-Stars.[86] Bob, now 22 and a Yale graduate, accompanied his father during an appearance and speech at the Wisconsin State Fair.[87] Herbert drove his half-brother home from Milwaukee following two speeches in September.[88] The whole Kohler family was present at a rally in Sheboygan that same month that attracted 8,000 people and featured a six mile parade route.[89] Charlotte and Walter Sr.'s sisters continued to entertain and educate throngs of tourists who arrived regularly at Kohler.

But the brunt of the labor in the campaign, again, fell on the Governor's shoulders. By mid-September he had flown more than 7,000 miles and given speeches in 58 counties.[90] Giving five and six speeches a day, he estimated that he addressed more than 200,000 people, not counting those who heard him on the radio.[91] Walter later wrote to an official in the Governor's office, "I shall always remember your remarks about the 1930 campaign, that the Governor 'lived on lozenges and throat spray.' It was characteristic of him doggedly to do the job ahead without sparing himself in any way."[92]

The State Republican Chairman, and close Kohler adviser in 1930, was Thomas E. Coleman of Madison. Tom, as he was known by friends, was born in 1893 in Aurora, Illinois. His father was president of the Madison-Kipp corporation in Madison, a company that manufactured die castings and die castings machinery. After graduating from the University of Chicago, Coleman joined the family company as a sales representative. At the death of his father, in 1927, Tom became the company president. He was also the president and director of a Madison bank for many years.

Coleman entered Wisconsin politics in 1928, helping secure Walter Sr.'s election. Both men were industrialists who believed that government should be run like a business, for the benefit of all. And they liked each other. Tom stood next to the Governor in the reception line at the inauguration.

A slim, good-looking gentleman of moderate height, Coleman was especially good at party organization and fund raising. He was a tireless and highly skilled operator and manipulator who knew everyone important and wealthy in the state. He did not welcome opposition to his will; political columnist John Wyngaard called him a 'deadly serious young Republican leader." Tom was also ambitious. In time, he was to become "Boss Coleman," ruler of the GOP in Wisconsin, and a major figure in the political careers of Walter, Joe McCarthy, and scores of others. Staunchly conservative, he was an implacable enemy of the Progressives, and later of GOP moderates.[93]

But no matter how well organized and funded the Kohler campaign was, or how hard the candidate and his supporters labored, the spread of the Great Depression threatened to destroy the reelection bid. Phil La Follette and the Progressives placed the full blame for the economic disaster on Kohler and Hoover, constantly warning of allegedly secretive and powerful plots in high places to exploit the average man.[94]

Between August, 1929 and November, 1930, employment in the state's manufacturing industries fell by almost a fourth. By October, 1930 employers were receiving 178 applications for every 100 job openings. By one account 20,000 unemployed were looking for work in Milwaukee by March, 1930. At about the same time, Milwaukee police arrested a father of six for stealing four loaves of bread from a grocery store.

Wisconsin's gross farm income fell from $438 million in 1929 to $357 million a year later; this at a time when half the state's nearly 3 million people lived in rural areas and a fourth of Wisconsin's work force was engaged in agricultural employment. Milk production was dropping, the value of agricultural real estate was falling, and according to one study, 59 of every 100 Wisconsin farms were mortgaged in the year Kohler ran for re-election.[95]

The Governor dealt with the depression as best he could, calling for optimism, the full use of state construction funds, and lower taxes. (The legislature rejected his attempt to reduce income taxes for people of average means, and he vetoed a Progressive bill that would have increased all income taxes 25%.) Fearing a widespread dependence on the dole system and big government bureaucracies, he encouraged cooperative activities to restore prosperity. He created the Wisconsin Citizens' Committee on Employment, chaired by a distinguished University of

Wisconsin economist, and he asked the secretary of the Wisconsin Manufacturers' Association to conduct a survey on the availability of jobs in the state.[96]

The Governor could also boast that he was doing his best to handle state finances in a responsible way. He and the legislature were able to eliminate a state deficit estimated at $3.5 million and create a surplus in the state's operating funds of $500,000. He could also point to successful efforts to streamline state bureaucracy and to vetoes of pork barrel bills. In short, Kohler had made good on his promise to run the state like a business.[97]

Walter Sr. talked often in campaign speeches about the rights of labor and of the fact that he signed the first state anti-yellow dog contract bill. (Yellow dog contracts prohibited workers from joining a union.) In fact, in his two years in office, Kohler signed some 20 bills sought by labor unions.[98] He boasted that by careful planning, he was able to keep his own employees on the job. "We have increased our payroll 50 times in 25 years. We have paid out $46,000,000 in wages in the last 10 years."[99] He railed at Progressives for offering nothing specific to help working people, and he jeered at his youthful opponent, Phil La Follette, for never having worked with his hands for a living.[100] He told a crowd of workingmen at the Allis-Chalmers Company plant in Milwaukee that he stood ready to do anything that would relieve unemployment, and that no matter what might happen, wages should not be cut. "I want the standard of living in Wisconsin to be better than any other place in the world."[101]

But it was all to no avail. The Depression was too severe, and the vague promises of radical change too appealing. Phil La Follette, who had campaigned furiously and enjoyed the active support of both Progressive United States Senators, won the primary decisively. He would proceed to win 70 percent of the total vote in the general election.[102]

Walter and other family members were at Riverbend on election night, listening to the sad news on the radio. When it became clear that Kohler had lost, a crowd of 3,000 gathered at the recreation hall of the Kohler plant and marched to the governor's home. The Eagles fife and drum corps from Sheboygan led the parade. Girls Scouts presented Mr. and Mrs. Kohler a wreath of flowers and Boy Scouts gave the Governor a scout emblem. The crowd then broke into song, serenading the family that meant so much to the entire region.[103]

In January, there was a second song fest outside Riverbend to celebrate the formal return of the Governor to his home. More than 1,000 people sang "Happy Days Are Here Again."[104] Later in the month, after returning from Governor La Follette's inauguration, the Kohlers gave a party at the lavishly decorated recreation hall for about 1,500 residents of the Village, including dinner and entertainment. The crowd demonstrated its loyalty and friendship by greeting Walter Sr.'s remarks with loud applause.[105]

Peace did not return to the G.O.P. after the primary. The proceedings of the Republican State Convention, held in Madison, revealed the bitter hatred Progressives had for Stalwarts and especially the "reactionary" Governor Kohler. Progressives defeated a minority report lauding the Kohler administration for sound business practices, the new children's code, and other social legislation by a vote of 69 to 38.[106]

Soon after the primary election, with his father's approval and no doubt financial assistance, Walter set off alone on his second European trip, a vacation that had been delayed by campaigning. He drove through France, Germany, and Central Europe. He flew to Greece and wound up in Egypt, enjoying "a month or so of sunshine in Luxor."[107]

Walter apparently returned to the East Coast for a time and then returned to Kohler to continue in sales at the factory. He took a cut in pay in early 1930, from $350 a month to $315, a sign of the increasing impact of the Depression on the company.[108]

In December, 1930 Walter Sr., Charlotte, and Herbert traveled to the East Coast for a week. One stop was the White House for a social call on President Hoover. It was no secret that Hoover had offered Kohler a government position, but Walter Sr. declined, saying that he had too much to do in Wisconsin. The Governor also met with national GOP leaders and attended an annual banquet sponsored by Washington correspondents. The party then traveled to New York.[109]

In late June, 1931, Walter, along with Herbert, John, Evangeline, Marie, and Lillie Kohler, greeted Walter Sr. and Charlotte at the train depot in Milwaukee following the couple's three-week, seven nation tour of Europe. In impromptu remarks to reporters, Walter Sr. told of desperate financial conditions in Germany and urged approval of a proposed war debt moratorium. "How Germany goes, the world will go." He also observed that the Depression had severely limited American tourism in Europe.[110]

In 1932, as the world-wide economic catastrophe deepened, business at the Kohler Company continued to plummet. Walter took three pay cuts between January and April, winding up at $175 a month.[111] Between 1929 and 1932, the average annual income for American workers fell 40%, from $2,300 to $1,500.

By the summer of 1932, some 200,000 Wisconsinites were unemployed, and another 200,000 worked only part-time. The Chevrolet and Fisher Body plants in Janesville announced that they were closing down, putting 1,400 men out of work. Governor La Follette and his Progressive allies in the legislature increased state spending by $20 million, raised taxes, passed the nation's first unemployment compensation act, and frightened many business leaders by promoting public power, public works, and expensive relief programs.[112]

Privately, Walter Sr. was greatly worried that he might have to begin laying people off. For Christmas, 1931, he had been able to give every married man in the factory a dressed goose; single workers received pipes; nine men were given gold watches.[113] Optimism prevailed, at least in public. But only a few months later, Kohler was wrestling with the unthinkable. Supplies were stacked up to record heights, the construction industry was in severe distress, and the company's plumbing industry sales had plunged 89 percent. Work schedules were reduced to three days a week in some areas of the company, and then dropped to a mere eight hours a week. The company was borrowing money to stay afloat.[114]

❧ ❧ ❧ ◉ ❦ ❦ ❦

There was no Stalwart as popular and well-known as Kohler, and in March, 1932 a Kohler for Governor club opened in Milwaukee, intent on persuading the industrialist to re-enter politics.[115] Pressures grew throughout the spring, furthered by concern that Phil La Follete and a pro-La Follette legislature might press for sweeping tax increases. And the Democratic Party seemed to be stirring in the state; some Republicans were even considering running as Democrats.[116]

For months, Walter Sr. resisted these efforts, even after a "draft Kohler" movement started, arguing that his family opposed another political campaign and that he was needed at his company. When the state convention of Stalwarts gave clear indication that it would endorse him, however, he changed his mind and entered the race.[117]

With Charlotte at his side, Walter Sr. launched his campaign in early August before an audience estimated at between 7,000 and 10,000 in Beaver Dam. He excoriated the La Follette administration for extravagant spending, inept handling of the Depression, and corruption. Kohler noted that since he left office farm prices had dropped by one half, bank failures had increased by nearly 25 percent, and the percentage of tax delinquency had doubled. He called for reduced spending, less bureaucracy, lower taxes, and government based on sound business principles. Kohler's audience was enthusiastic, but it was obvious to many, including the La Follettes, that Kohler's solutions to the Depression sounded much like President Hoover's.[118]

Walter and his brother Bob were assigned the duty of accompanying the candidate throughout the state and handing out campaign literature. Throughout the summer, they took turns driving the five-passenger, Wisconsin-made automobile, stopping at hundreds of cities, towns, and villages.[119] The car broke down on one occasion, forcing the candidate to hike a quarter of a mile to a telephone to cancel his talk.[120] After a breakdown in Port Washington, late in the campaign, the candidate and Walter hitch-hiked their way home to Kohler.[121]

One day, the candidate and his sons drove 170 miles, a day in which the candidate delivered three speeches and spoke for four hours.[122] Walter Sr. had to take throat medicine, sleep with an ice pack, and limit his cigar smoking.[123] On another day, the trio drove 160 miles, and Walter Sr. gave five speeches, addressing 4,800 people. In the first two weeks of campaigning, the Kohlers traveled 1,650 miles.[124] On a day in late August, the Kohlers used two cars to drive 320 miles in six hours to begin a day of speech making.[125]

The candidate read newspapers and studied speech materials during these automobile trips. At times, he marveled at the beautiful Wisconsin countryside. "Walter," he would say, "stop a minute." He told a reporter, "I've seen most of the beautiful places all over the world, but we have things in Wisconsin you don't see anywhere else."[126]

The candidate and his sons managed to spend a few campaign weekends at Riverbend. The Kohler Company was never far from the candidate's mind. During a speech in Janesville, Walter Sr. blasted La Follette and other "radicals" for failing to understand basic principles of business. "Radicals claim that under their rule Wisconsin has progressed industrially, but I tell you it has progressed in spite of the radicals. It has progressed," he said, "because of the character of our men and women and because of the management of industry. Radicals cannot understand the friendly relations between management and men in the shop. They cannot understand that there is no class feeling, no class hatred."[127] He told a crowd of 5,000 in Fond du Lac, "When they attack my attitude toward labor I ask you to consider my record as governor and I ask you to come to the village of Kohler and learn from the men there about their relations with me. We are fellow workers at Kohler; we work out our problems together."[128] Haunted by the possibility of layoffs he might himself have to make, Walter Sr. said in South Milwaukee, "Nothing can be more tragic than the plight of the working man who, unable to get a job, first exhausts his savings and eventually is helpless to protect his family from cold and hunger."[129]

In Kenosha, Walter Sr. endorsed relief and public works, but said that the funds devoted to these purposes had to be handled efficiently and be free of political purposes.[130] This tack stemmed from genuine concern by the candidate, but it was also designed to counteract Progressive claims that he was the "millionaire candidate" who cared nothing about the welfare of most Wisconsinites. Moreover, the La Follette administration was dispensing relief at record levels as the election neared. In Milwaukee, Kohler told a crowd of 4,000 that the Progressives should create their own party "instead of masquerading as Republicans."[131]

Kohler's audiences were often large; 12,000 turned out in Madison to cheer the Stalwart candidate and hear him dismiss the *Madison Capital Times* as "a propaganda sheet."[132] A crowd of 18,000 turned out in Sheboygan, their enthusiasm bringing tears to the candidate's eyes.[133] In Milwaukee, at a large Stalwart rally, a young girl sang the Kohler campaign song, "Let's Put Him Back Where He Belongs," distributed across the state by Walter and his brother at campaign stops. The first verse went, "Folks are happy, smiles on their face; Smiles that you or I can't erase; We know what they're smiling about; That's just why they shout." The chorus: "Kohler's the man for Governor; Onward with Kohler and win. Let's put him back, let's put him back, U-RAH-RAH-RAH. On Wisconsin, Kohler has proven tried and true; Honest and fearless and fair; Hip hip hurray, he's on his way; Back to the Governor's chair."[134]

Kolher won the September 20 primary election, taking 57% of the vote. He would again face the Democratic Mayor of Madison Albert G. Schmedeman in the November election. The Stalwarts were over-

joyed; beating a La Follette in Republican Wisconsin was tantamount
to election.[135]

Walter and his brothers spent election night at Riverbend, poring
over the results showing substantial margins of victory for their father.
"Wow," Walter exclaimed, when one precinct reported 25 votes for
Kohler and eight for La Follette. A visitor told him, "It looks like you
drove your dad to the right places on his speaking tour." Walter replied,
"It certainly does!" At the village community hall, some 4,000 people
cheered, paraded, and engaged in a "snake dance" to express their joy.
At 1:15 a.m. the crowd, led by a band from Sheboygan, marched to
Riverbend to cheer the successful candidate and his family.[136]

After a month-long break, Kohler went back on the campaign trail,
for the first time openly endorsing the Hoover Administration. It was
a calculated risk, but one that Walter Sr. was willing to make, for he
greatly admired the President and believed that his policies would restore
the nation's prosperity. His very first public endorsement of the GOP
national ticket drew some boos from a crowd in Appleton. During the
same speech, Kohler called himself "a constructive liberal," expressing
deep concern for the ten or eleven million unemployed in the nation
and agreeing to endorse the 30 hour work week if necessary.[137]

Phil and Robert La Follette, Jr. came out for Democratic candidate
Franklin D. Roosevelt, as did William T. Evjue at the *Madison Capital
Times*. There were growing hints on the campaign trail that voters
throughout Wisconsin were leaning in that direction as well. But Republicans dismissed all such evidence, insisting that there was a public
groundswell for Hoover.[138]

Walter and Bob again traveled with their father during the final push
of the campaign. One day in late October, a storm delayed a scheduled
radio broadcast, and Walter spoke for 15 minutes until his father arrived. A reporter observed, "It was young Kohler's first experience in
making a political speech, but he got away with it."[139]

As the campaign climaxed, doubt crept into the Kohler camp for the
first time. The Democratic candidate for governor, Mayor Schmedeman, was an ineffectual opponent with a weak record; he was the not
the problem. The Kohler decision to back a most unpopular president,
a president who rejected Republican pleas to make an appearance in
Milwaukee before the election, seemed to be doing grave damage. At
an election eve rally in Milwaukee, the turnout for Kohler and Republican senatorial candidate John B. Chapple of Ashland was embarrass-

ingly small. When Walter Sr. said he was for Hoover, loud booing was mingled with the applause. Several hundred got up and walked out after a Chapple harangue against the *Milwaukee Journal* and assorted Reds and atheists. While all G.O.P. candidates were invited to the platform, Kohler was alone on stage during Chapple's talk, which he applauded and claimed to enjoy.[140]

On election day, Schedeman beat Kohler by a vote of 590,114 to 470,805. It was a reflection of the Democratic landslide. Led by Franklin D. Roosevelt, Democrats swept the national elections, taking 22.5 million votes nationally, while Hoover could not quite gain 16 million. FDR carried Wisconsin with a whopping 63.5 percent of the vote. Beside the governorship, Democrats won the senate race, took control of the lower house of the state legislature, and their candidates for lieutenant-governor, attorney general, and state treasurer were also victorious. This in a state that had not voted for a Democratic presidential candidate since 1912, a state in which a Democrat had not held the governorship since 1892, a state in which Democrats had not controlled either house of the state legislature since 1894.

The election of 1932 was a political revolution in Wisconsin. And the La Follettes and many of their Progressive followers were on the winning side, along with the Democrats.[141]

A large and jubilant crowd, gathered at Riverbend to celebrate a Kohler victory, grew increasingly quiet and then sad as the election results poured in over the radio. A participant later recalled a sense of shock that went through the crowd.[142] Walter Sr. was gracious in defeat. He was exhausted and disappointed; this was his last political campaign. He now turned his attention full-time to the effort to save what he could of his company and keep his men employed.

Once the election returns were in, Walter left politics behind him completely. Perhaps, like other members of his family, he was delighted to be free from the rigors and anxieties of campaigning. He was not yet persuaded to run for office himself. Walter's immediate attention was on another matter, known only to family members and close friends. He was making preparations to be married.

Notes

[1] See Richard C. Haney, *A Concise History of the Modern Republican Party of Wisconsin 1925-1975* (Madison: The Republican Party of Wisconsin, 1976), 3-4; Richard C. Haney, "The Rise of Wisconsin's New Democrats: A Political Realignment in the Mid-Twentieth Century," *Wisconsin Magazine of History* 58 (1974-75): 91-92. See also comments by William J. Morgan of Milwaukee from the 1946 GOP State Convention, Republican Party Papers, 97: "…the seeds of disunion sown in that 1926 convention well nigh wrecked the administration of one of the finest men that ever sat in the Governor's chair in the history of the State of Wisconsin."

[2] "While the Clock Strikes the Hour," *The Wisconsin Alumni Magazine*, October, 1928, 12.

[3] Fred C. Sheasby, "Kohler to Run for Governor; Won by 'Draft,'" *Milwaukee Journal*, June 17, 1928.

[4] Editorial, *ibid.*, June 18, 1928.

[5] Fred C. Sheasby, "Slaps by Bob Helping Kohler," *ibid.*, July 20, 1928. Kohler had met with Hoover in May, pledging his full support in the presidential race. But leading Wisconsin Republicans urged Hoover to stay out of the fray between the two factions of the GOP. "Kohler Tells How He Came to Make Race," *ibid.*, June 18, 1928.

[6] "Kohler Voices Political Creed," *ibid.*, June 21, 1928.

[7] "Kohler's Foes Right, He's Not a Politician," *ibid.*, July 19, 1928.

[8] "State a Business, Kohler Tells Club," *ibid.*, July 10, 1928.

[9] "Kohler Promises No Housecleaning," *ibid.*, August 11, 1928.

[10] "Pay, Chief Item, Kohler Explains," *ibid.*, July 20, 1928.

[11] Uphoff, *Kohler on Strike*, 10-13.

[12] E.g., "Mr. Kohler Host to Booster Party," *Milwaukee Journal*, July 12, 1928.

[13] "500 Plan to Visit Kohler Tuesday," *ibid.*, August 6, 1928; "Kohler Chats While He Eats," *ibid.*, August 8, 1928. See "Winnebagoes Invade Kohler, Greet Walter," *ibid.*, August 12, 1928.

[14] "Women in Politics: Invited to Kohler, Work, for Governor," *ibid.*, August 26, 1928.

[15] "Kohler Lauded by Schoenfeld," *ibid.*, August 13, 1928.

[16] "Kohler Schedule for Week Heavy," *ibid.*, August 12, 1928; Walter J. Pfister, "Wisconsin Rivals Seek Office by Air," *New York World*, August 26, 1928. Pfister noted that Governor Fred Zimmerman used an airplane in politics even earlier than Kohler, but not to the extent that Walter, Sr. did.

[17] "Kohler Flies to Reach Places, Not for Stunt," *Milwaukee Journal*, August 30, 1928.

[18] "Kohler Accepts a Pipe but Won't Be Indian," *ibid.*, August 6, 1928. A year later, however, he was made a Chief of the Winnebago Indians at Pittsville,

Wisconsin and wore an Indian war bonnet while posing for photographers. "Governor Kohler," *Kohler of Kohler News*, May, 1940, 25.

[19] On the airplane, see "The 'Spirit of St. Louis' Had a Sister in Kohler," *Sheboygan Press*, May 21, 1977, and Walter Sr.'s testimony in the John Doe hearing of 1928, file 19, box 39, Walter J. Kohler, Sr. papers.

[20] Fred C. Sheasby, "Kohler Meets Issues Firmly," *Milwaukee Journal*, July 28, 1928.

[21] "Kohler's High Hat," *ibid.*, August 6, 1928.

[22] "Threaten Ducking for Kohler Attack," *ibid.*, August 28, 1928.

[23] "Kohler Burns Up Politicians," *ibid.*, August 29, 1928; "Kohler Draws Record Crowd," *ibid.*, August 31, 1928.

[24] "Kelley and Kohler Speakers at Beloit," *ibid.*, August 6, 1928.

[25] "1,500 Hear Kohler's Talk at Appleton," *ibid.*, August 25, 1928.

[26] "Kohler at Slinger Sunday," *ibid.*, August 26, 1928.

[27] "Labor Chief Raps Kohler," *ibid.*, August 8, 1928.

[28] "Kohler Replies to Labor Chief," *ibid.*, August 10, 1928.

[29] "Union Defends Kohler Record," *ibid.*, August 26, 1928.

[30] Fred C. Sheasby, "Kohler Grows as Big Hurdle," *ibid.*, August 20, 1928.

[31] Fred C. Sheasby, "Kohler Talks Like a Winner," *ibid.*, August 21, 1928.

[32] "Kohler Opens Plant to Foes," *ibid.*, August 24, 1908.

[33] "Kohler Names Needs of State," *ibid.*, September 1, 1928; "Kohler Draws Record Crowd," *ibid.*

[34] "Rival Candidates Both Get Crowds," *ibid.*, September 2, 1928.

[35] Fred C. Sheasby, "Workers Used Heads at Polls," *ibid.*, September 7, 1928.

[36] "Business Rule, Kohler Pledge," *ibid.*, September 5, 1928.

[37] "Editors Write of Kohler Vote;" "Kohler Victory Stirs Comment," *ibid.*, September 6, 1928.

[38] "Kohler Is Glad to Rest After His 200 Speeches;" "When News of Victory Came," *ibid.*

[39] "Kohler Offers Business Rule," *ibid.*, September 18, 1928; J. C. Ralston, "Ekern Chosen Over Goodland;" Editorial, "The Primary Humbug," *ibid.*, September 19, 1928.

[40] "Fund Inquiry Called Biased," *ibid.*, October 10, 1928; "Kohler Again Denies 'Slush,'" *ibid.*, October 17, 1928; "Kohler Describes Malicious Attacks," *ibid.*, October 19, 1928.

[41] Fred C. Sheasby, "Political Foes Amuse Kohler," *ibid.*, October 30, 1928.

[42] "Kohler Drive Cost $50,000," *ibid.*, September 6, 1928; "Kohler Barrel Will Be Target," *ibid.*, September 13, 1928.

[43] "Kohler Ordered Before Supreme Court," *ibid.*, October 2, 1928.

[44] Walter, Sr. Campaign file, Terry Kohler papers.

[45] "Kohler, Wapperman Ordered to Inquiry," *ibid.*, October 3, 1928; "Use of Kohler Cash Defended," *ibid.*, October 4, 1928; "Demands Quiz in La Follette Campaign," *ibid.*, October 5, 1928.

[46] "Kohler Wins Petition Fight in High Court," "Row Disrupts Party Parley," *ibid.*, October 9, 1928.

[47] "Defend Kohler in High Court," *ibid.*, October 8, 1928.

[48] "$105,000 Was Kohler's Fund," *ibid.*, October 21, 1928.

[49] "Hoan Challenges Kohler to Debate Expenditures," *ibid.*, October 24, 1928.

[50] "Democrat Hits Kohler Funds," *ibid.*, October 31, 1928.

[51] "Kohler Broke Laws—Ekern," "Call in Books of Kohler Co.," *ibid.*, October 23, 1928.

[52] "Kohler Wants Sweeping Quiz," *ibid.*, November 1, 1928.

[53] "Flier Injured in Plane Meet," *ibid.*, October 22, 1928; "Wisconsin Is Likely to Discover," *ibid.*, January 4, 1929. Walter Sr.'s youngest son, Jim, also became a pilot. Peter Kohler, Jim's son, owns a photograph showing Jim at the controls of a primitive looking little airplane with his proud father standing nearby.

[54] "Dry League Backs Kohler," *ibid.*, October 23, 1928. Wisconsin was largely a wet state; the Germans especially disapproved of prohibition. Kohler remained silent on the issue, and both camps assumed he was on their side.

[55] "764 to 29," *ibid.*, November 7, 1928.

[56] "Kohler Strong in Legislature," *ibid.*

[57] See Paul W. Glad, *The History of Wisconsin: War, Vol. 5, a New Era, and Depression, 1914-1940* (Madison: State Historical Society of Wisconsin, 1990), 320-321.

[58] Fred C. Sheasby, "Kohler Hazing Bout Proposed," *Milwaukee Journal*, December 18, 1928.

[59] "Kohler's Wife Has Great Day," "Frigid Blasts off lake Add Zip to Parade," *ibid.*, January 7, 1929; "Governor Rites Will Go On Air," *ibid.*, January 3, 1929..

[60] "Broom Sent Kohler for Cleanup," *ibid*, January 6, 1929.

[61] J. C. Ralston, "First message to Legislature Recites Needs," *ibid.*, January 10, 1929.

[62] On Kohler and women, see "Business Women Win High Tribute From Gov. Kohler," *ibid.*, March 14, 1929. For a strong statement on conservation, see "Kohler Sets Week for 'Conservation,'" *ibid.*, April 6, 1929. On Kohler's Herculean work habits, see "Governor Confers Over Office Lunch With Lawmakers," *ibid.*, February 7, 1929, and Sheasby, "Kohler Setting Pace for Aides," *ibid.*, February 10, 1929.

[63] "Long Struggle on Liquor Law Finally Ended," *ibid.*, May 29, 1929; "Plain Ginger Ale is as Strong as Kohler Will Go," *ibid.*, March 5, 1929.

[64] Blodgett, *A Sense of Higher Design*, 82.

[65] John F. Sinclair, "No Tax Penalty in State," *Milwaukee Journal*, August 15, 1929.

[66] "Reverts," *ibid.*, July 3, 1929.

[67] "Richard S. Davis, "Governorship Is First Kohler Political Job," *ibid.*, November 9, 1950.

[68] "Kohler Enjoys Frolic in Snow," *ibid.*, February 11, 1929.

[69] "Home in Madison Gets Mrs. Kohler's Attention," *ibid.*, January 9, 1929.

[70] Walter Kohler interview, Oral History Research office, Columbia University, 1971, 2.

[71] "Kohler Heads Parade Again," *Milwaukee Journal*, January 15, 1953. See box 37, folder 4, Walter J. Kohler, Sr. papers for correspondence surrounding the presidential inauguration.

[72] *Decennial Record of the Class of 1925, Yale College*, in the Yale University Archives; Steinberg, "Is This the Man to Beat McCarthy?" 77.

[73] "Moses Kohler Finds Need for Fast Roads," *Milwaukee Journal*, December 8, 1929.

[74] "Kohler is Patient at Mayo Hospital," *ibid.*, December 19, 1929; "Governor at Clinic for Periodic Visit," *ibid.*, December 20, 1920; "Governor Enjoys Dinner of Turkey," *ibid.*, December 26, 1929; "Kohler is Gaining Steadily, Bulletin," *ibid*, December 30, 1929. For primary sources on the hospitalization, see folder 2, box 6, Walter J. Kohler, Sr. papers.

[75] Davis, "Governorship is First Kohler political Job," *Milwaukee Journal*, November 9, 1950.

[76] "Kohler to Run if Endorsed," *ibid.*, March 29, 1930.

[77] A copy of the testimony is in file 19, box 39 of the Walter J. Kohler, Sr. papers.

[78] State of Wisconsin, In Supreme Court, January Term, 1930, State Ex Rel. La Follette and others, Appellants, vs. Kohler, Respondent, December 7, 1929-February 4, 1930, *passim*.

[79] Copy, press release of February 18, 1930, folder 19, box 30, Walter J. Kohler, Sr. papers.

[80] "Governor Kohler on the Stand," *Milwaukee Journal*, May 13, 1930; "Jury Finds for Governor W. J. Kohler," *Sheboygan Press*, May 15, 1930; "3 La Follette State Officials Facing Removal," *Chicago Daily Tribune*, February 27, 1930. See Donald Young, ed., *Adventures in Politics, The Memoirs of Philip La Follette* (New York: Holt, Rinehart, and Winston, 1970), 125-128; Patrick Maney, *Young Bob, A Biography of Robert M. La Follette, Jr.* (Madison: Wisconsin Historical Society Press, 2d ed., 2003), 72-73.

[81] "Kohler Cheered at Lion Parley," *Milwaukee Journal*, May 27, 1930.

[82] "Kohler Keeps Distant Dates," *ibid.*, June 14, 1930.

83 See press release, "Opening Campaign Address by Governor Walter J. Kohler, Milwaukee Auditorium, Monday Evening, August 11, 1930, 8:00 p.m.," Terry Kohler papers, and the account by Fred C. Sheasby in the *Milwaukee Journal*, August 12, 1930.

84 "…any thinking man or woman, we believe, will find in it compelling reasons for retaining Mr. Kohler in the high office which he has filled with such ability and distinction." Editorial, "Gov. Kohler's Address," *ibid.*, August 12, 1930.

85 See Don Anderson to Walter Kohler, Jr., August 21, 1930, Walter J. Kohler, Sr. Campaign file, Terry Kohler papers.

86 On March 29, 1951, the *Racine Journal Times* ran a photograph taken on September 15, 1930 of the Governor and his son at Horlick Athletic field.

87 "Fair Crowds Hear Kohler," *Milwaukee Journal*, August 27, 1930.

88 "Kohler Talks to Two Crowds," *ibid.*, September 13, 1930.

89 "Torches Flare at Kohler Rally," *ibid.*, September 7, 1930.

90 "Kohler Talks to Two Crowds," *ibid.*, September 13, 1930.

91 Fred C. Sheasby, "Throngs Grasp Kohler's Hand," *ibid.*, September 11, 1930.

92 Copy, Walter J. Kohler, Jr. to Arthur Tiller, April 30, 1940, Condolence file, Terry Kohler papers. See "Heckler Fails to Jar Kohler," *Milwaukee Journal*, September 9, 1930.

93 See the biography in the Thomas Emmet Coleman papers, prepared by archivists at the Wisconsin Historical Society. See also Robert H. Fleming, "Top GOP Job for Coleman?," *Milwaukee Journal*, October 17, 1951, and William F. Thompson, *The History of Wisconsin, Volume VI, Continuity and Change, 1940-1965* (Madison: State Historical Society of Wisconsin, 1988), 414-415.

94 See Glad, *The History of Wisconsin, Volume V*, 323. Progressive campaign literature may be sampled in the Walter J. Kohler, Sr. Campaign file, Terry Kohler papers.

95 Glad, *The History of Wisconsin, Volume V*, 356-363.

96 *Ibid.*, 377; "Governor's Talk Covers Unemployment, Chain Banks," *Milwaukee Journal*, August 12, 1930; editorial, "Kohler Talks Right Out," *ibid.*, August 12, 1930.

97 "Kohler Links Foe to Ring," *ibid.*, November 2, 1932. Cf. Blodgett, *A Sense of Higher Design*, 81.

98 *Ibid.*, 82; "Kohler Recalls Labor Record," *Milwaukee Journal*, September 9, 1932.

99 "Big Crowds Hear Kohler," *ibid.*, September 6, 1930.

100 "Kohler Warns of Family Rule," *ibid.*, September 5, 1930.

101 "Kohler Tells Labor Record," *ibid.*, September 9, 1930.

[102] See Glad, *The History of Wisconsin, Volume V*, 323, 325, 334.

[103] "Governor is Serenaded by Kohler Home Folks," *Milwaukee Journal*, September 17, 1930.

[104] "Kohler, Home Again, Looks to Happy days," *ibid.*, January 6, 1931.

[105] "Kohlers Host to 1,500 at Homecoming Feast," *ibid.*, January 25, 1931.

[106] "Minutes of the Republican State Convention Held in the Assembly chamber in the State Capitol in the City of Madison, Wisconsin, on Tuesday, September 30, 1930, Box 13, Republican Party papers.

[107] *Dicennial Record of the Class of 1925, Yale College.* Walter's French driver's license is in the Leslie Kohler Hawley collection.

[108] Walter J. Kohler, Jr. employment record, Kohler Company archives.

[109] "Kohlers Call On Hoover At White House," *Sheboygan Press*, December 13, 1930.

[110] "Kohler Here After Voyage," *Milwaukee Journal*, June 25, 1931.

[111] Walter J. Kohler, Jr. employment record, Kohler Company archives.

[112] Glad, *The History of Wisconsin, Volume V*, 380-397.

[113] "Kohler Workers Get Gifts," *Milwaukee Journal*, December 23, 1931.

[114] Blodgett, *A Sense of Higher Design*, 87; "Kohler Favors Shorter Hours," *Milwaukee Journal*, February 19, 1931.

[115] "Kohler Boosters Open Clubroom," *ibid.*, March 11, 1932.

[116] "Good Support Awaits Kohler," *ibid.*, April 18, 1932.

[117] "Kohler Is Told of Endorsement," *ibid.*, June 12, 1932.

[118] The full speech is in "Kohler Opens Fighting Campaign," a campaign flyer in the Terry Kohler papers. See also Fred C. Sheasby, "Kohler Opens his Campaign in Fiery Style," *Milwaukee Journal*, August 9, 1932.

[119] "Kohler Takes Advice of Coolidge on Fairs," *ibid.*, August 10, 1932. It seems likely that friendly *Milwaukee Journal* reporter Fred C. Sheasby traveled much or part of the time with the Kohlers in their automobile. His newspaper endorsed the candidate.

[120] Fred C. Sheasby, "Kohler Picks 'Tough Spots,'" *ibid.*, August 21, 1932.

[121] "Kohler Hitch-Hikes Back to Home City," *ibid.*, September 19, 1932.

[122] Fred C. Sheasby, "Kohler Draws Large Crowds," *ibid.*, August 11, 1932.

[123] Fred C. Sheasby, "More Co-ops, Kohler urges," *ibid.*, August 12, 1932.

[124] Fred C. Sheasby, "Thousands out to Hear Kohler," *ibid.*, August 20, 1932.

[125] Fred C. Sheasby, "Kohler Attacks State Fund Use," *ibid.*, August 24, 1932.

[126] Fred C. Sheasby, "Kohler Is Now Real Politician," *ibid.*, August 14, 1932.

[127] Fred C. Sheasby, "Kohler Pounds Gov. La Follette," *ibid.*, August 16, 1932.

[128] Fred C. Sheasby, "Kohler Recalls Labor Record, *ibid.*, September 9, 1932.

[129] Fred C. Sheasby, "'Ghost' tactics Rouse Kohler," *ibid.*, September 18, 1932.

[130] Fred C. Sheasby, "Kohler Pledges Aid for Needy," *ibid.*, September 14, 1932.

[131] Fred C. Sheasby, "4,000 Cheer Kohler Here," *ibid.*, September 15, 1932.

[132] Fred C. Sheasby, "12,000 Cheer Kohler in Madison Stadium," *ibid.*, September 8, 1932.

[133] Fred C. Sheasby, "Great Crowd Greets Kohler," *ibid.*, September 11, 1932.

[134] Fred C. Sheasby, "Kohler, La Follete Talks Stress Issue of Economy," *ibid.*, September 17, 1932. The words and music of the campaign song were by Eric Karl of Milwaukee. Copies can be found in the Terry Kohler papers and in the Mary Kohler Ahern papers. Henry A. Mass also composed a band march called "Walter J. Kohler For Governor" which is in the Terry Kohler papers.

[135] Glad, *The History of Wisconsin, Volume V*, 336, 401.

[136] "Villagers Up All Night to Congratulate Kohler," *Milwaukee Journal*, September 21, 1932.

[137] Fred C. Sheasby, "Kohler Urges Hoover Vote in Final Drive," *ibid.*, October 20, 1932. On the Hoover endorsement, see Fred C. Sheasby, "Kohler to Keep Own Platform," *ibid.*, September 22, 1932.

[138] Fred C. Sheasby, "Kohler Flays Foe's Record," *ibid.*, October 27, 1932; Fred C. Sheasby, "Kohler Attacks Madison Ring," *ibid.*, October 28, 1921; Fred C. Sheasby, "Kohler Talks Relief Plans," *ibid.*, October 30, 1932.

[139] Fred C. Sheasby, "Cheese Plank Called Illegal," *ibid.*, October 26, 1932.

[140] "Leaders Talk at G.O.P. Rally," *ibid.*, November 5, 1932.

[141] See Glad, *The History of Wisconsin, Volume V*, 399-404

[142] Walter J. Vollrath, Jr. interview.

Chapter Four
Romance & Rebellion

Walter enjoyed the social life of the wealthy; the dinner parties, the balls, the exclusive private clubs, the most fashionable nightclubs. To one degree or another, all four Kohler brothers became involved in high society. A son later described Bob as something of a playboy in his youth, a pleasant, agreeable man of shallow tastes and minor intellectual interests who would have enjoyed remaining a playboy for the rest of his life.[1] A daughter later described young John as "a gay blade, with his big car and white suit."[2] Three of the four married society women from highly prosperous families.

As in most matters, Walter was the leader, setting the pattern of style and comportment that his brothers emulated. Good looking, wealthy, well-dressed, socially adept, roaring about in expensive automobiles, Walter and Bob especially were no doubt dashing figures in the eyes of a large number of the women who encountered them during the Roaring Twenties and the early years of the Depression. Walter once made a pass at the beautiful young woman his brother John was courting, and she slapped him for his effort. The young woman later told her daughters that Walter had been a flirt and a ladies' man.[3] But there is no evidence suggesting that his youthful conduct was unusual or unseemly. He resembled his father too closely to be more than casually frivolous and flirtatious.

At some point, probably as a teenager, Walter met Celeste Holden. (Celeste used to brag that all three of her husbands were present at her coming-out, which would have taken place in Chicago about 1918.)[4] In the late 1920s, she was an attractive, intelligent, sophisticated, and outgoing socialite. Four years older than Walter, she was estranged from her husband and had a daughter. One Kohler family story has it that Walter fell deeply in love with Celeste, pursued her diligently, and was greeted at first with a lukewarm response.[5]

She was born Marie Celeste McVoy in Chicago in 1900. Her father, Eugene Joseph McVoy, headed the McVoy Sheet and Tin Plate Company in Chicago, a firm founded by his father that had brought considerable wealth to the family. A daughter later described Eugene as a handsome, generous bon vivant, eager to gamble and womanize. Celeste's mother was the former Pauline Celeste Aymond, a beautiful, emotionally cold, and severely neurotic woman from Missouri who was "socially obsessed," in the words of a daughter, and proud of her French ancestry. She would bear four children: Marie Celeste, Corinne, Jean Dor, and Eugene. An impersonal mother, Pauline Celeste left the children largely in the hands of nannies during their formative years.

The McVoys were of Irish descent and Roman Catholic. All four children were sent to Catholic schools. But it was their wealth that principally defined the McVoys. The whole family was often in Europe, especially in Paris and Italy. The children learned to speak French and were exposed to the finest cultural exhibits and events. Corinne, a talented artist, attended the Sorbonne, but did not graduate. In Chicago, the McVoys lived in stately mansions on fashionable Sheridan Road and Lake Shore Drive, enjoying constant parties and social gatherings with their wealthy and worldly peers. A son of Corinne's would later label the social life of the McVoys "The Great Gatsby."[6]

Celeste attended the Convent of the Sacred Heart in Chicago. She, along with her brother and sisters, seemed to shed their Catholic faith as quickly as they graduated. Aside from their father's generosity toward Catholic charities, Catholicism was at best a formality to the McVoy family; Mrs. McVoy never attended Mass, and her husband snored through the services. Bitter quarrels between their parents, and their father's wandering eye toward the ladies, did not help the children's spiritual growth. And their experiences in Catholic schools seem to have been counterproductive. Celeste was wholly secular from an early age.[7] She apparently graduated from high school at Briarcliff School, a public institution on Lake Avenue.[8]

It was common at the time to send wealthy young women to finishing school rather than college. There they would be prepared for society rather than given the sort of rigorous education their brothers might receive. Jean Dor, Celeste's sister, later said of her own experience, "I realize now, as the teachers later did too, that I should have taken college-slated studies, but this was a finishing school for girls not interested in higher math or science or more education."[9]

Celeste attended Miss Spence's School in New York City, graduating in 1920 in a class of 41. Her yearbook declared, "She dresses divinely, and dances quite finely. There's naught she can't do. And she's pretty too!"

In the class prophecy, she was described as "anti-everything—Especially joy." She was captain of the basketball team, headed "Spence Publications," and placed second in the senior class vote for "Most Attractive."[10] Her son would later describe Celeste as "very well read" and "extremely intelligent—a match for any man."[11]

Celeste was, or quickly became, a flapper, a "new woman" of the 1920s. She and millions like her, especially in the nation's largest cities, expressed their liberation from traditional female morality and social relations with bobbed hair, short skirts, silk stockings, gaudy cosmetics, cigarettes, liquor, racy and cynical conversation, daring dancing, and a relaxed attitude toward sexuality. Noble womanhood, as it had been defined in the Gilded Age, including the corset and heavy clothing, the stern sense of personal and public morality, the centrality of the home and family, the willingness to endure self-sacrifice in marriage, was a thing of the past to what one historian has described as the "giddy flapper, rouged and clipped, careening in a drunken stupor to the lewd strains of a jazz quartet."[12]

After graduation, Celeste came home and joined the family at Pentwater, the large family summer home built on eight acres in 1918. Located 15 miles south of Ludington, Michigan, Pentwater was (and is) on Lake Michigan and provided ample opportunities for boating, swimming, hiking, and horseback riding. At times, family members and guests also engaged in sometimes wild and dangerous conduct, drinking, partying, and romancing. In her autobiography, Jean Dor recalled several examples of her own escapades.[13]

Society friends poured into Pentwater during the summer. In 1921, Celeste hosted a large house party, having the woods decorated with Japanese lanterns and taking guests aquaplaning in her large motor boat on nearby Pentwater Lake. On one trip out with some Canadian friends, a rope caught in the propeller and sank the boat. The Coast Guard rescued the group, but some of the guests—who could not swim—lost jewelry they had worn while clinging to life cushions. Locals dived for years in the hope of finding the valuables.[14]

At some point, perhaps several years earlier in the swirl of Chicago's high society, Celeste met Edward W. J. (Jack) Holden, a wealthy Toronto railroad official's son. The couple was married in 1922 in Canada. They were living in Toronto when their daughter Jacquelin Minerva (Jackie) was born in 1924.[15] Soon afterward, the marriage failed. Holden was an alcoholic who often physically abused his wife.[16] Celeste moved back to

Chicago and occupied the fourth floor of the McVoy mansion. There were seven or eight servants at the time, and Jean Dor later recalled the long and detailed list of duties Celeste posted for each servant. Organized and aggressive, the young woman was running the house.[17]

Tim Gorham, who knew Celeste most of her life, said that she was "dynamic, educated, well-read, and well spoken." She would walk into a room like Katherine Hepburn, and all eyes would turn to her.[18]

Tim's wife, Barbara Gorham, met Celeste later in her life and was greatly impressed. She recalls that Celeste was very attractive, always well-dressed, often rather quiet, and at all times intimidating. She spoke with "an upper class accent," could make "cutting remarks," and was "something of a snob." She seemed to plan events to focus on herself, Gorham thought. She remembers seeing Celeste enter a room, tossing a long scarf over her shoulder with much dramatic effect.[19]

Celeste's son would later say of her, "She had an inner toughness."[20] A granddaughter would recall, "She was vivacious. She loved life."[21]

Celeste tried for several years to get a divorce, but English law in Canadian courts prolonged the case and required Jackie to remain for a time on English soil. Before she was five years old, Jackie was sent to the ultra-progressive Bertrand Russell School to live, ride her pony, and study. One day, on a vacation in France, Jackie began screaming on a city street, "I don't believe in God… There is no God." She had learned that lesson well at her fashionable English school. Brilliant, neglected, and spoiled outrageously, Jackie was to be a problem for many family members and others for the rest of her life.[22]

In the fall of 1929, Jean Dor visited Celeste and her father in New York. They were preparing for a trip to Egypt. Pauline Celeste had thrown her husband out of the house, even though he was recovering from a heart attack, for allegedly having a nurse read him the Anita Loos novel *Gentleman Prefer Blondes*. Eugene did not expect to survive his trip to Egypt, but he went in any case. A photograph shows Celeste riding a camel, her father nearby, with the Sphinx in the background.

Eugene died of a heart attack in Cairo at age 56. The funeral was held a month later in Chicago. His widow, while driving in a limousine to the cemetery, seemed largely interested in trivia about those who attended. In 1931, she married an Italian gigolo, Fortunato Jerace, one of three handsome young men who escorted her around Rome during a stay there to recover from cancer. Jerace, an architect, was only three years older than Celeste. He lived under the total control of his demanding and wealthy wife until her death in 1939. (Thereafter he wooed, won, and married his own daughter-in-law.)[23]

In the summer of 1930, Celeste vacationed in France with friends and her younger sister, Jean Dor. After partying in Paris and visiting Chartres, Celeste settled down in a rented villa in Normandy with Jackie, an English nurse, a cook, and a maid. Jean Dor was given a fake wedding ring so that she could accompany Celeste and friends to the local casino to gamble. One night Celeste distributed hashish and liquor to her guests. She had smuggled the hashish out of Morocco in her Chrysler coupe convertible.

On another evening, after smoking hashish with Celeste, Jean Dor brought up the subject of their difficult mother, and broke into tears. Celeste advised Jean Dor to treat Pauline Celeste the way you would a cat, as she did: let her come and go as she pleased and pay no attention to her. When Jack McVoy, a cousin, visited the villa, he, Celeste, and Jean Dor swam nude in the Atlantic and chased fireflies on the beach.[24]

In 1931, Celeste was in New York. She rented an apartment on the East River. Six-year-old Jackie was in a school some miles away up the Hudson. A nearby day school had rejected her application because she was too radical. Jean Dor was in a local finishing school.

It was here, in 1931, that Jean Dor first met Walter Kohler. By this time, Celeste and Walter were planning to be married. Jean Dor said later that the two had known each other for some years, a recollection that confirms Celeste's later comment about her husbands being present at her coming-out.[25] Celeste was studying composition at the Julliard School of Music while she waited for her divorce to become final. At about the same time, Jean Dor also met Bob Kohler, who was courting his future wife, Margaret (Peggy) Brewster Taylor.[26]

Celeste and her sister attended concerts, lectures, and plays, and visited museums and galleries. Jean Dor said later that Celeste gave her a solid appreciation of art. Artist friends of Celeste's dropped by the apartment on occasion. One, a St. Louis relative, was an alcoholic who drank so much that Celeste and Jean Dor left her unconscious on a window seat. She urinated on one of Jean Dor's books. Not long afterward, the woman committed suicide.[27]

Walter, referred to as "K" at the time, visited Celeste in New York on several occasions. Jean Dor remembered the three of them enjoying George Gershwin's musical "Of Thee I Sing."[28]

The divorce from Holden finally came through in August, 1932, while Walter was campaigning with his father.[29] Arrangements were made for the wedding to take place in November, after the election. Walter purchased a home at 605 West Park Lane in Kohler, becoming a resident of Kohler Village.[30] He chose an attractive, two-story house, painted white, constructed a few years earlier on a corner across from Ravine Park in an area of equally attractive and middle class homes. It was the most modest residence Celeste had ever called home, but there was room upstairs for one or two live-in servants.[31]

Walter's monthly salary was only $228, and his official title at the company was Milwaukee Heating Salesman. But Walter could count on family financial resources to provide Celeste with the style of life she had long enjoyed. By this time he and his brothers had no doubt been given preferred stock in the Kohler Company, which meant not only a sizable improvement in their net worth but an annual subsidy of considerable size to augment their salaries. Celeste knew well that she was marrying into the Kohler fortune. Indeed, given his talent, charm, and drive, Walter might well one day hold the reins of the entire company.[32] But Celeste was no gold digger. Though her family had lost a lot of money in the stock market crash, she and her siblings still enjoyed ample wealth.[33] Eugene McVoy, Celeste's brother, never had to work a day in his life.[34]

On Saturday, November 12, John Kohler gave a large dinner party in honor of Walter and Celeste and of his own fiancée, Julia Lilly House of Evansville, Indiana. On the Sunday before the wedding, 200 guests attended a pre-nuptial party. The wedding took place on November 14 in what the newspapers called "the Jerace home" on Lakeshore Drive in Chicago. A minister, probably an Episcopalian, conducted the service. Only immediate members of the family were present, including Walter Sr. and Charlotte, and Charlotte's sister, Mrs. Matthew W. Berriman, along with Celeste's mother, step-father, and siblings. John was Walter's best man, and Celeste's brother-in-law, attorney Sidney Gorham, Jr., gave away the bride. Celeste was dressed in a blue velvet gown with a high collar and low neckline. In the wedding photograph of the seated couple that appeared in a Milwaukee newspaper, Walter, in dark blue jacket with carnation and pinstripe trousers, is smiling and gazing lovingly at his bride. Celeste, with only a suggestion of a smile, is looking straight into the camera.[35]

The newlyweds went to Mexico for their honeymoon. Walter said later that during the motor trip they "loafed" for six weeks.[36] The couple returned in time for the annual Christmas celebration at Riverbend. The *Sheboygan Press* published a large photograph of Celeste, taken several years earlier, declaring that "a charming new matron" would soon be welcomed by Sheboygan and Kohler society.[37] That may not have excited a woman who had known Paris and New York.

Jackie lived with Walter and Celeste for a time, attending a local Catholic school. When that didn't work out, for no doubt predictable reasons, she was sent to the Ethel Walker School in Farmington, Connecticut. Her mother and step-father saw her largely during the summers at Pentwater.[38]

In 1933, Jean Dor, Celeste's younger sister, became pregnant, and she turned to Celeste for help. The new Mrs. Kohler quietly arranged an abortion, conducted by a Sheboygan physician while he and Jean Dor were on a date. It was the second abortion for the 19-year-old.[39]

That same year, Celeste became pregnant herself. Both she and Walter were no doubt eager for an heir to carry on the Kohler name. On May 14 of the following year, Celeste gave birth to a healthy baby boy they named Terry Jodok. A large number of family photographs show Walter enjoying the company of his infant son.[40]

✦✦✦✦✦✦✦

By 1934, all four of the Kohler brothers were married and working for the company. Three lived in the area of the plant and John lived in Glencoe, Illinois and worked in Chicago. Jim had been the first of the four to marry. His bride was Dorothy Lorraine Dings. She was born in La Porte City, Iowa in 1904, the daughter of a hardware store owner, Peter Conrad Dings, who invested in oil and through much effort became a wealthy banker. In time, he and his family moved to Chicago. His wife, Alice, died when Dorothy was 13. A few years later, Walter Sr. met Dings in Chicago and invited him to visit Riverbend. He brought Dorothy along, and there she met Jim, a student at MIT. They married in 1925, when Jim was 20 years old.

Dorothy, whom a granddaughter later called "a pampered only child," attended Ferry Hall in Lake Forest, Illinois, and Pine Manor in Wellesley, Massachusetts. She also studied abroad. In the words of a daughter-in-law who knew her well, Dorothy was "a woman of the future," being intelligent, bold, active, and outspoken. She was a glider pilot (as was her husband), an expert rifle and pistol shooter, and a GOP activist who often went to party meetings, locally and nationally, on her own. As was the custom of the Kohler women, she let nannies, in large part, raise her children. Her aversion to cooking was such, that her husband acted as family chef.[41]

The couple's first child, Carl J. (Jim) Kohler, Jr., was born in 1926, while Jim was finishing his degree at MIT. Three other sons would follow: Conrad (Connie), Walter III (Wally), and Peter. All would go to Andover and would follow their father into areas of science after college.[42] (The young women in the Kohler families would often attend Abbott Academy, across the street from Phillips Andover, and then proceed to a distinguished college or university.)[43]

"Jimmy," as he was affectionately known, was quiet and friendly, largely devoted to his scientific work. He would hold seven patents during his many years with the Kohler Company. But he also found time to be highly active in community affairs and politics. He would become known as "Mr. Republican" in the Sheboygan area, and Dorothy would be an ardent supporter of Joe McCarthy. His son Peter later remembered his father for his "absolute integrity" and loveable nature.[44]

John Kohler married Julia Lilly (Julilly) House in 1933 in Evansville, Indiana, the bride's home town. Julilly was not a society woman. She was born in Cincinnati, and her family, of modest means, had its roots in Kentucky. Her father died young, and she was an only child. Still, she was able to raise enough funds to graduate from Wellesley, where she majored in French. During the Depression she was forced to be a sales clerk at Marshall Fields Department Store in Chicago, where John met her. She later told a daughter that some members of the Kohler family looked down on her because of her Kentucky origins. (Her mother, proud of her roots, had her birthplace in Morganfield, Kentucky carved on her tombstone at the Kohler cemetery.)

Julilly was brilliant, creative, outspoken, and charming. Well-read, she could carry on an intelligent conversation with anyone. Julilly loved parties and dominated them by the radiance of her good looks, energetic conversation, and strong will. A son later called her "an amazing woman" and "a driving woman, very focused." Mike Weber, who knew Julilly when he was a youngster, described her as "sparkling." Julilly would become an expert on plants and flowers and write ten children's books.[45] She was also to become a civic leader. After her marriage, she was the Kohler family's only political liberal. She was also the family's most serious Christian, being a devout Methodist.

So luminous was his wife, that John usually faded into the background at social events and was thought by some, despite his university degree, to be a bit dull and timid. But this was a misleading view of Walter's brother, who was the branch manager of the Kohler Company in Chicago at the time of his marriage. A daughter remembers him as "very smart, and an original thinker." Another calls him "a lovely, sweet man." A son remembers him as a quiet, intelligent, gentle man of complete integrity.[46]

The couple's four children—John Michael, Jr. (Michael), William (Collins), Julilly, and Marie—would all be attractive, highly educated, and accomplished. (Collins, however, has suffered from schizophrenia much of his life.)[47]

Margaret "Peggy" Brewster Taylor met Bob Kohler in Bermuda, and they were married in New York in 1933. She was born in Brooklyn in 1908 and raised in New Jersey. A son later described her roots as "Brooklyn bourgeois" rather than upper class. Her father was a wealthy civil engineer and inventor who invested well and got out of the stock market before the crash.

Peggy was a graduate of Smith, where she majored in Dutch and Flemish art. Beautiful and intelligent, she was more intellectual than her husband, loved opera, and enjoyed visiting museums. Peggy had a better sense of humor than Bob, and was even more extroverted. She enjoyed golf and in later years would play with Walter and his wife.

A daughter later recalled a family story of action in a fashionable New York nightclub, "21," on the evening before her parents' wedding. Walter was there with Robert and his fiancé. When a drunk began harassing Walter, knocking off his hat and stepping on it, Bob intervened, getting socked in the face for his bravery. He showed up at the church the next day with two black eyes. His bride, who had tried to prevent the fight, was furious.[48]

After their wedding, Bob and Peggy moved to West Park Lane, two doors away from the Walter Kohlers. At first, having enjoyed the culture of metropolitan New York, Peggy had a difficult time living in tiny Kohler. She slowly adjusted, but a son recalled that his mother never felt she had realized her potential.[49]

Bob and Peggy would have a son, Robert, Jr., and two daughters, Victoria (Vicki) and Gillian (Jill). All rivaled their cousins in high intelligence and good looks. Vicki and Jill would attend Smith, and Robert, after Yale and Harvard, was to become a distinguished historian of science at the University of Pennsylvania.

Three of the four Kohler marriages lasted until death intervened. Walter's divorce, as we shall see, was not something he desired. (The children of these marriages, however, would experience numerous divorces, as would their own children.)

The Kohler wives were never close friends, even in the small community in which they lived. But then their husbands were not that close either. At family gatherings, which included Walter's half brother Herbert (who would marry in 1937), one could sense a measure of competitiveness and a slight aloofness that, while it was not disruptive and was often well concealed, kept a distance between brothers, wives, and children.[50] But in the early 1930s, with Walter Sr. still at the helm of the company and his half brother and four sons working their way up in the factory, the family pulled together to retain their economic prosperity. The difficulties were formidable.

❖❖❖◆❖❖❖

Despite a whirlwind of activity by the President and Congress, in 1934 the Great Depression still had America firmly in its grip. The New Deal had devised new and expensive ways to put people to work; Harry Hopkins, head of the Civil Works Administration had spent about a billion dollars in less than five months to give people jobs and salaries. But at least 9 million men and women remained unemployed, and hundreds of thousands suffered from severe poverty.

As the country struggled with want and despair, increasing numbers of Americans turned to the Democratic Party for help. The elections of 1934 nearly destroyed the GOP as a national political force. Forty one of the 48 states elected Democratic Governors. Democrats led in the House 322 to 103, and in the Senate 69 to 37. Voters wanted change, and the party of Herbert Hoover, despondent and without effective leadership, seemed to be blocking the way.

In Wisconsin, the Progressive wing of the GOP, unwilling to join the state's deeply conservative Democratic Party, struck out on its own in 1934, creating the patchwork Progressive Party. The La Follettes promised voters to work with the President for dramatic change. They were soon to control the state.

Rural Wisconsinites continued to suffer greatly from falling prices and drought. In 1930, only 16% of homes had indoor plumbing, only 8% had bathrooms, and only 26 % had electricity. Wisconsin farms lost 40,000 people during the 1930s. Those in Wisconsin cities were hurting too. The value of manufacturing in the state fell by two-thirds between 1929 and 1933. The number of industrial jobs plummeted from 370,000 in 1929 to 232,000 in 1932. Wage payments fell almost 60%.

In 1934, Sheboygan was a city of 40,000. Largely Germanic, its streets were clean and its houses well-kept. It was an industrial town, largely unorganized by labor unions, proud of its independence, thrift, and commitment to hard work. The Depression, as it continued, squeezed workers and their families economically in a way they had never experienced. Layoffs and reduced hours became commonplace in industries that made furniture, toys, machines, shoes, and enamel ware, and many laborers found themselves depending on relief to sustain themselves and their families. Misery was compounded by shame.

With the construction industry in collapse, the Kohler company, the area's largest employer, lost over two million dollars in the first four years of the Depression. Walter Sr. made every effort to economize and increase sales. He stockpiled products and even had products destroyed to keep men employed. But in January, 1932 the company president was forced to cut wage rates, and in the fall of 1933 he was forced to cut production, order layoffs, and begin reducing the hours of remaining employees. Those workers who lived in the Village were given a few extra hours to help them pay their mortgages, but there was growing unrest throughout the company as incomes continued to drop.[51]

In 1933, as part of the New Deal's Hundred Days, Congress passed the National Industrial Recovery Act. Designed to avoid wasteful economic competition and strikes, the legislation permitted manufacturers, in consultation with union leaders and consumers' groups, to devise industry-wide codes of "fair business practices" and provide workers with minimum wage and maximum hours regulations. Section 7-A guaranteed the right of employees "to organize and bargain collectively through representatives of their own choosing" without interference from their employers. It said also that "no employee and no one seeking employment shall be required as a condition of employment to join any company union or to refrain from joining, organizing, or assisting a labor organization of his own choosing." The legislation also created the

National Recovery Administration (NRA) to supervise the drafting of the business codes and grant or deny government approval.

The meaning of Section 7-A was open to different interpretations. The right of workers to organize was already established in law. So what was new about the legislation? Did it mean that a majority of employees could legally obtain the sole bargaining power in a company, representing not only themselves but all other employees? That was the interpretation of labor leaders. But this view of the legislation was bitterly opposed by the nation's major employers; it meant, they argued, that labor bosses would rule all of business, virtually destroying the capitalistic system. Most employers were willing to work with the government to restore prosperity and profits, thus earning the Blue Eagle symbol of the NRA, which announced to all that "We Do Our Part." The Kohler Company readily signed on. But business leaders were not enthusiastic about encouraging the growth of trade unions.

In February, 1934, the National Recovery Administration sided with the employers on Section 7-A, ruling that "to organize and bargain collectively" did not restrict the rights of individuals. This meant that employees were free to join or not to join a union, to bargain for themselves or leave the process in the hands of organized labor.

Walter Sr. openly embraced this "open shop" position. He did not object, he said, to workers organizing, but he refused to permit labor leaders to speak for all Kohler employees. In August, 1933, with subtle but solid company support, some 1,800 employees joined the Kohler Workers' Association, one of many so-called "company unions" that were created across the country to ward off more militant labor groups. It was a functioning union: the Association initially handled some 180 cases, 155 of which were settled to the satisfaction of the workers. Critics noted, however, that the KWA was created shortly after the American Federation of Labor (AFL) formed a local union, and was clearly designed to ward off outside influence.[52]

AFL leaders objected strongly to the current interpretation of Section 7-A. In strikes all across the nation, they continued to press for the exclusive right to represent all workers when a majority chose to unionize. A strike by longshoremen on the San Francisco waterfront, for example, nearly shut down the city for four days, and Minneapolis and Toledo suffered similar incidents. All three of these major strikes of 1934 involved violence, destruction of property, and the presence of both Socialists and Communists.[53]

In the spring of 1934, AFL leaders turned their attentions to the Kohler Company. It was selected as a test case, a union attorney later admitted, because Walter Sr. was a benevolent employer. "Grievances more or less the same as in other cases will look different against that man's reputation. Then, of course, Kohler had a tradition to defend—the tradition of happy and contented labor in an open shop."

AFL leaders sent paid organizers to Sheboygan, who were joined by a number of Milwaukee militants. They created a weekly newspaper called *The New Deal*, and called meetings to tell workers that organized labor was carrying out the wishes of President Roosevelt. The federal government, they said, was trying to restore the health of the nation by raising wages, shortening work hours, and increasing spending power. That heroic effort, they argued, should not be hindered by selfish and greedy employers. "Pay your union dues," they said in effect, "and tell your bosses to go to hell." Sorely lacking money and dignity in the pit of a national economic collapse, many workers found the case for organized labor appealing.

Several strikes broke out in Sheboygan; tear gas was used, arrests were made. A mob of 3,000 overwhelmed police during a strike in the shoe industry. The strikers won, and the police were demoralized. Next on the agenda was the major target: the Kohler Company.[54]

On June 22, 1934, AFL leaders issued fourteen demands to Walter Sr., a list that included a 62 ½ percent increase in wages and a 25 % reduction in hours.[55] But the demand for sole bargaining power over the company was the heart of the matter. Whether this was called a "union shop" or a "closed shop," the result would be the same: every Kohler Company employee would be required to join the union and be represented in all matters by union leaders. Four days later, the plant shut down completely. Company officials could see serious trouble ahead. After a fruitless meeting with Walter Sr., union leaders decided to strike.[56]

When word of the proposed strike became known, more than 200 Village citizens (about half of the Kohler workers living there) rushed into the factory, eager to defend their place of occupation. Herbert Kohler, Executive Vice President of the company and the official in charge of security forces within the plant, was among them. So were John, Jim, and Bob Kohler, who were in the plant throughout the strike.[57]

The strike began at 4:00 a.m. on July 16. Violence erupted almost immediately. About 1,000 pickets virtually sealed off the factory with long ropes held by strikers in close formation. Employees trying to get to their jobs were roughed up. Strikers stopped trolley cars from Sheboygan, and blocked six trains delivering coal, dumping coal and blocking train wheels with railroad ties in the process. Since the Kohler Company provided the Village with its water, the attack on the trains was potentially critical to nearby residents, who would be deprived of sanitation and fire protection. Special deputies hired by the company fired two gas bombs and clubbed one striker. Strike leaders soon agreed to permit a limited supply of coal to enter the plant after Walter Sr. pledged that it would not be used in production.[58]

The company president did not make an appearance during the first day of the strike. But Walter was on the scene. He had been with Celeste in Chicago and upon returning home went immediately to the plant. Pickets barred his entrance, but former Milwaukee labor leader Maude McCreery, editor of *The New Deal*, intervened and escorted him to the door, no doubt revealing a personal respect for the Kohler family. A photograph of Walter chatting with McCreery made the pages of both Milwaukee newspapers. By now about 2,000 spectators were on hand to cheer the strikers.[59]

Once in the office building, Walter could not leave; he was among the employees trapped by the strikers outside. The rumor spread that he had been in Sheboygan lining up transportation for strikebreakers.[60] During the night, after the pickets had gone home, company officials had 60 cots and a truckload of provisions sent into the plant. A cook was smuggled in later.[61]

On the following day, Walter Sr. was the only person strikers would let through the picket line. He was booed and jeered. But later in the day, he was also permitted to leave. A great many of the pickets still held "the Governor" in esteem, and no one laid a hand on him.

Herbert, Marie, and Charlotte Kohler expressed their anguish to a reporter over what they thought was the shocking conduct of people they had befriended and helped for decades. Even now, said Herbert, group insurance was being continued for those on the picket line. "Throughout the depression, 95 per cent of our people have been getting earnings higher than the minimum" approved by the National Recovery Administration for the plumbing fixtures industry.[62]

In a statement issued on July 18, Walter Sr. blamed the strike on "outside labor agitators," and withdrew an offer to negotiate. Not more than four or five pickets, he said, were from Kohler Village.

Fr. J. W. Maguire, a member of the Chicago regional labor board, was on the scene trying to mediate the strike. He had addressed strikers on the first day, urging them to be peaceful. At his request, strike leaders agreed to open the picket lines to essential maintenance men and some "non-industrial" office workers. But the agreement lasted only briefly. Walter and the others remained trapped in the plant. Company guards, also in the plant, made their presence known to strikers for the first time, swinging their billy clubs in a threatening way. All employees knew that they had access to weapons.[63]

Strikers soon learned that food prepared in the American Club, across the street, had been bundled into packages that looked like mail, stamps and all, and was delivered to the people inside the plant in a mail truck. All vehicles were subsequently barred from entering the plant. One woman drove up to the factory fence and threw over a package of clothing to her husband. Pickets chased her in their cars until police intervened.[64]

On July 23, the president and 20 members of the Kohler Workers' Association joined the picket lines. There seemed to be no question any longer about the heavy involvement of Kohler workers in the strike. In blazing heat and high humidity (the national death toll was 275, and a Milwaukee woman collapsed and died), about 1,000 people trudged around the plant, hoping to hear word that a settlement had been reached. Workers from other unions joined the crowds, waving banners expressing encouragement. They donated funds to the strike effort.

But the scene grew increasingly tense. Kohler Village Mayor Anton Brotz (the Kohler Company's chief research engineer since 1898) deputized more than 300 men, most from the Village but a few from surrounding communities. Each of these special deputies received a billy club made of wood and fortified with lead, weapons made at the plant. They soon closed all of Kohler Village to traffic. Strikers and spectators had to walk as much as two miles to get to the picket lines. Company guards inside the plant said that the facility was well protected against possible attack.[65] One can imagine the extent of the protection surrounding Riverbend.

Following a round of talks with federal mediators, Walter Sr. contended that his interpretation of Section 7-A was the correct one; majority as well as minority groups had the right to bargain collectively. Therefore, he would not negotiate with AFL strike leaders. In an official statement, he stated: "...the company is determined to stand by its loyal employees, including both those who have remained inside for the maintenance of the plant, and those on the outside who have refrained from unlawful activities."

At midnight, 30 or 40 special deputies showed up in front of the plant, driving sleeping pickets off the property. They moved to a position across the street, and both sides shouted obscenities and threatened to use their clubs. The special deputies soon revealed clubs equipped with a trigger to release tear gas. After more shouting, the confrontation ended. But it was clear that, barring a settlement, serious violence was not far off. Families were split over the strike, savings were dwindling, and bitterness against the Kohlers had reached unprecedented heights.

On the morning of the thirteenth day of the strike, in a surprise move, 75 special deputies, armed with shotguns and tear gas bombs, and riding in four Kohler Village trucks, swooped down upon picket lines, ordering strikers to surrender all weapons. Awed pickets complied, giving up clubs, stones, and slingshots. Thirteen windows had been smashed during the night, and strikers were told that such conduct would no longer be tolerated. This move was officially in response to an order by Mayor Brotz limiting picketing groups to no more than three people and forbidding them to prevent persons from entering or leaving the plant. A petition signed by 1,500 employees, eager to return to work, had requested such a move.

Special deputies then moved to the rear of the plant, tearing down strikers' shacks and confiscating more weapons, including railroad spikes, and iron washers and slingshots. They also destroyed a small fort of railroad ties and permitted a coal car from Sheboygan, that pickets had blocked, to enter the plant. The special deputies patrolled the streets in four trucks wrapped with sheet iron, to ward off bullets and prevent strikers from easily climbing aboard. A crowd of 3,000 booed the patrol trucks.

People in the Village were growing desperate with fear. As Walter later reported, "For nearly two weeks the residents of the Village were subjected to loud shouting and foul language throughout the day and night. Women and children were so terrified that some of them were sent away from home."[66] After Celeste and Walter received kidnapping threats, Terry, only a little over two months old, was placed in a bucket topped with clothes and smuggled from the family home to a nearby hospital under an assumed name.[67] Jim's new born son Peter could not be brought home from the hospital because of the threats of violence.[68]

A Kohler Company newspaper advertisement announced that the normal payroll would not be issued. Checks would reappear, said company officials, as soon as employees enjoyed their legal right to return to work. The American Club was turned over to the special deputies, and two striking union members who lived there were evicted.

The Mayor of Kohler Village issued a statement warning everyone, especially women and children, to stay outside the danger zone. Nine unarmed workers were situated at key observation posts around the factory, including the office tower and mill building roof, equipped with telephones, field glasses, and in some cases flood lights and spotlights. War appeared near.[69]

On Friday, July 27, at about 8:00 p.m., a group of male teenagers began hurling stones and bricks through windows of the foundry, on the south end of the plant. Men and women, young and old, joined in. Soon a shouting, screaming mob of several thousand formed, breaking every window they could find. The Kohler Company display rooms were destroyed. Walter Sr., Herbert, and Walter were in the main office building as the glass came pouring in upon them. Armed guards were prepared to resist attackers with bullets if they broke through the main doors. A portion of the mob attacked the rear fence of the plant and were threatening the front gate[70]

The assault spread throughout the immediate area. The mob wrecked a police car, and stoned the automobile owned by a female probation officer. The Kohler Showrooms in the business section of the city had its windows shattered, and several adjacent businesses were attacked. Twenty one plate glass windows in the Village Recreation Center were smashed, and an effort was made to set the building on fire. (Women and children lived in upstairs apartments.) The very survival of the Kohler Company and Kohler Village was at stake.[71]

At 8:30, from the American Club, the special deputies began shooting tear gas into the crowd. Guards inside the plant joined the counterattack by throwing tear gas bombs. The air was filled not only with gas but with rocks and bricks. Men, women, and children ran in all directions seeking escape.

Shooting started quickly. Both sides later blamed the other for initiating it.[72] The some 400 special deputies and plant guards, some of them armed and many wearing steel helmets, waded into the crowd, using their clubs. Herbert and Walter Kohler marched out of the building with the guards. Walter was reported as being "with the special police on the firing line," and it seems likely that he was armed in some way, if only for self-protection.[73] No one ever proved, however, that any top Kohler Company official fired a weapon or injured anyone. (In 1950, a Democrat would tell an audience, "Most of you know of the strike at the Kohler family plant and how two strikers were killed, presumably by armed deputies. Did you know that Walter Kohler was an armed deputy in that strike?" During the same campaign, a Kenosha labor paper stated, "He cannot deny that he was part of the strikebreaking gang which clubbed and shot at a group of hungry workers not so long ago….He remains forever associated with violence and thuggery rather than with enlightened statesmanship and human intentions." A strike committee chairman claimed that Walter roughed up one of the older union pickets.)[74]

Bullets flew in all directions. Some special deputies hid behind the armored trucks to avoid being hit. Some, as one photo showed, aimed their weapons carefully before shooting. One truck sported a machine gun, but it was not used. The panic increased when a keg of dynamite blew up.

The sheriff of Sheboygan County wired the Governor to send the National Guard to restore order. Walter Sr. and Fr. J. W. McGuire, the mediator, joined the plea. By the dawn of the next day, two men in their twenties, a six-year company employee and a spectator, had been killed, and 43 others were injured, many from gunshot wounds. (Walter's detailed analysis of riot victims soon revealed that no women were casualties, as reported, and only two juveniles were injured. Not a single special deputy was wounded, despite a newspaper report of a bloodied deputy being assisted by Bob Kohler.)[75] The entire community was outraged at this unprecedented mayhem.[76]

The next morning, 250 national guardsmen from Milwaukee were on the scene to serve as police. The special deputies surrendered their badges and went home. Another 300 troops arrived on Sunday to patrol the streets. Union leaders were furious, demanding that Governor Schmedeman end "martial law."[77]

Union lawyer David Rabinovitz put the full blame for the riot and the bloodshed on the company's president. His refusal to negotiate had prompted the strike, the attorney declared, and "Every act of violence that has occurred has been perpetrated by the deputies of the village of Kohler."[78] It soon became known that Bob and John Kohler both served as special deputies during the melee. [79]

Once peace was restored, Walter Sr. issued a public statement blaming outsiders and people with "communistic affiliations" for the violence. He noted the presence of Al Benson, state secretary of the Socialist Party, who had addressed strikers on July 17, urging them, Kohler said, to seize the plant. "Fewer than 2 percent of those who participated in the strike were residents of Kohler village....The men who resisted the attack after the trouble started last night were deputy sheriffs and deputy marshals of the village, residents of this county. No outsiders were brought in to deal with the mob. The village police tried in every way they could to avoid bloodshed."[80]

A *Milwaukee Journal* reporter revealed that of the 43 wounded or injured in the rioting, only 17 were employees or former Kohler Company employees.[81] A later analysis by Walter found that of 35 gun shot victims, 15 were employees or former employees, and 20 were non-employees.[82] On the other hand, the head of the striking union, Arthur F. Kuhn, had worked for the Kohler Company for 19 years and was a resident of Kohler Village. His home was under foreclosure due to his inability to make mortgage payments.[83] (The Kohler Building and Loan Association held 268 mortgages. Between 1930 and 1935, it had 13 judgments taken on homes, and other foreclosure actions were started.)[84] The strike committee, including Kuhn, contained seven members who had worked for the Kohler Company an aggregate of 82 years.[85]

The influential *Milwaukee Journal*, which had supported Walter Sr. in three election bids, now backed the strikers, condemning Kohler for "paternalism" and a failure to acknowledge the spirit of the times.[86] Socialist Al Benson agreed, denying any attempt to stir up anyone while on the scene and contending that the killing and wounding of strikers "rests squarely on the shoulders of Walter Kohler and on him alone." The Sheboygan Central Labor Council sent an open letter to the Governor protesting the appointment of Walter Sr. to a newly created housing commission. "These delegates, representing all local labor unions, hold that Mr. Kohler has definitely proven that he is wholly incapable of caring for the people of this state."[87]

Some 10,000 people turned out for the Sheboygan funeral of one of the men slain in the riot. It was the largest such service ever held in the city. Henry Ohl, Jr., president of the state AFL, invoked the name of President Roosevelt in his remarks. Of all the victims in the riot, he said, "Our brothers were slain or injured in a contest between human rights and profits. Surrender by labor would mean slavery." In Milwaukee, Communist pickets marched in front of the Kohler Company showrooms, one sign reading: "The hands of Kohler Co. officials are stained with the blood of murdered strikers."[88]

Famed Catholic economist Msgr. John A. Ryan was publicly critical of Kohler officials. Fr. J. W. McGuire, the labor mediator, declared, "I have been in many strikes, but I never saw such needless and ruthless killing by supporters of the law." Most of those wounded by bullets, he said, were shot in the back.[89]

Picket lines resumed, strikers saying they were committed solely to "peaceful picketing." The last of the National Guard troops left the area on August 20, but Mayor Anton Broz said that the Village was training an armed guard for any emergency.[90] Wooden barricades remained at every entrance to the Village. The plant was closed. On the outside it looked like a ruined fortress.

While Walter was trapped in the main office building for twelve days, he prepared or helped prepare brief historical and analytical accounts of the strike that were the basis for company press releases and stories in the August issue of *Kohler of Kohler News*. The company monthly also contained photographs of the devastating damages inflicted on the plant by the mob. The historical accounts were later circulated among business leaders. Recently discovered copies of these documents reveal them to be, however partisan, carefully researched, factual, and well written.[91]

Negotiations between company and labor officials continued to falter on the issue of the Open Shop. Walter Sr. continued to believe that his interpretation of Section 7-A was legally correct, and he refused to permit AFL leaders to speak for all his employees.[92] The company president claimed that the strike was hurting the nearly 1,600 members of the Kohler Workers' Association who had the constitutional right to earn a living without being molested by anyone. Until that right was established, he said, the plant would remain closed.[93]

In late August, Walter Sr. was summoned to appear and testify at a public hearing in Sheboygan. The proceeding was in response to a formal union complaint that the company had violated Section 7-A and should be stripped of its National Recovery Administration membership. The AFL also sought the dissolution of the Kohler Workers' Association.

On the stand as the first witness in the hearing, Walter Sr. revealed interesting financial data about his company. It had issued, he said, $4 million worth of preferred stock and 200,000 shares of no par value common stock, all owned by 8 or 10 stockholders, "six or seven" of whom were his relatives. (The book value of a private company's stock is determined by management and company auditors.) In 1933, the company did a $5 million business, having steadily declined since 1928. Altogether, he said, the company employed 2,114 people, 1,800 at the plant.[94]

While the hearing was underway, the new National Labor Relations Board, contradicting both the President and the National Recovery Administration, ruled for labor, contending that Section 7-A declared majority rule to be all-inclusive. This was a major blow against America's employers. Walter Sr. declined to accept the ruling, saying he awaited a decision by the courts.[95]

In a second appearance on the stand, Walter Sr. denied union allegations that he had encouraged workers to join the Kohler Workers' Association and had penalized and fired those who were organizing the AFL. Under questioning, he revealed more financial data about himself and his company. Kohler's personal salary in 1928 was $40,000. It remained at that level through 1929 and 1930. The following year he worked for no salary. In 1932 and 1933 he earned $22,000, the level it remained in the year of the strike. (He acknowledged, however, that his preferred stock had brought in between $20,000 and $30,000 between 1928 and 1934.) All salaries were cut during the Depression, he said. Walter Sr. again expressed his lifelong devotion to the working man and his desire to see his employees happy and prosperous. "It is my opinion that we have kept from 1,000 to 1,500 more men employed at work since the depression hit us than we actually needed to."[96]

On September 15, the National Labor Relations Board ruled against the Kohler Company, stating that the company had interfered with the "free and unhampered self-organization" guaranteed by Section 7-A of the National Industrial Recovery Act. It granted the request by organized labor to conduct secret, supervised elections at the plant to determine representatives for collective bargaining. This was a battle between the AFL and the Kohler Workers' Association; the winner would represent all employees.[97] Walter Sr., agreed to the election while rejecting the NLRB's decision. By now the company had resumed operations on a reduced scale.[98]

When the ballots were counted on September 27, the Kohler Workers' Association defeated the AFL handily, 1,063 to 642 (with over 500 votes being challenged by both sides and not yet counted). The union filed a protest, alleging an assortment of complaints, and the picketing contin-ued. But Walter Sr. was the clear victor in this struggle. KWA workers and others drove to Riverbend for a spontaneous celebration.[99]

When the national convention of the American Federation of La-bor met in San Francisco in mid-October, an effort was made by the Wisconsin State Federation of Labor to adopt a resolution protesting the results of the election at the Kohler Company. Henry Ohl, Jr. told delegates that company officials had created a majority by bringing in workers from outside the company, including city employees. The resolution failed by a narrow margin.[100]

In March, 1935, the National Labor Relations Board upheld the supervised election, rejecting AFL allegations. Wisconsin union lead-ers, claiming nationwide support, said nevertheless that they would continue the strike.[101] Kohler Company officials gleefully pointed to the irony of this position: union leaders were refusing to abide by their own principle of majority rule. Union leaders then called for a national boycott of Kohler products.[102]

In July, the widow of one of the slain men and several others filed lawsuits against the Kohler Company, Walter Sr., Herbert, Walter, Bob, and four other company employees. The complaint sought total dam-ages of $285,000, alleging a conspiracy by the defendants to do them physical injury in the course of the riot on July 27, 1934.

The lawsuits were originally filed in Milwaukee County, and then transferred, according to law, to Sheboygan County, the residence of all parties concerned. The attorney for the plaintiffs asked for a change of venue, arguing that a fair trial could not be held in Sheboygan. When a judge ruled otherwise, the complaints were dropped and the lawsuits dismissed.

The conservative *Green Bay Post-Gazette* jeered at the unwillingness of the plaintiffs to prove their case before area citizens. The dismissal of the damage suits "brings to a public end perhaps as great an error as labor ever made in Wisconsin."[103]

But it was not to be the end. In 1935, the Supreme Court declared the National Industrial Recovery Act unconstitutional. Congress then passed the National Labor Relations Act, commonly called the Wag-ner Act. This "Magna Carta" of the labor movement gave workers the right to bargain collectively and prohibited employers from interfering with union organizational efforts. A National Labor Relations Board was created to supervise plant elections. And the principle of "majority rules," long sought by labor, was now established. Walter Sr. and other business leaders had lost their battle as the country moved to the left in an effort to defeat "old man depression."

There was a union in place at the Kohler Company, created by majority rule in a fair election. But organized labor was determined to destroy it. (Picketing from the 1934 strike continued until 1941.) The intense bitterness between Kohler management and the AFL would reappear in 1954, when Herbert Kohler ran the company and his nephew was Governor of Wisconsin. The second Kohler strike would continue the longest labor-management dispute in American history.

Notes

[1] Robert E. Kohler, Jr., interview.

[2] Marie Kohler interview.

[3] *Ibid.*; Julilly Kohler interview, October 7, 2003.

[4] E-mail, Leslie Kohler Hawley to the author, March 25, 2005, in Celeste Kohler file.

[5] Julilly Kohler interview, October 7, 2003. This was a recollection of Julilly Kohler, John's wife, handed down to her daughter. Typically, Walter never discussed this matter with his son. Terry Kohler interview, June 12, 2003.

[6] Tim and Barbara Gorham interview, October 24, 2004; Jean Dor Sarabia, *Eighty Years of My Wandering Spirit*, 1-13, an unpublished autobiography in the possession of Tim Gorham.

[7] *Ibid.*, 11-13, 16; Terry Kohler interview, March 25, 2004.

[8] Photographs of Celeste and classmates at Briarcliff are in the Leslie Kohler Hawley collection.

[9] Sarabia, *Eighty Years of My Wandering Spirit*, 26.

[10] Celeste's personal copy of *Miss Spence's School Class of 1920* is in the Terry Kohler papers. Among those signing her yearbook was Consuelo Vanderbilt of 666 Fifth Avenue, New York. Officials of The Spence School did not reply to a request for Celeste's academic record.

[11] Terry Kohler interview, March 25, 2004.

[12] Fass, *The Damned and the Beautiful*, 25.

[13] Sarabia, *80 Years of My Wandering Spirit*, 33-34.

[14] *Ibid.*, 15.

[15] Jackie was born on May 28, 1924. (Her death certificate says May 29.) She was always to remain a Canadian citizen. Later in life, she altered the year of her birth to make herself seem younger by three years, and she claimed to be born in Chicago. The Jacquelin Kohler papers are in the Terry Kohler papers.

[16] Holden (1895-1940) remains something of a mystery. Jean Dor, Celeste's sister, could not describe him physically years later, and no one today seems to know his occupation. Jean Dor called him a businessman. Terry Kohler was told simply that he was a millionaire. While Celeste saved hundreds of photos, not one that has survived contains her first husband. See Terry Kohler interview of June 12, 2003, and Jean Dor Sarabia interview.

[17] Sarabia, *80 Years of My Wandering Spirit*, 18.

[18] Tim and Barbara Gorham interview, October 24, 2004.

[19] *Ibid.*

[20] Terry Kohler interview, June 12, 2003.

[21] Leslie Kohler Hawley interview.

[22] Sarabia, *Eighty Years of My Wandering Spirit*, 29.

[23] *Ibid.*, 27, 30; interview with Tim and Barbara Gorham, October 24, 29, 2004. Fortunato (1897-1995) and Mary F. McVoy Jerace (1918-1995) lived in Michigan, near Pentwater, for many years, he working as an architect. Mary divorced Eugene, Celeste's brother, to marry her Italian lover. Ancestry.com incorrectly cites Jerace's given name as "Fortuno." He and Pauline Celeste made an around-the-world cruise in 1936, and their names appear on a San Francisco passenger list that can be found on Ancestry.com. A photograph of the couple, appearing in Jean Dor Sarabia's autobiography, clearly shows the nineteen year age gap between the two. Jean Dor was the only family member who refused to attend the wedding of Jerace and her mother. Sarabia, *80 Years of My Wandering Spirit*, 30. On Jerace's architectural credentials, see *Il Nuovo Stile Littorio* (Milano-Roma, S. A. Arti Grafiche Bertarelli, 1936), 247.

[24] Sarabia, *80 Years of My Wandering Spirit*, 28.

[25] Jean Dor Sarabia interview, November 2, 2004.

[26] Sarabia, *80 Years of My Wandering Spirit*, 31.

[27] *Ibid.*, 32.

[28] *Ibid.*

[29] "Kohler-Holden," *New York Times*, November 15, 1932.

[30] See T. B. Engelking to W. J. Ireland, November 15, 1932, Personnel file. This internal Kohler Company memorandum dates the purchase November 11.

[31] Interview with Peter and Nancy Kohler, May 6, 2005.

[32] Walter's salary is from his employment record in the Kohler archives. His job description is in the Personnel file.

[33] Tim and Barbara Gorham interview, October 24, 2004; Terry Kohler interview, June 12, 2003; Sarabia, *80 Years of My Wandering Spirit*, 35-36.

[34] Interview with Tim and Barbara Gorham, October 24, 2004.

[35] "Walter Kohler Jr. and Bride," *Milwaukee Sentinel*, November 15, 1932; "Kohler-Holden Wedding at Chicago," *Milwaukee Journal*, November 14, 1932. The Associated Press photograph has both Kohlers smiling.

[36] *Decennial Record of the Class of 1925, Yale College.*

[37] "Bride of Walter Kohler Jr.," *Sheboygan Press*, November 14, 1932.

[38] "Jacquelin Bender Kohler," *ibid.*, January 15, 1982.

[39] Sarabia, *Eighty Years of My Wandering Spirit*, 39, 42.

[40] The photographs are largely in the Leslie Kohler Hawley collection.

[41] Peter and Nancy Kohler interview, May 6, 2005.

[42] *Ibid.*

[43] Abbott and Andover have merged and become known simply as Andover.

[44] Peter and Nancy Kohler interview, August 11, 2003, May 6, 2005; "Carl J. Kohler Found Dead In Summer Lodge," *Sheboygan Press*, November 17, 1960; "Mrs. Kohler is Trustee At Lakeland," undated clipping in the Carl

Kohler file. For the granddaughter's statement, see e-mail, Ann Fichtner to the author, February 7, 2005, Genealogy file.

[45] Two of her books remain in print: *Plants and Flowers to Decorate Your Home* (Racine, Wisconsin: Golden Books, 1977), and *Collins And His Rabbit* (Chicago: Children's Press, 1969). The latter was titled *Farmer Collins* when it first appeared in 1949.

[46] Julilly Kohler interview, October 7, 2003; Michael Kohler interview; Marie Kohler interview; e-mail, Michael Kohler to the author, January 12, 2005, John Michael Kohler III file; Mike Weber interview.

[47] Julilly Kohler interview, October 7, 2003.

[48] Vicki and Jill Kohler interview. The story was told by Jill.

[49] *Ibid*; Robert E. Kohler, Jr., interview.

[50] This perception came from many interviewees.

[51] Garet Garrett, "Section Seven-A at Sheboygan," *Saturday Evening Post*, October 27, 1934, 5-7; Blodgett, *A Sense of Higher Design*, 87.

[52] Uphoff, *Kohler on Strike*, 28-29.

[53] See David F. Selvin, *A Terrible Anger: The 1934 Waterfront and General Strikes in San Francisco* (Detroit: Wayne State University Press, 1996).

[54] Garett, "Section Seven-A at Sheboygan," 79-81.

[55] For the full list of demands and the company's reply, see "Issues in Kohler Strike," *Milwaukee Journal*, July 28, 1934.

[56] See Uphoff, *Kohler on Strike*, 30-34.

[57] Peter and Nancy Kohler interview, August 11, 2003.

[58] See Uphoff, *Kohler on Strike*, 43-44.

[59] "Gas Bombs Hurled on Kohler Strikers," *Milwaukee Journal*, July 16, 1934.

[60] Uphoff, *Kohler on Strike*, 47.

[61] Strikers would have let some people out of the plant if they used passes issued by the union and gave reason for their exit. Unwilling to acknowledge that strikers had that legal authority, company officials said that the employees would stay put. *Ibid.*, 46-7. On the cook, see "Strike Started Almost Gaily," *Milwakee Journal*, July 28

[62] "Kohler Alone Passes Pickets," "'The Governor' Is Sad and Worried; Strike Destroys Dream of Harmony," *ibid.*, July 17, 1934. The NRA Code, approved in January, 1934, provided a minimum wage of 40 cents an hour (35 cents in the South) and maximum week of 40 hours. Ninety five percent of Kohler Company employees received wages in excess of the 40 cent per hour minimum. See "A Statement by Kohler Co.," *Kohler of Kohler News*, August, 1934, 5-6.

[63] "Kohler, Priest Discuss Peace," "Kohler Near Water Limit," *Milwaukee Journal*, July 19, 1934.

[64] "Coal Passes Kohler Lines," *ibid.*, July 20, 1934.

[65] "More Pickets at Kohler Co.," *ibid.*, July 23, 1934. On Bratz, see Blodgett, *A Sense of Higher Design*, 78. On pickets from other unions on the scene, see Uphoff, *Kohler on Strike*, 48.

[66] See copy, "A Statement by Kohler Co.," August 9, 1934, Riot Data file, Terry Kohler papers.

[67] Terry Kohler interview, June 12, 2003.

[68] Peter and Nancy Kohler interview, August 11, 2003.

[69] "Deputies Raid Kohler Pickets, Stones and Clubs Confiscated," *Milwaukee Journal*, July 27, 1934; "Strike Started Almost Gaily," *ibid.*, July 28, 1934. On the observation posts, see the copy of Walter's undated paper "Defense of the Kohler Plant," 1, Riot Data file, Terry Kohler papers.

[70] *Ibid*, 3

[71] See "Village Head Blames Union," *Milwaukee Journal*, July 30, 1934. See also copy, "Firearms in the Mob," 2, Riot Data file, Terry Kohler papers.

[72] See *ibid.*

[73] Walter's presence was reported only in a *Milwaukee Sentinel* article of July 28. He did not mention it in his written accounts of the strike. At no time, however, did he deny the *Sentinel* description. See "The Attack on Kohler Village, Friday, July 27, 1934," Second Draft 8-16-34, 17, Riot Data file, Terry Kohler papers. Here Walter's account suggests the presence of firearms, assuming he was among the group described.

[74] "Opponents Rip Kohler, Wiley," *Milwaukee Journal*, August 22, 1950. The speaker was Charles P. Green of Milwaukee, who was seeking the Democratic nomination for Governor. See also "The Past Haunts GOP Candidate," "Wisconsin Remembers The Kohler Massacre," *Kenosha Labor*, July 27, 1950. The hitherto standard source on the Kohler strike of 1934, by Walter H. Uphoff, quotes a labor official who contended that Herbert "and other Kohler officials and supervisors" were "all carrying rifles, guns, pistols or clubs." However that may be, the entire account of the strike is biased in favor of the strikers. Uphoff, *Kohler on Strike*, 63.

[75] Copy, "Riot Casualties of July 27, 1934," September 20, 1934, Riot Data file, Terry Kohler papers. This was confirmed by an inquest. See Uphoff, *Kohler on Strike*, 80-83. On Bob Kohler, see "Thud of Crashing Stones, Billies Resounds Through Kohler Night," *Milwaukee Journal*, July 28, 1934..

[76] "Two Dead, 38 Hurt in Kohler's Night of Strike Rioting Terror," "Labor Heads Blame Kohler," *ibid.*, July 28, 1934. See also "Two Dead and 39 Injured," *Sheboygan Press*, July 28, 1934.

[77] "Kohler Quiet as More Troops Are Moved In," "Governor Upholds Calling of Troops," *Milwaukee Journal*, July 29, 1934. See the photos on page 3.

[78] "Labor Heads Blame Kohler," *ibid.*, July 28, 1934.

[79] "Thud of Crashing Stones, Billies Rounds Through Kohler Night," *ibid.*

[80] "Kohler Blames Agitators; Strike Chief Accuses Him," *ibid.*

[81] "Kohler Peace Again Sought by Mediators," *ibid.*, July 30, 1934.

[82] Copy, "Riot Casualties of July 27, 1934," Riot Data File, Terry Kohler papers.

[83] "Kohler Union Leader Talks," *Milwaukee Journal*, August 3, 1934.

[84] Payments were automatically deducted from paychecks, often leaving workers with little extra money. In 1934, more than 90 percent of the 450 homes in Kohler Village were occupied by Kohler employees. About 200 of the homes were occupied by rank-and-file workers. Fewer than 10% of the factory workers lived in the Village. Uphoff, *Kohler on Strike*, 7-8.

[85] *Ibid.*, 37.

[86] Editorial, "Blindness and Tragedy at Kohler, *Milwaukee Journal*, July 28, 1934.

[87] "Benson Denies Urging Pickets to Seize Plant," "Workers Demand Ouster of Kohler," *ibid.*, July 30, 1934.

[88] "10,000 Bow in Tribute at Bier of Kohler Victim," *ibid.*, July 31, 1934.

[89] "Priest Attacks Kohler's Stand," *ibid*; "Board to Ask State Guard Be Kept at Kohler," *ibid.*, August 2, 1934. Mc Guire was soon removed from the mediation process, angering labor leaders.

[90] "Deputies Rule Kohler Strike," *ibid.*, August 20, 1934; "Kohler Village Trains Force," *ibid.*, August 25, 1934.

[91] The reports are in the Riot Data file of the Terry Kohler papers. See also copy, O. A. Kroos, to "The Wholesale Trade," October 20, 1934, *ibid* .

[92] "Text of Board's Terms and Proposal of Kohler," *Milwaukee Journal.*, August 16, 1934; "Kohler Defies Labor Set-Up," *ibid.*, August 17, 1934; "Guard Troops Are Ordered Out of Kohler," *ibid.*, August 19, 1934.

[93] "Kohler States Plant Policy," *ibid.*, August 22, 1934.

[94] "Kohler Fought Organization of Union a Year Ago, Ohl Testifies," *ibid.*, August 30, 1934.

[95] Editorial, "Labor Majority Shall Rule," *ibid.*, September 1, 1934; "Kohler Explains Ideals of Company," *ibid.*, September 2, 1934.

[96] *Ibid.*

[97] "Plant Election Ordered in Kohler Strike," *ibid.*, September 16, 1934.

[98] "Kohler Co. Yields to Employee Election Order," September 20, 1934. Those guilty of violence during the strike were excluded from the vote by the NLRB.

[99] "A. F. of L. Union Beaten in Kohler Vote," *ibid.*, September 28, 1934.

[100] "Shuns Rebuke of Kohler Co.," *ibid.*, October 13, 1934.

[101] "Kohler Co. Wins Decisive Victory," *Sheboygan Press*, March 28, 1935.

[102] Uphoff, *Kohler on Strike*, 93-94.

[103] "Court Dismisses Damage Suits," *Kohler of Kohler News*, January, 1936, 3-4.

Chapter Five

Change of Command

After the turmoil subsided and the Kohler Company resumed a regular schedule of production, Walter began to ascend in the corporate structure. In 1936 he was named to the Board of Directors, and a year later he became Secretary of the Company.[1] It was clear that Walter Sr. was planning a bright future for his 32-year-old son, the son who most resembled himself in style, intellect, and ambition.

Walter joined the Sheboygan Country Club in 1936. Members later recalled him as one who rarely came out for golf and was always keen on solving the Club's financial problems. He played excellent poker but refused to play for more than modest stakes. The Club became the exclusive Pine Hills Country Club in Sheboygan, and Walter would serve as its president for several years. He appeared to townspeople to be quiet, confident, relaxed, dignified, agreeable, and friendly, but few doubted that he was at the same time a man of strong will and determination. There was nothing weak or vulgar about him.[2]

Relatives Peter and Nancy Kohler later recalled that throughout his life Walter was reserved, cautious, and very proper. He almost never appeared in casual clothes, preferring at informal times to wear khaki pants and a blazer, perpetuating the Andover look. At the same time, he was a bright, well-read man who "had the nicest smile when you talked with him."[3]

On March 29, 1936, Walter and Celeste became the proud parents of a daughter they named Charlotte Nicolette (Niki). Jackie, Celeste's daughter from her first marriage, was in her Connecticut boarding school during these years. Her father, Jack Holden, was still alive, but he had disinherited Jackie when the divorce became final, and probably made no further contact. Twelve years old in 1936, Jackie thought of Walter as her father and years later would call herself Jackie Kohler, although that was never her legal name.[4]

A handsome photograph, found on the walls of some Kohler family homes to this day, was taken in July, 1936 in the gardens at Riverbend. Walter Sr. and Charlotte are seated, the family patriarch holding infant

Niki in his arms, and Terry seated at his feet. Five other grandchildren and Julilly's mother, Lilly Waller House, are seated and standing around the couple. The occasion was a "mass christening ceremony" of the younger Kohlers. Walter Sr.'s face shows traces of the several years of economic disaster, the firestorm at his company, and the impact of recent political developments. The young, vibrant, optimistic Governor now seemed grayer and more pensive.[5]

In the election struggles of 1936, Walter Sr. publicly railed against the New Deal, which he thought was corrupting the nation. In a speech at Faneuil Hall in Boston, on Constitution Day, 1935, he had blasted the rise of big government's authority over the economy and its impact on individual freedom and initiative.[6] He was seriously mentioned as a possible GOP presidential candidate at the time but did nothing to encourage backers.[7] FDR's overwhelming re-election victory in November over Alf Landon must have been a severe blow. Even more galling, perhaps, was the Progressive control of state government in Wisconsin. Kohler's bitter enemies, the Wisconsin Federation of Labor and the Socialist Party, were prominent members of the Progressive alliance.

But change soon relieved Kohler's anxiety. In 1938, Governor Phil La Follette, eager to achieve even greater power, created his own national political party. It was stillborn, in part due to the Governor's campaign tactics, which some thought resembled Nazi activities. La Follette abandoned Wisconsin politics and began devoting his energies to the cause of American isolationism. Milwaukee industrialist Julius Heil, supported by a Republican-Democratic coalition, won the gubernatorial race for the GOP, and vowed to reverse the leftist course set by Progressives. Republican Alexander Wiley won a Senate seat, and Republican Walter Goodland became Lieutenant Governor. Thus began two decades of Republican domination in Wisconsin.[8]

❖⟶❖⟶❖⟶◉⟵❖⟵❖⟵❖

In the late 1930s, both Jim and Walter Kohler began laying plans for family estates of their own in Kohler. It seems certain that these highly expensive projects were financed by Walter Sr.[9] Jim constructed a beautiful three story, 8,500 square foot home on eight acres west of Riverbend that resembled the Kohler family home. He and Dorothy called the estate Elmwood, and they would raise their four children there.[10]

Walter and Celeste were planning something different, a 7,000 square foot, ultra-modern home on 53 wooded acres that they initially called the Windway Farm Residence. The architect was William F. Deknatel of Chicago, a Princeton graduate who had studied under Frank Lloyd Wright and was also a friend of Celeste's family. Deknatel completed his plans for the sprawling, two-story home in February, 1937, stunning both Walter and Celeste with the proposed cost. To save money, a flat, tar and gravel roof was substituted for a pitched copper roof. (It was a costly mistake, for leaks began almost immediately and would plague the house for decades.) A construction contract was signed in May with a Fond du Lac company that had built the pottery building for the Kohler Company in the 1920s.

Walter and the contractor then began a long series of disagreements about costs. Walter scrutinized the price of virtually every component in the home, and the architect made many changes as construction proceeded. The quarreling became so severe that Walter consulted the Kohler Company attorney, and a labor arbitrator had to be consulted. Both Walter and Celeste told Terry that the general contractor bid too low and went bankrupt during construction. The house had to be completed on a cost-plus basis. Terry said later that Windway was "... built like a fort with LOTS of poured concrete and steel."[11]

Some expensive items were not questioned. An engineer who worked on the house later recalled Deknatel investigating the thick, white living room carpet with a jeweler's eyepiece, studying the fibers. The cost was $75 a yard, "a fabulous price in the 1930s." Existing documents do not reveal Windway's total cost, but Celeste later told Terry that the house and land together totaled $250,000 (or about $3.5 million in 2005 dollars.) That figure may be higher than the actual cost. In any case, Walter and Celeste each paid half the sum.[12]

The Kohlers moved in during the spring of 1938.[13] Almost immediately Windway was featured in the *New York Herald Tribune* and an assortment of other newspapers and magazines. It attracted attention in large part for its "cutting edge," Frank Lloyd Wright-Prairie School design and magnificent setting. The house featured sunken rooms, low ceilings, and distinctive brick work. Architect Deknatel also designed the Wright-like furniture, which was more attractive and distinctive than comfortable.

Views outside the large windows of the home were stunning. Just a few yards to the east was a sharp drop-off that opened into a wooded valley, through which ran the Pigeon River. Vast lawns and a garden increased the property's beauty. An attached garage had upstairs rooms for servants.

The entire complex, some thought, was a showplace for Celeste; more of a permanent exhibit than a home. But Walter too enjoyed Windway, and lived there the rest of his life. Both were conscious of the house's contribution to their socio-economic status. To send a letter to Walter or Celeste, one needed only to write on the envelope "Windway, Kohler, Wisconsin." It was a distinctive and impressive address. The Kohlers entertained frequently, and Windway was often filled with visiting relatives and friends, many from Chicago. The charming, wealthy young plumbing company executive and his attractive, sophisticated wife were going places in Midwestern high society, and had friends and acquaintances of similar rank in cities around the country and in Europe. Celeste, more than Walter, reveled in the constant swirl of social events.[14]

Dorothy Engleman lived in the upstairs garage apartment for 13 years, coming in 1938 when Windway opened. She was the cook and maid, and her husband, Fred, was the family chauffeur and gardener. Celeste hired both of them when they were unemployed and desperate. Mrs. Engleman later remembered Mrs. Kohler as "wonderful and beautiful," an intelligent woman devoted to entertaining, writing, and charity work. Walter, she said, was gentle, warm, and kind. Engleman has photographs of Walter wrestling on the floor with Terry and her son Wayne. "He did this with them almost every night."

The Kohlers had three dogs, two of them German Shepherds named Wotan and Freia. (These names are characters in *Die Walkure*; Walter often enjoyed the music of Richard Wagner.)[15] When guests arrived, Engleman recalled, extra cooks and kitchen help were sometimes hired. Dinners might be served to a dozen or even a hundred people. In the evenings, Engleman said, Walter and Celeste read and listened to opera and classical music. She once saw them fascinated by the tango. Their devoted servant thought the Kohlers "the ideal couple."[16]

The Kohlers spent the Labor Day weekend, 1939, at Pentwater. Celeste's sister Jean Dor was being married, and there was golf for the men and sailing for the women. Jean Dor later recalled seeing Celeste sweep sand under the rugs while cleaning the house. Jackie telephoned from Canada where she had been arrested for smuggling a gun across the border.[17]

At the end of March, 1940, Walter was stunned to read blazing newspaper headlines reporting that a federal grand jury had indicted

104 companies, trade associations, unions, and individuals on charges
of criminal conspiracy to freeze plumbing prices above normal levels,
thus violating the Sherman Anti-Trust Law. Among those indicted were
Walter Sr. and the nation's three largest plumbing manufacturers, the
Kohler Company, the Crane Company, and the American Radiator and
Standard Sanitary Corporation. He undoubtedly knew that his father
would be deeply upset by this challenge to his integrity and would
probably hold FDR and his union allies to blame.[18]

Walter and Celeste had made reservations at a fashionable ski resort
in Sun Valley, Idaho, and they proceeded on their trip. Although he had
skied since his youth, Walter fell and broke his right leg. On April 21,
while convalescing at Windway, he received the news that his father had
died of a sudden heart attack.[19] Walter Sr. had been in Milwaukee on
Friday to post a bond of $1,000 to insure his appearance in the federal
court in Cleveland. He spent Saturday in his office. On Sunday morning,
Charlotte found him dead, lying next to his bed.[20] He was 65.

Newspapers throughout Wisconsin and across the nation recalled the
history of Walter Sr.'s rise to wealth and fame, stressing his devotion to
his employees and the people of Wisconsin. Tributes poured in, even
from long-time enemies. Governor Heil declared, "A great enterprise
is a monument to his business ability. He was a public spirited citizen
whose mind labored for the upbuilding of his fellow men. He was a
good governor. His life is an inspiration for the best in citizenship."
Senator Wiley stated, "He was a builder, not only creating jobs and
material wealth, but a man of ideas in statecraft, squaring performance
with promise; a man who got things done; a man who had faith in
America." Former Governor Schmedeman said, "I think he was one
of the greatest governors the state has ever had." Phil La Follette said,
"He was an able and distinguished governor and citizen of Wisconsin."
Industrialist Herman Falk stated, "We had been close friends for many
years. During this long relationship I came to have great admiration for
his character and ability. I feel that industry, state and national, has lost
one of its outstanding figures."[21]

Governor Heil soon expanded upon his initial remarks, saying "Former Governor Walter J. Kohler died of a broken heart and everybody
knows it. He was crucified by organized labor in an unjustified strike,
when he had done more for labor than any man in Wisconsin. He was
crucified by the politicians when they rigged a charge of violating the
State Corrupt Practices Act, of which he was found innocent, but only

after a long, distressing trial. He was being crucified by the New Deal, which was trying to smear him with charges of violating the Anti-Trust Act."[22]

Many average citizens also declared their admiration for Walter Sr. Carl Berlin, who retired in 1931 from the Kohler Company after 29 years, told a reporter, "Ja, he was a good friend to everybody. I remember when the mama and I had our golden wedding he came, and he drank beer with us, and he sang like all the rest. And every little while he would stop by the house here and talk about flowers and trees." Richard Held said, "I've been with the company 30 years—I was a moulder when I was a young man, but now I'm in the finishing department—and it won't seem right not to have 'the governor' coming around in his jumpers to look things over." Kohler worker William Range told a reporter, "You know what I'll always remember best about him? The night of the strike when they broke all the windows. He came around to me and he said: 'Never mind, Bill, just don't get too close. All this can be repaired, Bill, but if we lose a human life...' He was all broken up and that's all he could say. I guess that shows what kind of a man he was."[23]

As the deceased's son and Secretary of the Kohler Company, Walter personally handled scores of private messages of condolence that poured into his office.[24]

The open coffin was placed in the great hallway at Riverbend just before the funeral, and hundreds lined up to say farewell. One veteran Kohler Company employee, on his way to the bier, came face to face with Walter. Without a word being spoken, the two burst into tears and clasped each other as they wept.

Almost 15,000 people attended the funeral service at Riverbend on April 24, all but about 700 in the house listening over loudspeakers set up on the lawn. "Wisconsin has never seen a funeral like this one," said a Milwaukee reporter. The Governor, and seven Supreme Court Justices, were among the dignitaries. The service was led by Episcopal Bishop Harwood Sturtevant of the Diocese of Fond du Lac. The Kohler high school choir sang. Afterward, a color guard from the American Legion and from St. John's Military Academy presented arms as the hearse set out for the Village cemetery. On its route, some 3,700 Kohler Company employees and their wives stood bareheaded at the curb of the main street in Kohler. They had been waiting there for more than two hours to pay their last respects.[25]

Herbert, John, and Walter were executors of Walter Sr.'s will. Charlotte received the largest single share of the estate, held in trust during her lifetime. A portion equal to her share was divided between the four sons, who would inherit their mother's share at her death. Charlotte was guaranteed an income of $50,000 a year and a life residency at Riverbend. (Outsiders were unaware that Charlotte, 71, was suffering from Alzheimer's Disease.)[26] The will also contained several generous bequests to local charities and household servants. While the sum of the estate was not made public, it is clear that Walter and his brothers now enjoyed considerable wealth and authority within the privately held company.[27]

There was also the question of Walter Sr.'s successor as president of the company. Walter Sr. had told the John Doe inquiry in mid-1928 that he owned 43% of Kohler stock.[28] He did not believe that one who ran a company should completely own it.[29] His wife, sisters, half-brother Herbert, and his sons were the other major stockholders. Leadership, as was the company tradition, would surely come from within the family.

Herbert was the logical choice. He had started working at the Kohler Company when he was 16, laboring during his summer vacations in the foundry as an enameler and moulder. He joined the company full time in 1920. A year later, at the age of 30, he was elected to the Board of Directors. The following year he became company treasurer, and in 1928 he was named to the newly created post of Executive Vice President. During the 1934 strike, Herbert led the company forces within the plant and no doubt coordinated efforts with the special deputies housed at the American Club. Walter Sr. ran the company, but Herbert was surely second in command. In 1937, Walter Sr. assumed the title of Chairman and gave the title of President to Herbert. At Walter Sr.'s death, Herbert knew more about the company than anyone else.

Herbert Vollrath Kohler, as we have seen, was born in the family home in Sheboygan in 1891, the only child of John Michael Kohler's second wife, Minnie Vollrath. He was, then, 16 years younger than Walter Sr., and 13 years younger than the youngest of Walter's three sisters. After the death of their father in 1900, Walter Sr. made the major decisions in Herbert's life, including his schooling. Highly intelligent, Herbert graduated from Yale in 1914 with a Bachelor of Philosophy degree. He had taken the science option and was employed at the plant in its engineering department.

Herbert was six feet tall, handsome, muscular, and aggressive. He was a champion wrestler at Yale and was also on the track team. After college, he spent two years in the army, rising to the rank of Captain of field artillery in the 32nd division and taking part in four major campaigns in France. Back at the Kohler Company, he kept in shape by joining five other young members of the Kohler Volunteer Fire Department in running eight miles to and from Sheboygan each noon, pulling a hook-and-ladder truck.[30] By anyone's estimation, Herbert V. Kohler was a formidable man.

In 1937, at the age of 45, Herbert married for the first time. Ruth Miriam De Young, 30, was attractive, intelligent, and charming. She had been born in Illinois, the daughter of a chief justice of the Illinois Supreme Court. She was a graduate of Smith, where she majored in history, and had spent a year studying at the Sorbonne in Paris and the University of London. When Herbert first saw her at a woman's conference in Chicago, she was the women's editor of the *Chicago Tribune*. Herbert introduced himself to Ruth that very day, telling an assistant "I'm going to marry that girl." He proceeded to send her a bouquet of red roses each day for the next three months, until they were wed.[31] Throughout his life, Herbert almost always got what he wanted.

When the newlyweds settled down in Kohler, in a large house in the Village, Ruth quickly became active in civic and cultural affairs.[32] She would have three children, write two books on Wisconsin history, and become a major figure in historic preservation within the state. None of the Kohler women dared look down upon her, and many, in and outside the family, thought she had a highly positive impact on her husband.[33] A son recalled that Herbert was "very, very devoted" to his wife.[34]

Herbert was widely known to be a moody, passionate man with a fearsome temper. Some thought him tyrannical and obstinate. It is certain that he was a man of strong convictions with an iron will.[35] On the other hand, Herbert could be gracious, relaxed, and jovial.[36] A company attorney described him as being "very dignified, solid, a man of integrity," and recalled his employer's consistent affection toward his employees.[37] Peter and Nancy Kohler remember Herbert's delight in playing with and spoiling their four young daughters when the family lived a couple of blocks from the elder Kohler's home.[38]

Herbert V. Kohler, Jr. described his father as thoughtful, kind, warm, funny, and a man of principle. "He loved to paint landscapes and joined his daughter Ruth, who enjoyed drawing, on excursions into the mountains of Alberta." Herbert was also an expert horseman. His son recalled, "His fondness for horses and horsemanship began as a child, developed in the Cavalry of the First World War, and continued for sixty years thereafter."[39]

Soon after Walter Sr.'s death, the Board of Directors chose Herbert to be both the company President and CEO.[40] This was not good news for Walter's sons, for Herbert did not like or respect his nephews. One relative reports that Herbert was a rather private person, and that Walter Sr.'s sons, over the years, had snickered at him during social events.[41] There were no doubt other, deeper family issues involved which cannot be documented at this time. It seems likely that Walter and his brothers knew of their uncle's negative attitude toward them well in advance of their father's death but underestimated the depth of his animosity.

Herbert also undoubtedly saw his nephews as competitors. They were already major stockholders, and at their mother's death they were to inherit a sizable portion of additional company stock. They might at any time garner the votes of other stockholders to challenge his position, or they might use their name and influence, individually or collectively, to resist his decisions.[42] Walter, especially, must have posed a threat, for he, more than the other three, most closely resembled his father and might always be considered seriously as a possible replacement or successor. Herbert wanted no less than absolute authority. That was his nature.

The Kohler company head told his nephews that they could stay on the payroll, but he refused to give them any meaningful work. The message was clear: Walter Sr.'s sons had no future at the company. All four decided initially to stick it out, if only to hold onto their valuable stock and hope that their uncle might eventually treat them more favorably. Besides, they had all been employed at the Kohler Company since their early teens; it was their life.[43]

John was permitted to remain in his position as Treasurer. In 1947, he would be promoted to Vice-President. But in fact Herbert gave him virtually nothing to do. As a result, he sometimes became depressed, a situation which was compounded by colon cancer when he reached his fifties.[44] John was to spend the next 28 years, until his death, whiling away the hours in his office, determined to be faithful to what duties he had and make the best of his situation. His children admired him for what they thought was his courage and tenacity.[45]

John's wife, Julilly, in the words of her son Michael, "worshipped Walter Kohler Sr." She just as fervently disliked Herbert, not only for his treatment of her husband but because of his politics. Herbert was as far to the Right as Julilly was to the Left, and the two sometimes quarreled openly, increasing family tensions.[46]

Jim labored in the plant until his death in 1960, at age 55. He became Director of Research in 1945, and his work generally satisfied him. A niece recalls him being marginalized, kept in a factory basement, content to live in his own little world of engineering.[47] A son recalls him dressing in khaki and green, never wearing a tie, often driving a jeep. He was much loved by co-workers.[48]

Jim had created a local company for his four sons, hoping to keep them in the vicinity, and he intended to join them at some point. While his early death spoiled that plan, three of the sons continued to work at the successful Kohler-Joa (later Kohler General) company the rest of their lives.[49]

Bob Kohler chafed at his meaningless job. His daughter Jill later described it as "Vice President of Nothing."[50] For the first few years after his father's death, he was probably waiting to see what course of action Walter would take.

In the fall of 1940, Walter took his mother, Celeste, Terry, and Niki to Hawaii. Charlotte suffered not only from grief but was succumbing to Alzheimer's Disease, and this change of scenery was designed in part to help ease her pain. It was also a working trip, for Walter was setting up distribution rights for Kohler products in the islands, which were anticipating a big tourist boom. The Kohlers stayed in Hawaii for about six months.[51]

Back home in the spring of 1941, Walter was involved in a serious automobile accident that occurred near Plymouth, Wisconsin, not far from Sheboygan. He, Celeste, her brother Eugene, and his wife were in a convertible when it went off the road on a curve and rolled over. Walter broke his collar bone, and Celeste suffered lacerations that ingested poison ivy. Terry later recalled that his mother "was VERY affected by that for awhile!" Eugene was badly hurt, having been thrown from the car and landing on a barbed wire fence. He was in traction for a time to heal several broken bones and recuperated at Windway with a private nurse for the best part of a year.[52] Walter's fortunes improved greatly, however, in July when he was named to the Board of Directors of the Vollrath Corporation, replacing his late father.

❖❖❖❖◆❖❖❖

It will be recalled that at the death of Jacob J. Vollrath in 1873, his entire estate was left to his wife, Elisabetha. At her death, the estate was to be divided in six equal parts: one to each of the five remaining sons and daughters and one to Lillie's children. Because John Michael Kohler had married two of the Vollrath girls, he stood to become a major Vollrath heir. Elisabetha Vollrath died in 1906, six years after John Michael. Walter Sr., 31, now president of the Kohler Company, became a leading figure in the Jacob J. Vollrath Manufacturing Company. He controlled his own stocks, those of his sisters, and those held by his step-mother, Minnie.

In April, 1908, company stockholders met to incorporate under the laws of Wisconsin what was now called The Vollrath Company. The initial capital stock was $10,000. Since Andrew Vollrath had been bought out, the five descendants of Jacob J. Vollrath held most of the authority, and they were the most active in purchasing shares. The largest shareholder was the company President Carl A. W. Vollrath, the founder's fifth child and second son, who had worked with his father at the factory since the age of 12. (When he died in 1932, he had served the company for 58 years.) He purchased 136 ⅔ shares. Minnie Kohler had 13 ⅓ shares, while Walter Sr. and his sisters each held only 3 ⅓ shares. Still, Walter Sr. was on the three-man Board of Directors, drew up the company's new constitution and by-laws, and was elected vice president, a post he would retain until his death.[53] The Vollraths and the Kohlers were committed as relatives, friends, and business associates to making the company prosper.

Under this leadership the company's line of pots, pans, kettles, dishes, cups, pitchers, and strainers proved increasingly popular. In 1910 The Vollrath Company began to construct a new plant at 18th and Michigan in Sheboygan (its current site). The following year its net assets totaled more than $600,000 and stockholders purchased $500,000 in stock. In 1912, Vollrath family members still dominated the investors, Walter Sr., his sisters, and Minnie owning just over 8% of the 5,000 shares of stock. But Walter Sr. remained a major figure in the business decisions of the company. Now in its new facility, Vollrath employed some 200 men.[54]

Throughout the prosperous 1920s, company sales and profits continued to rise. Capital stock was increased to a million dollars in 1920. In 1923, the advertising budget rose to $60,000. Two years later, sales shot up to more than $1.8 million. By 1928 the company was selling over 800 different items, including colored cooking utensils. In January, 1930, Vollrath displayed its wares at the prestigious Third Annual House Furnishing Exhibit in Chicago. In the mid-1930s, the company began producing non-enameled stainless steel kitchen and hospital items.[55]

When Minnie Kohler died in 1929, her stock was distributed to Walter Sr., his three sisters, and Herbert. This amounted to only a slight adjustment in the economic authority of the Kohlers in the company. Herbert, however, unlike his half-sisters, did not give Walter Sr. his proxy, a fact that may have revealed some tension between the two men. In early 1932, Herbert received permission to attend Board meetings, to see for himself what was going on.[56]

The Great Depression had a profoundly negative impact on Vollrath. In the first three years, the company lost nearly half a million dollars. Workers were fired, salaries were slashed, hours were cut, pensions were reduced, corporate memberships were cancelled, charitable donations were curtailed, and the plant operated at only 53% normal capacity. A huge inventory of unsold goods stacked up inside and outside the plant. Loans from company officers and a Sheboygan bank kept the factory going. The book value of each share fell from $213 in 1931 to $152 in 1936.[57]

Walter Sr. served throughout these years of turmoil as Chairman of the Board, in addition to his tenure as Vice President. He was absent from Board meetings only during the Kohler strike of 1934. Jean C. Vollrath succeeded his late father, C. A. W. Vollrath, as company President, grappling as best he could with economic disaster. In 1934, he paid for his own $50,000 life insurance, the company being unable to part with the necessary funds.[58]

In 1935, there were encouraging signs of the company's economic recovery. But they soon faded, and losses again began to mount. The net loss for 1938 was over $73,000, and stocks slumped to $145 a share.[59] The net loss for 1939 was over $36,000.[60]

Walter Sr., whose own company was prospering, was given increasing authority over Vollrath. Herbert was often at his side when key decisions were made.[61] In 1940, the Board officially thanked both men for reorganizing the company, its products, and its marketing. Neither had received any compensation for their extensive and successful efforts. Net sales for 1939 were 6.3% higher than a year earlier, and the future seemed brighter. Herbert now joined the Board as a full-fledged member.[62]

Walter Sr. had grown powerful at Vollrath in another way by controlling a huge block of shares, carried on the books as one of two C. A. W. Vollrath Estate accounts that stemmed from debts owed the company by the late President's heirs. Moreover, he continued to control his own shares and those of his three sisters. "The Governor," as he was still called, was the single most important official in the company.

Walter Sr.'s death on April 22, 1940 left Board members in deep mourning. The deceased was not only a beloved relative and friend, he had served The Vollrath Company selflessly and with much energy and dedication for 33 years.[63] His reforms bore immediate fruit, as the company showed a profit for the year.[64] Before long, war orders would restore full prosperity and enable company growth.

Soon after Walter Sr.'s death, Herbert produced a document that he said was signed by his late half-brother in early 1933 giving him full authority to vote on his behalf should he be absent. Board members and stock holders did not object, and Herbert assumed Walter Sr.'s full authority at the company. At stockholders' meetings, he commanded more than 2,600 of the total 9,212 shares.[65]

Walter and his brothers, inheriting their father's personally owned shares, were now invited to shareholders' meetings. Their authority was limited, as each only owned 47 shares. Walter alone was selected, of the four, to join the Board of Directors, serving with Herbert and three members of the Vollrath family. It was clear that he had the respect of the shareholders, many of whom no doubt saw him as a reflection of his father. Walter played an active role at his first two meetings as a Board member. He was not to be his uncle's puppet.[66]

The rise of German and Japanese militarism in the mid and late 1930s prompted most Wisconsin citizens, especially those with German ancestral roots, to be sympathetic toward isolationism. (There is no evidence revealing a position taken by any member of the Kohler family.) Prevailing opinion within the state favored cutting economic ties with European nations and working toward the improvement of America's own welfare and security. Direct military intervention in the Woodrow Wilson years, many thought, had failed to bring world peace, and a similar policy during the Great Depression could spell economic disaster for the nation, as well as needless loss of American lives. After a tour of Europe in 1938, Phil La Follette was persuaded that the United States could escape war by simply refusing to become involved, by demonstrating to the world that work and freedom were compatible. Fascism might well wither, he preached, in the light of America's example.[67]

After Hitler's invasion of Poland in 1939, the fall of France in 1940, and the bombardment of Great Britain, the case for direct American intervention became more powerful. Moreover, it began to be clear that helping our allies assisted prosperity rather than hindering it. In 1940, average Wisconsin payrolls increased 41%, and in the following year workers earned more than they ever had. (Unemployment was still almost 14% in 1940; a decade later it stood at 3%.) State farmers received similar gains as Wisconsin became a key producer of dairy products, peas, and eggs in the "Food for Defense" program. In late 1941, the Vollrath Company began to convert almost all of its facilities to defense work. Kohler Company officials carefully observed international affairs, for it was clear that major production changes would be in the works if America entered the war.[68]

The Japanese attack on Pearl Harbor, and the same-day assault on U. S. bases at Guam, Midway Island, and in the Philippines, persuaded virtually all Americans that this was their fight as well, and that World War II deserved every ounce of their energy in order to stop fascism, both in Europe and Asia. December 7, 1941 marked the end of American isolationism. Those of German descent, in Wisconsin and elsewhere, pitched in with Americans of all nationalities to defeat an evil that was threatening to devour the world.

When Walter and his family were in Hawaii for six months, they had to be well aware of the military buildup in the area. The American Pacific fleet and a large number of aircraft were on hand, along with some 43,000 soldiers. As Walter read the tragic list of Pearl Harbor casualties—2,403 Americans dead, 1,178 wounded, eighteen warships sunk or crippled, 204 planes on the ground damaged or destroyed, five airfields damaged extensively—he knew what he had to do. It was a matter of principle.

The day after Pearl Harbor, Walter joined the long lines of men, seen all across the country, eager to get into the Armed Forces. He signed up for the Naval Reserve, seeking active duty. Celeste was deeply upset by the decision. Her husband could easily have avoided military service. In April, 1942, Walter would be 38 years old. He had dependents. Moreover, with the Kohler Company certain to convert its facilities into war production, his regular duties would be of at least some service to the Allied cause.[69] His brothers stayed at home during the war. (Jim served in the Armed Forces for three months starting in May, 1945.)[70] Walter might have continued to enjoy the comforts of wealth and the pleasures of family life right through the conflict. Celeste "grieved" (in the words of her son) about her husband's sense of honor and self-sacrifice; it was something she had never experienced and could not share. But her pleas were in vain.

Walter easily passed his physical (a slight astigmatism in one eye was corrected by glasses) and soon prepared to report for duty. He became a lieutenant on April 29 and took his oath of office on May 19. He wanted from the start to serve in the South Pacific.[71]

Notes

1 See Personnel file. The appointment was made on April 10, 1937.

2 Sternberg, "Is This The Man to Beat McCarthy?," 77; Walter J. Vollrath, Jr. interview. This is a general description that appears consistently in my oral interviews.

3 Peter and Nancy Kohler interview, August 11, 2003.

4 Tim and Barbara Gorham interview, October 24, 2004. Her death certificate lists her surname as Kohler, and she can be found on Ancestry.com under that name. See the Jackie Holden papers in the Terry Kohler papers.

5 A copy of the photograph is in the Mary Kohler Ahern collection. It was published in the *Milwaukee Journal*, July 6, 1936. Terry Kohler was christened earlier, the *Journal* caption read.

6 See copy, "Constitution Day Speech by Walter J. Kohler at Faneuil Hall, Boston, Massachusetts, September 17, 1935," Terry Kohler papers.

7 "State Mourns Walter Kohler, Leader in Politics and Industry," *Milwaukee Journal*, April 22, 1940.

8 For balanced accounts, see Robert C. Nisbet, *Wisconsin, A History* (Madison: the University of Wisconsin Press, 1973), 492-494, and Haney, *A Concise History*, 5-7.

9 There is no certain explanation for Walter's policy of funding projects for Jim and Walter, Jr. and doing nothing for John and Bob. One possible explanation concerning John is that he, as the oldest, was offered first choice at purchasing Riverbend in Walter Sr.'s will. See Julilly Kohler interview, October 7, 2003, and e-mail, Michael Kohler to the author, May 7, 2005, John Michael Kohler III file. John and his family lived on a company farm in Sheboygan Falls, west of Kohler. John rented the modest farm house from 1938, when he returned to Kohler from Chicago, until 1949. Bob and his family stayed in their West Park Lane home until building near Walter in 1958. See the Mary Kohler Ahern interview.

10 See Peter and Nancy Kohler interview, May 6, 2005.

11 E-mail, Terry Kohler to the author, March 8, 2005, Windway file.

12 *Ibid.* Remaining documents suggest a cost for constructing the house to be in the neighborhood of $104,000, but one can't be certain. Moreover, that figure does not include architectural fees and the purchase of land. Terry acknowledges that the conversation about the cost of Windway occurred "years later (after WW-II) and my mother may well have been trying to push the number up in my head." Celeste implied also that she had loaned her husband part of his half of the total sum. But this was said after the divorce, and Celeste's bitterness may have been reflected in the statement. See e-mails to the author, March 9, 2005, *ibid.* Relevant documents are in the Windway files in the Terry Kohler papers. See also the Terry Kohler interviews of August 13, 2003, March 25, 2004. For many years the flat

roof was flooded with water to provide a sort of air conditioning. The engineer quoted was Robert Gordon Jones of Kohler, Wisconsin. See a copy of his letter to Terry Kohler, February 7, 1988 in the Terry Kohler papers. Photographs of Windway, as it was being constructed, are in the Leslie Kohler Hawley collection.

[13] Jackie was in Canada in the fall of 1939 and graduated from Central High School in Sheboygan in 1941 (the only degree she was to acquire). One can rarely be certain about Jackie's whereabouts until much later in her life.

[14] Terry Kohler interview, March 25, 2004; Peter and Nancy Kohler interview, August 11, 2003.

[15] E-mail, Terry Kohler to the author, April 28, 2005, in the Miscellaneous file.

[16] Dorothy Engleman interview.

[17] Serabia, *80 Years of My Wandering Spirit*, 44.

[18] "Kohler and Others Indicted in Probe of Plumbing Costs," *Milwaukee Journal*, March 29, 1940.

[19] See Walter's physical examination report of July 23, 1942, Terry Kohler papers; copy, Walter J. Kohler, Jr., to William J. Matthews, April 30, 1940, Condolence file, *ibid*; e-mail, Terry Kohler to the author, May 18, 2004, Walter J. Kohler Sr. file.

[20] "State Mourns Walter Kohler, Leader in Politics and Industry," "Man With the White Carnation in Lapel Was Noted for His Splendid Hospitality," *Milwaukee Journal*, April 22, 1940.

[21] "Tributes Paid to Mr. Kohler," *ibid*.

[22] "Ex-Gov. Kohler, 65, Dies In Wisconsin," *New York Times*, April 22, 1940.

[23] "Kohler Village Workers Mourn Toiler Who Left Indelible Mark in Community," *Milwaukee Journal*, April 23, 1940.

[24] See the Condolence file, Terry Kohler papers.

[25] "Walter Kohler Is Laid to Last Rest in Village Where They Loved Him," *Milwaukee Journal*, April 25, 1940. The *Milwaukee Sentinel*, April 25, carried a large article on the funeral along with numerous photos. See also *Kohler of Kohler News*, May, 1940, for a solid biography and excellent photographs.

[26] See Michael Kohler interview.

[27] "Walter J. Kohler's Will Filed Today; Friendship House Bequest Included," *Sheboygan Press*, May 21, 1940.

[28] See file 19, box 39 of the Walter J. Kohler Sr. papers.

[29] Julilly Kohler interview, October 7, 2003.

[30] Blodgett, *A Sense of Higher Design*, 125-126. The truck is on display at the visitors' center in Kohler. See also "Kohler Dies; Headed Plumbingware Firm," *Milwaukee Journal*, July 29, 1968.

[31] Blodgett, *A Sense of Higher Design*, 126-127; Herbert V. Kohler, Jr. interview.

[32] The house, at 441 Green Tree Road, remained the Kohler residence throughout Herbert's life. His son, Herbert Jr., continued to live there for many years.

[33] Blodgett, *A Sense of Higher Design*, 126-128; "Mrs. Herbert Kohler Called Unexpectedly," *Sheboygan Press*, March 7, 1953; Bender, *At The Top*, 253.

[34] Herbert V. Kohler, Jr. interview.

[35] See Roland Neumann interview; Terry Kohler interview, June 12, 2003; Walter J. Vollrath, Jr. interview; Vicki and Jill Kohler interview; Uphoff, *Kohler on Strike*, 162, 175, 210, 293, 382-387;

[36] Walter Vollrath, Jr. interview; Mike Weber interview.

[37] Ken Benson interviews of May 17, 18, 2004.

[38] Peter and Nancy Kohler interview, May 6, 2005.

[39] Herbert V. Kohler, Jr. interview.

[40] Bob Kohler told his daughters that Walter Sr. thought his boys too young to run the company and that Herbert was his choice. Vicki and Jill Kohler interview. Walter told Terry that Board members chose Herbert because he was the oldest heir, and that they had more confidence in him than in his nephews. Terry Kohler interview, June 12, 2003.

[41] Walter J. Vollrath, Jr. interview.

[42] Corporate counsel Lucas P. Chase later told the Kohler family attorney of the narrow margin of Herbert's power in terms of stock shares under his control, a margin that might be topped by his nephews in alliance with other board members. Roland Neumann interview; e-mail, Roland Neumann to the author, January 9, 2005, Miscellaneous file.

[43] Roland Neumann interview; Julilly Kohler interview, October 7, 2003.

[44] Marie Kohler interview.

[45] Julilly Kohler interview, October 7, 2003; Marie Kohler interview; Michael Kohler interview.

[46] Marie Kohler interview; Julilly Kohler interview, October 7, 2003.

[47] Julilly Kohler interview, October 7, 2003. Cf. Roland Neumann interview.

[48] Peter and Nancy Kohler interview, August 11, 2003; Roland Neumann interview; "Carl J. Kohler Found Dead In Summer Lodge," *Sheboygan Press*, November 17, 1960.

[49] Peter and Nancy Kohler interview, May 5, 2005. The exception was the oldest son, Carl (Jim), who at one point owned a restaurant-bar near Mequon, Wisconsin.

[50] Vicki and Jill Kohler interview.

[51] Terry Kohler interviews of June 12, August 13, 2003.

52 Walter's physical examination report from 1942, Terry Kohler papers; e-mail, Terry Kohler to the author, May 18, 2004, Miscellaneous file; Serabia, *80 Years of My Wandering Spirit*, 47.

53 Vollrath Company Minutes, April 13, 1908.

54 *Ibid.*, February 14, 1912; *The Vollrath Story, Celebrating 125 Years*, 7-8.

55 *Ibid.*, 9-11; Vollrath Company Minutes, December 17, 1920; February 14, 1923; February 11, 1925; May 28, 1928.

56 *Ibid.*, February 11, 1931; January 28, 1932.

57 *Ibid.*, February 24, April 10, 1934; February 13, July 3, 1935; February 18, 1936.

58 *Ibid.*, April 10, 1934.

59 *Ibid.*, September 12, December 12, 1935; February 18, 1936; April 1, 1938; March 1, 1939.

60 *Ibid.*, February 22, 1940.

61 *Ibid.*, May 15, 1939; July 17, 1939.

62 *Ibid.*, February 22, 1940.

63 *Ibid.*, May 13, 1940.

64 *Ibid.*, July 2, 1941.

65 *Ibid.*, January 27, June 6, July 2, 1941.

66 *Ibid.*, July 2, December 20, 1941; March 5, 1942.

67 Glad, *The History of Wisconsin, Volume V*, 527, 560-564.

68 *Ibid.*, 564-565; *The Vollrath Story, Celebrating 125 Years*, 12. On unemployment data, see Nesbit, *Wisconsin, A History*, 517.

69 Terry Kohler interview, June 12, 2003.

70 Bob was actually given something to do during the war, serving as liaison between the company and the federal government regarding armaments manufacture. "Robert Eugene Kohler," *Sheboygan Press*, March 19, 1990.

71 Terry Kohler interview, June 12, 2003; Steinberg, "Is This the Man to Beat McCarthy?," 77; physical examination, July 23, 1942, and fitness report, October 26, 1942, Military files, Terry Kohler Papers.

Chapter Six

At War

Walter left the Kohler company on August 14, 1942. Four days later, Lieutenant Kohler reported to the Naval Air Station at Quonset Point, Rhode Island for what turned out to be 17 weeks of basic training. Navy officials chose to use him as an Intelligence Officer. Walter's fine education and learning skills, his pilot training, and his administrative experience acquired at the Kohler Company solidly qualified him in that field.

Celeste and the children rented a home in New Haven, Connecticut. Terry and Niki were enrolled in a nearby private school.[1] In a letter to his mother and his brothers and their wives, Walter described the demanding nature of the activity at Quonset Point and of a pleasant weekend he spent with Celeste, the children, and Jackie. One of his recent duties was to help staff officers in selecting billets for the 750 men who graduated. He noted that he was among the top students, both in I.Q. score and academic achievement, and thus could have his choice for assignment. He was almost sent on a temporary assignment to the Great Lakes Naval Training Station, outside Chicago, "it being the best billet in the class." But Walter did not want to spend the war or any part of it in Chicago, arguing strenuously for Air Combat Intelligence duty overseas. He soon got his way. The assignment required extra training, which accounts for the extraordinary length of Walter's time at Quonset.[2]

In early November, Walter wrote again to family members in Wisconsin. He observed that he had just graduated from indoctrination school and had enjoyed six days of leave with Celeste and the children in Newport. The additional training he received, he said, was interesting and demanding, the courses being taught by university professors. In a letter of December 9 (a continuation of his earlier letter to family members), Walter noted that he had not yet received a specific assignment but knew that he was one of several chosen to attend special seminars in the Pacific Area, "from which the inference could be drawn that that's where we're slated to be sent." Celeste, he noted, was studying drama, one day spending 13 hours building a stage set. "The kids are very anxious to get back to Windway."[3]

After a Christmas leave, Walter said goodbye to his family and left for San Francisco, gateway to the combat zone in the Pacific. He soon learned he had guessed correctly that his assignment would be in one of the most dangerous areas of the war.

After her husband's departure, Celeste and the children stayed in New Haven. In the summer of 1943, Celeste moved to Key Largo, Florida, rented a house, and placed Terry and Niki in a nearby boarding school. Terry later noted that this move marked the end of nannies in the family; from this point on, Celeste took a more direct involvement in the lives of her young children. She did not spoil them as she had Jackie. Terry later recalled his mother was a "strong disciplinarian," who would spank him on occasion "when I had it coming."[4]

Walter surely knew of his wife's move to Florida, but on all of his military forms throughout the war he continued to list her residence as Windway. (No wartime correspondence between the two has survived.) No doubt the lieutenant's family was often on his mind as he traveled out into the Pacific to meet an enemy he was resolved to help defeat.

The Japanese, following their attack at Pearl Harbor, had expanded their military operations rapidly. The nation needed oil and foreign markets for its industries. The immediate goal was to create a self-sufficient empire, and to do that the Americans and British, above all, had to be driven out of their Pacific strongholds. Japanese troops poured into Guam in the Marianas, where America had a major area base, and took strategic Rabaul at the northern tip of New Britain. Despite fierce resistance by U.S. Marines, they captured Wake island, site of another major U.S. base. They also took the British held Gilbert Islands, and attacked Midway. Within 70 days, Malaya and Singapore were taken from the British, and Hong Kong fell on December 25.

Before Pearl Harbor, President Roosevelt had created a new Army command in the Philippines, placing General Douglas MacArthur at its head. Fearing impending trouble with the Japanese, defenses of the islands were strengthened, and several huge, B-17 "Flying Fortress" planes were dispatched to the area. The Japanese attack began shortly after the strike at Pearl Harbor, starting at Luzon, the site of 250 American aircraft. At the end of three weeks, American air power was destroyed, and MacArthur and his forces retreated to Corregidor. The takeover of the Philippines seemed inevitable. The evacuation of MacArthur to

Australia in March, 1942, the surrender of American troops in April, the infamous Bataan "Death March," the siege of Corregidor, and the fall of Manila Bay in May were heavy blows to the United States.

In March, 1942 the Joint Chiefs of Staff gave the Navy responsibility for the "Pacific Ocean Area" and designated Admiral Chester W. Nimitz to head its forces. (The Army, under MacArthur, had control of the "Southwest Pacific Area," consisting of Australia and the Philippines.) Although President Roosevelt gave priority to the defeat of Germany, American forces in the Pacific increased rapidly in 1942. By the end of the year, more than a half of the overseas divisions and about a third of the air combat forces were engaged in war against the Japanese.

The bombing of Tokyo began on April 18, 1942. The daring daylight raid by 16 B25's marked the first time that bombers flew from an aircraft carrier. In May, the Battle of the Coral Sea boosted American morale by stopping Japanese expansion in the Southwest Pacific. The Battle of Midway in June was a major victory, insuring the retention of both Midway and the Hawaiian Islands and inflicting major damage to Japanese ships and personnel. The struggle also proved the effectiveness of dive bombers launched from carriers. The Allies were now on the offensive.

In early 1943, after a year and a half of fierce fighting, the Japanese gave up Guadalcanal, a crucial spot in the Solomon Islands. Suffering horrific casualties, the Japanese were also driven out of Buna, preventing their takeover of strategically important New Guinea.

By the time Walter was on his way to the Pacific, then, American, British, and Australian forces were growing increasingly confident that they could defeat the Japanese. But no troops of any nationality took their adversaries lightly, for they had suffered greatly at their hands and knew them to be fanatical and capable warriors. America suffered 6,000 casualties at Guadalcanal. At Buna, there were 2,848 American casualties, and 5,698 Australian casualties. At Midway, the United States lost a carrier, a destroyer, about 150 planes, and 307 men. Americans could not forget or forgive the Bataan Death March and the murder of about 600 Americans and some 5,000 to 10,000 Filipino prisoners by Japanese troops. Who could tell how many more years and tens, if not hundreds, of thousands of lives it would take to defeat Japan and crush its plans for empire?

In early 1943, 374,000 American troops poured into the Pacific area. In contrast, 298,000 were in the Mediterranean and about 107,000 in Europe. MacArthur, Admiral William F. "Bull" Halsey, and other top military authorities hashed over numerous plans for victory in the Pacific, seeking to conquer an assortment of islands and air bases with an eye on returning to the Philippines. At first, Walter was assigned to the staff of the Commander, Air Force, Pacific, based at Pearl Harbor. In April, 1943, he was transferred to Admiral Halsey's combat command in the South Pacific. Walter's orders sent him to Havalo seaplane base, on the Florida Islands, in the Solomons.

The Solomon Islands chain contains several hundred islands, thinly populated and only barely developed when the war came. The northern region was part of the Australian Mandated Territory of New Guinea, and the rest of the Islands were under the British Solomon Islands Protectorate. The entire chain is among the world's wettest areas; rainfall in some places can exceed 200 inches a year. From November to March, inhabitants can expect monsoons. The temperatures are tropical, ranging daily between 73 to 93 degrees, and the humidity is high. Troops suffered terribly from malaria and fungus infections and sores. During the struggle to conquer Papua, New Guinea, there had been 8,659 cases of infectious disease.

The Florida islands are east of the northern tip of Guadalcanal. Tulagi, the center of British government in the area, lay between the two bodies. It boasts the best harbor in the Solomons and was thus the scene of a major Allied buildup in 1942. Henderson Airfield on the northern shore of Guadalcanal, facing the Florida islands, was the center of another massive buildup when Walter arrived. A steady stream of aircraft zoomed in and out of the airfield, often fresh from conflicts with the enemy. In January there had been more than 50,000 American troops on Guadalcanal, and Walter was one of thousands who continued to come.

After their severely costly losses at Guadalcanal, the Japanese moved northward 200 miles to the New Georgia group, and American planes pursued them, bombing airfields and installations and watching for submarines. Although the Allies had clear air superiority, the Japanese fought back in a constant barrage of warfare on land, sea, and air. All around the beaches of the area lay the wrecks of ships, aircraft, tanks and landing craft. Fragmented palm trees and burned out patches of the tropical rain forests also bore evidence of the horrendous warfare that had transformed this once sleepy land of jungles, mountains, deep rivers, swamps, barefoot natives, and cocoa and coffee plantations into a strategic battleground.

Walter was the Combat Intelligence Officer at the Halavo seaplane base in a unit which had as its primary mission the rescue of American pilots shot down by the Japanese. These "Dumbo" missions, as they were called, had first been organized in December, 1942, and by April, when Walter arrived, the operation was running smoothly. By that time, there were actually six types of missions: "1. Rescue missions to a designated island where personnel were known to be ashore. 2. Sea searches for fliers reported down at sea or sighted at sea by other aircraft. 3. Ferry missions involving transport of supplies to Coastwatchers ('Grocery Hops') or transport of personnel ('Taxi Service'). 4. Missions to evacuate personnel from enemy held territory or wounded from combat zones. 5. Anti-submarine or convoy escort missions. 6. Sector patrols…"

In a historical report written on May 6, Walter noted that by the end of April, the Halavo base had 13 officers (11 pilots and two ground officers), 91 enlisted men, and nine seaplanes, one being used for parts. The physical range of activity by the men at Halavo was often extensive. One mission in February rescued a B-17 crew from an island more than 400 miles away from the spot they were reported down. The frequency of flights reflected the state of the warfare in the area. In June, twenty two flights, including ten rescue missions, were made. Forty six flights were made in July, and 395 men were rescued.

One flight in mid-July brought back a Japanese fighter pilot, now a prisoner of war, along with 35 American personnel. Many flights brought the wounded to the hospital at Halavo. At times, a pilot and crew could only recover dead bodies. One flight rescued not only a crew of nine and two passengers, but 22 Chinese men, women, and children and their belongings. The severely overloaded plane needed a three-mile run before it could be airborne.

Carrying out the Dumbo missions was demanding and often dangerous work. Rescue planes were often inside enemy lines and received fire from land and air. Walter noted in his May 6 report, "The slow speed, lack of defensive fire power, and limited maneuverability of float planes makes them extremely vulnerable to enemy fighters."

As Combat Intelligence Officer, Walter interviewed crew members and survivors and wrote reports of operations. He kept a copy of a collection of his reports, and the detailed and well-written accounts contain thrilling accounts of brave, sick, and often wounded men struggling to survive in shark-infested waters and on dangerous land, sometimes for days, until they could be rescued. A poem, written by an ensign and included in the confidential report, declared "You'll not judge the 'Dumbo' by sleekness and speed. You'll see its greatness in courage and deed."[5]

There is no record of how many flights Walter took part in, but he did participate as well as write reports. In 1951, he told a magazine reporter that coast-watchers, hidden throughout Japanese-held islands, radioed word to him about American fliers shot down behind enemy lines. Part of his job was to arrange rendezvous and accompany pilots sent to rescue downed fliers.[6] He kept a photograph of one of his personal encounters with downed pilots.

Olen Clements, an Associated Press reporter, went along on one of Walter's rescue missions. The goal was to find two Marine fliers who were forced to bail out near an island held by the Japanese. In a Navy plane en route to the point where the flyers were downed, Clements asked the lieutenant if he was connected with the company that manufactured Kohler products. Walter, sitting next to the reporter on a box of ammunition, said that he was, and Clements replied, "I know your product well." Walter soon spotted one of the Marines on a beach, the bomber landed, and the flier was taken aboard. The Marine reported that he had been forced to bail out seven miles from the island and had paddled ashore in his rubber raft. Natives told him of nearby Japanese, and he hid in the jungle. His fellow Marine was never found. When Walter spotted the rescued man, he was rigging up a craft to make an escape. The story was carried by newspapers all across the United States.[7]

It is not known if Walter knew young John F. Kennedy. In March, 1943, JFK reported for PT boat duty on Tulagi, just a few miles from the Halavo seaplane base. Walter may have heard of Kennedy's accident before he left the area. On August 1, Kennedy's PT boat 109 was rammed by a Japanese destroyer near Kolombangara island. Two men were killed, and for a few days the young lieutenant and his crew were reported missing. Sailors all over the area sniggered about the only PT boat in the South Pacific to have suffered such a deadly mishap.[8]

In late July or the first days of August, Walter was sent to a cluster of islands called New Georgia, north and west of Guadalcanal. In early July, Americans had begun to invade the Japanese stronghold with air strikes, artillery fire, tanks, flamethrowers, and other weaponry, meeting fierce resistance. It is impossible to trace Walter's exact movements and duties during this portion of his service. But he later told a reporter that he participated in the night cruiser bombardment of the Munda airdrome just before it was captured, on August 5, by the United States, and was among the first troops to land on and occupy the key Japanese air base of Vila on the southern shore of the island of Kolombangara. Walter was stationed at Munda during the period that Americans constructed a 6,000 foot runway for bombers, the most widely used airstrip in the South Pacific. The huge Allied attack on Bougainville, the largest island in the Solomons, was soon underway.[9]

Walter said he did reconnaissance flying and engaged in air technical intelligence during this period. He also interviewed many Japanese prisoners, observing later that much of what they told him was propaganda. In the course of his duties, he visited virtually every island in the area.[10] Walter later told a Yale publication that at Munda he was the officer in charge of a joint Army-Navy Technical Air Intelligence unit.[11]

Documents show that in September, Walter went to Brisbane, Australia to work with the Seventh Fleet in Crash Intelligence.[12] An identification card dated September 10 notes that the bearer was "an Intelligence Technical inspector for the Directorate of Intelligence, Allied Air Forces. He and his Section are to take complete charge of all crashed or captured enemy air force equipment as early as possible."[13]

Walter's performance records were excellent. On his evaluation of December 14, the reporting Colonel gave him scores of 3.9 out of a possible 4.0, rating him at the very top in intelligence, judgment, cooperation, and endurance. The Colonel concluded: "An outstanding Air Combat Intelligence Officer in all respects....His work throughout has been uniformly excellent."[14]

Three of Walter's letters home in 1943 have survived, all of them addressed to his sister-in-law Julilly Kohler. On February 23, writing from Pearl Harbor, he reported on correspondence from his wife. "Poor Celeste is apparently having her troubles, however—no oil, no shoes for the kids, no coffee, no meat and no household help. She writes she is doing all the cooking and housekeeping while she does her crew work at school. She seems to prefer it that way although she says the children are beginning to look peaked on her cooking (facetiously, I hope.)" On his own experiences, he declared, "I must say I'm not bored but I don't mean by that there's been any violent excitement. The warm weather is certainly pleasant and I still get a thrill out of driving a jeep and being near, and often on, the water." He added, "I am well, beginning to get a little exercise, and am not unhappy although I certainly miss Celeste, the kids, and you all."

In June, from the Solomons, Walter said that he and all the troops were suffering from extreme homesickness and that mail was appreciated. "This collective isolation gives you the feeling sometimes, that (in D. H. Lawrence's obscure phrase) we're 'pinpoints in infinity'—a nothingness ahead and nothingness behind." He wondered about the mental condition of his mother, Charlotte. "Does she ever talk about me or give any indication of worry or concern? Or is my absence too far in the past to perturb her now? I hope the latter." Walter also noted that censorship limited his written remarks. "The book you anticipate, will never be written. Aside from the fact that diaries are strictly prohibited, I spend too much of my time emphasizing the importance of not carrying notes or letters or other documents in planes, to make any notes of my own."

In November, Walter wrote, "your description of the October countryside quicked that old familiar nostalgia for Wisconsin's autumns with their color, the blue haze over the valley, and that strange, fugitive melancholy. Being in a place where there are two seasons—the rainy season and the more rainy season—certainly evokes an appreciation for the truly astonishing contrasts of Wisconsin's climate." He spoke of his "restless impatience at sameness," continuing "War has plenty of sameness, of course—but also many high moments of intense excitement, and, strangely, not infrequent moments of beauty. There's no beauty in the cold facts of death and wounded men, or tortured and burned earth. But these islands with the first flush of dawn coloring the towering and billowy clouds, or the unbelievable green of the water around coral reefs, or the geometric pattern of a flight of many planes seen through the fallen leaves, or an enemy plane at night, mortally hit, trailing long plumes of flame as it plummets down—all these things have a unique and ineluctable beauty of their own."[15]

Walter flew home for Christmas, 1943, spending a couple of weeks at Windway with his family. The *Sheboygan Press* ran a large story on the lieutenant, including several photographs of him at Tulagi and Munda, along with a Japanese translator and a number of soldiers and sailors. With his shirt off in the blazing sun, on a wrecked Japanese boat at Tulagi, the lieutenant looked every bit the experienced combat veteran that he was. He told a reporter, "From what I have observed, the United States is doing a superb job in the South Pacific. There has been a coordinated effort on the part of the Navy, Army, and Marines that is really remarkable."[16]

Jackie was on hand for a family photo. After briefly attending the University of Wisconsin, she decided to return to her native Canada, and join the Royal Canadian Air Force. She was in uniform when she spent time with Walter, Celeste, and the children in Rhode island in the late summer of 1942. Ever the eccentric, she became the CRAF's first female mechanic. Brilliant, uninhibited, and outspoken, standing 5 foot nine inches tall and being physically strong, Jackie believed herself to be the equal of any man.[17]

In January, 1944, Walter was assigned to the brand new aircraft carrier Hancock, as the ship's Air Combat Intelligence officer. The Hancock's destination was the South Pacific and what would undoubtedly be fierce fighting against the Japanese. The family's farewell must have been difficult. Published lists of wartime casualties produced acute anxiety all across the nation every day, and families of servicemen dreaded the "knock on the door" that would bear the bad news. Celeste and the children may well have wondered if they would ever see Walter again.

In a short time, back in Key Largo, Terry was introduced to a painter named Robin MacFadden. He lived in the house next door. Ten years old and only home on weekends, Terry did not sense anything special in the friendship between the painter and his mother. A bit later, Celeste, her children, and Robin moved into a houseboat in a Marina shed on the Miami River. Still, Terry suspected nothing. In fact, Robin was a childhood sweetheart of Celeste's from Chicago, and the two were having an affair.[18]

✦ ✦ ✦ ◈ ✦ ✦ ✦

Before Pearl Harbor, the United States had begun production of 24 large Essex Class aircraft carriers, 9 smaller Independence Class carriers, and a large number of small escort carriers. This unprecedented and costly effort was timely, for as America entered the Second World War, she had only four carriers to match Japan's ten. Seventeen of the Essex ships would see action.[19]

In 1942, a military strategy was devised in which each carrier would go into battle escorted by approximately two cruisers and three destroyers. The escorts surrounded the carrier in a "wagon wheel" formation, protecting the larger ship with anti-aircraft fire and serving as a shield against attacks from surface ships and submarines.

Each carrier had an air wing of some 90 planes, and they consisted of three kinds: torpedo bombers, dive bombers, and fighters. By August, 1944, 65% of the Navy planes on carriers were fighters. The Helldriver could carry 2,000 pounds of bombs, twice the amount a Japanese plane could hold. The new Hellcat fighter had a range of 1,300 miles. The Corsair fighter bomber, flown by Marines, could reach a speed of 417 miles per hour. It carried bombs and could shoot rockets.

Unlike the Japanese, Americans had radar, which compensated for an inability to send scout planes as far as the Japanese could. By 1944, radar was fitted on 5-inch, long range anti-aircraft shells. These "proximity shells" exploded when near a target and were highly effective. The medium range 40 millimeter anti-aircraft guns used exploding shells. The close-in, 20 millimeter guns were equipped with a gyroscope optical device which calculated a target's location, a great advancement over the old method of using a sight on a gun barrel.

In 1944 a task force sent into battle consisted of four carriers, three to five cruisers, and 12 to 14 destroyers. The Japanese, with fewer carriers (they had lost four at Midway), sent 12 escorts to protect two of their carriers.[20]

The USS Hancock was one of the Essex Class aircraft carriers produced in the United States between 1942 and 1944. There were two sub-classes: The Short Hull ships, each of which had a length of 876 feet, eight inches, and the Long Hull Group, each of which was 885 feet, five inches in length. The carriers could handle some 90 aircraft, each could host a crew complement of 3,448, and each had a maximum speed of 32.7 knots. The second "Essex Class" carrier, the USS Yorktown, got into the first major offensive by the Navy in early February, 1942 in raids on the Marshall and Gilbert Islands. The USS Hornet was used in Jimmy Doolittle's raid on Tokyo that April.[21]

When completed, the USS Hancock, or "Ol' Hannah" as her crew commonly called her, was of the Long Hull Group. This meant that the flight deck was shortened and the bow lengthened to accommodate a larger anti-aircraft battery; the width of the flight deck was 146 feet, eight inches. The Hancock was capable of holding 80 aircraft on the flight deck, and its hanger could accommodate 120 other aircraft. About 90 planes were usually aboard. Steel cables and catapults could accelerate aircraft up to 90 miles per hour. The ship carried a dozen five-inch anti-aircraft guns, as well as 72 40-millimeter guns and 59 20-millimeter guns.[22]

The 27,100 ton Hancock was launched on January 24, 1944 at the Bethlehem Steel Company in Quincy, Massachusetts. She was commissioned on April 15. The first Commanding Officer was 47-year-old Captain Fred C. Dickey, whose long and distinguished naval career included medals for service all across the world.[23] Lieutenant Kohler, who turned 40 in April, was named the Air Combat Intelligence Officer. He immediately began creating an efficient administrative unit that could handle the ship's needs in combat. He was also watch officer in port, Assistant Air Plot Officer, and a Division Censor.[24]

About 80% of the Hancock's personnel had never been to sea, and about 60% had no knowledge of ship machinery. Many weeks of intensive training lay ahead for the crew.[25] The ship's diary tells of several injuries and deaths in the course of the instruction. Plane crashes were all too common as pilots learned to make precision landings on the flight deck, by day and night.[26]

After shake-down training off Trinidad and Venezuela, the Hancock returned to Boston for alterations July 9. She was then dispatched to the Pacific, traveling via the Panama Canal and San Diego to Pearl Harbor. The ship traveled 10,188 nautical miles from America's West Coast to reach its destination, the Ulithi Atoll, near the Yap islands, east of the Philippines in the Western Caroline Islands. This was the home port of the Third Fleet.

U.S. troops had taken Ulithi from Japan in September. A Hancock sailor wrote later, "The name of the place was Ulithi, although most of us wondered why such a water-logged little atoll should have a name. This was not land as we were accustomed to speak of land. The multitude of ships…looked more like they were anchored in mid-ocean and there appeared to be more deck space in Ulithi Harbor than there was beach area anywhere in sight." Forty four fighter planes and 30 bombers were soon moved to the Hancock's flight deck.[27]

The Hancock was summoned to battle on October 10, four days after its arrival in Ulithi. The destination was the Ryukyu Islands, north of Okinawa, as part of a fleet operation. The pattern for future action was set on this first day: planes from the Hancock made 156 sorties over enemy targets and dropped 53 tons of bombs. During the next two days, between 90 and 100 Japanese planes attacked the fleet. Sailors on the Hancock were on alert for seven hours and fifteen minutes of constant attack. The ship's anti-aircraft guns proved effective, however, and little damage was done. Hancock's planes wreaked destruction on enemy planes, shipping, torpedo boats, midget submarines, industrial plants, barracks, and hangars.

The ship then turned southward toward Luzon to assist MacArthur's return to the Philippines. Her planes attacked Japanese fortifications and shipping on Luzon and Camiguin Island north of Luzon. The entire crew of the Hancock had much to be proud of, delivering heavy blows to the Japanese and returning to base with only minimal losses.[28]

On October 25 the Hancock was ordered to the offshore area of Samar, in the central Philippines, where her planes did some damage to Japanese shipping in the San Bernadino Strait. From there the ship traveled to the vicinity of Manila, sending her planes to support advancing Army troops and attacking Japanese shipping over a 350 mile perimeter.[29] Intense fighting continued almost daily. The ship returned to Ulithi for five days in mid-November before setting out again to engage the enemy at Manila Bay.

On November 19, the Hancock fell under particularly heavy enemy fire. On the 25th, the ship became the target of a Kamikaze attack. Antiaircraft guns exploded the suicide plane 2,000 feet above the ship, but parts of the aircraft hit the deck and caused fires that were skillfully and promptly quelled.[30] (The major design flaw in the Essex Class ships was a wooden flight deck.) Two other ships in the vicinity were soon hit and damaged by suicide planes. But all three ships remained in action.

Kamikaze suicide planes had begun attacking American ships on June 19, 1944. From October 24 on, this battle tactic was pursued vigorously, inflicting much damage. Between October 23 and 26, seven carriers and 40 other types of ships were hit. Five were sunk and 23 sustained heavy damage. The attack on the Hancock, then, was part of a larger effort that would intensify as Japanese air power decreased from battle attrition and American ships drew closer to Japan.[31]

During a layover at Ulithi, Admiral Halsey paid a visit to the Hancock for a presentation of awards to members of the Third Fleet.[32] The Hancock was then ordered to the Luzon area, where its planes again proved effective. A severe typhoon hit on December 17-18; waves broke over the flight deck, 55 feet above sea level. Two nearby ships were debilitated by the weather, and within the next two days officers learned of damage to nine more, including three that capsized. Numerous planes were destroyed, 48 on one ship, and seven men in the task force were swept overboard and lost. The Hancock sustained no damage or loss of life.[33]

Walter's fitness report at year's end was again glowing. Captain Dickey gave him near perfect scores, adding: "Lieut. Kohler is an outstanding officer in his abilities and a tireless worker in the performance of his duties. He has shown excellent judgment in his evaluation of information and in the dissemination of it. He is qualified for promotion."[34] Two days later, on December 3, Walter was promoted to the rank of Lieutenant Commander.[35]

After Christmas in Ulithi, the Hancock was sent to the South China Sea area to attack Japanese shipping and aircraft. Strikes were launched at Luzon, Formosa, Saigon, Hainan Island, the Pescadores Islands, and shipping in the harbor of Hong Kong.[36] Despite encountering some foul weather, deadly anti-aircraft fire, and attacks by enemy aircraft, the Hancock was part of a task force that rained terror on its enemy. At one point, carrier pilots carried out 11 consecutive days of strikes, dropping 1,865 tons of bombs, 100 torpedoes, and 8,770 rockets. Some 635,000 tons of enemy shipping were sunk or damaged. The task force shot down 148 enemy planes, and 464 more were burned or exploded on the ground. These actions were particularly effective in weakening Japanese control over Luzon and Formosa. A historian of these actions wrote, "January 1945 has added another ringing blow to the avalanche of blows which are gradually driving the enemy to the perimeter of his homeland defenses."[37]

On January 21, 1945, after the resumption of raids on Formosa, one of the Hancock's planes, having returned safely to the ship, suddenly exploded. The landing had jarred loose the plane's 500-pound bomb, which exploded on contact with the deck. The tragedy killed the three man crew and 52 deckhands, and injured 75 more, many with severe burns. Three airplanes were demolished and the ship sustained considerable damage.

Walter escaped injury, but all of the men in the compartment next to him were killed. Providentially, Walter was standing on the far side of a bulkhead that shielded him from the inferno. Crewmen quelled the fire in 36 minutes, and the ship promptly returned to formation. The next morning it participated in strikes against Okinawa before returning to Ulithi.[38]

In February, the Hancock was part of Task Force 58, an arm of the Fifth Fleet. She and other carriers launched attacks on airfields in the vicinity of Tokyo. On a single day, February 17, planes from the Hancock downed 71 Japanese aircraft, probably destroyed 19 more in the air, destroyed eight on the ground, and damaged twelve others. The following day, American flyers destroyed 12 Japanese planes, and shot down perhaps three others. Damage to Japanese airfields and shipping was extensive.

Much of the activity at this time was aimed at preparing the area for the invasion of Iwo Jima, and the Hancock was soon stationed offshore, attacking enemy airfields and strafing enemy troops ashore. Resistance was fierce, and the USS Saratoga was hit by four Kamikaze planes, causing extensive damage. The Hancock was under almost constant fire. But the overall effectiveness of the American offensive was obvious to all.

Congratulations poured in from top naval headquarters and from Congress. The Task Force Commander wrote in an official report, "in spite of bad weather the task group in two days of hard slugging has handed the little yellow bastards some punches that ought certainly to make him [sic] remember Pearl Harbor."[39]

On February 28, Captain Robert F. Hickey, the ship's new Commanding Officer, wrote a fitness report that gave Kohler near perfect ratings. "Lieutenant Commander Kohler has made the air combat intelligence office aboard this ship an indispensable information center through his initiative and administrative ability. He is mature in his judgment and has a high sense of responsibility. He will be qualified for promotion when due. His personal and military character are excellent. He is considered excellent material for eventual appointment to permanent commissioned rank in the U.S. Naval Service."[40]

While the Hancock was making a brief visit to Ulithi to take on supplies and fuel, two Kamikaze planes attacked the base, seriously damaging a carrier and its planes, killing at least 25 sailors, and destroying a boat repair center. There was no longer a safe refuge in this deadly struggle.

In March, the Hancock returned to Japanese waters, joining other Task Force 58 ships in strikes in the Inland Sea of Japan. Task force ships were under constant fire. One carrier, the USS Franklin, only a thousand yards from the Hancock, was hit by two bombs, causing enormous fires that ignited ammunition. The disaster claimed the lives of 724 men. Twenty six planes and twenty four officers and men from the damaged ship, including two Rear Admirals, were transferred to the Hancock.[41]

On March 20, while the Hancock was refueling a destroyer, a Kamikaze plane attacked both ships. Under fire from anti-aircraft guns, the plane began to disintegrate at 1,000 to 700 feet, but parts of it, and its bomb, crashed into the destroyer. The destroyer lost its steering, turned across Hancock's bow, and was nearly cut in two, missing disaster by only a few feet. A survivor later recalled, "It was a busy few minutes for Hannah. The surface ship's gunners and the CAP shot down 46 enemy planes this day. The enemy knew what the major target was—Okinawa—and they were not going to give it up easily." During the rest of March, the Hancock launched attacks on Japanese islands and provided support for amphibious landings at Okinawa. Americans were closing in on the enemy's home territory.[42]

The Japanese responded with a flurry of Kamikaze attacks. From March 25 to June, some 1,900 suicide planes damaged 250 ships, sinking 34 destroyers and a number of smaller ships. Some Japanese planes launched Baka piloted glide bombs at American ships. They were fueled by a jet engine or rocket and were loaded with a one ton warhead. One sank a destroyer off Okinawa in April.[43]

A young fireman on the Hancock, I. D. "Inny" Cerbini, said later, "The thing that used to scare the daylights out of us is when we're under attack, you'd hear on the system, the radar picked up a bogey, an enemy plane or a squadron, whatever. And as they got closer, you had combat air patrol up there that would try to shoot these planes down....When they got within a certain distance of the fleet, combat air patrol would break off and the ship's guns would start firing. And there was five inch guns on a carrier. They would start firing and you're pinned in a compartment inside the guts of the ship, right, and all you can hear is sound and you hear the five inch guns going off then you would hear the 40-millimeter guns going off because that told you the planes are getting closer to you. Then you had 20-millimeter guns and when them twenties went off that plane was in close. That's when you started going, 'Our Father who art in heaven, hallowed be thy name.' Really, you prayed until you heard, splash, one bogey. The gunner shot him down and you were safe for a time being."[44]

A colleague of Walter's, Intelligence officer John H. Adams, later recalled one Sunday of almost constant attacks upon the Hancock. In a letter to Walter, he wrote, "I was flat on my face in your room, with Hank Krause palpitating beside me. It was one of those times when we were using your room for an office. You were in your bunk smoking a cigarette and in a lull in the firing you said, pensively and to no one in particular, 'You know, I've just been thinking—isn't this a hell of a way to spend a Sunday afternoon?'" The comment broke the tension in the room, and Adams thanked Walter for raising his morale at a critical time.[45]

On April 1, the Army landed on Okinawa, and the Hancock and Task Force 58 were nearby, providing support. On April 7, a Kamikaze plane cartwheeled across the Hancock's flight deck, dropping its 550-pound bomb, which went off, and crashing into a group of planes. The force of the explosion was tremendous, killing 63 men and wounding 82 others. Seventy three men were blown off the ship by the explosion and rescued. Walter kept a photograph, taken on a nearby ship, of the Hancock engulfed in flames and smoke. The ship sustained major damage. Crew members, however, doused the fire within 30 minutes, and the ship returned to action within the hour. Four hours later planes were again landing on the flight deck.[46]

Again, Walter escaped injury. But the havoc wreaked by the suicide plane helped change the direction of his life. Throughout the voyages of the Hancock, Walter and his fellow officers had chatted about what kind of world they wanted once the war was over. Most of the talk, Walter said later, was cynical and expressed helplessness. The men didn't expect to be able to do anything personally to improve things. On April 7, badly shaken by death and destruction all around him, Walter vowed to himself that if he got out of the war alive he would go into politics and do what he could to make the world a better place. He said later, "I decided then that if I got back safely, I had a big debt to pay—especially since America had been better to me than to most."[47]

On April 18, Walter wrote a letter to his brother John, saying how much "this particular battle weary sailor" envied him for being able to vacation in Arizona. "Only I'd just as soon take Windway in late May or early June when hawthorn is in bloom, and violets and trillium are out, and lilac and apple blossoms are in bloom. The Wisconsin countryside is pretty special when you haven't seen it in three years." Without making specific reference to what he went through a few days earlier, he noted that the war was growing more intense "This close-in fighting gets tougher and tougher, though, and they [the Japanese] all seem glad to die for the Superior whereas our boys would like to come back and see their wives and kids. I don't see that very much can be done about it, however. If the job isn't finished now, Terry and Michael and Collins will do the finishing which is a dirty job to wish on those young kids." He thought that the war would last another year.[48]

Damage to the Hancock was such that it was forced to return to Pearl Harbor for repairs. At its departure, on April 13, the ship ensign was lowered to half-mast as word reached the ship of the death of President Franklin D. Roosevelt.[49]

The Hancock headed back into action on June 13, but without Lieutenant Commander Kohler.[50] He had earned enough service points to be granted an honorable discharge and, exhausted by months of intense battle, chose that option. The decision was made in late April, and when news of it spread, Intelligence officer Adams wrote a personal note to Walter."Just in case I miss you, however, I would like to say that (forgetting our respective positions just this one moment) my deep personal regard and sincere best wishes go with you. You are the one man I've known at all intimately so far in this Naval comedy who deserves the position of trust and responsibility, in all respects, which is thrust upon all the men who wear 'Gold Braid.' I hope our paths may cross again back in God's Country, in God's (peace) time, and I shall always keep a lookout for news of you."[51]

In early May, Walter received a staff position on shore. His final rankings by Captain Hickey were again extraordinarily high. "Lt. Comdr. Kohler is a thorough, competent officer who works well with all who have contact with him. He is conservative in his estimates of damage done to enemy installations and has a passion for accurate, complete reports. He has done an outstanding job as ACI officer on the USS Hancock. Lt. Comdr. Kohler is qualified and is recommended for promotion when due."[52]

Walter left Pearl Harbor on May 15 and on reaching the United States took a month's leave. Walter was confident that in a very short time he would permanently return to Wisconsin with his beloved family and could pick up his life where he left it.

In late June he reported to Quonset, Rhode Island for a three week refresher course. He was then sent to Washington, D.C. and given an administrative job. He left the nation's capital one day before the Japanese surrendered. From mid-August through September, he had administrative duties at the Navy facility in Glenview, Illinois. He was officially discharged on September 24.[53]

Now 41, Walter had served 37 months of active duty. Admiral M. A. Mitscher awarded him the Bronze Star Medal and Permanent Citation. "For distinguishing himself by meritorious achievement in connection with operations against the enemy during the period 10 October 1944 to 8 April 1945 while serving as Air Combat Intelligence Officer of the U.S.S. Hancock (CV19). He organized, from the start, a complete and efficient combat intelligence center which functioned with outstanding efficiency throughout these operations, and through his untiring and unceasing efforts, he made it possible for the squadron and ship personnel to combat the enemy at all times infallibly equipped and prepared. His intrepidity, devotion to duty, and intuitiveness were in keeping with the highest traditions of the United States Naval Service."[54]

Walter also won the Asiatic theater ribbon with five battle stars, the Philippine liberation ribbon with two battle stars, and the naval unit citation.[55]

The USS Hancock continued to fight in the Pacific until the war's end on August 15. Its scoreboard for World War II was 733 planes destroyed, 14 warships sunk, 34 merchant ships sunk, and 10 enemy planes downed by ship's guns. A total of 221 shipmates were either killed or missing in action. By the time of the Japanese surrender, the Hancock had traveled 119,822 nautical miles, far enough to go 39 times across the United States.[56]

Walter returned to Windway on the evening of September 24, and the next morning applied for work at the Kohler Company.[57] Soon, his elation at the war's sudden and successful ending and his return home had changed to deep sorrow. Herbert V. Kohler gave him another do-nothing job, Secretary of the company's Executive Department, and let him know that he would have no future responsibility.[58] Far more disturbing, however, was the news delivered by Celeste. She had fallen in love with another man and intended to get a divorce.[59]

Notes

[1] Notation in Kohler's employment record, Personnel File; fitness reports, October 26, December 19, 1942, paperwork and orders, Military Files, Terry Kohler papers (hereafter referred to as MFTK); Terry Kohler interview, June 12, 2003.

[2] Walter J. Kohler, Jr. to "Dear Mother, John, Jim, Bob & wives," September 30, 1942, Kohler Family Papers.

[3] Walter J. Kohler, Jr. to "Dear Mother, John Jim, Bob & wives," November 3, December 9, 1942, *ibid.*

[4] Terry Kohler interview, March 25, 2004.

[5] Copy "Dumbo Operations in the Solomon Islands, Jan. 1 to Aug. 15, 1943," 1-11, 27, et passim, MFTK. The account of the overloaded seaplane is in a report dated April 18, 1943. Walter later told Terry that he had played a role in the successful attack on Admiral Isoruko Yamamoto. On April 18, 18 planes took off from Henderson Field for the kill. See www.salute.co.uk/salutegames/yamamoto/Yamamoto.htm.

[6] Steinberg, "Is This The Man to Beat McCarthy?," 77.

[7] "Lieut. Walter J. Kohler Jr. Aids in Rescuing Stranded Flier," *Kohler of Kohler News*, June, 1943, 6. The photos are in MFTK. For more on the general topic, see *www.ibiblio.org/hyperwar/USN/ACTC/actc-9.html* and *www.army.mil/cmh-pg/books/wwii/GuadC/GC-02.htm.* On the Vought 0S2U-3 Kingfisher seaplane used at the Halavo base, see *www.caw15.com/aircraft/seaplanes.html.*

[8] See Thomas C. Reeves, *A Question of Character, A Life of John F. Kennedy* (New York: The Free Press, 1991), 61-68. Walter was apparently often at Tulagi. In fact, in 1951 he told a *Colliers* reporter that he was stationed there. Steinberg, "Is This The Man to Beat McCarthy?," 77.

[9] On this general topic, see *www.ibibio.org/hyperwar/AAF/IV/AAF-IV-7.html.*

[10] "Lieut. Walter J. Kohler Returns From year In Combat Zone Of The South Pacific," *Sheboygan Press*, December 29, 1943.

[11] See the copy of an undated response by Walter to a Yale publication inquiry, Miscellaneous file, Terry Kohler Papers.

[12] Documents in MFTK.

[13] *Ibid.*

[14] See fitness reports of April 30, 1943, March 8, 1944, *ibid.*; "Lieut. Walter J. Kohler Returns From Year In Combat Zone Of The South Pacific Area," Sheboygan *Press*, December 29, 1943.

[15] Walter J. Kohler, Jr. to Julilly Kohler, February 23, June 2, November 3, 1943, Kohler Family Papers.

[16] "Lieut. Walter J. Kohler Returns From Year In Combat Zone Of The South Pacific Area," *Sheboygan Press*, December 29, 1943.

[17] Terry Kohler interview, June 12, 2003; interrogatories in her 1979 divorce file, Terry Kohler papers. A photograph showing Jackie in her RAF uniform is on display at Windway. The Christmas, 1943 family photo is also on display.

[18] Terry Kohler interviews, June 12, 2003, March 25, 2004; e-mail, Terry Kohler to the author, March 23, 2004, Celeste Kohler file. On MacFadden, see also Tim and Barbara Gorham interview, October 24, 2004; Sarabia, *80 Years Of My Wandering Spirit*, 52.

[19] See Philip A. St. John, *USS Hancock, CV-19/CVA-19, Fighting Hannah* (Paducah, Kentucky: Turner Publishing Company, 2d ed., 2004), 10. Thirty two carriers were initially authorized, and 24 were completed.

[20] See *http://johnsmilitaryhistory.tripod.com/carriertactics.html.*

[21] Information on the Essex class ships often varies in detail. See *www.ehistory.com/wwii/USNCV3.cfm.* and *www.ehistory.com/wwii/USNCV4.cfm.*

[22] See St. John, *USS Hancock*, p. 8; *www.ushancockv19.com/specs.htm; www.dayofthekamikaze.com/hancock_danfs.html.* I am also indebted to Hancock experts Ken Jaccard and Jim Bauer for data. See their e-mails to the author in the Military Record File. See also *www.globalsecurity.org/military/systems/ship/cv-19.htm.* For photographs of the Hancock, see *www.odyssey.dircon.co.uk/Hancock,htm,* and *www.usshancockcv19.com/navalmuseums.htm.* St. John's *USS Hancock* has a splendid assortment of photos.

[23] See *www.usshancockassociation.org/wwii%20history-3.html.* This is hereafter referred to as the Hancock Association history. The detailed chronology and narrative are invaluable guides to the ship's activities.

[24] Fitness report, December 1, 1944, MFTK. During the early months of 1944, before reporting for duty on the Hancock, Walter was in training at Quonset and at Boston. See the relevant documents in MFTK.

[25] Hancock Association history.

[26] USS Hancock War Diary, MFTK. This confidential document reports the ship's movements and actions day-by-day through May 1, 1945.

[27] *Ibid.* The Hancock would serve as part of Admiral Halsey's Third Fleet and, for a time, the Fifth Fleet headed by Admiral R. A. Spruance.

[28] Hancock Association history; *www.dayofthekamikaze.com/hancock_danfs.html.*

[29] *Ibid.*

[30] *Ibid.*

[31] See *www.ww2pacific.com/suicide.html.*

[32] Hancock Association history. I have at all times checked these Internet sources against the ship's diary and made occasional alterations in my narrative favoring the diary.

[33] Hancock War Diary; St. John, *USS Hancock*, 37-39.

34 Fitness report, December 1, 1944, MFTK. This report includes a chronology, signed by Commander Dickey, of the Hancock's travels between October 10 and November 30. A second such chronology for subsequent activity is contained in Walter's fitness reports.

35 Lieutenant Commander in the Navy is the equivalent of Major in the Army. See the relevant documents in MFTK.

36 Hancock Association history; _www.dayofthekamikaze.com/hancock_danfs. html_.

37 See the unsigned copy of the history, along with data and photographs, in Task Force 38 file, MFTK.

38 Hancock War Diary; St. John, _USS Hancock_, 41-43; Hancock Association history; _www.dayofthekamikaze.com/hancock_danfs.html_; Sternberg, "Is This The Man to Defeat McCarthy?," 77.

39 Hancock War Diary. The quotation is in the fitness report of February 28, 1945, MFTK.

40 _Ibid._

41 St. John, _USS Hancock_, 47.

42 Hancock War Diary; Hancock Association history; _www.dayofthekami-kaze.com/hancock_danfs.html_, and _www.usshancockcv19.com/gallery.htm_. There are slightly conflicting stories of the March 20 incident, and I chose to follow the Hancock War Diary account. See St. John, _USS Hancock_, 47-48.

43 See _www.ww2pacific.com/suicide.html_.

44 _www.dayofthekamikaze.com/cerbini.html_.

45 John H. Adams to Walter J. Kohler, Jr., July 1, 1945, MFTK.

46 Hancock War Diary; Hancock Association history; _www.usshancockcv19. com/gallery.htm_, 6-7. For photographs of the disaster, see St. John, _USS Hancock_, 51-55.

47 Sternberg, "Is This The Man to Defeat McCarthy?," 77.

48 Water J. Kohler, Jr. to John Kohler, April 18, 1945, Kohler Family Papers.

49 St. John, _USS Hancock_, 56.

50 _www.dayofthekamikaze.com/hancock_danfs.html_.

51 John Adams to Walter J. Kohler, Jr., April 23, 1945, MFTK.

52 Fitness report of May 8, 1945, MFTK. A formal photograph of Walter in his lieutenant commander uniform is in the Leslie Kohler Hawley collection.

53 He was officially released from duty on October 24. The relevant orders are in MFTK. The Kohler family later funded a small display featuring Walter and his wartime record at the EAA Air Venture Museum in Oshkosh, Wisconsin. It is in the WWII era Eagle Hanger.

54 The statement and records of Walter's post-Hancock assignments are contained within the fitness reports, MFTK. Walter learned of his medal on

July 6. See *ibid*. The Bronze Star was first established in 1944, "For Heroic or Meritorious Achievement of Service, not involving aerial flight, in connection with Operations Against an Opposing Armed Force."

[55] "War Gave Us New Governor," *Milwaukee Journal*, November 9, 1950.

[56] Hancock Association history. Cf. *www.usshancockassociation.org/hancock-history.html*, 1-2. See St. John, *USS Hancock*, 62. The Hancock saw duty in Vietnam and was scrapped in 1976.

[57] See the relevant documents in MFTK.

[58] Roland Neumann interview. A magazine article, based on interviews with Walter, later reported, "And at the Kohler Company, he discovered that future plans would not give him as much to do as he would like." Sternberg, "Is This The Man to Defeat McCarthy?," 77.

[59] Walter J. Kohler, Jr. Oral History, Columbia University, 1971, 1.

Chapter Seven
Transitions

By all accounts, Walter was devastated by the breakup of his family and his home. He had had no warning about the romance between Celeste and Robin MacFadden, and the sudden realization that his thirteen-year marriage was over left him, for a time, in shock. For the rest of his life he could not quite shake his bitterness, and chose never to discuss Celeste, even privately. Later communications with his ex-wife were usually impersonal and terse. He would not attend her funeral.

Walter broke the news of the impending divorce to his children at Windway, asking them which parent they would like to live with in the future. Though they had barely seen their father during the past three years, both Terry and Niki chose Walter. Celeste apparently balked at this arrangement, and in a day or two, Walter told the children that Terry would stay at Windway and Niki would go to live with Celeste.[1]

The divorce was granted in Florida in 1946. Terms of the settlement were never made public, but it is certain that Celeste remained in financial comfort.[2] Shortly afterward, she and Robin MacFadden were married; it was her third wedding and his second. She was 46 years old, and it seems that he was too. MacFadden had at least one daughter from his earlier marriage.[3]

Little is known of MacFadden. He was slightly taller than Celeste, making him perhaps five foot eight, and he sported a mustache. In 1945 he was employed as a professional "loadmaster" for the military/ Pan American Airways flights going out of Coral Gables, Florida. Terry Kohler remembered him as friendly, casual, and smart. MacFadden taught Terry the basics of sailing and fishing. "He certainly behaved as a surrogate father to me during the war years," Terry wrote later.[4] Michael Kohler, who knew MacFadden about the same time, remembered him as "a friendly but sophisticated man who liked the good things in life."[5]

Being a childhood friend of Celeste's, MacFadden was surely a product of Chicago's high society. His views on marriage and the opposite sex were no doubt laced with the cynicism and opportunism common to that social set at the time. Whatever achievements he made as a painter have long been lost and forgotten. He seems to have had no other occupation after the war. It is doubtful that he brought much income to his new marriage. Celeste purchased the couple's 50-foot yacht.

After their marriage, the MacFaddens lived in Florida, New York City, and Oakland, New Jersey before moving to the Virgin Islands in 1951. Celeste was no doubt pleased to be out of tiny, provincial Kohler, Wisconsin. Robin and Celeste remained together about ten years, often taking Terry and Niki with them in their yachting adventures throughout the Caribbean. Then one day, at St. Thomas, MacFadden, accompanied by a young woman, stole a newer, 56 foot yacht Celeste had purchased, and was never seen again. Celeste, for the third time in her life, filed for a divorce.[6]

During the first few years after the war, Terry saw his mother and sister for about a month each summer, largely at Pentwater, the McVoy home on Lake Michigan. At some point, probably in 1950, Niki was diagnosed as having a slight mental disability requiring her to attend a special boarding school. The decision to send her away from home was very difficult, Terry said later. Niki, in her early teens, was much loved by all who knew her. The family found what they were convinced was the best place available: the Woods School in Langhorne, Pennsylvania, a suburb of Philadelphia.

Thereafter, Niki saw her father mostly at Christmas and Easter, when she traveled to Windway for brief holiday visits.[7] According to Niki, her father visited her often in the early years of her life in institutions. But the visits declined over the years and stopped altogether.[8] Celeste, on the other hand, saw Niki often and sought to spend as much time as possible with her away from the institution. Niki's parents clashed over the issue of her personal freedom. It may be that tensions between Walter and Celeste over Niki were reflections of their bitter divorce.[9]

The evidence suggests that Walter took Niki's diagnosis very hard. He never mentioned his daughter publicly, and when he became Governor, obliging reporters said merely that she was away at school. Peter and Nancy Kohler hypothesized that Walter was embarrassed by his daughter's incapacity; it was the fashion in those years, Nancy said, to avoid even discussion of children with such problems.[10]

During 1946, numerous women hovered over Walter, again a most eligible bachelor.[11] Celeste's sister later noted that Walter had an affair after the war with Ti Carbonnier, who had been married to the Swedish consul in New York.[12] A cousin, Walter J. Vollrath, Jr., who knew Walter most of his life and during this period, later recalled that he was "a charmer with women."[13] In early 1947, Walter was dating a Sheboygan teacher.[14]

Jackie moved into Windway in 1946, and later told Terry that she helped Walter overcome a lot of pain and sorrow over the divorce.[15] That same year, Walter Vollrath and his father bumped into Walter and Jackie at a train station and invited them to the senior Vollrath's home for the evening. Kohler, said the younger Vollrath, was "a nice guy to know." Jackie struck him as "kind of wild and boisterous."[16]

In 1946, Walter had to decide what to do about his dead-end job at the Kohler Company. He was stunned to learn that during the war Herbert Sr. had assumed control of the voting rights of stock held by his three half-sisters and now controlled the company and the Board. How exactly Herbert achieved this gift from Evangeline and Lillie (Marie died in 1943) cannot be documented at this time. Walter simply stated the fact of the takeover to Terry without giving details. John Kohler told his wife another story, and so did Jim when explaining matters to his son Peter.[17] It is certain, however, that all four brothers resented Herbert's new authority, and a breach in the family developed that would last for many years.[18]

Walter knew that if he stayed with the company, as John and Jim were prepared to do, he would be totally under his uncle's thumb and without purposeful employment until his retirement. He pondered this situation for awhile, as he adjusted to civilian life and the personal turmoil of his family's breakup. He went to work each day, no doubt thinking about the future and hoping that something would soon change.

Leaving his job was especially difficult in 1946 because the Kohler Company had prospered during the war, which meant that its stock continued to grow in value, making all four of Walter Sr.'s sons increasingly wealthy. The company sold artillery shells, submarine torpedo tubes, aircraft controls, piston rings, and other military goods to the government, winning a coveted Army-Navy E Award for exceptional performance in wartime production. Herbert wisely decided to stay in the precision controls business after the war, and the company was soon to become a major supplier of aeronautical valves and controls.[19]

Herbert himself won praise for his wartime efforts at local fund raising. In 1942, for example, he was elected chairman of the Sheboygan County citizens war fund, heading a campaign that raised $125,000.[20]

Walter was also faced with the question of how to begin in politics. He chose to start at the top, wanting to be a United States Senator. With his credentials and name recognition, he thought he had at least a chance to win the seat currently held by Robert La Follette, Jr., a Progressive whose party was in shambles and who was thinking of seeking reelection as a Republican. One formidable man stood in Walter's way: Joe McCarthy.

McCarthy had been born on a farm outside Appleton, one of seven children. He stood out from his siblings from his earliest youth, being exceptionally bright, extraordinarily personable, and intensely aggressive and ambitious. After elementary school, he had stayed on the farm for a few years raising chickens. When the business went broke, he decided to go back to school. Using to the full his incredible energy and near photographic memory, McCarthy completed a four year curriculum in nine months. From there he went to Marquette University in Milwaukee, where he was a successful boxer, popular fraternity member, and active womanizer. He took a law degree, but emerged without achieving much in the way of a solid education. He had largely memorized the lectures and the discussions of more studious friends to get through, and had not grappled with serious books or ideas. People who knew the good-looking, powerfully built young Joe McCarthy thought of him as a totally extroverted, fun-loving, generous, energetic, blarney-spewing Irishman, who loved to gamble and bluff and was not above cheating a bit to have his way.[21]

After struggling as a small-town lawyer during the Depression, McCarthy went into politics. A Democrat, he was active in local party groups and lost a race to become district attorney. Undaunted, in 1939 he won election as the Tenth Circuit judge. During the campaign, McCarthy revealed a ferocious capacity for sustained effort, a powerful ability to charm voters (he campaigned most effectively in the region's many taverns), and a willingness to lie and use underhanded tactics.

Urban Van Susteren of Appleton, who became a close friend of McCarthy's about this time, said later that Joe was absolutely fearless, loved a fight, and could be fierce in combat. "You could watch Joe's eyes light up," said Van Susteren, "as he figured out almost immediately how to screw an opponent." At the same time, McCarthy could be selfless,

sentimental, funny, and religious. Friends accepted him for what he
was: an anomaly. Most people who met him were dazzled by his charm
and drive.[22]

In 1941, Van Susteren was shocked one evening when McCarthy
told him that he planned to run for the United States Senate. He was
without funds and had practically no knowledge of national or international issues. But that didn't matter to McCarthy. He said that he
would join the Republican Party, which dominated politics in Wisconsin,
tour the state while filling in for other judges, and campaign tirelessly.
He proceeded to do just that. In the course of his whirlwind travels,
he often played poker with local citizens. One who was part of such
a game later described the experience as 'wild." The judge would raise
the ante until the other players dropped out in fear. No one could tell
when McCarthy was bluffing.[23]

When America entered the Second World War, McCarthy joined
the Marines. An Intelligence officer, he was sent to the South Pacific
in 1943 and served at Henderson Field, Guadalcanal, just a few miles
from where Lieutenant Kohler was conducting similar duties. Outside
the course of his regular work on the ground, Joe McCarthy enjoyed a
few relatively safe flights with pilot friends. He soon had photographs
taken of himself in the gunner's cockpit, claimed falsely to have been
wounded in battle, and apparently forged a superior's signature to win a
citation for heroism. These were the ingredients in the myth of "Tailgun-
ner Joe," which McCarthy created for use in future election campaigns.
(McCarthy's military record would not be questioned for several years,
and was not fully examined until after his death.)

McCarthy ran for the Senate in 1944, while still in the Marine Corps.
He came home on leave to display his uniform and tell of his "war
wound" and daring exploits overseas. He also played some tricks with
the numbers when reporting campaign expenses. He lost the bid for
the Republican nomination to incumbent Senator Alexander Wiley,
but was undaunted. His sights were set on 1946, and the race against
Senator La Follette.[24]

McCarthy spent 16 months overseas, resigning from the Marines
in December, 1944. He came home during the following month, won
reelection as judge, and immediately began preparations for the 1946
Senatorial campaign. He gained the avid support of the Young Republican Federation of Wisconsin. He campaigned tirelessly throughout
the state, reaching out to people individually (he could call thousands

of people by their first name) and rarely discussing issues. Progressive critic Miles McMillin observed, "It is doubtful whether Wisconsin has ever seen a politician who is more ambitious politically or more untiring and unremitting in his campaigning. He never ceases to campaign. He seems to have no other interest than political power."[25]

The biggest selling job McCarthy had to pull off was with Tom Coleman, now the leader of the Stalwarts, who controlled the GOP. "Boss Coleman," as Progressives called him, hated the La Follettes for dividing and opposing regular Republicans for decades, and he dreamed about defeating the incumbent Senator. But McCarthy was not his style of person; the youthful backslapper was not a gentleman of good breeding and wealth.[26] Moreover, he had been a Democrat only a few years earlier, and no one was quite sure what he stood for. When La Follette and his backers reentered the GOP, Coleman was even more determined to find a candidate who could defeat him.

Joe just kept on campaigning furiously across Wisconsin. On one of these trips, he came to Windway for the evening and a chat with Walter. McCarthy had gotten wind of Kohler's desire for the Senate seat, and he wanted to talk. He had paid similar visits to other potential candidates, prompting them to drop out of the race.[27]

We do not know exactly what was said at the Windway meeting. According to Terry, McCarthy simply told Walter what he had told Tom Coleman and every other Republican who stood in his way: He would win the primary and the election, and that was that. He enjoyed total self-confidence. In any case, after McCarthy's visit, Walter abandoned his candidacy. He said later that he quit the race for fear of splitting one bloc of votes in the Republican primary, paving the way for La Follette's reelection.[28] That seems likely, especially in light of the strong support McCarthy had already acquired by the time he visited Windway.[29] Walter had not begun to organize a campaign and had not traveled anywhere in the state to meet and win over GOP officials. He hadn't played cards in scores of lodge halls, knocked on doors, or bellowed Irish songs in hundreds of taverns. Walter probably responded to McCarthy the way Tom Coleman had, considering him a rather amusing, uncouth, overly-aggressive, and potentially effective GOP candidate.[30]

McCarthy convinced most Republicans of his ideological orthodoxy after he delivered a staunchly conservative speech at the state convention of the Young Republicans. That profession of the faith, as well as the legions of zealous McCarthy supporters, especially young veterans, encountered everywhere in the state, persuaded Tom Coleman to back the "Fighting Marine." The Republican Voluntary Committee endorsed McCarthy overwhelmingly on the first ballot. Still the state GOP remained seriously divided between Stalwarts, Progressives, and a number of mavericks.

As the primary neared, McCarthy began to contend that La Follette was playing into the hands of Communists and benefiting from war profiteering. The Senator, shy, moderate, moody, and ill, refused to debate McCarthy and did very little on his own behalf. He was convinced that his name and his record stood for themselves. When he finally returned home for a week of campaigning, he discovered Democrats and Republicans alike strongly opposed to his reelection bid. Democratic candidate Howard J. McMurray, who enjoyed the support of organized labor, railed against the Senator's isolationist record and claimed that he had Nazi and fascist support. The Senator's decision to back a gubernatorial candidate opposed by many Republicans, including Coleman, boosted support for McCarthy.[31]

McCarthy won the primary by a margin of only 5,378 votes. His election in strongly Republican Wisconsin now seemed certain. But in clashes with his hapless Democratic opponent, Howard J. McMurray, McCarthy went beyond the standard rhetoric about opposition to Big Government, Big Labor, and isolationism, and proceeded to smear the political science instructor with charges that he was pro-Communist. And the allegation didn't stop there. In Janesville, he said, "All Democrats are not Communists....But enough Democrats are voting the Communist way to make their presence in Congress a serious threat to the very foundation of our nation."

Republicans throughout the country were using the soft-on-the-Reds tactic in 1946 to win election, and McCarthy, who knew virtually nothing about Communism except that it was bad, no doubt saw such charges as simply part of the game of political warfare. A young veteran in California named Richard Nixon was employing red-baiting in a more sophisticated and effective way, and he was not alone. Catholic organizations, naturally sympathetic to Catholic McCarthy and mortally opposed to Communism, added their authority to a growing concern about Reds in high places. Some newspapers, including the *Chicago Tribune* and the entire chain run by the Hearst publishing empire, had learned that charges of treason in government increased readership.

On election eve, McCarthy predicted victory by 227,000 votes. He won by a margin of 241,658. At 38, Joe McCarthy would be the youngest member of the United States Senate, a decade younger than the average incumbent, and more than 25 years younger than the average committee chairman. Moreover, McCarthy now had the support of Tom Coleman and the vast majority of Wisconsin Republicans. Anyone, including Walter J. Kohler, Jr., who aspired to political office in the state would have to win his approval.[32]

Walter undoubtedly realized the implications of McCarthy's victory. Pondering the general intellectual vacuity of the recent campaign and seeing the almost fanatical zeal of the Senator-elect's supporters, he must have wondered what it would take to win the confidence of such people. Was it too late for a candidate to employ calm reasoning, a solid knowledge of issues, a gentlemanly approach to campaigning, and a commitment to intellectual independence in a successful election campaign? Even though the GOP won solidly, in Wisconsin and throughout the nation in 1946, Walter could not have been elated by the irrational and emotionally-charged mood that was increasingly haunting American politics in the post-war period.

Still, this setback did not destroy Walter's political hopes. There would be other races and other opportunities to serve the public. He began reading and collecting articles on state and national politics to better inform himself. And, in 1947, in part no doubt to increase his public visibility, he ran the Wisconsin fund campaign for the American Cancer Society. The following year he became Director of Region IV of the Society, and in 1949 he became a member of the Society's national Executive Committee.[33]

❧ ❧ ❧ ❦ ❧ ❧ ❧

Walter's mother, Charlotte, died on February 2, 1947 at age 77. She had been ill with Alzheimer's for several years and had been confined at home for the last six months. Her immediate family was at her bedside when the end came. The obituaries in the local press lauded Charlotte's artistic contributions to Kohler Village and Riverbend, her service as the First Lady of Wisconsin, and her generally sunny disposition. Jackie and several of Celeste's Chicago relatives attended the funeral, held at Riverbend, along with close family members. Two local Episcopal priests, whose parishes had benefited from Kohler benevolence over the years, presided at the service.[34]

Two issues now faced Charlotte's four sons. The first was what to do with Riverbend. The cost of maintaining the mansion, its staff, and its landscaped 40 acres would be high, and Walter and Jim had already constructed their own estates. After much indecision, John decided to bear the burden that his brothers did not seek. The move, although it made no financial sense, was taken largely out of love and respect for his parents. John could not bear to see the family estate sold.

John and Julilly and their four children lived off John's relatively modest salary and stock dividends. One of the children, the younger Julilly, said later that people in the community thought her father the cheapest man in town, not knowing that he was often strapped for funds because of the demands of Riverbend. To make matters worse, when Charlotte was alive, the Kohler Company provided the home's steam heat and electricity. Herbert cut off that subsidy in 1947, and John's bank account was strained that much more. Moreover, Julilly recalled, since all Charlotte's sons inherited the Riverbend movables, including furniture, John had to purchase these things from his brothers. Over the next almost three decades the estate deteriorated for lack of maintenance.[35]

Still, a brother and sister of Julilly's have more favorable recollections of the family's finances. There were servants in the house, however poorly paid; John drove a Cadillac, even it was second-hand; and the Kohler children attended some of the nation's finest and most expensive schools. Mike followed the traditional family route for males of Andover and Yale; Marie and Collins went to Harvard; Julilly went to Wellesley and Washington University, before going on to the University of Wisconsin for a law degree.[36] (At John's death in 1968, he left an estate worth $3.7 million, largely represented by Kohler stock and Riverbend.)[37]

The annual Halloween and Christmas parties at Riverbend, long a family tradition, continued to be well-planned and popular celebrations. A large number of Kohlers, Vollraths, and others in the community appreciated the efforts by John and Julilly Kohler to entertain and solidify family relations. In 1950, Julilly initiated a reunion of the Waller clan at Riverbend, a nine-day event that set a precedent so positive that it is continued to this day. The Wallers were related to Julilly on her mother's side; they had originally emigrated from England to Kentucky. Some 20 different families participated in subsequent reunions that, over the years, would feature piano recitals, songs, skits, a mock political convention, a bathing beauty parade, story telling, family movies and displays, and an assortment of tours.[38] Riverbend, while under the direction of its vivacious hostess, was rarely quiet and never glum.

The second issue facing the four Kohler sons, after the death of their mother, was their inheritance. They now were able to divide equally the largest single block of money and stock in their father's estate. Should they now attempt to regain control of the Kohler Company or was this new wealth to be treated as a ticket to independence? Challenging the authority of Herbert Sr. was an option they did not pursue. To be free of the company and start a business of their own, the Kohler sons would no doubt be required to sell their valuable family stock, which might risk the future security of their families. And perhaps, outside the comfortable environs of the company, they would fail. Not one of the sons had independent business experience. As we have seen, John and Jim decided to stay put.

Walter soon decided that the risk was worth taking. Not long after his mother's death, he used his own funds, borrowed $200,000 from the Security National Bank in Sheboygan, employed his influence with Board members, and made a bold bid for leadership of the Vollrath Company.[39]

The Vollrath Company, like the Kohler Company, had prospered during the Second World War. From August 1, 1942 until the end of hostilities it worked full time for the war effort, producing 12 million canteens, mess trays, meat cans, irrigators and basins, and other materials. It received the Army-Navy "E" Flag for its production record, and 764 Vollrath employees received lapel pins in recognition of their wartime effort.[40]

But some stockholders were concerned about what they feared was weak leadership. Walter said later that after the war the company was in poor shape.[41] In 1946, the company suffered a seven-week strike.[42]

Jean C. Vollrath was the company President. He had been with the company his entire adult life and had assumed the top office when his father, C.A.W. Vollrath, the founder's son, died in 1932. Robert P. Vollrath, Jean's brother, was the company Secretary. The Chairman of the Board and Treasurer was John M. Detling. An attorney, Detling had married one of the founder's granddaughters, Minneline Reiss, in 1911 and had been with the company since that time. Herbert Kohler, who commanded a large block of stockholder votes and sat on the Board, was also an important and outspoken Board member.

When Walter returned to the Board of Directors in November, 1945, the Vollrath Company's net profits were lower than in 1943, despite a sizeable sales increase. A year earlier, the federal government had required the company to refund what it considered to be excess profits, a sum that eventually rose to $136,674. Throughout 1946, no doubt to his uncle's extreme irritation, Walter increasingly became a prominent voice on the Board.[43] During February and March, 1947, Walter made his move to assume control of the company. The key to his successful effort, according to Kohler family sources, was 66-year-old Minneline Reiss Detling.

Minneline's mother Mary (or Marie as she was called) was the fourth child of Jacob Johann Vollrath. Lillie and Minnie Vollrath, who both married John Michael Kohler, were her sisters. Her father was John Reiss (1852-1906), who had been taken into the factory by Jacob Vollrath, as John Michael Kohler was, and became a leading figure in the business. Minneline inherited considerable stock in the family business from her father and grandmother and was in on the ground floor when the Vollrath Company was incorporated in 1908. She served as Secretary-Treasurer in 1908 and 1909, and was on the Board of Directors from 1915 to 1920. The Detlings would devote the rest of their lives to the company, John as an employee and Board member and Minneline as an increasingly powerful stockholder.

In 1932, Mineline's brother, De Witt Reiss, who had also inherited major family stock, died at the age of 46. His shares were transferred to his estate and then to his mother. Mineline's mother, Mary, died in 1937. At the shareholders' meeting of March 1, 1939, Minneline owned 2,895 shares, a large block of stock that she continued to hold after World War II when Walter returned to the company's Board of Directors. John Detling cast her votes at meetings, along with the votes of several other relatives. Only one block of shares in the company was larger: the Vollrath Estate shares held by Jean and Robert Vollrath. Herbert Kohler controlled a collateral estate that held 1,989 shares.

Minneline and her husband John were among the 13 trustees of that collateral estate. Walter wanted to purchase these shares, and Minneline reportedly encouraged him. She obviously saw great potential in the young man, and perhaps she was moved by his considerable charm. She had known him all of his life, and she and her husband were present at Terry's first birthday party.[44] In any case, company president Jean C. Vollrath approved the sale. Herbert and his sisters, for whom he was the proxy, lacked the voting power to stop it. When the transaction became inevitable, Herbert quickly resigned from the Board and severed his ties with the company. Three days later, on March 31, Walter quit his job at the Kohler Company.[45]

At the Board meeting of April 1, 1947, Walter J. Kohler, Jr. owned 2,036 shares (47 previously owned plus the newly purchased shares), and Minneline gave him her proxy. (She also privately gave Walter the option of buying her shares at her death.)[46] Together, they held a majority of the 9,212 company shares. With the support of Jean and Robert Vollrath, who controlled the main body of Vollrath Estate stocks, there was virtually no opposition. Walter owned 22% of company stock and had the support of virtually all the rest of the stockholders. The 43-year-old Lieutenant Commander was now at the helm of the Vollrath Company.

At the same April 1 meeting Walter and his allies led a move that resulted, by unanimous vote, in a stock split. Walter's 2,036 shares became 40,720 shares of the 200,000 issued. With each stock worth $7.50 each, his direct holdings had a value of $305,400. (It is not known what he paid for his shares originally, but it seems reasonable to assume that the split cost no one any money.) Walter was elected President, Jean Vollrath became Vice President, John Detling remained Chairman of the Board and Treasurer, and Robert Vollrath remained as secretary. Minneline was elected to replace Herbert Kohler on the Board of Directors. A change in the corporate laws moved the center of company power from the Chairman of the Board to the President.[47]

The revolution of April 1 soon bore fruit. Walter plunged himself into the management of the company. Through study, experience, and sheer intelligence he made necessary reforms and correct decisions. At a Board meeting in December, he received congratulations on the company's balance sheet. Sales and profits were at record highs, despite increases in wages and costs. Company sales were now almost at the $5 million level, and net profits before taxes were $969,257. The company was able to contain prices of its stainless steel products and was expanding into the dairy supply area. Walter received a Christmas bonus of $5,000 from his highly pleased colleagues.[48]

Still, Walter's authority in the company caused dissention among some members of the Vollrath family, who resented the domination of the family firm by a Kohler. Philip K. Vollrath, Robert's son, later reported that Jean was the sparkplug of this resentment. He and others also had a strong feeling of regret that the company moved into the commercial stainless steel and refrigeration business. But Robert had great admiration for Walter and worked to heal strains within his family. Walter held no ill will toward any Vollrath. In 1948, he hired Jean's son, Carl, who eventually became corporate secretary and did not retire until 1984, the last descendant bearing the Vollrath name to work for the company.[49]

For many years a mammoth tea kettle on a 25-foot platform symbolized the company's manufacture of simple, basic kitchen utensils. It came down with Walter's takeover of the company. The new President had larger plans. By 1950, the Vollrath plant was 500,000 square feet in size, and employed 750. Between 1945 and 1950, the net worth of the plant virtually doubled. Many new products in aluminum and bronze, such as boat hardware and some food service products, were added. The marine accessory line, including stainless steel boat hardware, expanded. Then came lawn mowers, portable power saws, and a vertical drill press. Sales in 1951 reached $8.5 million, the highest in company history.[50]

Walter was now a very wealthy man. His annual income rivaled that of the state's major industrialists who headed the GOP. Political opponents would later study his income tax returns, open by law to the public, and provide voters with the details. In 1946, Walter's total income was $126,650. It increased to $185,554 in 1947 and remained about the same the following year. Since most of his earnings came from tax-exempt dividends on his Kohler and Vollrath stock, he paid only $718 in state income taxes in 1946, $1,458 in 1947, and $1,160 in 1948. In 1949, when his income dipped slightly to $164,183, he paid $703.79 in state income taxes. So, in a four year period, Walter's taxable rate was a mere 11.4%. Democrats, ever eager for high taxes and income redistribution, howled about what they saw as the injustice of it all.

Walter's stock from the Kohler Company was the largest money maker. (However Herbert might have wished to separate Walter completely from the Company, he lacked the legal authority to compel him to sell his stock.) Between 1947 and 1949, the stock brought in about $135,000 a year. Walter's Vollrath dividends increased from $273 in 1946 to $13,749 and $19,749 in the next two years, reflecting his purchase of stock. Walter's Vollrath Company salary of $12,650 in 1947, $17,200 in 1948, and $19,000 in 1949, was only a small part of his annual income.

Thus between 1946 and 1949, Walter enjoyed a total of income of $662,032. Setting the figure at 1949, this equals almost $5.5 million in 2005 dollars. And he was able to shelter a good deal of it from the Wisconsin department of taxation.[51] (Walter's major critic, William T. Evjue of the *Madison Capital Times* admitted using the same tax-exemption law to his own benefit. In his defense, he employed the standard argument he criticized others for using: "I don't pay any taxes that aren't levied. I do pay every dollar in taxes which I am asked to pay under the law.")[52] There was no avenue of escape from the federal income tax, however. No government authority ever questioned any of Walter's tax returns.

※ ※ ※ ✦ ※ ※ ※

At some point in early 1947, while he was still employed at the Kohler Company, Walter was in Philadelphia on business and met Charlotte McAleer, the owner of a local company that distributed Kohler products and manufactured metal goods.[53] Walter was deeply impressed by the slim, attractive, elegantly dressed, brunette who was to become his second wife.

Charlotte Martha Wiley was born in Philadelphia on October 14, 1912. Her father was Dr. John Joseph Wiley, a 29-year-old local physician. Her mother, 26 year-old Nellie McAleer, was the daughter of a Philadelphia industrialist. The couple had been married by a Justice of the Peace on October 26, 1911. Soon after Nellie became pregnant, the couple separated. Nellie moved back into her family home, where Charlotte was born. Eugene J. McAleer and his wife Martha lived in Mt. Airy, an upscale community in northwestern Philadelphia.[54]

The federal census of 1920 notes that Nellie was divorced and had resumed her original surname, McAleer. Her 7-year-old daughter, however, was listed as Charlotte M. Wiley. A summer camp photo taken when Charlotte was about ten is signed Charlotte McAleer.[55] So between 1920 and about 1922, for a reason that is unknown, Charlotte's surname was changed to match that of her mother and maternal grandparents. Charlotte would never speak about her father.

The McAleers were of Irish descent. In 1889, Eugene founded E. J. McAleer & Company, a metal manufacturing firm in Philadelphia that specialized in making steel cabinets.[56] The business prospered, and in time the McAleers became wealthy. Eugene and Martha were Quakers, and their two children, Eugene Jr. and Nellie, were raised in the faith.

Charlotte, her mother's only child, loved small dogs and horses and became a skilled equestrienne. She was accustomed to summoning servants to attend to her needs. Several formal photographs of Charlotte during this period reveal the family wealth and suggest that the only little girl in the house was the spotlight of much attention.[57]

After completing grade school at the Friends School in Germantown, a Philadelphia neighborhood, Charlotte was sent to Friends Central School, a small Quaker, co-educational school in Wynnewood, a Philadelphia suburb. There she was nicknamed "Mac," and was described in the yearbook of the Class of 1931 as "the champion knitter of the class." She served as class president one year, acted in three plays, and wrote for the school newspaper. She was a quiet and physically attractive young woman, known as "the generous owner of the famous green Buick." Her affluence was also evident in the thanks paid to her in the yearbook for hosting two dances and co-hosting a New Year's Eve party.[58]

After graduation, Charlotte went to New York and tried her hand at acting. Her photograph collection contains numerous publicity shots. She landed a few small parts, including one, she said, in the Broadway play "Death Takes a Holiday."[59] Charlotte later described her years in New York under the heading of "education." Not highly intelligent or motivated academically, she chose not to go on to college.

Charlotte's grandfather died in 1936, and her uncle died the following year. That left Nellie to head the family firm. When she died in 1942, Charlotte, at age 30, found herself a corporation owner and president. Charlotte had started learning the business after her uncle's death, and took an accounting course in order to read the company balance sheets. Company engineers taught her how to read blueprints. But she was not a skilled executive. After trying to run the company for a year, she turned the presidency over to a veteran employee, became the vice-president, and took to the road as a saleslady. It was during a call at the Army's Chemical Warfare unit in New York that she met Lt. Col. Albert Edmund Link. They were married in 1943. Three photographs in Charlotte's collection apparently show Link, a solidly built, good-looking man of average height with blonde wavy hair.[60]

During the war, Link was sent to the Dugway Proving Grounds in Utah. DPG was officially established in early 1942, 85 miles southwest of Salt Lake City, Utah. During the war, the Army used the facility to test toxic agents, flame throwers, chemical spray systems, biological warfare weapons, antidotes for chemical agents, and protective clothing.[61]

When not on the road, Charlotte lived in Chestnut Hill, a Philadelphia community near Mt. Airy, with her elderly grandmother, a butler,
and her prize-winning cocker spaniel. Her company's 295 employees
were busily engaged in manufacturing casings for incendiary bombs,
Navy pie plates, toolboxes, and cluster holders for jelly fire-bombs. A
newspaper photograph published in 1945 featured Charlotte standing
next to a 500-pound incendiary bomb casing made for the Royal Air
Force. She told a reporter that whenever possible, she traveled to the
Dugway Proving Grounds to visit her husband. Obviously impressed
by this attractive young business executive, the reporter noted that she
"has long been known as one of the best-dressed women in town."[62]

At some point after the war, Charlotte and Lt. Col. Link were divorced.
Charlotte would never discuss her first marriage, and a later attempt by
a Kohler family attorney to locate any information about Link proved
unsuccessful.[63] In many later articles about Charlotte, her first marriage
would not be mentioned. She told her long-time personal maid that
her husband had died during the war.[64]

When the war ended, the E. J. McAleer company found itself without
war contracts and in a financial quandary. On August 14, 1945 there
was $1 million dollars worth of work; in two days, the contracts were
cut to $15,000. Quickly readjusting to peacetime production, McAleer
began making commercial display cases, metal kitchen cabinets, and
vegetable bins for food stores. Charlotte supervised the design of
modernistic kitchen cupboard units.[65] Prosperity had returned by the
time Charlotte met Walter.

Charlotte later told an interviewer that she did not see Walter for a
year and half after their first meeting. He returned to Philadelphia and
looked her up. "People say he'll go to any length to keep a customer,"
she joked. Charlotte had not forgotten her initial meeting with Walter.
She said later, "He's far more extroverted than I, and I thought he was
attractive as soon as we'd met."[66] A Kohler family attorney later recalled
seeing Walter's love letters to Charlotte, noting, "He was infatuated
with her."[67]

The couple was married on November 8 in the New York apartment
of Charlotte's cousins, Mr. and Mrs. Merton Squires. A clergyman, apparently an Episcopalian, officiated. (Charlotte was as secular, however,
as Walter.) John, Jim, and Bob Kohler flew in for the wedding. There
were no attendants. Two photographs shows a small wedding, done in
good taste. Charlotte, in a dark blue suit, wore a large orchid, a strand

of pearls, and a small black hat with a short veil. The newlyweds left immediately for a Caribbean cruise and were back at Windway on December 1.[68]

Charlotte said later that she had not been in Wisconsin until she visited the Kohler family a week before the marriage.[69] (In fact, she appears in a formal photograph taken in Sheboygan on January 11, 1945.)[70] Walter's relatives and friends were soon stunned to discover that the new Mrs. Kohler was a person who immensely disliked virtually everything about her new environment and almost all of the people in it. Charlotte was considered, at best, a "difficult" woman by virtually everyone who met her.

In the first place, Charlotte detested Windway, and was eager to tell visitors for many years that this was not "her" house or "her" furniture. She collected antiques, and had some family furniture; as they had no place in the ultramodern, brick home, she put them in storage.[71] Charlotte also disliked the Windway staff. She expected total obedience and efficiency, and treated servants on an impersonal basis that bordered on contempt. Charlotte's long-time maid, Bernice Blanke, said later, "She was a very strong woman. You were working for her. Do it the right way or you are gone."[72] Dorothy Engleman, who had come to Windway in 1938, stayed for only a short time after Charlotte's arrival before submitting her resignation. The new Mrs. Kohler, she said later, was "too regimented" and "not as warm" as Celeste had been. She asked an interviewer, "Don't you know about people from Philadelphia?"[73]

Charlotte thought the Sheboygan area, Wisconsin, and the entire Midwest intolerably provincial. She traveled several times a year to the East Coast, loved to spend winters in hot climates, and yearned to travel abroad. She made little or no effort to win friends in Wisconsin, and paid only perfunctory social calls upon members of the Kohler family. She complained endlessly about living in an area she couldn't stand and having to deal with people who were hopelessly uncouth. (She changed her tune in public after Walter's election, however, telling one reporter, "It's beautiful country here, and I love it. Northern Wisconsin with its lakes and huge pine trees reminds me of certain sections of Pennsylvania.")[74]

The younger Julilly Kohler remembered Charlotte as "really catty and arrogant."[75] Margery Uihlein, a GOP activist in the late 1940s, said that Charlotte was "frozen" and "a pain."[76] When Michael Kohler, John's son, first met Charlotte, she seemed "a little chilling, a little forbidding," and she didn't warm up much afterward.[77] Vicki and Jill Kohler, Bob's daughters, described Charlotte as "stylish," "snobby," "outwardly cold," and "stiff and straight." Jill recalled that at family gatherings, she would sometimes see Charlotte staring at her from across the room. "She reminded me of a cobra, ready to strike or slink back into a hole." Charlotte often told people, said Jill and Vicki, that she was from Philadelphia.[78] Robert E. Kohler, Jr., remembered Charlotte as "stupid, boring, and demanding."[79]

Jackie Holden lived at Windway when Walter arrived home with his new bride. Charlotte took an instant dislike to the 24-year-old woman and one day ordered all of her belongings put out in the driveway, a clear notice of eviction. Walter did nothing to defend his step-daughter from the wrath of his wife. Perhaps he saw Jackie as a last link with Celeste. And he may have been relieved to be free from his step-daughter's often erratic behavior. One day she hurled an overly-amorous young man into a wall at Windway, doing such damage to the wall that a large map of the world was placed over the indentation.[80]

Homeless and dejected, Jackie drove to Chicago and moved in with relatives of her mother, Tim and Barbara Gorham. She stayed with them four years, holding various jobs (department store investigator, airplane mechanic), and keeping everyone in laughter with her often hilarious and wild ways. While she never complained, the Gorhams clearly saw a dark side to the young woman. It was based largely, they believed, on the pain and humiliation of being tossed out of Windway and being abandoned by Walter. She was also sensitive about a physical handicap she endured, a pronounced limp resulting from a motorcycle accident in Mexico. The Gorhams became concerned about Jackie's drinking.[81]

What most irritated and amused the Kohlers and others about Charlotte was her superficiality. Aside from some light fiction, she had no intellectual life. Windway was filled with serious books, and Charlotte showed no interest in them beyond the dust they accumulated—a matter best handled by the servants. Although she had long been a Republican, she freely and repeatedly stated her hatred of politics. She clearly wanted no part of her husband's aspirations for public service.

Charlotte could converse only on a limited range of topics, usually centered upon her own jewelry, clothes, antiques, dogs, and knitting. She stayed at home much of time, spending many hours a day in knitting and needlepoint. Charlotte explained to one interviewer that this activity helped her cut down on smoking by keeping her hands busy.[82]

Beyond this hand work, Charlotte had no domestic talents (she once tried in vain to fry eggs when a cook failed to show up), leaving all that to staff members. Still, she designed dinners and luncheons in detail. She almost fired maid Bernice Blanke for her reply to a question raised at a dinner by one of the guests. "Don't you ever, ever speak to my guests again," she barked. Blanke apologized profusely and never again spoke to a visitor at Windway. She knew her place.[83]

Charlotte had closets packed with expensive garments and shoes. By 1970, and surely earlier, she traveled to New York four times a year to purchase the most recent fashions from the most prestigious clothiers. She explained to Blanke, who accompanied her, that she paid for the trips and clothes out of "my money," meaning the generous funds she regularly received from her stock in Mrs. Paul's Frozen Foods, which purchased the McAleer company.[84]

Charlotte was five feet four and a half inches tall; she seemed taller because of high heels and the straight posture she always displayed. Consistently trim, she could look attractive in a wide variety of clothes, but she was conservative in her tastes. She would buy ten expensive dresses and five or six even more expensive suits at a time while in New York. At one point she owned "way over 100 pairs of shoes of every color and style." She had special handbags and jewelry for each season.[85]

In 1950, Jeanne Lungren, from the *Milwaukee Journal* visited Charlotte at Windway, conducting an extensive interview. The reporter was immediately impressed. "She has short, fluffy, dark brown hair and eyes, and sometimes wears smart gold rimmed glasses and uses a long red cigarette holder." Charlotte had on a handsome, gray suit by Irene, the famous movie costume designer. When asked about her clothes, Charlotte exclaimed, "I adore formal clothes. I wear my clothes until they drop off my back, but even so, I always like the newest ones best. So my pet evening dress is always my newest one. I love hats, too, and buy them all the time. But I don't wear them very much. I don't have any favorite designers, either. But as I think about it, it seems that of the original clothes I've had, there have been more by Hattie Carnegie than any other."

Charlotte also enjoyed discussing the two dogs she and her husband owned. "We have two Scottie dogs, Birkie and Cissie. I've shown Birkie in dog shows. I had him before my marriage. If you have a good dog, it's fun to show him, so I did for two years. But I haven't since I've been in

Wisconsin, and Cissie was never shown. They're both too hopelessly spoiled now, anyway."[86]

Walter J. Vollrath, Jr. later recalled a time when Charlotte was put off a train after she became belligerent over a ruling that her dog couldn't eat with her in the dining car.[87]

No one could understand the chemistry that bound Walter to Charlotte, as they were so different in many ways. But all the evidence points to a happy marriage. Charlotte did her best to make Windway a comfortable and pleasing environment for her husband. She told Lungren how much she and Walter enjoyed listening to classical music together at home, and going to concerts and the theatre. She said she played golf with her husband, and took tennis lessons. "I hadn't touched a racket in 20 years, but Mr. Kohler plays tennis and I had beautiful thoughts about playing with him. But I'm afraid I wasn't so good and it petered out." Charlotte also noted that she traveled with Walter on occasion when he was on business trips.[88] Terry Kohler said later, "She was good for Dad."[89]

Robert Selle, a family investment consultant, later recalled the time that he and Walter arrived at Windway, to be greeted by Charlotte with a tray, two drinks, and a candle. She hadn't expected Selle but quickly adjusted, having a three-candle dinner that Selle said was "all very romantic." He remembered Walter and Charlotte in the front room of Windway, year after year, sitting in their accustomed places, enjoying quiet evenings together.[90]

Charlotte showed kindness to both Terry and Niki when they returned to Windway on vacations. But she didn't pretend to be their mother, telling reporter Lungren, "A few people have written as though I have complete charge of the children. I haven't, and their mother might well take exception to such ideas, and I don't blame her."[91] Many years later, Charlotte told a Windway staff member that she wanted to have children by Walter, but that he refused, fearing the birth of another child with a mental disability.[92]

Charlotte was capable of considering the needs of others outside her home. During the war she had done volunteer work for the Red Cross. She knitted clothes at times for other family members. Her gifts at Christmas and birthdays were often expensive. During her stint as First Lady of Wisconsin she would work with the Red Cross and blood bank, and collect Christmas gifts for patients at the state mental hospital. In the mid-1970s, she was the leader of a large-scale needlepoint project that provided Grace Episcopal Church in Sheboygan with a stunning collection.[93]

Charlotte also exhibited extraordinary generosity toward her dutiful and devoted personal maid, Bernice Blanke. While these benefactions began in the 1970s, they surely reflected something deep and positive in Charlotte's character that Walter may well have sensed from the beginning of their relationship.

Blanke has acknowledged that Charlotte paid a $16,000 hospital bill owed by one of her daughters, paid another daughter's college tuition for four years, helped a third daughter with school costs, and attended all of the family's wedding receptions, bringing gifts. (She bought silver for one daughter, a 12 piece china set for another, and wrote a check for $500 to a third.) She sent similar birthday presents to all members of Blanke's family. One Christmas, Charlotte presented her maid with a mink jacket, and three years later gave her a full length mink coat. Believing that everyone should play golf, Charlotte paid for Blanke's golf lessons and clothes. "When I left," the maid said later, "I had eleven pairs of golf shoes." Since Bernice and Charlotte both wore a size 6, the maid enjoyed receiving the many expensive clothes that Charlotte purchased but then chose not to wear.[94]

We also know that when Erna Schwartz, a long-time personal secretary of Walter's, became seriously ill, Charlotte invited her to Windway to spend several months of expense-free recuperation. Schwartz later remembered Charlotte telling her sadly, "I am an orphan and have no sisters or brothers."[95]

Janet Raye, who cared for Charlotte in her old age, later called her "compassionate." Beyond the "hard shell," Raye said, Mrs. Kohler was "a very gentle, loving woman. I was very attached to her. Every girl who worked for her got very attached to her....She had to be compassionate for Walter to have married her."[96]

Notes

[1] Terry Kohler interview, March 25, 2004.

[2] The property settlement, reached in September, 1945, obligated Walter to maintain Windway. Walter did not purchase Celeste's half of the property. By early 1963, after the desertion of her third husband, Celeste was reportedly hurting financially, and Terry asked his father if he would purchase his mother's half of Windway, as he had promised two years earlier. Walter declined, saying that the home was a "in the white elephant" category and would not bring in much money. He did not send Celeste money, he explained, because of the gift tax. Walter Kohler to Terry Kohler, January 15, 1963, Leslie Kohler Hawley collection. When Celeste moved to St. Thomas in 1958, she built a new home and had a cook, maid, gardener, and laundress. Celeste Macfadden to Terry Kohler, undated but probably 1959, *ibid.*

[3] E-mail, Terry Kohler to the author, March 24, 2005, in Celeste Kohler file.

[4] E-mail, Terry Kohler to the author, March 23, 2005, *ibid.* See Terry Kohler interview, August 3, 2004.

[5] E-mail, Michael Kohler to the author, March 18, 2005, in Celeste Kohler file.

[6] Terry Kohler interview, March 25, 2004; e-mail, Terry Kohler to the author, March 23, 24, 2005, Celeste Kohler file; Jean Dor Sarabia interview, November 3, 2004. Celeste's husband is no doubt the "Robin McFadden" listed in Ancestry.com as having been born in 1900 and died in Kaloa, Hawaii in June, 1975. On the other hand, Celeste's death certificate of 1974 says that she was "widowed." The certificate is in the Leslie Kohler Hawley collection.

[7] Terry Kohler interview, March 25, 2004; Niki Kohler interview, May 6, 2004.

[8] *Ibid.*; Terry Kohler interview of May 7, 2004.

[9] See the undated (probably 1961) letter from Celeste to Terry in the Leslie Kohler Hawley Collection.

[10] Peter and Nancy Kohler interview, May 6, 2005.

[11] Terry Kohler interview, June 12, 2003.

[12] Sarabia, *80 Years of My Wandering Spirit*, 48.

[13] Walter J. Vollrath, Jr. interview.

[14] Roland Neumann interview.

[15] Terry Kohler interview, March 25, 2004. See Sarabia, *80 Years of My Wandering Spirit*, 52.

[16] Walter J. Vollrath, Jr. interview.

[17] The story alleges that Herbert V. Kohler, Sr. used underhanded methods to bend his sisters to his will. The official company history does not address the issue directly, noting only that the three sisters "adored" their younger

half-brother, who was brought up in their house and under their tutelage. The implication is, of course, that the sisters voluntarily turned over their shares. Blodgett, *A Sense of Higher Design*, 123, 126. I have been unable to document the anti-Herbert story many Kohler family members believe. One interviewee sent me to a Kohler company physician who, she said, could verify the most serious allegation. Dr. Donald Rowe flatly denied it and expressed his total admiration for Herbert Kohler. Donald Rowe interview. Lillie died in a Milwaukee hospital in 1965, her death barely being mentioned in the press. The funeral service was held in Herbert's home. *Milwaukee Journal*, April 18, 1965. No information about the last two decades of her life or her financial status is available. Evangeline's obituary noted that she changed her will in 1944, naming her brother, Herbert V. Kohler, executor of her nearly million dollar estate. "Miss Evangeline Kohler's Will Is Filed For Probate," *Sheboygan Press*, November 13, 1954. See also "Miss Evangeline Kohler Is Laid To Rest After Rites," *ibid.*, August 30, 1954. Marie left most of her estate to the Kohler Foundation, created in October, 1940, which Herbert controlled. See "Marie Christine Kohler," *Kohler of Kohler News*, November, 1943, 19. See also "Death Takes Marie Kohler," *Milwaukee Journal*, October 11, 1943.

[18] Terry Kohler interview, August 13, 2003. See also Peter and Nancy Kohler interview of August 11, 2003 and May 6, 2005; Roland Neumann interview; Vicki and Jill Kohler interview; Marie Kohler interview; Robert E. Kohler interview.

[19] Blodgett, *A Sense of Higher Design*, 138-40.

[20] "Herbert V. Kohler, 76, Dies: Rites Wednesday," *Sheboygan Press*, July 29, 1968.

[21] Reeves, *The Life and Times of Joe McCarthy*, 1-18.

[22] *Ibid.*, 19-38.

[23] *Ibid.*, 38-39.

[24] *Ibid.*, 45-61.

[25] *Ibid.*, 65-68.

[26] Political journalist John Wyngaard wrote in 1945 that veteran Republicans were skeptical about McCarthy's youth and Democratic background. Still, "McCarthy has the physical qualifications. He is young and vigorous, a fair orator, an indefatigable campaigner. He has been proved in that respect." John Wyngaard, "McCarthy and Philipp Are Only Potential Candidates to Oppose Bob La Follette," *Janesville Gazette*, July 6, 1945.

[27] Reeves, *The Life and Times of Joe McCarthy*, 68-74; Terry Kohler interview, June 12, 2003.

[28] Terry Kohler interview, December 2, 2005; "Hard Work by Friends Helped Kohler to Win," *Milwaukee Journal*, June 11, 1950.

[29] Walter's admiring journalist friend John Wyngaard later supported this explanation for Kohler's departure from the 1946 race. "Kohler: The Man, Politician," *Sheboygan Press*, March 30, 1976.

[30] See the Margery Uihlein interview. A Wisconsin GOP activist, she knew both McCarthy and Kohler after the war, saying they had very little in common. McCarthy was an "Irish Mick" who, after a few drinks, would join a couple of pals and sing Irish songs. "I adored him." Walter was "courtly, sort of elegant, and gentle; a gentleman." He was not at all a politician, she said, and disliked campaigning. Politics to Kohler was a matter of duty and public service, she added, reflecting the influence of his governor-father.

[31] Reeves, *The Life and Times of Joe McCarthy*, 74-92.

[32] *Ibid.*, 92-109.

[33] "Walter J. Kohler, Jr." *Cancer News*, July, 1954, 11; e-mail, American Cancer Society to the author, August 31, 2004, American Cancer Society file.

[34] "Mrs. Walter J. Kohler Is Summoned Sunday," editorial, Mrs. Walter J. Kohler, Sr.," *Sheboygan Press*. February 3, 1947; "Impressive Funeral Rites Are Held For Mrs. Walter J. Kohler," *ibid.*, February 6, 1947.

[35] Julilly Kohler interview, October 7, 2003; Marie Kohler interview.

[36] Julilly Kohler interview, October 7, 2003; Michael Kohler interview.

[37] See e-mail, Julilly Kohler to the author, August 7, 2004, Julilly Kohler file.

[38] See e-mail, Michael Kohler to the author, January 12, 2005, John M. Kohler III file; Michael Kohler interview; Philip K. Vollrath interview; Walter J. Vollrath, Jr. interview; Ken Benson interview. See also "The John M. Kohler Family Returns From Waller Reunion," *Sheboygan Press*, June 29, 1965. The Sheboygan County Historical Society has a collection of printed Christmas invitations sent out by John and Julilly Kohler, revealing a commitment to good times and the family's secular emphasis for the holiday. Christmas cards from the John Kohler family are in the Leslie Kohler Hawley collection. They featured family photographs and news. Nancy Kohler later observed that a failure to be invited to the Christmas parties was a sign of being of little social value in the community. Peter and Nancy Kohler interview, May 6, 2005.

[39] On the bank loan, see Steinberg, "Is This the Man to Beat McCarthy?," 78. I assume the loan came from the Sheboygan bank. Walter and bank president Clarence Weber were long-time friends and business associates. See the James Raffel interview.

[40] *The Vollrath Story*, 13.

[41] See the e-mail Terry Kohler to the author, November 8, 2003; Steinberg, "Is This the Man to Beat McCarthy?," 77.

[42] See copy, J. M. Detling to John G. Kamps, July 2, 1946, Vollrath Company file. This document was provided by long-time Vollrath employee Bill Kessler.

[43] Vollrath Company Minutes, September 5, 1944; November 21, 1945; July 29, December 17, 1946. On stockholder apprehensions, see Roland Neumann interview; Walter J. Vollrath, Jr. interview.

[44] Terry Kohler's baby book is in the Leslie Kohler Hawley collection.

[45] Walter J. Kohler, Jr. personnel file. On Minneline's role, see e-mail, Terry Kohler to the author, December 29, 2003, Vollrath Company file; Julilly Kohler interview, October 7, 2003, and Walter J. Vollrath, Jr. interview. See Minneline's obituary in the Vollrath Company Minutes of September 23, 1952.

[46] See e-mail, Terry Kohler to the author, December 29, 2003, Vollrath Company file.

[47] This summary, beyond the references to Minneline's possible motives, was based on the Vollrath Company Minutes.

[48] *Ibid.*, December 18, 1947. Walter's initial salary was $850 a month. He was making $600 a month at the Kohler Company.

[49] Philip K. Vollrath interview; *The Vollrath Story, Celebrating 125 Years*, 22. The Robert Vollrath family was invited to Riverbend for the annual Halloween party. On dissention between some of the Vollraths and Kohlers, see e-mail, Julilly Kohler to the author, December 28, 2003, Vollrath Company file.

[50] *The Vollrath Story Celebrating 125 Years*, 16; Philip K. Vollrath interview; copy, Phillip T. Drotning to E. J. Williams, January 14, 1952, box 50, Walter J. Kohler, Jr. papers; Vollrath Company Minutes, April 12, 1952.

[51] "Kohler Income $662,032, Pays Tax on $75,739," *Madison Capital Times*, July 28, 1950.

[52] "Kohler Should Have Paid $40,000 Instead of $4,040," *ibid.*, August 21, 1950. Wisconsin corporations paid a 3% tax on dividends paid to shareholders. That law was passed in 1934 under the administration of Governor Phil La Follette.

[53] See Charlotte's account of the initial meeting in Jeanne Lungren, "Wisconsin's Future First lady at Home," *Milwaukee Journal*, November 12, 1950. This lengthy and revealing interview with Charlotte was the first given to a reporter after her husband's election as governor of Wisconsin. The article featured only a single sentence on Charlotte's first marriage, without names or dates. On the date and place of the initial meeting between Walter and Charlotte, see Steinberg, "Is This The Man to Beat McCarthy?," 78. The account in Nancy Greenwood Williams, *First Women of Wisconsin: The Governors' Wives* (Kalamazoo, Michigan: ana Publishing, 1991), 191, is clearly incorrect. Terry Kohler is of the opinion that Walter and Charlotte met at the National Housewares Show at McCormick Place in Chicago. Terry Kohler interview, June 12, 2003. See "Charlotte McAleer Kohler," *Sheboy-*

gan *Press*, July 5, 1995 and e-mail, Terry Kohler to the author, March 25, 2005, in the Charlotte Kohler file.

[54] The Wiley/McAleer marriage certificate reveals that Wiley was born in Philadelphia on May 4, 1883. Nellie was born in Philadelphia on July 11, 1886. Marriage certificate, Charlotte Kohler file. Wiley was a member of the Philadelphia County Medical Society and the Pennsylvania Medical Society. The last time his name appeared on the list of the latter organization was 1921. See e-mail, Sue Scordo to the author, March 24, 2005, in *ibid.* Wiley appears in the census of 1900. His father, John S. Wiley was born in Philadelphia in 1858, and he was at least partly of Irish ancestry. Father and son appear again, living together, in the census of 1930. Census reports are available on Ancestry.com. Charlotte's birth certificate is in the Charlotte Kohler file.

[55] The signed camp photo is in the Leslie Kohler Hawley collection. See Williams, *First Women of Wisconsin*, page 191, which is inaccurate on the name change. In the census of 1920, Nellie's uncle Eugene J. McAleer, Jr. (1888-1937), a hardware store manager, was also living at the same address. Nellie McAleer remained in the family home for the rest of her life and did not remarry. In her old age, Charlotte told a nursing assistant that her mother was "weak." Ann Kraft interview.

[56] The census of 1900 and 1910 report that Eugene was born in 1873, which would have made him only 16 when founding his company. The census of 1920 has Eugene born in 1868, which seems more likely.

[57] Eugene's Irish connection comes from the census of 1930. For further details of Charlotte's early life, see Rex Rittenhouse, "Mrs. McAleer's Plant Converted To War Products Before Pearl Harbor," *Philadelphia Record*, January 25, 1945. Charlotte's death certificate, giving her father's full name, is in the Terry Kohler papers. Many photographs of young Charlotte are in the Leslie Kohler Hawley collection.

[58] Page 39 of Charlotte's yearbook, describing her years at Friends Central School, is in the Terry Kohler papers. The full yearbook, *The Record*, and her diploma are in the Leslie Kohler Hawley collection.

[59] Williams, *First Ladies of Wisconsin*, 191. In the yearbook, see pages 39, 57, 59, 60, 73, 77, 100, 114. She was not listed among the top students.

[60] See Rittenhouse, "Mrs. McAleer's Plant Converted To War Products," about her company experiences and her marriage. The photographs are in the Leslie Kohler Hawley collection. Perhaps Charlotte destroyed other photos after the divorce. One envelope labeled "Mrs. Link" contains several stunning photos of Charlotte during the war.

[61] See *www.globalsecurity.org/wmd/facility/dugway.htm.*

[62] Rittenhouse, "Mrs. McAleer's Plant Converted To War Products."

[63] Roland Neumann interview. Despite numerous requests of military and political authorities, I too have been unable to secure much information on Link. His records may have been destroyed by a fire. See Nick Katers to the author, April 3, 2005 in the Charlotte Kohler file.

[64] Bernice Blanke interview, August 25, 2004. At a Philadelphia benefit show in April, 1948, in which she was a model of costumes by Hollywood designer Irene, Charlotte was listed as Mrs. Charlotte McAleer Link. This was unusual in that she did not use her married surname during the war at the factory, no doubt to show that she was the boss. Perhaps the divorce from Link took place in 1948, between the time of the article and her marriage to Walter. Evidence is unavailable. *Philadelphia Inquirer*, April 18, 1948.

[65] "Effects of War and Its Sudden Ending in Some Local Industries," *The Evening Bulletin* [Philadelphia]. August 24, 1945.

[66] Lungren, "Wisconsin's Future First Lady at Home."

[67] Roland Neumann interview.

[68] "Miss McAleer Weds Kohler," *Milwaukee Journal*, November 10, 1948. Charlotte's first marriage went unmentioned in this article, although Walter's earned a full paragraph. A photograph of Charlotte appeared in the newspaper the next day. Two informal wedding photographs are in the Leslie Kohler Hawley collection.

[69] Dorothy Parnell, "Mrs. Walter Kohler Jr. Calm About 'First Lady' Role," *Milwaukee Sentinel*, September 4, 1950.

[70] The photograph, in which she is likely surrounded by Kohler Company personnel, is in the Leslie Kohler Hawley collection.

[71] Roland Neumann interview; Lungren, "Wisconsin's Future First Lady at Home."

[72] Bernice Blanke interview, August 25, 2004. Blanke was Charlotte's personal maid for 22 ½ years, starting in 1970.

[73] Dorothy Engleman interview.

[74] Parnell, "Mrs. Walter Kohler Jr. Calm About 'First Lady' Role."

[75] Julilly Kohler interview, October 7, 2003. See also the Bernice Blanke interview, August 25, 2004.

[76] Margery Uihlein interview.

[77] Michael Kohler interview.

[78] Vicki and Jill Kohler interview. See the Marie Kohler interview.

[79] Robert E. Kohler, Jr., interview.

[80] The map is still there. It formed the background for a classic photograph of Walter and his brothers, taken in the early 1950s. I have heard the story of Jackie's physical rejection of her suitor several times from both Terry and Mary Kohler.

81 Tim and Barbara Gorham interview, October 24, 2004. See Terry Kohler interview, August 3, 2004. Peter Kohler later remembered Jackie as masculine, gregarious, and loud. "And she could get angry." Nancy Kohler recalled hearing about a traffic accident in New York after which Jackie, in the wreckage of her car, held her wounded head erect with her hands for some time to minimize her own physical damage. This revealed the woman's physical strength and mental perseverance, Nancy said. Peter and Nancy Kohler interview, May 6, 2005.

82 Lungren, "Wisconsin's Future First Lady at Home." See also Terry Kohler interview, June 12, 2003, and Julilly Kohler interview, October 7, 2003.

83 Bernice Blanke interview, August 25, August 28, 2004.

84 Roland Neumann interview.

85 Bernice Blanke interview, August 25, 2004.

86 Lungren, "Wisconsin's Future First Lady at Home."

87 Walter J. Vollrath, Jr. interview.

88 Lungren, "Wisconsin's Future First Lady at Home."

89 Terry Kohler interview, June 12, 2003.

90 Robert and Katherine Selle interview.

91 Lungren, "Wisconsin's Future First Lady at Home."

92 Ann Kraft interview.

93 Williams, *First Ladies of Wisconsin*, 192; "Mrs. Kohler to Head Services of Red Cross," *Milwaukee Journal*, November 23, 1951; Jeanette Kliejunas, "Grace Church Begins Needlepoint Project," *Sheboygan Press*, January 25, 1974. Charlotte trained 26 women in needlepoint at Windway for the project, and labored at great length herself on the 27 piece collection. The priedieux in Our Lady of Walsingham chapel is a product of Charlotte's personal effort. Mrs. Kohler was the only one of the women involved who was not a member of the church. A plaque at the church commemorates the work of the stitchers. See Pat von Rautenkranz interview, May 7, 2005.

94 Bernice Blanke interview, August 25, 2004.

95 Erna Schwartz interview.

96 Janet Raye interview.

Chapter Eight
The Man Wisconsin Needed

In early 1948, Republicans were confident of winning the White House for the first time since Roosevelt's defeat of Hoover sixteen years earlier. The Truman Administration had grown increasingly unpopular. Newspapers regularly carried charges of corruption, cronyism, and ineptitude at the federal level. Many business leaders were furious with the President for attempting to defeat the anti-labor Taft-Hartley bill. The House Un-American Activities Committee railed at the President for allegedly ignoring subversives in high places of the government, despite the Administration's strict new loyalty-security program. Southerners were restless over Truman's emerging commitment to racial equality, especially after the President ordered the desegregation of the military and established a committee designed to end racial discrimination in the federal civil service. Many Eastern intellectuals were nervous about the Missourian's hawkish approach to the internal security issue and his militant stand against the Soviet Union, as revealed in the Truman Doctrine and the Marshall Plan. Soaring postwar inflation and housing problems rattled millions. The President's fiery temper and blunt speech irritated many across the political spectrum. To millions, Truman appeared to be an unworthy successor of FDR.

The first major Republican presidential candidate was Harold Stassen. The tall, good-looking, 40-year old former Governor of Minnesota announced his decision to jump into the race in the winter of 1947. In fact, he had been campaigning in neighboring Wisconsin for four years. Among Stassen's earliest supporters was Senator Joe McCarthy, a personal friend. Both Stassen and McCarthy were widely thought to be moderate Republicans. Tom Coleman, finance chairman for the state GOP, personally favored conservative Ohio Senator Robert Taft, but he backed Stassen, thinking him capable of winning in Wisconsin. Some Republicans farther to the Right (and a few Progressives) favored General Douglas MacArthur, who was still on duty overseas. Others, in the middle and toward the Left, backed Thomas Dewey, the party's presidential candidate in 1944.

Walter J. Kohler, Jr. joined the Stassen team not long after the Minnesotan declared his candidacy. Both men were young, attractive, vigorous, ambitious, and of the same general frame of mind about political and economic matters. Moreover, Walter had determined that this was the time to make his move into the political arena; to meet people, to make valuable contacts, to be associated with a candidate who might well become the next President. In this campaign, he was working side by side with both Coleman and McCarthy, and the former in particular was a man Walter needed in future political races. Industrialist and party leader Wayne Hood was also a Stassen supporter.

By mid-March, 1948 Stassen was already on his third campaign trip of the year through Wisconsin. Walter introduced him at a large rally in Sheboygan. Stassen was applauded for defending the importance of agriculture and asserting that farmers should receive "a full 100% of parity," meaning that the federal government should be responsible for maintaining a high level of farm income. Following the rally, about 75 people attended a reception for the candidate at Windway.[1]

In the statewide Republican primary election held in early April, Stassen delegates swept the returns. Walter topped all delegate-at-large candidates, including Joe McCarthy and Phil La Follette. Stassen delegates won 19 of Wisconsin's votes and MacArthur supporters had eight.

Robert H. Fleming, an astute political reporter for the Milwaukee Journal, observed that Kohler's victory raised eyebrows all over the state. "The widely known Kohler name had great pulling power and it is natural to speculate that the handsome, personable son of the former governor may try for something big in Wisconsin politics now that he has passed this test." Kohler was known to be considering a run for high political office, and it was rumored that he might attempt to be elected governor. Republican Oscar Rennebohm, who, as Lieutenant Governor, had become Governor in March, 1947 at the death of Walter Goodland, had many critics, inside and outside his party. Some young Republicans hoped Kohler would run for the Senate two years later against the incumbent, Republican Alexander Wiley.[2]

At a meeting in early June, Wisconsin delegates met to select a chairman. In a contest between Kohler and McCarthy, the two top vote getters in the election, the MacArthur delegates decided to back

Kohler, angry over a McCarthy speech against the General that noted his divorce and remarriage and derided claims that he was a "native son." Behind the scenes, Tom Coleman, with the assistance of young Republican Melvin Laird and his mother, pulled strings to get Kohler elected. Laird said later that Coleman was grooming Kohler for a later gubernatorial race.[3] Sensing his likely defeat, McCarthy opted out of a direct contest with Kohler, saying he had plans to be busy on the floor of the Philadelphia convention. Indeed, McCarthy nominated Kohler for the chairmanship and defended him when a maverick delegate tried to keep the vote from being unanimous.[4]

At the GOP state convention in Milwaukee, warfare again broke out between personalities and factions, the result being that no official slate of candidates was endorsed. This was a defeat for Tom Coleman and other party leaders who had endorsed Governor Rennebohm for reelection and other specific candidates for state office. Progressive Ralph Immel, who wanted to be Governor, led the victorious struggle. It was clear to all that disunity within the GOP was hampering its effectiveness.[5]

As the GOP convention in Philadelphia neared, there was again considerable talk about Kohler as a gubernatorial candidate. Supporters thought he could defeat both Rennebohm and Immel. A reporter observed, "Kohler's friends point to his name, his father's reputation and his general pleasant personality and good looks as assets. They concede he is lacking in political experience." The reporter continued, "It is known that ever since he got out of the navy he has been interested in running for political office. It may be of importance that he is making no effort here to discourage discussion of himself as a possible candidate for governor." Walter himself made no comment.[6] Warren P. Knowles, a 40-year-old attorney from New Richmond and Republican majority leader in the State Senate, formed a Kohler for Governor Club, which started a "Draft Kohler" movement.[7]

Stassen's bid for the presidency soon collapsed. He lost to Dewey in Oregon and then suffered defeats in New Hampshire and Ohio. Dewey swept to victory at the national convention, leaving Wisconsin GOP leaders disappointed and frustrated, but still confident of victory. Rennebohm and Immel waged vigorous gubernatorial campaigns. Walter decided not to enter the contest, in part, no doubt, because of the intensity of the competition and also because Tom Coleman and other party leaders were intent on reelecting Rennebohm. His time would come, no doubt two years later. There was also talk of Kohler taking on McCarthy in 1952.[8]

In November, Wisconsin Republicans were pleased to see Rennebohm reclaim the governor's office. The GOP won eleven congressional seats and large legislative majorities. But Republicans were stunned when Truman carried the state by 56,331 votes. The shock was felt nation-wide when the President came from behind and won an upset victory over Dewey. Walter said later, "I make no pretense here tonight that I anticipated the results of the election of 1948. I admit, with considerable chagrin, that I shared the complacency of most members of our Party. I believed that Dewey would win."[9] Rival candidates in the South and on the Left should have sealed Truman's fate. Pollsters had abandoned their efforts, concluding that the incumbent couldn't win. The Chicago Tribune had declared a Dewey victory in huge headlines. Ballrooms were rented for election night victory celebrations. But Truman's friendship with organized labor and a highly effective nationwide campaign trip by train won the President enough votes to enjoy a narrow victory.

The impact of the election was such that many Republicans vowed to bring down Truman and win the next presidential election at all cost. They had lost five times in a row, and this was to be their final humiliation. The primary weapon was to be the Reds in Government issue. In the rage and anguish that stemmed from their defeat in 1948, many Republicans became zealous proponents of what has been called the Second Red Scare.

One of the staples in the GOP arsenal was the Alger Hiss case. It played only a minor role in the 1948 campaign, but it showed promise as an election issue. Hiss was the embodiment of the Eastern, Ivy League, liberal establishment that had supported the New Deal and become prominent in the State Department. The slim, attractive, impeccably dressed gentleman was charged with being a Soviet spy by Whittaker Chambers, a short, stout, rumpled intellectual who had admittedly been a Communist since 1924 and part of a government Red spy ring in the mid-1930s. In August, in a dramatic showdown between the two men before the House Committee on Un-American Activities, Hiss had shown an evasiveness that helped convince Congressman Richard Nixon that Chambers' charges were true. He also was enjoying leaks from FBI officials who had evidence to substantiate the allegations.

After the election, Chambers led investigators to a pumpkin patch on his farm and produced microfilms of State Department documents which he said Hiss had transmitted to him. The revelations caused a sensation in the media. In December, a federal grand jury indicted Hiss on two counts of perjury for claiming not to have seen Chambers (whom he knew as George Crosley) after January 1, 1937. Chambers' documents were from 1937 and 1938. The charge would have focused on espionage but the statute of limitations had run out years earlier.

In 1949, the storm of charges increased with revelations that Judith Coplon, a Department of Justice employee, had been a Soviet spy. In August, Secretary of State Dean Acheson, who had defended Hiss, declared that China was about to fall to the Communists. In September, Russia suddenly exploded its first atomic bomb. In December, Chiang Kai-shek and the Nationalist government of China fled to the island of Formosa, and all of Asia seemed prey to the Reds. Some Republicans were convinced, or at least said they were convinced, that these tragedies had been planned by Communists working in high government positions, aided and protected by Democrats. State governments throughout the nation passed laws cracking down on all allegedly seditious conduct, associations, and speech. Spy stories were everywhere in the press.

The Second Red Scare, growing in intensity throughout 1949, exploded after the conviction of Alger Hiss on January 21, 1950. Republican Congressman Karl Mundt, a leader in the GOP crusade, called upon the President to begin to weed out government employees "whose Soviet leanings have contributed so greatly to the deplorable mess of our foreign policy." Congressman Nixon said that the Hiss case was only "a small part of the whole shocking story of Communist espionage in the United States."

More shocks were soon felt across the nation. On January 31, President Truman announced that the Soviets were developing a hydrogen bomb, a weapon scientist Albert Einstein said could destroy life on the planet. Four days later, the press announced in screaming headlines that Dr. Klaus Fuchs, a British physicist who had worked on the American atomic bomb project during the war, had been arrested as a Communist spy. On February 7, FBI Director J. Edgar Hoover talked to Senators about Fuchs and contended that the United States contained about 540,000 Reds and fellow travelers. All across the nation, Republicans filled their Lincoln Day speeches with warnings about Communists and Democrats.[10]

Senator Joe McCarthy, who had dallied during his political career with charges that his opponents had been Reds or pro-Communists, now stumbled into the Second Red Scare and became the focus of the entire GOP effort. At his Lincoln Day speech in Wheeling, West Virginia, on February 9, he claimed, quite irresponsibly, that he had a list of 205 Communists in the State Department, names known to the Secretary of State. His hastily and sloppily prepared speech quickly drew national attention, and McCarthy returned the fire of critics with a brazen volley of bluff and lies. The warfare was such that a *Washington Post* cartoonist coined the term McCarthyism, which soon entered the dictionary as "a mid-twentieth century political attitude characterized chiefly by opposition to elements held to be subversive and by the use of tactics involving personal attacks on individuals by means of widely publicized indiscriminate allegations, especially on the basis of unsubstantiated charges." The Second Red Scare and the Republican effort to brand Democrats as subversives became, above all, the struggle to defend or condemn Joe McCarthy.

McCarthy loved the attention. He had been trying since entering the Senate to identify an issue or a cause that would vault him into the headlines. Now he found himself under attack by the entire liberal establishment, and his psychological makeup was such that he found the struggle exhilarating. Better informed conservatives filled his head and his office with tons of information to assist him in his battle. A battery of right-wing assistants helped him wade through the materials, write speeches, and reply to critics. Never a sophisticated or well-educated man, despite his high intelligence, Joe was transformed in 1950 from a cynical blowhard into a much more dangerous and destructive true believer. Heavy drinking did not aid his use of evidence and sense of political balance. The former Wisconsin farm boy was now one of the most famous—and infamous—men in the nation. Among those required to deal with his boisterous personality and shaky data were the Republicans from his home state, including Walter J. Kohler, Jr. Their political futures seemed tied to the Senator and his often outrageous allegations whether they liked it or not.

Tom Coleman was a quiet leader in securing financial support for McCarthy and protecting him when Democrats began a probe of the Senator's charges. He told members of his Finance Committee, "...if just one or two cases can be proved, I think that the political results for the Republican Party will be good."[11]

In 1949, Walter stayed in the public eye by chairing the Wisconsin Committee on Hoover Commission findings. We do not know how he obtained this position, but Tom Coleman, who saw a great political future for the young executive, may have played a role. The Commission on Organization of the Executive Branch of the Government, popularly known as the Hoover Commission, was created by President Truman to propose recommendations for greater efficiency and economy in the federal government. Truman and former President Herbert Hoover shared a desire to trim the government of waste and stop bureaucratic infighting. Part of the plan was to create citizen committees throughout the nation to promote public understanding of the Commission's findings. Wisconsin was the first state to create such a committee, and Walter worked busily, meeting people, attending meetings, giving speeches, and issuing statements to the media.[12]

In December, Walter posed for a photograph with Mrs. Oveta Culp Hobby, war-time commander of the Women's Army Corps, and Dr. Robert L. Johnson, chairman of the Citizens' Committee for the Hoover Report. All three were active participants in a "Cracker Barrel" conference in Washington on the Hoover Report. The New York Herald Tribune carried the photo on its front page.[13]

The State Republican Voluntary Committee, now for all intents and purposes the GOP in Wisconsin, met in convention in 1949. Walter, Charlotte, and Jim Kohler were delegates, and John Kohler was an alternate. Walter was elected chairman of the Committee on Rules and Order of Business, a clear sign that he was a member of the party's inner ring.[14] Walter helped Tom Coleman push through a motion that would require the organization, when meeting in election years, to endorse, by majority vote, one candidate for each of the five constitutional offices and for United States Senator. Endorsement for other offices would remain optional. This was an obvious attempt to bring order to the party and increase Coleman's ability to help select qualified people for office who would pursue GOP objectives.[15]

The new rule became important in May, 1950 when Governor Rennebohm announced that, for reasons of health, he would not seek reelection in the fall. Three Republican candidates immediately jumped into the race for endorsement by the Republican Voluntary Committee: Walter, Frank Keefe of Oshkosh, and Gordon Bubolz of Appleton. Walter's competitors had a definite edge in political experience: Keefe had been in Congress since 1939, and Bubolz had been in the state senate since 1944. Moreover, both men also had excellent educational credentials: Keefe was a graduate of the University of Michigan Law

School, and Bubolz had degrees from Lawrence College, the Wharton School of Finance at the University of Pennsylvania, and the University of Wisconsin Law School. With the Republican Voluntary Committee meeting only two weeks away, GOP officials predicted a strenuous battle for the nomination. Still, these same officials, a Milwaukee reporter observed, thought Kohler the favorite in the race.[16]

Two more candidates soon entered the race. Harvey V. Higley of Marinette was a veteran GOP insider and former chairman of the Republican Voluntary Committee. Storekeeper Erwin L. Benjamin of St. Croix Falls, another veteran GOP campaigner, became the fifth candidate and was taken seriously by no one.[17]

When Keefe pulled out of the race on June 3, Kohler became the odds-on favorite to win the nomination. His surname, youth, attractive personality, and vote-getting achievement as a Stassen delegate in 1948 were often mentioned. Rumor had it as well that Tom Coleman favored him.[18] GOP insiders knew that this was true. State GOP chairman Wayne Hood explained to another party leader, "I think his interest in Walter Kohler, Jr. goes back to the day when he was campaign manager for Walter's father."[19] But Coleman kept busily raising money for the party and stayed out of the convention struggle. He was already an avid McCarthyite and was actively assisting the Senator in his efforts to defend himself against critics.[20]

A roadblock to Walter's selection seemed to appear when Governor Rennebohm came out for Higley. Insiders said that this reflected a struggle for power between Rennebohm and Coleman.[21] When asked, Walter told a reporter, "I have no knowledge that Coleman is working for me. It would be wonderful if he was, but I have no commitment from him, and I certainly have none to him."[22]

Two days before the convention convened in Milwaukee, Kohler, Higley, and Bubolz spoke before 500 people in the city Auditorium. Bubolz threw some jabs at Kohler, principally for his lack of experience in public office. "Being governor and the titular head of the Republican party is no job for an amateur," he said. When Walter's turn came, he chose to ignore the barbs and expressed what he believed were the qualities needed for a governor, including personal integrity, character, intelligence, a deep sense of justice, and "a high regard for the fundamental liberties of mankind." With a nod to the supporters of Senator McCarthy, who was scheduled to give the keynote address at the convention, Walter added, """In short, he should be as far from a Fascist or a Communist as any human being can get."[23]

Support for Joe McCarthy was at a fever pitch when the convention assembled. The fiery speech by the "Fighting Marine" ("I know of not one single reason why Communists should be handled with kid gloves. They don't use kid gloves or powder puffs on us") prompted Republicans from all corners of the state to sing the Senator's praises. A resolution passed commending and encouraging McCarthy's attacks on the State Department. A delegate was booed down for warning that the Senator's campaign was divisive and dangerous to the country and to the GOP.[24]

McCarthy himself took no position on the gubernatorial race, but one of his closest friends, Tom Korb of Milwaukee, was at work for Kohler, as was McCarthy loyalist Lloyd Tegge of Waukesha, Chairman of the Young Republicans.[25] Dorothy Kohler, Walter's McCarthyite sister-in-law, belonged to the Friends for Kohler Organization that raised funds for the candidate.[26]

State Senator Warren P. Knowles, who had supported Kohler for Governor in 1948, placed Walter's name in nomination, declaring, "Walter Kohler is the only candidate who has demonstrated vote-getting ability in the State of Wisconsin."[27] Knowles would soon be Kohler's campaign manager. Melvin Laird, another State Senator and former Stassen supporter, was also active.

In a brief speech before the convention, Walter again listed the qualifications required of the next governor and made his independence known. The next governor, he said, "should be bossed by no man or group of men. But he should work cooperatively with the legislature and should cooperate with local party leaders in the selection of men for offices. We should be Americans first and Republicans second." Delegate Thomas Bentley, declared, "We know Walter Kohler in Sheboygan County; we honor him, and we love him....He has made good in Sheboygan County; he has made good in the State of Wisconsin, and everybody in the State of Wisconsin not only knows his name but respects him.... There may be some little attempt to defeat him, but Walter Kohler is going to be our next Governor."[28]

Kohler won the Voluntary Committee's endorsement on the first ballot, securing strong support from Milwaukee and Madison delegates. Higley placed second and Bubolz third. When the result was announced and the cheering died down, Charlotte, no doubt with much trepidation, walked to the rostrum and said, "I can't help but feel that you have all chosen very wisely and very well. I know you will all be very proud of Mr. Kohler in November and in the years to come." The couple was mobbed by well-wishers. (Charlotte would later tour the State Fair with her husband, but played no other role in the campaign.)[29]

The Madison vote suggested support from Tom Coleman, but Walter continued to deny that he was tied to anyone. He told a reporter, "Tom Coleman has been my friend for many years. I expect he'll continue to be my friend. But I meant what I told the convention—that I would welcome advice from all competent persons, that I would need their assistance, but that no man would be my boss."

Robert H. Fleming attributed Kohler's victory largely to the candidate's strong personal appeal. "Some of those who had known him for years did the heavy work of winning delegate support at the state convention, Friday and Saturday. But there were many more who felt a feeling of friendship though they'd known him only a few days or even hours before the balloting began. Kohler is a man who showed there that he can make friends quickly. Men liked his firm handshake and straightforward manner. Women found him handsome, and liked his ready laugh. His friendly manner will be a major asset as he campaigns for governor."[30]

A Milwaukee Journal editorial observed that Kohler had come into the convention with obvious political advantages over his rivals. "He offered a name known in every corner of the state. He had no past political record vulnerable to Democratic attack or objectionable to any voter faction. He made a sensational run in the 1948 presidential elector race, showing political allure. He had a record of leadership in welfare drives and in the state campaign in support of the governmental reorganization proposals of the Hoover commission." In his pre-convention speeches, the editorial added, "Kohler was careful not to commit himself specifically on state issues. That, too, was politically wise strategy."[31]

Within the span of two weeks, then, Kohler had emerged, along with Senator McCarthy, as one of the two top stars in Wisconsin's Republican party. He would still have to win the state primary, held on September 19, to become the official GOP candidate, but with the blessings of the Republican Voluntary Committee leaders and delegates his selection seemed certain.

Some thought that Kohler's political inexperience, while a mixed blessing in the initial GOP runoff, would pose a formidable problem, for the candidate would be required to grasp a wide assortment of state issues, quickly learn effective campaign tactics, and find a body of trusted advisers who could be wisely employed. But these hurdles were not as large as they appeared. Walter had been watching political maneuvering since his youth and had been with his father during a grueling campaign trek across the state. He knew a great many key Republicans in the state on a first-name basis from his years as a participant in party meetings and through his business and charitable activities. He followed the press, was in touch regularly with party leaders, and had a broad understanding of the state's needs. Moreover, Kohler did not rely extensively upon advisers and aides; he was committed to doing much of the hard work himself. Walter's keen intelligence and capacity for sustained labor, long distinctive features of the Kohlers, were to serve him well as he rose to power in the GOP.

Running as a Republican in Wisconsin was a considerable advantage. After 1938, when voters grew tired of Progressive promises to restore prosperity, voting Republican had become more or less routine. During the 1940s through the mid-1950s Republicans held impressive majorities in both houses of the state legislature and controlled from two-thirds to three-fourths of the state's county offices. In 1946, the GOP could claim both United States Senators, all ten of the state's delegation to the House of Representatives, and 27 of the 33 state senators

The GOP tended to be comprised of affluent, native-white Protestant voters, including business and professional leaders and prosperous farmers. German and other Catholics began coming into the party in significant numbers during the 1940s. The Republicans were better organized and financed than any of their competitors. In the 1940s and early 1950s, major business leaders headed the party's fund-raising and campaign activities, operating almost exclusively through the Voluntary Committee. Tom Coleman was the principal figure, but there were others, including F. J. Sensenbrenner, chairman of the Kimberly-Clark Corporation; Henry Ringling of the Baraboo circus family; Wayne J. Hood, vice-president of the Trane Company of La Crosse; Cyrus L. Philipp, president of the Union Refrigerator Transit Company of Milwaukee; and Pierpont J. E. Wood, general counsel of the Parker Pen Company in Janesville. Imperious Walter Harnischfeger, who headed his own Milwaukee corporation and was a director of the National Association of Manufacturers, was also a powerful figure in the party.[32]

After many decades of torpor, the Democratic party began to show life in 1944. Once the La Follette party disintegrated, Democrats enjoyed an infusion of votes from organized labor, Socialists, and younger Progressives. Industrial Milwaukee, Racine, and Kenosha counties showed special interest in the new, liberal image of the party, as did Dane County, home of the University of Wisconsin. New, often young, party leaders, many of them lawyers and office-seekers, were committed to revitalizing the party. Among their ranks were State Senator Robert Tehan of Milwaukee; attorney Gaylord Nelson, whose father had been a leading Progressive; Madison attorney James E. Doyle, who had served in a law firm headed by Phil La Follette; Madison attorney Horace Wilkie; attorney Carl Thompson, an activist from Madison; Milwaukee attorney Henry Reuss; former Progressive John W. Reynolds of Madison, who came from a distinguished family of Progressive leaders in Green Bay; former Socialist Milwaukee mayor Daniel Hoan; State Assemblyman Patrick Lucey of Crawford county; veteran Socialist and labor leader Andrew J. Biemiller; and Attorney General Thomas Fairchild, an ex-Progressive.

In 1948, liberal leaders created the Democratic Organizing Committee, designed to raise money and conduct campaigns as a body separate from party regulars. It defined itself as liberal and anti-communist, to distinguish itself from the far Left backers of Henry Wallace. Truman's victory in Wisconsin gave Democrats renewed hope and resolve. Robert Tehan was awarded a federal judgeship in 1949.

In 1950, the party had four candidates in the race for Governor. The leader from the start was Carl Thompson, who ran an impressive if unsuccessful campaign against Governor Rennebohm two years earlier. Thompson, 36, had been a Progressive leader as a student at the University of Wisconsin and was now an attorney and real estate broker in Stoughton, his home town. He was a vigorous activist, instrumental in creating the new Democratic Party. The DOC, now organized throughout the state, promised an issues-oriented campaign, supporting Truman's Fair Deal and the centrist Americans for Democratic Action, and opposing McCarthy and his "ism."[33]

Kohler and his allies knew they had to wage an all-out campaign. Party members were delighted when Governor Rennebohm gave his support. "While another candidate was my personal choice for endorsement, this fact does not detract in the slightest from the respect which

I have for the character, integrity and ability of Walter Kohler."[34] Other GOP leaders quickly followed suit.

A few days after Walter's nomination, the Socialist Party nominated a candidate for Governor, William O. Hart of Baraboo. The Socialists had a long history in Wisconsin, collecting their biggest vote in 1920, when its gubernatorial candidate won 71,103 votes. Party support had been dropping ever since; in 1946, fewer than 9,000 people voted for the Socialist candidate for governor. Milwaukee elected a Socialist ticket in 1910, and party chairman Frank P. Zeidler was the city's mayor in 1950. But the Socialists now held little public appeal across the state. Only 25 people showed up for the opening of the party's two day state convention.[35]

Organized labor in Wisconsin was not yet wholly in the Democratic Party. Most Vollrath employees, who belonged to the CIO, and the Kohler Workers' Association were both solidly behind Walter's candidacy.[36] Almost no one in the labor camp paid any attention to the People's Progressive party, which also nominated a gubernatorial candidate. The far Left party had been formed in 1948 to support Henry A. Wallace for president. Ninety three delegates from 24 counties turned out for the party's state convention to draft a platform and endorse candidates.[37]

On July 10, Walter and the four other major Republican candidates for state office began a ten-day tour of 51 cities and towns. The purpose was to meet, greet, and talk to people; no major campaign speeches were planned. The initial emphasis was on the western part of the state where rural voters had gone for Truman in 1948.[38]

Former Progressive and now Republican maverick Leonard F. Schmitt of Merrill wanted to debate Kohler in La Crosse, hoping that it would boost his independent candidacy for the governorship. He wanted a completely open primary and charged that Kohler was the tool of industrialists and millionaires who had captured the GOP. Walter quietly rejected the debate offer and supported party endorsement.[39] In Rice Lake, he said, "There is no bossism in Wisconsin. At the Republican convention that nominated me, the Republican governor, the national committeeman for the state and the former Republican state chairman were all united for another candidate. Yet I won that nomination because the delegates made a free and unbossed selection. I reject any claim that bosses guided the delegates."[40]

While in La Crosse, Walter portrayed the GOP as the authentic party of the people. He said, "The Republican party was formed in the 1850s to fight the entrenched party of privilege, and to protect the freedom of the common man. It has that same duty today, as a boastful, arrogant Democratic party, powerful enough to make good its boasts, forgets individual freedom to create ever growing dominance of our central government. The Democratic Party is one of reaction." Vernon Thomson, the GOP candidate for Attorney General, added, "We are a liberal state, and your Wisconsin Republican party has written that liberal record. We must win the elections this fall so that we can carry on in the tradition of that great liberal leadership."[41] References to the previous popularity of Truman in the region were unnecessary.

Walter spent much of every day during the tour shaking hands. Several people told him, "I knew your father." One man said, "I thought you were an older man," thinking that he was addressing Walter's father. Walter was effective at this obligatory political activity; people responded warmly to his friendly and gentlemanly manner. A newspaper columnist in Eagle River wrote, "A Real Thrill—That's what I got Sunday night when I was introduced to Water J. Kohler, Jr. One look at his handsome face and two minutes conversation with him convinced me that I was talking to the next Governor of Wisconsin. Maybe I talked to a future President of the US. He certainly has all the qualifications plus some to spare. Mr. Kohler has a captivating personality, that makes you realize you are in the presence of a great man."[42]

People also seemed to react positively to Walter's often sharply partisan remarks, made during luncheons, dinners, and rallies of all kinds. In River Falls, he criticized Democrats for debasing the coinage, inflating the currency, practicing profligate spending, and burdening people with a crushing mixture of taxation and inflation. The Truman Administration, he charged, demanded the subservience of Congress and sought the same sort of domination over the Supreme Court."[43]

Reporter Robert Fleming, traveling with the cavalcade, observed that Kohler "was showing himself a hard working campaigner, able to stir the enthusiasm of party members. Last week he seemed to thrive on schedules that keep him going 16 hours a day, visiting 8 to 10 western Wisconsin towns.[44]

In late July, union leaders brought up the Kohler strike, attempting to connect Walter with the violence and death that marked the event.[45] The Madison Capital Times, now solidly in the Democratic camp, displayed Walter's tax returns, noting his wealth and claiming that he legally avoided taxation.[46] Kohler, the newspaper editorialized, was the "boss-endorsed candidate," who "seems allergic to the people."[47] Leonard Schmitt told audiences throughout the state that Kohler was guilty of "deceitful double talk" about the primary election law and warned that his Republican opponent was spending more than the legal limit. The Democratic Party's state chairman, Jerome Fox, spoke of the "Republican silk stocking boys," the sort of language Truman had used effectively against Dewey.[48]

Veteran GOP leaders thought that Walter needed help. To handle publicity and to manage the entire Kohler campaign, State Senator Warren Knowles hired Phillip Drotning, a former newspaper reporter who was serving as executive secretary to Governor Rennebohm.[49] Thirty-year-old Drotning, a Marine Corps veteran, was slim, personable, highly intelligent, and extremely hard working. He was to become Walter's most active and trusted political aide throughout his years in politics.[50]

Throughout the summer, Walter and a caravan of his supporters traveled across the state in a grueling search for votes. In Kenosha, the candidate told a group of businessmen that "the Democratic party has put this nation in a hell of a mess—no one even knows if we're in the third world war or not."[51] This was a reference to the outbreak of the Korean War in June, a new brand of conflict for Americans in which they fought without a formal declaration of war and under the flag of the United Nations. Truman couldn't win: While claiming that the Administration was "soft" on the Reds, Republicans also condemned it for entering the struggle to prevent the spread of Communism. Treason in high places was one partisan explanation for America's bloody and seemingly unsuccessful involvement. But Walter had not gone to that extreme.[52]

In Racine, Walter pledged to reapportion state legislative districts if elected. The Constitution requires states to take this action every decade following each federal census. In Wisconsin, redistricting had not been achieved fully since 1921, and Republicans, in control of the legislature, had taken no such steps in a decade. Rural districts were politically more powerful than their numbers permitted, and the GOP liked it that way. Kohler's pledge took courage, for he knew that a great many in his party desired to leave district lines untouched.

On that same day in early August, Kohler promised to make the state's veterans' housing law more effective, came out for better roads in southeastern Wisconsin, pledged to enforce antipollution laws, and said he favored the open primary. Major speeches featuring specific data, issues, and promises to take action were now replacing mere pleasantries in the campaign.[53]

As he began detailing his political agenda, Walter said repeatedly that the Republican Party was a liberal party. There was evidence to substantiate the claim. The Rennebohm administrations, for example, had pushed a building program at the University of Wisconsin greater than had been seen in a century. State aids for mental hospitals and public schools had also been increased substantially.[54] In 1950, two agencies, the university and the department of public welfare, accounted for half or more of all state employees.[55] Assemblyman Vernon W. Thomson, traveling with Walter as a candidate for Attorney General, stated that other state governments had received credit for progressive legislation, but that Wisconsin's laws were better. "The Republican party has provided dynamic, forward looking government in Wisconsin," he said.[56]

In Milwaukee, Walter endorsed a state liberal arts college in Milwaukee, a concept explored and soon supported by the Rennebohm administration. "The high cost of maintaining a student away from home prevents many young people in this area from obtaining a college degree," he said. "I believe in equal educational opportunity. A college degree is becoming increasingly important." Kohler also promised to help stamp out "Bang's Disease" that threatened the entire dairy industry in the state and required herd testing for brucellosis.[57]

Not all of the campaigning was as constructive and peaceful. Both Kohler and Attorney General candidate Thomson accused the Democratic Party of violating the state's corrupt practices law. Thomson claimed that leading Democrats had failed to report $100,000 in campaign funds raised at Jefferson-Jackson Day dinners in 1949 and 1950. Secretary of State Fred Zimmerman soon declared that the Democrats had violated no law. This led to countercharges by Democrats about "fat cat" Republicans. Carl Thompson said, "Kohler is building a phony smoke screen in a desperate attempt to obscure the fact that the Republican voluntary committee, whose creature he is, will this year, as in past campaigns, spend five to six times as much as all the other parties combined."[58] Charles P. Greene, another Democratic candidate for Governor, endorsed all partisan charges against Kohler (tax avoidance, the Kohler strike, being

a puppet of Tom Coleman) and declared, "I say it's time to quit pushing inexperienced millionaires into the governor's chair."[59] Such heated
blather by both sides continued throughout the campaign.

In Milwaukee, in late August, Walter made his first comments on
foreign affairs, no doubt in response to a request by Guy Gabrielson,
Republican National Committee Chairman, that all party candidates
and workers unite in criticizing the Truman Administration's far eastern
policy. Walter noted correctly that Secretary of State Dean Acheson
had stated publicly in January that the United States would not defend
Formosa and Korea."I fought in those waters and I knew Formosa was
the key to their defense. I was sick at this virtual invitation to Stalin to
move in." He approved of Truman's military response to Communist
aggression in Korea, "the policy we should have had from the start," but
blasted the "incompetence" of the Administration's overall foreign policy.
McCarthy and his allies, meanwhile, were charging treason rather than
incompetence. Kohler also criticized the Administration for allegedly
handicapping the development of civil defense in Wisconsin.[60]

In a speech before a Polish audience in Milwaukee two days later,
Kohler became bolder, claiming that American soldiers had inadequate
training and equipment, adding that "the whole [Administration] record
has been one of selling out free nations, including our own."[61] This was
McCarthyite language, part of the deliberate attempt, largely by Republicans, to stress the presence of Communists and pro-Communists
in Washington. As the September 19 state primary drew near, Walter
called the Korean War "the third Democrat war in a generation." He
again pointed to "blundering," a milder form of McCarthyite lingo that
stressed human error rather than subversion.[62] However inflammatory,
Kohler's language was actually more moderate than much campaign
rhetoric employed by GOP candidates throughout the nation.

Making it clear that he was not a reactionary, Walter pledged to
continue and expand Wisconsin's welfare program if elected. He told
a Milwaukee audience that the last legislature had appropriated more
than 13 million dollars for improvements at welfare institutions, a
record that placed Wisconsin ahead of other states in this important
category.[63]

By September 17, two days before the state primary, Walter had
campaigned in all but one of the state's 71 counties and delivered 230
speeches.[64]

A large GOP ad published in the Milwaukee Journal backing the entire ticket featured photos of Kohler and Alexander Wiley, a moderate and former isolationist who had served in the United States Senate since 1938. It emphasized the Korean War, claiming that Democrats had "stumbled through Asia into their third World War in a generation" and charged that they had "coddled Communists." The "Pinkish New Dealers" reference was basic McCarthyite campaign language, although relatively mild by comparison with Senator McCarthy's charges. In a separate ad paid for by Citizens for Kohler, the language was restrained and said nothing of foreign policy. It stressed the candidate's youth, vigor, and success in business, concluding, "Walter Kohler isn't a politician looking for a job. He is the man Wisconsin NEEDS in the difficult years to come."[65]

In the primary election, Kohler easily defeated Leonard Schmitt 272,139 votes to 150,315, carrying 62 counties. Other candidates endorsed by the Republican Voluntary Committee were also victorious. The Democratic gubernatorial candidate was Carl W. Thompson, who won his race by a large margin. Democratic Attorney General Thomas E. Fairchild, 37, was chosen to oppose 66-year-old Senator Wiley. Democrats were elated by an increase in their vote from 18% to 29% in just two years.[66]

Thompson promised the "fightingest campaign ever made."[67] Setting the tone for the conflict, CIO United Automobile Workers union president Walter Reuther soon told an audience in La Crosse, "What does Walter Kohler know about raising a family? He was born with a silver spoon in his mouth." He followed this with a rumination on foreign policy. Republican leadership in the early 1940s, he said, would have cost the nation victory in the Second World War. "If we follow their leadership now we will lose the fight against communism." Extremism was to be found on both sides of the political fence.[68]

Walter had declared his independence from the beginning of his election campaign, but after winning his party's nomination at the polls he went a step farther, publicly calling for changes in the GOP platform, urging revisions in "nearly every plank." He intended to be a party leader as well as a candidate for office. The initial proposal that drew the most attention was Walter's request for an alteration of the state law that exacted a 3% tax on dividends of Wisconsin corporations and exempted stockholders from income tax on those dividends. Democrats had been howling for months about the high, tax-free Kohler dividend

income of the past few years, and this was a direct response to his critics. Carl Thompson, obviously flustered by his opponent's removal of
a key campaign issue, accused Kohler of adopting "the old adage that
'if you can't lick 'em, jine 'em.'"[69]

Walter later admitted that his difficulties with State GOP leaders
began with his demand for changes in the party platform. Tom Coleman, Wayne Hood, and Henry Ringling said he had no right to do so.
But he stood his ground.[70]

The GOP platform convention met in Madison in early October. Both
parties had a statutory obligation to hold such a meeting, attended by
nominees for state administrative offices and for the legislature, charged
with electing a state central committee and releasing a platform. One
hundred and three nominees attended the opening Republican conclave.
Walter presented delegates with a 14 page draft of proposed planks he
called "suggestions." He told an interviewer years later, "The Republican
party platform of June, 1950 was weak and innocuous. I had no hand
in it at all. However, once I had been nominated, Phil Drotning and I
sat down one day at my home in Sheboygan and drafted a whole new
platform."[71]

Sitting on the platform committee, headed by his friend State Senator
Melvin Laird, Walter was instrumental in obtaining most of his recommendations. Reapportionment was endorsed, and so was the preservation
of the open primary, a bow to those who feared that nominees might
be designated by party "bosses." The delegates approved of increased
expenditures to end Bang's Disease, sought creation of a new agency to
work for the conservation of water resources, endorsed legislation to
enact an adequate civil defense program, agreed to continue highway
construction programs, and endorsed a boost in the limit on housing
loans for veterans. At Walter's request, a veterans' bonus proposal, based
upon a financial plan developed by the Veterans of Foreign Wars, was
to be given careful study by the legislature.[72]

But Walter did not win every battle. The platform did not take a stand
on a liberal arts college in Milwaukee, and the controversial revision of
the dividend tax was deemed worthy only of further study.[73]

Democrats, meeting in a similar convention, called for increased taxes
on corporation dividends, backed the UN action in Korea, supported
the reapportionment of legislative districts, and rejected a veterans'
bonus proposal.[74] They were soon delighted when Leonard Schmitt,
who had won more than 150,000 votes in the Republican primary as the

"non-boss" candidate, announced that he would vote for the Democratic ticket. Party leaders hoped this defection would help persuade more La Follette Progressives to become Democrats. It might also weaken the GOP in the northern part of the state, where Schmitt had been most effective in winning votes.[75]

When final primary financing figures became available, a Milwaukee Journal reporter's compilation of data revealed that Republicans had outspent Democrats by a wide margin, $146,097 to $109,531. Most interesting were the numbers broken down by specific campaigns. Republicans had spent $16,692 on the Governor's race, while Democrats had spent only $6,208. A total of $12,219 was spent by and for Kohler. Democrats had allocated much more money to the Senatorial contest: $42,869 to the Republicans' $16,527. It seemed that Democrats had virtually conceded the Governor's race and were focusing their attention on the defeat of Senator Wiley.[76]

In early October, Walter launched his first major swing in the general election campaign. In economically depressed Ashland, in the far north of the state, he proposed a cut in the waiting time for unemployment compensation and a boost in benefits. He said he would support continued work in reforestation and forest fire protection.[77] In Richland Center, Kohler criticized the Truman Administration for neglected dairy farming and favoring the producers of oleomargarine and processed cheese foods.[78] In Platteville, he defended his tax paying record and used a quotation attributed to the late New Dealer Harry Hopkins, who allegedly said that Democrats should "tax and tax and tax and spend and spend and spend and elect and elect and elect."[79] In ten days of campaigning, Walter traveled more than 2,500 miles through more than 30 counties, giving as many as a dozen talks a day, most of them on street corners.[80]

In a campaign meeting on the campus of the University of Wisconsin, Walter was faced squarely with the issue of Joe McCarthy and his "ism." Democrats had been hammering Republicans about the controversial Senator, particularly in Madison, where the liberal Madison Capital Times was conducting in-depth research on McCarthy and his claims. This was a subject both Walter and Senator Wiley wanted to evade; both men, as insiders knew, had private reservations about the state's junior Senator, but they were well aware that he enjoyed near unanimous support from GOP leaders in the state. To attack McCarthy meant joining the assault undertaken by Democrats and leftists of all sorts. And such an attack would no doubt destroy their own political aspirations.

Kohler told his audience that he was "suspending judgment" on McCarthy's charges of Communist infiltration in the State Department until the Senator received a fair hearing. The investigation into McCarthy by the Tydings Committee, he said, was designed "apparently to conceal truth instead of exposing it." Walter continued, "I am against Communists and communism. I think it important that these charges be investigated fairly." But he added that he hadn't "the slightest doubt that there are thousands of Communists in key places of the government. The case of Alger Hiss proves that." When asked if his appearance on the same stage with McCarthy constituted an endorsement of the Senator, Walter replied, "I have been on the platform with several people and at no time did an appearance imply an endorsement of anyone's views."[81]

The campaign remarks in Madison probably satisfied no one, for Walter distanced himself from McCarthy and yet endorsed McCarthy's thesis that the federal government was filled with Communists. This contention came very close to accepting the next step in the McCarthy argument that those Reds in high places were servants of Stalin actively engaged in treason. In questioning the integrity of the Tydings Committee investigation, which annihilated McCarthy's Wheeling speech and in normal times would have destroyed the Senator's reputation, he was siding with McCarthy supporters. At the same time, he was agreeing with contentions raised by the Republican minority on the Tydings Committee, following a line of thought that a great many Republicans and some conservative Democrats all across America were repeating at the time.

Were the candidate's comments sincerely held or merely expedient? Walter was not given to lying, in private or in public. Still, reason can be easily manipulated by desire, and the passions aroused in political battles can often lead one to believe, do, and say regrettable things. It seems reasonable to conclude that Walter was following his party's rhetoric and that his views were based on the best partisan evidence he had seen. Walter had certainly not studied the carefully researched and detailed Tydings Committee report itself. Few Americans had.

The intense heat of partisan politics in the fall of 1950 tended to polarize both major political parties in a way that colored even the most careful study of evidence. McCarthy himself, in an unceasing and passionate barrage of charges and countercharges, continued to fuel the warfare. At an Isaac Walton League picnic in Fond du Lac, he labeled the Tydings Committee majority report "dishonest" and called its authors "well-meaning little men—men without the mental or moral capacity to rise above politics in this hour of the nation's gravest danger." The audience of 4,500 roared its approval.[82]

McCarthy campaigned in Wisconsin in more than a dozen cities, consistently drawing large crowds and endorsing all Republican candidates. He called Democrats the "party of the puppets of the politburo" and labeled Secretary of State Dean Acheson a "procurer of pinks and punks." He came up with new evidence against the loyalty of the *Milwaukee Journal*, which was consistently critical of the Senator. The chairman of the newspaper's editorial board, he said, was married to a lady whose sister was married to a New York attorney who was once the lawyer for a now-defunct left-wing periodical.[83]

From August 6 through November 6, McCarthy traveled to at least fifteen states, delivering scores of speeches and sometimes speaking several times a day. Tens of thousands cheered him ecstatically, confident that they now had heard a solid, factual explanation for America's international and domestic problems: Reds and pro-Reds were to blame, and they were everywhere in America, especially in the highest echelons of the Truman Administration and in the Democratic Party. In a booklet widely distributed by McCarthy, called *The Party of Betrayal*, a blurb on the cover stated, "The record points unmistakably to one fact—no one can be for the Administration Democrat Party and at the same time against Communism." Republicans were especially eager to invite McCarthy to their area to tar their opponents with a Red brush. Mc-Carthyite campaigns by Richard Nixon in California, Robert Taft in Ohio, Everett Dirksen in Illinois, John Fine in Pennsylvania, Homer Capehart in Indiana, and many others all across America prompted *Washington Post* cartoonist Herblock to ask, "Is Joe Stalin running in all these elections?"[84]

To his opponents, such as Herblock, McCarthy was a creature, a fearsome ape-man, a monster who knew only how to lie, cheat, and smear. Norman Cousins, editor of the influential Saturday Review of Literature, contended that the Senator employed Communist techniques against his victims. "I can't think of anyone who has helped Communism more than Joe McCarthy." Some critics thought him eager to run for the presidency or vice-presidency in 1952.[85]

Carl Thompson, whose rather lame gubernatorial campaign focused largely on the issue of his opponent's wealth, used the McCarthy issue skillfully. In a speech in Hortonville, the Democrat blasted Kohler for "fence sitting." He said, "In a recent talk, my opponent took a vigorous and determined stand of 'suspending judgment' on the tactics of smear and slander used by Joseph McCarthy. It's a good Republican trick. In refusing to endorse McCarthy—while appearing on the same platform with him—my opponent apparently wants to eat his cake and have it, too. He is mustering all the votes which McCarthy may get him while refusing to assume responsibility for linking his name with McCarthyism....He realizes it isn't politically expedient to cuddle up with McCarthy and that thousands of independent voters won't vote for him if he formally endorses McCarthyism."[86]

The crucial issue facing Kohler was a simple question that worried a great many in American politics: Was it possible to be both for and against McCarthy? Wasn't McCarthyism one of those great issues in history about which neutrality was impossible? That remained to be seen.

When the State Republican party widely distributed a McCarthyite tabloid called "Blunders Mean Blood," Walter said publicly that he had had nothing to do with its creation, and his campaign committee objected to the publication. But in fact Walter was still in the Coleman camp. During his campaign speeches he spoke often of the "Democrat War." (McCarthyites always referred to the Democratic Party as the Democrat Party.) To his credit, he did not mention in his speeches any of the scores of people McCarthy was recklessly claiming to be spies and dupes.[87]

Senator Wiley, ranking GOP member of the Senate Foreign Affairs Committee, swallowed his personal reservations about McCarthyite tactics and attacked the Truman Administration for letting pro-Communists and fellow travelers influence its policies. At one point he praised McCarthy for alerting the nation to "the danger of Communist penetration" and condemned Democrats for "seventeen years of coddling Communists."[88] The alternative, he feared privately, was defeat in the November election.

A few GOP candidates in Wisconsin, notably attorney Charles Kersten of Milwaukee, were proud McCarthyites who had no intention of moderating any of the Senator's language and contentions. The former Congressman, seeking reelection after a two-year hiatus, boasted often of his personal friendship with Senator McCarthy. Kersten's success at the polls would show clearly how appealing local voters found the Reds in government issue.[89]

In his campaign speeches, Walter preferred to focus upon governmental issues, especially taxes and spending. In Monroe, he called for the creation of a department of administrative services to eliminate waste in state government. The unification of such services as mailing, office space assignments, and the entire operation of state publications could save Wisconsin taxpayers a great deal of money, he said.[90] In a radio speech, he defended Wisconsin's last two Republican governors, observing that the state had always had a balanced budget and that in 1950 the treasury would have a surplus of at least $35 million. He criticized Democrats for "falsehood and deception" in condemning the GOP governors, saying that it was an attempt to divert voters' attention from "the waste, extravagance and deficit spending of their national administration."[91] In a Wauwatosa speech, Walter lashed out at Democrats for consistently seeking high taxes, noting that the federal government took $800 million in taxes out of Wisconsin during the past year and that 90% was extracted from middle and low income families.[92]

Two days before the election, Democrats again listed the names of ten affluent Republicans, citing, from public records, their total income for five years and stressing their tax-free dividends during the same period. They were playing the class card, their biggest weapon in the campaign. A new column listed contributions to the Republican party in five years. Industrialist Reuben N. Trane had given $2,850. Tom Coleman's total was $1,150. Kohler's was a mere $150, the least of any donation on the list. Walter's frugality, hammered into him by his father from an early age, extended even to politics.[93]

In a last-minute radio address, Kohler said that his major election pledge was "the continuation of businesslike, forward-looking government in Wisconsin." By "forward-looking" he meant liberal, and his speech provided specific proposals he had stressed during his campaign, including increases in workmen's compensation and unemployment benefits, better care for the elderly, aid to veterans in their search for affordable housing, the continuation of the state's expanded highway construction program, and a study of a proposed veterans bonus plan. He also endorsed two new state departments designed to maximize efficiency and reduce expenses. He did not mention foreign policy, although conditions in Korea were apparently turning from bad to worse.

China had entered the war in early October, and United Nations troops were being driven back south of the 38th parallel.[94]

Wisconsin Republicans scored major victories in the November 7 elections. In a record turnout, Kohler won 59 of 71 counties , and received 605,649 votes to Thompson's 525,319. Wiley won reelection by almost the same margin. (Both Kohler and Wiley proved highly popular in Joe McCarthy's Outagamie County.) GOP candidates swept all other state offices by comfortable margins. Republicans won nine out of ten Congressional contests, including the Milwaukee race which Charles Kersten won by a narrow margin.[95]

As big a victory as it was, careful observers soon noted that Kohler did not match Rennebohm's victory margin over Thompson in 1948 and that he lost in Madison, Milwaukee, Eau Claire, Kenosha, and La Crosse. Moreover, Kohler attracted fewer votes than each of the GOP candidates for Lieutenant Governor, Secretary of State, State Treasurer, and Attorney General. The four top vote-getting Republicans, however, were all well-known political veterans facing weak Democratic opponents.[96]

On election night, Windway was filled with guests, including Walter's three brothers and a number of friends from Kohler Village. There were no demonstrations or outbursts. The Kohlers were celebrating their second wedding anniversary when the election results came pouring in on the radio. Walter flashed a victory smile to reporters and Charlotte posed with her two Scotties, Cissy and Birkie. Walter went to bed about 3:30 a.m. when Carl Thompson formally conceded the election.[97]

Charlotte soon granted an interview to a woman reporter (who did not receive a byline) from the Milwaukee Journal. The state's new first lady made selective comments about her past and dwelled on her hobbies. The reporter noted, "She is as happy as a college girl when knitting argyle and other fancy socks for her husband." Stories of Charlotte's difficult personality had obviously reached the reporter, who wrote tactfully, "Her interests do not run to large groups." She added, "Some persons who have described her as haughty probably do not realize that she is extremely near-sighted."[98]

A similar human interest article appeared on Walter in the same newspaper. Beyond contributing a useful sketch of Kohler's history, reporter Richard S. Davis made some often interesting observations about the newly elected governor. "A friendly smile that frequently flashes across his face is one of his political and social assets. His quiet laughter comes largely in chuckles and he is frequently amused. He can, however, be fairly stern, as some of his political lieutenants discovered in the campaign that triumphantly ended Tuesday. He is not known to be a man of temper." Davis also noted that Walter was given to dressing modestly in dark suits, that he smoked about a pack of cigarettes a day, that his best golf game ever was an 86, and that he was a social drinker "distinctly on the modest side." Some saw the new Governor's personality as "warm," Davis wrote, and some didn't, but during the campaign he showed that he could make friends quickly. Davis also credited the 46-year-old first-time candidate with a touch of subtle political savvy: "He and Mrs. Kohler both own a Cadillac, but in the campaign he rode in the small cars of associates. This was taken as an indication that he learns quickly."[99]

Nationally, the elections of 1950 were a triumph for the GOP, especially for those candidates who embraced Joe McCarthy. Richard Nixon won in California by nearly 700,000 votes; Everett Dirksen defeated Senator Majority Leader Scott Lucas; Robert Taft cruised past his opponent in Ohio; James Duff in Pennsylvania ousted House Majority Whip Francis Myers; Homer Capehart won reelection in Indiana, and so did Eugene Millikin in Colorado. Journalist Marquis Childs observed, "In every contest where it was a major factor, McCarthyism won."[100] Altogether, the GOP gained five Senate seats, 27 House seats, and six governorships.

The most stunning election occurred in Maryland, where Joe McCarthy and his staff personally led an attack on Senator Millard Tydings, who had investigated and shattered the initial McCarthy charges against the Truman Administration. McCarthy's unprecedented act of revenge smeared the incumbent's integrity and patriotism in a flood of literature, postcards, advertisements, and speeches that reached all corners of the state. One tabloid featured a "composite" photograph that portrayed Tydings listening attentively to Communist leader Earl Browder. McCarthy himself gave two speeches in Maryland on behalf of Tydings' opponent, John Marshall Butler, and delivered a third in the District of Columbia that was broadcast by several Maryland radio stations. A nephew of Booker T. Washington, who lived in Chicago, was imported to Maryland where he was paid to give 56 speeches intended to sway the Black vote. McCarthyite radio commentator Fulton Lewis, Jr. attacked Tydings repeatedly on his nationally syndicated programs. So much money poured into the Butler campaign from the far Right that in the last three days of the campaign its leaders purchased 460 radio advertisements. Butler's big win in November, by a majority of 43,100 votes, cheered the McCarthy forces all across the nation.

In fact, when the election results were studied carefully, Joe McCarthy's influence over the election returns was exaggerated. For example, of 21 Democratic congressman who voted against the McCarthyite McCarran Act, passed in September, only five were defeated, two of those trying to move to the Senate. Twenty three of the 28 Democrats beaten in the election had supported the bill. Senator Lucas's defeat in Illinois was in large part attributable to scandals revealed by an investigation headed by Senator Estes Kefauver. Robert Fleming of the *Milwaukee Journal* pointed out that in Wisconsin Democratic candidates for senator and governor received an impressive 47 percent of the vote, and noted that where Joe McCarthy personally attracted the largest audience, in Kenosha, GOP votes fell by nine percent.[101]

But these analyses failed to shake the belief by many politicians, especially the Republicans, that McCarthyism was the hammer that could smash the Democrats in 1952. Tom Coleman and the top leadership of the Wisconsin GOP firmly believed that victory was within reach and that the Reds in government issue that would take their party to the White House. How the newly elected Governor would respond to this bold and irresponsible political strategy was anyone's guess, but it was clearly a matter he could not evade no matter how he tried.

Notes

[1] Robert H. Fleming, "Stassen Uses a Parity Base for Farm Plan," *Milwaukee Journal*, March 16, 1948.

[2] Robert H. Fleming, "Shutout Seen for Dewey in Delegate Test," *ibid.*, April 7, 1948.

[3] See Reeves, *The Life and Times of Joe McCarthy*, f. 35, 697.

[4] Robert H. Fleming, "Choice No. 2 Seekers Woo GOP Group," *Milwaukee Journal*, June 8, 1948; "McCarthy to Yield to Kohler on Post," *ibid.*, June 11, 1948; "Name Kohler as Chairman of Delegation," *ibid.*, June 13, 1948.

[5] See Thompson, *History of Wisconsin, Volume VI*, 536-537.

[6] Laurence C. Eklund, "Heavy Going for Governor," *Milwaukee Journal*, June 23, 1948.

[7] W. P. Knowles to unknown, June 25, 1952, Warren P. Knowles papers.

[8] "Governor to Quit After Term; Three Jump Into GOP Race," *Milwaukee Journal*, May 25, 1950.

[9] Copy, Walter J. Kohler, Jr. address of April 13, 1951, Wayne Hood papers.

[10] See Reeves, *The Life and Times of Joe McCarthy*, 211-222.

[11] Copy, Thomas Coleman to Finance Committee, March 18, 1950, Wayne Hood papers.

[12] E.g., "Hoover Backing urged, *Milwaukee Journal*, May 26, 1950.

[13] "A 'Cracker Barrel' Conference on the Hoover Report," *New York Herald Tribune*, December 13, 1949.

[14] 1949 delegate list and transcript of proceedings, box 4, Republican Party papers.

[15] 1949 state convention transcript, box 3, *ibid.*; Thompson, *History of Wisconsin, Volume VI*, 537-538.

[16] "Governor to Quit After Term; Three Jump Into GOP Race," *Milwaukee Journal*, May 25, 1950; "GOP Expects Rough Battle," *ibid.*, May 26, 1950.

[17] "Higley Among GOP Hopefuls," *ibid.*, May 29, 1950; "Another Race in GOP Race," *ibid.*, May 31, 1950.

[18] Edwin R. Bayley, "Kohler GOP Favorite as Keefe Drops Out," *ibid.*, June 4, 1950.

[19] Wayne J. Hood to Mrs. Foster E. Blackburn, June 1, 1950, Wayne Hood papers.

[20] See copy, Thomas E. Coleman to Finance Committee, March 18, 1950, *ibid.*

[21] Edwin R. Bayley, "Rennebohm Supports Higley in GOP Rivalry for Governor," *Milwaukee Journal*, June 7, 1950; Robert H. Fleming, "Battle Is Expected," *ibid.*

[22] Bayley, "Rennebohm Supports Higley in GOP Rivalry for Governor," *ibid.*, June 7, 1950.

[23] *Ibid.*

1. Charlotte Schroeder Kohler and Walter, Jr., 1904.
Windway collection.

2. Charlotte Schroeder Kohler and her four sons, about 1911.
Leslie Kohler Hawley collection.
From left to right: Walter J. Kohler, Jr., Carl James (Jim), Robert (Bob) in the
lap, Charlotte Schroeder Kohler, and John Michael Kohler II.

3. Walter J. Kohler, Jr. in about 1917.
Windway collection.

4. Pilots in 1928: Walter, J. Kohler, Jr., Terry Brotz, Anton Brotz, and Jim Kohler. Leslie Kohler Hawley collection.

5. Walter J. Kohler, Sr. the candidate, 1932.
Leslie Kohler Hawley collection.

6. From September 20, 1932, the Kohler family plus one political friend counting votes, top row, left to right: Jim Kohler, Bob Kohler, State Senator Herman Boldt from Sheboygan Falls, and Walter Kohler, Jr. Bottom row, left to right: Dorothy Dings Kohler, John Michael Kohler II, Walter J. Kohler, Sr., and Charlotte Schroeder Kohler. Leslie Kohler Hawley collection.

7. Celeste Holden and her father Eugene Joseph McVoy in Egypt, 1929.
Leslie Kohler Hawley collection.

8. Celeste McVoy Holden Kohler at her wedding, November 14, 1932.
Leslie Kohler Hawley collection.

9. Left to right: Marie Kohler, Evangeline Kohler, Lillie Kohler, unidentified woman, Herbert V. Kohler, Walter & Celeste Kohler.
In the foreground: Walter Kohler, Sr., Terry (in his arms), & Charlotte Schroeder Kohler, 1934, at Riverbend. Windway collection.

10. Some Kohler family members in 1936. From left to right, Walter J. Kohler III, Walter J. Kohler Sr, Niki Kohler (in his arms), Terry Kohler (seated), Carl James Kohler (standing), Julia House (standing) holding John Michael Kohler, Jr., Charlotte Schroeder Kohler, Conrad Dings Kohler, and Peter Galt Kohler (seated) Mary Ahern collection.

11. Walter and Terry, 1934.
Leslie Kohler Hawley collection.

12. Celeste and Terry, 1935.
Leslie Kohler Hawley collection.

13. Walter in the South Pacific with two Navy buddies, 1943.
Leslie Kohler Hawley collection.

14. Niki Kohler
in about 1943.
Windway
collection.

15. The Walter J. Kohler, Jr. family at Christmas, 1943, Windway. Left to right: Jackie, Walter, Niki, Celeste, Terry. Leslie Kohler Hawley collection.

16. Jackie in her Canadian Air Force uniform, 1943.
Windway collection.

17. The USS Hancock under attack by Kamikaze planes, April 7, 1945. Leslie Kohler Hawley collection.

18. Lt. Commander Walter J. Kohler, Jr., a formal photo taken in 1949.
Leslie Kohler Hawley collection.

19. Charlotte McAleer golfing in the late 1930s.
Leslie Kohler Hawley collection.

20. Charlotte and Walter, wedding photograph, November 8, 1948. Leslie Kohler Hawley collection.

21. Oscar M. Fritz swears in Walter as governor, 1951. Windway collection.

22. The four Kohler brothers in 1951:
left to right, Jim, Walter, John, Bob, at Windway.
Mary Ahern papers.

23. Niki Kohler in the early 1950s.
Niki Kohler collection.

24. General Douglas MacArthur and Governor Kohler, April 27, 1951, traveling through Kenosha. Leslie Kohler Hawley collection.

25. Governor Kohler and presidential candidate Dwight D. Eisenhower on the campaign train through Wisconsin, 1952. Leslie Kohler Hawley collection.

26. Charlotte and Walter at Windway in the early 1950s.
Leslie Kohler Hawley collection.

27. Ben Gage, Walter, Charlotte, Esther Williams Gage, March, 1954.
Leslie Kohler Hawley collection.

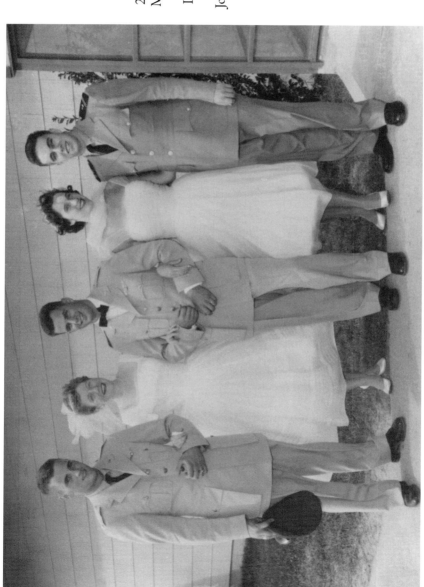

28. Wedding photo, May 29, 1956. From left to right, Jim Lang, Danny, Terry, Nancy Meissner, John Michael (Mike) Kohler, Jr. Leslie Kohler Hawley collection.

29. Terry Kohler family in the mid-1960s, from left to right: Diana (Danny), Leslie (standing), Michelle, Terry, Danielle. Leslie Kohler Hawley collection.

30. Terry and Danny's daughters in the late 1960s, from left to right:
Michelle, Leslie (standing), and Danielle.
Windway collection.

31. Danny and daughters in 1981, from left to right:
Michelle, Danny, Danielle, Leslie.
Leslie Kohler Hawley collection.

32. Terry and Mary Kohler with Newt Gingrich in the late 1987. Windway collection.

33. Terry and Mary traveling. Windway collection.

34. Rosemary Miley and Walter in about 1975.
Windway collection.

[24] See Reeves, *The Life and Times of Joe McCarthy*, 326; transcripts of the proceedings, box 4, Republican Party papers.

[25] Edwin R. Bayley, "GOP Parley Brings Many to Milwaukee," *Milwaukee Journal*, June 8, 1950.

[26] Copy, Warren P. Knowles to Mrs. Carl J. Kohler, June 25, 1952, Warren P. Knowles papers.

[27] Transcripts of the proceedings, box 4, Republican party papers.

[28] See *ibid.*

[29] *Ibid.*; "Kohler Gets Lesson at Fair:'Placing Second Isn't Good,'" *Milwaukee Journal*, August 28, 1950.

[30] Edwin R. Bayley, "Kohler Endorsed for Governor by GOP," *ibid.*, June 11, 1950; Robert H. Fleming, "Hard Work by Friends Helped Kohler to Win," *ibid.*

[31] Editorial, "The Republican Slate," *ibid.*, June 12, 1950.

[32] Thompson, *History of Wisconsin, Volume VI*, 408-410, 528, 533.

[33] *Ibid.*, 561-575. See Haney, "The Rise of Wisconsin's New Democrats," 91-98. For a biographical sketch of Thompson, see "Governor," *Milwaukee Journal*, September 17, 1950.

[34] "Rennebohm Jumps to Kohler's Support; Rules Out a Split," *Milwaukee Journal*, June 12, 1950.

[35] "Hart Will Run for Governor," *ibid.*, June 13, 1950.

[36] "Kohler Co. Union Supports Kohler," *ibid.*, June 20, 1950. For more on Vollrath support for Kohler, see Robert H. Fleming, "Fairchild Raps at Kohler Gate," *ibid.*, October 13, 1950.

[37] "'Peace' Is Issue of Wallaceites," *ibid.*, June 19, 1950.

[38] See Wayne J. Hood to Earl Hale, June 27, 1950 for a discussion of the strategy of the tour. Political expert Leon Epstein has noted that in the 1950s the farm vote comprised less than 20% of the total state vote. "This proportion is not what is responsible for the lavish attention which politicians of both parties give to farmers and farm issues. Rather it is the demonstrated capacity of Wisconsin farmers for wholesale switching of party allegiance." Leon Epstein, *Politics in Wisconsin* (Madison: University of Wisconsin Press, 1958), 72.

[39] "GOP's Slate to Tour State," *Milwaukee Journal*, July 9, 1950; Robert H. Fleming, "Kohler Avoids Rival Schmitt," *ibid.*, July 12, 1950.

[40] Robert H. Fleming, "Deficit Policy Hit by Kohler," *ibid.*, July 14, 1950.

[41] Fleming, "Kohler Avoids Rival Schmitt," *ibid.*, July 12, 1950.

[42] Robert H. Fleming, "GOP Political Tour Is Fast,'Neighborly," *ibid.*, July 13, 1950; Albert Mitchell, "It Says Here," *Vilas County News*, July 20, 1950.

[43] Fleming, "GOP Political Tour Is Fast,'Neighborly," *Milwaukee Journal*, July 13, 1950.

[44] Robert H. Fleming, "GOP Outlook in State Mixed," *ibid.*, July 16, 1950.

[45] "Wisconsin Remembers The Kohler Massacre," *Kenosha Labor*, July 27, 1950.

[46] Cedric Parker, "Kohler Income $662,032, Pays Tax on $75,739," *Madison Capital Times*, July 28, 1950.

[47] Editorial, *ibid.*, August 1, 1950.

[48] "Kohler Plans Talks Here," *ibid.*, August 3, 1950; "GOP Spending Hit by Schmitt," *ibid.*, August 4, 1950; "Kohler Raps at Democrats," *ibid.*, August 8, 1950. Warren Knowles soon told Walter that he and other friends were seeing another Dewey campaign, and he urged the candidate to seek more actively the independent vote. Copy, W. P. Knowles to Walter J. Kohler, Jr., August 16, 1950, Wayne Hood papers.

[49] Warren F. Knowles to Wayne Hood, July 10, 1950, *ibid.*

[50] For a biography of Drotning, see Willard R. Smith, "Departure of Drotning Will Leave a Big Void," *Milwaukee Journal*, November 11, 1956. More details are in his obituary in the *Wisconsin State Journal*, June 12, 1993.

[51] Edwin R. Bayley, "Lively GOP Caravan Invades Sleepy Village," *Milwaukee Journal*, August 4, 1950.

[52] See Reeves, *The Life and Times of Joe McCarthy*, 327-329.

[53] Edwin R. Bayley, "Kohler Says He'll Rezone," *Milwaukee Journal*, August 5, 1950.

[54] Haney, *A Concise History of the Modern Republican Party of Wisconsin*, 11.

[55] Thompson, *History of Wisconsin, Volume VI*, 616.

[56] "Kohler Urges New College," *Milwaukee Journal*, August 11, 1950.

[57] *Ibid.*

[58] "GOP Charge Called 'Phony,'" *ibid.*, August 14, 1950; "Thomson Raps Party Expense," *ibid.*, August 15, 1950. The Republican Party of Wisconsin reported collecting $48,332 and spent $33,143 on pre-primary and primary campaign projects. Citizens for Kohler received $8,000. "GOP Reports Its Expenses," *ibid.*, September 11, 1950.

[59] "Opponents Rip Kohler, Wiley," *ibid.*, August 22, 1950.

[60] "Candidates Hit Foreign Policy," *ibid.*, August 30, 1950.

[61] "Kohler Raps Foreign Policy," *ibid.*, September 1, 1950.

[62] "A 'Democrat' War, He Says," *ibid.*, September 17, 1950.

[63] "Kohler Pledges To Expansion Of Welfare Program," *Oshkosh Northwestern*, September 13, 1950.

[64] "What Candidates Said and Did," *Milwaukee Journal*, September 17, 1950; "Talks of State, Kohler Insists," *ibid.*, October 6, 1950.

[65] Both advertisements are in *ibid.*, September 18, 1950.

[66] "Democrats Pick Fairchild to Race Wiley," *ibid.*, September 20, 1950.

[67] "GOP Promises Big Campaign," *ibid.*, September 21, 1950.

[68] "Reuther Raps Wiley, Kohler," *ibid.*, September 29, 1950.

[69] Robert H. Fleming, "Kohler to Ask for Repairs in GOP Platform," *ibid.*, October 2, 1950; "Gibes Kohler for Tax Stand," *ibid.*, October 3, 1950.

[70] David Carley, "Legal and Extra-Legal Powers of Wisconsin Governors in Legislative Relations—Part II," *Wisconsin Law Review*, 1962 (March, 1962), 315. Carley interviewed Walter in 1958.

[71] David Carley, "Legal and Extra-Legal Powers of Wisconsin Governors in Legislative Relations—Part 1," *ibid.*, 1962 (January, 1962), 43. Kohler told Carley, "I believe that the governor should be the chief architect of the platform, especially for the first time he runs." *Ibid.*, 45. On the status of voluntary committees and the statutory conventions held in October, see *ibid.*, 44, f. 144.

[72] Walter was a member of the American Legion, Veterans of Foreign Wars, American Veterans of World War II, and the Military Order of the World Wars. Richard S. Davis, "Governorship is First Kohler Political Job," *Milwaukee Journal*, November 9, 1950.

[73] Edwin R. Bayley, "Republicans use Many Kohler Suggestions; Pledge to Reapportionment," *ibid.*, October 4, 1950. See the printed GOP platform in box 4, Republican Party papers.

[74] Robert H. Fleming, "Democrats Turn Down Plank for Veterans' Bonus After a Bitter Convention Debate," *Milwaukee Journal*, October 4, 1950.

[75] Edwin R. Bayley, "Lost to Kohler, L. F. Schmitt to Vote Democrat," *ibid.*, October 25, 1950.

[76] "GOP Primary Outlay Leads," *ibid.*, October 12, 1950.

[77] "Kohler Vows Benefit Boost," *ibid.*, October 10, 1950.

[78] "Lag in Defense Laid to GOP," *ibid.*, October 12, 1950. Both gubernatorial candidates and Senator Wiley criticized repeal of the federal tax on oleomargarine, a topic dear to dairy farmers.

[79] "Kohler Talks of His Taxes," *ibid.*, October 13, 1950. In fact, Hopkins did not make that statement, but it was widely used at the time by Republicans.

[80] "Kohler is 'Encouraged,'" *ibid.*, October 15, 1950.

[81] "Kohler Cagey on McCarthy," *ibid.*, October 17, 1950.

[82] Reeves, *The Life and Times of Joe McCarthy*, 314.

[83] *Ibid.*, 335.

[84] *Ibid.*, 332-334.

[85] *Ibid.*, 313-322. The Venona Papers, first made available to Western scholars in 1995, were secret messages between Soviet KGB officers reporting on American informants in the 1930s and 1940s, intercepted and decrypted by U. S. intelligence personnel. The cables revealed the presence of many Soviet spies in the government of the United States. But this has little to do with charges raised by McCarthy and other leaders of the Second Red Scare. McCarthy himself found no Communists in Washington, although his conclusions about a few widely celebrated suspects such as Alger Hiss

and Julius and Ethel Rosenberg proved correct. The emphasis by McCarthyites, largely for political gain, was on the false allegation that Communists and pro-Communists dictated self-destructive American foreign and domestic policy. See John Earl Haynes and Harvey Klehr, *Venona: Decoding Soviet Espionage in America* (New Haven: Yale University Press, 1999) and Harvey Klehr, John Earl Haynes, and Kyrill M. Anderson, *The Soviet World of American Communism* (New Haven: Yale University Press, 1998).

[86] "Kohler Called a Fence Sitter," *Milwaukee Journal*, October 25, 1950.

[87] Edwin R. Bayley, "Vote of State on Nov. 7 Still Is Big Puzzle," *ibid.*, October 29, 1950. See also "GOP Tabloid Is Under Fire," *ibid.*, October 18, 1950.

[88] Reeves, *The Life and Times of Joe McCarthy*, 333.

[89] See "Wisconsin Key State Tuesday," *Milwaukee Journal*, November 5, 1950. On Kersten, see "Kohler Tells His Program," *ibid.*, November 9, 1950, and Reeves, *The Life and Times of Joe McCarthy*, *passim*. Kersten had been elected in 1946 but was defeated two years later, in large part because the state department of taxation revealed his failure to pay taxes over a three-year period. In 1950, Kersten defeated the man who had earlier taken his Congressional seat, liberal Andrew Biemiller.

[90] "Wiley Attacks Big City Law," *Milwaukee Journal*, October 24, 1950. It was a common practice of the *Milwaukee Journal* to include several articles under a single headline.

[91] "Kohler Strikes at 'Falsehoods,'" *ibid.*, October 29, 1950.

[92] "Wiley, Kohler Blast Critics," *ibid.*, October 31, 1950.

[93] The ad appears in *ibid.*, November 5, 1950.

[94] Horace Wilkie, a Democrat ran unsuccessfully for Congress in 1950, said later he thought that Chinese entry into the Korean War on the brink of the election hurt Democratic candidates. Haney, *A Concise History of the Modern Republican Party of Wisconsin 1925-1975*, 11.

[95] Robert H. Fleming, "Kohler, Wiley Win in State's Heavy Vote," *Milwaukee Journal.*, November 9, 1950; Arthur Bystrom, "Kohler, Wiley Win by Over 80,000," *Madison Capital Times*, November 8, 1950; "State Vote for Senator, Governor," *Milwaukee Journal*, November 9, 1950.

[96] For official election results, see *The Wisconsin Blue Book, 1952* (Madison: the Wisconsin Legislative Reference Bureau), 739-751.

[97] "Victory Welcomed Happily in Kohler Home at Kohler," *Milwaukee Journal*, November 8, 1950.

[98] "Voters Gave Mrs. Kohler 'Anniversary Gift' by Electing her husband Governor of State," *ibid.*, November 9, 1950.

[99] Richard S. Davis, "Governorship is First Kohler Political Job," *ibid.*, November 9, 1950.

[100] Reeves, *The Life and Times of Joe McCarthy*, 343-344.

[101] *Ibid.*, 314-346.

Chapter Nine
Steps to the Left & Right

On New Year's Day, 1951, some 3,000 people attended the inauguration ceremony in the east section of the capitol rotunda. Walter wore a dark blue suit, in line with his request that the event be a little less elaborate than in the past. Charlotte, wearing a large corsage of camellias on her garnet velvet dress, stood at the rear of the platform while her husband was sworn in as the state's new governor. She was accompanied by Earl Johnson, Assistant Secretary of the Army and a long-time friend of Walter's. All of the top state officers were on hand, including former governor and newly re-elected Secretary of State Fred R. Zimmerman, the state's top vote-getter in the last election. He was conspicuous by dressing in a cutaway suit and striped trousers, perhaps causing Chief Justice Oscar M. Fritz, while administering the oath of office, to ask if Zimmermann would uphold the laws of Wisconsin "as Governor." The ceremony was televised for the first time by a Milwaukee station. Twenty two years earlier, the same station had broadcast Walter J. Kohler Sr.'s inauguration for the first time on radio.[1]

In his brief address, Walter began by emphasizing the international tension of the period that called for self-sacrifice by all Americans. His own task in Wisconsin, he said, was comparatively easy because of the "forward-looking stewardship of Governor Oscar Rennebohm," whose policies he swore to continue. Walter then stressed his personal commitment to principle, warning against the influence of special interests, vowing to appoint "the most conscientious and able individuals who are available," and promising to stand above partisan politics. "We must be motivated by fairness, justice and impartiality rather than by political considerations. We must remember that he who would play politics and place party above state or nation, betrays not only state or nation but betrays party as well."[2] One can well imagine Tom Coleman wincing at that bold declaration.

When Walter moved into the governor's office at the state capitol, he placed a large, stern portrait of his father, sitting in the same chair, on the wall under the clock. He was proud of his father's many achievements and was determined to uphold the standards of integrity and efficiency that had long been associated with the first Governor Kohler.

Visitors soon learned that Walter disliked working according to schedule, never bothered with protocol, often worked in his shirt sleeves, and chain-smoked his way through the many meetings that were part of his job. He liked an uncluttered desk and did most of his business at a long conference table. The governor had a filing system containing national and international data that he began after the war, and he regularly referred to its contents and supplemented older materials with the latest information.[3]

The 70th state legislature opened its proceedings on January 10. Both houses were dominated by Republicans, as they had been since 1938; the margin in the Senate was 27 to 7, and in the Assembly 75 to 24. In the previous session, in 1949, Democrats had held one more Assembly seat and one less Senate seat. The Republican floor leader in the Senate, Warren Knowles, predicted a five month session; the last few had lasted six or seven months. (Unlike in many other states, Wisconsin's legislative sessions were not limited to a certain period of time. The legislature met every two years and after a winter and spring session could return in the fall to deal with gubernatorial vetoes and handle other matters that had arisen unexpectedly.)[4]

The following day, the governor delivered his first message to a joint session of the legislature. About 200 guests were on hand in the galleries. Walter surprised all by presenting a 7,000 word address containing requests for 46 specific pieces of legislation in 19 different fields. The *Milwaukee Journal* complemented the new Governor on his quick grasp of the state's complex needs, adding that the message was "not a speech, but a *clear blueprint.*"[5]

Walter began by calling for civil defense legislation, including the creation of a state agency in the adjutant general's office that would organize and administer all defense activities. His audience shared his deep concern for the safety of the nation, for the Chinese had recently driven U.N. troops out of Seoul, and the Cold War seemed about to erupt on a massive scale. Walter thought that the severity of the world situation was such that "We need to cut ruthlessly the requests for luxuries of government," and yet continue to "provide adequately for the needs of those citizens who must look to the state for aid. We must see that essential state services are maintained."

The governor then backed a series of administrative proposals to consolidate state government and maximize its efficiency. Many of these proposals came from the state's Legislative Council, a body created in 1947 to study complex state issues and make recommendations to the legislature. The Council was composed of fifteen appointed legislators, nine from the Assembly and six from the Senate, assisted by a staff. It had the authority, with a two-thirds vote, to introduce bills, but members usually preferred to support a proposal it sanctioned when made by an individual legislator so as not to become a "little legislature." From the beginning of his governorship, Walter respected the judgment of the Council and supported its studies and recommendations.[6] Walter also backed several of former Governor Rennebohm's proposals, including a constitutional amendment extending the terms of the state's top officials from two to four years. (Twenty four states had shifted to the four year term, and one or two more were adopting the change each year.)

The governor urged further study of the state's Bang's Disease program (a brucellosis outbreak threatened Wisconsin's dairy industry), called for an updated code of food laws, requested further study of the needs of the elderly, recommended the creation of a four-year college in Milwaukee (favored in 1950 by an American Council of Education survey team and a commission appointed by Governor Rennebohm), backed the creation of a committee of state agencies to coordinate state conservation activities, called for tougher highway laws against trucks, sought increased housing loans for veterans, called for stronger gambling laws, approved the Legislative Council's proposal to repeal the dividend tax that had become an issue in the last election, and backed reapportionment. On the last topic, noting that both parties had formally endorsed the principle, he said, "Every member of this legislature is formally committed to pass a reapportionment act consistent with the constitution before the 1951 legislature adjourns." It was clear that the second Governor Kohler was a leader who wanted action and wanted it soon.[7]

A top state Republican, Cyrus Philipp, wrote to GOP colleague Harvey Higley, "I think the Governor has gotten off to a good start. His message was widely and favorably received, and even though some of his tax plans are not too popular, they are being accepted even by some of the most conservative."[8]

By this time, the Kohlers had moved into the Executive Residence in Madison. The three-story Maple Bluff mansion had been completed in

1928. In 1949, the state purchased the home, on a 3.7 acre parcel of land on Lake Mendota, from Madison businessman Carl A. Johnson. With 34 rooms and 20,777 gross square feet, it worthily complemented the grandeur of the marble state capitol building not far away. The mansion was designed in the Southern classic revival style, with painted stucco over sandstone and a hollow clay tile facade. A six column portico welcomed the many visitors and guests.[9]

Charlotte had some of the furnishings at Windway brought to the Residence, including furniture and china.[10] She also used this opportunity to display some of the antiques she had stored when moving to Wisconsin. While Charlotte continued to despise politics and no doubt disliked her obligations as First Lady, Terry Kohler was convinced that she did a good job of "faking it."[11] Always concerned for her privacy, Charlotte carried out her social duties with an absolute minimum of press coverage.

The Kohlers spent a three or four day week in Madison, often Tuesday through Friday, and then returned to Windway. In the tradition of his father, Walter not only handled his duties as governor but also continued to run the Vollrath Company. Erna Schwartz, Walter's personal secretary at Vollrath, worked furiously to keep up with the increased flow of correspondence, typing many political as well as personal and business letters. (First employed at Vollrath in 1938, Schwartz worked for Walter until his death. Years later, she had only the highest praise for her boss, stressing his kindness and integrity.)[12] Walter would be the last Wisconsin governor to attempt to handle two full-time jobs simultaneously. On Sundays, the Kohlers tried to relax, play golf, and listen to the symphony on the radio.

During the first few weeks of 1951, Walter immersed himself in his new duties. In an article he later wrote on his office, he said that a governor was at once a party spokesman and a formulator of policy; the director of the executive branch, which included more than 40 departments, boards, commissions, and agencies, comprising more than 14,000 employees; and the ceremonial head of the State, expected to attend all sorts of dedicatory celebrations and convocations, give speeches, and issue proclamations. He found the last duty the most taxing, as he received about ten speaking invitations a day.

Thousands of letters poured into the governor's office each month, and Walter took upon himself the task of reading each one. He also made it his policy to make himself available to every visitor to the executive office and to every citizen who attempted to reach him by telephone. Of course, Walter had assistants to help him with correspondence, speeches, proclamations, and financial and legal matters. And not everyone who tried to reach the governor was successful, as aides screened applicants about the nature of their request, often handling problems themselves and sending people to other relevant state officials.

Working with the legislature was a major responsibility of the governor. He reported his views on issues and promoted policies he believed essential. He had the authority to call a special session and could veto any legislative enactment and any item of an appropriation measure. (The line item veto was passed in 1930 and remains in force to this day.) Still, the Wisconsin constitution did not give governors any specific administrative power, and legislatures over the years had roped off government agencies from their direct control. Governor Rennebohm had been a strong leader, but legislators usually preferred governors to be weak. "The idea," said a *Milwaukee Journal* editorial, "is that a bad governor can't do much harm. The result is that a good governor eager to do a job must go about it somewhat deviously. Since he can't give many orders, he must consult and suggest and persuade. His success depends mainly on the knowledge and intellect and force of personality he can bring to bear."[13]

Walter soon made it his regular policy to attend party caucuses in the two houses only when invited to do so, but he later admitted that he sometimes requested an invitation. He met regularly with party leaders in his office to discuss proposals and strategy. Legislators soon learned that they had a good deal of freedom in making their own voting decisions, as it was not in the governor's makeup to make deals or issue threats to get bills passed. Indeed, Walter purposely avoided such tactics, making it clear that he preferred to be a statesman and a gentleman rather than a professional politician.

When departments wanted a law introduced, the governor expected it to be presented to his office first. If Kohler liked the proposal, it was often incorporated into his own program. If he disliked it, he expected the department to refrain from introducing the bill. Walter's personal proposals were discussed with key legislators and sent to the State's Legislative Reference Library, where skilled staff members drew up a bill that would be introduced by top senators and assemblymen.[14]

The governor also served as chairman of the State Investment Board and chairman of the State Building Commission. He presided at budget hearings and was responsible for reviewing biennially most of the requests for spending tax money. He had pardoning power and worked carefully with his legal counsel to study requests from convicted persons. He was commander-in-chief of the National Guard, and could summon troops during emergencies. He was required to approve the orders of the conservation department, the department of agriculture, and the State Board of Health. He had to approve any federal grants made available to the State. The governor also made appointments to an assortment of bodies, including the University of Wisconsin Board of Regents.

The authority of the governor to appoint was limited, as most of the positions on the state payroll came under civil service regulations and were tied to a merit system. Of 395 positions that could be filled by the governor, only 36 could be described as full-time, salaried appointments. Twenty five of the 36 came under Senate purview and three were under civil service regulations. Moreover, most of the governor's appointments were for terms of four, six, and ten years, making it difficult to construct a politically loyal bureaucracy. Walter inherited most of his immediate subordinates; agency heads served six-year terms and were not removable except for gross misdeeds. The heads of several State departments, including conservation, agriculture, and public welfare, were selected by boards and were not appointed directly by the governor.[15]

At the end of February, the *Milwaukee Journal* applauded the governor's appointment practices, noting that he had announced his choices for appointive offices and boards and commissions well in advance of a term's expiration date, assuring smoother and less frustrating transitions and avoiding struggles over senate confirmation.[16] One case stood out. Organized labor opposed the renomination of Lawrence E. Gooding as chairman of the Wisconsin employment board. Kohler had confidence in him, however, and summoned senators to his office, one by one, to discuss the matter. In this way, he won 24 of the 33 votes in the Senate for the renomination. Political columnist John Wyngaard called this "an administration triumph."[17]

To Kohler, one of his most important appointees was Phil Drotning, named to the combined posts of executive secretary and press secretary. Walter said later, "No governor ever had a better executive secretary than Phil has been to me." He praised Drotning's "innate integrity and honesty" and credited him with "a sixth sense in politics. He knows what is wise and what is unwise, both to say and to do." Two-thirds of his

time, Drotning said later, was spent listening to the appeals of visitors
to the governor's office, trying to send them away happy or at least angry
at him and not the governor. He was also a key figure in legislative proceedings. "The big satisfaction comes from going into a legislative session
with a program in which you have confidence, a program which means
something to the state and achieving success with it. Both governors
I've served with have remarkable records in that respect."[18]

Arthur E. Wegner was the governor's financial secretary, and would
serve him throughout his years in Madison. Earlier, Wegner had been
a part of the Walter Goodland administration (1943-1947) and was
thoroughly experienced in government and politics as well as fiscal
matters.[19]

Early in his administration, Kohler stressed fiscal responsibility. After
a study made by his staff, the governor altered state investment policies
in a way that increased returns by some $700,000 a year.[20] In his initial
biennium budget message, he trimmed $11.5 million of departmental
requests and urged continuation of a current 25% surtax on all state
incomes in order to retain state fiscal reserves. (The surtax had been
passed in 1949 to promote building projects.) Still, the governor recommended a record executive budget of $211,109,018, which was $1.5
million higher than the budget appropriations made by the legislature
in 1949. His recommendations contained increases for both the fair
employment practices commission and the human rights commission,
and included salary and bonus increases for all state workers. Walter said
that the state enjoyed the "soundest financial position in its history."[21]

Democrats were flustered by the governor's prudent and humane
proposals. "That was a good Democratic speech," said a party member.
"It doesn't leave anywhere for us to go." Democratic minority floor leader
George Molinaro of Kenosha declared, "Why, I'd be proud to introduce
the bills he talked about myself." Another Democrat complained, "he's
stealing our stuff. He's a lot smarter than I thought." A colleague moaned,
"What can you do with a guy who is elected as a conservative and then
takes two steps to the left?"[22]

Walter experienced almost the full range of his duties within the first
several months. In mid-February, he and Major General Ralph J. Olson,
Wisconsin adjutant general and state civil defense director, traveled to
Washington for a nation-wide, closed door civil defense meeting. The
Truman Administration was pushing a $3 billion program to construct
bomb shelters and other facilities in strategic centers on a federal-state

matching basis. Governor Kohler caused a sensation by declaring publicly that he disapproved of the proposal. It would not be possible, he contended, to construct enough of the extremely expensive underground shelters, and in the event of an attack, the existing shelters would be difficult to reach in time. He favored making existing buildings as safe as possible and believed that states should take care of their own needs. "We should be sensible in our approach to this problem," he said.[23] In a speech in Milwaukee a few weeks later, Kohler outlined in some detail the different responsibilities of the federal and state governments. Civil defense was not a matter of buying vast quantities of equipment or building huge bomb shelters, he said. The problem "is essentially one of organizing available equipment and personnel and training everyone sufficiently to avoid panic."[24]

In early March, the governor traveled to Portsmouth, Virginia to celebrate the reactivation into the Atlantic fleet of the battleship Wisconsin, which had served in five campaigns against the Japanese in World War II before being put in mothballs. The huge ship, which originally cost $100 million, now appeared more impressive than ever, sporting nine 16 inch guns and 20 five inch guns, and its decks bristling with antiaircraft weapons. Walter told an invited audience that during his service in the South Pacific, the Wisconsin was an "old and trusted friend." "The recommissioning of this vessel," he said, "should serve plain notice to any enemy of the United States that our patience is wearing thin. As a combat veteran in the naval service, as governor of Wisconsin and as an American citizen, I am proud to take part in thus serving this plain notice: The people of our nation will not be conquered, nor will they permit the rest of the world to be conquered without a mighty struggle."[25]

Shortly after returning to Wisconsin, Walter spoke in Milwaukee before the North American Wildlife conference, urging the pursuit of conservation measures. "There was a time," he said, "when people could move from wornout land to new territory. That fact is a part of our own history. It has been the same story from the wheat lands of Tunisia in the time of Carthage, which fed the Roman empire, but which are now drifting sands, to the abandoned farms of the east coast states and also of Michigan, Minnesota and Wisconsin." He urged his audience not to feel "frustrated and discouraged" when the public failed to respond to conservation efforts. That feeling, he said, "assails all who ever crusaded for a cause in the common good."[26]

Back in Madison, Walter agreed to host a series of four television broadcasts entitled "From the Governor's Office," to be filmed in the capitol by a Milwaukee television station. The programs were designed to acquaint citizens with their state officials and the major issues they faced. On the first live program, aired on March 18, Kohler, two state senators, and an assemblyman discussed the 25% surtax in light of increased revenue estimates. This was the first encounter Walter had with the newly elected assemblyman from Madison, Democrat William Proxmire.[27]

In early April, Walter spoke in Milwaukee before the annual convention of the Wisconsin Press Association, urging editors to "strive for utmost fairness." As an example of unfairness, he said, one newspaper called another "Kohler's stooge" for printing the text of the governor's recent speech delivered at the recommissioning of the battleship Wisconsin. (Everyone knew that his target was the shrilly partisan *Madison Capital Times*, which had criticized the moderately liberal *Milwaukee Journal*.) "That speech was printed in the *New York Times*," Kohler said. "I don't think the *New York Times* has become 'Kohler's stooge.'"[28]

The *Madison Capital Times* was now beginning to bear down on Kohler for his apparent sympathy toward Joe McCarthy, and others on the Left were joining in. Walter had appeared with the Senator at a Lincoln Day dinner in early January, and soon delivered a strongly anti-Communist speech at the State Historical Society of Wisconsin.[29]

In early April, Walter went farther. In a speech before the Big Ten Young Republican conference in Madison, the governor charged that Democrats "tolerated, sponsored and encouraged the infiltration of Communists and fellow travelers" into high government positions. That was indisputably McCarthyite rhetoric, being used by Republicans all across the nation. Democratic State Senator Henry W. Maier of Milwaukee contended that Kohler had become a political "blood brother" of Senator McCarthy, and contending that Kohler was probably "on orders" from Republican bosses to join in the smear campaign."[30]

The speech in question could not be defended by Walter's moderate GOP admirers. But this was a time when passions were overruling reason, when political victory seemed to many Republicans to be the most important issue on earth, indeed affecting the very survival of the human race. The Cold War seemed to be spiraling out of control, and the Truman Administration seemed to millions to be either helpless or in league with the enemy.

When the President dismissed General Douglas MacArthur in early
April, Republicans all over the nation were outraged. Speaking of Truman, McCarthy told a *Milwaukee Journal* reporter, "The son of a bitch
should be impeached." He continued, "He is surrounded by the Jessups,
the Achesons, the old Hiss crowd." MacArthur's dismissal was a victory
for the Communists, "homemade and foreign made," he cried, "a victory
achieved with the aid of bourbon and Benedictine." Senator Taft spoke
of the new "appeasement." Senator William Jenner said, "We must cut
this whole cancerous conspiracy out of our government at once. Our
only choice is to impeach President Truman and find out who is the
secret invisible government which has so cleverly led our country down
the road to destruction." The Republican Policy Committee's consultant
on national defense, Brigadier General Julius Klein, said that the United
States had not known such humiliation since Bataan and suggested that
the Kremlin fire a 21-gun salute in celebration.

The Gallup Poll showed two-thirds of the American people opposing MacArthur's dismissal. Some 60 million watched on television as
MacArthur delivered a self-serving and McCarthyite address before the
joint houses of Congress. Truman's popularity plunged to a low never
before experienced by a president.[31]

Soon after the televised speech, the Wisconsin legislature adopted a
joint resolution condemning the Truman Administration's foreign policy
and inviting the general to address a legislative session. Governor Kohler
said he would invite General MacArthur to make such an address.[32]
MacArthur agreed only to appear in his home state on a brief tour that
began in Chicago. He had already been hailed in massive demonstrations in New York, Washington, and San Francisco.

Some 50,000 people turned out at Chicago's Soldier Field to cheer
the famed general and hear him defend his "realistic" Korean War policy
and dramatically declare the close of his public life. Then the General
and a huge motorcade headed for Wisconsin.

Walter and Charlotte met the MacArthur motorcade at the state
border, and Walter rode the rest of the way to Milwaukee in the general's
red convertible, sharing the back seat, amid a din of sirens and nearly 100
police motorcycles. Both men smiled at the thousands of people who lined
the streets to cheer, wave flags, and display signs supporting the general.
(Charlotte rode in the car that followed with Mrs. MacArthur and her
13-year-old son, Arthur.) At Racine and Kenosha, workers had been
excused from their jobs to join in the welcome. Some 100,000 people

met the party in Racine. In Milwaukee, the frenzied reception was so overwhelming that a reporter claimed there had been no equal since young Colonel Charles Lindbergh landed his plane at the local airport. Fire sirens, aerial bombs, factory whistles, and church bells added to the festivities. The 71-year-old general, dressed in his familiar trench coat, khaki uniform with tie, Eisenhower jacket, and the celebrated garrison cap with the large quantity of gold braid, made only brief and solemn expressions of thanks.[33]

MacArthur's larger message was clear, and was expressed succinctly in Chicago: The Truman Administration was needlessly causing the death of thousands of American troops. This was Joe McCarthy's position on the Korean War. The junior Senator from Wisconsin was soon charging publicly that Secretary of Defense George Marshall and Secretary of Defense Dean Acheson were part of "a conspiracy on a scale so immense as to dwarf any previous such venture in the history of man. A conspiracy of infamy so black that, when it is finally exposed, its principal shall be forever deserving of the maledictions of all honest men."[34]

The MacArthur family quickly left Milwaukee and returned to New York. More than a few Republicans, in Wisconsin and throughout the United States, agreed with the general's private but transparent opinion that he would make an outstanding Chief Executive. Several MacArthur for president groups began assembling all across the state.

Governor Kohler's first legislative defeat came as the result of a popular referendum in which voters rejected the idea of extending the terms of office for the governor and other top state officials from two years to four. As a result of the election, plans were abandoned by legislators to advance the issue.[35] On the other hand, pay increases for all state employees were passed almost unanimously, and the governor reappointed 17 major officials whose terms of office had to be ended briefly for the raise to be in harmony with state law. Walter's salary was raised from $12,500 to $14,000 a year. The Director of Public Welfare's salary went up from $10,000 to $11,000. Professors in the state schools got $20 to $30 more a month. The total cost of the salary increases was estimated to be about $8 million a year.[36]

A major reason for the legislature's generosity was the healthy economy Wisconsin enjoyed. On May 1, the state had an estimated surplus of $17 million more than forecast in January. Kohler told a joint session of the legislature that the State could now afford to reduce the 25% surtax to 10% and still have enough money to fund his own $10 million building plans, which included major improvements in higher education facilities and in public welfare institutions.[37]

While the legislators grappled with the scores of bills before them, Walter took some time away from his immediate duties to fulfill a number of speaking requests. Before the strongly pro-McCarthy Young Republicans of Wisconsin in May, he spoke of the Truman Administration's "moral degeneration" and said that the GOP "must be a party of principle and not of expediency."[38] Kohler told members of the Republican National Committee, meeting in Tulsa, Oklahoma, that the party must take "clear and unequivocal positions on issues" and must offer "specific remedies for evils it objects to."[39] On receiving an honorary doctor of laws degree from Beloit College, he advised graduates to bring "idealism, enthusiasm, energy and moral courage into civic life."[40] Despite occasional lapses, the governor's rhetoric remained at a reasonably high moral and intellectual plain and did not descend into the Red Scare mudslinging that was a common feature of Republican politics at this time.

McCarthy led the way in volatile rhetoric. When Democratic Senator William Benton decided that he had become a national menace and that steps should be taken against him, the junior Senator from Wisconsin issued a statement denouncing Benton as "Connecticut's mental midget" and charged him with having "established himself as the hero of every Communist and crook in and out of government."[41]

When Senator Robert Taft of Ohio came to Milwaukee to deliver a speech before a large GOP audience, he lauded McCarthy, denounced Secretary of State Dean Acheson, and blamed the Soviet threat to world peace on "the weak and wrong headed policies of this and the preceding administration at Teheran, Yalta, Potsdam and in China." The Korean War, he said, "is a Truman war," and "the whole theory of punishing aggression has become a joke." Taft's fund-raising speech was interrupted 18 times by applause. Walter sat at the head table—by chance, he on the left side and McCarthy on the right.[42]

For Kohler, being governor was far more than politics. In Madison, he worked hard to persuade the predominantly Republican legislators to pass his proposals. A *Milwaukee Journal* reporter observed, "Unlike his recent predecessors, Kohler did not merely generalize in his recommendations to the legislature; he urged specific measures. Also unlike his predecessors, he did not then sit back and see what happened. He lobbied for all he was worth—attending caucuses, conferring with key legislators, summoning dissenters and trying to persuade them."[43]

Toward the end of the legislative session there were reports of friction between himself and several leading GOP members of the assembly and senate. Friends urged the governor to appeal to the public to put pressure on those opposing him. Assemblyman Elmer Genzmer stormed, "'They crucified Christ and that's what they did to Kohler. They rode on his coattails to victory and then wrecked every bit of his program along with the Republican platform. They'll be sorry. Everybody in the state is back of Kohler except a half dozen of these self-anointed leaders in here." But Walter did not go public; indeed, he chose to keep the struggles as private as possible. Edwin R. Bayley observed, "He has tried to get along with everyone."[44]

In the end, this strategy proved wise. When the legislature adjourned in mid-June, the governor said that the session was "one of the most fruitful since Wisconsin achieved statehood." He praised "the high level of agreement between the governor and the legislature" and reported that 47 of his 55 specific proposals for legislation had been passed. He considered the achievements a triumph for the GOP majority.[45]

Looking at a $44 million surplus to begin the next biennium on July 1, the legislature let the entire 25% surtax expire, a move that had been favored by Democrats from the start. It agreed to eliminate the 3% privilege tax that had come under fire during the recent election campaign, choosing instead to tax dividends as regular income. Legislators passed several reforms in budget procedures and administrative mergers and improvements, created a state civil defense organization, and approved the governor's entire building program. They also increased old age pensions and authorized a study of the problems of the elderly, established a new Bang's Disease control program, approved pure food regulations and truck weight restrictions, strengthened laws against gambling, passed two major civil rights measures (resorts could no longer advertise "Gentiles only"), and improved unemployment and workmen's compensation benefits. A score of measures strengthened and improved the state's conservation policies.

Kohler's losses were minimal. His major disappointment was his failure to persuade members of the Assembly to go along with the Senate in approving a four-year college in Milwaukee. But he resolved to keep working for this proposal. To keep reapportionment alive, he agreed to place the issue before voters in an advisory referendum. There were smaller issues such as weed control and authority for municipalities to control rents that failed to win approval. Kohler vetoed a bill to permit county-wide referendums. But none of this detracted from the governor's elation over the achievements he and the legislature had contributed to the welfare of the State. The $211,844,000 biennial budget passed by lawmakers was the largest in Wisconsin history.[46]

The *Milwaukee Journal* concluded editorially that this had been an outstanding legislature. "Healthiest feature of all was the close relationship between the governor's office and the lawmakers. Even many who differ with Gov. Kohler's politics can respect the qualities he brought to his office—a good mind for government, personal persuasion, courage to take a stand and fight for it, capacity for hard work, skill and ingenuity in 'handling' a legislature." The editorial noted that legislators adjourned instead of recessing until fall and saving a chance to override vetoes, the practice in the last four sessions. "The clear inference is that this legislature trusted Gov. Kohler."[47]

John Wyngaard wrote in his state-wide syndicated column of Walter Kohler's way of dealing with a legislature, "which is earnest and helpful collaboration, persuasion without coercion, and friendly understanding. Kohler probably maintained a closer contact with members of his party in the legislature this year than any other governor in a generation....The lawmakers quickly learned that he knew what he wanted, and why he wanted it, and that he was serious about his program. They appreciated the fact that he understood their right to disagree and held no grudge against them for it. A gentleman, Kohler appreciated the dignity of his colleagues and the independent responsibility of the legislative branch. In the long run, Kohler won more through his tactful and diplomatic way than some of his more assertive predecessors did in spite of their heroic publicity."[48]

After delivering a warm and appreciative farewell address to the legislature, Walter was physically and mentally exhausted. Phil Drotning told reporters, "He's just plain tired. His physician has ordered him to limit his activities to his official duties for several weeks." The governor cancelled all public speeches for 30 days.[49] Wyngaard noted that the legislature placed more than 350 bills on Kohler's desk, which he had to examine, consider, and sign or veto. On one recent day, he waded through 61 such legislative enactments. The ten-hour work day was all too common in the governor's schedule. (By early August, Walter had signed 735 new laws.)[50]

In late June rumblings were heard of a struggle from within the GOP
Voluntary Committee. Tom Coleman was behind a move to replace
long-time party activist Cyrus Philipp from his post as national committeeman. The real issue was control; Philipp had quarreled with the
"Boss" over the selection of a national Republican chairman, and now
he was scheduled to pay the price when the Republican Voluntary
Committee held its annual convention in Wisconsin Rapids on July
7. Governor Kohler and Senator McCarthy were both set to speak at
the convention, and McCarthyite Senator Everett Dirksen of Illinois
was also on the program.[51]

The day before the convention, four state Democrats—Henry Reuss,
James Doyle, Gaylord Nelson, and William Proxmire—sent a public
telegram to the governor, urging him to use the meeting at Wisconsin
Rapids to clarify his position on Senator McCarthy. "As governor
and as leader of the Republican party in Wisconsin, you have the responsibility of declaring whether your party embraces McCarthyism."
Kohler ignored the message. Three of the four Democrats (Reuss, from
Milwaukee, was the exception) were members of "the Madison ring," a
small group of youthful ex-Progressives who, through sheer energy and
determination, were becoming party leaders. Each of the four telegram
signers was being mentioned as a possible senatorial candidate against
McCarthy in 1952.[52]

About 1,800 delegates were on hand for the convention, held in a
local high school field house. The governor opened the meeting with
an address that lauded the state legislature's achievements, claiming
that independent voters would find its performance laudable and help
the GOP at the polls. In contrast, he said, the Truman Administration
was "unbelievably and intolerably incompetent." One state representative who addressed the delegates said, "Governor Kohler preaches and
practices honesty, decency, and morality."[53]

It was just as well that Walter said nothing at all about McCarthy,
for it was clearly evident that anything but praise would have been met
with hostility. Coleman's dispatch of Philipp, in favor of the more loyal
Henry E. Ringling, was achieved quickly. Senator Dirksen of Illinois
used McCarthyite language to blast the Administration and the opposition party. And McCarthy himself was given a rousing welcome
to the convention. Delegates also applauded when a group of Young
Republicans broke into song: "Fighting Joe McCarthy, We're one and
all for you. Our land you'll save, The flag will wave, The true red, white

and blue." The Senator hurled names and claims freely, much to the delight of his audience.[54] (Walter later recalled of McCarthy, "In fact, I've seen tears come to people's eyes and they kiss[ed] his hand when he was campaigning.... His was an emotional constituency. They believed he was saving us from Communism.")[55]

Delegates passed resolutions commending General MacArthur, deploring the Administration's "lack of morality, principle and integrity," and condemning "secret diplomacy" which led America into the Korean War. They also sent expressions of gratitude to Senator Wiley, Governor Kohler, and the 1951 legislature. When a resolution to commend Senator McCarthy was made, Arthur Peterson, a young, first-term state senator, objected, saying that "certain public men have not practiced the public morality and honesty essential to America." The boos and shouts from the crowd became so loud that Peterson couldn't continue his remarks. Several men approached the microphone to demand that he "sit down" and "get out of the Republican party." People threw wadded programs at the speaker. A second such speaker was treated similarly. Walter had left the convention to return to Kohler when these incidents occurred.[56]

The four Democrats who sent the telegram to Kohler about McCarthy proceeded to hold street corner meetings, labeling their effort "Operation Truth." After the GOP convention, they issued a statement criticizing the governor for failing to take a stand against the Senator and defending the two anti-McCarthy speakers who were booed down on the convention floor. "Governor Kohler is certainly aware that political leadership in Wisconsin has always carried with it the duty to repudiate those within one's own group who fight decency in public life. He has now demonstrated that he will not fulfill this duty and furthermore that he will not help those Republicans with the courage to repudiate McCarthy to obtain an open and honest hearing in GOP circles."[57]

Walter did not remain silent in the face of this attack, and he soon called the action of the Republicans who booed down the two anti-McCarthy delegates "disgraceful." He added, "Had I been present, I would have taken the floor to insist upon the rights of properly accredited delegates to present their views fully and without interruption. Freedom of speech is a fundamental part of the American system and should be preserved at all costs. The Republican party of Wisconsin should be most zealous in asserting the rights of all citizens to declare their views." He did not choose to respond directly to the Democrats, labeling their challenge "an obvious bid for publicity."[58]

Some top GOP officials in the state did not appreciate Kohler's remarks. State Chairman Wayne Hood, who was close to Tom Coleman, said, "I thought the governor used a poor choice of words," and contended that delegates were reacting to one speaker only because he had gone over his allotted five minutes. Lloyd Tegge, Waukesha state Young Republican chairman, was more frank, saying, "Sure, I booed and I thought it was the right thing." He added, "We are just as enthusiastic for McCarthy as they are against him and we have a right to show our contempt the same as they show theirs."[59]

Under fire from both Left and Right, Walter wrote a 700 word letter to his four Democratic detractors, released to the press. While not embracing McCarthy, he said again that the Tydings Committee had not given the Senator's charges an impartial hearing, adding, "It is certain that Senator McCarthy's activities pleased neither the Communists nor certain Democratic leaders." That came fairly close to linking the two, and Democrats could make the case, as they promptly did, that the governor was now guilty of engaging in McCarthyism. Kohler continued, "Like Senator McCarthy and like all loyal American citizens, I am emphatically opposed to the infiltration of Communists into our government, as I am unequivocally opposed to communism anywhere. However, the infiltration of Communists into the federal government is not the only major problem of federal personnel. I am equally opposed to government by crony and to government by mediocrity, both of which characterize the present Democratic national administration."[60]

The four Democrats called the letter a "bitter partisan attack" and urged voters to think of their party as the only effective vehicle for opposing McCarthyism. The governor, they charged, had succumbed to the pro-McCarthy forces within the GOP. Kohler was well aware, they asserted, "that McCarthy's cowardly use of his senatorial immunity to revile patriots like General Marshall has offended millions of Americans who are neither Communists nor Democrats, including Republican Senators Margaret Chase Smith, Wayne Morse, Irving Ives, and Charles Tobey, and independent newspapers like *The Milwaukee Journal*, the *Madison Capital Times*, the *New York Times*, the *Washington Post* and the *St. Louis Post-Dispatch*."[61] This was a reference to a firestorm of criticism by Democrats and a few liberal Republicans, mounting all across the nation, against the increasingly irresponsible allegations by McCarthy.

In an editorial titled "Kohler Fails in a Test," the normally friendly *Milwaukee Journal* called the governor's letter "a dissembling diatribe," echoing some of McCarthy's attacks and rhetoric and bestowing "fainthearted approval" of McCarthyism. In addition, the editorial provided one of the best definitions of McCarthyism ever written: "It is the technique of the big lie. It is the use of half truths and untruths for personal and political advantage. It is character assassination. It is the cynical use of the technique of 'guilt by association' to arouse suspicion against worthy men. It is treacherous, vile and appalling opportunism."[62]

The fact of the matter remained, however, that the GOP hierarchy was standing by the Wisconsin Senator, expecting him to lead them to victory in the next presidential race. Moreover, Republicans in Wisconsin were almost solidly in favor of their native son. While Kohler's friends continued to assure insiders like journalist John Wyngaard that the governor despised McCarthy and all that he stood for, Kohler himself was required, if he was to have a political future, to follow the party line as closely as he dared. Moreover, he was completely sincere in his opposition to Communism, his disgust with the Truman Administration, and in his strong desire for a GOP victory in 1952.

If Kohler's letter antagonized many on the Left, few on the Right expressed any opinion at all, perhaps reflecting the realization that the document said nothing directly for or against McCarthy. A wire of support from the chairman of the Milwaukee County GOP statutory committee was the sole exception.[63] The question remained: Was anything resembling a middle ground possible in the Republican Party in the early 1950s? It was conceivable in Oregon, where maverick Senator Wayne Morse could express his anti-McCarthy views freely and without political danger, and in Maine, where Margaret Chase Smith held a secure Senate seat. But what about Wisconsin?

In late July, a group of Wisconsin Republicans announced an Eisenhower for president drive. The spokesman demanded anonymity when talking to a reporter. The group's members were largely liberal and anti-Coleman, including people who backed Thomas E. Dewey in 1944 and some who supported Harold Stassen four years later. They had been working with similar Eisenhower groups in Kansas and Nebraska. The major hurdle for the Wisconsinites was a new state law requiring "consent" by a candidate before his name could appear in the primary presidential ballot. Eisenhower was not a declared candidate. When asked if he would appear on the ballot as a "favorite son" pledged to Eisenhower,

Governor Kohler declined. Walter had taken no public position on the presidential race except to rule himself out of the running.[64]

It now seems clear, however, that behind the scenes Walter was engaged in private conversations about an Eisenhower candidacy. The press learned about one such dialogue when Harold Stassen visited Windway. Stassen expressed his support for Eisenhower and hinted that he might head a slate in Wisconsin to boost the general's candidacy. Governor Kohler seemed very supportive, Stassen told reporters.[65] In late August, two prominent Republicans, State Senators Warren Knowles and Melvin R. Laird, said they would probably back Kohler if he ran as a "favorite son."[66]

At about this time, Tom Coleman came to the Executive Residence and had a private conversation with the governor about the 1952 presidential race. Coleman was supporting Taft and wanted to know if Kohler would join him. Walter said that he had reservations about the Ohio Senator, especially in the field of foreign relations, and would prefer to support Eisenhower. It was the beginning of a serious breach between Coleman and Kohler, as Walter later admitted.[67]

On September 2, Walter and Charlotte departed for Europe for a three week vacation. They planned to visit Geneva, Vienna, Berlin, Paris, London, Madrid, and Lisbon. It was the first vacation the Kohlers had enjoyed since the election, and Walter had not been to Europe in 20 years. While there, he would view developments in America's economic and military aid programs. What he did not tell reporters was that he had an appointment with General Eisenhower. His visit would be personal and unofficial, but it had the potential of being of major importance, perhaps revealing Ike's political intentions.

During a two-day visit to Rome, the governor told reporters that the Korean war, European reconstruction, and the North Atlantic Treaty Organization were "the three most important things going on in the world." The American taxpayer, he said, would be staggered to learn the cost of rearmament, but he "is fully aware of the importance of facing up to Russia." Charlotte remarked that she and her husband "have been moving so fast I haven't had time for window shopping."[68]

The couple made a brief trip through the Russian sector of Berlin, Walter being impressed, he said later, by the "somber" expressions on the face of East Germans who faced scarcity in the shops and an abundance of political advertising. He later wrote, "In Berlin the quantity and quality of the destruction is indescribable. Six years after the war there are places where nothing but hollow walls and rubble can be seen in any direction. It is an appalling and depressing sight." Within the city's four sectors, "the last six years have seen an endless sequence of both major and minor maneuvers by the Russians, all calculated to embarrass, discourage, exasperate and in fact strangle and destroy the American, French and British occupations. Only one effective counter-weapon exists—and that is prompt and severe retaliation."[69]

At Marly-le-Roi, near Versailles, Walter had about a half hour private conversation with General Eisenhower, Supreme Allied Commander in Europe. The discussion was extremely amicable, and each man was impressed by the other. There was no doubt some conversation about Soviet intentions and American defenses, but Walter had come to talk primarily about the presidential race. He wanted to know if Ike would run. Eisenhower said that he would become a candidate if NATO were jeopardized and he alone could save it. This statement, revealed by Walter upon returning home, won the attention of moderate and liberal Republicans all across America.[70] In Wisconsin there was re-newed interest in running Governor Kohler as a "favorite son" pledged to Eisenhower. Wilbur Renk of Sun Prairie, a Stassen supporter in 1948 and a close friend of Kohler's, said that such a campaign would start immediately if the governor "gave the word."[71]

The Eisenhower visit obviously invigorated Walter, giving him hope that an immensely respected, charismatic, and moderate leader might be heading the GOP ticket in 1952 instead of McCarthyite Senator Taft, favored by Tom Coleman and his influential friends. Walter soon admitted encouraging the general to run and was convinced that Eisenhower "will do it if he feels it his duty."[72]

The governor's new confidence was such that he told reporters he had never stated he would refuse to run against Joe McCarthy. The possibility of a Kohler-McCarthy battle produced huge headlines in state newspapers and attracted attention throughout the country. The Senator said simply, "Walter's been a good governor and would be a good senator, but I hope he doesn't run."[73]

One can well imagine McCarthy aides scurrying to find evidence of Kohler ties with known Communists or Red dupes. All who threatened or criticized McCarthy were treated in this way, and if the danger became serious the information collected, no matter how flimsy, would be con-tained in the Senator's speeches or leaked to sympathetic reporters. At times, McCarthy would tell a critic that he could expect to be exposed for what he truly was. And then he would laugh, slap the victim on the back, and invite him to have a drink. Joe was just that way, friendly as a puppy one minute and as dangerous as a wounded bull the next.

Letters poured into the governor's office in Madison, and by a three-to-one margin they favored a Kohler challenge to McCarthy. A poll of 641 state farmers showed Kohler ahead of the incumbent in the race for the GOP nomination by a small margin. Walter said he would make his decision in January. One of his considerations, he cautioned, would be his business in Sheboygan, noting that it would be more difficult to keep on top of it if he were in Washington. Walter took the occasion to say that while America's Far Eastern policy was once wrong, leading to the fall of China, it was now on the right track. "If you didn't fight in Korea, you'd be fighting in Indo-China or Malaya." That was in sharp contrast to the campaign rhetoric coming from semi-isolationists and conspiracy theorists on the far Right. A reporter observed, "The governor was in good spirits and appeared fit and rested."[74] He was soon off to a Governors' conference in Gatlinburg, Tennessee.

In early October, John Bennett of Washington, D.C., was in Milwaukee and conferred with Kohler. Bennett was touring the country testing Eisenhower sentiment, and was working with Pennsylvania Senator James Duff, a top planner of the Eisenhower backers. At the same time, Tom Coleman and 13 other major Wisconsin Republicans were urging Robert Taft to enter the state's 1952 presidential primary. The governor tactfully encouraged Taft to enter the race, but it was no secret that Kohler and his party's leadership in the state were on a collision course.[75]

On October 11, the press learned that MacArthur had declared himself out of the race and was urging his supporters to back Taft. A few days later, Taft formally declared his candidacy, the first Republican to do so, and announced that Tom Coleman was to be one of his three top advisers. Taft soon said that when he entered the Wisconsin primary, he would welcome support from Senator McCarthy.[76]

Walter bowed out as a "favorite son" candidate. But it was widely known that Harold Stassen was likely to run in the Wisconsin primary as an Eisenhower backer. He formally announced this intention on October 27. The Eisenhower candidacy was gaining steam; New York Governor Thomas E. Dewey and Senator Wayne Morse both gave their support. When the general would make his candidacy public was anyone's guess, and some thought it wouldn't happen at all. But backers such as Morse were confident that the announcement would be forthcoming at an appropriate time.[77]

Surely Walter's telephone was much in use during this period, as a great many moderate and liberal Republicans were eager to know about Eisenhower's intentions. Revealing his fear of a victory by the far Right, Walter told a conference of newspaper editors that during his European travels he became convinced that Europeans favored a continuation of the Democratic administration. "I think they are afraid that our foreign policy might change and abandon them."[78]

But that approach could be pursued only so far, as the reality of the present required the governor to remain in the good graces of his party's pro-McCarthy leadership. When appearing on a "Town Meeting of the Air" radio broadcast with liberal Senator Paul Douglas of Illinois and liberal historian Arthur Schlesinger, Jr., Walter was pressed to give his views on Senator McCarthy's charges. After trying unsuccessfully to evade the issue, he said, "I'm not in position to know if the charges are justified. Only the FBI knows that. As for whether the charges were properly presented, I would say they were presented properly if they are correct, but I can't know that." When pressed further, the governor said, "There is a man named Finnegan [James Finnegan, St. Louis collector of internal revenue who had been discharged and indicted] who says the president urged him not to resign. Attorney General McGrath is under some suspicion from a federal judge for his actions on tax matters. I don't know what happens in the Democratic administration. It would take a bold man to say that McCarthy is in every respect wrong. I just don't know." This mixture of allegations about Truman Administration corruption and charges by McCarthy of treason in high places, spoken off the cuff, was somewhat embarrassing. Top Wisconsin Democrat James E. Doyle said of the governor that he "never had the courage to utter one single syllable of criticism of McCarthyism where all can hear." But Walter was walking a tightrope and was perfectly aware how extremely dangerous it was to fall off.[79]

During the fall of 1951, Joe McCarthy was running into trouble. Enemy reporters were digging deeply into his past, and Senator William Benton was attempting to have him expelled from the Senate on grounds that ranged from "perjury, fraud and deceit" to accepting "influence money." A Senate subcommittee had condemned McCarthy's "despicable, back street" campaign in Maryland against Senator Tydings. *Time* magazine ran the Senator's photograph on its cover over the caption "Demagogue

McCarthy," noting that he had failed to produce a single name of a State Department Communist since charging at Wheeling that there were 205. (Joe's response was to charge that there were some 400 active Communist Party members holding positions in the American media, and he condemned *Time* magazines "degenerate lying." As for Benton, he was acting "as the megaphone for the Communist party-line type of smear attack on me.") Even Senator Taft criticized McCarthy's "extreme attack" on General George C. Marshall."[80]

But most Republicans were still backing the Fighting Marine, and in Wisconsin he was as popular as ever. Harold Stassen, in a Wisconsin press conference, expressed a "high regard" for McCarthy and defended his attack on liberal Philip C. Jessup's appointment as a delegate to the United Nations general assembly.[81] Stassen, who may well have been angling for his own candidacy as well as Eisenhower's, was also on the tightrope.

In late November, *Collier's* magazine published a major article on Kohler entitled "Is This The Man to Defeat McCarthy?" The author, Alfred Steinberg, provided the nation with a flattering and revealing biographical sketch of the Wisconsin governor, probing especially his views on politics and McCarthy. An aide, no doubt Phil Drotning, was quoted as saying that "at one time Kohler believed McCarthy would prove to be either a great American or one of the worst scoundrels in national politics. But he refused to pass judgment on McCarthy before the senator's sensational charges—against many government officials, both big and little, regarding their alleged Communist sympathies or connections—were examined. Today, I'd say the governor doesn't think that McCarthy is a great American." Walter himself, however, was not so blunt. Steinberg wrote that "his mind keeps mulling over McCarthyism."[82]

When Robert Fleming of the *Milwaukee Journal* soon pressed him about running for the Senate, Walter said "I honestly don't know."[83] During a business-vacation trip to Los Angeles with Charlotte in late November, he said he had not made up his mind.[84] The *Eau Claire Leader* declared editorially, "State Republican leaders are horrified" by a possible Kohler-McCarthy contest "as they visualize a party split right down the middle like few parties have been split."[85]

When a large testimonial dinner for McCarthy was held in Milwaukee, bringing the Senator to tears, Walter was conspicuously absent. He was attending an Indian affairs conference in Helena, Montana, but it was generally believed at the dinner, said a knowledgeable reporter, that he was avoiding the event.[86] Oshkosh attorney and former congressman Frank B. Keefe, who served as toastmaster at the dinner, said that he was considering running for governor if Kohler ran against McCarthy.[87] The pro-McCarthy Young Republicans of Wisconsin started a letter-writing campaign to urge Kohler not to run for the Senate.[88]

In December, former Milwaukee mayor Daniel W. Hoan and his wife, a Democratic Party official, visited President Truman, telling him that only a Democrat could beat McCarthy. "The machine is supporting McCarthy," said Mrs. Hoan, "and Kohler won't buck the machine." Her husband added, "He hasn't got the guts."[89]

After visiting General Eisenhower in Paris, Harold Stassen returned home and announced his own candidacy for the presidency. He would not divulge what Eisenhower told him about his own plans, but the clear implication was that the General had chosen not to run. Senators Duff and Henry Cabot Lodge of Massachusetts, both leading Ike backers, said that Stassen's decision would not effect the Eisenhower candidacy. Kohler apparently had no idea what Eisenhower planned to do, and so he said publicly that he had made no commitment on the presidential race and had no present plans to take a public position.[90]

If Walter chose to run against McCarthy and Eisenhower stayed out of the presidential race, he would surely be committing political suicide, for he knew that only with a popular moderate heading the national ticket, drawing votes from the far Right and lending credibility to those opposing McCarthy, did he have a chance to win the senate seat. Ike might be the perfect candidate, but the last time the five star general discussed the matter, he said publicly that he had no political aspirations; he refused even to say which political party he favored.[91] Walter also knew that the longer he stayed silent about his Senate intentions, the more animosity he caused among state Republicans, especially the McCarthyites. At year's end, the GOP, in Wisconsin and elsewhere, was confused and divided.

The situation changed suddenly and dramatically on Monday, January 7, 1952 when Dwight David Eisenhower, still in France, publicly declared himself a Republican and said that he would accept the GOP nomination if it were offered. But he said also that he would remain in the army and would not actively campaign for the presidency until nominated. The statement was prompted by an announcement by Senator Henry Cabot Lodge, national chairman of the Eisenhower for president movement, that he would enter Eisenhower's name in the March 11 New Hampshire primary, the nation's first.

Many Republicans cheered the long-awaited news. Democrats, who had tried to woo Eisenhower since 1948, were reportedly dejected. The *New York Times* and *Chicago Sun Times* quickly endorsed Eisenhower. The *New York Herald Tribune* and *Life* magazine had already expressed strong support for the World War II leader.[92]

Over the weekend, reporters learned, Eisenhower campaign leaders had asked Walter to run as a favorite son in Wisconsin. If Ike was to enter the state primary on April, 1, they said, he needed to mount the strongest campaign possible, and that pointed to Kohler.[93]

Notes

[1] "State Officers Inaugurated at Capitol Rites," *Milwaukee Journal*, January 2, 1951.

[2] "Gov. Kohler's Speech," *ibid.*

[3] Steinberg, "Is This the Man to Beat McCarthy?," 78.

[4] "Batch of Bills Waits for Start of Legislature," *ibid.*, January 7, 1951.

[5] Editorial, "Governor's Excellent Message," *ibid*, January 11, 1951.

[6] See copy Earl Sachse to William B. Alexander, August 12, 1954, and copy Walter J. Kohler to W. B. Alexander, August 17, 1954, Box 84, Walter J. Kohler, Jr. papers.

[7] "Marshaling of Strength Urged by Gov. Kohler," *Milwaukee Journal*, January 11, 1951. See the editorial "Kohler Faces Reapportionment Issue as Whole State Should," *ibid.*, January 23, 1951.

[8] Copy, Cyrus Philipp to Harvey V. Higley, January 19, 1951, Cyrus Philipp papers.

[9] See *www.doa.state.wi.us/pagesubtext_detail.asp?linksubcatid=328&linkcatid =18&linkcid*. As incredible as it now sounds, the state provided no security forces or systems for either the Executive Residence or Windway. Walter drove himself to and from Madison, and was easily recognizable because of the single digit "1" on the license plate of his black Cadillac. On occasion, state troopers drove him to specific events. E-mail, Terry Kohler to the author, May 16, 2005, Windway file.

[10] "Kohlers Start Moving Task," *Milwaukee Journal*, November 25, 1956.

[11] Terry Kohler interview, June 12, 2003.

[12] *Ibid.*; Erna Schwartz interview;

[13] Editorial, "Good Governor's Role Difficult," *Milwaukee Journal*, October 23, 1951.

[14] Carley, "Legal and Extra-Legal Powers of Wisconsin Governors in Legislative Relations—Part II," 308-314.

[15] Walter J. Kohler, Jr., "The Governor's office," *Wisconsin Magazine of History*, 35 (Summer, 1952), 243-246, 311-312; Carley, "Legal and Extra-Legal Powers of Wisconsin Governors in Legislative Relations—Part I," 16-19.

[16] Editorial, "Excellent Appointment Practices," *Milwaukee Journal*, February 26, 1951.

[17] John Wygaard column in the Janesville Daily Gazette, March 5, 1951. Wyngaard's columns were syndicated throughout the state. 24. Wyngaard was a personal friend of Walter's and served as a member of what Melvin Laird later called the governor's "brains trust." This informal group consisted of Laird, Phil Drotning, University of Wisconsin Political Science professor Bill Young, Carl Zielke of the Wisconsin Newspaper Association, and Wyngaard. The men met infrequently, sometimes at Laird's cottage in northern Wisconsin, to discuss political issues. Melvin Laird interview.

[18] Smith, "Departure of Drotning Will Leave a Big Void," *ibid.*, November 11, 1956. Early in his administration, Walter named his former Yale roommate, Guido Rahr, to the state conservation committee. "Kohler Appoints Smith and Rahr," *ibid.*, January 12, 1951. Melvin Laird said later that Walter was "highly sensitive" about pleasing people and had a powerful desire to be liked. He chose not to confront legislators directly, giving that assignment to key aides, including Drotning. Drotning was "very important" to the Kohler administrations, Laird recalled, and was unpopular with quite a few legislators. Melvin Laird interview.

[19] Three boxes of Wegner's papers are in the Walter J. Kohler, Jr. papers.

[20] "Kohler Sees Big Savings," *Milwaukee Journal*, January 18, 1951.

[21] "Keep 25% Surtax, Kohler Urges State," *ibid.*, January 31, 1951.

[22] Edwin R. Bayley, "Kohler Wins Praise, Envy," *ibid.*, February 1, 1951.

[23] "Kohler Urges Defense Policy of Self-Reliance," *ibid.*, February 13, 1951.

[24] "Civil Defense Needs Stressed," *ibid.*, March 27, 1951. In April, Kohler and Olson returned to Washington to attend a national civil defense staff college conference, covering all phases of civil defense. "Kohler and Olson to Attend Session," *ibid.*, April 24, 1951.

[25] Laurence C. Eklund, "Big Wisconsin Rejoins Forces on Active Duty," *ibid.*, March 4, 1951.

[26] "Predicts Test for Resources," *ibid.*, March 7, 1951.

[27] "TV Series Set From Capitol," *ibid.*, March 11, 1951; "Surtax Topic of TV Panel," *ibid.*, March 18, 1951.

[28] "'Use Power,' Editors Told," *ibid.*, April 7, 1951.

[29] The photograph of McCarthy, Cyrus L. Philipp, and Kohler is in *ibid*; January 23, 1951. See "Kohler Hails History Center," *ibid.*, January 28, 1951.

[30] "Maier Raps Gov. Kohler," *ibid.*, April 9, 1951.

[31] Reeves, *The Life and Times of Joe McCarthy*, 370-371.

[32] "Gov. Kohler to Ask General to Address Legislature Apr. 27," *Milwaukee Journal*, April 20, 1951.

[33] "Home Town Greets MacArthur," *ibid.*, April 27, 1951.

[34] See Reeves, *The Life and Times of Joe McCarthy*, 372-374.

[35] "4 Year Term for Governor turned Down," *Milwaukee Journal*, April 4, 1951.

[36] "State Officials and Workers to Get Raises," *ibid.*, April 19, 1951; "Kohler to Appoint a Record Number, *ibid.*, April 30, 1951.

[37] "Governor Urges Legislature to Reduce State surtax to 10%," *ibid.*, May 2, 1951.

[38] "'Rebel' Seeks GOP Position," *ibid.*, May 5, 1951.

[39] Editorial, "Kohler's Advice to His Party," *ibid.*, May 15, 1951.

[40] "Kohler Addresses Beloit Graduates," *ibid.*, June 11, 1951.

[41] Reeves, *The Life and Times of Joe McCarthy*, 375.

[42] Robert H. Fleming, "U.S. Foreign Policy 'a Joke', Taft Charges in Speech Here," *Milwaukee Journal*, June 10, 1951.

[43] "Gov. Kohler Got Most of Program He Asked," *ibid.*, June 15, 1951.

[44] Edwin R. Bayley, "Top Legislators in GOP Block Kohler Program," *ibid.*, June 3, 1951.

[45] Willard R. Smith and Edwin R. Bayley, "Legislature Ends '51 Session, Kills 10% Surtax on Incomes," *ibid.*, June 15, 1951.

[46] *Ibid.*; "Spending Up, Taxes Down," *ibid.*, June 15, 1951; "Big Strides by '51 Legislature," *ibid.*, June 17, 1951.

[47] Editorial, "An Outstanding Legislature," *ibid.*, June 17, 1951.

[48] John Wyngaard's column, *Appleton Post-Crescent*, June 22, 1951.

[49] "Take It Easy for 30 Days Kohler Told," *Milwaukee Journal*, June 20, 1951.

[50] John Wyngaard column, *Green Bay Press Gazette*, July 24, 1951; "Bill Is Signed on Districting," *Milwaukee Journal*, August 6, 1951. On his vetoes, see John Wyngaard column, *Green Bay Press Gazette*, July 30, 1951; "Governor Signs Building Plan, Vetoes Seven Bills," *Milwaukee Journal*, July 25, 1951.

[51] Edwin R. Bayley, "GOP Leader Called 'Boss'," *ibid.*, June 22, 1951; Edwin R. Bayley, "Philipp Aided by Gabrielson," *ibid.*, June 28, 1951.

[52] "Prod Kohler on McCarthy," *ibid.*, July 6, 1951. On "the Madison ring," see Edwin R. Bayley, "Madison Runs State Politics," *ibid.*, July 25, 1951.

[53] Edwin R. Bayley, "Kohler Sees GOP Victory in '52 Election," *ibid.*, July 7, 1951.

[54] "Weigh Rivals for McCarthy," *ibid.*, July 8, 1951.

[55] Walter J. Kohler, Jr. Oral History, Columbia University, 1971, 24.

[56] Robert H. Fleming, "State GOP Endorses Ringling for National Committee Post," *Milwaukee Journal*, July 8, 1951.

[57] "Kohler Scored by Democrats," *ibid.*, July 10, 1951.

[58] "Booing at GOP Parley Is Rebuked by Kohler," *ibid.*, July 12, 1951.

[59] "Kohler's Stand Is Not Backed," *ibid.*, July 13, 1951.

[60] Robert H. Fleming, "Kohler Blast at Democrats Is His Reply," *ibid.*, July 19, 1951.

[61] *Ibid.*

[62] Editorial, "Kohler Fails in a Test," *ibid.*, July 22, 1951.

[63] "Kohler Silent on Debate Plea," *ibid.*, July 20, 1951.

[64] Edwin R. Bayley, "GOP Backers of Eisenhower Busy in State," *ibid.*, July 25, 1951. On Kohler's view of the presidential race at this time, see "Weigh Rivals for McCarthy," *ibid.*, July 8, 1951; Robert H. Fleming, "Kohler Talked as 'Native Son'," *ibid.*, August 26, 1951.

[65] Edwin R. Bayley, "Stassen Talks With Kohler," August 1, 1951.

[66] Fleming, "Kohler Talked as 'Native Son'," *ibid.*, August 26, 1951. During this period Laird volunteered to serve as Kohler's part-time executive sec-

retary while Phil Drotning was recovering from surgery. "Laird Volunteers as Aide to Kohler," *ibid.*, August 21, 1951. Walter named Laird's mother to the University of Wisconsin Board of Regents. "Doubts Kohler Senator Race," *ibid.*, October 3, 1951.

[67] Walter J. Kohler, Jr. Oral History, Columbia University, 1971, 2, 7.

[68] "Kohler Lauds Aid Programs," *ibid.*, September 19, 1951.

[69] "Gov. Kohler Might Run Against Joe McCarthy," *ibid.*, September 25, 1951. See Kohler's report on his European trip, written for the *Milwaukee Journal*, in *ibid.*, October 7, 1951. A copy of the manuscript is in box 50, Walter J. Kohler, Jr. papers.

[70] When interviewed years later, Walter said that Eisenhower was "non-committal" about his nomination. Walter J. Kohler, Jr. Oral History, Columbia University, 1971, 3-4.

[71] "Gov. Kohler Lands in U.S.," *ibid.*, September 25, 1951.

[72] Edwin R. Bayley, "Kohler Might Run Against McCarthy," *ibid.*, September 26, 1951.

[73] "'Hope Kohler Doesn't Run,'" *ibid.*, September 27, 1951.

[74] "Letters Advise Kohler to Run," *ibid.*, September 28, 1951. On the farmers' poll, see "Doubts Kohler Senator Race," *ibid.*, October 3, 1951. The numbers were Kohler, 37%; McCarthy, 32%; and undecided, 31%.

[75] Robert H. Fleming, "Taft Reply Friendly to State GOP Bid," *ibid.*, October 5, 1951.

[76] Edwin R. Bayley, "MacArthur Declares Self for Taft, Seems Out of GOP President Race," *ibid.*, October 11, 1951; "Taft Says He Will Run for President Next Year," *ibid.*, October 15, 1951; Robert H. Fleming, "Top GOP Job for Coleman?," *ibid.*, October 17, 1951.

[77] Robert H. Fleming, "Kohler Refuses Favorite Son Role in Presidential Primary," *ibid.*, October 12, 1951; "Taft Says He Will run for President Next Year," *ibid.*, October 16,1951; "Contend Taft Is 'Too Early,'" *ibid.*, October 17, 1951. On Stassen's formal announcement as a candidate in the primary, see Robert H. Fleming, "Three in State Primary Race," *ibid.*, October 28, 1951.

[78] "'Europe Wants Democrats In,'" *ibid.*, October 13, 1951. In fact, Taft made clear from the start his intention, if elected, to continue anti-Communist policies established in Korea and in Western Europe. "Taft Says He Will Run for President Next Year," *ibid.*, October 16, 1951. Joe McCarthy, on the other hand, had recently challenged the funding of European economic aid.

[79] Robert H. Fleming, "Kohler is Coy on McCarthy," *ibid.*, October 24, 1951. On Doyle, see "DOC Demands Kohler's Stand," *ibid.*, November 7, 1951.

80 Laurence C. Eklund, "McCarthy is No. 1 Man in the Headline Ratings," *ibid.*; October 28, 1951; Reeves, *The Life and Times of Joe McCarthy*, 384-385.

81 "See McCarthy in Spring Race," *Milwaukee Journal*, November 6, 1951; Reeves, *The Life and Times of Joe McCarthy*, 388-392.

82 Steinberg, "Is This the Man to Beat McCarthy?," *passim.*

83 Robert H. Fleming, "Kohler to Run for Some Post," *Milwaukee Journal*, November 20, 1951.

84 "GOP Timber Good, Says Gov. Kohler," *Los Angeles Times*, November 28, 1951.

85 Reprinted in the *Milwaukee Journal*, November 30, 1951.

86 Robert H. Fleming, "Tributes Paid to McCarthy," *ibid.*, December 12, 1951.

87 "Keefe Awaits Kohler Word," *ibid.*, December 13, 1951.

88 "Urge Kohler Not Run, Plea," *ibid.*, December 24, 1951.

89 "Vision Defeat of McCarthy," *ibid.*, December 19, 1951.

90 "Stassen Gets Into Race; is Silent on Wisconsin," *ibid.*, December 28, 1951.

91 "Eisenhower Insists That He Still Has No Political Aspirations," *ibid.*, November 3, 1951.

92 Jack Bell and Marvin L. Arrowsmith, "'Ike' Willing to Accept GOP Nomination," *ibid.*, January 7, 1952.

93 "Race in State by 'Ike,' Hint," *ibid.*, January 7, 1952.

Chapter Ten
For Eisenhower & McCarthy

Eisenhower backers began to mobilize quickly in Wisconsin, and they were joined by moderates and liberals who had formerly backed California Governor Earl Warren. At the same time, Taft headquarters were opened in Milwaukee, headed by attorney Thomas W. Korb, a long-time personal friend of Joe McCarthy's. Harold Stassen was already campaigning in Wisconsin. When asked about the possibility of Kohler running as a favorite son, heading a pro-Eisenhower slate of delegates, Stassen said, "I am advised that will not happen."[1] A few days later, Walter reaffirmed his decision, announced in October, not to run as a favorite son. Undaunted, the Eisenhower people said they would go elsewhere to find leadership for their campaign.[2]

Walter's tightrope seemed to be swaying uncontrollably. He wanted to enter the senatorial race, but he was faced with his state party's pro-Taft, pro-McCarthy leadership and McCarthy's strong popularity in public opinion polls.[3] He wanted to support Eisenhower, but there was no certainty that the General would declare his desire for the White House or that the campaign by his supporters would get off the ground; at this point it was certain only that an endorsement would alienate tens of thousands of Wisconsin voters, not to mention Tom Coleman. And then there was Walter's old friend Harold Stassen. Every vote Kohler might receive in the primary would detract from Stassen's total, making Taft's victory that much more certain. Moreover, former governor Phil La Follette and others continued to back the candidacy of liberal Earl Warren.[4]

At the end of January, 1952, Walter stated publicly in a letter that he would not oppose McCarthy and instead would seek re-election as governor. He said that he wanted to follow through on his state legislative program and introduce new measures. (He was currently engaged in a struggle to win congressional approval of legislation to build the St. Lawrence Seaway.) Quoting Thomas Carlyle, he wrote, "Do the duty that lies nearest you." Democrats jeered at the governor's decision, some claiming that he lacked courage and others contending that he secretly favored McCarthy. One Milwaukee reporter asserted that Tom Coleman had been advising the governor for months that he could not beat McCarthy at the polls. Walter emphatically denied ever discussing the matter with Coleman or any other top Republican. It was a fact, however, that units of the Republican Voluntary Committee in three congressional districts had adopted resolutions asking the governor not to run against McCarthy.[5]

In early March, William Proxmire, 36, announced his candidacy for the Democratic nomination for governor. He was running for the state's top position after living in Wisconsin only three years and serving only a single term in the Assembly. He pledged, "I shall campaign in every precinct, ward, village and township in Wisconsin." Proxmire had impressive credentials. He was a graduate of Yale, and had received graduate degrees in business administration and public administration from Harvard. He had served five years in the Army in World War II, completing his service as a First Lieutenant in military intelligence. He had been a newspaper reporter in Madison and now operated a farm implement business in Sun Prairie and Arlington. Since 1950, no one had worked harder to promote his party throughout the state.

In a statement on his candidacy, Proxmire talked about taxes and honesty in government, but he attracted the most attention when he declared, "Finally, the Republican legislature and the Republican governor have identified themselves with this evil thing that is Mc-Carthyism. If Wisconsin is to rid itself of the national disgrace that is Senator McCarthy, it is clearly up to the voting, vigorous Democratic party to do it."[6]

The results of the New Hampshire primary, the nation's first, made headlines all over the world: Eisenhower easily beat Taft. This unexpected victory triggered much Republican interest in the Eisenhower candidacy. Meanwhile, the Democrats seemed equally committed to internal warfare. In New Hampshire, the president was upset by Senator Estes Kefauver of Tennessee, who had became famous for his congressional investigations into organized crime. Truman's defeat was such that it threatened his hold on Democratic party machinery, and he soon took himself out of the race.[7]

In Washington D. C. to testify before a House expenditures subcommittee on federal taxing power, Walter told reporters that he thought the New Hampshire primary would have little impact on Wisconsin and that he would remain neutral before his state's April 1 presidential primary.[8]

During the campaigning that followed, the governor introduced all three major GOP candidates on different occasions in equally glowing terms and denied newspaper allegations that he favored any of them.[9]

Taft's national campaign began to falter after another poor showing in the Minnesota primary and his withdrawal from the New Jersey primary. In Minnesota, 110,000 voters wrote in Eisenhower's name, deeply cutting into Stassen's narrow victory. Wisconsin McCarthyite John Chapple said he was "shocked" by the write-in vote. "I sincerely hope Wisconsin and Nebraska will make a better showing against the pro-Soviet New York bank crowd behind General Eisenhower."[10]

Write-in ballots were illegal in Wisconsin. Eisenhower backers, failing to persuade any Republican to run as a favorite son and unable to put the general's name on the ballot, were encouraged when Earl Warren's supporters said that Ike was their second choice.[11] Then, in late March, Stassen offered to commit half of the delegates he won in Wisconsin to Eisenhower.[12] Political experts had cause to wonder if these were acts of desperation, for all liberal and moderate Republicans knew the strength of the far Right in the state and were well aware that the Taft forces were outspending their opponents by a large margin.[13]

Joe McCarthy was not often in Wisconsin during the first six months of 1952. He traveled a great deal giving speeches and was busy in the Senate, where he routinely confronted critics with a measure of slander and bullying that left many colleagues gasping in disbelief. (Insiders knew that his behavior was due in part to the fact that he was succumbing to alcoholism.) Wisconsinites were not ignorant of the struggles of their junior Senator, however, for the stories of his battles appeared almost daily in the media. And McCarthy came home on occasion to alert and inspire his legions of fans. An audience in Fond du Lac heard him call the nation's leadership "almost completely morally degenerate." President Truman, he declared, was "a puppet on the strings being pulled by the Achesons, Lattimores, and Jessups."[14] While announcing his candidacy for re-election, he told the Wisconsin Young Republican convention in Racine to help him rout out "treason."[15] Reds and their allies were everywhere, said McCarthy in his speeches, focusing their fire especially upon the one man, himself, determined to fight them most effectively.

Wherever the Senator traveled he was greeted with huge, wildly cheering crowds. He was even more popular in New England than in Wisconsin, in part because he spoke more often there than in his home state. McCarthy was known to be very friendly with Joseph P. Kennedy

262   *Distinguished Service: The Life of Walter J. Kohler, Jr.*

and his family. Republican Senator Leverett Saltonstall of Massachusetts was up for reelection in 1954 and did not dare to oppose McCarthy publicly, even though he personally despised him. Massachusetts Senator Henry Cabot Lodge, now an Eisenhower supporter, had defended McCarthy during and after the Tydings Committee hearings. Out of sheer partisanship, he had been unwilling to acknowledge the fact that the probe destroyed Joe's initial claim to have found 205 Reds in the State Department.[16]

In the Wisconsin primary, Taft won 24 of the 30 delegates to the GOP national convention. He placed first in the balloting, receiving about 41% of the Republican vote, followed by Warren, Stassen, and two others. *Milwaukee Journal* reporter Edwin Bayley lauded Tom Coleman and his colleagues for assembling "what probably was the most efficient and best financed political machine ever unlimbered in Wisconsin."[17] Taft also eked out a narrow win in Nebraska, and now jubilantly declared himself the leading candidate for the nomination.[18]

Four days after the Wisconsin primary, Walter publicly declared his support for General Eisenhower. His statement said in part, "I have the highest respect for the abilities of Senator Taft, Governor Warren and Governor Stassen and believe they would lead our nation far more soundly, honestly and constructively than has the present Democrat administration. At the same time I believe that General Eisenhower's demonstrated talent for organization, his impressive record as an administrator, and his experience and proven skill in the most delicate negotiations particularly equip him for the task of the presidency in these difficult times."[19] *Life* magazine listed Kohler as one of ten Republican governors pledged to Eisenhower.[20]

Even though Walter promised to back any GOP convention nominee, his commitment to Ike was risky, for it was a direct break with Coleman and McCarthy. (Walter chose not to serve as honorary state chairman of the Wisconsin Citizens for Eisenhower group, headed by his friend Wilbur Renk, and donated only a couple of hundred dollars to the effort.)[21] And yet there was a strong tide in the country for Eisenhower, as the *Life* magazine article pointed out, listing leading Americans in politics, diplomacy, the media, business, and academia who were declaring for the general. Moreover, in Wisconsin the combined vote for Warren and Stassen exceeded that won by Taft. Republicans knew, of course, that many Democrats and independents, especially in urban areas, had crossed party lines to vote for their liberal and moderate candidates. Kohler had long urged upon the GOP the necessity of appealing to such voters and believed that if given the chance they would back Eisenhower.

State Democratic chairman James E. Doyle, who had earlier said "The governor was AWOL when the Lord passed out backbones," now declared that the governor's statement after the primary election "entitles him to the undisputed championship among pussyfooters of his height and weight." He continued, "Wisconsin Republicans apparently hope to combine Kohler's lack of nerve and McCarthy's lack of scruples into a winning team."[22] Such rhetoric competed with McCarthy's for headlines and was representative of the tone state Democrats set for the upcoming campaign.

Walter soon had a taste of the animosity his declaration for Eisenhower produced among many Republicans. At a luncheon of the Wisconsin Federation of Women Republican Clubs, the governor faced several hostile questions and negative reactions from his audience. When asked why he had endorsed Eisenhower, he said, "That's a fair question. I came out because I repeatedly and constantly was asked where I stood. I have an innate dislike for ducking or dodging questions." He again explained his commitment to Eisenhower, saying at one point, "I think he's a good man. That's fundamentally the question." Kohler assured party members that Eisenhower's positions on a variety of issues would become clear when the general returned to civilian status. In response to a claim that his endorsement was dividing the party, Walter said he hoped that there would be no division in the GOP after the national convention. He exclaimed, "If I made a mistake it was an honest one and not a malicious one. If I have made mistakes it's because I have tried to lean over backward to be honest and forthright. I have made mistakes and I probably will continue to make them as long as I live and breathe." Soon a voice piped up, "Not another one like that!"[23]

Walter invited further trouble by telling his audience that he had not yet made up his mind on whether to support or oppose the advisory referendum on constitutional reapportionment. While he had long called for redistricting, he learned during the legislative session how fiercely many rural Republicans opposed the attempt to reduce their political authority. Wayne Hood, chairman of the Republican Voluntary Committee, came out against the referendum, arguing that the state should be represented on an area as well as population basis. The State Federation of Republican Women's Clubs voted not to support the referendum, one delegate receiving applause by saying that redistricting helped Democrats, who lived in big cities. So while Walter was hammered for making a decision on Ike, he was also attacked for avoiding a decision on the referendum. The usually friendly *Milwaukee Journal* blasted the governor on reapportionment, saying he had "strengthened his bid for the pussyfooting championship."[24]

Three weeks later, the governor came out unequivocally for the referendum, admitting that he should have reaffirmed his position on the issue earlier. "I went far beyond it to discuss area population versus population only representation. When I told the Republican women I had not made up my mind, I was referring to my position on a specific constitutional amendment to consider area."[25] In any case, Walter was again at odds with his party leadership on a major issue. Wayne Hood was stumping the state, urging GOP opposition to the referendum. In Milwaukee, two groups of delegates to the state convention backed the referendum, and one group booed Hood when he spoke. There was much turmoil during the meetings, and Lieutenant Governor George Smith said that he noted disunity in the party "with regret." Kohler spoke to both groups, urging Republicans to come together in the fight to end "20 years of Democratic misrule."[26] Eight other GOP caucuses, however, supported Hood and opposed the referendum.[27]

In early June, prior to the GOP state convention, the governor appeared before the platform committee, urging members to avoid a recommendation on reapportionment that would provoke party disunity. He and a Milwaukee Republican advocated a position that would recognize "persuasive arguments" for area representation and leave the outcome to the voters. Walter was trying to smooth over differences rather than alter his position, no doubt confident that in the end voters would implement the constitutional rule of equal votes for all citizens.[28] The proposed platform plank that emerged was worded so that it took no specific stand. Phil Drotning and two others, each representing opposite sides of the issue, wrote the plank.

State party chairman Hood was not mollified. He soon claimed that the proposed platform plank called on the party to reject the referendum. When Kohler disagreed publicly, Hood told reporters that the governor might not be nominated for reelection if he entered the convention struggle over reapportionment.[29] It was a threat to be taken seriously.

Kohler further alienated fellow Republicans by signing a public statement, endorsed by eight other pro-Eisenhower governors, criticizing tactics employed by Taft backers in the South.[30] In sharp contrast, on June 11, Tom Coleman became Senator Taft's floor manager for the GOP national convention. He said confidently that his candidate might win the presidential nomination on the first ballot. Victor A. Johnson, former executive secretary of the Wisconsin Republican party, was named Taft's national campaign director.[31]

United States Senator Richard Nixon was the keynote speaker at the Republican Voluntary Committee convention in Milwaukee. He pleaded for party unity and urged Republican candidates to use the Reds in government issue as the major weapon in their campaigns. The young Californian, his shrewdness laced with zeal and apparent earnestness, impressed everyone as a rising star in the party. Senator McCarthy made a dramatic appearance, warning the some 3,000 delegates that the *Milwaukee Journal* distorted the news (it was publishing accurate and highly damaging information on McCarthy's past), lashing out at corruption in the Truman Administration, and telling Republicans of their duty to see that people understood the "tragic blunders" and "high treason" in the nation's foreign policy. Other speakers followed the same theme. McCarthyite Congressman Charles J. Kersten said that bitterness and disagreement similar to that present in the GOP was keeping anti-Communist elements in Russia from "throwing out the Stalin regime." The strongest applause was awarded to McCarthyite Congressman Alvin J. O'Konski, who shouted demands that Republicans "drive the Reds out of America.... This is a holy crusade. This is a day of judgment."[32]

Senator Warren Knowles introduced the governor, saying "he has become to the citizens of Wisconsin the very symbol of honesty, character and integrity in public office."[33] Kohler's speech stood in sharp contrast to some of its competitors, being subdued and reasoned. The governor listed and praised the accomplishments of the recent session of the legislature and said that his party deserved the credit. On reapportionment, he expressed his personal position but supported the compromise plank and did not advocate a party position on the referendum. He was the only speaker at the convention to raise the issue. (The *Milwaukee Journal* soon editorialized, "Support of such a plank is Kohler's burnt sacrifice to the golden calf of 'harmony.'") Walter ended his talk with a plea for unity.[34]

Delegates accepted the proposed plank on reapportionment by voice vote. Wayne Hood then declared that it permitted Republicans to spend money opposing the referendum, and opponents of reapportionment began buttonholing delegates on behalf of their cause. The convention's resolutions included one that lauded Senator McCarthy, stating that despite "unmerciful abuse, he has had faith in his convictions and has put his country ahead of himself in continuing to bring public attention to all subversive elements in government." Only a few "noes" were heard. Another resolution, backed by Taft forces, criticized Senator Wiley for supporting a bipartisan foreign policy and making remarks praising Secretary of State Dean Acheson. Wiley did not appear at the convention.

Delegates swiftly re-nominated both McCarthy and Kohler. Walter used his acceptance speech to pledge support for "the Republican ticket, the Republican platform and the Republican candidate for president." McCarthy was particularly popular with convention goers. An estimated 2,000 people filed in and out of a room in which he was signing copies of his 50 cent paperback *The Story of Gen. George Marshall*; at one point, the wait in line to meet the Senator stretched to 45 minutes.[35]

Former Governor Fred R. Zimmerman, Secretary of State for 18 years and consistently the top-voter getter in the state, was denied renomination. Voluntary Committee officials stated that the 71-year-old Republican was guilty of "party irregularity." Zimmerman soon told supporters that he was rejected because of his opposition to McCarthy and Taft. He vowed to run anyway.[36]

After the convention, William Proxmire challenged Kohler to "tell the people of Wisconsin why he is supporting Senator McCarthy." He vowed to repeat the question every day until the governor answered. Noting that Kohler had never publicly criticized the Senator, the Democratic gubernatorial candidate declared, "Whether Kohler supports McCarthy because he is afraid to stand up to him, whether Kohler thinks McCarthy can help Kohler win re-election as governor, or whether Kohler genuinely believes in McCarthyism, the facts are overwhelmingly clear. Kohler is serving McCarthy exceedingly well."[37] James Doyle soon chimed in, "One hardly knows whether it would now be smarter for McCarthy to repudiate Kohler or vice versa. But they are stuck with one another this year in fond embrace—McCarthy, the uncompromising wretch, and Kohler, the wretched compromiser."[38]

This sort of personal and partisan challenge to his integrity and courage must have deeply angered Walter. But he was determined to see Democrats swept from office, and knew that only a united GOP could do it. That meant that all Republicans, from the Left, Center, and Right, had to be recruited to defeat a Democratic party that he believed was plagued with corruption and guilty of inflating federal authority and bungling the Cold War.

But what if Taft, not Eisenhower, won the GOP nomination? On June 18, the Ohio Senator praised Joe McCarthy during an appearance at the National Press Club in Washington. "Senator McCarthy dramatized a fight that was started by the House un-American investigating committee," Taft said. "He accomplished a successful public service. The word McCarthyism, like isolationism, is a smear word."[39] Walter still thought Taft preferable to any likely Truman successor. The three time presidential candidate was brilliant, honest, and conservative, and he could boast of having initiated and supported a long list of important laws. But how could Taft win? A study showed that 41% of American voters were Democrats, 32% were Republicans, and 27% were independents. To win the White House, the GOP would have to attract some four million more votes than it had ever totaled. Those votes would have to come from independents and Democrats, and it was clear to Kohler that Eisenhower, not Taft, could win them. Walter believed strongly that Eisenhower would win the GOP nomination and the election, and he intended to do whatever he could to help assure those victories.[40]

In late June, Walter traveled to Houston, Texas for the annual governors' conference. At a joint news conference with Republican Governor Alfred E. Driscoll of New Jersey, he said, "I don't think any Republican is going to have an easy chance to get elected president this year." Governor Driscoll agreed, declaring "Fighting an entrenched machine, which has patronage and the power of the federal pay roll, we Republicans will have to work." When the subject of McCarthyism came up, Walter said that he backed the decision of the Republican convention to support the Senator's reelection. "You can't write McCarthy off. You can like him or dislike him but the fact remains that all of the things he has said about the Communists in government stack up to the point where there is too much smoke to repudiate McCarthy." Walter endorsed Senator Wiley's view that foreign policy should be bipartisan, but he chose not to comment on the Senator's remarks critical of McCarthy.[41]

Kohler was bowing to reality: there could be no Republican victory in November without the far Right. To attack McCarthy was to embrace the Democrats, who were crying for the Senator's scalp in virtually every speech. And because of McCarthy's popularity in the party, opposition was futile. Merrill, Wisconsin attorney Leonard F. Schmitt declared his candidacy for the GOP senatorial nomination, condemning McCarthy and saying that he was in "a fight to retire from high public office the most dangerous and irresponsible demagogue to despoil the political scene in many years.[42] No one gave Schmitt the slightest chance of success.

No matter how important McCarthy was to the GOP and to victory in November, Walter must have privately regretted having to support a man he neither liked nor respected. The charge that he was placing party above principle no doubt stung. Walter was not, like some of the professional politicians in both parties, a cynical person. The four sons of Walter Kohler, Sr., while sophisticated, worldly, and ambitious, were never cynics or misanthropes; indeed, as we have seen, they were trained from youth to be exactly the opposite. It seems clear that at this early stage in the campaign the governor rationalized his conduct on the ground that Republican victory was a higher goal than the condemnation of a single Senator, no matter how demagogic his conduct. It was a matter of accepting reality rather than abandoning moral principle.

Walter could find some solace in the fact that liberal and moderate Republicans all over the country were wrestling with the same problem of how to win in November while holding hands with the devil. Eisenhower himself, if he was to win the GOP nomination, would have to find a way to embrace or at least tolerate McCarthy. To attack him meant certain defeat.

In a news conference on June 5 at Abilene, Kansas, Eisenhower was asked directly if he favored McCarthy's reelection. He declined to "indulge in any kind of personalities," but added, "No one could be more determined than I am that any kind of communistic, subversive influence be uprooted from responsible places in our government, make no mistake about that. On the other hand, I believe that can be done...without besmirching the reputation of any innocent man."[43] That was to be Ike's solution to the McCarthy problem: Be strong against internal subversion but carry on the fight responsibly. It implied criticism of McCarthy, but the impact of the criticism could be minimized by refusing to condemn McCarthy directly and by accepting a basic tenet of McCarthy's crusade, that the Truman Administration had been insufficiently attentive to the question of Reds and their sympathizers in government. It was an approach designed to appeal to all Republicans and a great many Democrats.

Millions of Americans, in both parties, believed that the federal government continued to harbor people working against the best interests
of the nation. The media had been featuring spy stories, often daily, for
the past five years. Such names as Hiss, Judith Coplon, Klaus Fuchs,
Bentley, Louis and Elizabeth Budenz, Julius and Ethel Rosenberg,
John Carter Vincent, John Stewart Service, and Owen Lattimore were
familiar throughout the country. Congressional and state investigating
committees were in constant pursuit of people they labeled Reds and
Red sympathizers. FBI Director J. Edgar Hoover warned Americans
repeatedly about the dangers of internal subversion. Several movies,
following a much-publicized investigation of communist subversion
in Hollywood, featured the struggle of courageous patriots against
Soviet spies.

The Truman Administration, aggressively anti-Communist at home
and abroad, had launched a tough loyalty-security program that drove
hundreds from government service. In late April, 1951, the President,
no doubt to deflect the accusations of critics who continued to call him
"soft" on the Reds, signed an executive order strengthening the loyalty
program. By March 1952, 2,756 of the 9,300 employees who had been
cleared under the old standard were again under investigation.[44] But
Republicans were unconvinced that liberals could be trusted to root
out all of the subversives; after all, they had hired and promoted them
in the first place, and had howled about a "witch hunt" every time an
investigating committee named a suspect.

How was one to explain the fall of China to the Reds, the rapid
Soviet possession of nuclear technology, and the seemingly endless
Korean War? For a variety of reasons, McCarthy and his many allies
in Congress, state government, and in the media had a simple explanation: the enemy within. Millions of Americans, the sophisticated and
the gullible, sincerely believed the charge. As Walter put it, with all that
smoke there had to be fire. The Second Red Scare was in full flame in
1952. It was a movement largely of Republicans, and in many ways, like
politics in general, it was ugly.

On June 30, the GOP announced that its keynote convention speaker
would be General Douglas MacArthur. And Senator McCarthy was to
be one of its principal speakers. Several others on the far Right were also
scheduled to speak, including Senator Styles Bridges, Senator James P.
Kem, former Secretary of War Patrick J. Hurley, Representative Walter
H. Judd, Senator Harry P. Cain, and former President Hoover, a critic

of Truman anti-subversive efforts. Taft and Coleman had done their work well.[45]

Five days before the GOP convention opened in Chicago, a "fair play" manifesto supported by 23 of 25 Republican governors meeting at a conference in Houston called on the party not to permit disputed, pro-Taft delegates from five southern states to vote on whether they or the competing Eisenhower delegates should be seated. (Two Republican governors not in attendance later added their endorsement after the document became public.) Kohler was among those who agreed. The document began, "We, as Republican governors believe that our party this year has the opportunity to provide the American people with a national administration based upon the noblest concepts of public service, honor, integrity, justice and equality." The mostly pro-Eisenhower governors wanted the GOP presidential nominee to enter the campaign "with clean hands." Both Taft and Coleman fumed, for they needed the votes of the disputed delegates to insure a swift victory. *New York Times* reporter William S. White called the manifesto "a profound and possibly mortal blow" to Taft's candidacy.[46]

In Denver, General Eisenhower quickly declared his intention to come to the Republican convention in person and oppose the seating of the pro-Taft delegates.[47] A full-scale battle was promised when GOP National Chairman Guy Gabrielsen rejected the governors' manifesto and sided with Taft.[48] In Ohio, on his way to Chicago, Ike told a cheering crowd, "If anybody overrides the surge for clean politics, they are going to have to put up a fight. As we go on into Chicago, in a way I find it another D-day." Taft said bitterly that "the New Deal faction of the Republican party and the Democratic press, show their fear of the election of anyone who really represents the majority of the Republican party."[49]

The GOP platform, especially in the vital area of foreign affairs, sounded a bit more like Eisenhower than Taft. (Its main architect was Ike supporter John Foster Dulles, and Eisenhower personally approved the tentative draft of the foreign policy plank.) While the far Right could cheer the document's charge that the Truman administration had contributed to Soviet expansion by squandering the nation's power and prestige, and agree fully with the allegation that the administration was responsible for the Korean war, the platform also accepted the treaty commitments signed by Truman and Roosevelt, promised continued support of the United Nations and NATO, and vowed to continue assistance to allies throughout the globe. There was to be no repudiation of the Yalta accords and no retreat into "fortress America," two common themes of the Taft-McCarthy wing of the party.

The platform's most controversial pledge laid great stress on the importance of giving hope and encouragement to the "captive peoples" now under the domination of the Kremlin. This implied, especially to ethnic voters in America's large cities, that the United States would take action of some sort to liberate all or portions of Soviet-held Eastern Europe. It was not widely known at the time that this vague and ultimately meaningless proposal came from Congressman Charles Kersten of Milwaukee, and was undoubtedly a concession made by Ike to appease McCarthyites.[50] Eisenhower knew as well as Kohler that only a united party could defeat the Democrats.

Governor Kohler and former governors Rennebohm and La Follette came to the convention on their own, not being members of the Wisconsin delegation. All three immediately became engaged in the "stop Taft" movement, Kohler and Rennebohm working for Eisenhower and La Follette backing Earl Warren. Tom Coleman, laboring night and day for his candidate, met privately with his state's 24 delegates (including Dorothy Kohler) pledged to Taft, and continued to express confidence. His prominent role among the Taft forces prompted some top Eisenhower aides to float his name as a possible Eisenhower campaign manager.[51]

On the first day of the convention, after heated exchanges, delegates voted 658 to 548 to back Eisenhower's view of the southern delegate dispute over Taft's. The vote showed the Ohio Senator's vulnerability and ended talk about a first ballot win. Eisenhower called the rules victory "heartening news" to himself and millions of Americans. Walter and Charlotte, visiting the general in his suite along with several other Wisconsinites, heard the candidate express his delight in even more jubilant terms, believing that it expressed the sentiment of the convention as a whole in an Eisenhower nomination. To a group of Warren delegates from the Badger State, the general said, "It was a great moral victory. I felt like letting out a great big war whoop." He likened the experience to his reaction in March, 1945 when the 9th Armored Division took the Remagen bridge over the Rhine, which served as an avenue for American troops to pour into Germany.[52]

Still, the Taft-McCarthy forces remained powerful, and that could be heard in the rhetoric from convention speakers, beginning with General

MacArthur, and in the enthusiastic and prolonged displays of affirmation by delegates to right-wing allegations. Temporary chairman Walter S. Halanan, the Taft man who invited Joe McCarthy to speak, introduced the senator with a fervor that left no question about where he stood on the ideological spectrum: "The Truman-Acheson administration, the Communist press and the fellow travelers have all joined hands in a tremendous propaganda campaign to discredit and destroy an able and patriotic United States senator because he had the courage to expose the traitors in our government. They have not succeeded and they will not succeed. The fact that he is the object of such violent hatred is a badge of honor in the eyes of every patriotic American."

McCarthy walked to the microphone accompanied by a band playing "On Wisconsin." Thunderous applause and cheers almost drowned out the music. The Senator's half hour speech was interrupted 28 times by admirers. Ten Wisconsinites led a parade during the talk, carrying their state's convention standard. Soon eight McCarthyites paraded back and forth at the front of the hall waving signs that displayed "red herrings" labeled Acheson, Hiss, and Lattimore.

The speech itself was classic McCarthy, talking about his service in the Marines, alleging treason in government, pointing to Soviet expansion in the world, and railing against the "Acheson-Truman-Lattimore party" he had earlier labeled the "Commiecrats." At one point, he cried out:

"My good friends, I say one Communist in a defense plant is one Communist too many. (Applause)

One Communist on the faculty of one university is one Communist too many. (Applause)

And even if there were only one Communist in the State Department, that would still be one Communist too many (applause)"[53]

Reaction outside the convention hall was predictable. The Hearst newspaper chain showered McCarthy with praise. The *New York Times* stated editorially that with the speech the GOP convention had "reached rock bottom." When President Truman was asked about McCarthy's charges, he replied sharply, "If McCarthy said it, it's a damned lie, you can be sure of that."

Inside the hall, a *Milwaukee Journal* reporter noted restlessness during the latter part of McCarthy's speech. Perhaps that was because a large number of delegates were already aware that the tide was turning strongly for Eisenhower. His awesome military reputation, glowing smile, and winning ways with delegates who visited his suite at the Blackstone

Hotel, had won the hearts and minds of a great many. His solid group of convention supporters, including the governor of Wisconsin, had also made an important impact on delegates.

Shortly after McCarthy's speech, the platform writers released copies of their foreign policy plank, endorsing collective security. It amounted to a direct counterattack on the Taft-McCarthy wing of the party. That evening, the Eisenhower camp won a long and bitter struggle over the credentials of southern delegates. Now there was not only talk of an Eisenhower victory on the first ballot, but a story was floating about that 41-year-old Richard Nixon had been chosen to run with Ike, a move obviously designed to win the allegiance of the far Right in the election.[54]

We do not know in detail what Walter did on Eisenhower's behalf, but the Associated Press reported that he and Oscar Rennebohm were "working feverishly." On the fourth day of the convention, Walter was said to be closeted with uninstructed delegate groups from eastern states, attempting to win their votes for Ike. "He was not seen all day among midwestern delegations." Rennebohm, a personal friend of Earl Warren, was urging the California governor to release his delegates to Eisenhower if, after the first ballot, there seemed no chance of his winning the nomination.[55] What is certain is that Tom Coleman resented every move made by Kohler. The two had never before worked so intensely for opposite goals.

On the first ballot, Eisenhower won 614 votes, ten more than was necessary to win the nomination. Wisconsin stuck with its pledged 24 votes for Taft and 6 for Warren. As state after state turned to Eisenhower to make the nomination unanimous, Dorothy Kohler and Mrs. Virginia Braun of Antigo shouted "no" when Wisconsin joined the procession. (Walter's sister-in-law, ever the McCarthyite, was never to support Eisenhower.) When asked to comment on Ike's swift victory, Tom Coleman shook his head, and replied, "I have nothing to say." Looking dazed and haggard, he turned and left the amphitheater.[56]

Walter and Charlotte may well have been in the Eisenhower suite, among staff members and friends, when the first ballot put the general over the top. Shortly thereafter, Walter's friend Wilbur Renk, chairman of the state Eisenhower club, held a dinner-meeting for Wisconsin delegates to cement party harmony. Governor Kohler was the main speaker. But the dinner was not enthusiastically supported. Some bitter Taft delegates who had left the International Amphitheater after the first ballot failed even to return for the candidate's convention appearance.[57]

Eisenhower himself had better luck at the unification effort. He visited Senator Taft soon after his nomination, and Taft supporters reciprocated by streaming through the Eisenhower suite in large numbers expressing their support. Vice-presidential candidate Richard Nixon was on hand, as was Tom Coleman, Senator McCarthy, and several others on the far Right. Very quickly, Republicans rallied behind Ike. McCarthy told the press, "I think that Eisenhower will make a great president. One of the finest things I've seen is Eisenhower going to Taft's headquarters and accepting Taft's offer of cooperation." Governor Kohler said, "I think he would make an excellent president. I will give him all the aid I can and I will campaign actively for him." Wayne Hood said, "Eisenhower's the nominee, and we'll have to support him."[58]

Wisconsin Democrats were hoping, of course, that the call for unity would fail. James E. Doyle wondered aloud how state residents could vote for both Eisenhower and McCarthy. If George Marshall had been, as the Senator claimed, part of a conspiracy to sell out to the Russians, Eisenhower would surely have been a party to the treason, said Doyle. "So far, only that Flexible Flier Walter Kohler has reconciled this conflict; Kohler is for both McCarthy and Eisenhower, the accuser and the accused." Thomas E. Fairchild, who hoped to oppose McCarthy in the senate race, said, "My impression is that there is a serious split on some fundamental issues within the Republican party no matter who was nominated."[59]

Back in Wisconsin, Walter met with Wayne Hood, Wilbur Renk, and Henry Ringling at the Executive Residence. "We are all united," Kohler told reporters afterward. "Renk will be head of the Eisenhower clubs in the state, and there will be complete co-operation between these clubs and the state party organization."[60] Wayne Hood was soon appointed Executive Director of the Republican National Committee, a leading GOP position that was obviously aimed at further promoting party unity. The post was reportedly first offered to Tom Coleman, but he was still licking his wounds after the convention and did not respond to the invitation.[61]

Although unopposed in the GOP primary, Walter began his re-election campaign on August 1. Between then and the September 9 primary, he toured much of the state, delivering speeches, making appearances at county fairs, and attending a variety of Republican events.[62] When

William Proxmire challenged him to a debate, Walter employed some rarely used sarcasm in reply, no doubt revealing the extent to which the personal attacks by Democrats had stung. "I believe it would be unfair of me to take advantage of your prominence in Wisconsin politics by sharing your audiences for my campaign appearances." And if that were insufficiently nasty, he added: "People are entitled to an accurate report on these problems rather than the distorted and inaccurate information which has been circulated in Democrat campaign speeches and the state platform."[63]

With Joe McCarthy recovering from a hernia operation, Walter agreed to take some of his campaign schedule. In Eau Claire, he told an audience of 200, "As far as I know, he has been completely endorsed by the state [Republican] organization. It is supporting him as I am, and as I said I would at Milwaukee when the state GOP convention was held."

William Proxmire sneered, "Governor Kohler's decision to appear on behalf of Senator McCarthy is a major political tragedy. It is an act that should make Wisconsin voters think long and hard about the character of their governor." Henry Reuss of Milwaukee, another Democrat interested in running against McCarthy, declared, "For some weeks Walter Kohler has been dabbling with McCarthyism. Now he has embraced all the indecency for which the McCarthy name is known. The tragedy of it all is that Walter Kohler knows better. He has many times told liberal newsmen that he considers McCarthy a disgrace. Now, in the hope of catching a few votes, he has turned his back on everything that was honorable in his character....Kohler's all-out endorsement of McCarthy will not only, in the end, hurt the cause of clean government. In the end it will also hurt Walter Kohler."[64]

Stung by such personal attacks and wholly convinced of the need to support all party members against Democrats, Walter soon went a step farther, showing that he was prepared to accept not just generalities about Reds and their sympathizers in government but also to endorse some of McCarthy's highly controversial charges against specific individuals. In a public statement issued by Phil Drotning, the governor said, "I have not always agreed with Senator McCarthy in the past, nor do I expect I shall in the future. However, the factual foundations of many of his charges has already been demonstrated." He then mentioned three highly controversial cases (Edmund Clubb, John Stewart Service, Owen Lattimore), that had been pushed into headlines by McCarthy and the McCarran Committee, a Congressional ally headed by an ultraconservative Democrat. He also cited minutes of the Loyalty Review Board condemning the State Department for refusing to discharge employees for disloyalty.

This was a turning point in Walter's political life, one driven primarily, it seems certain, by his passion to elect Eisenhower. Other Eisenhower moderates throughout the nation were taking similar steps at about the same time. McCarthyism was now the rage of the GOP.

Drotning issued the gubernatorial statement only after the governor refused to talk directly with a *Milwaukee Journal* reporter about support for McCarthy. The statement did not assuage the newspaper's wrath. That same day, an editorial condemned Walter for failing to live up to his father's high standards of morality and accused him of "condoning irresponsible demagoguery and falsehood."[65]

Kohler made good his pledge to campaign for Eisenhower. In Milwaukee he appeared with Charles Kersten, contending that Democratic presidential candidate Adlai Stevenson, the liberal Governor of Illinois, could not wipe out corruption in Washington because he was too closely linked with Truman and Chicago political boss Jake Arvey. Kohler and Kersten also attacked Arthur Schlesinger, Jr., the liberal Harvard University history professor and aide to Governor Stevenson. Walter called the liberal, anti-Communist organization Americans for Democratic Action, to which Schlesinger and Democratic campaign manager Wilson Wyatt belonged, "as left wing as an organization can be and still stay in the Democratic party." This was now standard Republican rhetoric. Notably, Kohler did not join Kersten and another McCarthyite at the event in praising McCarthy, railing about appeasement, attacking George Marshall, and calling for the liberation of the peoples of Eastern Europe.[66]

On August 22, vice-presidential candidate Richard Nixon said that both he and Eisenhower were backing Joe McCarthy, if he was renominated, without necessarily endorsing his methods.[67] Insiders knew that Eisenhower despised McCarthy, and they were not surprised when, the day after Nixon's announcement, the presidential candidate declared in a news conference that he would never campaign for nor give a blanket endorsement to McCarthy. He said furthermore that he differed sharply with the "un-American" methods he implied that the Senator had employed. Still, Eisenhower declared that he would support any Republican against any Democrat for election to the Senate in 1952. His explanation was that the GOP needed every seat possible in Congress.

At one point the presidential candidate left his chair and walked into the center of the room to defend the patriotism of General George Marshall. "If I could say any more, I would say it, but I have no patience with anyone who can find in his record of service for this country anything to criticize." When asked if he would appear in Wisconsin with McCarthy, Eisenhower smiled and said that he didn't think it was "such a heinous crime" to be on the same platform with the Senator.[68]

Kohler quickly told reporters that his position on McCarthy was identical to Eisenhower's. "I have disagreed with [McCarthy] over many things in the past and I expect to disagree with him over others in the future. I am certainly not endorsing everything he has said."[69] Still, as a candidate for political office in Wisconsin, the governor was required to draw a bit closer to McCarthy than Ike had. On August 25, in a campaign speech at Stevens Point, Walter said that he was supporting McCarthy because he believed him "more than half right" in his "crusade against Communism." He said that the Senator had "exposed" John Stewart Service, O. Edmund Clubb, Owen Lattimore, and the Institute of Pacific Relations. And that, apparently, amounted to "more than half" of the many scores of McCarthy claims since the Wheeling speech, two and half years earlier.

Each of the cases cited by Kohler involved the fall of China to the Communists, an event the far Right had for years attributed to traitors in the State Department. The very shaky case against "China Hand" Service had been around for years before McCarthy took it up, and his dismissal by the State Department in 1951 resulted from a finding by the Loyalty Review Board only that there was a "reasonable doubt" as to his loyalty. Clubb, another State Department official involved with Chinese affairs, was first investigated by the House Un-American Activities Committee and cleared by Secretary of State Dean Acheson. Pro-Soviet Lattimore had been attacked for years by the far Right, long before McCarthy, in a wild bluff during the Tydings Committee investigation, named the Asian expert "the top Russian espionage agent in this country." Charges were investigated thoroughly by the Tydings committee and demolished; four secretaries of state denied in writing that Lattimore had anything to do with Far Eastern policy. The leftist Institute of Pacific Relations was well known to investigators before McCarthy and the Senate Judiciary Committee made it famous. It was shown to have had no demonstrable impact on the White House, the State Department or American foreign policy.

But these cases were in the headlines constantly during the early 1950s, and casual or partisan readers could easily have assumed the guilt of those so often attacked. Moreover, some of McCarthy's reckless charges were supported by the McCarran Committee, another Senate body which worked hand in hand with the Wisconsin Senator. It labeled Lattimore "a conscious articulate instrument of the Soviet conspiracy" and cited him for perjury. McCarran hearings on the Institute of Pacific Relations ran from July 25, 1951 to June 20, 1952, giving the media the false impression that it had uncovered vast deposits of information on Reds in America.[70]

From McCarthy's charges in Wheeling through the election of 1952, Republicans often acted reflexively, feeling it both proper and politically advantageous to believe allegations that Democrats had aided and abetted the Soviet Union, deliberately at times due to Reds in high positions of authority, and at other times through stupidity and error. Just as reflexively, Democrats rejected these attacks. Facts were not as important in this political struggle as emotions; even people with fine minds and good character chose to overlook evidence in favor of ideology and the smell of victory in November.

President Truman tended at times to minimize accusations of treason under his watch, often dismissing charges as mere Republican partisanship. Of course, much of his belligerence reflected his anger at extremist accusations against the likes of such distinguished Americans as George Marshall and Dean Acheson. The partisan struggle was such that at times Truman failed to acknowledge evidence of espionage. For example, he no doubt erred in vociferously defending Harry Dexter White, a high-ranking Treasury Department official in both the Roosevelt and Truman administrations, against charges made by former Communist spies Whittaker Chambers and Elizabeth Bentley.[71] Still, Truman was not at all blind to internal subversion, and supported efforts made by officials of his loyalty-security program. Moreover, he was correct in contending that the Soviet spy apparatus in this country did not formulate or directly effect national policy making, a key McCarthyite claim.

At the same time, Republicans, even moderates such as Eisenhower and Kohler, tended increasingly to accept the most extreme right-wing fantasies. If moderates objected to accusations against George Marshall, they nevertheless perpetuated the McCarthyite view of thousands of disloyal government employees actively in the service of Joseph Stalin and a Communist Party in America still a danger to the republic. (In fact, the Communist party by 1952 was an eviscerated shell of its former self, its personnel and every move known in detail by the FBI.) The zeal for office was at the root of much of their behavior. In 1950, Robert Taft publicly encouraged McCarthy and allegedly advised him to "keep talking and if one case doesn't work out he should proceed with another."[72] *New York Times* columnist James Reston quoted Tom Coleman as saying that same year, "The issue is fairly simple, and it was made by the newspapers. It is now a political issue, and somebody is going to gain or lose politically before it's over. It all comes down to this: are we going to try to win an election or aren't we?"[73]

Almost no one active in politics or in the major media at the time was neutral or wholly objective in this intense ideological and political struggle. That was especially true in Wisconsin where public admiration for McCarthy clouded the minds of those Republicans who sought at the same time to be responsible and to win elective office. Governor Kohler's allegation, then, that McCarthy was "half right" is understandable if wholly outside the general framework of his life before and after the campaign of 1952. Reason is all too often the servant of desire, and Kohler was wholly persuaded that Republicans had to do everything in their power to sweep the Democrats out of state government and Congress and put Ike in the White House. The politics of this extraordinary time prevented him, as well as others, from rising above the partisan clamor. (Nearly two decades later, Walter would admit that McCarthy's batting average was "probably pretty low," especially during the last years of his life.)[74]

On September 3, Senator McCarthy made his first campaign appearance in Wisconsin. A high school auditorium in a Milwaukee suburb was packed with about 1,700 supporters, and 300 others listened to loudspeakers in nearby classrooms. To a roar from the crowd, Joe strode to the podium, his arm around Governor Kohler, also scheduled to speak. McCarthy's address, interrupted 16 times with applause, castigated the Truman Administration, presented a distorted view of Adlai Stevenson's endorsement of Alger Hiss, and gave a fictitious account of a personal friendship with the late Secretary of Defense James Forrestal, who allegedly warned McCarthy about "the plans to betray America through incompetence or treason."

Walter's speech also blasted the Truman Administration, but its emphasis was on social gains made by Republican legislators in Wisconsin. Audience applause was faint and halting. Unlike McCarthy, the governor boosted the Eisenhower candidacy, saying that Ike would be "a president with the ability and the will to clean house in Washington." At the conclusion of the speech, following a whispered conversation with Charles Kersten, who had introduced McCarthy, Walter again took the microphone and said, "If any of the press might read something into my speech because of the omission of any endorsement of candidates on the endorsed Republican ticket, I want to make it clear that I am supporting the endorsed candidates, including Senator Joseph McCarthy." However reluctantly, the two were a team.[75]

In the September 9 Republican primary, McCarthy crushed Leonard F. Schmitt by a 2 ½ to 1 margin, winning more than a half million votes. Many Democrats crossed party lines to vote for the controversial Senator. Edwin R. Bayley of the *Milwaukee Journal* called it "the largest crossover vote in the state's history." On the other hand, Fred R. Zimmerman, the former governor who criticized McCarthy, won renomination for Secretary of State over the endorsed candidate. (Zimmerman remained, for reasons not even he fully understood, one of the most popular politicians in state history.)[76]

Kohler, who was unopposed in the primary (but had campaigned furiously all through August), placed second to McCarthy in vote-getting, winning well over a half million votes.[77] He declared of the Senator's victory, "Clearly, the people were not diverted by the injection of synthetic issues in the campaign, but were determined to endorse Senator McCarthy's fight to expose subversion. The large vote reflects great credit on the people of Wisconsin, and the huge Republican totals auger well for a sweeping Republican victory for national, state and local offices in November." He soon told a Milwaukee audience that "we should elect not only a Republican president but a Republican congress, and we should re-elect Joe McCarthy."[78]

Senator Wiley, from Washington, gave McCarthy a warm and sweeping endorsement, saying, "I shall speak and vote for Senator McCarthy and urge every Republican and independent voter of our state to do likewise."[79] The GOP state executive committee passed a resolution commending the voters who backed Republican candidates. "These citizens believe the Democratic party has sought to shelter Communists and to protect corruption and office buying at all levels of government."[80] Senator Frank Carlson of Kansas, a top Eisenhower adviser, told reporters that an invitation to McCarthy to speak throughout the country on the Communists-in-government issue was "in the works." The invitation was quickly accepted.[81]

Democrats received low vote totals in the primary, making their chances in the fall appear negligible. In 1952 the party was able to field only 159 candidates for all state offices and legislative seats, compared with 250 two years earlier. Still, state Democrats were excited about the Stevenson-Sparkman national ticket, and they hoped that an all-out attack on high state taxes and McCarthyism would pay dividends in Wisconsin by November. They were strong in Milwaukee, Madison, and other smaller urban areas, and they had some newspaper support.[82]

Thomas Fairchild won the Democratic nomination for the Senate. The 39-year-old Verona attorney was a former Progressive who had been elected Attorney General in 1948, the only Democrat to win a statewide office between 1932 and 1957. He had come into the race in early July declaring, "The fight against McCarthy is a crusade for American liberties."[83] After the primary, he assured Stevenson and Truman that he had "a good fighting chance" to defeat McCarthy.[84] It was difficult for objective observers to make the same claim with a straight face. McCarthy's power was now such that Democratic national chairman Stephen A. Mitchell told reporters that the Senator "was not a prime target" of his party in 1952. "Our party's platform and candidates are strongly opposed to communism. We don't want that to be obscured by controversies about a personality."[85]

On September 16, Kohler met with Eisenhower in St. Paul, Minnesota, joining the candidate in a motor tour of the Twin Cities and conferring briefly with Ike and top strategists aboard the candidate's plane. There they discussed the campaign effort in Wisconsin. Walter soon told reporters that Eisenhower would make a one day "whistle stop" crossing of the state and give six campaign speeches. He said also that Ike termed McCarthy's primary victory "remarkable" and admitted that he and the general discussed the use of the "Reds-in-government" issue in Wisconsin. "I suggested that he point it out," Kohler said, although "I didn't press it."[86]

The following day, Walter assured Wayne Hood that the GOP primary victories had not make him complacent. "I had a speech every night last week; I have one every night this week; and I expect to continue that pace during the seven weeks which remain before general election day."[87]

Kohler was more interested in the national election than in his race against Proxmire. In mid-September he gave the keynote address at the Minnesota Republican state convention, contending that every major program of social welfare enacted nationally within the last two decades originated with the GOP. He termed "completely fraudulent" Adlai Stevenson's contention that a Republican victory in November would mean the abandonment of all social progress in the nation.[88]

Kohler was soon one of several Republican governors giving a nation-wide radio speech on behalf of Eisenhower. In his talk, he hammered Stevenson for the presence of crime in Illinois.[89]

After Richard Nixon was caught with a private "slush fund" and defended himself over national television with his maudlin "Checkers" speech, Walter questioned the integrity of Adlai Stevenson, demanding that the presidential candidate make a "full, frank and complete disclosure" of the "extralegal fund which he has collected and disbursed in the state of Illinois."[90] This standard GOP defense of the Vice Presidential candidate smacked more of partisanship than investigation and moral indignation.

The Eisenhower campaign train was scheduled to make stops at Green Bay, Appleton, and Milwaukee on October 3. The day before, McCarthy, Kohler, and Henry Ringling flew to Peoria for a private conference on the details of the trip. Of paramount importance, of course, was how the presidential candidate would treat McCarthy. The meeting was arranged by Tom Coleman, now an important figure on Eisenhower's staff. Coleman had met with Ike earlier, attempting to convince him of the righteousness of McCarthy's cause.

The presidential candidate spent a half hour with McCarthy in his Peoria hotel suite, telling him in no uncertain terms what he thought of his attacks on George Marshall and others. McCarthy had his own agenda: he learned that an Eisenhower speech scheduled for Milwaukee contained a positive reference to Marshall, and he did not want it delivered. The exchange between the two men was intense; an aide later said that it was the only time he had ever heard Eisenhower speak "in red-hot anger."[91]

What is uncertain about the exchange is whether or not the Senator expressed his desire to have the reference to Marshall omitted. Walter said later that McCarthy told him after the meeting that the general had not mentioned his Milwaukee speech, which implies that McCarthy did not get his message across.[92] In any case, the decision to omit the tribute was not made in Peoria.

That evening, the presidential candidate was in a better mood when he had dinner with Walter and Eisenhower aide Bobby Cutler. Years later, Walter said of the general, "Well, I think congenitally and chronically he was an optimist....He always had this contagious grin, and he was a very personable man." Table conversation featured "an agreeable conversation, that's all." McCarthy was not invited.[93]

Eisenhower knew that with its 12 electoral votes, Wisconsin was a vital state, and he agreed to details worked out between state Republicans and aides about the careful strategy that was to be followed during the campaign trip aboard the train "Harmony."

At Green Bay, where McCarthy was extraordinarily popular, Republican Congressman John Byrnes introduced dignitaries from the train platform. Governor Kohler was greeted with polite applause. Senator McCarthy received wild cheers. He waved but did not speak, and left the platform before Eisenhower was announced. In his speech, Ike said that differences among Republicans were to be expected. "The differences between me and Senator McCarthy are well known to others. But what is more important, they are well known to him and to me and we have discussed them. I want to make one thing very clear. The purposes that he and I have of ridding this government of the incompetents, the dishonest, and above all the subversive and the disloyal are one and the same. Our differences, therefore, have nothing to do with the end result that we are seeking. The differences apply to method." Eisenhower asked support for the entire GOP ticket, but he would not agree to pose for photos of himself with McCarthy.

In Appleton, some 8,000 people turned out to cheer their native son, and McCarthy was permitted to introduce Eisenhower with a single sentence. He said nothing else. McCarthy was allowed to remain on the platform, but Kohler was placed between the Senator and the general. Ike again spoke of the need to elect all Republicans but made no specific reference to McCarthy. The train then moved southward with stops at Neenah, Oshkosh, and Fond du Lac, where there was no more talk about the Reds in government issue. At Neenah, McCarthy received rousing cheers from the crowd of some 4,500, but he left the platform before Eisenhower appeared, and Attorney General Vernon W. Thomson introduced the presidential candidate.[94]

As the train headed toward Milwaukee, Walter pleaded with Eisenhower strategist Sherman Adams to delete the planned reference to Marshall, arguing that it would be a needless insult to the Senator and might cost votes. Adams agreed, and brought Walter to Eisenhower, along with Major General Wilton B. "Jerry" Persons, who sympathized with Walter's argument. Ike quickly conceded, snapping, "Take it out." An aide later described him as "purple with rage."[95]

It would later be said that Eisenhower had capitulated to McCarthy. In a sense that is correct, for the Senator wanted the tribute omitted. But at the time Ike was actually capitulating to Kohler and two of his most highly trusted advisers, who were eager to cement the wings of the GOP and win in November.

Years later, Walter thought the entire incident blown greatly out of proportion, reflecting not at all on Eisenhower's character or leadership ability. "...changing this, deleting that paragraph, did not in any way leave the impression, to me at least, that Eisenhower was retracting any of his defense of General Marshall. Not at all." Of his own role, he said, "Again, we're trying to win an election. We think Wisconsin's 12 electoral votes may well be decisive. We don't know. We don't want to take any chances....The General had made this spirited defense of General Marshall just two weeks before, and it seemed just gratuitous to come here and re-pick a fight with a man who was extremely popular in Wisconsin at that time."[96]

An estimated 20,000 Milwaukeeans greeted the Eisenhower train and viewed a parade along Wisconsin Avenue. Charlotte was on hand at the train station and was one of two women to enter the private car first, bearing flowers for Mrs. Eisenhower. During the parade, the general sat atop a convertible, flashing his famous smile to the enthusiastic crowd. Both the governor and his wife were in the parade, along with scores of GOP dignitaries.[97]

At the Milwaukee Arena, before a cheering crowd of 8,500, Walter introduced Eisenhower, calling him "a man whose personal integrity has never been questioned." The speech, even without the Marshall reference, was enough to please the most adamant McCarthyite. A national tolerance of Communism, Eisenhower said, had "poisoned two whole decades of our national life" and insinuated itself in our schools, public forums, news channels, labor unions, "and—most terrifyingly—into our government itself." Reds had penetrated virtually every department, Eisenhower said, and it meant "a government by men whose very brains were confused by the opiate of this deceit." The candidate attributed the fall of China and the "surrender of whole nations" in Eastern Europe to Reds in the federal government. The impact was felt at home, as well. "This penetration meant a domestic policy whose tone was set by men who sneered and scoffed at warnings of the enemy infiltrating our most secret councils." In short, he declared, "It meant—in its most ugly triumph—treason itself."[98]

At the conclusion of the rally, photographers snapped a very awkward handshake between Eisenhower and McCarthy; both men were six feet apart and neither would move closer, so each was forced to lean far forward in the direction of the other. Some of McCarthy's supporters rejoiced, saying "Joe made Ike come to him."[99]

Reporters received full copies of the speech and quickly saw the Marshall deletion. When the *New York* Times learned of Ike's concession, several top Eisenhower officials and McCarthy himself denied that anything of the sort had happened. Tom Coleman lied to reporters. Others who knew about the matter refused to talk.[100]

When Walter was asked if McCarthy had requested Eisenhower to eliminate the Marshall reference, he snapped, "I don't believe it." This was technically correct, for the Senator had told him that Ike didn't bring the speech up when the two men met in Peoria. Still, Walter was not providing the press information on the editing of the speech.[101]

This was to be Eisenhower's only visit to Wisconsin during the campaign. He and his aides had seen quite enough of McCarthy and the Reds-in-government issue for a while. Columnist Joseph Alsop wrote that members of Eisenhower's personal staff privately referred to the Wisconsin trip as the "terrible day."[102]

Adlai Stevenson, in Milwaukee five days later, condemned his GOP rival for an "opportunistic grasping" for votes. In nearby Waukesha, he labeled the GOP's right wing, "the most accomplished wrecking crew in this country's history" and said that Eisenhower had given it a first, second, and third mortgage "on every principle he once held." Cartoonist Herblock, who worked for the pro-Eisenhower *Washington Post*, published a cartoon of McCarthy as a leering ape-man, standing in a pool of filth, holding a sign that read "ANYTHING TO WIN." Next to him, Ike explained to a horrified voter, "Our differences have nothing to do with the end result we are seeking." A *New York Post* headline declared, "He has met the enemy, and he is theirs."[103]

Walter spent the rest of the election campaign on the road, speeding from one village, town, and city to another, shaking hands on street corners and delivering scores of speeches. He was primarily concerned about the presidential election, and made only a single reference to William Proxmire, calling him a "visitor" to Wisconsin.[104] Walter spoke of several state issues, however, and clashed with the state GOP hierarchy by coming out strongly for reapportionment.[105]

In his efforts for Eisenhower, Kohler sometimes employed the extremist language being used all over the nation by both parties. When Harry Truman said that Eisenhower had "moral blindness" and would use Nazi methods if elected, Walter declared that the president was guilty of "a monstrous fabrication which reveals Harry Truman as a spiteful, embittered and unprincipled politician deserving only public contempt."[106] When a Veterans For Ike caravan reached Madison, the governor told them if Eisenhower were elected he would not just "deal sternly" with corruption and communism in government, he would "kick 'em the hell out."[107] At Lawrence College in Appleton he dismissed the Fifth Amendment, saying, "If a United States citizen under oath refuses to say he is not a Communist, then in my book he is."[108]

One of the nasty features about the national campaign was the determination of Republicans to persuade voters that Adlai Stevenson was an "egghead," which is to say an intellectual. A photograph revealed that the Democratic presidential candidate had a hole in one shoe, and that led GOP candidates to conclude that he was somehow effete, ineffectual, and unpractical—which is to say, almost if not entirely "un-American." Many Republicans, especially the McCarthyites, derided top academic credentials in general, sneering at people with Harvard degrees as symbols of Alger Hiss, Dean Acheson, and the many disloyal Ivy Leaguers presumably still in the federal government.

At one point, Walter joined this effort, calling a leading Democrat "a Harvard professor" and employing a stale campaign joke that labeled Stevenson "Harry Truman with a Harvard accent." A terse editorial in the *Milwaukee Journal* commented, "It is incongruous to find Gov. Kohler resorting to the demagogic device of playing upon the supposed mob distrust of educated men....To keep things straight, Stevenson actually is a Princeton man. And Kohler [is] Yale '25."[109]

William Proxmire campaigned at his normal, almost superhuman pace. On October 27, he began with a factory visit at 5:30 a.m. and went to bed at 1:00 a.m. the following day, a day in which he made campaign appearances in five cities.[110] Proxmire had little of value to offer in the way of constructive alternatives to state government; he was interested primarily in introducing himself to as many voters as possible. On a Marinette radio station broadcast, however, he lashed out at Kohler, calling him the "official apologist" for McCarthy and blaming the governor for Eisenhower's retreat on the George Marshall reference during his Milwaukee speech. Walter chose not to comment on this embarrassing historical fact, revealed by columnist Joseph Alsop in the *New York Herald Tribune*.[111]

Just before the election, Proxmire talked on the radio to a statewide network of stations for 30 consecutive hours, refusing all stimulants, including tea and coffee. One of the signs posted in the Milwaukee radio studio in which he sat read "Good-by Wishy Washy Walter—Hello Battling Bill."[112]

Joe McCarthy, confident of his reelection, paid little attention to his Democratic opponent. Aided by a huge campaign fund, he spoke in ten states on behalf of ultraconservative candidates, linking their opponents with Communist subversion. In Montana, he called Democrat Mike Mansfield "either stupid or a dupe" because the Congressman had once been praised by the Communist *Daily Worker*. In Indiana, McCarthy called friendly Senator William Jenner "a great American" and the target of "Eastern bleeding hearts." Jenner repaid the compliment by declaring that McCarthy had been "marked for liquidation by an administration which...consorts openly with Reds and pinks." In Connecticut, McCarthy said that his arch-foe William Benton was "worth a hundred million dollars to the Kremlin on the floor of the United States Senate." Democrat Joseph P. Kennedy saw to it that McCarthy stayed out of Massachusetts, part of an all-out effort by the multi-millionaire businessman to elect his son John to the Senate.[113]

On October 27, McCarthy himself paid for time on 55 television stations and 550 radio stations to carry a Chicago speech designed to "expose" Adlai Stevenson. Nervous GOP leaders wondered to what extremes the Senator would go. Rumor had it that McCarthy intended to brand Stevenson both a Communist and a homosexual. Eisenhower quietly sent a trio of representatives—Governor Kohler, General Wilton B. Persons, and General Robert E. Wood—to Chicago to confer with McCarthy about his intentions. Don Surine, a zealous and often careless McCarthy staff member, showed his visitors a large pile of anti-Stevenson materials he had collected and presented to the Senator. He said later that the three Republican insiders were impressed by his evidence.

In the widely noted speech, delivered before a cheering crowd of 1,700, McCarthy accused many Stevenson associates of being soft on the Reds, falsely claimed that the *Daily Worker* had endorsed the Democrat's candidacy, and contended, "I do not state that Stevenson was a Communist or pro-Communist, but I must believe that something was wrong somewhere." At least four times, he said, "Alger—I mean Adlai," deliberately linking Stevenson and Hiss, much to the delight of his audience.

Democratic Party researchers soon studied the speech and discovered "at least 18 false statements, distortions or quotations wrenched from context." Northwestern University law professor Willard H. Pedrick, who checked the Senator's documentation, called the Chicago speech, "a most amazing demonstration of studied inaccuracy." A later analysis by a McCarthy biographer confirmed Pedrick's conclusion.[114]

No major Republican criticized McCarthy's attack on Stevenson. Those who chose to comment applauded. Tom Coleman praised the Senator, saying that the speech made a "great many" votes for the party.[115] Kohler described McCarthy's speech as "interesting and well documented," and thought it presented "a rather convincing and persuasive case." Walter said he did not believe Stevenson to be a Communist or a Communist sympathizer, but agreed with the assertion that the Illinois governor had shown "a softness toward Communists."[116] It was a delicate task to distinguish a sympathizer from one who was merely "soft," but during an election campaign like this many things were possible.

As the election drew closer, McCarthy-like attacks became commonplace. Vice President Nixon, now back in Eisenhower's good graces after the Checkers speech, supported McCarthy's reelection and called Stevenson "Adlai the appeaser" who "carries a Ph.D. from Dean Acheson's Cowardly College of Communist Containment." In Billings, Montana, Eisenhower promised, "We will find the men and women who may fail to live up to these standards; we will find the pinks; we will find the Communists; we will find the disloyal." He soon called for the repudiation of the Yalta agreements, and he blamed the Administration for the Korean War, promising to travel to the scene of the protracted bloodshed if elected.

Everywhere one saw a sea of "I Like Ike" buttons and bumper stickers bearing the GOP campaign theme K1C2, meaning "Korea, Communism, and Corruption."[117] Eisenhower was a national celebrity, a hero for the hour who, it was thought, might not only conquer the White House but sweep thousands of Republicans into office in the process.

The estimates were fairly accurate. Eisenhower won nearly 55% of the nation's vote, carrying 39 states, including Wisconsin. All of the major GOP candidates in Wisconsin were elected. Kohler received 1,009,171 votes, crushing Proxmire, who collected 601,844. Walter placed second in the number of votes, trailing only Fred Zimmerman, and he carried 69 of the state's 71 counties. His vote total was an all-time high for a gubernatorial candidate in Wisconsin and surpassed the 979,744 won by Eisenhower.[118] Friends said that Kohler saw in his reelection a vindication of the defeat his father had suffered 22 years earlier when he first tried to regain the governorship following a distinguished first term.[119]

McCarthy defeated Fairchild, collecting 870,444 votes to the Democrat's 731,402. Charles Kersten won his Congressional race, scoring a rare Republican victory in Milwaukee. Walter's friend Melvin Laird also won a seat in the House of Representatives. Voters approved redistricting, 753,092 to 689,915. Republicans kept a firm grip on the state Assembly, holding 75 seats to the Democrats' 25. There were no party changes in the Senate, and the GOP controlled 26 of the 33 seats.

The Republican sweep, in Walter's eyes, was worth the compromises made with McCarthy and his followers. Unity had prevailed, and Eisenhower's victory was especially rewarding. Years later, looking back on the campaign of 1952, Walter told an interviewer that Ike "won handily, and won handily in Wisconsin. So you can't fault success. It was a good campaign if it got good results."[120] Had he thought longer about that comment, he might have distinguished "good" from "honorable," but partisan passions frequently have a way of blending those two often antithetical concepts.

Democrats faced their election losses with a minimum of bitterness. James E. Doyle, state chairman of the Democratic Organizing Committee, sent congratulations to Eisenhower, Kohler, and Stevenson, but added, "To Senator McCarthy: War unto the death."[121] At 6:00 a.m. the day after the election, Bill Proxmire stood at a factory gate in the rain, shaking hands and thanking workers for their support. His 1954 campaign for governor was underway.[122]

After the votes were counted, Walter's role in the July 2 "fair play" letter signed by 25 Republican governors became widely known. Ed

Arndt of Kansas had come to the governors' conference in Houston seeking signatures for an endorsement of Eisenhower. Kohler sympathized with the effort but advised Arndt that some of the governors were committed to other candidates and would not sign. To avoid this divisiveness, Walter proposed a different approach. After consulting with several governors, he had Phil Drotning write a draft of a letter focusing on the issue of the disputed pro-Taft delegates in the South. With the approval of Sherman Adams, and after the determined efforts of Colorado's Dan Thornton to persuade colleagues, the statement received the support of all the governors. When published, the letter did much to stimulate interest in Eisenhower all across the country. Even after his friend Thomas Dewey made the story public, and Phil Drotning filled in most of the details, Walter maintained a discreet silence about his important role in rallying the GOP governors for the general.[123]

Some political analysts soon pointed to GOP weaknesses in the 1952 "Eisenhower landslide." Republicans barely won control of Congress, having only a one vote lead in the Senate and an eight vote margin in the House. McCarthy's victory was not as impressive as predicted; of the eleven Republicans on the ticket, he ran last. He was especially damaged by revelations of his often shady past published in the *Milwaukee Journal, Madison Capital Times,* and the *Sheboygan Press.* One pollster, Louis H. Bean, later concluded that McCarthy would have lost in Wisconsin had it not been for the Eisenhower sweep. Moreover, of the ten Senatorial incumbents and challengers McCarthy backed, four were defeated. Bean discovered that McCarthy's support actually damaged the campaigns of his allies. The election returns showed that moderate Republicans who supported Eisenhower fared better in the elections than did their colleagues on the far Right.[124]

But in the immediate flush of GOP victories, McCarthy's stature seemed greater than ever. The Senator himself was elated, saying, "The election of Eisenhower and most probably a Republican senate and house more than justifies my faith in the intelligence of the American people. This is a new day for America." He was particularly delighted when his foe William Benton was defeated in Connecticut. On election night at the Hotel Appleton, where the Senator and his supporters were celebrating, the election board announced proudly, "Benton went to hell at 8:30." Heard throughout the evening was the remark, "Joe won in Connecticut." When asked if he would continue the search for Reds in government with his party in control, he replied, "very definitely."[125]

How long GOP moderates and McCarthyites would remain at peace was anyone's guess. During the campaign, it had often been difficult to tell one from the other.

Notes

[1] Robert H. Fleming, "Stassen Will Run in the State in GOP Presidential Primary," *Milwaukee Journal*, January 8, 1952; "Taft Has Office Here," *ibid.*

[2] "Kohler Rejects Ike Slate Role," *ibid.*, January 13, 1952.

[3] E.g., "GOP Women Applaud Taft," *ibid.*, January 17, 1952. See "Taft Delegate Slate Listed," *ibid.*, February 13, 1952. On Taft and McCarthy, see James T. Patterson, *Mr. Republican: A Biography of Robert A. Taft* (Boston: Houghton Mifflin Co., 1972), 503, 530-531.

[4] Robert H. Fleming, "Gov. Warren Invited to Run in Wisconsin," *Milwaukee Journal*, February 17, 1952.

[5] Edwin R. Bayley, "Kohler Spurns Senate Race, Wants to Remain Governor," *ibid.*, January 30, 1952. Walter recalled in 1971 that he had been urged to run largely by Democrats, "and certainly there was no point in my playing into their hands. They all assured me of considerable support and I don't doubt for a second in a primary I'd have had their support, but not in the general election....If I ran against McCarthy it would split the Wisconsin Republican Party right down the middle and could quite conceivably result in the election of Stevenson." While acknowledging that McCarthy was "a very devious character," he denied rumors that the Senator had threatened to make much of Walter's divorce if he governor campaigned against him. Walter J. Kohler, Jr. Oral History, Columbia University, 1971, 17, 30. Warren Knowles said later that in his judgment Kohler's thoughts about running against McCarthy were never very serious. Haney, *A Concise Hitory of the Modern Republican Party of Wisconsin*, 12.

[6] Edwin R. Bayley, "Enters Race for Governor," *Milwaukee Journal*, March 8, 1952.

[7] Jack Bell, "Eisenhower, Kefauver Win N. H. Vote," *ibid.*, March 12, 1952.

[8] Laurence C. Eklund, "Governors Hit 'Tax Stealing,'" *ibid.*, March 13, 1952.

[9] "State GOP Reprints Jab at Warren While 'Neutral' Kohler Praises Him," *ibid.*, March 28, 1952; "Misconstrued, Kohler Claims," *ibid.*, March 29, 1952.

[10] "Chapple Is 'Shocked,'" *ibid.*, March 20, 1952.

[11] Edwin R. Bayley, "Warren Slate Says Ike Is Its Second Choice," *ibid.*, March 20, 1952.

[12] "Stassen Offers to Turn Over Half of His Wisconsin Delegates to 'Ike,'" *ibid.*, March 25, 1952.

[13] On campaign spending, see Willard Smith, "State Election Spending Led by Taft's Backers," *ibid.*, March 25, 1952; editorial, "Wisconsin Votes and Dollars," *ibid.*, April 27, 1952.

[14] Reeves, *The Life and Times of Joe McCarthy*, 397.

[15] Robert H. Fleming, "Senator Says He's Running," *Milwaukee Journal*, May 3, 1952.

[16] See Reeves, *The Life and Times of Joe McCarthy*, 305-312, 401-402; Reeves, *A Question of Character: A Life of John F. Kennedy*, 87, 101-102, 120, 157; Donald F. Crosby, *God, Church, and Flag: Senator Joseph R. McCarthy and the Catholic Church, 1950-1957* (Durham, North Carolina: the University of North Carolina Press, 1978), 102-113, 194, 205-215, 232-233.

[17] Edwin R. Bayley, "Taft Wins 24 of State's 30 Delegates, *Milwaukee Journal*, April 2, 1952.

[18] Democrats in Wisconsin voted overwhelmingly for Senator Kefauver over two favorite sons. *Ibid.*; Robert R. Fleming, "Kefauver Wins Easily Over Democrats' 'Favorite Sons,'" *ibid.*; Laurence C. Eklund, "Taft Now Feels Himself in Lead for Nomination," *ibid.*

[19] "'I Am for Eisenhower,' Gov. Kohler Declares," *ibid.*, April 6, 1952.

[20] "Ike's Roster Lengthens," *Life*, 32 (April 7, 1952), 40.

[21] Kohler, former governor Oscar Rennebohm, and Renk each gave a couple of hundred dollars to the effort, which collected a total of only about $6,000 prior to the GOP national convention.

[22] "Kohler Called a 'Pussyfooter,'" *ibid.*, April 7, 1952. On the "backbone" statement, see Edwin R. Bayley, "Kohler Move is Applauded," *ibid*, January 31, 1952.

[23] "Women Outnumber Kohler in an Argument About Ike," *ibid.*, May 2, 1952.

[24] Robert J. Doyle, "Women Kick Redistricting," *ibid.*; "Redistricting Stand Is Hit," *ibid.*, May 5, 1952; editorial, "Is GOP Going to Fight Equal Votes for All?." *ibid.*; editorial, "Governor Wobbles Around," *ibid.*, May 6, 1952.

[25] "Governor Urges a 'No' Vote on Redistricting Referendum," *ibid.* May 27, 1952. See the editorial "Vote 'No' to Save Constitution's Guarantee of the Equal Vote," *ibid.*, May 28, 1952.

[26] Edwin R. Bayley, "'No' on Redistricting, Stand of City GOP," *ibid*, May 28, 1952.

[27] "May Sidestep Redistricting," *ibid.*, June 10, 1952.

[28] Willard R. Smith, "GOP Platform Group Skittish on Districting," *ibid.*, June 8, 1952. A transcript of Walter's remarks is in the Republican Party papers.

[29] "May Sidestep Redistricting," *Milwaukee Journal*, June 10, 1952; Robert H. Fleming, "GOP Plank Okays a Drive for Area Voting, Hood Says," *ibid.*, June 13, 1952.

[30] "Taft Leaders 'Flout Rule,'" *ibid.*, June 3, 1952.

[31] Robert H. Fleming, "Coleman Gets Big Taft Post," *ibid.*, June 12, 1952; Robert H. Fleming, "Badgers Play Weight Roles," *ibid.*, July 2, 1952.

[32] Edwin R. Bayley, "Stay Together, Speakers' Plea to State GOP," June 13, 1952.

[33] See page 117 of the transcript of the meeting in the Republican Party papers.

[34] Robert H. Fleming, "GOP Plank Okays a Drive for Area Voting, Hood Says," *Milwaukee Journal*, June 13, 1952; editorial, "The Hypocritical GOP Plank on Value of Each Man's Vote," *ibid.*, June 16, 1952. A copy of the state platform and a transcript of Kohler's speech are in the Republican Party papers.

[35] Edwin R. Bayley, "Reapportionment Foes Hail GOP 'Compromise' Plank," *Milwaukee Journal*, June 14, 1952; Edwin R. Bayley, "Zimmerman Denied GOP's Endorsement," *ibid.*, June 15, 2005.

[36] "Zimmerman Raps at Foes," *ibid.*, June 23, 1952. The 4th ward Republican club in Milwaukee banned local attorney Edward J. Yockey from speaking to it because of his criticisms of McCarthy. Raymond E. McBride, "Agree to One Principal Foe for McCarthy," *ibid.*, June 29, 1952.

[37] "Proxmire Insists Governor Explain," *ibid.*, June 20, 1952.

[38] "DOC's Districting Plank Uges 'No' Vote on Area," *ibid.*, June 28, 1952.

[39] "Repeats Praise for McCarthy," *ibid.*, June 19, 1952.

[40] Editorial, "The GOP Cannot Possibly Win Without Independent Votes," *ibid.*, June 20, 1952.

[41] "Kohler Tells of GOP Task," *ibid.*, June 30, 1952. See Walter J. Kohler, Jr. Oral History, Columbia University, 1971, 24.

[42] Edwin R. Bayley, "Schmitt Is In Senate Race," *Milwaukee Journal*, June 25, 1952.

[43] "GOP to Hear Joe McCarthy," *ibid.*, July 1, 1952.

[44] See Reeves, *The Life and Times of Joe McCarthy*, 354-356.

[45] "GOP to Hear Joe McCarthy," *Milwaukee Journal*, July 1, 1952.

[46] The *New York Times* story by William S. White was published under the headline "23 GOP Governors Assail Taft's Delegate Vote Stand," *ibid.*, July 3, 1952. At the governors' meeting, Walter also proposed that the states bargain with Congress about offering to surrender federal aid in return for all taxes from cigarettes, liquor, beer, and gasoline. The governors adopted a resolution declaring that taxpayers would be better served if certain federal taxes were abandoned to the states in lieu of federal grants in aid. "Pass Resolutions," *ibid.*, July 3, 1952.

[47] "Ike 'to Fight' for 'Fit' GOP," *ibid.*

[48] "Governors' Bid Turned Down," *ibid.*

[49] "Verbal Punches Traded by Eisenhower and Taft," *ibid.*, July 5, 1952.

[50] "Plank Writers Back Treaties," *ibid.*, July 6, 1952; Reeves, *The Life and Times of Joe McCarthy*, 428.

[51] Robert H. Fleming, "Kohler works to 'Stop Taft' at Convention," *Milwaukee Journal*, July 7, 1952; Martin S. Hayden, "Nixon Urged for Ike 'Ticket'", *ibid.*, July 7, 1952. Rennebohm spent ten days in Chicago working for

Eisenhower. Robert H. Fleming, "New Leader for State GOP," *ibid.*, July 13, 1952. Walter and Charlotte arrived in Chicago on the first day of the convention.

52 Robert H. Fleming, "Ike Is Lured by State Fish," *ibid.*, July 8, 1952.

53 Laurence C. Eklund, "Big Reception Given Speech by McCarthy," *ibid.*, July 10, 1952. See also Reeves, *The Life and Times of Joe McCarthy*, 424-426.

54 Ecklund, "Big Reception Given Speech by McCarthy," *Milwaukee Journal*, July 10, 1952; Martin S. Hayden, "Nixon Urged for Ike 'Ticket,'" *ibid.*, July 7, 1952; Reeves, *The Life and Times of Joe McCarthy*, 424.

55 "Kohler Works Feverishly for Victory by Ike," *Milwaukee Journal*, July 10, 1952.

56 Robert H. Fleming, "Badger GOP Urged to Get Back of Ike," *ibid.*, July 12, 1952; "Views Differ on Ike's Win," *ibid.*

57 Fleming, "Badger GoP Urged to Get Back of Ike," *ibid.*

58 "Views Differ on Ike's Win," *ibid.*

59 *Ibid.*

60 "Kohler Sees GOP United," *ibid.*, July 17, 1952.

61 "Wayne Hood Appointed to High Position in GOP," *ibid.*, July 30, 1952. Coleman vowed to spend the summer in Europe if Taft lost the nomination, and he was keeping his word. Walter J. Kohler, Jr. Oral History, Columbia University, 1971, 28.

62 "Kohler Plans a Campaign," *Milwaukee Journal*, August 1, 1952.

63 "Asks Debate With Kohler," *ibid.*, July 15, 1952.

64 Robert H. Fleming, "Kohler Gives Full Backing to McCarthy," *ibid.*, August 7, 1952.

65 "'Facts' Back of McCarthy, Kohler Says," *ibid.*, August 8, 1952. The *Milwaukee Journal* then said in an editorial that the current governor failed to live up to standards set by his esteemed father. "Politically, Governor Kohler has now shown the same strong qualities. Some of his more kindly critics would say he was wishy-washy; the less generous would say that he simply lacked political guts....In campaigning for Senator McCarthy, the governor is not espousing even a half truth. He is condoning irresponsible demagoguery and falsehood. He has debased himself by this association." Editorial, "Kohler Embraces McCarthy," *ibid.*

66 "Give Lashing to Democrats," *ibid.*, August 20, 1952.

67 "Ike and I Will Back Joe McCarthy—Nixon," *ibid.*, August 22, 1952.

68 W. H. Lawrence, "Ike Defends Marshall, Withholds Blanket Endorsement of McCarthy," *ibid.*, August 23, 1952.

69 "Same Position as Ike: Kohler," *ibid.*, August 23, 1952.

70 These cases are discussed at length in Reeves, *The Life and Times of Joe McCarthy, passim.* On Lattimore, see also Ted Morgan, *Reds: McCarthyism in*

Twentieth-Century America (New York: Random House, 2003), 397-401, 405.

[71] John E. Haynes and Harvey Klehr, "Two Gentlemen of Venona," *The Weekly Standard*, May 13, 1966, 16-17; Haynes and Klehr, *Venona: Decoding Soviet Espionage in America*, 9-10, 125-126, 138-143 Arnold Beichman, "Guilty as Charged," *www.hooverdigest.org/992/beichman.html*. Cf. R. Bruce Craig, *Treasonable Doubt: The Harry Dexter White Case* (Lawrence, Kansas: University of Kansas Press, 2004), *passim*.

[72] Reeves, *The Life and Times of Joe McCarthy*, 263.

[73] *Ibid.*, 283. Walter's friend and GOP colleague Warren P. Knowles also pressured the governor to work for party unity by backing McCarthy. See copy, Warren P. Knowles to Bill [sic] Drotning, September 2, 1952, Warren Knowles papers; copy, Warren P. Knowles to Walter J. Kohler, Jr., September 10, 1952, *ibid.*

[74] Walter J. Kohler, Jr. Oral History, Columbia University, 1971, 34.

[75] Edwin R. Bayley, "McCarthy is Cheered by Overflow Crowd," *Milwaukee Journal*, September 4, 1952.

[76] Robert H. Fleming, "McCarthy Defeats Schmitt by 2 ½ to 1," *ibid.*, September 10, 1952; "Victory Goes to Zimmerman," *ibid.*; Edwin R. Bayley, "Democrats Helped Pick McCarthy, Votes Show," *ibid.*; "Issues Won for McCarthy," *ibid.*

[77] For a schedule of Kohler's campaign appearances August 6 through 16, see the Warren P. Knowles papers. Walter shook hands in eight different towns on August 8, 7, and 15. Warren Knowles was active in creating Kohler campaign groups throughout the state. Jim Kohler headed one in the Sheboygan area, a group wracked with dissention. See copy, W.P. Knowles to Charles Erasmus, June 25, 1952 Warren P. Knowles papers; copy, W. P. Knowles to Carl J. Kohler, June 15, 1952, *ibid.*; copy [W. P. Knowles] to Henry Ringling, August 13, 1952, *ibid.*

[78] "Kohler Hails Vote," *Milwaukee Journal*, September 10, 1952; "Warns GOP of Optimism," *ibid.*, September 13, 1952.

[79] Laurence C. Eklund, "Wiley to Give McCarthy Aid," *ibid.*, September 10, 1952.

[80] "GOP Unit Hails Vote," *ibid.*, September 13, 1952.

[81] "Republicans Will Ask McCarthy to Carry His 'Red' Campaign Into Other States," *ibid*, September 17, 1952; "Will Make Speeches," *ibid.*, September 18, 1952.

[82] Edwin R. Bayley, "Democrats Have to Go a Long Way in State," *ibid.*, August 22, 1952.

[83] "Fairchild Enters Race; Angers Reuss' Backers," *ibid.*, July 8, 1952. See Haney, "The Rise of Wisconsin's New Democrats," 98.

84 "'I Have a Good chance,' Fairchild Tells Truman," *Milwaukee Journal,* September 17, 1952.

85 "'Not a Prime Target,'" *ibid.,* September 18, 1952.

86 "Republicans Will Ask McCarthy to Carry His 'Red' Campaign Into Other States," *ibid.* See Walter J. Kohler, Jr. Oral History, 1971, 32-34.

87 Walter J. Kohler, Jr. to Warren P. Knowles, September 17, 1952, Warren P. Knowles papers.

88 "Kohler Says GOP Led in Reforms," *Milwaukee Journal,* September 17, 1952.

89 "GOP Governors to Speak for Ike," *ibid.,* September 21, 1952; Robert J. Doyle, "Kohler Slaps at Stevenson," *ibid.,* September 26, 1952.

90 "Kohler Pokes at Stevenson," *ibid.,* September 24, 1952.

91 See Reeves, *The Life and Times of Joe McCarthy,* 438. Official copies of the Eisenhower speeches delivered in Green Bay and Milwaukee are in the Wayne Hood papers.

92 Walter J. Kohler, Jr. Oral History, Columbia University, 1971, 21

93 *Ibid.,* 18-21.

94 Edwin R. Bayley, "Eisenhower Supports McCarthy in His First Two Talks in State," *Milwaukee Journal,* October 3, 1952; Robert H. Fleming, "State GOP Happy as Ike Speaks," *ibid*; Walter J. Kohler, Jr. Oral History, Columbia University, 1971, 21-23.

95 *Ibid.,* 23-32; Reeves, *The Life and Times of Joe McCarthy,* 439.

96 See Walter J. Kohler, Jr. Oral History, Columbia University, 1971, 23-32. The quotations are on pages 23 and 26.

97 Doyle K. Getter, "20,000 line Route for Ike's Motorcade," *Milwaukee Journal,* October 4, 1952. This seems to have been the full extent of Charlotte's participation in the campaign. She did, however, attract some minor attention by christening the new Lake Michigan ferry, the S. S. Badger, on September 6. The Badger is still in service. See *www.carferries.com/pm/43/* .

98 "Text of Eisenhower's Speech in Milwaukee," *Milwaukee Journal,* October 4, 1952.

99 Robert H. Fleming, "Ike, McCarthy Shake Hands," *ibid.*

100 *Ibid.*

101 *Ibid.*

102 Reeves, *The Life and Times of Joe McCarthy,* 440.

103 *Ibid.*

104 James C. Spaulding, "Kohler Calls Foe 'Visitor,'" *Milwaukee Journal,* October 16, 1952.

105 "Kohler Asks a Vote of 'No,'" *ibid.,* October 16, 1952.

106 "Kohler Blasts Truman Talk," *ibid.,* October 19, 1952.

107 "'Ex-GI's for Ike' Talk to Governor," *ibid.,* October 21, 1952.

108 "Kohler Blasts 'False Issue,'" *ibid.,* October 21, 1952.

[109] Editorial, "Harvard, Princeton and Yale," *ibid.*, October 29, 1952.

[110] Harry S. Pease, "Cites GOP's 'Tax Laxity,'" *ibid.*, October 28, 1952.

[111] "Proxmire Rips Kohler Stand," *ibid.*, October 16, 1952. See Sykes, *Proxmire*, 54-58.

[112] "No Stopping for Proxmire," *ibid.*, November 3, 1952. The candidate went without dinner on the last evening of the event. Afterward, he drank a glass of milk and ate about three-quarters of a sandwich. Proxmire claimed to have answered some 1,000 questions during the marathon. "30 Hours on the Air, Proxmire Closes Drive," *ibid.*, November 4, 1952..

[113] The Kennedys were not above using McCarthyite tactics. JFK's campaign literature portrayed him as a staunch opponent of "atheistic Communism" and criticized incumbent Senator Lodge for failing to nab more Reds in government by failing to attend most of the Tydings Committee hearings. The *Chicago Tribune* called JFK a "fighting conservative" and condemned Lodge as a "follower of the Truman-Acheson-Lattimore foreign policy." Some Democrats, including Harry Truman, also used McCarthyite language against opponents. See Reeves, *The Life and Times of Joe McCarthy*, 440-444.

[114] *Ibid.*, 444-447.

[115] "'GOP Helped by McCarthy,'" *Milwaukee Journal*, October 30, 1952.

[116] Paul M. McMahon, "'Not in Bag,' Kohler Says," *ibid.*, October 30, 1952.

[117] Reeves, *The Life and Times of Joe McCarthy*, 449-452.

[118] See "Kohler Tops Ballot for Ike," *Milwaukee Journal*, November 21, 1952. Official state voting figures are in *The Wisconsin Blue Book, 1954* (Madison, Wisconsin: The Wisconsin Legislative Reference Bureau, 1954), 756.

[119] Paul M. McMahon, "Proxmire Defeated by a Record Vote," *Milwaukee Journal*, November 5, 1952. See Walter J. Kohler, Jr. Oral History, Columbia University, 1971, 35. Here Walter attributed some of his voting strength to a quirk in the voting machines and thought Eisenhower's support a key factor in his victory.

[120] See Walter J. Kohler, Jr. Oral History, Columbia University, 1971, 32.

[121] "'It's War to the Death,' DOC Tells McCarthy," *Milwaukee Journal*, November 5, 1952.

[122] Sykes, *Proxmire*, 63.

[123] "Ike Indebted to Kohler for Governors' Letter," *Milwaukee Journal*, November 5, 1952; Walter J. Kohler, Jr. Oral History, Columbia University, 1971, 8-14.

[124] See Reeves, *The Life and Times of Joe McCarthy*, 453-455.

[125] *Ibid.*, 456-457.

Chapter Eleven
The Aim & End of Government

Not long after the election, Eisenhower wrote a warm public letter thanking Walter for his many campaign efforts.[1] At some point during the campaign, Eisenhower had mentioned several persons he considered to be of presidential material, and Kohler was one of them.[2] Few doubted that the Governor of Wisconsin was highly respected in Washington.

For several weeks there were rumors of offers of top administrative and diplomatic posts. Walter said later that he was offered many jobs, including a position on the White House staff. He was at no time interested, however, because in Washington, "you're not your own man any more."[3] Unspoken was the fact that he could hardly have persuaded Charlotte to move to Washington, where she would be surrounded constantly by politics and politicians.[4] Moreover, he was extremely reluctant to leave the Vollrath Company in the hands of others. From the start, the governor made it clear that he intended to remain in Madison and serve out his entire term.[5] There was unfinished work to be done, especially in higher education and highway planning and construction, and the budget needed urgent attention.

During budget hearings in late November, Walter demanded that the board of regents of both the University of Wisconsin and the state colleges (the teacher training institutions that had just begun to offer a four-year liberal arts degree) be merged into a single body. The consolidation was necessary, he said, to quell the competitive bidding by these boards for funds and students and to bring down costs. So adamant was he that he recommended giving neither body a cent until they agreed to merge.

Kohler declared that a merger would also lead to a full four year liberal arts college in Milwaukee that would be part of the University of Wisconsin. He wanted to prevent the Madison campus from ballooning to a projected 25,000 students, which he considered too large to be effective, and he sought to enable students in the state's largest city to be able to earn a UW degree without leaving home. At the same time, he envisioned no graduate or professional schools outside of Madison.[6] Currently, there were two state supported campuses in Milwaukee: the University of Wisconsin in Milwaukee, which offered a two year degree, and the Wisconsin state college, which had recently been authorized to offer a four year degree. A single UW college in the city meant a merger of some sort for the two institutions, and top officials on both campuses opposed the change.

In the past two years, the state general fund surplus had decreased from $49 million to a projected $15 million. Kohler blamed the federal government for the drop; federal excise taxes were currently imposed on gasoline, distilled spirits, malted beverages, cigarettes, and motor vehicle equipment, taxes that might well have been left to the states. The only solution to the vanishing surplus, the governor was convinced, was to reduce state expenditures. In the hearings, Walter went through the UW budget in detail, demanding specific spending cuts even down to a request for 200 new typewriters.[7] He soon complained that not a single department head was helping him create a balanced budget. During a Milwaukee speech, he declared, "It appears that I am fighting a lone battle for the forgotten man—and that forgotten man is the taxpayer."[8] While one leading Democrat jeered at the governor's efforts as "soap opera," the *Milwaukee Journal* loudly applauded Kohler's leadership.[9]

The year 1953 began pleasantly for Walter and Charlotte. Following a governors' conference in Phoenix, they traveled to Pasadena, California to head the official Wisconsin delegation to the Rose Bowl. They participated in the Rose Parade and saw the University of Southern California Trojans defeat the University of Wisconsin Badgers 7-0.[10] The Kohlers had been apart, most of the time, for the past several months, and the brief trip to Arizona and the West Coast was something of a vacation.

A few days later, back in Madison, Walter delivered a brief and eloquent inauguration address. He declared, "It is in our finest tradition to pioneer legislation to improve education, to aid the unfortunate, to banish corruption, to mete out justice and to improve the economic and social well-being of all our citizens. That is the aim and end of government to which we here today rededicate ourselves." He expressed personal pride in being selected by the people of Wisconsin to help carry out these tasks. "I shall not betray the faith, breach the trust nor violate the confidence. I shall execute the duties and responsibilities of the office of governor faithfully, in accordance with my oath and my pledges to the people. With God's help and with the people's help we shall continue to go forward."[11] Already it seemed apparent that Walter had shed at least some of the shrill partisanship of the last election campaign and was again exercising the calm, determined leadership that had distinguished his first two years in the state's capitol.

On January 15, in a formal message delivered in person to the 71st Wisconsin legislature, the governor stressed the need for a stringent highway safety program and a much larger state patrol; 893 persons had died on the state's highways in 1952, and more than 30,000 suffered injury. Kohler also recommended college board integration, better benefits for retired teachers, salary increases for top administrative officials, an increase in the governor's authority over certain administrative matters, and a study to consider the feasibility of a cross-state toll road. Walter stressed the need for fiscal caution, and urged legislators to resist the temptation to raise taxes.[12] Conspicuously absent was any reference to reapportionment, the most divisive issue facing the GOP. Rural Republicans remained adamant in opposing any change in their legislative representation.

The governor's proposed budget soon recommended reducing state expenditures by $7.6 million for the two years beginning July 1, 1953, bringing the spending total to $247,201,000. State institutions of higher education faced heavy cuts, receiving 13.6% less than they requested. Reaction at the University of Wisconsin was particularly bitter. (The state paid about 38% of the university's budget.)[13] Public welfare institutions fared better in the budget. "This more generous treatment is fair and reasonable, I believe, because we are dealing with the care, comfort and treatment of citizens who cannot help themselves, and whose needs were overlooked for many years," Kohler wrote. He also requested that an increase in the cigarette tax be devoted to mental hospital construction.[14]

Later that month, Walter and Charlotte attended the inauguration festivities in the nation's capital, being honored at the governors' reception, attending an inaugural ball and stage shows featuring Hollywood and New York celebrities, riding in the parade, and watching the swearing-in ceremony.[15] Kohler and Governor Dan Thornton of Colorado, the two leaders in the pre-convention "fair play" manifesto, were the first luncheon guests of the new president at the White House. After regaling his guests with amusing stories and listening to a pitch about the need to reduce federal intrusion on state taxing authority, Eisenhower took the two governors on a personally conducted half hour tour of the "renovated" White House (which had been almost totally reconstructed during the Truman administration).

Kohler then joined six other governors who comprised the inter-governmental relations committee of the Conference of Governors, a body planning a campaign to urge Congress to leave certain fields of taxation to the states.[16] Perhaps partly from exhaustion, Walter soon came down with a case of the flu and retired to Windway where his temperature reached 103.[17]

A few days later, the governor began a series of weekly radio talks over the state FM radio network designed to explain government problems and in particular what he called his "exceedingly lean" budget for fiscal 1953-1955.[18] The joint finance committee of the legislature, also eager to avoid a tax increase, soon submitted a budget that lopped nearly $2 million from Kohler's budget.[19]

On April 14, Walter was present at the stadium in Milwaukee, along with some 35,000 enthusiastic sports fans, to officially welcome the new Milwaukee Braves baseball team. The team had been moved from Boston a month earlier, and it returned Milwaukee to the major leagues after 52 years in the minors. Ford C. Frick, the commissioner of baseball; Warren Giles, president of the National League; Mayor Zeidler, and an assortment of other notables spoke to the crowd before the game. During his turn at the microphone, the governor told jokingly of his desire a day earlier to call the team the Wisconsin Braves. That set off a chorus of boos. But he quickly added, "I'm reconciled now to leave it the Milwaukee Braves," and the crowd cheered. Walter threw out the first ball from a box slightly to the right of home plate. Pitching great Warren Spahn and rookie star Billy Bruton led the team to a 3 to 2 victory over the St. Louis Cardinals.[20]

The rest of April was not as kind to the governor. The University of Wisconsin Board of Regents, led by his own appointees, came out against merger.[21] The legislature's joint finance committee predicted that the state was headed for a $7 million deficit by June 30, 1955.[22] And the legislature passed a law that called for limited redistricting, giving 70% recognition to population and 30% to area. Walter was willing to sign the compromise legislation on redistricting but said that the issue would have to be settled by the state supreme court. He clearly doubted that the new law conformed to the constitutional mandate to reapportion legislative districts immediately after each federal census.[23] Secretary of State Fred Zimmerman said flatly that the law was unconstitutional and intended to ignore it when preparing for the next election.[24]

The governor worked hard for the university merger bill, appearing before the Assembly Republican caucus for the first time, and calling legislators into his office. He told the caucus that the bill was "a cornerstone of my program," and said at one point in the deliberations that he knew "all my friends will vote for the bill."[25] But opposition from University of Wisconsin regents, alumni, and students, an assortment of important GOP committee chairmen, former governor Rennebohm, and Tom Coleman, who made telephone calls portraying himself as simply "a friend of the university," led to the defeat of the bill in the Assembly. (It had earlier passed in the Senate.) Republicans voted 41 to 30 against the merger plan, revealing that for the first time Governor Kohler had been dealt a severe defeat by his own badly divided party.

This was not a Left/Right split. Some opponents in the legislature objected to the determined methods the governor used to win support; others noted that too many Democrats and labor union officials backed merger; others expressed serious doubt about the details of the proposal (University of Wisconsin backers were afraid that the proposal, making state colleges branches of the University, would damage or destroy the University's reputation as an elite institution); and some were still bitter about Kohler's endorsement of reapportionment of the legislature. Walter himself said that he probably failed to explain the merger fully, but added that his efforts were handicapped by "misstatements and specious arguments of the opponents. It was a case of being unable to catch up with all the errors in their arguments." The unaccustomed bitterness was duly noted by Republicans and Democrats alike.[26] Proxmire crowed in a weekly radio talk that the defeat of the bill was a "grass roots rebellion against Governor Kohler's sleight of hand promise of a $100 million improvement in higher education on an empty state treasury and with no new state taxes."[27]

GOP legislators soon added to Kohler's humiliation by killing a proposal to increase the size of the state patrol. In a talk before the state convention of the Republican Voluntary Committee in June, the governor noted the two failures and indicated that some of the legislature's appropriation measures would be vetoed when they reached his desk.[28] Robert H. Fleming observed, "Party loyalty is not a binding tie in the legislature these days."[29]

Walter made more enemies on the far Right by publicly opposing the Bricker Amendment. This was a McCarthyite attempt to impose controls on the power of the Chief Executive to negotiate international treaties and limit the scope of such agreements. On April 6, Secretary of State John Foster Dulles declared the proposal "dangerous to our peace and security." Senator Wiley also opposed the constitutional amendment, earning him a rebuke at the Republican party's state convention. Wiley called the action against him "a stab in the back," prompting the editor of an unofficial Wisconsin Republican periodical to denounce him as a "cry baby who stoops to fascist tactics" in criticizing those who have expressed "their sincere beliefs" about his "limited qualifications."[30]

It was dawning on liberal and moderate Republicans that the far Right had not significantly reduced its frenzy after the election. Even though the new administration was firing hundreds of federal employees who were in some way thought to be dangerous to the nation's security, ultraconservatives were now beginning to shoot negative glances at their own White House and State Department. Critics who had long condemned them for being cynical vote-getters might well have wondered why they were now going after their own party members.

Early in the year Don Surine told HUAC officials that Senator McCarthy, new chairman of the Committee on Government Operations and chairman of the committee's permanent Subcommittee on Investigations, did not plan to limit his probes to any one field. He was not even reluctant to subpoena Harry Truman. "Senator McCarthy isn't afraid of anyone or anything," said Surine. "He means business. You watch and see what he does. It will make history."[31]

McCarthy and his allies were soon condemning the president's selections for United States High Commission for West Germany and ambassador to the Soviet Union. A probe into the Voice of America set off a panic of "anti-subversive" activity in the State Department and raised hackles all over Europe. McCarthy, at the peak of his powers by mid-year, even attempted to make a personal impact on international trade by making a deal with Greek ship owners. Eisenhower was privately furious about the activities of the Wisconsin Senator but remained determined not to confront him officially. He told close associates, "I just will not—I refuse—to get into the gutter with that guy."[32]

Governor Kohler was forced to deal directly with the far Right for it continued to control the Republican Voluntary Committee in the state and command the allegiance of many legislators. Even though he won more than a million votes in the last election, and the man in the White House was his friend and ally, Walter was still something of an outsider in his own party. (A few months earlier, at a meeting of the Milwaukee Women League of Voters, Walter was asked if he, as head of the Republican party in the state, would use his political influence on the reapportionment issue. He replied, "Who thinks I'm the head of the Republican party in Wisconsin?")[33]

The legislature recessed on June 12, and by the end of July the governor had signed a total of 622 bills and vetoed 34 (an all-time high). All of his vetoes, it seems, were based on sound reasoning, evidence, and the judgment of experts rather than mere partisanship.[34] One veto, of a $2.8 million appropriation for an addition to the University of Wisconsin medical school, did not help his relations with top UW officials, but it was based on the state's fiscal crisis, as many understood.

One bill Walter was particularly pleased to sign ended open inspection of income tax returns. No other state had ever had such a law, and neither had the federal government. Kohler's own finances had been featured in the press and used against him by political opponents, even though no wrongdoing was found. The governor called the bill a victory for personal privacy and a boost to state industry.[35]

In early August, Kohler played a prominent role at a governors' meeting in Seattle. He was also appointed to the important resolutions committee of the conference. Walter took the occasion to praise the truce in Korea, calling it a "qualified victory" because Reds had not seized the whole of the country. But he was not above citing the possible Republican gains that might arise from the settlement and criticizing the former administration: "There could have been a complete victory in Korea if it hadn't been for the Acheson and United Nations policies of fighting with one arm behind our back there."[36] The fiery campaign of 1952 had left its scars on the governor, as it had on most Republican leaders.

In early October, Walter traveled to the 9th Congressional district to spend four days campaigning for Arthur L. Padrutt. A special election had been called after the incumbent's death, and the governor declared the election of his friend Padrutt "a test case of whether the Eisenhower administration is going to have the support of the people of the nation." Kohler's campaign was aided by the fact that the predominantly rural district in the south central part of the state had never elected a Democrat to Congress.

But Democrats badly wanted this Congressional seat and believed they could win it. Farm prices had fallen 20% in the past couple of years, and there was noticeable discontent in the region. Democrats nominated Lester Johnson of Black River Falls and sent Estes Kefauver and former Democratic secretaries of agriculture Charles F. Brannan and Claude Wickard into the area to campaign for him. Kohler blamed almost all of the drop in farm prices on the Truman administration and spent much of his time touting the Eisenhower administration's achievements in other areas, including foreign relations, where the policy of "passive containment" had been replaced by one of "constructive pressure" against the Communists in Europe.[37]

To Walter's chagrin, the Democrat won the election. The victory prompted James E. Doyle to pour ridicule and scorn upon the governor, telling one group of elated Democrats, "Don't laugh. How would you like it if you had spent your way through Governor Goodland's cookie jar until you finally had to raise state taxes and then you found no ambassadorship was being offered and you had to run for governor again on a Republican economy ticket? Some say Kohler will run in 1954 like he ran against McCarthy—away."[38]

When the state legislature reconvened on October 25, the governor asked it for special authority to curtail spending by permitting him to share authority with the director of budgets and accounts to evaluate fund allotments and amend or disapprove them if there was insufficient revenue. The budget director was now forecasting a deficit of nearly $3 million in the current biennium. With the new authority and the upholding of his vetoes, Kohler said, the state could make its way through the current crisis and possibly wind up with a small surplus.[39] While Democrats predictably opposed the plan, Republicans were split on the issue. The Assembly quickly overturned six of the governor's vetoes, and the one Senate move to override passed on a vote of 30-1. The *Milwaukee Journal* called for a tax increase. Democrats gleefully predicted a series of landslide victories for their party in 1954.[40]

On October 27, the Joint Finance Committee twice turned down Kohler's bid for special authority. The votes were preceded by an angry, closed door session of the Committee that included the governor. A Republican member of the Committee afterward told a reporter, "The governor shouldn't have lost his temper, so I don't want to talk about it." Kohler was especially upset by members of his own party who refused to support him, and declared that unless the legislature agreed to his request he would not assume responsibility for balancing the budget. It was a matter of principle with him. Following a sharp debate, a caucus of GOP assemblymen voted 28-23 to ask the Finance Committee to report the Kohler request for Assembly consideration. The Joint Finance Committee rejected the request.[41]

On November 4, a compromise was worked out by the governor and legislative leaders, and it soon passed in both the Senate and Assembly by large numbers. With assurances from Kohler that revenues would be higher than anticipated, legislators declared the budget "balanced" without new taxes. In doing this, they rejected the estimated deficit but directed the budget director to cooperate with the governor in cutting already budgeted allotments if necessary. In short, Walter received the authority he wanted and avoided new taxes. Moreover, the deal also gave the legislature's emergency board the power to raise or lower salaries, within a $15,000 maximum, for 54 state department heads. The governor was one of three men on the board. Walter had every reason to believe that his firmness and patience had paid off. While some veteran Republican legislators had reportedly sniffed at the governor's lack of political savvy—he was not given to small talk, arm twisting, and political deals—they now had to acknowledge that he could get results.[42]

Democrats were furious about what they called a "financial sleight of hand." One leading Democrat declared, "This was a proposal for one man government in the Nazi and Soviet system." More accurately, he called the resolution "a peace treaty after a week of Republican civil war."[43]

Thereafter, the governor largely had his way with the legislature during its nine day session. Legislators sustained 32 Kohler vetoes and overrode only three. The *Milwaukee Journal* called that "remarkable." When the governor vetoed a bill passed in the current session, legislators accepted the veto and reworded the item so that Kohler would sign it.

The largest failure of the legislature was to accept the governor's requests for highway safety measures. The ten month total of traffic deaths in Wisconsin was 701, but this fact insufficiently impressed legislators.[44] Still, a bill was passed and signed to create a five man Expressway Commission for Milwaukee County to plan and build the county's proposed 73 mile expressway system. Voters had approved two bond issues totaling $8 million to ease traffic congestion, and a third for $3 million more would soon be voted on. The governor was authorized to make the appointments. Kohler's choices, made promptly, were widely applauded by Milwaukee leaders, beginning with Mayor Zeidler.[45]

In December, Walter was back in Washington to speak at a luncheon of the national conference on highway financing, sponsored by the United States Chamber of Commerce. He traced the history of the federal gasoline tax, first imposed on an emergency basis in 1932. Twenty years later, the federal government was collecting about $850 million in gasoline taxes, but federal highway aid allotted to the states from that revenue was only $575 million. Federal motor vehicle excise taxes in 1952 amounted to $1.2 million. The governor called on the federal government to get out of the gasoline taxing business, leaving that function entirely to the states. When a Congressman raised objections to the proposal, Walter conceded that he wanted the federal government to continue to be interested in the national system of interstate highways.[46]

At this conference, the governor's interest in a major Wisconsin toll road increased, as he learned of the rapid progress of toll road expansion all across the country. There were 809 miles operating in ten states; 1,083 miles in several states were under construction; 3,146 miles were authorized in 18 states; and 2,423 miles were proposed and under study.[47]

During the first few days of 1954, syndicated columnist and Kohler admirer John Wyngaard was granted an interview in the governor's office. It was the third anniversary of Walter's governorship, and the journalist was interested in obtaining views on a variety of people and issues. Wyngaard noted that, "As always, the governor was reluctant to talk about himself" and desired only to discuss his political experiences.

Walter was as unwilling to talk about his family as he was about himself. His relations with Charlotte were entirely private. He wanted no public attention paid to Niki, who had just returned to her institution outside Philadelphia after the Christmas holiday. And he did not desire to discuss 19-year-old Terry, with whom he had experienced some rather strained relations.

Terry had been a bright, fun-loving youngster whose independent ways did not fit in well with the schools to which he was sent. After attending the Kohler public schools, he went to Andover, as was the family custom. After a summer preparatory course to evaluate candidates, he was denied admission. This was a serious blow to Terry's self-confidence, and his father was not at all pleased. Terry was then sent to The Gunnery, another private school, in Connecticut. He stayed there three years, enjoyed competitive skiing, and was kicked out in his

junior year for smoking. In April, 1951, Terry enrolled in the Oakland
Military Academy in Oakland, New Jersey, near his mother's residence.
In June, 1952, he graduated from the Admiral Farragut Academy in New
Jersey. He enjoyed the military regimen there and wanted to attend the
U.S. Naval Academy.

After a year of private study, Terry applied to the Academy and was
accepted. But in 1953 he decided not to attend. He had met a lovely
young Sheboygan woman who would become his wife and desired to
remain near her. In June, Terry went to Northwestern University to
study civil engineering. Bad grades forced him to leave 8 months later.
During 1954, the governor's son lived at Windway, joined the crew of
a Milwaukee racing boat, served as a surveyor's assistant, worked on
local farms, and was a paid driver in his father's political campaign.
Walter demanded that Terry work if he wanted to eat; that was the
Kohler way.[48] Years later, Terry said that his father's mandate was given
"out of love."

Terry's difficulties, caused admittedly by a lack of maturity, served
as a roadblock between himself and his father, who had personally
known only success. Still, Walter made every effort to understand his
son; he never expressed general disappointment in Terry nor compared
him unfavorably with other members of the Kohler family. Terry believed that his father respected him, despite his troubles in school. But
there was a distance between him and his father that he continued to
acknowledge decades later. Walter was warm but quite formal; kind
rather than censorious, but also firm and demanding. Father and son
were close but not intimate.[49]

Terry first made the press in early 1955 when he was sworn into the
Air Force, saying that he wanted to become a jet fighter pilot. At his
father's suggestion, he had applied for cadet training the previous May
and passed the air force's mental and physical tests. He was soon on his
way to Lackland Air Force Base in San Antonio, Texas to begin a 12-week
preflight training course. This was the beginning of a resurgence in the
young man's life that was to bring his father considerable pride.[50]

There was something else that Walter did not want to discuss with
John Wyngaard. On February 20, 1953 Walter had quietly sold all of
his 21,415 shares in the Kohler company back to the company for $115
a share, receiving a total of $2,462,725. (Walter's brother Bob had sold
his shares in 1951, buying a struggling plastics firm in Sheboygan.)[51]
He could see serious labor trouble looming at the plant and thought

it would be politically inadvisable to own the stock. In May, 1952 the Kohler Workers Association had lost an employee referendum to the UAW-CIO, and bitterness was boiling up against Herbert V. Kohler, who actively campaigned for the KWA. The recent law making income tax data confidential was passed just in time to keep the public from knowing how very wealthy Walter was.[52]

On the subject of politics, the governor told the journalist that looking back on the past three years, he was content with "a sense of duty performed." He was especially proud of the legislative achievements. There were things he would have done differently but he was confident that his "failures" in political matters were not "failures of conscience." He had not yet decided, he said, about running for a third term.

Wyngaard observed that the governor, at 48, was in good health and along with his gubernatorial duties was operating a company that did a $9 million business in 1953. Walter said that while he was terribly busy, he probably worked no harder that others who had served in the office. Wyngaard also noted that Kohler was more easily available to callers, even casual callers to his office, than most of the state department heads who were his subordinates. The governor's popularity in Madison, said the journalist, was widespread.[53]

Soon, however, defiant Republican lawmakers again made an unfriendly statement to the governor. In what appeared to be a premeditated rebuke, the two prominent legislative members of the emergency board voted against salary increases. Sanford Goltz of the *Wisconsin State Journal* observed, "To Capitol observers, it seemed a needless, even arrogant, action. The amount of money involved was tiny, with no bearing on the budget situation. It was a matter on which the governor set great store, affecting the possible retention of at least a few top administrators and the chances of recruiting others in the next year or two." When added to Kohler defeats on the highway safety recommendations and the higher education integration bill, it seemed clear that more than a few leading GOP legislators failed to respect the governor's wishes, confident that Walter was not the kind of man who would attempt to punish them for their independence. (GOP legislator Harry Franke said years later that Walter was never vindictive like Attorney General and future governor Vernon Thomson, a "tough guy" who "never forgave a slight.") If this attitude continued into 1955, Goltz stated, it could be an unhappy year for any occupant of the governor's chair.[54] State conservation director Ernest Swift soon resigned to take a better paying job with the federal government, and Walter said that he didn't blame him for his departure.[55]

In early 1954, Walter and Charlotte vacationed in the West Indies. This winter-time escape would continue annually, and a few years later the couple would build a home in Antigua, in the Windward islands south of St. Thomas about 300 miles. The cabana was constructed at the ultra-exclusive Mill Reef Club. The Kohlers would use it two months a year and rent it out for the rest of the year.[56] Walter loved these visits to the tropics, and in 1954 he returned to Madison tanned and rested.

In mid-March Walter and Charlotte were in California, where the governor attended a meeting of the American Cancer Society. In Hollywood, he served as godfather to the three children of movie star Esther Williams. The actress and the governor had met at Eisenhower's inauguration. She was pregnant at the time, and Kohler, hearing that she had two boys at home, predicted a girl. Williams told Walter that if the child were a girl, he could be the godfather. Three of the handsome photos taken at the service were carried by wire services and distributed all over the country. After the service a reporter asked Walter about Senator McCarthy. He replied, "It's a nice day, isn't it? Beautiful weather out here."[57]

On May 6, Walter announced his bid for a third term, stressing his desire to improve the state's highways and schools and wanting to assist the dairy industry, in turmoil since the federal government slashed parities from 90% to 70% on April 1.[58] John Wyngaard, noting the "essential contentment of the electorate" thought Kohler's reelection highly likely. "His principal assets are dignity, a strong feeling for personal propriety, a natural integrity of outlook and spirit, and a keen intelligence." His liabilities "are not of the mind, but of the personality. He is an inept politician, knows it, and chooses to do nothing about it."[59]

The conservative *Wisconsin State Journal* endorsed the candidate immediately, stating in an editorial, "Gov. Kohler has done a good job for Wisconsin. He has worked hard. He has shown patience and understanding in the manifold tasks of the office. In such fields as mental welfare, and in pushing the state's long-neglected building program, he has shown vision. The improved treatment programs for the state's unfortunate citizens and the new buildings rising on every campus and every institution grounds in Wisconsin are Walter Kohler's best answer to those who now accuse him of 'dissipating' the generous surplus he found on taking office in 1951."[60]

James E. Doyle, the former co-chairman of the Democratic Organizing Committee, became a candidate for his party's nomination for governor. It was his first bid for office. He was opposed by William Proxmire, whose non-stop campaigning had been going on since the day he lost the election to Kohler.

❧ ❧ ❧ ✦ ❦ ❦ ❦

At the time of Walter's campaign announcement, Joe McCarthy was in a mortal conflict with the Eisenhower administration. He had stepped up his attacks on the State Department and was claiming to have found traitors in defense plants, the Central Intelligence Agency, and in the Army. His increasingly wild attacks were aided by Roy Cohn, a brilliant and unscrupulous young attorney who joined McCarthy's staff on the first day of 1953. With the Senator increasingly prey to alcohol, Cohn increased his personal influence and helped involve McCarthy in a severe conflict with Army officials that led to the Army-McCarthy hearings, featured on national television from April 22 to June 17.

By the spring of 1954, McCarthy's popularity was in sharp decline. In early March, his poll numbers sagged dramatically. President Eisenhower was becoming increasingly audible about his distaste for the Senator's methods. Senator Ralph Flanders of Vermont denounced McCarthy on the floor of the Senate. Several of the nation's major newspapers and magazines routinely attacked the Wisconsin senator.

On March 9, famed television commentator Edward R. Murrow devoted his entire "See It Now" program on CBS to an attack on McCarthy, making a profound impression on the American people. Murrow's daring and unprecedented program infuriated McCarthyites. One letter writer suggested a new, Murrow-like Statue of Liberty with the inscription: "Send me your Commies, pinkos, and crackpots, and I will put them on television." A Hearst newsman referred to the broadcaster as "Egghead R. Murrow." A Murrow associate, attacked repeatedly by the Hearst press as a "pinko," committed suicide.[61]

At about the same time, former McCarthy supporter Leroy Gore, editor of the weekly *Sauk-Prairie Star* in tiny Sauk City, Wisconsin, about 30 miles from Madison, attracted attention throughout the world by launching a drive to recall McCarthy. This "Joe Must Go" campaign soon attracted the support of the Wisconsin Federation of Labor and the Wisconsin state CIO.[62]

Gore was of the opinion that Governor Kohler would back his movement, giving this assurance to State Senator Harry Franke, a moderate
Republican who lent his signature to the recall drive. The nature of any
agreement between Gore and the governor remains unknown and may
not have existed at all. When Gore sent a public telegram to Kohler,
urging him "to speak your conscience and step outside Republican state
political circles which are aligning themselves with the McCarthy-Mc-
Cormick-Wood axis of Midwest isolationists," the governor did not
reply or make any public statement.[63]

There was a good reason for Walter's silence. When Franke's name
appeared in the initial "Joe Must Go" ad in the *Milwaukee Journal*, the
Milwaukee legislator was besieged with hate mail and telephone calls
and was invited to resign from his local Republican organization.[64] No
major Republican officeholder in Wisconsin supported Gore. It was
political suicide.

By the end of the Army-McCarthy hearings in mid-June, thoughtful
people all over the Western world knew that Joe McCarthy was finished. He had self-destructed before the television cameras, revealing
himself to be a crude and insufferable bully and bluffer whose principal
contribution to history was calumny. McCarthy's colleagues on both
sides of the aisle began an investigation leading to his censure. Refusing
to recant anything he had said or done, Joe rejected all attempts to save
his political career. A cynical man would have acted otherwise

Still, McCarthyites all across the nation rose up to defend the Senator, and many Wisconsin Republicans continued to revere their native
son. Again running for office, Walter needed every vote and chose to say
nothing about the colossal controversy that had rent the GOP and was
leading to McCarthy's demise. William Proxmire and the Democrats
had a field day with attacks on the governor for "surrendering" to the
far Right and abetting the scandal of McCarthyism.[65]

❖❖❖◉❖❖❖

On April 4, workers at the Kohler Company went on strike. Above all,
they were seeking the union shop (requiring all production employees
to join the UAW-CIO local 833 after a specified period of time). Anyone who knew Herbert V. Kohler knew that he would never accede to
such a demand. On the night of April 25, Herbert had approached the
picket line carrying a truncheon. When questioned by pickets about his
legal right to carry a club, he said testily, "I am the law!"[66] During the

second week in June, Herbert expressed extreme annoyance at pickets interfering with the progress of his car at the office entrance, telling the men, "When I get through with you, you'll come crawling back on your bellies, begging for jobs!"[67] The company hired detective agencies to spy on strikers and evicted eight employees from the American Club and two from Company-owned homes.[68]

In late June, Harvey Kitzman of Milwaukee, director of the U.A.W.'s region 10, contacted Governor Kohler for assistance in settling the strike. The labor leader suggested that the governor name a fact-finding panel to study the conflict and make recommendations. Walter told him, Kitzman later recalled, that "he was no longer officially connected with the company and that they had booted him out and that maybe his intervention would be more of a hindrance than good." Kitzman suggested some distinguished panel members, assuring the governor of his intention to seek objective judgment. When two perspective panel members turned down the governor, he decided to take action on his own.

In early July, while at a governors' conference in Lake George, New York, Walter issued a public letter to both Herbert Kohler and Allan W. Graskamp, president of the local union, calling for binding arbitration of the strike. The letter stressed the governor's neutrality in the issue and pointed to the economic consequences of the strike. "I need not tell you how disturbed I am over the severe personal hardship being endured by those who are unemployed because of this dispute. Extension of the conflict is good for neither the company nor the union. It is emphatically not good for the community nor for the state." The governor said that "little prospect exists that these disagreements can be speedily resolved through collective bargaining procedures." Kitzman quickly recommended to the local union that it accept the governor's proposal. The *Sheboygan Press* also endorsed the plan.[69]

There were no doubt two other reasons for the governor's letter. Herbert's militant obstinacy was tarring the family's surname, and Walter used this opportunity to distance himself from his uncle. Many Wisconsinites perhaps still thought that the governor had close connections with the Kohler Company, tempting Democrats in the forthcoming campaign to link the two relatives as "fat cats" who cared only about corporate profits. In the third sentence of his letter, Walter stated, "As you know, I have no financial interest in or other connection with Kohler Company." Moreover, there was the element of revenge. Walter knew full well that his uncle would never accept binding arbitration, and this letter was a way of needling him in public for the treatment all four of Walter Sr.'s sons had received at his hands.

The next day, in a blistering public letter to the governor, Herbert rejected the proposal, saying that binding arbitration would reward "an illegal picket line which by coercion and violence prevented employees who desired to come to work from doing so." Herbert stated, "We will not grant to anyone outside the company...the ultimate authority to prescribe such vital elements of cost as wages, working schedules, fringe benefits, etc.", and he flatly rejected the concept of the union shop. In a slap at his nephew, Herbert called attention to the wage increases the Kohler Company had granted over the past two years. "Our wages, including our present offer to the union, exceed the average for Sheboygan, where the plant you head is located, by 43.4 cents per hour and by $23.30 per week." The bad blood between the two Kohlers was made extremely clear in the last sentence of the letter: "You are so far wrong in your suggestion that our refusal to let an arbitrator write a contract for us will embarrass us before the public, that we shall see to it that the stand we have expressed in this letter gets the fullest publicity."[70]

Union leader Graskamp termed Herbert Kohler's rejection of the governor's proposal "a public be damned attitude which every thinking person in Wisconsin must despise. Governor Kohler acted in the finest sense of statesmanship and the Kohler Company virtually told him and the public to go to hell."[71]

Striking employees, whose actions during the strike were often violent, both on and off the picket line, soon passed a resolution urging Herbert Kohler to resign.[72] "The effort of Herbert V. Kohler to maintain his private dictatorship has been a great drain on this community....It has seriously damaged the company which he, and others, inherited."[73]

Walter's proposal had been effective: He had clearly attempted to distinguish himself from his uncle in the public's eye and had made an effort, applauded throughout the state, to settle a nasty, costly, and dangerous strike. In short, the governor had again proved that he was a better politician than many thought. Even so, Democrats observed correctly before the election that the governor was still being blamed by many voters for the Kohler strike.[74]

❧~❧~❧~◉~❧~❧~❧

Throughout the summer of 1954, Democratic candidates William Proxmire and James E. Doyle pummeled the governor with an assortment of charges as they crisscrossed the state in search of votes. Proxmire said at one point that Wisconsin state government was "living the life of an improvident playboy," contending that the Kohler administration had "pushed spending far beyond state revenues" and predicting tax increases.[75] On one of his regular radio programs from Madison, he declared that Kohler was fighting Eisenhower's highway plan by proposing that the federal government return its share of the gas tax to the state.[76] In Oshkosh, he declared, "I defy anyone to cite one action Governor Kohler has taken to promote dairy products." He also scored the governor for using the "enormous prestige of his office to help Senator Joseph McCarthy."[77]

Doyle said in Madison that assertions by Republicans about the state debt were "at best fiscal ignorance and at worst calculated deceit."[78] He charged at one point that Kohler showed "a coldness bearing on hostility toward the University's financial problems" and was "languishing on the sands of Jamaica" when Secretary of Agriculture Benson cut dairy support prices.[79] When Walter acknowledged publicly that it was he who urged Eisenhower to alter his Milwaukee campaign speech, Doyle declared, "'Countless Wisconsin citizens are deeply shocked to learn that it was Governor Kohler alone who knifed that great American patriot, General George C. Marshall...'"[80]

Kohler, unopposed in the primary, campaigned only slightly during the summer months. In early September, at Chippewa Falls he told 300 township chairmen that state finances were in excellent shape. He noted the reduction in state income taxes under his administration and the completion of a $90 million building program since World War II, and he dismissed the "stupidity" of the Proxmire charge that he had squandered the state surpluses. Walter used his authority as chairman of President Eisenhower's committee of governors working on development of a nationwide highway program to defend the state's road improvement efforts.[81]

In Milwaukee, the governor urged the election of his friend State Senator Warren Knowles as lieutenant governor. The post was currently held by Republican George M. Smith, who had lost the party's endorsement to the popular Knowles. Kohler spoke of Knowles as his likely successor; both of his immediate predecessors, Oscar Rennebohm and Walter Goodland, had followed the route from lieutenant governor to governor.[82]

Following a light primary turnout in mid-September, Knowles was selected to be the governor's running mate and William Proxmire again became the Democratic candidate for governor. The combined total of votes for Doyle (85,187) and Proxmire (141,548) fell more than 104,000 votes short of the governor's 331,006. Indeed, Kohler was the top vote-getter in the primary.[83] Democrats promised an all-out effort to defeat the governor, blaming him, among other things, for the 40 percent drop in the price of milk since the GOP victories in 1952.[84]

Throughout the fall, Proxmire traveled frantically across the state, loudly condemning the governor for an assortment of alleged failures, calling him a McCarthy appeaser, and demanding a public debate on "any issue whatsoever that you may select."[85] This approach got under Walter's skin. He replied angrily, "Debate is impossible when one of the parties consistently refused to be bound by the facts." The governor accused his challenger with "cynical contempt for the truth about Wisconsin....in fact, to the best of my knowledge you have never said anything good about the state which you so recently adopted."[86] (The two were not to debate during the campaign, appearing together only once, in a Milwaukee television studio, where each made a brief presentation.)[87] Speaking at a GOP rally in Fond du Lac, the governor vowed to visit every corner of the state to "expose every misrepresentation, half truth and falsehood uttered by the Democratic gubernatorial candidate during the current campaign."[88]

In October, Walter participated in nine district GOP rallies throughout the state, along with Warren Knowles and Attorney General Vernon Thomson. In Milwaukee the rally took place at the Eagles Club before an audience of about 200. The governor took the high ground, boasting of Republican achievements, and left the rough stuff to his colleagues. Thomson accused "Foxy Proxy" of being a "foreign candidate" sent to Wisconsin by the Jake Arvey interests in Illinois, the Texas oil and gas interests, the oleo interests, and the southern foes of the St. Lawrence seaway to corrupt Wisconsin, dissipate its treasury, and drain off Lake Michigan water into the Chicago river, "the biggest open sewer in the world." Democratic "carpetbaggers" Estes Kefauver ("old coony Kefauver"), Congressman Sam Rayburn of Texas, and former Secretary of Agriculture Charles Brannan, he said, were also campaigning in the state on behalf of the peanut and cotton trust and other foreign interests. Thomson called Adlai Stevenson "that fugitive from a horse meat scandal."

Knowles used the McCarthyite technique of castigating the "Harvards." "E. William Proxmire was born in Lake Forest, Illinois, and educated in the east, in a plush finishing school in Pennsylvania. He went on to Harvard and Yale, then got a position with the J.P. Morgan Company. He married into the Rockefeller family—the Wall Street Rockefellers. He finally wound up working for the Capital Times over in Madison. He was dismissed from his duties as a reporter and took up some other employment. We haven't been able to find out just how he has been making his living since then. He has been too busy running for office."[89]

All through October, Walter stumped through the state, slogging through mud on the outskirts of Manawa to speak to people at the state plowing championship, giving the keynote address at the Republican state platform convention in Madison, addressing a school boards association meeting in Boscobel, speaking to the Wisconsin Indianhead association in Spooner, and so on throughout all ten congressional districts.[90] He had the advantage of presenting a largely positive message. At a homecoming celebration in Bonduel, he lauded the state's administrative efficiency and noted that Wisconsin was one of only eight states in the union without a state debt and one of only 16 states without a state sales tax.[91] In one of several televised campaign speeches from Madison, he said that Wisconsin stood in the front rank of states in the fields of highways, education, public welfare, agriculture, and labor education.[92]

Senator Wiley also stumped the state on behalf of the GOP ticket. Senator McCarthy did not participate in the campaign, the official story being that he was in a naval hospital in Maryland being treated for a sinus condition. In fact, almost no one wanted his support in the fall elections. He had not been in Wisconsin since the Watkins Committee in the Senate unanimously recommended censure.[93] Still, his point of view was present. Walter's friend and now Congressman Melvin Laird spoke at a rally in Antigo, saying that if Democrats won control in Congress they would recognize Communist China. "The Truman-Acheson approach always has been and always will be pro-Red China."[94] Congressman Charles Kersten remained a proud McCarthyite throughout his reelection campaign against liberal Democrat Henry Reuss.

In late October, Kohler and Proxmire got into an intense conflict over the Democrat's contention in a television ad during the summer that dairy farmer Oscar Holte of Stoughton suffered a big loss in milk check income between November, 1952 and May, 1954. The governor went on the air over a 28 station network to charge Proxmire with having distorted Republican farm policies. Holte's 1952 check, said Walter, represented the full production for his farm. But in 1954, he had gone into partnership with his son and his check represented only the farmer's 60% share. Moreover, said the governor, Proxmire had compared wartime milk prices with peacetime prices, concealed a drop in the milk test of Holte's herd, and made two other distortions. These facts, Walter said, "raise the question whether a man [Proxmire], so careless with the truth, has a right to ask for support for the highest office in the state." He called Proxmire's claim "the most scandalous hoax I have ever seen in a Wisconsin political campaign."

The governor added that it was false for Democrats to contend that farm prosperity could be achieved by imposing strict production controls on dairy farmers in exchange for 90% price supports. And he reminded his listeners that under the Democrats the national debt had climbed to $270 billion "and the names of 1,200,000 American boys, many of them Wisconsin farmers' sons, were casualties in World War II and the Korean war." These were, of course, conflicts Kohler had supported fully.[95]

Proxmire fired back, saying that "Governor Kohler's extravagant and false charges of lies and hoaxes have demeaned the office of governor" and announced that he would go on the radio to offer "undeniable, shocking proof that Governor Kohler's hoax charge is false."[96] Holte, a Democrat, sided with Proxmire and said he would vote for him. The *Madison Capital Times* soon became involved in the uproar, predictably siding with Proxmire.[97] The complexities of the dairy price squabble were such that probably no one fully understood what was being debated. It was certain, however, that Wisconsin dairy farmers were not at all pleased with the Eisenhower Administration's policy toward their price supports and that Kohler was taking some of the blame.[98]

A few days before the election, at a rally held in Milwaukee's American Serb Memorial Hall, the governor boasted that Wisconsin Republicans had a "record of legislative accomplishment unmatched by any state in the union." He detailed efforts to modernize and expand state welfare agencies and facilities, said that the state had produced more labor legislation than any other, and noted progress in such fields as unemployment and workmen's compensation, aid to the disabled, and aid to dependent children. Observing that the Eisenhower Administration had made the St. Lawrence seaway a reality, he proposed to create a new program to help the state benefit from the new development.

Still, despite the positive bent of his talk, Walter felt obligated to dip a bit into the mud of McCarthyism. He said that the Republicans had "eliminated" 6,000 federal employees as "Communists, fellow travelers or security risks" and warned, "If you elect a Democratic Congress, you will see an end to the investigations of Communists and an end to investigation of corruption in government."[99]

To his credit, Walter's use of this campaign tactic had decreased greatly over the past two years. And other Republicans throughout the country, notably Vice President Nixon, were saying the same things, and worse. McCarthy the man may have been nearly eliminated as a force in American politics, but the Second Red Scare was still very much alive during the campaigns of 1954. In August, Senate Democrats, terrified that their opponents might brand them as "soft on the Reds," had passed the Communist Control Act, which attempted to outlaw the Communist Party in the United States.[100]

Proxmire was not above using Red Scare tactics either. On a day in Milwaukee in which he campaigned for 16 hours, he linked the governor's stance in the dairy price squabble with McCarthy's "big lie" techniques and contended that a Kohler defeat would be a "tremendous blow" for Senator McCarthy.[101]

On November 2, Kohler defeated Proxmire by an unexpectedly narrow margin, 596,158 to 560,747. This was the closest gubernatorial race in the state since 1932. The Wisconsin State CIO announced that it would demand and finance a recount in all 71 counties, and the *Madison Capital Times* said that Proxmire gave Kohler "the scare of his political life."[102] The Democrat won in Milwaukee by a large margin and carried the urban areas of Racine, Kenosha, and Madison. The governor won by a two to one ratio in McCarthy's Outagamie County and enjoyed a commanding lead in traditionally Republican Waukesha County. In Sheboygan County, where 33,333 votes were cast, Walter's victory margin was only 3,691. (The governor said later that the Kohler strike had "considerable effect" on his election race. "It is not generally known that I have no connection with the Kohler company.")[103] Democrats made strong gains in rural areas.

While all the major GOP candidates for state office won, three of them—Fred R. Zimmerman (secretary of state), Warren R. Smith (treasurer), and Vernon W. Thomson (attorney general)—collected more votes than Kohler. Walter's friend and apparent successor Warren P. Knowles (lieutenant governor) won 2,638 fewer votes than the governor.[104]

Democrat Henry Reuss narrowly ousted Charles Kersten in the 5th District's congressional race. Democrats won 36 of the state assembly's 100 seats, a gain of 11, and increased their number in the senate from six to eight. Not since 1934 had Democrats controlled this many seats.[105]

In a sense, this was a typical off-year election, with the party in power losing some of its strength to the opposition. But Democrats were more vigorous and successful than had been predicted. Nationally, they wrested control of both the Senate and the House, and toppled seven Republican governors.[106] Moreover, analysts pointed to defeats by McCarthyite candidates in more than a half dozen states.[107]

Joe McCarthy, about to be censured in what he called a Senate "lynching bee," blamed Eisenhower, among other party leaders, for Democratic gains in the election.[108] In May, in a rage about the Eisenhower Administration's defense of the Army against his charges, he had added the first year of the Republican reign to the era of Democratic rule, referring to "the past twenty or twenty-one years" of treason in government.[109]

After his censure, McCarthy apologized for having supported Eisenhower in 1952 and accused the president of a "shrinking show of weakness" toward the Reds. White House Press Secretary James Hagerty responded by citing the number of Communists the Administration had discovered and fired, assuring reporters that the Attorney General was working to keep the figures current.[110]

The Wisconsin Republican State Committee soon issued a statement commending the president for "working carefully, diligently, and aggressively" to remove subversives from the federal payroll. Governor Kohler called the "shrinking show of weakness" charge against the president "nonsense."[111] This marked his first specific criticism of Senator McCarthy in public.

Notes

[1] "Eisenhower Writes Congratulations, Thanks to Kohler," *Janesville Daily Gazette*, November 20, 1952.

[2] Arthur Bystrom, "State GOP Delegates Plan Boom for Davis," *Milwaukee Journal*, August 22, 1956.

[3] Walter J. Kohler, Jr. Oral History, Columbia University, 1971, 47.

[4] When it was contended in the press that Mrs. Kohler was eager to move to Washington, an associate of the governor, probably Phil Drotning, said, "Mrs. Kohler would prefer that the governor give up politics entirely because she dislikes the demands of public life on his time, so she is not anxious that he take a federal position. But she is no more interested in him getting to Washington than in having him remain as governor." Robert J. Fleming, "Will Kohler Quit to Take a Federal Job With Ike?," *Milwaukee Journal*, February 22, 1953. See the Melvin Laird interview.

[5] "Madison Is Only Goal for Kohler," *Milwaukee Journal*, November 13, 1952; Willard R. Smith, "Kohler Won't Leave Office," *ibid.*, January 24, 1953; "Kohler Rejects U.S. Job Offer," *ibid.*, February 28, 1953.

[6] "Kohler Urges Ultimatum on College Plan," *ibid.*, November 22, 1952; "Kohler Tells College Stand," *ibid.*, November 23, 1952. Since the war, the university board had received about $20 million and the state college board about half that amount in building appropriations. In 1952, the university board was seeking another $11 million for buildings over a two-year period, and the state colleges were asking for $16 million. Editorial, "Kohler Tries Hard to Get Unity in Educational Setup," *ibid.*, November 25, 1952.

[7] Robert J. Doyle, "Kohler, UW Officials Battle Over Budget," *ibid.*, December 17, 1952.

[8] "Ballooning State Fund Requests, Federal Handouts, Irk Governor," *ibid.*, December 18, 1952.

[9] "Kohler's Budget Outbursts Called 'Soap Opera' by Foe," *ibid.*, December 19, 1952; editorial, "Uniform State College Fees," *ibid.*, December 23, 1952.

[10] "Alice, Kohlers in Bowl Group," *ibid.*, December 13, 1952.

[11] "Kohler, in Inauguration Address, Pledges to Work for Well-Being of 'All Our Citizens,'" *ibid.*, January 5, 1953.

[12] "Text of Message Delivered by Governor to State Legislature," *ibid.*, January 15, 1953; "Kohler Speech Comment Split," *ibid.*, January 16, 1953. See "Areacrat "Bill in Assembly," *ibid.*, January 15, 1952.

[13] State funds covered about 72% of the state college budgets. John M. McLean, "Big Potential Enrollment Poses Problem to State," *ibid.*, February 25, 1953.

[14] "'Exceedingly Lean Budget' Recommended by Kohler," *ibid.*, January 27, 1953. On reactions to the decision to slash $5 million from the University of Wisconsin's requests, see John Hunter, "'Miserable' Case Presented for

UW," *Madison Capital Times*, February 10, 1953; "Kohler Budget to Bring U.W. 'Decay,'" *ibid.*, February 13, 1953; Robert H. Fleming, "Proposed Cut in Budget for UW Stirs Bitterness," *Milwaukee Journal*, February 15, 1953.

[15] See "Governors Feted At Inaugural Bow," *New York Times*, January 29, 1953; "The Stars Shine At Capital Fetes," *ibid.*, January 20, 1953. Invitations and acceptances (a box at the inaugural ball cost $300) are in the Terry Kohler papers.

[16] "Kohler Guest of Eisenhower," *Milwaukee Journal*, January 21, 1953; "Hints a Visit to Wisconsin," *ibid.*, January 22, 1953; Walter J. Kohler, Jr. Oral History, Columbia University, 1971, 36. The luncheon invitation is in the Terry Kohler papers. In the White House Central Files at the Eisenhower Library, there are some 100 pages of references to contacts to and from Governor Kohler. For copies, see the Eisenhower Library file. On March 6, these files reveal, Kohler had an autographed photograph of the president sent to his McCarthyite sister-in-law, Dorothy Kohler, no doubt to appease her wrath. On March 11, the president agreed to a request by the Wisconsin governor to become Honorary Chairman of the American Cancer Society's educational and fund-raising drive. Walter was chairman of the Board of the American Cancer Society from 1953-1959. Walter made several recommendations to the White House for federal positions, including one for Harvey Higley.

[17] "Kohler Plan for UW Told," *Milwaukee Journal*, January 28, 1953.

[18] "Kohler to Explain Budget Cut on Air," *ibid.*, February 7, 1953. On the first broadcast, the governor pointed out that his allocation to the University of Wisconsin was actually about $1 million higher than was required for general campus operations during the current biennium. Editorial, "Kohler Puts UW Budget Into Its Proper Light," *Waukesha Freeman*, February 9, 1953. See the supportive editorial "The Right Spirit 'Twixt Capitol, Hill," *Wisconsin State Journal*, February 9, 1953. In a later talk, Kohler pointed out that twelve other states had already integrated their higher education systems, and 19 more had partially done so. "Kohler Tells College Stand," *Milwaukee Journal*, March 23, 1953.

[19] "Finance Body Cuts Requests by Governor," *ibid.*, February 24, 1953.

[20] "Baseball Leaders, Public Officials Hail Milwaukee Braves," *ibid.*, April 14, 1953; Doyle K. Getter, "Day Was historic for the City and Game a Baseball Classic," *ibid.*, April 15, 1953. The ball thrown by Kohler went to the baseball Hall of Fame in Cooperstown, New York to commemorate the launching of the new team.

[21] Robert J. Doyle, "Regents Buck Colleges Bill," *ibid.*, April 11, 1953.

[22] "Doyle Hits Kohler on State Economy," *ibid.*, April 22, 1953; "Kohler Proud of Buildings," *ibid.*, April 27, 1953.

[23] "Upstate Will Gain One Seat in State Body," *ibid.*, April 29, 1953.

[24] "Study Moves on Districting," *ibid.*, June 8, 1953; "Seeks Speedy district Test," *ibid.*, June 24, 1953.

[25] "College Merger Bill Tests Kohler Strength," *ibid.*, May 3, 1953; "Kohler Visits GOP Caucus to Ask Votes," *ibid.*, May 6, 1953; Robert H. Fleming, "Kohler Has a Big Stake in Remainder of Session, *ibid*, May 17, 1953.

[26] "Kohler's Plan for Integration of Colleges Is Killed, 55-41," *ibid.*, May 7, 1953.

[27] "College Merger Defeat Is Hailed," *ibid.*, May 18, 1953.

[28] "Hopes Economics Will Enable State to End Biennium Without an Increase in Taxes," *ibid.*, June 14, 1953.

[29] Robert H. Fleming, "Kohler Faces New Test Educational TV Bill," *ibid.*, May 24, 1953.

[30] "Kohler Backs Wiley Stand," *ibid.*, June 27, 1953.

[31] Reeves, *The Life and Times of Joe McCarthy*, 462.

[32] *Ibid.*, 467-491.

[33] "Kohler Notes Major Tasks," *Milwaukee Journal*, February 17, 1953.

[34] "Kohler Clears Desk of Bills," *ibid.*, July 24, 1953.

[35] "Contends That Closing Tax Returns Is Restoration of Rights," *ibid.*, June 18, 1953. George Haberman, president of the Wisconsin State Federation of Labor, criticized the bill, arguing that it hurt unions. Collective bargaining, he said, was based in part on a knowledge of corporate income. Kohler said that labor unions could still determine by a simple calculation the amount of corporate income. "I don't believe that labor has been deprived of any resource." "Kohler, Labor Head Tangle," *ibid.*, August 19, 1953.

[36] "Kohler Urges Tax Cut Delay," *ibid.*, August 3, 1953.

[37] David A. Runge, "Kohler Goes Gunning for Votes for Padrutt," *ibid.*, October 8, 1953.

[38] "Doyle Swan Song Given Ovation by Democrats," *ibid.*, October 25, 1953.

[39] Willard R. Smith, "Kohler Asks Power to Control Spending," *ibid.*, October 26, 1953.

[40] Willard R. Smith, "Kohler Won't Get Spending Curbs Easily," *ibid.*, October 27, 1953; "UW Building Veto Upheld," *ibid*; editorial, "We Used Up $14,000,000," *ibid.*; Edwin R. Bayley, "Victorious Democrats Look to Governorship," *ibid.*

[41] "Kohler, Legislators Battle Over Spending Power Plea," *ibid.*, October 28, 1953; Robert H. Fleming, "Kohler and Legislators Fight Over Two Words," *ibid.*, October 29, 1953; "Tap Building Funds, Finance Unit Urges," *ibid.*, November 4, 1953.

[42] "State Senate Approves Plan Calling Budget 'Balanced,'" *ibid.*, November 5, 1953; "'Balanced Budget' Plan Gets Final Approval," *ibid.*, November 6, 1953.

[43] *Ibid.*

[44] Robert H. Fleming, "Legislature Bequeaths '55 Session 'Legacies,'" *ibid.*, November 8, 1953; "On Wisconsin," *ibid.*; editorial, "The 'Oops, Sorry' Legislature," *ibid.*, November 9, 1953. The legislature rejected a bill increasing the pay of state university and college teachers by $10 a month. Teachers at all levels in the state received low salaries. Still, the average annual salary for Wisconsin public schoolteachers was $3,721, just four dollars below the national average.

[45] "Expressway Commission is Created by New Law," *ibid.*, November 26, 1953. See "Gov. Kohler Names Five to Expressways Posts," *ibid.*, December 19, 1953; "Expressways' Backers Laud Kohler's Choices, *ibid.*

[46] "Give Gasoline Tax to States, US Is Urged," *ibid.*, December 10, 1953.

[47] "Urges Building of Toll Roads," *ibid.*, December 11, 1953.

[48] Terry was put to work in the summers at age 16, doing a variety of jobs, often at Windway. His father had left the Kohler Company when Terry was 13, so he did not share the other Kohler boys' burden at the plant. Walter did not have his son work at Vollrath because he was newly in charge and thought that Terry's employment might seem awkward. Telephone interview with Terry Kohler, June 16, 2005.

[49] Terry Kohler interviews, June 12, 2003 and March 25, 2004. Peter Kohler, Jim's youngest son, went with Terry to Andover. The two were the same age. Peter's success only intensified Terry's misery at being rejected. Moreover, he was the first Kohler to meet such a fate at Andover.

[50] "Kohler's Son Set to Join Air Force," *Milwaukee Journal*, February 10, 1955; Terry Kohler interview, June 12, 2003. Terry disguised his failing grades at Northwestern, telling a reporter that he left the university because he "didn't like it."

[51] Bob purchased Vinyl Plastics, maker of tile floors, and headed it the rest of his life. See Vicki and Jill Kohler interview, December 19, 2003, and Robert E. Kohler, Jr., interview.

[52] "Kohler Sues His Uncle, Claims $214,156 Loss," *Milwaukee Journal*, December 10, 1956. On Kohler Company labor problems, see "Kohler Union Concedes Loss," *ibid.*, May 2, 1952, and "Kohler Union Joins the CIO," *ibid.*, May 12, 1952.

[53] John Wyngaard, "Governor Looks Back at Three Years in Office," *Green Bay Press-Gazette*, January 6, 1954.

[54] Sanford Goltz, "Governor Finds Friends Not Supporters," *Wisconsin State Journal*, February 3, 1954. See also John Wyngaard, "Kohler Salary Defeat Direct Slap in Face," *Waukesha Daily Freeman*, January 18, 1954. For Franke's assessment, see Harry Franke interview.

[55] "Plans in Air, Kohler Says," *Milwaukee Journal*, March 4, 1954.

[56] Terry Kohler interview, March 25, 2004.

57 "Kohler Godfather for Youngsters of Esther Williams," *Milwaukee Journal*, March 15, 1954. The swimming star later presented the Kohlers with an engraved photograph book commemorating the service. It is in the Leslie Kohler Hawley collection. For an assortment of clippings on the service, see the Esther Williams file. One published account said that the Kohlers and the Gages (the star was married to Wisconsin native Ben Gage) had met in Hawaii several years earlier. Walter told a Madison resident that the Gages were "friends of many years standing." Copy, Walter J. Kohler, Jr. to Ira Langlois, March 19, 1954, box 34, Walter J. Kohler, Jr. papers.

58 "Governor Kohler Announces He Will Seek Third Term," *Sheboygan Press*, May 6, 1954.

59 John Wyngaard, "Kohler Favored to Win Third Term as Governor," *Eau Claire Leader-Telegram*, May 14, 1954. Wyngaard pointed out that only six men had tried and succeeded to win the governorship of Wisconsin three times.

60 Editorial, "A Good Governor Runs Again," *Wisconsin State Journal*, May 7, 1954.

61 Reeves, *The Life and Times of Joe McCarthy*, 564-566.

62 Ibid., 584.

63 "Gore Urges Kohler To Step Out Of State Pro-Joe GOP," *Sheboygan Press*, May 12, 1954.

64 Harry Franke interview. Franke never discussed the matter with Kohler.

65 See for example, "Raps Kohler In 'Recall' Legal Case," *Madison Capital Times*, July 6, 1954. Still, state Democrats, knowing how popular McCarthy remained in Wisconsin, decided that he would not be a campaign issue in 1954. George Rodgerson, "State Democrats Ignore McCarthy Issue, But Major Speaker Doesn't," *Wisconsin State Journal*, July 11, 1954.

66 Herbert and five close employees were deputy sheriffs during the strike. The Village of Kohler was stocked with tear gas and machine guns. Uphoff, *Kohler on Strike*, 162-167.

67 Ibid., 175.

68 Ibid., 206-207.

69 Ibid., 172-173; "Plan Is Told by Governor to End Strike," *Milwaukee Journal*, July 9, 1954. See "Kohler Strike Stirs Up House," *ibid.*, January 14, 1955.

70 "Firm Rejects Kohler's Plan to End Strike," *ibid.*, July 10, 1954; Uphoff, *Kohler on Strike*, 174-175.

71 Ibid.

72 On union violence, see *ibid.*, 213-249. After spending about $10 million in strike benefits without much effect, the UAW launched a nationwide secondary boycott of Kohler products. See *ibid.*, 249-261. Peter Kohler, Jim's

son, carried a gun under the driver's seat of his car during the strike. Peter and Nancy Kohler interview, August 11, 2003.

[73] "Union Wants Kohler to Quit," *Milwaukee Journal*, July 11, 1954. Uphoff's account of the strike, the standard source, should be balanced with Blodgett, *A Sense of Higher Design*, 140-145. This official account does not, however, note the National Labor Relations Board finding of 1960 holding the company guilty of unfair labor practices. See Uphoff, *Kohler On Strike*, 303. The strike did not end completely until 1965, when a federal court ordered the Kohler Company to rehire almost all of the strikers and to pay wages and benefits, lost during the strike, amounting to $4.5 million.

[74] Edwin R. Bayley, "Strangle Hold of GOP Fades," *Milwaukee Journal*, October 6, 1954.

[75] "Proxmire Compares State Government to 'Playboy,'" *Janesville Gazette*, July 31, 1954.

[75] "Says Kohler Fought Ike's Road Plan," *Madison Capital Times*, July 19, 1954.

[77] "State Faces Huge Deficit, Proxmire Says," *Appleton Post-Crescent*, August 18, 1954.

[78] "State Government Failing To Meet Costs, Says Doyle," *Sheboygan Press*, August 5, 1954.

[79] "Doyle Cheered As He Blasts Kohler Record," *Madison Capital Times*, August 28, 1954.

[80] "Doyle Raps Kohler For Part in Gen. Marshall Incident," *Sheboygan Press*, July 13, 1954. In May, Doyle had claimed that Kohler was "pro-McCarthy" and "anti-Eisenhower." "Doyle Declares Kohler is 'Pro-Joe, Anti-Ike,'" *ibid.*, May 14, 1954.

[81] "Kohler Claims State Finances 'Excellent,'" *Milwaukee Sentinel*, September 5, 1954.

[82] Edwin R. Bayley, "Nomination of Knowles Urged by Gov. Kohler," *Milwaukee Journal*, September 9, 1954.

[83] *Wisconsin Blue Book, 1956*, 703.

[84] "Dems Pledge All-Out Vote Drive to Elect Proxmire," *Madison Capital Times*, September 20, 1954.

[85] "Proxmire Out of Plow Fight," *Milwaukee Journal*, September 24, 1954.

[86] Copy, Walter J. Kohler, Jr. to William Proxmire, September 24, 1954, series 10, box 1, Walter J. Kohler, Jr. papers. Proxmire's invitation of September 23 is in the same file. Walter used almost the exact same language in public in a speech delivered the following day in Milwaukee. "Larkin Blasts Kohler Talks," *Milwaukee Journal*, September 25, 1954.

[87] "Voters Hear Issues on TV," *ibid.*, November 1, 1954.

[88] "Larkin Blasts Kohler Talks," *ibid.*, September 25, 1954.

[89] William R. Bechtel, "State GOP Opens War to Stop the Democrats," *ibid.*, October 1, 1954.

[90] Copies of Kohler's speeches before the Republican State Platform Convention and the Wisconsin School Board Association Regional Meeting are in box 2, "Executive Department, Governor's Secretaries' files," Walter J. Kohler, Jr. papers.

[91] "'Hoover Unit' Demands Hit," *Milwaukee Journal*, October 10, 1954.

[92] "TV Audiences See Politicians," *ibid.*, October 18, 1954.

[93] "GOP 'Big Three' May Share Dais," *ibid.*, October 12, 1954. See Reeves, *The Life and Times of Joe McCarthy*, 653. That same month, Walter and Terry Kohler did a half-hour program on Milwaukee television featuring conversation about an assortment of campaign issues. This question and answer format was rather unique at the time. Terry Kohler interview, December 5, 2005.

[94] "Kohler Blasts Foe's Tactics," *Milwaukee Journal*, October 13, 1954.

[95] "Kohler Claims 'Hoax' by Foe," *ibid.*, October 21, 1954.

[96] "'Hoax' Claim Answer Is Set," *ibid.*, October 23, 1954;

[97] *Ibid.*; Harold E. Entwistle, "Kohler Hid Vital Facts in Radio Blast at Proxmire," *Madison Capital Times*, October 22, 1954; editorial, "Who's Pulling the 'Hoax'?", *ibid.*

[98] Edwin R. Bayley, "Strange Political Drive Nine Days From Finish," *Milwaukee Journal*, October 24, 1954. Proxmire called the governor's support of the administration farm policy "an incredible betrayal." "Raps Kohler on 'Betrayal,'" *ibid.*, October 29, 1954. In Sykes, *Proxmire*, 68-70, the author neglects to note the fact that Holte was a Democrat and naturally disposed to support Proxmire in this clash. See also page 70 for another, less important, campaign clash between Kohler and Proxmire.

[99] "Leaders of State GOP Praise Party's Record," *Milwaukee Journal*, October 27, 1954.

[100] See Reeves, *The Life and Times of Joe McCarthy*, 647, 654.

[101] "City Toured by Proxmire," *Milwaukee Journal*, October 28, 1954.

[102] Arthur Bystrom, "Kohler Wins By 34,000," *Madison Capital Times*, November 3, 1954; "Recount May Not Be Asked," *Milwaukee Journal*, November 7, 1954. Proxmire did not choose to request a recount, even though, he contended, there were "mysteries to be cleared up." "No Proxmire Recount Bid," *ibid.*, November 9, 1954. Not long after the election, Proxmire's wife divorced him. The perpetual candidate said, "Doubtless, the exacting demands of political life provoked enduring conflicts in our marriage. Therefore I would have given up political activity completely and finally, if this action could have saved our family life together." "Divorce Given to Proxmires," *ibid.*, February 10, 1955.

[103] "Kohler Plans Race if Ike Does Not File," *ibid.*, August 11, 1955.

[104] *Wisconsin Blue Book, 1956,* 745-746.

[105] Edwin R. Bayley, "1954 Unfolded in State as a Big Political Year," *Milwaukee Journal,* January 2, 1955.

[106] "Democrats Win House; Senate Close," *ibid.*

[107] Reeves, *The Life and Times of Joe McCarthy,* 654.

[108] "Senate Meets on McCarthy," *Milwaukee Journal,* November 8,1954.

[109] Reeves, *The Life and Times of Joe McCarthy,* 624.

[110] *Ibid.,* 666-667 .

[111] *Ibid.,* 667; Edwin R. Bayley, "1954 Unfolded in State as a Big Political Year," *Milwaukee Journal,* January 2, 1955.

Chapter Twelve
Matters of Principle

After the election, Walter and Charlotte took a vacation in Spain. Just before they were to return home, on December 30, Secretary of State Fred Zimmerman died. He had been hospitalized throughout the election campaign. Outgoing Lt. Governor George Smith, acting in the governor's absence, named one Louis Allis, Jr. to the post. When Walter returned home, he reversed the appointment. (John Wyngaard soon observed that Smith had "no innate skill as a politician.")[1] He selected Glenn Wise of Madison, who became the first woman in Wisconsin history to hold a constitutional state office. Mrs. Wise, 58, was the wife of John E. Wise, an electrical engineer with the state industrial commission. She was currently active in her second term as secretary of the national women's Republican organization.[2]

Two years later, Walter said of Mrs. Wise, "...of all the appointments which I have made as governor, the one which was most right, and the one in which my judgment has been most thoroughly proved correct, and the one of which I am most proud, was made on January 1st of 1955." He chose her, he said, "first, because I believed that the great and unselfish work of women in the Republican party deserved recognition." The second reason was "because the candidate in question probably had done as much in the cause of better government in Wisconsin as any woman in our history." And thirdly, "I made it...because she was a woman of great intelligence, great stature in her community and State, great devotion to the highest principles of government and politics, and the highest standards of personal honesty and integrity." The Secretary of State was third in the line of governmental authority, and on two occasions, when Kohler and Knowles were both unavoidably absent for a short time, she became the first woman to serve as acting-governor of Wisconsin.[3]

Governor Kohler, Mrs. Wise, and the three other constitutional officers were sworn in at a brief inauguration ceremony in Madison on January 4, 1955. Appearing slightly more formal than earlier, the governor was attired in a black coat, striped pants, and a gray tie. His inaugural address was only 320 words in length, warning that "the tasks ahead of us are greater in magnitude than any that lie behind." Charlotte and some 500 visitors, friends, and state employees observed the ceremony.[4]

In his address to the joint session of the 1955 legislature, the governor said that he expected close harmony and productivity. "If each of us holds fast to our commitments to the people of the state, there should exist in this session remarkable cooperation, not only between the legislative and executive branches of the government, but within the legislature itself."

Quoting from party platforms, Kohler said that both Republicans and Democrats wanted legislation in highway safety and development, merger of the higher education boards of regents, and a variety of economic development programs. He emphasized traffic safety, pointing to a study by the Northwestern University Traffic Institute recommending a State Patrol of 609 officers with responsibility for enforcement on all rural roads. (The State Patrol currently had a staff of 70.)[5] Both parties, he said, had also agreed to recognize 2,200 miles of state highways as an arterial system, which would be improved to meet modern requirements.

Among the governor's other recommendations was an extension of unemployment compensation coverage; increased disability compensation; increased state scrutiny of health and welfare funds maintained by trade unions; a revised civil defense law, requiring local units of government to establish civil defense systems; revision of administration rule-making processes, providing for greater public participation and information; creation of a division of economic development within the executive office; continuation of the brucellosis control program; and a study of annexation laws by the legislative council. He also requested broader authority for the governor, particularly in administering "housekeeping" matters within state departments. Such a move, he said, could reduce overhead costs by $500,000 a year.[6]

On January 20, Assemblyman Al Ludvigsen, co-chairman of the legislature's joint finance committee, predicted that a 25% surtax on incomes would be necessary even if no new spending were voted because income tax revenues were expected to be lower than previously estimated. Such a surtax had been in effect in 1949-1950, and had brought in $14 million. (For eight years prior to 1943, the state had endured a 60% income surtax.)[7]

Ludvigsen's estimate soon turned out to be overly cautious. In his budget address to the legislature, the governor proposed a budget of $278 million, the largest general fund request in state history. It was needed to make up for a $9 million deficit for the current biennium and to pay for state government in the 1955-1957 biennium. Kohler told legislators that revenues from existing sources were to fall short by $58 million. He suggested, based on an estimate by state financial experts, that a surtax of 40% or a boost in the income tax would be necessary. He also called for an interim study of state finances and state taxes.

The governor presented a $208 million budget for the highway department and an $18.5 million conservation department budget, neither being part of the general spending program contained in the general fund message.[8] Kohler had himself reduced the conservation request by $1.4 million.[9]

Predictably, Democrats pounced on the governor's budget address. It proved, said a party statement, "that if the truth had been told last fall, there would now be a Democratic governor."[10] State Senator Gaylord Nelson said that Kohler and Attorney General Thomson had "pulled a fraud" on the people during the last campaign. Senate Democrats sponsored a resolution declaring the budget in balance, a satiric move using much the same language Republicans employed in 1953. Then they joined Republicans in defeating the proposal 30 to 0.[11]

Walter replied to critics by noting that state finances had changed rather dramatically since the previous October when he said that the state could operate without reinstating a surtax. The earlier estimate "was an accurate statement of facts as we then knew them." Of late, anticipated revenues had declined and operating costs were up. "It was not until the budget hearings in November that these increased costs amounting to more than 20 million dollars became apparent." He continued, "We have learned that requirements for educational aids will be over 10 million dollars higher than were anticipated for the current biennium. Increased enrollments at the institutions of higher learning added 4 million dollars and increased population at our welfare institutions added another $4,500,000 to the operating costs of the current biennium."

The governor also called attention to William Proxmire's flawed estimates of state finances during the past two campaigns, citing in detail the Democrat's incorrect deficit predictions. Proxmire, however, claimed that the governor's budget was "a confirmation to the letter of the charges I made repeatedly in the last campaign..."[12]

Leaders of both industry and labor were unhappy about the prospect of tax increases.[13] The *Milwaukee Journal*, declared in an editorial, "Governor Kohler, to be sure, did prudently ask to keep some part of the 25% income surtax in 1951. But the legislature gaily dropped the whole of it, which is one big reason why we're in the soup now. And the governor ever since, up to and including Tuesday, has been pointing with pride at this same tax 'saving' that he had counseled *against*."[14]

To assure state residents that no fiscal crisis was on the horizon, Lieutenant Governor Knowles told a Knights of Columbus gathering that Wisconsin enjoyed a financial condition superior to virtually every other state. "Wisconsin has built up a 262 million dollar physical plant; it has more than 30 million dollars in trust funds; it has cash in the bank and is without public debt." He noted also that state income tax rates had been reduced 40 percent since 1943 while state expenditures for education, public welfare, and other purposes had steadily increased.[15]

The governor was soon delivering speeches with the same message. Even a 25% surcharge, he said, would simply return taxes to the level that were in place in 1949-1950.[16] He refused to cut the budget by curtailing the construction of state buildings, pointing to severely dilapidated and outdated facilities throughout the state serving the mentally handicapped and youth.[17]

In mid-February, after weeks of meetings with educators and staff members, the governor unveiled a new plan for merging all of Wisconsin's institutions of higher education. The essentials were the same and continued to call for a four-year institution in Milwaukee. But in this "gentler" version of the integration proposal, the state colleges would retain their names and not be branches of the University of Wisconsin; instead of a single chancellor ruling over the combined boards, an administrative officer would be selected by the board to coordinate activities of state college officials; and the bill entrusted "the immediate government" of the state colleges to their respective faculties. Despite initial approval by a bipartisan committee of the legislature, and approval in principle by state college regents, a committee of the University of Wisconsin Board of Regents denounced the new proposal, declaring: "The state cannot afford to take any action which might lower the effectiveness, the quality or the reputation of the University of Wisconsin."[18]

Revealing his shattered relations with the governor, Tom Coleman announced publicly that he was strongly opposed to the college integration bill, arguing that the case for merger was poor, that the University of Wisconsin had "flourished" under its own board, that the new proposal's principles might lead to the surrender by local governments of their authority over their own school systems, and that Kohler might have the opportunity to appoint the entire board of regents. In a well-reasoned and strongly worded reply, Kohler dismissed the objections point by point. He dismissed one of Coleman's contentions as "totally without merit."[19] This animosity between these two leading Republicans, now known to all, could not be helpful to Walter's political future.

When a substitute amendment was introduced in the legislature a short time later, placing the proposed new campus in Milwaukee under the UW Board of Regents and maintaining separate boards for the two systems, the governor called the proposal "wholly inadequate." He added, "It is actually a kind of pretense and a fraud that pretends to go to the heart of the problem but doesn't in any sense at all." He called a similar substitute amendment "a fraud and a deceit." This sort of response angered many on both sides of the merger proposal, especially those who objected to Kohler's innovation on the ground that it would harm the University of Wisconsin. Former Governor Rennebohm, in a hearing before Senate and Assembly education committees, cried out, "Don't bring down the university. Do not spoil the plan that has been in existence for 106 years." (His anger against Kohler was such that he soon vowed to run for governor in 1956.)[20] The University's Board of Regents voted 6 to 2 to support the substitute amendment.[21] It soon became clear that the governor was dependent upon Milwaukee Democrats to pass his program, his own party being deeply split on the issue.[22] He indicated that he would veto any plan other than his own.[23]

In early March, Walter was in Washington, testifying before the Senate roads subcommittee as chairman of the governors' conference special committee on highways. When asked how the states could raise the funds required of them by Eisenhower's proposed $101 billion, ten year highway program, Kohler suggested increases in gasoline taxes as high as ten cents a gallon.[24] Back in Madison, the governor personally delivered a special message to a joint session of the legislature calling for a two cent increase (from four to six cents) in the state's gasoline tax. He also requested increases in drivers' license renewal fees and license fees for heavy trucks. Still, the proposal envisioned the first gasoline tax hike in 24 years and did not increase the state's low automobile registration fee. The tax hikes were to be used to finance a unified highway improvement and highway safety program.[25]

However laudable the intention, this proposal increased voter opinion that Kohler was working full time to raise their taxes. In fact, even though state revenues had jumped from $172 million in 1946 to $426 million in 1954, government expenses had grown so large that more had to be taken out of the public's pockets. Reducing these expenses was not as easy as some voters thought. A careful analysis of state expenditures by a *Milwaukee Journal* reporter pointed out that the governor and legislators were limited by statute and constitution in making budget reductions. "Unless there are drastic cuts in spending for highways, education and public welfare or sizable reductions in aids to local communities, no big dent can be made in the over-all state government costs." (About 41% of the entire executive budget recommended by the governor for the next biennium went for various aids to local communities, aids that were established by law, with their method of distribution prescribed by statute.) In progressive Wisconsin, both parties currently saw such reductions as virtually unthinkable. The yearly cost of state government jumped by $270 million in the decade ending June 30, 1954, soaring at a rate that soon could mean spending a billion dollars each biennium.

One of the state's leading tax researchers said that he believed the governor's budget to be "fairly tight." Even William Proxmire acknowledged that the need for more revenue reflected the "inevitable expansion of the state's responsibilities to its citizens, from its school children to its aged," adding that "The governor deserves credit for manfully measuring up to this fact in his budget address." A study by state budget officials showed that other states were facing the same problems of increased spending and taxation. Still, it was clear that a great many Wisconsinites were unhappy about the governor's proposals.[26] A Milwaukee Democratic assemblyman accused the governor of a "tragic betrayal" on state finances and charged that Kohler was asking the legislature "for the biggest tax increase by far in the history of Wisconsin government."[27]

More trouble within the state GOP came to light on March 11 when Assembly Speaker Mark Catlin, Jr. declared that he would run against Senator Wiley if "no other better qualified Republican" announced by June 1. Wiley had been sharply criticized by McCarthyites for ducking the censure vote on Joe McCarthy (he was conveniently out of the country) and for supporting Eisenhower's foreign policy. Catlin, a good-looking, smooth-talking McCarthyite from Appleton, thought by some to have flexible ethics, also had a grudge against Wiley for criticizing his lobbying activities in Washington a year earlier. Catlin had been a $100 a day lobbyist for the American Pyrotechnic Association, a business organization trying vainly to defeat a bill co-sponsored by Wiley to keep bootleg fireworks out of Wisconsin. Wiley responded to Catlin's current declaration with a speech, placed in the *Congressional Record*, attempting to link himself and his party with complete support for the Eisenhower administration.

Catlin also suggested that Attorney General Vernon W. Thomson, a Taft supporter in 1952, should be the party's candidate for governor in 1956, a deliberate slap at Kohler and Knowles. Kohler himself was rumored to be considering a Senate race against Wiley, but chose not to announce anything at this early point in his third administration. He did not comment on Catlin's declaration; he faced enough problems without asking for more.[28]

After more than a month of speeches, lobbying, parliamentary maneuvering, name-calling, and frayed tempers, both sides of the governor's merger proposal agreed to a compromise. The merger would occur, as Kohler sought, but the new board would be divided into two "sub-boards" to handle "day by day" affairs (personnel, student affairs, and other local matters) of the University of Wisconsin and the state colleges. The bill also provided for merger of the University of Wisconsin extension in Milwaukee and Wisconsin State College, Milwaukee, creating a single, four-year campus. On April 13, the bill passed the Senate 28 to 4, with both sides congratulating the governor for his leadership and willingness to compromise. The new board was scheduled to begin operations in a year.[29]

After a month of delay in the Assembly, and a great deal of politicking by University of Wisconsin officials, the merger bill was defeated 60-32. A big majority of Democrats supported Kohler while Republicans solidly opposed their governor. The leader of the opposition was Speaker Mark Catlin, who reneged on his promise to back Kohler's legislation, saying that he thought the bill unconstitutional. The minority floor leader in the Assembly claimed that Catlin and other Republicans were eager to scuttle the governor's bill for fear that Democrats would get the credit for passing it.

A counterproposal by Catlin passed the Assembly 60-34: There would be separate regent boards and a coordinating committee consisting of members of each board that would make recommendations on various matters and report directly to the legislature on budget questions. There was no reference to a Milwaukee merger in the bill. Democrats, especially those from Milwaukee, were furious. Kohler, it seemed, was not the leader of his own party.[30]

On the day of the Assembly vote, Walter told a group of Milwaukee high school essay contest winners in Milwaukee that politics often was "frustrating, exasperating and bitterly disappointing." And yet, "Politics is also richly rewarding, in the sense that sometimes you are able to accomplish things for the good of a great many people." The governor said that he deplored the attitude "that politics is a dirty business that decent people don't get mixed up in."[31] Quickly learning of the Assembly votes, defeating his months of labor on behalf of merger, Walter might have temporarily had second thoughts about the nobility of his current occupation.

The governor's highway traffic package was greeted positively. The legislature passed requests for a two cent a gallon gas tax hike, a state driver licensing examining system, and a measure establishing a 2,200 mile state arterial highway system to be given priority in the highway construction program. On June 21, however, the Assembly killed the effort to boost the size of the State Patrol from 70 to 250. (Kohler had asked for 610.) The vote was 56-43. The bill died swiftly without a word of debate. Party lines were split.[32] On the last day of the legislative session, under considerable pressure from the governor, the Assembly changed its mind and both houses of the legislature passed a bill to increase the State Patrol to 250. County traffic officials, who were to be absorbed into an expanded State Patrol in Kohler's plan, were now to remain in their current occupations. This was a compromise Kohler accepted.[33] He would try to later to expand his gains.

As the legislators began to become eager to pack up and go home, they defeated further attempts to merge the two systems of higher education in the state. The governor soon vetoed a bill passed by both houses to create a four year campus in Milwaukee without the proposed merger. (The action was publicly deplored by several legislators and approved by state college officials.) He also tabled building requests of the university and state colleges totaling $9 million pending legislative action on merger. The entire Kohler proposal would be awaiting further consideration when the legislature reconvened in October.[34] Walter was determined; it was a matter of principle.

In a final joint session of the legislature, the governor said "It is my pleasure to tell you today, without reservation, that I regard the 1955 session not only as the most fruitful during my three terms as governor but as the most constructive session in at least a quarter of a century."[35] Observers quickly realized that, for all the squabbling, the governor had been highly successful in his dealings with the legislators. Of Kohler's 50 specific recommendations, delivered in three messages, 43 passed, four were held over for consideration in the fall, three were defeated, and two were never offered in bill form. Not one of the five outright failures was of major importance. (One was a requested increase in appropriations for 4-H Club work.)

The governor's biggest successes included the highway and state patrol gains, a 20% income tax surtax, increased salaries for top state officials, liberalized and extended benefits in both unemployment benefits and workmen's compensation, a tree disease bill and a strong conservation department budget, revisions in the Children's Code, strengthening of the state's civil defense act, a $3 million brucellosis program, and a building fund compromise that included a new industrial school for boys at Waukesha.[36]

The two most controversial items of the five and one-half month legislative session were campus merger, which would be reconsidered, and the Catlin Bill, which banned political contributions by labor unions. Senate Democrats introduced 16 amendments and filibustered against the labor bill for 24 hours. Their counterparts in the Assembly talked for six hours in an attempt to slow down progress of the bill. Firebrand Senator Gaylord Nelson of Milwaukee charged that its passage would make the GOP "the party of calumny, confusion and Catlinism."[37] The Assembly passed the bill 54 to 35, and the Senate passed it 19 to 14.

When the governor signed the bill, he said, "This measure decides a very simple question. Shall the individual union member have the right to decide what candidate or party to support, and how much he is willing to contribute financially to that candidate or party, or shall that decision be made for him by others." Labor officials were furious with Kohler, who had "given his blessings to this gross injustice."[38] They were all the more willing to link the governor with his uncle and the Kohler Company and condemn him for being "anti-labor."[39]

On July 5, 15 weeks into the Kohler strike, an angry crowd of about 2,500 prevented Kohler Company workers from unloading a Norwegian freighter bearing a load of British clay. Top regional and national labor officials declared that thereafter all ships attempting to unload clay for the Company would be picketed. Municipal dock workers in Sheboygan said they would honor the picket line. A shutdown of plant supplies seemed imminent. After meeting with his executive counsel and Sheboygan civic and police officials, the governor announced that he would see to it that no "unlawful interference with lawful commerce" would occur. He would not say if he was willing to call out the National Guard. Again, Walter made it clear that he personally had nothing to do with the Kohler Company or the strike. He expressed regret about the prolonged labor dispute and contended that he had exhausted the means at his disposal to bring about a peaceful settlement.[40]

The governor soon pledged not to call out the National Guard unless it seemed that local officials were unable to handle disturbances. He then summoned labor leaders to Madison, one of whom threatened trouble if the Guard were summoned, and had a frank discussion with them about rights and responsibilities. It yielded a public pledge by the union men to instruct pickets to be peaceful and orderly. At the same time, Kohler assured his guests that he would protect the right of workers to picket peacefully.[41] This even-handed and public-spirited treatment of the strike minimized the impact of organized labor's condemnation of the governor. But it did not prevent pro-union Sheboygan Mayor Rudolph Ploetz from later declaring, "If you put Governor Kohler, Herbert Kohler and [Mark] Catlin in a bag, shake it up and reach in and pull out any one of the three you would have the same anti-labor individual."[42]

It was also difficult for labor officials and Democrats to portray the governor as a heartless reactionary, for he was plainly proud of the social welfare contributions he and the Republican dominated legislature had produced. Addressing delegates to the regional conference of the American Public Welfare Association in late June, Walter described Wisconsin's public assistance program as "among the leading in the nation." The State's old age assistance program, aid to dependent children, the blind, and the totally and permanently disabled were all well above the nation's average. The people of Wisconsin, Kohler said, had long believed that providing economic security for its citizenry was "a rightful function of government." He continued, "It is questionable if this free American economy could exist without public welfare programs which provide the organized machinery for coming to the rescue of those individuals who get hurt in the competitive process."

One of his proudest achievements in the last session of the legislature, Walter said, were the reforms in the Children's Code, the first since his father was governor in 1929. The trend was now toward state subsidized foster homes and away from orphanages, and he cited the amount of funds sent to foster parents. In the area of delinquency the emphasis was now on prevention rather than just juvenile court justice, and Kohler pointed to the $6 million appropriation for the new school for boys in Waukesha. Wisconsin's social welfare programs, he said, were aimed at "preventing social and personal maladjustments, particularly by focusing on the strengthening of family life." Still, the governor advised, social welfare should be the concern of every citizen and not be left exclusively to government and the professionals.[43]

President Eisenhower had often said that his philosophy was "liberal where people are concerned and conservative where their money is concerned." That seemed to be exactly the point of view Wisconsin's governor had followed since taking office.

In late July, Kohler joined Milwaukee's socialist Mayor Frank Zeidler and the liberal organization Americans for Democratic Action in deploring a vote in the House of Representatives to consider a bill that would free natural gas producers from federal control. The governor appealed to Wisconsin members of the House to fight the measure. Wisconsin was a natural gas consuming state, and the legislature, the attorney general, and the public service commission, as well as the governor, opposed the bill. Walter warned the state's Congressmen that passage of the legislation would give the Phillips Petroleum Company "all the monopolistic advantages" it had earlier enjoyed before a successful Wisconsin lawsuit affirmed the right of the Federal Power Commission to regulate the price of natural gas paid producers at the wellhead.[44]

In early August, Kohler again earned the praise of Mayor Zeidler by vetoing two bills that would have sharply curtailed the powers of the Milwaukee Housing Authority. The measures were sponsored by the Wisconsin Association of Real Estate Boards and had been solidly opposed by Democrats in the legislature. The governor exercised his veto after a series of conferences between proponents and opponents, saying afterward, "I return the bill because of the conviction that it would effectively halt any future slum clearance or housing projects in the city of Milwaukee..." Not only was this a matter of principle to Walter, but his approach to the issue followed a pattern approved in Washington. Mayor Zeidler said, "In his action I believe the governor has put himself solidly alongside the president in his announced national program for the rebuilding of cities. Thoughtful Milwaukee citizens will be grateful to the governor."[45]

Walter was extremely concerned about preserving the Eisenhower coalition of liberal and moderate Republicans, and was already a strong supporter of the president's reelection. At an August press conference in Chicago, where he was attending a governors' conference, he said that he would run as a favorite son in the following spring's primary if the president had not filed his candidacy by March 2, the state deadline. He emphasized the point that as a favorite son he would merely be serving as a stand-in for Eisenhower. (Nevertheless, the *Milwaukee Journal* ran a huge front page headline: "Gov Kohler May Run For President.") When asked about Joe McCarthy, often a harsh critic of the president, Walter said politely that "the intensity of feeling" about the senator had diminished on both sides, and that his attacks on Eisenhower were only self-defeating.[46]

In early September, Walter conferred in Washington with top White House and Agriculture Department officials on agricultural policy and the farm vote. The drop in farm prices appeared to be the biggest campaign problem facing the GOP in 1956. The governor remained convinced that two decades of rigid farm price supports under the Democrats had damaged the largely dairy farm economy of Wisconsin. He was also persuaded that "The transition from a wartime to a peacetime farm economy is being skillfully handled by this Republican administration."[47] The argument was plausible, but it must have seemed to many, especially farmers, to be wholly partisan.

On September 24, President Eisenhower suffered a heart attack while on vacation in Denver. Kohler expressed shock at the turn of events but hoped that Ike would recover quickly and be a candidate for reelection.[48] Over the next few weeks, as silence about the president's intentions worried many Republicans, Kohler said that other party leaders were capable of leading the ticket effectively, including Vice-President Nixon, Treasury Secretary George M. Humphrey, and Milton Eisenhower, the president's younger brother, who was president of Pennsylvania State University.[49]

The best news of the summer for Walter involved his plans for higher education in the state. In late August, the boards of the University of Wisconsin and the state colleges worked out a compromise that pleased almost everyone, including the governor. The new plan established a powerful 15-member coordinating committee, created from both boards, and the founding of a new four-year campus in Milwaukee. The compromise varied only slightly from the original Kohler plan for merger, and was a tribute to the governor's persistence.[50] On October 1, the University of Wisconsin regents voted 7 to 0 in favor of a plan to coordinate all tax supported higher education in Wisconsin.[51]

The fall session of the legislature opened on October 3 and lasted three weeks. The governor had several good reasons to be pleased. All 28 of his vetoes were sustained, which was a record. The merger plan for higher education passed the Assembly 95 to 0 and was approved by the Senate 29 to 1, prompting the *Milwaukee Journal* to editorialize, "If one individual were to be singled out for laurels, it would have to be Governor Kohler. He kept up his fight for a broad, meaningful merger bill even when hopes burned dim and where there was no political profit in pressing the matter further."[52] An improving economy and the impact of recent tax increases put the state on stronger fiscal ground, enabling legislators to resist a sales tax that several business groups were pushing.[53]

Dissension within the GOP, led by Speaker Catlin, was the most worrisome feature of the session. Always brusque and sometimes tricky, Catlin at times seemed to be losing his psychological composure. During a debate on Kohler's veto of the bill limiting public housing projects in Milwaukee, the Assembly Speaker attacked the governor's intelligence and character and delivered a 40 minute, desk-pounding tirade against the press, suggesting that his newspaper critics should have their throats cut.[54] Perhaps to embarrass the governor, Catlin unsuccessfully pushed a bill to restore the right of towns and villages to provide their police and constables with machine guns. This was an obvious reference to the bitter Kohler strike, the intended beneficiary of the weapons being Kohler Village.[55] Catlin engineered an unexpected defeat of a small salary increase for state employees, implying that the governor was uninterested in the state's taxpayers.[56] He was forced to withdraw a bill, defeated earlier, to allow motorists to exceed speed limits if they thought they were justified. Amused legislators made much of the Speaker's five convictions for speeding.[57] At one point, in the course of a 35-minute oration, Catlin called William Proxmire dumb, a fake, a fraud, and a phony.[58]

A reporter observed that Catlin's influence in the Assembly had slipped noticeably since the spring session, and that a number of Republicans were in open rebellion against him.[59] It was obvious to all that Catlin was no friend of the governor's.

Critics thought that Catlin seemed extraordinarily connected to a number of special interest groups, including real estate and liquor companies. As the legislative session came to a close, the *Madison Capital Times* revealed that the Speaker had received almost $5,500 in 1954 from the Time Insurance Company of Milwaukee, noting that Catlin had drafted and introduced a bill which the company strongly desired, a bill opponents argued would save big stock insurance companies a lot of money. The bill was killed in the spring session, and the Assembly refused to reconsider it during the current session.

Catlin called charges of illegal conduct "hogwash" and told reporters that in 1954, while in Washington lobbying against a ban on bootleg fireworks, he merely served as an observer for the insurance company during hearings on private health insurance plans. He could not explain why the company listed $2,499 as "expenditures in connection with matters before legislative bodies" and $3,000 as "general legal" with the state insurance department. Catlin did not report the fees as lobbying receipts. When contacted, the president of the Time Insurance Company said that Catlin was "lobbying for us in a sense" in Washington, D.C., adding that "I thought his charges were high." He denied, however, that the Speaker was paid for pushing the bill his company sought.[60]

Catlin presented another problem for Kohler by pushing through the Assembly a bill that gerrymandered the Fifth Congressional District, encompassing Milwaukee and some of its suburbs, to favor the GOP's chances in future elections. It passed the Senate 18-14 only because party leaders demanded it. The action caused an outcry by Democrats all over the nation, Democratic National Chairman Paul M. Butler calling it a "steal." If Kohler signed the bill, he would alienate independents and tarnish his reputation for veracity. If he vetoed it, he would rile many members of his party, especially the ultraconservatives, some of whom were already pushing Attorney General Thomson for governor. (The list of Thomson supporters included Tom Coleman and Dorothy Kohler.) Walter had threatened to veto a similar bill in 1953, effectively killing it.[61] A major Milwaukee Democrat and Mayor Frank Zeidler both made personal appeals to the governor to veto the gerrymander bill.[62]

On November 26, the governor vetoed the bill, arguing that all of the state's congressional districts should be redrafted, in order to make them equal in population, and urging legislators to take such action in 1957. Many Republicans were angered by the move, as Walter knew they would be. At the same time, he signed a bill that said in effect that the Milwaukee Housing Authority should sell a public housing project to the highest bidder if directed to do so by the voters in a referendum or by the common council. The bill resembled the legislation Kohler had vetoed earlier, and was considered by Milwaukee officials and Democrats to be a blow against the cause of public housing construction and a victory for the real estate lobby and private landowners. The governor, however, clearly described the differences between the housing bills he vetoed and signed, noting that the new legislation had been studied extensively by his legal counsel and would "create no valid legal barriers to any future projects which the Milwaukee Housing authority may wish to undertake, nor will it jeopardize presently pending urban redevelopment projects."[63]

Within a single day, then, Governor Kohler, adhering to principle and heeding legal over political advice, managed to alienate a large portion of the GOP and at the same time anger Democrats and independents throughout the Milwaukee area. Mark Catlin said that the governor's veto "completely begs the question" and was "completely fallacious."[64] Mayor Zeidler called the public housing decision a "body blow" to Milwaukee's slum clearance, urban renewal, and housing plans. He said that Kohler "has made it clearly evident that he has little sympathy for Milwaukee, its housing projects or its low income families."[65]

Still, not everyone was critical. State Senator Allen J. Busby, a Republican from the Milwaukee area, declared: "Governor Kohler demonstrated a high degree of leadership and statesmanship in vetoing the gerrymander bill. I believe he has instilled renewed courage in the Republicans of Milwaukee county, if not the state and nation, that the Republican party stands for principles of fair play and morality in government." William Proxmire, still actively campaigning, sent a telegram to the governor congratulating him for his "commendable courage." He continued, "Wisconsin citizens, regardless of party, must recognize that you firmly resisted severe pressure and the temptation of partisan advantage in choosing the way of conscience." The *Milwaukee Journal* said editorially, "The governor will receive credit for having obeyed his own instincts of decency in thwarting the iniquitous attempt to steal a seat in congress by the misuse of legislative power." Philleo Nash, state Democratic Party chairman also praised the governor's veto. "We are happy that he resisted the pressures within his own party and upheld the integrity of the state government." But he added, "We wish he had found it possible to veto the housing bill as well, which was opposed by the people most intimately affected."[66]

Among the governor's final actions of 1955 was signing into law a revised criminal code, a bill that stemmed from six years of study and was the first comprehensive revision of the statutes in this field since Wisconsin became a state. It was to take effect on July 1 of the following year.[67]

Just before Christmas, Walter appeared before the state building commission to defend the legislature's intention of constructing a new school for boys in the Kettle Moraine forest in Sheboygan County. Objections were raised by the Izaak Walton League, which argued that the school would destroy the recreational value of the area. The governor told a welfare department official that "any opposition to the construction is without merit and should be resisted vigorously." The state legislature in this matter, he said, declared its wishes and should be obeyed. "It acted legally, morally, and ethically."[68] Those concepts were still paramount to Walter, and they would haunt him as he prepared to make a decision about his political future.

In early 1956, Mark Catlin decided to run for the United States Senate against Alexander Wiley. He had the support of many in the McCarthyite wing of the GOP, the same group coalescing behind Attorney General Thomson for governor. Catlin said of Kohler, "I like him personally, but as far as his Republican party responsibility is concerned, I don't like him." The Assembly Speaker had been traveling across the state speaking on the Republican record. "If you can read or recall any occasion where the governor of the state of Wisconsin has been doing anything vaguely resembling what I am doing, then I apologize to him."[69]

On March 8, Walter announced that he would not seek any public office in 1956. The timing no doubt had to do with Attorney General Thomson, who was scheduled to launch his candidacy for governor at a dinner in Milwaukee two days later. In his official statement, Kohler cited a Wisconsin "tradition" against fourth terms and said, in part, "On three occasions, my fellow citizens have entrusted me with the leadership of their government, an honor for which I shall always owe them a deep obligation of gratitude. I have taken my responsibilities seriously, and I know I shall be pardoned for the pride I feel in the accomplishments which, with the help of the legislature and countless citizens, have been achieved during my three terms as governor."

Walter said that he was not leaving politics and did not intend to take a federal position of any kind. When asked if he would run against Senator McCarthy in 1958, Walter said, "That is too far ahead, but don't rule out anything." Reporters took this to mean "tentatively yes." Reporters knew that several friends of the governor had been urging him to run against Wiley, but they assumed he chose not to because it would have meant an open struggle with Catlin and the far Right, as well as pro-Eisenhower Wiley, a battle that would inevitably weaken the party in a major election year. The governor said that he would continue to serve during his term of office and would work to help re-elect President Eisenhower.[70]

William Proxmire unexpectedly expressed sorrow that Kohler was leaving public office. "Although we have disagreed on many public issues, I like and respect him. He has served Wisconsin earnestly and honestly. The Wisconsin Republican party will sorely miss Governor Kohler's moderate, middle of the road leadership. As a Wisconsin citizen, I hope that this great party will not fall under the control of its ultraconservative element."[71] If Thomson became governor and Catlin won the Senate seat, McCarthyites would indeed rule the GOP in the state. And Tom Coleman would no doubt again become its "boss."

Even at this point in 1956, reporters were no doubt correct in think-ing that Kohler's next race would be against Senator McCarthy. Joe was cracking up, physically and mentally. Although unreported in the press (as was the custom), his drunken condition was widely known. Walter last met McCarthy at the Milwaukee ballpark on opening day, where they shook hands. The Senator's deterioration must have been obvious.[72] Joe might have the political clout to be reelected in 1958, as his fans in Wisconsin and elsewhere remained numerous and zealous. But the more interesting question was how long he could physically survive his self-destructive behavior.

In any case, assuming that Eisenhower was reelected, Walter would have wanted to run against McCarthy to preserve the GOP, locally and nationally, from the far Right. And a Senate seat, it will be recalled, was his first ambition after the war.

Reporters still didn't know about the resistance Charlotte might give her husband if he ran for the Senate. She was a quiet but powerful force in his decisions to decline several offers from the Eisenhower administration. (He was soon being considered for Secretary of the Interior.)[73] If she refused to live in Washington in 1953, why would she change her mind six years later? Walter no doubt thought he would worry about that when the time came. For now, he had to continue his work as governor and do whatever possible to see a united GOP reelect a very popular president.

Notes

1. John Wyngaard, "Former Lieutenant Governor May Be heard From Again," *Waukesha Daily Freeman*, January 12, 1955. Wyngaard speculated, no doubt correctly, that Kohler chose to select Mrs. Wise rather than order a special election because he wanted to deny Smith the opportunity to run for the office. Smith had seriously alienated GOP insiders, who had forced him to run against Knowles, and they did not care to revive his political career.

2. "First Woman Sworn In as State Officer," *Milwaukee Journal*, January 3, 1955. The Republican Party has an interesting history of opening opportunities for women, both in the party and in government. See *www.nfrw.org/republicans/women/2.htm*.

3. Copy, speech by Walter J. Kohler at the 1956 state convention, box 5, Republican Party papers, 117. On Wise serving as governor, see Richard S. Davis, "Our Lady Governor Still Cooks Breakfast," *Milwaukee Journal*, August 22, 1956.

4. Aldric Revell, "State Officers Sworn In," *Madison Capital Times*, January 4, 1955. The governor's assistants at this time were: Executive Secretary, Phillip T. Drotning; Personal Secretary, Mrs. Evelyn M. Tranmal; Legal Counsel, Edwin M. Wilkie; Research Aide, Robert D. Siff; and Legislative Secretary, Arthur E. Wegner. Copy, Phillip T. Drotning to Frank Bane, February 8, 1955, Box 25, Walter J. Kohler, Jr. papers.

5. The governor soon told a safety conference in Milwaukee that in the previous decade, traffic accidents had caused 7,631 deaths and injured 167,557, "making the total number of persons involved nearly equal to the combined population of Racine, Kenosha and Green Bay." "Asks Support of State Patrol," *Milwaukee Journal*, January 21, 1955. In 1954, Wisconsin had 1,334,000 registered motor vehicles. In 1955, the state established a new record for traffic deaths: 932. Between 1941 and 1956, more than 12,000 people died on Wisconsin streets and highways. "Traffic Safety Drive Begins in Wisconsin," *ibid.*, December 2, 1956.

6. "Highway Safety Legislation Emphasized by Governor," *ibid.*, January 13, 1955; "Text of Message Delivered to State Legislators by Governor," *ibid.* The "housekeeping" proposal was a plan to create a division of administrative services in the executive office. This was the third legislature in a row to hear Kohler's request. See editorial, "How State Can Save Money," *ibid.*, February 11, 1955.

7. "Need for 25% Surtax on Incomes Forecast," *ibid.*, January 21, 1955.

8. Willard R. Smith, "Kohler Asks Total of 278 Millions, Proposes State Income Tax Boost," *ibid.*, February 1, 1955.

9. "Highway Bill for Biennium Is 208 Million," *ibid.* See "State of Wisconsin General fund—Executive Budget," *ibid.* In fact, the executive budget repre-

sented less than one third of the state's total spending, but it was the budget most familiar to taxpayers.

[10] "Trouble Seen by Democrats," *ibid.*

[11] "Kohler Is Hit for Statement," *ibid.*, February 3, 1955.

[12] "Kohler Defends Report on Finances Last Fall," *ibid.*, February 2, 1955; "Asks Apology From Kohler," *ibid.*

[13] "State Business Leaders Glum at Tax Prospects," *ibid.*

[14] Editorial, "Kohler's Kidding is Ended and We Face Grim Fiscal Facts," *ibid.*

[15] "Knowles Praises State's Finances," *Waukesha Daily Freeman*, February 12, 1955. By late April, Knowles had made 35 speeches and was called the "man in motion" for the Kohler administration, speaking largely on behalf of the governor's legislative program, particularly his financial plans. Arnold Swislak, "State, For Most Part, Favors Tax Increase, Knowles Says," *Portage Daily Register*, April 29, 1955. This was further evidence, no doubt, that Knowles was being groomed to be Kohler's successor.

[16] "Finances of State Seen by Governor as Sound," *Milwaukee Journal*, March 23, 1955.

[17] "No Sales Tax Now, Word of Gov. Kohler," *ibid.*, March 24, 1955; "Boy's School Crisis Told," *ibid.*, March 25, 1955.

[18] "Offers College Merger Plan," *ibid.*, February 18, 1955. On the evolution of the proposal, see "New College Plan Outlined," *ibid.*, February 3, 1955;

[19] "Coleman Hits at College Bill," *ibid.*, March 4, 1955.

[20] "Kohler May Race Wiley for Senator," *ibid.*, April 17, 1955.

[21] John McLean, "Battle Lines Forming on College Merger Bill," *ibid*, March 10, 1955; "UW Regents Back Merger," *ibid.*, March 13, 1955. Both Rennebohm and Coleman, who wrote a second public letter to the governor, objected to Kohler's strong language. See "Coleman Renews School Plan Fight," *ibid.*, March 13, 1955.

[22] "College Merger Plans to Be Tested This Week," *ibid.*, March 27, 1955.

[23] "Minority Vote Delays College Bills Debate," *ibid.*, March 30, 1955.

[24] Laurence C. Eklund, "Gasoline Tax Boost is Seen," *ibid.*, March 2, 1955.

[25] Willard R. Smith, "Higher Fees for Drivers Also Sought," *ibid.*, March 3, 1955.

[26] Paul McMahon, "State Taxpayer is Cinch to Pay More Next Year," *ibid.*, March 6, 1955. The number of state employees rose from 12,158 in 1940 to about 20,000 in 1955. The average state salary in 1954 was $3,400. In 1940, it had been $1,400. See also Paul M. McMahon, "State Surplus All Spent, New Sources Needed," *ibid.*, March 7, 1955, Paul M. McMahon, "Budget Hard to Trim, So Levy Must Go Up," *ibid.*, March 8, 1955; Paul M. McMahon, "Aid to Localities Limits State Control of Budget," *ibid.*, March 9, 1955. The latter article pointed out that Wisconsin taxpayers

paid $282 million in property taxes in 1954, a gain of $175 million in nine years. "If the state government were to reduce aids to local units or retain a greater share of taxes now shared with them, the communities probably would be forced to boost local property taxes to compensate for the loss." Paul M. McMahon, "Pay as You Go Policy Seems to Spell Surtax," *ibid.*, March 10, 1955, noted that 33% of the state's population paid income taxes, amounting to about $100 million a year. "Scarcely a state in the nation relies as heavily upon the income tax as does Wisconsin....Considerably more than one-third of all the taxes raised for the general fund come from income taxes." The state highway department spent only $25.6 million dollars in 1930. A quarter century later, it was anticipating an expenditure of $93 million in a single year. It envisioned spending $100 million a year by 1957. Paul M. McMahon, "Highway Levy Boost Appears Quite Likely," *ibid.*, March 11, 1955. On other states with similar problems, see Paul M. McMahon, "State finds Company in Financial Miseries," *ibid.*, March 13, 1955.

[27] "Finances of State Seen by Governor as Sound," *ibid.*, March 23, 1955.

[28] "Catlin's Bid for Senate Sparks Wiley Fireworks," *ibid.*, March 11, 1955.

[29] "United Regents Bill Voted, Proposes UW Control Here," *ibid.*, April 13, 1955. In early May, Walter was one of 46 governors invited to the White House for discussions of international, national, and state problems. He was one of a half dozen governors to arrive in advance to share their views on radio and television programs. He appeared on NBC with three other governors, expressing his support for Eisenhower and GOP chances in 1956. "46 Governors at Conference," *ibid.*, May 2, 1955.

[30] "Kohler College Merger Bill Is Killed in Assembly Vote," *ibid.*, June 14, 1955; "UW Was Winner, Rest of State Lost, College Bill View," *ibid.*, June 14, 1955. In early June, Attorney General Vernon Thomson had raised legal questions about the college merger proposals, but he did not say that they were unconstitutional. "Doubts Raised on College Bill," *ibid.*, June 3, 1955. Catlin's concern was undoubtedly more political than legal.

[31] "Kohler Tells of Frustration; Assembly Proves His Point," *ibid.*, June 15, 1955.

[32] "Bill to Boost Traffic Patrol Is Killed 56-43 by Assembly," *ibid.*, June 21, 1955. On the gas tax hike, see "Gasoline Tax Split Okayed," *ibid.*, June 15, 1955. On the driver licensing examiner system, see "Kohler Gets License Bill," *ibid.*, May 27, 1955.

[33] "250 Man State Traffic Patrol Passed by Assembly 61-39," *ibid.*, June 23, 1955; "Senate Okays Patrol Boost," *ibid.*, June 24, 1955. The national death toll in 1955 was nearly 36,000, some 2,500 more than the 33,417 American soldiers, sailors, marines, and airmen killed during the 37 months of

the Korean War. "Travel Rush Begins Amid Auto Warnings," *ibid.*, December 30, 1955; "'55 Road Toll Set at 38,500," *ibid.*

[34] "Kohler Vetoes School Merger," *ibid.*, July 21, 1955; "UW Building Funds Tabled," *ibid.*, July 14, 1955. On reactions to the veto, see "Kohler's Veto Called Breach," *ibid.*, July 22, 1955.

[35] "Kohler Calls Session Best in Long Time," *ibid.*, June 25, 1955.

[36] Willard R. Smith, "Kohler Batting Average Is High in 1955 Session," *ibid.*, June 26, 1955; "Actions of 1955 Legislature Made Session a Historic One," *ibid.* Some 500 bills cleared both houses during the session. The legislature was uninterested in area redistricting, defeating efforts by rural Republicans to amend the state's constitution

[37] Willard R. Smith, "Catlin Labor Bill Is Passed After Senate Filibuster Ends," *ibid.*, April 29, 1955.

[38] "Catlin Bill Is Signed; Kohler Praises Law," *ibid.*, May 21, 1955.

[39] See, for example, John D. Pomfret, "Labor Unity Seen as Boon," *ibid.*, August 16, 1955.

[40] "Kohler Vessel Truce Blows Up; Governor Vows to Enforce Law," *ibid.*, July 11, 1955; "Kohler Vows to Back Law," *ibid.*, July 14, 1955. See Uphoff, *Kohler On Strike*, 226-235.

[41] "Calling Guard Dependent on New Trouble," *Milwaukee Journal*, July 22, 1955; "CIO Pledges No Violence in Picketing," *ibid.*, July 25, 1955.

[42] "Ploetz Lashes at 'Kohlerism,'" *ibid.*, September 6, 1955.

[43] "State's Public Aid Plan Called one of the Best," *ibid.*, June 27, 1955. Kohler pointed out that Wisconsin's average grant in the old age assistance program was $62.96, compared with the national average of $51.71. Aid to dependent children was $40.43 a person, compared with a national average of $23.90. Aid to the blind was $67.06, while the national average was $56.63. The state gave an average of $90.70 to totally and permanently disabled persons, while the national average was $54.60. In April, 1955 there were 1,617 children in 1,038 homes under the children's code. Total payment for that month was $87,162, or an average of $53.90.

[44] Laurence C. Eklund, "House Okays Gas Bill Study," *ibid.*, July 28, 1955.

[45] "Governor Vetoes Bills Curbing Housing Unit," *ibid.*, August 6, 1955.

[46] "Gov. Kohler May Run for President," *ibid.*, August 10, 1955. On the "favorite son" issue, see also "Governor's Day at Fair Costs Governor $1.50," *ibid.*, August 24, 1955.

[47] "GOP Studies Farm Voting," *ibid.*, September 9, 1955.

[48] "Illness of Ike Shocks Kohler," *ibid.*, September 25, 1955.

[49] "Kohler, Kuehn 'Favor Nixon,'" *ibid.*, October 6, 1955.

[50] "Regents Agree on Proposal for Merger of Colleges Here," *ibid.*, August 31, 1955. Each board would elect five members to the committee, and the governor would appoint four non-regent members. State Superintendent

of Public Instruction, George E. Watson, a member of both boards, would also serve.

51 "UW Gives Okay to Co-ordination," *ibid.*, October 1, 1955.

52 Editorial, "College Merger to Bring New Era in Education," *ibid.*, October 13, 1955. For more on the merger from the perspective of a state college administrator and future Chancellor of the University of Wisconsin-Milwaukee, see J. Martin Klotsche, *Confessions Of An Educator: My Personal and Professional Memoirs* (Milwaukee: n. p., 1985), 61-64, 84-100, 119.

53 For a session summary, see "Short Session of Legislature Worked Hard," *Milwaukee Journal*, October 23, 2005.

54 "Housing Bills Veto Upheld," *ibid.*, October 4, 1955; "Public Housing Curbs Okayed by Assembly," *ibid.*, October 18, 1955.

55 "Machine Gun Bill Defeated," *ibid.*, October 11, 1955. The bill was rejected in the Assembly 70-25, without a word spoken on its behalf.

56 "Assembly Rejects State Pay Raises," *ibid.*, October 20, 1955.

57 "Catlin Withdraws Do it Yourself Bill on Speeding Laws," *ibid.*, October 7, 1955.

58 "Assembly Vaudeville Features 'Oratory?'," *ibid.*, October 19, 1955.

59 William R. Bechtel, "Kohler's Report on State Finances Comes as Surprise to Legislators," *ibid.*, October 9, 1955.

60 William R. Bechtel, "$5,500 Paid to Catlins by a Risk Firm," *ibid.*, October 22, 1955; "Catlin's Fees Called 'High,'" *ibid.*, October 23, 1955.

61 Edwin R. Bayley, "Gerrymander May Be National issue in 1956," *ibid.*, October 23, 1953. On Thomson supporters, see "Thomson Holds His Hat Out of Ring—for Present," *ibid.*, November 1, 1955.

62 "Walter Kohler's Decision on Housing and 'Gerry,'" *ibid.*, November 6, 1955.

63 "Kohler Signs Housing Bill Aimed at City," *ibid.*, November 27, 1955. The gerrymander's immediate target was Henry S. Reuss, the liberal Democrat who defeated Charles Kersten in 1954. In his memoirs, Reuss thanked Kohler for his integrity displayed in the veto. Henry S. Reuss, *When Government Was Good: Memories of a Life in Politics* (Madison: University of Wisconsin Press, 1999), 41. Two other references to Kohler in the book, on page 39, are historically inaccurate.

64 "Republican Chiefs Cool to Gerrymander Veto," *Milwaukee Journal*, November 27, 1955.

65 "Housing Supporters Hit as Governor Okays Bill," *ibid.*

66 "Republican Chiefs Cool to Gerrymander Veto," *ibid*; editorial, "Kohler Points the Way to State-Wide Redistricting," *ibid.*, November 28, 1955. Many newspapers throughout the state supported the veto. See "State Press Backs 'Gerry' Veto," *ibid.*, November 29, 1955.

67 "New Crime Code Signed by Kohler," *ibid.*, December 16, 1955.

[68] "Kohler Raps Walton Stand," *ibid.*, December 22, 1955.

[69] "Catlin Attacks Wiley, Kohler and Thomson," February 15, 1956. Wayne Hood wrote privately to a member of the Republican National Committee, "If Walter Kohler decides to run against Wiley for the Senate we really are going to have some problems in Wisconsin, as if Walter's name is on the ballot as a candidate we will have some money problems, as well as problems within the organization." Copy, Wayne Hood to Robert Humphreys, March 8, 1956, Wayne Hood papers.

[70] Edwin R. Bayley, "Kohler Steps Out of All Contests; 'To Seek No Public Office in 1956,'" *Milwaukee Journal*, March 8, 1956.

[71] *Ibid.* The sympathetic statement is especially interesting because it was widely known that the Democrats considered a McCarthyite much easier to defeat than a moderate like Kohler, who attracted independent voters.

[72] "Fans and the Famous Get 1955 Season Under Way," *ibid.*, April 13, 1955.

[73] Laurence C. Eklund, "Cabinet Post for Kohler?," *ibid.*, March 29, 1956. Douglas McKay was leaving the cabinet on April 15 to run for the Senate in Oregon.

Chapter Thirteen

A Standard of Propriety

In mid-May, 1956, Walter traveled to the Marshall Islands in the South Pacific where he was an official civil defense observer at a series of thermonuclear weapon tests. The center of the testing was on Eniwetoc atoll, where the first American hydrogen bomb had been exploded on November 11, 1952, and Bikini Atoll in the same island chain where another hydrogen bomb had been exploded on March 1, 1954. Walter saw one nuclear device go off that was twice as powerful as the bomb that devastated Hiroshima. But an even larger explosion was delayed to the point that the governor came home without seeing it. During the tests he spoke with scientists about the meaning and future of these weapons.

Walter came away from the two and a half week experience convinced of the need to emphasize technical skills in education and to continue nuclear testing as a deterrent in the Cold War. In a talk at the Milwaukee Press Club, he said, "We as Americans have got to learn as much as we possibly can about fusion. Because, if we don't, by gosh, somebody else is—and it can be the Russians as well as anybody else." While he made no specific reference to Adlai Stevenson, who had urged the United States to call off nuclear tests in the Pacific, Walter said he thought that anyone who urged cessation of the tests "either is crazy in the head or is for the Russians."[1] That echo of McCarthyism was to be one of the last of its kind from Kohler.

On May 22, the governor hosted 250 business, professional, labor, civic, financial, and governmental leaders at the first annual governor's conference on industrial development. The event was held at the American Baptist Assembly grounds on Green Lake. One of Walter's most prized legislative achievements in 1955 was the creation of an industrial development division in the governor's office, and in a speech he called it "a turning point in terms of the official policy of the state of Wisconsin toward industrial activity." (This conference was organized by its director, Robert Siff.) If the State could expand its production of manufactured goods and services sufficiently, Walter stated, the rising cost of government would not be accompanied by higher taxes. But action by private citizens had preceded the new legislation, Kohler continued, noting a study showing that more than 10,000 new jobs, with an annual payroll in excess of $30 million, had been created in the State's smaller cities and villages with financial assistance from 122 local industrial corporations and foundations.

Walter took this occasion to express some deep feelings he had for the people of his native state. Wisconsin, he said, had many natural resources that could attract industry, "but the most precious and most valuable asset is the basic integrity of our citizens." He continued, "Wisconsin government, state and local, is synonymous throughout the world with honesty and efficiency. The absence of graft, the swift and searching disposition of corrupt officials, the steadfast refusal to condone or even to permit debasement of public office—all of these characteristics of Wisconsin government—are only reflections of the character of Wisconsin people."[2] The reference to "corrupt officials" was no doubt a jab at Mark Catlin, who was again making headlines.

On May 16, the State Supreme Court announced that a complaint had been filed by the state board of bar commissioners, after several months of secret investigation and hearings, charging Catlin with accepting $5,725 from state prison inmates and their families to use his political influence to get prisoners released. There were three counts, including the case of a Kenosha man, Louis Fazio, a convicted murderer sentenced to life imprisonment. His appeals for a pardon had been rejected by Kohler three times, so the family turned to Catlin. A tape recording existed of the cash transaction between members of the Fazio family and Catlin. A witness in another case said he turned over $500 to Catlin in a men's room of a parking garage and later paid him $225 more upon request. Another said she gave $500 to Catlin in a Chicago airport and another $500 a month later. Catlin, for all of his efforts, had been unable to release anyone, which undoubtedly contributed to the willingness of those who had paid him to testify.

A fourth count involved Catlin's activities on behalf of five other convicted felons "and others" who had paid him. A guilty verdict by the Court would almost surely result in Catlin's disbarment and end his political career.

The governor had first learned of the charges in January. He had them investigated by Edwin M. Wilkie, his pardon counsel, and then turned them over to the Attorney General and the bar commissioners for further study. "At the time," said a reporter, "it was known that the governor was agitated over the evidence." A criminal law expert in Attorney General Thomson's office, however, reported that he found no evidence of a criminal offense.[3]

Catlin vigorously denied the allegations and complained that there were "motives behind the charges," using the words "persecution" and "character assassination." The Assembly Speaker complained specifically about the governor's actions in the case. Catlin did not, however, deny accepting the money, and acknowledged that the payments were mostly made in cash. The places for receiving the funds, he said, were chosen by relatives of the prisoners. In his defense, Catlin noted that he was the attorney of record for six of the people cited in the allegations, including all five listed in the fourth count. He would not divulge his fees. At no time, he said, did he attempt to use his political influence on behalf of anyone.[4]

Some Republican leaders wanted Catlin to drop out of the Senate race in favor of Lieutenant Governor Warren Knowles. They worried that far Right delegates might be successful in winning the nomination for Catlin at the oncoming state convention with the charges against him still unresolved.[5]

Politics soon dominated the story as Catlin publicly condemned Kohler for "personal animosity" in the allegations facing him. He told a GOP gathering, "The charges were conceived, initiated and carried out as a political smear by Walter Kohler and Ed Wilkie, his political counsel. For whom they are doing it, I don't know. If Kohler thinks I can't fight back, he's badly mistaken, and I will prove it before this is over." After his talk, he told a reporter that the bar commissioners' report was deliberately timed to be announced just before the state Republican convention. He again blamed Kohler for a "deliberate political smear."[6]

Walter dismissed Catlin's contention and issued a statement describing how the information about the Speaker's questionable activities had first come to his attention and the steps he had taken to investigate the charges before turning them over to the proper authorities on January 13. (The initial charges had stemmed from Allen C. Hubanks, executive director of the Wisconsin Service Association in Milwaukee, an organization that aided prisoners. It was Hubanks who first heard rumors sweeping the state prison at Waupun that Catlin, for a fee, was the man to see to arrange favorable action upon applications for parole and pardon. He informed the governor.) At no time, Walter said, did he discuss the issue with the jurists weighing the case, adding that it was "ridiculous in the extreme to suspect that so distinguished a group of Wisconsin attorneys would act for political reasons." The governor also noted that he had apprised Catlin of the charges against him and that the Speaker had appeared before the board of bar commissioners to present his case.[7]

The far Right was now up in arms. Charles Kersten, seeking the GOP nomination for United States Senator, charged publicly that Kohler was in league with Knowles, and that the charges against Catlin were part of a "miserable plot" led by most major Republican leaders in the state to crush Catlin and Kersten in 1956 and Joe McCarthy in 1958. In going after McCarthy, these political "bosses" sought "to control a seat in the United States Senate for the obvious purpose of reading real Republicans out of the party and an effort to curry favor with the pro-Communists, Socialists, the ADA, and the Walter Reuther cult."[8] Philip G. Kuehn, GOP state chairman, named by Kersten, replied to the allegations with, "Poppycock. So asinine as to hardly merit comment. Period." Robert L. Pierce, national committeeman, said that Kersten's charge was "absolutely ridiculous. He must be talking in his sleep."[9]

On the eve of the state convention, Catlin sponsored a smorgasbord dinner for a crowd of 500 at the Ambassador hotel in Milwaukee. The audience booed when Kohler and Wiley were mentioned, and there were shouts of "Give 'em hell, Mark!" Catlin again declared that the charges against him were initiated by the governor, contending that the animosity stemmed from the Speaker's failure to support all of Kohler's legislative program. Catlin said he had acted at all times only as an attorney, never as an influence peddler, and contended that he had turned down "upward of 50" requests to represent prisoners whom he thought unworthy of obtaining pardons. In a new twist, Catlin claimed that the governor had known of his representation of the clients in question and at one point had suggested that he represent a certain prisoner.[10]

When the Republican state convention opened in Milwaukee on May 25, the governor attracted mild applause by declaring in his address that the GOP must nominate candidates who are "models of integrity and honesty." Senator Wiley followed, making the same point: "I am proud to say that there has not been the slightest whisper against my honor or integrity." He added, "The Republican party will be reelected if we can keep hate out of the campaign. I look forward to the Republican party carrying the torch of light, not getting down in the gutter."

McCarthyites got the message. They were busily distributing a mimeographed pamphlet, written by a Catlin supporter, containing a bitter attack on the governor. A second pamphlet being passed out to the 5,000 delegates was written on behalf of Charles Kersten and called Wiley a "one worlder and internationalist." It declared that the GOP, like the Democratic Party, had been taken over by "pro-Communists."[11] When Mark Catlin addressed the delegates, he drew cheers by attacking Wiley for his failure to vote on the McCarthy censure. "I will never run out on a fellow colleague on a controversial issue," he said. The reference to Kohler was obvious.[12]

Attorney General Vernon Thomson won the nomination for governor. That was another sign of the strength of the far Right. Lt. Gov. Warren Knowles and State Treasurer Warren R. Smith were endorsed for re-election. Kohler appointee Glenn Wise won the endorsement for Secretary of State.

Senator Wiley had four competitors, all of them pointing to his age, 72, and allegedly tepid credentials as a patriot. When Assemblyman Eugene Toepel of La Crosse nominated Catlin, he tore into Kohler, receiving a storm of applause in return. Toepel said that Catlin was "a public servant of impeccable integrity" who was being persecuted by a governor who had links with Democrats, La Follette Progressives, labor bosses, and Americans for Democratic Action. "Political connivers both within and without our party are responsible for having filed charges aimed at the destruction of a man, his family and his life. These charges are aimed at the destruction of the conservative wing of our party.... This convention must condemn the connivers." Toepel continued, "We must decide whether we will be men or mice. We must decide whether we will face up to this political assassination by the foes of our philosophy or give in to the pitiless pawns of the pink liberals in both parties." In short, Walter J. Kohler, Jr. was soft on the Reds.

The far Right showed its muscle at the convention by repudiating Senator Wiley and nominating Representative Glenn R. Davis of Waukesha for senator. Davis's name was raised when the four opponents of the incumbent seemed unable to win a majority of the delegates. Davis was a protégé of Tom Coleman, who allegedly headed a group of businessmen that guaranteed a war chest of $150,000 if Davis were endorsed. Catlin was at first stunned by news of the backroom maneuvers said to be behind Davis's selection on the third ballot. "I did not know we had kingmakers in the party." But he was soon persuaded to pave the way for Davis's nomination. Wiley vowed to run for reelection without the GOP endorsement.[13]

Walter must have been greatly shaken by the power of the McCarthyites. What chance had he now for a political future? The consortium of big money men, who paved the way for Davis, had the support of his old friend Melvin Laird, and heralded the return of Tom Coleman as the true head of the GOP in Wisconsin.[14] Walter's close relations with Eisenhower were no doubt actually held against him by a majority of Republicans at the state convention. Wiley had linked himself with Ike during his convention speech to no avail. The veteran Senator was even loudly booed at one point in his address. Charles Kersten got a better response when he promised, if elected, to introduce a resolution in the Senate repealing the censure of Senator McCarthy.

But Walter kept his mouth shut, and delegates to the national GOP convention had the courtesy to continue the tradition of choosing the governor as their chairman.[15] All five of the constitutional officers in Wisconsin were named delegates-at-large. Kohler was likely to play a prominent role in the San Francisco convention. Whether the far Right liked it or not, Eisenhower had recovered from his heart attack and was intent on winning re-election.

On May 29, Walter and Charlotte were in the chapel at Laughlin Air Force Base in Del Rio, Texas to witness the marriage of Terry and Diana Prange of Sheboygan. (Best man Michael Kohler later described Del Rio, Texas as "a barren place where vultures circle in the skies" and not at all a romantic setting.)[16] Celeste, her husband Robin MacFadden, and Jackie Holden were also present. Terry had been in the Air Force since February, 1955 and had graduated seventh in his pre-flight basic training school. He received his Wings and his commission as a second lieutenant on the day of his marriage.

Prange, an attractive strawberry blonde, two years older than Terry, was the daughter of a Kohler factory worker. Terry had first met her at the Ford agency in Sheboygan where she was employed. Diana (Danny, as she was known) had only a local high school diploma, and several members of the family thought that Terry married beneath him. "They were not, however, unkind to her," Terry later recalled.[17]

Terry was soon off to Waco, Texas for six months of training to become a bombardier and navigator, as well as a pilot. In January, 1957 he began a three year stint on an air combat crew at The Mountain Home Air Force Base in Idaho, flying Strategic Air Command B-47s all over the world. Walter had good reason to be proud of his son's achievements. In his early 20s, Terry had at last blossomed, and his full potential was just beginning to appear.[18]

From Texas, Walter and Charlotte traveled to New York. At a press conference in mid-June, Walter sidestepped attempts to have him take a stand on whether he would support Senator Wiley or Representative Glenn Davis. He praised the Eisenhower foreign policy and said that the opposition to Wiley was personal and did not involve the Senator's disavowal of the Bricker Amendment. Kohler said of Davis that he had "a fine record in Congress. He's a hard campaigner. He's honest, able, and he has courage." Walter added, "Actually, Davis' record—foreign and domestic—in support of the administration is better than Senator Wiley's." But he again refused to endorse either man. Walter was still on the tightrope, which obviously meant that he continued to be interested in running for office.[19]

Walter was in New York to serve as the main speaker at a "Pulse of the Nation" forum dinner co-sponsored by the Republican National Committee and the national Republican Club. He used the occasion to repeat a theme he had used during the last election: Republicans had long been champions of social progress in the United States. He cited old age assistance, first enacted by Montana in 1923 under Governor Joseph M. Dixon; aid to dependent children, first enacted under the Republican governors of Illinois and Missouri in 1911; aid to the disabled, first enacted under Governor Goodland of Wisconsin in 1945; and workmen's compensation and unemployment compensation, initially enacted under Wisconsin Republican governors in 1911 and 1932. He then turned to the achievements of the first Eisenhower administration. They included, he said, the removal of government controls that had "shackled our economy," the creation of high national security standards, the ending of the Korean War, the creation of a balanced budget, cuts in the federal payroll, the largest reduction in federal taxes ever made, a halt to inflation, and leadership in developing a national highway system.

"Finally, however," Walter declared, "the Republican administration has restored decency, honor, integrity and honesty to the federal government." The GOP in Wisconsin, he added, had the same goal. "We have demanded that our candidates for office be models of integrity and honesty and when they have failed in this respect we have not sought to conceal it, rather we have conceived it our duty to expose it for all the world to see." Many in his audience no doubt recognized the reference to Mark Catlin.[20]

❧ ❧ ❧ ◉ ❦ ❦ ❦

Catlin, who dropped out of the Senate race and sought reelection to the Assembly, attempted several legal maneuvers to free himself from the charges raised by the Wisconsin board of bar commissioners.[21] But he was unsuccessful, and a hearing on the case, supervised by a referee named by the state supreme court, began in Milwaukee in August. The first witness was Frank Fazio, who said he gave $5,000 in a cloth bag to Catlin to free his brother. Catlin had told him, Fazio said, that he had influence with the governor, who owed him a favor. The Speaker "said he could guarantee to get my brother out."[22] A secretary to the Fazio brothers soon testified that she heard Catlin say that Governor Kohler would not grant pardons except through him.[23] A Milwaukee businessman testified that Catlin initially asked $8,000 to try to win pardons for the man's brothers.[24]

When the hearing shifted from Milwaukee to Madison, the governor was summoned to the stand. He testified that he warned Catlin of his disapproval of legislators serving as paid attorneys for state prisoners seeking clemency, and told the Speaker that he would deny any such applications "automatically." On cross-examination, Kohler was told that there was nothing in the canon of legal ethics to prevent a lawyer-legislator from representing clemency applicants. Walter replied, "If there is no such provision, let me say I think there should be one." An attorney elected to the legislature, he said, if he was a man of "utmost integrity," should lean over backward to avoid giving the impression that he was bringing pressure on any department. When asked if he was activated by any political motive in bringing the Catlin case to the legal authorities, Walter replied that he would have gone ahead if "my own son" had been involved.

Kohler also told of being stunned to learn from Catlin that the attorney had urged one of the men involved in the case (sentenced to life for murder and armed robbery) to lie about being represented by the Speaker in his petition for clemency. The governor was both shocked and angered, he said, to learn from Catlin, in the spring of 1955, that he had accepted money for his services. Edwin Wilkie, the governor's legal counsel, gave testimony that corroborated Kohler's account of his actions in the matter.[25]

The normally anti-Kohler *Madison Capitol Times* editorialized, "In an era when the pay-off and giveaway have been accepted cynically by many as the norm in American politics, the stand taken by Gov. Walter Kohler in the Catlin hearing is refreshing reassurance to those who still believe there should be some standard of propriety in government.... On his forthright handling of this Catlin case...we must join with all citizens interested in good government in an expression of admiration and gratitude. It has certainly been the 'finest hour' of Gov. Kohler's administration."[26]

A third session of the hearing was held in Juneau, in Dodge County, where the Warden of the prison in Waupun and four inmates Catlin represented in clemency appeals were summoned to testify. The convicts and their relatives told of Catlin's promises, fee demands, and excuses for failing to gain executive clemency. Under cross-examination, however, Louis Fazio backed Catlin's charge that he had not promised to use political influence on his behalf. This was a direct contradiction of earlier testimony given by his brother Frank, who had paid Catlin.[27]

Back in Madison, in his own defense, Catlin claimed, "I have absolutely no recollection of ever suggesting a fee to a prisoner," and he called Frank Fazio "an unmitigated liar." Catlin summoned three Appleton lawyers and two judges to vouch for his good character.[28] The twelve days of the hearing concluded with the Speaker claiming that he had "earned every penny" and acted honorably in each of the convict cases.[29]

But Catlin's constituents were not impressed, and they defeated Catlin's bid for reelection that fall, ending his 14-year stint in the Assembly.

On February 8, 1957, the referee in the hearing, retired judge Frank Bucklin, found that Catlin had charged excessive fees and recommended that he be reprimanded and fined by the state supreme court for unethical conduct. "The practice of allowing lawyer-legislators to appear in any manner in either pardon or executive clemency petitions before the governor," he said, "is a vicious one, and should be promptly and effectively stopped. If the practice is stopped, the case will have a very good purpose." This was, of course, the governor's position. Bucklin found Kohler guilty of nothing. Still, Bucklin was amendable to Catlin's profession of good character and said he was guilty, in the Fazio case, of a "mistake."[30]

The state supreme court, on November 5, 1957, went farther than Bucklin, suspending Catlin's license to practice law for six months for misconduct as an attorney. It also ordered him to pay $1,500 toward the cost of the investigation. In a 14-page opinion, the court found the heart of the case against Catlin to be valid: he had promised to use political influence on behalf of prisoners and had taken inappropriate fees for this service, fees that were kept secret and for which no receipts were given. Catlin had also concealed his activity as an attorney for prisoners seeking executive clemency.

The court stipulated that the suspension would not end automatically in six months; Catlin's license would be restored when he showed a willingness to comply with state bar regulations. By that the court referred to Catlin's countercharges against the governor and the board of bar commissioners and his lack of contrition.[31]

Six months later, the state supreme court reinstated Catlin's license. While nothing was said publicly, this had to mean that Catlin had dropped his charges against Kohler and the board of bar commissioners and had asked forgiveness for his conduct.[32] In any case, his political career was over. Catlin ran twice more for election but could not regain his Assembly seat. In 1987, a home town obituary remembered him largely as a lawyer and politician who was "controversial."[33]

❧❧❧❦❧❦❦

In the September primary of 1956, Alexander Wiley stunned GOP insiders by defeating Glenn Davis. Once again, a veteran politician had shown that endorsement by Republican insiders was not a necessity. (Wisconsin primaries are open, and Democrats clearly aided Wiley's cause.) Tom Coleman and the right-wing of the state party undoubtedly considered Wiley's victory a serious blow, increasing their determination to keep Joe McCarthy's senate seat out of the hands of anyone but themselves.[34]

That same month, Wisconsin sent 30 delegates and 30 alternates to San Francisco for the national GOP convention.[35] (Dorothy Kohler, still angry at the president for his treatment of McCarthy, was not included.) At a cocktail party on the eve of the convention, the delegates warmly greeted Vice President Nixon and his wife. Kohler had been especially critical of his old friend Harold Stassen for suggesting that Nixon be dropped from the national ticket in favor of Governor Christian Herter of Massachusetts. Walter now predicted that the Eisenhower-Nixon ticket would run even stronger in Wisconsin than it had in 1952, when it won by a margin of about 300,000 votes.[36]

When Republicans gathered in San Francisco, the Democrats had already met, nominating Adlai Stevenson again, this time with Estes Kefauver. On the currently hot issue of civil rights, the party had elected to appease Southerners by failing to take a stand on legislative or executive "implementation" of the landmark United States Supreme Court decision of 1954 banning racial segregation in public schools. This left what was thought to be an especially important opening for Republicans, ever eager to lure blacks away from their well-established habit of voting for Democrats.

The final draft of the GOP platform "accepted" the Supreme Court decision and ignored the "implementation" issue. But it endorsed the court's admonition to accomplish desegregation with "all deliberate speed," which made it, in the judgment of a top NAACP official, "slightly" more advanced than the Democratic version. Walter charged that Democrats had "weaseled" on desegregation. "The Republican attitude is unequivocal," he said, "although we believe that the execution of the Supreme Court decision should be moderate. We should have a provision to implement the decision, but in a moderate way."[37]

Enlightened moderation was a term that could summarize the vision and aspirations of both Eisenhower and Kohler. Both men sought peace, prosperity, and social justice, but they had a keen sense of the possible and a great respect for the rights and wishes of others. This restrained and yet positive approach to government was widely respected and admired at the time, making an indelible mark on the entire decade. It seemed to be in harmony with the large body of common moral assumptions Americans enjoyed in the 1950s, rooted, in Robert H. Bork's words, "in our original Anglo-Protestant culture, and expressed in law."[38] This enlightened moderation would be greatly missed by people of that generation when another era, beginning in about 1965, chose a path often leading to confrontation, violence, and moral anarchy. The 1950s would then become the "Ike Age," and its politicians often depicted as stodgy, self-satisfied, and unenlightened. In 1956, however, the GOP convention in San Francisco seemed to represent the hearts and minds of the majority of Americans, Eisenhower appeared to embody the best this country had to offer, and the Republican ticket seemed unbeatable.

The GOP platform, passed by the convention, was hailed as both liberal and internationalist. Among other things, it called for the expansion of social security, vigorous support of the United Nations, federal aid for school construction, support for federal and local public housing programs, a generous immigration policy, aid to undeveloped countries, and a preference for "public bodies and cooperatives" in the marketing of public power. Walter thought the platform excellent and said he strongly supported both the public housing and immigration planks, both of which had drawn some grumbling from right-wing Wisconsin delegates. "I see no reason," he said, "to stop immigration. This country was founded on an open door immigration policy. America wouldn't be America if it hadn't been for the influx of so many people." He also commented favorably on the public power plank and a plea for extending reciprocal trade. Wisconsin delegates shouted their approval of the entire platform. If they hadn't read every line of it, they trusted the man they hoped would remain in the White House and firmly believed that the GOP was leading the country in the right direction.[39]

Walter was visible on several occasions during the convention. While announcing Wisconsin's unanimous support for the president, he called Wisconsin "the birthplace of the Republican party and America's dairyland." On the vote for vice president, he introduced Vernon Thomson as "the next governor of Wisconsin" and let him announce the delegation's support. Kohler also received attention by being one of those selected to help escort Thomas E. Dewey to the rostrum. Dewey and Kohler, largely due to their interaction at meetings of the governors, were close friends.[40]

At one point during the convention, Walter appeared on a television program with Glenn Davis, Wayne Hood, and Robert Pierce. Hood spoke on behalf of Davis (Wiley was largely ignored by Wisconsin delegates), and Kohler and Pierce discussed Wisconsin's economic future.[41]

Walter was delighted by the ease with which delegates from all across the nation responded to both candidates and issues. He considered the convention "the most harmonious in history," conducted "with a spirit of tremendous enthusiasm."[42] Walter termed Eisenhower's acceptance speech at the final session of the convention "magnificent." He said that he particularly liked the president's point about the GOP being the party of principle, not expediency. He also approved the liberal overtones of the message. "I liked his emphasis on the party's need to be forward looking and not brooding on the success of past years."[43]

When asked if he expected to play a role in Eisenhower's second administration should the GOP ticket win, Walter said, "I have no idea.

I'd rather not comment on that." When asked the question in another way, Walter thought a while before replying, "I have no such plans."[44]

Being a lame duck governor, Kohler was not called upon to campaign extensively for either the local or national GOP candidates. On October 1 he was present, along with other Republican dignitaries, when Vice President Nixon came to Milwaukee on a campaign swing. (Walter had another opportunity on that occasion to get a good look at Joe McCarthy, now being hospitalized periodically for detoxification.)[45] Walter also made several radio talks of a general nature, prompting speculation that he, along with other party insiders, was less than enthusiastic about the gubernatorial aspirations of Vernon Thomson.[46]

For the most part, the governor tended to his state duties during the fall. He was particularly pleased to appear in Milwaukee for ceremonies marking the creation, on September 1, of the University of Wisconsin-Milwaukee, a campus for which he was largely responsible. The initial daytime enrollment was about 4,500 full-time students, and another 4,500 part-time students were enrolled in evening courses. Kohler described the new university campus as a "great and valuable asset to the city," one that would enrich the cultural life of the community and "bring to tens of thousands of young people fine educational opportunities they would not otherwise have had. And inasmuch as a state or nation advances or declines in direct ratio to the knowledge and wisdom of the citizenry, so also will all of Wisconsin reap the benefits from this institution."[47]

On November 6, Wisconsin Republicans enjoyed a stunning victory. Eisenhower took 61.6% of the vote, a slightly higher percentage than he enjoyed four years earlier, winning 954,844 votes to Adlai Stevenson's 37.8% and 586,768 votes. Senator Wiley won 58.6% of the vote, easily defeating Democrat Henry Maier of Milwaukee, who took 41.2%. Vernon Thomson won 52% of the vote, edging William Proxmire (who finished 206,000 votes ahead of Meier and 312,000 votes ahead of Adlai Stevenson). Warren Knowles was reelected Lieutenant Governor. Stewart Honeck won the Attorney General's race. And Robert Zimmerman (son and assistant of his perennially popular father) became Secretary of State. The legislature remained firmly in Republican hands.

Nationally, Eisenhower crushed Stevenson, winning all but seven southern states and racking up an electoral college margin of 457 to 73. This time, however, Ike did not have such large coattails, and the Democrats continued the control of Congress they achieved in 1954.[48]

Two weeks after the election, top leaders in the state GOP made it known that they would like to dump Joe McCarthy. The Senator had announced his desire for another term, and party heads decided to try to put a halt to any campaigning. Speaking anonymously to Milwaukee reporter Edwin R. Bayley, the officials attributed their decision to McCarthy's belligerent attitude toward the President and his policies. Moreover, they said, the Senator was no longer a vote-getter. They had rejected his bid to campaign for the GOP ticket in 1956.[49]

Unspoken, to many, was the obvious: McCarthy was in perilous physical and mental condition. Watching Joe go through a bout of delirium tremens in front of his wife and friends, his long-time pal Urban Van Susteren made inquiries, learning that McCarthy had a serious liver condition and that death was imminent unless he stopped drinking. The next morning, Van Susteren confronted Joe with the issue. The response was "Kiss my ass." Angrily, Van Susteren shoved a bottle of whiskey in front of his old friend, telling him to end things quickly without further disgracing himself and his family.[50]

By this time, Walter had reportedly told friends that he was interested in running for McCarthy's Senate seat. (The first Kohler for Senator club opened in West Bend in late November, urging Walter to run.)[51] But he was making no public statement on the matter. The other candidate mentioned widely throughout GOP circles was Glenn Davis, who had lost to Wiley in the September primary but continued to enjoy Tom Coleman's favor. Kohler was far more widely known than Davis and had a better chance of winning, given his appeal to independent voters. But Davis held the ideological position that attracted both a majority of party leaders and those clinging to the last remains of the Second Red Scare. Among the Democrats, State Senator Gaylord Nelson of Madison and Congressman Henry S. Reuss of Milwaukee were being considered. William Proxmire, having lost three elections in a row, was thought to be a spent force. Except that even now, after his latest failure to be elected governor, he continued to campaign feverishly all over the state.[52]

The Kohlers began to move out of the Executive Residence before Thanksgiving.[53] Phil Drotning had tendered his resignation two weeks earlier. The governor's executive secretary and press secretary had been the governor's only close advisor during all three terms. One reporter was puzzled, thinking that Drotning's departure would harm Kohler's political future. But Walter had helped the trusted aide land his new job, vice-president in charge of public relations for Northwest Orient Airlines.[54]

On November 28, the governor conducted his last ceremonial function, dedicating three new buildings at Mendota state hospital, a facility for the mentally disabled. The main building was 94 years old, and from 1904 until Kohler's first term there had been no new buildings constructed on the site. Walter had early declared his desire to tear down the main structure, and his wish was soon to come true. Harold W. Story, vice-chairman of the state board of public welfare, praised the roles played by governors Goodland, Rennebohm, and Kohler in the evolution of the state welfare program. Kohler, he said, gave his department "such tremendous impetus…that it is now recognized as one of the outstanding departments in the nation." (The next day, Walter received an honorary life membership in the Wisconsin Welfare Council "in recognition of an outstanding contribution to social welfare in Wisconsin.")[55]

During his remarks, Walter might have won considerable applause and media praise by mentioning his own daughter, in a similar institution, using her plight to help explain his strong desire to improve the state's primary mental health facility. But he chose not to. Niki's welfare was a private matter.[56]

Soon after the election, a state study committee recommended that the legislature pass both a 2% sales tax (with food exempt) and an increased personal income tax in 1957 to meet the rising costs of state and local government.[57] The sales tax issue was political poison for the incoming administration; William Proxmire quickly announced that he was forming an organization to fight the new tax.[58] Vernon Thomson said that there would be no sales tax during his first administration. Kohler, on the other hand, stressing the very real need for more state funds, and rejecting a hike in the income tax, property tax, and personal property tax, endorsed the sales tax, the one untapped source for revenue. However realistic, this move made enemies, especially among businessmen and the far Right, who would again link Kohler's name with tax-and-spend Democrats. Republicans of all persuasions were puzzled by the fact that the outgoing and incoming governors held opposite views on the critical issue of taxation.[59]

At year's end, newspapers all across the state paid tribute to the outgoing governor. The *Milwaukee Journal*, in a glowing farewell, listed several major achievements that could be attributed to Kohler's leadership. The first was redistricting. "That a resisting legislature did pass the basic measure was certainly Gov. Kohler's doing. While he did not resist the ensuing effort to overturn it, still that initial passage was the key to the ultimate victory for the rule of equal votes." Secondly, he was almost solely responsible for the merging of the state boards of higher education and the creation of the University of Wisconsin-Milwaukee. "This is an historic gain, both for efficient management in a prime tax consuming area and for educational service." The governor also won applause for his efforts in highway construction and safety programs, governmental efficiency and integrity, conservation (five of the six present commissioners were Kohler appointees "and they seem to have restored, on the whole, a harmonious and sound situation"), construction of the state school for boys at Waukesha, and modernizations in the criminal and children's codes. The editorial also noted that 89 out of the governor's 92 vetoes were sustained during the three terms. Milwaukeeans were particularly pleased by Kohler's veto of the gerrymander of the city's congressional districts.[60]

The *Wisconsin State Journal* made a similar list, further stressing Kohler's excellent appointments and his achievements in public welfare. But what particularly struck the editorial writer as commendable was Walter's character. "The list could be yards longer. But beyond the cold, written record there remain the personal attributes of this man—his high, unbendable sense of integrity, his courage, his sense of public duty, his unstuffed but deep dignity. If there is to be one criticism of Walter Kohler, it is that he was 'too nice a guy'....He didn't know how to exert pressures, crack heads, make deals. And when others tried to teach him, he would have none of it. He might have accomplished even more if he had, but then—that was Walter Kohler....He won the public's attention and trust in another way, a way that has proved good for this state for six productive years."[61]

The *Monroe Evening Times* declared, "There have been few periods in the history of Wisconsin—or any other state for that matter—in which the personality, integrity and leadership of a governor have been reflected in such a fine record of accomplishment in state government."[62]

Just before Christmas, the Piscatorial and Inside Straight Society held a farewell dinner for Walter. The Society, comprised of politicians and media people, met about twice a year. They would sometimes gather at Wisconsin Dells, for example, to play cards, smoke, eat, drink, and talk politics. The emphasis at all times was on relaxation and fun. Among the 41 men who attended the black tie Kohler dinner were Vernon

Thomson, Warren Knowles, Phil Drotning, Stewart Honeck, Melvin Laird, Robert Pierce, Robert Siff, Guido Rahr, and newspaper reporters John Wyngaard, Robert Fleming, and Arthur Bystrom. Throughout the 1940s, Walter had belonged to a similar group that was part of the GOP's State Finance Committee. His charming manner and even temperament made him popular with members of both these groups.[63]

On January 2, 1957, as he prepared to turn over authority to Vernon Thomson, Walter held an informal news conference in his office. He declined to discuss his political future, saying only that he would not accept a position in the Eisenhower administration. His immediate plans, he told reporters, included returning to the Vollrath company, working to raise funds for the American Cancer Society, and vacationing in the West Indies. And "if we want to make a world tour later, there's nothing to stop us now."

Walter called his six years as governor a "tremendous, richly rewarding experience." He praised staff members, administrators, and a number of legislators. "The human relationships are the things I have enjoyed the most." Walter said that he was particularly pleased of late to see the effectiveness of an enlarged state patrol. After it was increased from 70 officers to 250, he said, 84 lives were saved in the following five months. The point system for drivers, put into effect a year earlier, had also acted "as a brake" on drivers, he said, and played a role in enhancing traffic safety.[64] In one of his last official statements before leaving office, Kohler urged a continued strengthening of the state patrol.[65]

Charlotte was delighted to leave Madison and the political formalities that occupied her time as first lady. She and Walter would now be able to travel more freely, and she could devote even more time to knitting and needlepoint. A photograph shows one of her pillows boasting needlepoint that exclaimed "You can't be too rich or too thin," a statement that expressed more than a little of Mrs. Kohler's philosophy of life.[66]

We do not know if Charlotte was aware at the time of her husband's continued political aspirations. Walter had yet to declare for any office, and perhaps he simply told his wife that the future would take care of itself. Not long after the new governor was sworn in, the Kohlers were off to Antigua for their winter vacation. Walter was only 53, and Charlotte was 45; a long and happy future appeared to await the handsome and wealthy couple.

Walter became interested in the work of the American Cancer Society, as we have seen, in 1948. It was a humanitarian commitment above all, but the effort was no doubt also designed to enhance Kohler's political prospects by enabling him to make valuable acquaintances throughout Wisconsin and keep his name in the press. In 1950, he became an ACS Director-at-Large, and three years later he became ACS Board Chairman. In 1957, after leaving office, he was the ACS National Campaign Chairman, heading a drive to raise $30 million.

During the five week period of March 20 to April 25, 1957, Walter traveled 12,000 miles and visited 16 cities, from Providence, Rhode Island to San Francisco, California on behalf of the fund drive. "The Governor," as Walter was called by almost everyone, including his son, delivered major addresses in every scheduled city, held 48 news conferences, gave 25 radio interviews, and made 11 television appearances. Charlotte accompanied her husband during most of his travels.

The tour began with a kickoff luncheon at the White House, where photographs were taken with the president. Another photograph shows the Kohlers in White Plains, New York on March 31; Walter is wearing his glasses to read his speech. In Atlanta, Georgia the Governor posed with actress Susan Hayward. In Chicago he was photographed with track star Jesse Owens, and he and Charlotte posed for photographs at the airport with actress Lauren Bacall. At a luncheon at Paramount Studios in Hollywood, Walter was photographed with film producer Cecil B. DeMille and actress Debra Paget. He declined to comment when a Los Angeles reporter asked if he would run against Joe McCarthy.

In a speech in Milwaukee, Walter pointed out that 250,000 Americans died of cancer each year. Over the previous five years, he noted, the American Cancer Society had raised more than $100 million for education, research and service. The funds were having results, as a third of all cancer victims were currently being saved from death. Wherever Walter traveled, he called for more research and education, described the great complexity of the problem, and expressed optimism. His basic speech was embellished with local cancer data. From the first, the Kohler campaign tour was a resounding success, and it eventually raised more than $2 million more than the ACS had ever brought in.[67]

On April 9, while Walter and Charlotte were still on their tour, Wisconsin GOP chairman Philip G. Kuehn told reporters that health might prevent Joe McCarthy from seeking reelection the following year. His illness was said to be "acute hepatitis," an "acute illness resulting from various forms of liver damage." The hospital in which McCarthy was confined would not elaborate. On May 2, the Senator died.

Walter told reporters, "My heartfelt sympathy goes out to Mrs. McCarthy as I am sure does the sympathy of all people regardless of whether they were friends or foes of the senator." This was somewhat more restrained than the comment by State GOP Chairman Philip G. Kuehn: "He shall go down in history as one of the most courageous and outspoken senators of all time. His vigorous anti-Communist fight was carried on without regard to the mental and physical punishment he endured. He awakened America to the horrible inroads communism had made. Many times he stood alone but carried on his fight to the bitter end." GOP insider Wayne Hood stated, "I think his fight on the Communist problem for the United States will make the historians mark him very high among the men who have served in the senate."[68]

Walter declined comment when asked about his political intentions, saying that "now would be the worst possible time" to discuss such things. But he would soon have to make a commitment, for Wisconsin law prohibited the governor from appointing a replacement, and Vernon Thomson was about to call a special election that would be scheduled not less than 55 days nor more than 70 days from the date of the governor's order. State law also dictated that if there were more than one candidate in either party, a primary election was required. Reporter Edwin R. Bayley observed that special elections to fill vacancies "usually bring out a large field."[69]

Notes

[1] "Kohler Backs Bomb Testing," *Milwaukee Journal*, May 23, 1956. Walter was observing Operation Redwing. See http://nuclearweaponarchive.org/Usa/tests/Redwing.html.

[2] "Kohler Notes Plants' Value," *Milwaukee Journal*, May 22, 1956.

[3] "Catlin Charged with Accepting Cash to Influence Prison Releases," *ibid.*, May 16, 1956; "Four Counts in Complaint Given in Full," *ibid.* "Probe Began After Rumors Were Heard," *ibid.* Governor Kohler had denied Fasio's applications for pardon in 1950, 1951, and 1952. The Fasio family turned to Catlin in late 1953.

[4] "'Persecution,' Replies Catlin," *ibid.*, May 16, 1956.

[5] "Knowles Draft Seems Likely," *ibid.*, May 17, 1956.

[6] "Catlin Charges 'Smear'; Kohler Says 'Incorrect,'" *ibid.*, May 18, 1956.

[7] *Ibid.* On Hubanks, see "Catlin Aid Termed Hope of Prisoners," *ibid.*, August 7, 1956.

[8] "Kersten Calls Count Against Catlin Part of 'Miserable Plot,'" *ibid.*, May 18, 1956.

[9] "Kersten Rips 'Party Bosses,'" *ibid.*, May 19, 1956. Watching their political opponents engaged in struggle, some Democrats sought to benefit from the turmoil. State Senator Henry Meier of Milwaukee said that Catlin was 'the very symbol of Republican leadership in Wisconsin," being the author of "every foul bill" the GOP leadership sought to pass in the 1955 legislature. "Help Catlin, GOP Is Urged," *ibid.*

[10] Edwin R. Bayley, "Catlin Lashes at Kohler, Shows He's Still in Race," *ibid.*, May 24, 1956.

[11] "'Models of Integrity Party Goal'—Kohler," *ibid.*, May 25, 1956.

[12] Edwin R. Bayley, "Catlin Appears to Be Strongest Challenger to Incumbent," *ibid.*, May 26, 1956.

[13] Edwin R. Bayley, "Gets Victory After Catlin Swings Votes," *ibid.*, May 27, 1956. Coleman said privately that the story of a guaranteed campaign fund was false, and he blamed the *Milwaukee Journal* for creating and spreading it. Copy, Thomas E. Coleman to Steve J. Miller, June 4, 1956, Thomas E. Coleman papers; copy, Thomas E. Coleman to Richard J. H. Johnson [of the *New York Times*], June 7, 1956, *ibid.*

[14] For an example of Coleman's fund-raising prowess, see copy, Thomas E. Coleman to William J. Grede, August 15, 1956, *ibid.* In one week, he raised nearly $4,500 by making eight telephone calls.

[15] "Kohler Is chairman of State's Delegates," *Milwaukee Journal*, May 27, 1956.

[16] E-mail, Michael Kohler to the author, July 7, 2005, Miscellaneous file. Flying to San Antonio after the wedding, Jackie, Terry's ever-eccentric half-sister, told Michael she was not wearing panties.

[17] Peter Kohler, Jim's son, married a local beauty whose father was a barber. Such class free marriages in the Kohler family have been rare, however. Peter and Nancy celebrated their 50th wedding anniversary in 2004.

[18] Terry Kohler interviews, June 12, 2003; March 25, 2004; undated clippings of the engagement and wedding are in the Leslie Kohler Hawley collection. This collection also contains many wedding photographs, the marriage certificate, and Diana's wedding garters.

[19] Wade H. Mosby, "Kohler Avoids Senate Choice," *Milwaukee Journal*, June 13, 1956. There was truth in the view that Wiley's personality was important in the GOP decision to abandon him, but ideology was even more important. See copy, Philip G. Kuehn to Dora D. Marshall, August 15, 1956, Thomas Coleman papers.

[20] Wade H. Mosby, "Kohler Lists GOP 'Firsts,'" *Milwaukee Journal*, June 14, 1956.

[21] See "Catlin Wants Counts Clear," *ibid.*, June 12, 1956, and "Justices Hear Plea by Catlin," *ibid.*, June 15, 1956.

[22] See "Sticks to Story About Vow To Use Influence," *ibid.*, August 6, 1956. A week earlier Kohler had again denied executive clemency to Louis Fazio and the three men convicted with him for murder. Six months later, he again denied clemency to Fazio and John Mandella but commuted the sentence of Jerome Mandella and Dominic Lampone, convicted with Fazio and also a part of the case against Catlin. "Point is Won, Catlin's View," *ibid.*, December 21, 1956. Governor Thomson was more amenable, and John Mandella was paroled in June, 1957. "John Mandella Is Out on Parole," *ibid.*, June 3, 1957.

[23] "Catlin Aid Termed Hope of Prisoners," *ibid.*, August 7, 1956.

[24] "Businessman Says $4,000 Finally OK'd After Capitol Talks," *ibid.*, August 7, 1956.

[25] Willard R. Smith, "Kohler Warned Catlin About Parole Activities," *ibid.*, August 14, 1956; "Kohler's Pardon Aide Resented Catlin Action," *ibid.*, August 15, 1956; "Parole Board Backs Catlin," *ibid.*, August 16, 1956.

[26] Reprinted in *ibid.*, September 10, 1956.

[27] "Fazio Relates Catlin's Visits," *ibid.*, August 17, 1956; Robert J. Boyle, "Fazio Backs Catlin Stand," *ibid.*, August 18, 1956.

[28] "Catlin Tells Why He Hid His Pardon Action Role," *ibid.*, August 22, 1956; "Catlin Calls Frank Fazio an 'Unmitigated Liar,'" *ibid.*, August 23, 1956.

[29] "He 'Earned Every Penny' in Prison Cases, Catlin Says," *ibid.*, August 25, 1956.

[30] "Fine, Reprimand for Catlin Urged for Ethics Violations," *ibid.*, February 8, 1957.

[31] "Catlin's License Suspended for Action in Pardon Cases," *ibid.*, November 5, 1957.

[32] "Catlin Given License Back," *ibid.*, May 7, 1958.

[33] "Former Assembly Speaker Dies at 76," *Appleton Post Crescent*, January 24, 1987.

[34] For an insiders' view of the Glenn campaign, see copy, George E. Rodgerson, "Publicity, Davis-Wiley Campaign of 1956," Wayne Hood papers.

[35] "Wisconsin Delegate List," *Milwaukee Journal*, August 19, 1956.

[36] William R. Bechtel, "Nixon Saluted by State GOP," *ibid.*, August 20, 1956. Nixon was known to be a close friend of Davis. For more on the Stassen flap, see "William R. Bechtel, "Stassen Bid to Dump Nixon Chilled by Ike Grin for VP," *ibid.*, July 24, 1956. This eccentric move spelled the end of Stassen's credibility. Kohler responded to Stassen's action by saying, "Incredible—absolutely unbelievable." At the GOP convention, Stassen gave a nominating speech for Nixon. Walter commented, "Everybody except Stassen knew that this convention wanted Nixon—we're happy to see he saw the light.""State's Delegates Snipe at Stassen, *ibid.*, August 23, 1956.

[37] Edwin R. Bayley, "Moderation is the Guide in Plank on Civil Rights," *Milwaukee Journal*, August 21, 1956.

[38] Robert H. Bork, "Their Will Be Done," *Wall Street Journal*, July 5, 2005.

[39] William R. Bechtel, "Didn't Read Platform They Voted to Adopt," *Milwaukee Journal*, August 22, 1956. Walter emphatically denied rumors that he wanted to be on the ticket, replacing Nixon, and he made this point in a statement on the convention floor. Arthur Bystrom, "State GOP Delegates Plan Boom for Davis," *ibid.*, August 22, 1956.

[40] William R. Bechtel, "Wisconsin Delegates Get Into the Limelight," *ibid.*, August 23, 1956.

[41] Arthur Bystrom, "Predict State Will Go GOP," *ibid.*, August 23, 1956.

[42] *Ibid.*

[43] William R. Bechtel, "Kohler Lauds Speech by Ike as 'Magnificent,'" *ibid.*, August 24, 1956.

[44] *Ibid.*

[45] "Republicans Greet Nixon on Arrival," *ibid.*, October 1, 1956. See Reeves, *The Life and Times of Joe McCarthy*, 665-670.

[46] "Tax Statement Is Seen Result of GOP Pressure," *Milwaukee Journal*, October 27, 1956. See Walter J. Kohler, Jr. Oral History, Columbia University, 1971, 46, which seems to confirm Walter's lack of enthusiasm for his successor.

[47] "Kohler Lauds UWM Future," *Milwaukee Journal*, October 16, 1956.

[48] The president sent a personal letter to Kohler thanking him and Charlotte for their congratulatory telegram. See copy, Dwight D. Eisenhower to Walter J. Kohler, Jr., November 8, 1956, Eisenhower Library file.

[49] Edwin R. Bayley, "GOP Leaders in State Set to Dump McCarthy," *Milwaukee Journal*, November 25, 1956.

[50] Reeves, *The Life and Times of Joe McCarthy*, 669-670.

[51] Edwin R. Bayley, "Run Against McCarthy, Gov. Kohler Is Urged," *Milwaukee Journal*, December 4, 1956. The organization grew out of a Wiley for Senator group and was apparently spontaneous. Walter made no comment when news of the club made the press.

[52] Edwin R. Bayley, "GOP Leaders in State Set to Dump McCarthy," *ibid.*, November 25, 1956.

[53] "Kohlers Start Moving Task," *ibid.*, November 25, 1956.

[54] Willard R. Smith, "Departure of Drotning Will Leave a Big Void," *ibid.*, November 11, 1956. See Melvin Laird interview. Another Kohler adviser from his third administration, state director of industrial development Robert D. Siff, quit at the end of the year to accept a banking position in New York. The governor called Siff "an extremely able man." He had been a research analyst for the Rennebohm administration. "Adviser to Kohler, Siff, Quits State Job," *Milwaukee Journal*, December 22, 1956.

[55] The certificate is in the Terry Kohler papers. A letter, accompanying the certificate, cited the revision of the Children's Code, more adequate buildings for welfare institutions, and a stronger Governor's Commission on Human Rights.

[56] "New Mendota Buildings Part of Kohler's 'Dream,'" *Milwaukee Journal*, November 29, 1956.

[57] "2% Sales Tax Endorsed by Study Group," *ibid.*, November 24, 1956.

[58] "Proxmire Starts Group to Defeat Sales Tax," *ibid.*, November 29, 1956.

[59] "Teen Ager Questions Kohler on Sales Tax," *ibid.*, December 9, 1956; Willard R. Smith, "Thomson Says No Sales Tax for State in Next Two Years," *ibid.*, December 20, 1956. Robert D. Siff's industrial development division issued a report in December declaring state taxes burdensome. The report was a reason Kohler backed a sales tax over increases in the already established taxes. "Adviser to Kohler, Siff, Quits State Job," *ibid.*, December 22, 1956.

[60] Editorial, "The Many Fine Fruits Will Do Him Lasting Honor," *ibid.*, December 30, 1956.

[61] Editorial, "Farewell to a Great Governor," *Wisconsin State Journal*, January 7, 1957.

[62] Quoted in a Walter J. Kohler for Senator brochure, Terry Kohler papers. The brochure contains a dozen such quotations from state newspapers.

[63] Terry Kohler interview, June 12, 2003. The program and a photograph of the event, held in Madison on December 13, are in the Terry Kohler papers.

[64] "No US Post, Says Kohler," Milwaukee Journal, January 3, 1957. In 1971, Walter told an interviewer than the only post that would have interested him was Secretary of Navy, "but it was never offered to me and I never

asked for it." Walter J. Kohler, Jr. Oral History, Columbia University, 1971, 47. According to Melvin Laird, Walter was indeed offered this post, along with an assortment of others. He believes that Charlotte was decisive in Walter's rejection of all offers. Melvin Laird interview. The Sherman Adams papers note that endorsements were received for Walter's appointment as an Associate Justice of the Supreme Court of the United States. See page 86 of my documents in the Eisenhower Library file.

[65] "Kohler Urges Bigger Patrol," *Milwaukee Journal*, January 8, 1957. A United Press poll of 35 legislators showed strong opposition to a large state patrol. Walter also commuted the first degree murder conviction of Milton J. Babich, a 26-year-old Milwaukee man, to second degree murder. The slaying had involved a teenage act of passion, Kohler said. "My own belief on the purpose of our prison system is that it is for rehabilitation and not solely punishment. I am advised that if paroled Babich will take a useful place in society." "Babich Eligible for Parole as Kohler Commutes Term," *ibid.*, January 4, 1957.

[66] The photograph is in the Leslie Kohler Hawley collection.

[67] This account is based on clippings, photographs, and letters contained in a large bound volume entitled "The Honorable Walter J. Kohler, Jr., America's Number One Crusader of 1957, Presented by The American Cancer Society, The Annual meeting, November 4, 1957," located at Windway. Notes are in the American Cancer Society file. On President Eisenhower's involvement, see copy, Walter J. Kohler, Jr. to Sherman Adams, January 14, 1957, Eisenhower Library file.

[68] "State Officials Express Their Shock and Grief," *Milwaukee Journal*, May 3, 1957.

[69] Edwin R. Bayley, "Predict Special Election to Pick His Successor," *ibid.*

Chapter Fourteen
Driving Ambition

In the speculation about a successor to Senator McCarthy, most of the attention was on the GOP, for Wisconsin had not sent a Democrat to the Senate in the past quarter century. It was known throughout the country that State Republicans were divided. No matter how accommodating Kohler had been toward the far Right in the election of 1952, and how deeply he was committed to party unity and victory, many McCarthyites considered him to be a dangerous liberal. Of course, they had the same view of the President of the United States. The national press often supported this point of view of Kohler by portraying him as a staunch opponent of McCarthy, who had considered running for the Senate in 1958 solely for the purpose of gaining further support for the Administration. The former governor was widely considered to be the favorite in the race.[1]

Walter said nothing until May 14, when he announced his candidacy. He was the first in either party to declare his intentions.[2] The following day, Warren Knowles and Glenn R. Davis entered the contest. The former was Walter's closest political friend, now looking out for himself, while the latter was bound to be favored by many on the far Right. In announcing his candidacy, Davis said that his views on all subjects would "compare quite closely" with those of McCarthy. But even Davis was too chummy toward the Left to suit some of the ultraconservatives. Milwaukee attorney Howard Boyle said, "The announced candidates are candidates for the White House social list. We need a man who will get in and fight like Joe McCarthy did." Representative Alvin O'Konski, a strong McCarthy supporter, soon entered the race. "I even voted against lend-lease to Russia during World War II," he boasted. Former state supreme court justice Henry P. Hughes also announced his candidacy, declaring that he had opposed Communists "long before McCarthy." Warren Knowles sighed, "It's going to be a hot summer."[3]

Governor Thomson pondered the possibility of changing the law and naming a McCarthy successor, a position favored by Senator Wiley and Tom Coleman.[4] A lumber company executive confided to Senator

Wiley, "If this goes into a special election it's going to be a hell of a dirty fight that will do the party no possible good."[5] But in early June the governor gave in to pressures from candidates of both parties to call a special election.

Kohler approved the decision. He also predicted that the state convention would fail to endorse anyone because the issue was not on the agenda. Walter knew that given the power of the far Right in the party, Davis was likely to win any endorsement given. McCarthy defender Senator Barry Goldwater of Arizona was scheduled to be the main speaker at the convention. Senator Wiley, assigned only three minutes to speak at the convention, declined to attend, blasting "isolationists" and "reactionaries" in the GOP.[6]

Five candidates worked the crowd when the GOP convention met in La Crosse for its one day session. Kohler said he would campaign on his record as governor and the record of the Eisenhower administration, which he promised to support "most emphatically." He was in accord with the president on foreign aid, civil rights, and the defense budget, he said, and differed with the Administration only on federal aid to education. "The Eisenhower foreign policy has been most effective in keeping us out of war," Kohler said. "He is one of the great Republican presidents. He ranks with Abraham Lincoln, Theodore Roosevelt, and Herbert Hoover."[7] This pro-Eisenhower stance was not shared by many delegates, however. When Governor Thomson paid tribute to the Eisenhower administration in his speech, the response was dead silence.[8]

The convention voted 2,526 to 801 to make no endorsement.[9] Nevertheless, each of the five candidates was invited to make a speech. Davis received loud and prolonged applause. The reaction to Knowles was slightly less favorable. Hughes and O'Konski earned some support. But when Kohler took to the platform, cheers were mixed with loud, sustained booing. Walter smiled, and waved. When the noise died down, he said, "I am particularly proud that my good friends and supporters in this audience have had the courtesy not to boo the other candidates who were introduced here, and I thank you for it." After a quick burst of applause, Walter proceeded to summarize the principles of the GOP and the achievements of the Eisenhower Administration, adding, "I might state that we as Republicans should fight against the Democratic Party...and we as Republicans should not dissipate our strength in fighting each other." A woman delegate commented to a reporter, "I feel sorry for him. Just like they did to Senator Wiley."[10]

On June 17, William Proxmire jumped into the race. After three defeats at the polls, he and his new bride, a long-time campaign worker in Madison, had decided to retire from politics, run their printing business, and enjoy life on the farm. Patrick Lucey, a major Democratic leader in the state, soon changed Proxmire's mind, however, telling him that he was the only party member with a chance of winning.[11] The whirlwind of campaigning soon began anew.

By this time, there were 11 candidates in the special election race—six Republicans, four Democrats, and a Socialist Labor Party candidate. State Senator Gerald Lorge, another McCarthyite, soon entered the contest promising to erase McCarthy's censure from the record. Supporters of Mark Catlin were urging him to run, contending that Kohler could not be elected if nominated.[12] Yielding to the power of the far Right, Warren Knowles said in Green Bay that he believed the McCarthy censure was wrong because it prevented the Senator from speaking his mind.[13]

The primary election was set for July 30. Kohler did not begin campaigning until June 29, three weeks after the GOP convention. There is no evidence to explain the delay. Perhaps he was blinded by self-confidence. He may have spent part of the time preparing intellectually, knowing that as a senatorial candidate he would face many delicate and complex national and international questions.

In West Bend, where he began, the response was warm and friendly. A reporter observed that "everyone seemed to recognize him, and voters came up to shake his hand without prompting." In a radio talk, Walter recited his record as governor and pledged to support the Eisenhower Administration, the twin themes of his campaign.[14]

Phil Drotning volunteered his part-time services, wrote some speeches and press releases, and made a small financial contribution. A statewide Kohler for Senator committee was announced on July 6. Its chairman was Everett Yerly, head of the GOP state central committee, and there were eleven vice-chairmen. But aside from Yerly and Cyrus Philipp, the list consisted of fairly obscure Republicans.[15] A fund raising effort was initiated in mid-July.[16] A Milwaukee campaign office was not opened until July 17, and its staff seemed to one reporter to consist largely of the Citizens for Eisenhower people of a year earlier.[17]

In contrast, Glenn Davis had a well-funded and tightly-organized campaign headquarters, and the candidate was traveling furiously across the state before Walter began. Milwaukee industrialist Walter Harnischfeger led an effort to raise $50,000 for the candidate. Reporter Edwin Bayley commented, "If organization can win an election, Davis will win this one. He showed up Monday with the smoothest functioning outfit since the late Senator Taft ran here in the presidential primary of 1952."

Davis situated himself ideologically between the McCarthyites and Kohler, saying of the latter, "The former governor is riding on Eisenhower's coattails. That is not the proper approach."[18] When Kohler said he would rather hang on to Eisenhower coattails than be "in Walter Harnischfeger's hip pocket" Davis replied that Kohler was one of the wealthiest industrialists in the state and could finance his own campaign, while he himself had to ask the citizens of Wisconsin for assistance. Eager to get in on the fray, Warren Knowles declared that he represented "no clique or faction within the party, nor am I a captive candidate of hand picked party bosses or industrialists."[19]

Kohler and Knowles sparred on Milwaukee television in early July, arguing about a variety of topics, including the meaning of "modern Republicanism." Knowles tried to position himself to the right of Kohler whenever he could. When Walter said he would like to see satellite countries free, but would not favor assistance that would generate war, Knowles declared, "I don't want to start playing footsie with any Communist either in this country or out."

When the debate turned to the federal budget, Kohler observed that the $71.8 billion federal spending package represented a reduction of $15 billion from requests made of the president. Lawmakers, he said, could make cuts "by limiting programs and not adding programs." Knowles said he thought that the administration's spending program was a "luxury budget on a global basis," and if elected he would "represent what I believe is the fundamental conservative philosophy of the people of this state."

On foreign aid, Kohler favored the arming of South Korea and military aid for South Vietnam and for "some middle-eastern countries too." Knowles said he did not "want to see anything in the way of entangling alliances."[20]

By mid-July Walter was in the thick of things in the campaign, shaking hands and making speeches tirelessly. One reporter described him as a "confident, buoyant candidate." A huge press corps now followed him, including representatives of three large national magazines, and newspapers in New York, Chicago, Milwaukee, and Madison.

In response to Davis's charge that Kohler was a millionaire and didn't need assistance from others, Walter reminded a Madison audience that state law limited the personal expense of all candidates to $10,000. For Davis to say otherwise, he said, was careless and deceitful. "Wisconsin doesn't need any deceitful men in the United States Senate." When asked if he was the only Eisenhower supporter in the race, he said, "I would judge so, yes." Commenting on his other GOP rivals, he said that Congressman O'Konski was promising voters the moon, and he paraphrased an old joke to ask: "Alvin, you durn fool, whose gonna pay for this?" He jabbed at the efforts by Knowles, Lorge, and Hughes to corral the McCarthy vote, saying that he didn't believe such a thing existed.[21] That was three parts campaign blarney and one part wishful thinking.

While the Republican candidates fought each other, William Proxmire denounced them all as McCarthyites and stooges of the rich. "Kohler, who is certainly one of the very richest of the tiny handful of enormously wealthy multimillionaires in Wisconsin, has attacked Davis because Davis enjoys the support of other big business boys," he said. "But Kohler was hand picked by the big industrialists who dominate the Republican party to run for governor in 1950..." Fellow Democratic candidate Clement Zablocki gibed at Kohler and Davis in a similar way, saying that he saw no difference between hanging on to "Ike's oil spotted coattails" and "being carried around in the hip pockets of big industrialists."[22]

In mid-July, the words between the Kohler and Davis camps grew even more heated. Winston Smith, chairman of the Milwaukee County Young Republicans for Davis, called Walter "a millionaire playboy," saying that Wisconsinites did not want this type of person as a Senator. He declared that "Kohler comes before the people with the blood of Mark Catlin on his hands and yet has the audacity to question the political integrity of Glenn Davis."[23] In Racine, Walter took a dig at his two Congressional opponents (Davis was the actual target), asking voters to judge whether they had disqualified themselves by "indifferent records, whether they vacillated, were unprincipled or exploited emotional causes to their own advantage." He said that the next Senator should be "personally honest," implying, of course, that some of his opponents were not.[24]

In a press conference prior to a rally that featured five of the seven GOP candidates, reporters grilled candidates about their stand on the late Senator McCarthy. Predictably, Davis showed more sympathy than scorn for McCarthy, and Knowles was equivocal, saying "I'm not taking a definite stand." Walter was the most critical, saying, "McCarthy was wrong in attacking the president." He continued, "McCarthy did focus attention on Communists in government. Probably it would have been done without him, though." When asked if the candidates thought McCarthy's total influence was positive or negative, Davis said, "The net result was plus." Knowles agreed. Walter replied, "Most of the exposures of communism were the result of other investigations. Still, the exposure had to be done." When the question was repeated, Walter shot back, "Neither one nor the other. He was unimportant in exposing communism. The man is dead." Kohler then cut off more questions. "Look," he said. "McCarthy is not an issue in this campaign. Let's drop it."[25]

But Walter knew perfectly well that for many Joe McCarthy was indeed a campaign issue. And among those were Democrats and independents Kohler hoped would cross party lines in the open primary and vote for him. In a speech at Sturgeon Bay, he charged that Davis was the "candidate of the super-reactionary wing of the Republican party." He continued, "Walter Harnischfeger would not only turn back the clock, but if he could he would return to the sun dial. The fact that Harnischfeger believes that Davis shares his views...should be of concern to every citizen who holds middle of the road political views and believes in progress."[26] Gone now was any pretense of a united party and the non-existence of a moderate/ultraconservative split. Walter said openly that he hoped to attract Democrats; everyone knew that Democratic votes had helped Senator Wiley in the 1956 GOP primary.[27]

The crossover vote was on the minds of several candidates. Proxmire thought that he could attract right wing Republicans by declaring in a Milwaukee radio address: "The Dulles foreign policy is losing ground to the Reds because it is paralyzed between appeasement of isolationists and fear of the Soviet Union." In short, Secretary of State John Foster Dulles, thought by normal people to be a militant anti-Communist, was soft on the Reds. Proxmire said also that the administration had muffed a great chance after the failed anti-Communist revolt in Hungary, and that the bungling served "as a frightful deterrent against a future drive for freedom by Russia's satellite colonies." Democrat Clement Zablocki joined in, charging that the Republican administration "seems to be under the impression that if they sit and wait long enough, and wish hard, communism will simply disappear of its own accord." Ironically, many liberal Democrats had charged in 1952 that the liberation of eastern European nations plank in the GOP platform was an example of right-wing extremism.[28]

When campaign clubs filed their financial reports with the secretary of state on July 22, the five GOP candidates had raised some $94,000. Glenn Davis supporters led the way with $39,341, spending virtually all of it. Contributors included the heart of the GOP state leadership: Tom Coleman, Walter Harnischfeger, and Wayne Hood. Kohler clubs placed second, raising $15,689 while spending only $5,345. That meant that Davis had outspent Kohler by more than seven times. Kohler backers included Cyrus Philipp and three members of the Vollrath family.[29] Walter soon reported that he spent $6,701.40 of his own funds in the campaign, the largest amount of any candidate.[30]

Part of the Kohler campaign funds were spent on the "Koeds for Kohler," a group of former "Ike girls" who carried signs and balloons and staged demonstrations during some of the candidate's rallies. Political enemies sometimes popped the balloons with cigarettes during Kohler speeches.[31]

Proxmire soon charged that more than two-thirds of Kohler contributions had come from wealthy industrialists and should be repudiated by the candidate and refunded. The former governor, said Proxmire, had criticized Davis for receiving backing from Walter Harnischfeger while at the same time collecting money from other rich businessmen. "Unless Kohler acts at once," said Proxmire, "he must stand convicted of brazen hypocrisy." Not to be outdone, Clement Zablocki told an Ashland audience that "the Eisenhower administration will go down in history as the administration which sounded the death knell for small business and independent enterprise in the American economy." Democrats had normally condemned Ike for being pro-business.[32]

As the primary election drew closer, Walter stepped up his attack on his ultraconservative opponents. In Milwaukee, he declared that "political control will be returned to the far right wing old guard of the Republican party" unless Wisconsinites elected a man who supported President Eisenhower. "The election of any of the other six Republican candidates would further handicap the president in his efforts to make of the Republican party a political organization that is in tune with the time." Davis countered by declaring that "One candidate has indicated he would rubber stamp everything from economic assistance to Monaco to higher interest rates on home owners."[33] Congressman O'Konski said that the easiest thing to do was to go along with everything that the administration did. But the nation's policies were wrong, he charged, and in eastern Europe they were driving nations into the hands of the Communists.[34]

The Eisenhower Administration itself stayed out of the primary contest, although it was widely known that the president and Sherman Adams, his assistant, had a high regard for Kohler. Senator Wiley was not invited to participate in the contest, but he too was known to be friendly toward Kohler and did not disguise his hostility toward the party leaders backing Davis.[35] Former Governor Oscar Rennebohm came out for Warren Knowles, no doubt a response to the battles he had fought with Kohler over the unification of higher education in the state.[36]

Two days before the election, the liberal *Milwaukee Journal* endorsed Kohler, declaring him to be the best qualified candidate. "His administration was the most outstanding in decades, it was productive of major and lasting achievements, particularly in the fields of higher education and highway safety, a revised children's code, a new code of criminal law and fair representative government. Kohler governed ably, honestly, efficiently and wisely. Good government, not politics, was his major concern."[37] This enthusiastic endorsement was a bitter pill for Proxmire and Zablocki to swallow, for the state's largest city had been fertile territory for Democrats, and both candidates expected it to anchor their victory in the primary. GOP ultraconservatives found it simply one more piece of evidence that Kohler was in league with the Left.[38]

The Milwaukee County Kohler for Senate clubs were criticized late in the primary race for distributing a letter of support by local 167, which represented workers at the Vollrath Company. The letter, an obvious effort to distinguish Walter from his uncle, still embroiled in the Kohler Company strike, claimed that 167 was an "IUE-CIO" local. The board of the Wisconsin CIO, however, pointed out that the Vollrath plant was represented by the independent United Electrical, Radio and Machine Workers of America, "which was thrown out of the CIO because of Communist domination." The error had been made by a staff aide, and it did not seem to hurt the Kohler campaign seriously. Moreover, the flap gave local 167 president Delbert Holtz another chance to endorse

Walter publicly. "I have great confidence in him. He is a fair minded man and deserving of support."[39]

On the eve of the election, eight of the nine senatorial candidates appeared on Milwaukee television to express their points of view. Very little was said that voters had not heard before. Proxmire condemned all Republicans as the tools of big business. Lorge said he was the only candidate pledged to continue "the fight against Communists and subversives." Davis said that experience in Congress was superior to state legislative experience. Kohler emphasized his record as governor, his support of the Eisenhower administration, and his personal character. But in a last minute speech in Fond du Lac, Walter went farther, predicting his own victory not only because of his credentials but also in part because of concern that the GOP was in danger of becoming "a vehicle for that handful of extreme reactionaries who would turn back the clock on social progress and make the Republican party a private club to serve their own selfish ends."[40]

Such language could not help but irritate and anger the Right. But Walter obviously thought this approach worth the risk, for if he won the primary he would no doubt have only hapless William Proxmire to face in the August 27 special election. Congressman O'Konski dismissed the perennial Democratic candidate as "Foxy, Proxy, Automatic Proxy" who had been running for governor for six years. Walter didn't talk about him at all during the primary race.[41]

On July 30, following a light turnout of almost a half million voters, Kohler defeated Davis by only some 9,000 votes. The margin of victory was apparently provided by crossover votes from Milwaukee independents and Democrats. Proxmire, on the other hand, won 69 counties and crushed Zablocki by about 30,000 votes. In Dane County, the state capitol and its neighbors, Proxmire won by the impressive margin of 9,344 to 1,169.[42]

While Kohler thanked supporters and called for party unity, McCarthyites seethed about this latest of their humiliations. A Milwaukee reporter now called the state GOP "riven by an almost unprecedented split." The national chief of the Always America First Committee sent telegrams to four of the defeated candidates stating that a "nationalist" Republican would run as an independent in August, and it urged them to withhold support from "internationalist" Kohler. O'Konski and Lorge both expressed suspicions about the vote in Milwaukee, where a harmless error had been discovered on primary ballots. Only a single

Republican rival, Warren Knowles, promptly pledged support for Kohler in the special election, less than a month away."[43]

It was also widely observed that Walter had not received a majority of the Republican votes in the primary. The *Madison Capital Times* trumpeted, "The votes of Davis and of Representative O'Konski, who was violent in his denunciations of the president, ran better than 50,000 ahead of Kohler."[44] Official figures soon showed that Davis won 31 counties, O'Konski 20, and Kohler 17.[45]

Senator Wiley, Republican National Chairman Meade Alcorn, and Warren Knowles issued statements urging all Republicans to rally behind Kohler. Wiley declared, "Walter Kohler made a fine governor and he will make a very fine United States senator. The Republican party must now close ranks behind him. With his fine business experience, his splendid background as governor and his sense of balance and judgment, I know that he is going to do a grand job for our state in Washington."[46] But was all this too late? Why should ultraconservatives back a man who had linked them with the stone age, impugned their integrity, and denigrated the achievements of Joe McCarthy?

Moreover, how could Kohler win Milwaukee County in the special election when Democrats, given the choice of only two candidates, would most certainly side with Proxmire? Organized labor was also pondering the advisability of throwing its full weight behind the Democrat.[47] The *Waukesha Freeman* spoke in an editorial of Kohler's "diminishing popularity as a vote getter," and noted that if the turnout in the special election was small (400,000 was a high estimate), the GOP's chances of sending Kohler to the senate were "in great jeopardy."[48]

The special election was important to both parties nationally as well as locally. The current composition of the United States Senate was 49 Democrats and 46 Republicans, with the Wisconsin seat vacant, and a victory was thought likely to have an effect on the 1958 races. Senator Kefauver and Michigan Governor G. Mennen Williams volunteered their services for Proxmire. James Sheldon of New York, public relations director of the nationalities division of the Democratic National Committee, and A. F. (Matt) Matthews of Washington, press secretary for the Democratic senatorial campaign committee, soon flew to Wisconsin to advise Proxmire.

Victor Johnson, Executive Director of the National Republican Senatorial Campaign Committee arrived in Milwaukee right after the primary to assist Kohler. He was uniquely qualified to heal party wounds

as he had worked under Tom Coleman and had been an administrative assistant to McCarthy. Vice President Nixon telephoned Kohler,
volunteering to come to Wisconsin to campaign. (The invitation was
declined for reasons that were never made clear.) Sherman Adams sent
his congratulations from the White House. Walter spoke confidently
of his impending election. Nixon, he said, looked forward to swearing
him in. Most political experts in the state thought Kohler the heavy
favorite.[49]

A few days after the primary, the Wisconsin Republican party began to come back together. The defeated senatorial candidates, with
the exception of ultra-McCarthyite Alvin O'Konski, officially backed
Kohler. Governor Thomson, at the designation of a monument desig-
nating Ripon as the GOP's birthplace, strongly urged party unity. The
Republican state executive committee voted unanimously to support
Kohler.[50] Secretary of the Interior Fred E. Seaton was dispatched to
Wisconsin to appear at a party unity meeting of some 200 leaders. He
emphasized how "terribly important" the election was to the party's
balance in the Senate, and he appealed to Republicans to abandon their
internal differences.

Still, the press picked up some angry rumblings from McCarthyites at
the meeting and elsewhere that raised a vital question: All of the leading
Republicans might say they were behind Kohler, but how vigorously
would they work for his election? Did anyone seriously think that Tom
Coleman and Walter Hernischfeger were prepared to labor intensely to
send Kohler to the Senate?[51] Reporter Edwin R. Bayley soon observed
a cool approach toward the election by former Davis supporters, several
declaring their intention to abstain from voting.[52]

On August 7, Howard H. Boyle, Jr., a 36-year-old Milwaukee attorney
who had run for the Senate in 1956, declared himself an independent
candidate for the August special election. He said he would run as a
"Joe McCarthy Republican," advocating adoption of the Bricker amendment, lower taxes, states' rights, and an end to subsidies and controls for
farmers. The regular party candidates, he declared, were unconcerned
with "principle and morality." By this time three other independent
candidates had entered the race, including one who also called himself
"a McCarthy Republican."[53]

Democrats had no problem falling in line behind Proxmire. Congressman Henry Reuss said that Proxmire's three defeats for governor
were unimportant. "Abraham Lincoln and old Bob La Follette failed in

politics several times before they succeeded—and how they succeeded after the voters finally recognized them!"[54]

Proxmire took the tack that he was the poor underdog, fighting against "These pink tea boys who always get everything they want." Kohler, he said, had never lost. "Let my opponent have the support of the man who has never proposed to a girl and lost. I'll take the losers. He can have the support of the man who has never owed a note he couldn't pay. I'll take the debtors. My opponent can have the votes of all those who have only pulled for all-winning teams like the Yankees. I'll take the Braves."[55] A physician's son, born into wealth; a graduate of an exclusive prep school, Yale, and Harvard; and a millionaire who did not have to support himself, Proxmire was portraying himself, as always, as the man of the people. He was, as he had told countless thousands of Wisconsinites in person, just plain Bill.

At an August 7 press conference in Washington, President Eisenhower declared himself a "Kohler man" in the upcoming election. He said also that he was one of the former governor's "great admirers."[56] Walter told reporters that he was "extremely pleased" by the president's endorsement, adding that he had not requested it.

Eisenhower's public support surely fed Walter's belief that he was unbeatable. This self-confidence was enhanced by the fact that virtually all of Wisconsin's newspapers, with the predictable exception of the *Madison Capital Times*, endorsed Kohler. Walter was far from complacent, however, vowing to campaign throughout the entire state and in every major city.[57] A schedule of the two senatorial candidates' appearances soon showed Walter working six days a week, flying and driving at a frantic pace.

But Proxmire worked seven days a week, campaigning in his usual fashion from dawn until late at night. Incredibly, he appeared to be more persistent and energetic than ever. John Wyngaard had written in 1956, "Nothing quite like Proxmire has turned up on the Wisconsin political scene in a long time....Proxmire has mobilized himself utterly for political campaigning. His daily pattern of activities is rigidly controlled. His personal budget, his eating habits; his sleeping, everything in his life is to conform to his political goals..."[58] A supporter noted in the same year that Proxmire was "a demon for work," who labored even while driving from one to place to another, typing letters, speeches, and press releases on his portable typewriter on a wooden board fitted to the back of the front seat. A night light let him continue the activity around the clock.[59]

At the Democratic Party's national convention in 1956, Proxmire had proposed to a beautiful young divorcee, Ellen Hodges Sawall, with whom he had worked on several campaigns. The couple decided to get married, but the service was delayed until after the election, for fear that a wedding service would remind voters that Proxmire was divorced.[60] Every aspect of his life was subordinate to his desire for political power. In 1957, Ellen dutifully accompanied her husband on many of his campaign ventures and served officially as his campaign manager. (Patrick Lucey, a close political associate of Proxmire's, said later, "Proxmire always ran his own campaigns.")[61] Charlotte Kohler, by contrast, was nowhere to be seen during the campaign.

Proxmire was not without assistance in spreading his message. Minnesota Congressman Eugene McCarthy, Michigan Governor Williams, and Tennessee Senator Estes Kefauver stumped the state for him.[62] Senator John F. Kennedy, who had made a brief splash at the Democratic convention a year earlier, was soon scheduled to appear in Milwaukee and Green Bay. Having avoided the vote on McCarthy's censure, he was thought especially capable of winning the votes of Catholics and ultraconservatives.[63]

Both the CIO and the Wisconsin State Federation of Labor endorsed Proxmire. This was unexpected, for harsh words had been exchanged in the past between labor leaders and the Democratic office-seeker. George A. Haberman, WSFL president, declared that "the Democratic candidate is the only liberal in the race, and it therefore behooves labor to lend its efforts in his election." So Walter could not win in the ideology department: he was too liberal for many Republicans and insufficiently liberal for organized labor and the Democrats. The WSFL statement, sent to 44 bodies throughout the state, also declared that Kohler was for big business and had "clearly demonstrated during his three terms in office, that he is not, and never was, a friend of labor."[64] This served to reinforce the idea that the former governor was of one mind with his widely reviled uncle at the Kohler Company.

In his talks throughout the state, Walter stressed his desire for stronger state authority and diminished federal power. In Beaver Dam, he declared, "There are few traditional state and local functions which cannot be administered more effectively and economically at the local, rather than the federal level." Kohler opposed federal aid to education and supported private power producing facilities. He also stood for a strong national defense, balanced budgets, low taxes, a sound currency, and business incentives. These were, of course, conservative positions. But he also spoke favorably of civil rights (on one Sunday, he spoke at four black churches in Milwaukee) and conservation efforts promoted by the Eisenhower administration. He also praised its successful efforts to squelch inflation and increase worker income. Kohler was "Ike's candidate," after all, a strategy compelled by personal conviction and the politically sound belief that the president's popularity in Wisconsin and elsewhere would be of incalculable benefit at the polls.[65]

Proxmire used his familiar strategy of stressing class and income. Kohler was for the rich and corrupt "big boys," he said at almost every opportunity, and had hiked state taxes (the 20% surtax) to a degree that the common people suffered. Moreover, he claimed at a dinner in Oconomowoc, the former governor had never once in six years obtained enactment of "even one economy measure." So Kohler, unlike the Democrats, was a taxer and spender. All his opponent had to offer, Proxmire declared, was uncritical support of the mistakes made by the current administration.[66]

When Walter traveled into the Fox River valley area, which had been strongly for McCarthy, he discovered, here as elsewhere, many citizens who had no knowledge of the coming election. "We've got the votes to win if we can only get them out," he said repeatedly. He also encountered supporters of McCarthyite Howard H. Boyle, Jr. At Neenah, he went to the home of Mrs. Emmy Barnett, 94, who said she had voted in every election since the 19th Amendment was passed. She told Kohler that she had supported him but also liked the late Senator McCarthy. "You and I might come to blows about that," she said. "No," Walter replied, "let's let McCarthy rest in peace." Kohler was of the opinion that Boyle backers were of no major importance to the campaign, conceding that there were some on the far Right he simply couldn't reach.[67]

In the waning days of his campaign effort, Walter was encouraged by repeated assurances that his election was "in the bag." He heard this so often that he warned audiences to beware of overconfidence and make sure that people were aware of the impending election. General interest in the senate race seemed so low that the *Milwaukee Journal* published a large cartoon on its front page showing the candidates seated alone in their parked automobiles reaching out of the car windows to introduce themselves to one another. The road was entitled "Lack Of Interest In Senate Election."[68]

While Proxmire and Boyle engaged in a radio debate, Kohler declined such invitations and barely mentioned his opponents during the campaign. This approach had long irritated Proxmire, and on August 21 he blasted the former governor for attempting to win a senate seat through a "billboard buildup" rather than by a frank discussion of issues. He told a Milwaukee audience that Kohler's face and name had been shown on 500 billboards at a cost of $15,000. "That's 500 more billboards than I have and about $15,000 more than I've got."[69]

The next day, Walter was in Milwaukee, telling members of the Milwaukee Junior Chamber of Commerce that he would vote with the Democrats in the United States Senate if a matter of "principle" were involved. This was a not-so-subtle way of appealing to local Democrats to cross party lines again and support him. When he was asked where he would place himself ideologically, he replied "Right square in the middle." The answer brought laughter as well as applause.[70]

Howard Boyle, Jr., in town on the same day, told supporters, "Kohler is an ideal anti-McCarthy person for them [administration leaders]. If they can get you to elect Kohler, they can claim to the whole nation that their whole program of Communist appeasement and welfare statism has the blanket approval of the people of Wisconsin."[71]

On August 23, the Secretary of State gave to reporters the expense accounts filed by the candidates for the entire campaign. They revealed that the Kohler forces had outspent Proxmire and his supporting groups by a margin of five to one. The GOP state organization had outspent its Democratic counterpart about ten to one. This data fed Proxmire's campaign theme of being the underdog and defender of the people against the "fat cats." The report showed the Democratic candidate personally funding the bulk of his campaign expenses.[72]

During the last days of the campaign, both candidates continued their furious efforts. Walter made a tour of northern Wisconsin by plane on one day and was in Milwaukee the next. But reporter Edwin R. Bayley observed that despite the hard work of the candidates, "the campaign has been dull. There is no sharp issue between Kohler and Proxmire, and neither has indulged in personalities. The voters are thought to be somewhat apathetic." He reported too that many voters would stay at home because their candidates had been defeated in the primary race. "One of the things that makes prediction difficult," Bayley wrote, "is that neither candidate is entirely popular in his own party. Some bitterness engendered in the Republican primary has persisted, and conservative-isolationist Republicans are unhappy with Kohler. Proxmire's driving ambition is resented by some Democrats who would like to see others run for major offices."[73]

Vernon Thomson reported privately to Senator Wiley, "I have just come from a Madison TV station where I was on a program to support the candidacy of Walter Kohler. It think it is essential that all Republicans take this election contest very seriously. I have in the past week been in most every part of the State, and I find disinterest and apathy all too prevalent."[74]

Both candidates displayed large, last-minute newspaper advertisements throughout the state. On August 25, Walter's ad was rather general and subdued, beginning, "former Governor Kohler's Record *proves* he had never taken the easy way in public office...." Proxmire's much larger ad promised improved social security, a $200 tax exemption increase, help for the farmers and small business, and action to contain inflation.

The Proxmire ad also claimed that Kohler had been silent on many "bread and butter issues." A list followed the contention: "Kohler has repeatedly denied that the rise in your cost of living is anything to be concerned about. Kohler is silent on a tax cut. Kohler has said almost nothing on social security. Kohler has never recognized the plight of small business....he has been silent on high interest rates, on price fixing, on tax relief for small business. Kohler has never recognized that the dairy farmer has any economic troubles. He warmly approves of Benson's policies and has said so repeatedly." That the overall charge and the specifics that supported it were false meant nothing to Proxmire. If he lost now, his political aspirations would be at an end.[75]

Shortly before the election, Patrick Lucey, a well-known Wisconsin Democrat, telephoned Ellen Proxmire to tell her not to be too disappointed when her husband lost the election. "I was trying to console her," he said later. Ellen replied, "But we're going to win!"[76]

On August 27, Proxmire defeated Kohler by 123,054 votes, winning 56 counties. Twenty nine of the 56 voted Democratic for the first time in any election for senator or governor in the postwar years. The tally was 435,985 to 312,931. The landslide victory shocked Republicans all over the nation. The magnitude of the defeat ended Kohler's political career. He almost lost Sheboygan County. Howard Boyle won only 20,581 votes and was not a significant factor in Kohler's loss.[77]

How was the stunning upset to be explained? The winner gave credit to the trade unions for bringing out the vote. That was undoubtedly an important factor, and journalists later described in detail the zeal with which union members worked to get people to the polls.[78] Overall turnout was better than expected, exceeding 772,000 and was 70% higher than the July 30 primary. Proxmire won every city, carrying every ward in the city of Milwaukee and winning there by a 2 to 1 margin. He won Milwaukee county by some 53,000 votes, Dane county by 11,000, and Kenosha and Marathon counties by 6,000 each. Kohler won only the small cities and villages, long GOP strongholds.[79]

Proxmire also thought that farmers and small businessmen helped him win, and the voting data proved him correct. The years of falling farm prices under Eisenhower had prompted many agricultural counties to turn to someone who promised change and prosperity.[80] Small business was irked at high interest rates and an inability to borrow funds. The Administration's path breaking civil rights bill of 1957 was also resented by some Wisconsinites, especially in the more rural north. This anti-Eisenhower feeling not only resulted in Proxmire votes but an unwillingness by many Republicans to go to the polls.[81]

Some Democrats credited the efforts by Senators Kennedy and Kefauver for assisting the victory. Almost everyone paid tribute to the winner for his Herculean campaigning. Kohler could not begin to compete with Proxmire's drive, zeal, and energy. No one could. He had shaken more hands than anyone in state history. Mayor Zeidler of Milwaukee said, "It was a victory for personal campaigning. If a candidate knocks on the door long enough, the voters finally say 'Come in.'"

Another major reason for Proxmire's victory was the failure of many Republicans to vote. Part of this, as noted, was a negative response to the Eisenhower Administration. But intra-party warfare was undoubtedly even more important. Glenn Davis had sulked for two days following his primary defeat and then refused to issue a personal statement of support. He chose not to send a letter to his chief supporters backing Kohler, and failed to campaign with Kohler in his home town of Waukesha after promising to do so. Davis supporters failed to get people to the polls, and some were even suspected of voting for Proxmire. One prominent Republican commented, "Davis doesn't deserve to be called a Republican. He's more of a maverick than Proxmire ever was."[82]

A Racine Republican later recalled hearing local party leaders express their unwillingness to vote for Kohler because he was an Eisenhower liberal. They were willing to concede the election to Proxmire, thinking that a conservative could easily beat him in 1958.[83]

The election returns showed that the total Republican primary vote, for all seven candidates, totaled 317,322. On August 27, Kohler received only 312,931. The Democratic total in the primary, for both candidates, totaled 143,320. That figure leaped to 435,985.[84]

Davis's sullen behavior and the Howard Boyle candidacy were legacies of the warfare around the life and legacy of Joe McCarthy. Mark Catlin crowed that Kohler's defeat "may be a great boon for the Republican party in the future." Urban Van Susteren said that Proxmire was elected because "the Republicans just didn't like Walter Kohler." McCarthy's widow told reporters that she was not at all surprised by the outcome and regarded the vote as a repudiation of the "modern Republicanism" advocated by Eisenhower.

Howard Boyle himself was aghast at the election returns. "I can't believe the people of Wisconsin realize they were voting for policies favoring destruction of our Constitution and in favor of Communist appeasement." He vowed to run again for the senate in 1958 when Proxmire's brief term expired.[85]

Vice President Nixon blamed Kohler's defeat on a lack of unity in the Wisconsin GOP. "The Republicans have no excuse for losing the Wisconsin election. It was the old story of a united, vigorous minority party, with a hard fighting resourceful candidate, defeating a divided, bickering, overconfident majority." Meade Alcorn, Republican national chairman, took the same approach and warned against disunity in 1958 and 1960. White House press secretary James Hagerty described the president as disappointed and feeling that the GOP 'took a bad licking.'"[86]

Then too, there was the issue of Proxmire's simplistic and often deceptive campaign appeals. Surely more than a few union members who voted and got others involved in the election were convinced they were making a statement about the Kohler strike and big business. A GOP county chairman had warned Senator Wiley in May that Kohler "is also guilty by name association of the most severe labor problem this state has had in many years. In this of course he has no actual hand, but the name will throw organized labor against him and could cause the party serious trouble. My personal prediction on this candidate is that if nominated, he would be defeated by a Democrat."[87]

Many senior citizens no doubt voted for Proxmire because he virtu-ally promised them a higher income. A Proxmire ad published the day before the election featured a drawing of two worried seniors with the message: "Do You Want Social Security Benefits Improved?...then you must take the time to VOTE on August 27th.".[88]

Many persons of all incomes surely supported Proxmire thinking they were voting against a new sales tax, which Kohler and the Wisconsin State Chamber of Commerce favored and the Democratic candidate opposed. (Proxmire claimed that the state could raise much-needed funds through unspecified cuts in spending.) The president of a hardwood company in Oconto wrote to Senator Wiley on the day of election, "There has been a tremendous amount of money spent by Mr. Proxmire with publicity on the TV every fifteen minutes throughout the day and evening, as well as on the radio, and also a claim, of course, that Mr. Proxmire beat the sales tax in Wisconsin. So far, and now it is too late of course, I have heard nothing from anyone trying to contradict this statement which has been on TV and radio for two days."[89]

And there was the "just plain Bill" image. Many voters undoubtedly felt they were voting for a man of the people—broke but unbowed, humble yet hopeful, earnest and hard working, behind in an uphill race against a well-heeled, powerful, and self-satisfied "Harvard." A Kohler ad that appeared the day before the election featured a photograph of Walter in a dress suit with vest, and it asked voters to examine the candidate's record and vote Republican. This was stuffy and bland, reminding one of Tom Dewey in 1948. Bill Proxmire, lean to the point of being emaciated, eager to spend a day working on an assembly line or in a cheese factory, dressed more like a white collar worker than a corporate executive while standing at factory gates, brimming over with empathy and promises to right wrongs, was simply a more appealing figure to many Wisconsinites. Just plain Bill was Jimmy Stewart in the movie "Mr. Smith Goes To Washington."

Surely the Secretary of State's report on campaign financing during the latter part of the campaign reinforced this image of Bill's uphill battle against the rich. Only after the election was it reported that Walter Reuther, president of the United Automobile Workers' union, had poured more than $10,000 into the Proxmire campaign as well as providing manpower to get out the vote.[90]

Aside from the issue of disunity, many state Republicans simply could not understand what had happened to them on August 27. Paul J. Rogan, state insurance commissioner and a top state Republican strategist said, "We were clobbered. If the turnout had been twice as large, Proxmire might have won by over 200,000 votes instead of his present margin." Madison attorney Claude Jasper, another GOP strategist, said that the Kohler campaign was handled correctly in every way. (A final campaign finance tally showed that Republicans had conducted one of their most successful fund raising efforts in history, collecting $153,944 on behalf of Kohler.)[91] He simply could not account for the defeat.[92]

Kohler issued a pro forma statement of congratulations to the winner and to his own supporters.[93] He did not send a personal telegram of congratulations to Proxmire.[94] Walter was stunned and crushed by the election returns and chose not to analyze his defeat in public. (In 1971, however, in an oral history interview, he attributed his loss to voter apathy, his identification with the Kohler strike, and the CIO's "hellbent" effort to get out the vote, especially in Milwaukee.)[95] Ever the gentleman, Walter preferred never again to discuss the Democrat who ended his political career, a man he did not like or respect.[96]

Starting at 6:15 a.m. on the morning after his victory, Bill Proxmire, accompanied by his wife and a campaign worker, stood bare headed in the rain outside Milwaukee factory gates, shaking hands and thanking workers for voting for him. He had enjoyed only 3 ½ hours sleep the night before. One worker with a big grin on his face told the senator-elect, "My wife told me that you'd never be here this morning. I bet her you would and, by golly, you are." "I sure am," replied Proxmire, "and I thank you for your support." He was already talking about his reelection campaign of 1958.[97]

Notes

[1] E.g., Godfrey Sperling, Jr., "Wisconsin Decision Awaited," *Christian Science Monitor*, May 6, 1957.

[2] Edwin R. Bayley, "Kohler Says He's in Race," *Milwaukee Journal*, May 14, 1957.

[3] Edwin R. Bayley, "Two to Enter Senate Race," *ibid.*, May 15, 1957; "Candidates Pleased by Call for Election," *ibid.*, June 3, 1957; Edwin R. Bayley, "Fierce Campaign for Senate Looms," *ibid.*, June 4, 1957; Edwin R. Bayley, "Endorsement Voted Down at State GOP Convention," June 8, 1957.

[4] See copy, S. M. Stebbings to Alexander Wiley, May 20, 1957, Alexander Wiley papers; copy, Thomas E. Coleman to Lisle F. Wallace, September 3, 1957, Thomas E. Coleman papers.

[5] S. M. Stebbins to Alexander Wiley, May 20, 1957, box 48, Alexander Wiley papers.

[6] "Candidates Pleased by Call for Election," *Milwaukee Journal*, June 8, 1957; Laurence C. Ecklund, "Wiley Irked by Bosses, Will Miss Convention," *ibid.*, June 6, 1957. See copy, Alexander Wiley to Ellis H. Dana, June 11, 1957, Alexander Wiley papers.

[7] Edwin R. Bayley "Endorsement Voted Down at State GOP Convention," *Milwaukee Journal*, June 8, 1957.

[8] *Ibid.*

[9] This was technically consistent with the GOP constitution which required endorsements only at conventions meeting in even-numbered years, i.e. regular election years. Epstein, *Politics in Wisconsin*, 94.

[10] Edwin R. Bayley, "GOP Boos Greet Kohler; No Candidate Is Endorsed," *Milwaukee Journal*, June 9, 1957. The decision not to endorse followed an earlier decision by the rules committee against endorsement. Party leaders were trying to minimize friction within the GOP. The text of Kohler's remarks was taken from the verbatim account of his speech in box 5, Republican Party Papers.

[11] Ellen Proxmire interview.

[12] "Drive Begun by Proxmire," *Milwaukee Journal*, June 17, 1957.

[13] "Davis' Campaign Bus Starts Tour for Votes," *ibid.*, June 24, 1957.

[14] "Kohler Busy in West Bend," *ibid.*, June 29, 1957.

[15] "Kohler Club Formed," *ibid.*, July 6, 1957. On Drotning, see "Drive Begun by Proxmire," *ibid.*, June 17, 1957.

[16] "Start Move for Kohler," *ibid*, July 12, 1957. On July 18, the Kohler for Senator committee reported $8,556 in contributions. The largest contributor, Harold Stassen's friend H. J. Johnson, President of S.C. Johnson and Son of Racine, gave $1,000. The Vollrath family donated $475. "Report Sums for O'Konski," *ibid.*, July 18, 1957.

[17] "Kohler Opens His Office Here With Bit of Ballyhoo," *ibid.*, July 17, 1957.

[18] Edwin R. Bayley, "Glenn Davis Meets Fred, Bill and Ernie," *ibid.*, July 2, 1957.

[19] "Davis Blasts Kohler View," *ibid.*, July 10, 1957.

[20] "Split Aired on GOP Aim," *ibid.*, July 8, 1957.

[21] William R. Bechtel, "Kohler Visits Capitol, Fires Political Salvos," *ibid.*, July 12, 1957.

[22] Edwin R. Bayley, "'Money' Talk Stirs a Sleepy Campaign," *ibid.*, July 14, 1957.

[23] "Senate Race Issue Is Cash," *ibid.*, July 17, 1957.

[24] "O'Konski Steals Show With Loud Politicking," *ibid.*, July 18, 1957.

[25] *Ibid.*

[26] "Kohler Blasts 'Far Right Wing,'" *ibid.*, July 21, 1957.

[27] Edwin R. Bayley, "Outcome in Primary is Difficult to Figure," *ibid.*, July 21, 1957.

[28] "Kohler Blasts 'far Right Wing,'" *ibid.*, July 21, 1957.

[29] "Clubs Raise $94,000 for GOP Races," *ibid.*, July 22, 1957. District Attorney Joseph Bluegood of Dane County cited 11 political clubs in both parties for technical violations of the state corrupt practices act. The infractions were largely technical, such as failing to cite complete names of donors and itemize some contributions. "Warns Clubs of Violations," *ibid.*, July 25, 1957.

[30] "List Expense for Campaign," *ibid.*, July 25, 1957. A later report showed that Walter spent $7,857 on his primary campaign. "Davis Committee Has New Report," *ibid.*, August 6, 1957.

[31] "John Schafer's Talk Is Hit of GOP Rally," *ibid.*, July 23, 1957.

[32] "Kohler Gets a Challenge," *ibid.*, July 22, 1957.

[33] "North, Goal of Candidates," *ibid.*, July 24, 1957.

[34] "Four GOP Aspirants Speak to 125 at Rally," *ibid.*, July 25, 1957.

[35] "Smith Denies Davis Claim," *ibid.*, July 26, 1957. During the election, Wiley told Governor Thomson that he was bogged down in Washington with legislative matters. Copy, Alexander Wiley to Vernon Thomson, August 5, 1957, Alexander Wiley papers. After the election, Wiley expressed irritation at not being invited to campaign for Kohler. Laurence C. Eklund, "Wiley Off for London, Proxmire Settles Down," *ibid.*, September 1, 1957. See also copy, Alexander Wiley to Sydney M. Eisenberg, October 19, 1957, Alexander Wiley papers, detailing the Senator's slight efforts on behalf of Kohler.

[36] "Rennebohm Supports Knowles in Campaign," *Milwaukee Journal*, July 28, 1957.

[37] Editorial, "The Republican Primary: Kohler—On The Record," *ibid.*, July 28, 1957.

[38] See the large, page 15 ad in *ibid.*, July 29, 1957.

39 "Letters Trip Kohler Club," *ibid.*, July 28, 1957. In a summary of qualifications, presented on page 7 of the same issue of the newspaper, Walter listed his religious affiliation as the Episcopal Church. That was a highly unusual step, no doubt a surprise to members of Grace Church, Sheboygan, that Walter must have thought necessary in a short and hard-fought campaign.

40 "Candidates for Senate Present Views on TV," *ibid.*, July 29, 1957.

41 On O'Konski, see "Rennebohm Supports Knowles in Campaign," *ibid.*, July 28, 1957.

42 Edwin R. Bayley, "Kohler and Proxmire Are Victors," *ibid.*, July 31, 1957. In Milwaukee county, Kohler received 34,325 votes to Davis's 15,105. Every major candidate won easily in his home area. In Sheboygan County, Kohler polled 7,633 to 885 for Davis. Zablocki, who was from Milwaukee, won 37,002 votes to Proxmire's 20,741. The turnout in Milwaukee topped 25%, considered good for a primary election. "County Vote Topped 25%," *ibid.*, August 2, 1957.

43 Harry S. Pease, "View Kohler Victory as Splitting the GOP," *ibid.*

44 Editorial, "State Comment on Elections," *ibid.*, August 1, 1957.

45 "460,552 Cast Vote July 30," *ibid.*, August 8, 1957.

46 "Rushes Wires to Candidates," *ibid.*, July 31, 1957.

47 John Pomfret, "Wooing by Proxmire May Win Labor Vote," *ibid.*

48 Editorial, "State Comment on Elections," *ibid.*, July 31, 1957.

49 "Kohler Sees Party Unity," *ibid.*, August 1, 1957; "Schafer Will Help Kohler," *ibid.*; "Aid Pledged by Kefauver," *ibid.*; "Proxmire Says Kohler Is Avoiding the Issues," *ibid.*, August 21, 1957.

50 "GOP Tablet Is Dedicated," *ibid.*, August 3, 1957; "GOP Leadership Supports Kohler," *ibid.*; "O'Konski Weighs Independent Try," *ibid.* O'Konski had won about 68,000 votes in the primary, ranking third among the seven GOP candidates.

51 William R. Bechtel, "Kohler Given Applause in GOP Drive for Unity," *ibid.*, August 4, 1957.

52 Edwin R. Bayley, "WSFL Nod to Proxmire," *ibid.*, August 11, 1957.

53 "Boyle Will Run as Independent," *ibid.*; August 7, 1957.

54 "Ike Gets Pat by Proxmire," *ibid.*

55 "Asks Votes of 'Losers,'" *ibid.*, August 7, 1957.

56 "Ike Backs Kohler," *ibid.*

57 "Kohler Hails Endorsement by President," *ibid.*, August 8, 1957. One key Kohler supporter soon found out that the Eisenhower endorsement was hurting his candidate in conservative areas such as the Fox River valley, where McCarthy had been strong. Kohler dismissed the idea. "Fears Kohler Hurt by Ike," *ibid.*, August 15, 1957.

58 Quoted in Sykes, *Proxmire*, 77-78.

[59] *Ibid.*, 78.

[60] *Ibid.*, 79-80,85-86, 90; Ellen Proxmire interview.

[61] Patrick Lucey interview.

[62] The week's schedule appears on page 28 of *Milwaukee Journal*, August 11, 1957.

[63] "Equal Time Asked," *ibid.*, August 18, 1957.

[64] Edwin R. Bayley, "WSFL Nod to Proxmire," *ibid.* The railway unions also supported Proxmire, lauding his "strongly progressive views and his outstanding record of fighting for the people's interest while a state legislator." "Rail Unions for Proxmire," *ibid.*, August 18, 1957.

[65] E.g., "Kohler Intimates He Likes Wiley Views," *ibid.*, August 13, 1957; "Kohler Proposes Curb on Federal Authority," *ibid.*, August 17, 1957; "Kohler Hails Ike's Record," *ibid.*, August 18, 1957; "Kohler Handshaking Shakes Up a Picnic," *ibid.*, August 19, 1957.

[66] E.g., "Points to Tax Boost," *ibid.*, August 15, 1957.

[67] Edwin R. Bayley, "Kohler Jolting Voters With News of Election," *ibid.*, August 20, 1957.

[68] See Edwin R. Bayley," Kohler Finds It Hard to Keep Himself Scared," *ibid.*, August 21, 1957. The cartoon is on the front page of the same issue.

[69] "Senate Race Debate Held," *ibid.*, August 21, 1957; "Proxmire Says Kohler Is Avoiding the Issues," *ibid.*

[70] "Stress Placed on Principles," *ibid.*, August 22, 1957.

[71] "Prediction of Boyle," *ibid.*

[72] William R. Bechtel, "Senate Race Spending Hits $212,536 Mark," *ibid.*, August 23, 1957. At this point, Walter had personally spent $7,856 on the campaign, while Proxmire had spent $6,119. Altogether, senate candidates and the state GOP had spent $184,508. Democratic candidates and their state party had spent $28,027.

[73] "Proxmire and Kohler Bid for County Votes," *ibid.*, August 24, 1957; Edwin R. Bayley, "Election on Tuesday Gets National Notice," *ibid.*, August 25, 1957.

[74] Vernon Thomson to Alexander Wiley, August 13, 1957, box 49, Alexander Wiley papers.

[75] The ads appear on pages 14 and 27 of the *Milwaukee Journal*, August 25, 1957.

[76] Patrick Lucey interview.

[77] Voting statistics are based on the official figures released in early September. "Senate Race Totals Given," *Milwaukee Journal*, September 5, 1957, corrected. See also Thompson, *The History of Wisconsin, VI, Continuity and Change, 1940-1965,* 609-611.

[78] E.g., Ira Kapenstein, "Unions Spurred Vote; Democrats Benefited," *Milwaukee Journal*, August 28, 1957.

[79] Leon Epstein points out that "The total vote was still only about two-thirds that of a regular November election in a non-presidential year, and the absence of a party ticket for lesser offices might have made the senatorial contest more personal than is usual at regular elections." Epstein, *Politics in Wisconsin*, 72. On Republicans and the urban vote, see *ibid.*, 75.

[80] See *ibid.*, 74. In September, 1956, a party official had warned his peers that if something was not done to placate angry farmers, the GOP could well lose Wisconsin and the Midwest. Copy, Steve J. Miller to Philip G. Kuehn, September 17, 1956, Wayne Hood papers.

[81] See S. M. Stebbings to Alexander Wiley, September 3, 1957, Alexander Wiley papers; S. M. Stebbins to Alexander Wiley, September 17, 1957, *ibid.* Stebbins, president of a lumber company in De Pere, traveled 3,000 miles across the state to discuss the election with voters. See also David A. Wilcox to Alexander Wiley, October 11, 1957, *ibid.* Wilcox was a county chairman who polled public opinion in his area after the election. Only about a third of the eligible voters in his county went to the polls. See also Alfred W. Gerhard to Alexander Wiley, August 28, 1957, *ibid.* Gerhard was a perceptive attorney and Republican from Wausau who added disgruntled World War One veterans to the list of those angry with the Eisenhower Administration.

[82] John Promfret, "Proxmire Is Victor by 122,000," *Milwaukee Journal*, August 28, 1957; Edwin R. Bayley, "Wins 56 Counties in Routing Kohler," *ibid.*; Robert H. Wells, "'Try, Try Again' Motto Proves to Be Right One for Proxmire," *ibid.* For more on Davis supporters and their lack of enthusiasm for Kohler, see Edwin R. Bayley, "GOP at Waukesha Diagnoses Its Troubles," *ibid.*, October 23, 1957. Both Vice President Nixon and Victor Johnston appealed unsuccessfully to Davis to back Kohler. Edwin R. Bayley, "Davis is in Front for 1958 'by Default,'" *ibid.*, October 27, 1957.

[83] Paul Weyrich interview, July 1, 2003.

[84] Editorial, "Victory of William Proxmire," *Milwaukee Journal*, August 28, 1957; "Senate Race Totals Given," *ibid.*, September 5, 1957, corrected.

[85] Robert H. Wells, "'Try, Try Again' Motto Proves to Be Right one for Proxmire," *ibid.*, August 28, 1957; "Eisenhower Admits Defeat 'a Bad Licking,'" *ibid.*

[86] *Ibid.* Historian William F. Thompson later wrote that the 1957 special election was "the last in a series of acts of self-immolation in which the party had indulged for a decade and a half." Thompson, *The History of Wisconsin*, VI, 560.

[87] David A. Wilcox to Alexander Wiley, May 23, 1957, Alexander Wiley papers. See the letter from "Duke" [at the Larson-Duncan advertising company in Milwaukee] to Alexander Wiley, June 26, 1957, *ibid*: "Kohler seems the best [candidate] but the Kohler name is not the magic it was. The strike

at the family plant hurts and the lack of human interest in Mr. and Mrs. Kohler getting to the level of all of us common people is the talk."

[88] The ad was on page 4 of the *Milwaukee Journal*, August 27, 1957.

[89] Donald S. DeWitt to Alexander Wiley, August 27, 1957, Alexander Wiley papers.

[90] John Pomfret, "Proxmire is Victor by 122,000," *Milwaukee Journal.*, August 28, 1957. The August 23 article in the *Milwaukee Journal* on the Secretary of State's report observed that labor union contributions played "only a small part in Proxmire's campaign funds to date. The only sizable amount listed is $828 reported by Labor's Political League of Milwaukee County. This was described as money raised in Proxmire's behalf through 'Labor day rally ticket sales.'" William R. Bechtel, "Senate Race Spending Hits $212,536 Mark," *ibid.*, August 23, 1957. Reuther's funds, then, must have been received in the last week or so of the campaign and were no doubt responsible for the extensive, last-minute media ads. The final campaign expense reports showed Proxmire spending $67,450. Labor unions contributed $12,000 to his campaign. Walter Harnischfeger contributed $1,200 to Kohler, but the list of contributors did not contain either Tom Coleman or Wayne Hood. "$372,500 is Total Cost of Filling Senate Seat," *ibid.*, September 22, 1957. Coleman privately said he played no part in politics after Senator Wiley defeated Glenn Davis in the 1956 primary. See copy, Thomas E. Coleman to Lisle L. Wallace, September 3, 1957, Thomas E. Coleman papers.

[91] "$372,500 is Total Cost of Filling Senate Seat," *Milwaukee Journal*, September 22, 1957.

[92] "GOP Chiefs Are Worried," *ibid.*, August 29, 1957.

[93] "Winner Sees Repudiation of Administration Policies," *ibid.*

[94] Sykes, *Proxmire*, 92.

[95] Walter J. Kohler, Jr. Oral History, Columbia University, 1971, 44.

[96] Terry Kohler had the impression that his father considered Proxmire something of an intellectual lightweight; a skilled political candidate but an opportunist. Terry Kohler interview, March 25, 2004.

[97] John Pomfret, "Proxmire is Victor by 122,000," *Milwaukee Journal*, August 28, 1957. After the returns were in, Proxmire and his wife were quickly flown to Washington, without even time for a change of clothes, so that the new Senator could be sworn in. Lyndon Johnson's authority in the Senate depended upon a Democratic victory in Wisconsin, and he needed Proxmire's vote as quickly as possible. A southern Senator was filibustering when the Proxmires arrived, and the process of being sworn in and introduced to others took four or five days. Ellen Proxmire interview.

Chapter Fifteen
After Politics

Soon after the election, Walter recuperated from the campaign at Windway and began thinking about life after politics. He knew that he wanted to make the Vollrath Company more prosperous. He wanted to increase his personal fortune. And he was intent on spending a lot more leisure time with Charlotte. Charlotte herself was no doubt delighted to be through with politics. She had not been a happy first lady. A relative heard that her relations with the staff at the Executive Residence and an assortment of politicos had been so stormy that many in Madison refused to vote for Walter in the senatorial election.[1]

During the early 1950s, the Vollrath Company had been healthy and growing. Its most profitable lines were stainless steel ware, stainless steel special manufacture, porcelain enameled ware, and a product called Lo-Heet Ware. The company had a foundry division engaged in developing stainless steel castings that seemed likely to flourish. (Cast iron cookware was dropped completely.) Saws and lawnmowers were now beginning to sell well. Net sales in 1950 amounted to $6,124,282, and the net profit was $390,610.[2] In 1953 sales had increased to $9,009,443, the net profit being $442,760.[3] In 1956, net sales had grown to $10,649,875, while the net profit had climbed to $648,461. When Walter returned full-time to the company, new products included insulated stainless steel restaurant and hospital items, stainless steel pots and pans with aluminum-clad bottoms, experimental heavy-gauge yellow ware, and a new line of marine items.[4] Increasingly, the company moved away from government contracts to private sales.

In 1954, Walter received an annual salary of $20,400 and a bonus of $7,500. This was the highest income of all Vollrath employees.[5] Soon, all top Company shareholders were receiving handsome profit sharing bonuses.[6] Still, the income from Vollrath was relatively small when compared to Walter's total personal fortune. In 1955, he purchased the late Minnie Detling's 60,816 shares, making him the largest stockholder.[7] In 1958, he increased the number of his shares to 101,867 (of some

181,000 total), having purchased shares from his brother Robert.[8] (That same year, Robert constructed a beautiful 7,000 square foot home near Walter named Thornhill.)[9]

The factory itself was run in large part by Paul Rohling, who became Vice President for Production in 1959. Rohling had joined Vollrath in 1944 after receiving an engineering degree from the University of Wisconsin. He had been a methods engineer, plant engineer, and assistant factory manager, and was widely admired for his integrity, hard work, and ability to communicate effectively with employees at all levels. Walter depended on him for many years and rewarded him with a good salary and Company shares. In 1964, Rohling would be elected to the Board of Directors, and three years later be promoted to Executive Vice President.[10]

Two veteran employees, Bill Kessler and Wally Gartman, said later that top management leaders always paid good wages, were honest and straightforward, and treated people with dignity. It was not at all uncommon for workers to spend decades at the Vollrath Company. Kessler stayed 60 years, and Gartman 47. (In 1969, the Quarter Century Club was founded, inducting 95 employees with a total of 2,942 years of service under their collective belts.)[11]

Many of the factory jobs at Vollrath were difficult. The foundry was noisy and dirty, and polishers and punch press operators had physically demanding jobs. Still, turnover was light and people from all over the Sheboygan area sought employment at the plant. "Everyone wanted in," said Gartman. Working conditions there were considered far superior to those offered at the Kohler Company, a few miles away.[12]

The United Electrical Workers, affiliated with and then expelled by the CIO, represented the some 650 workers in the early 1950s. When contract time approached, UE leaders would sometimes conduct short sit-down strikes and walkouts, and encourage workers to file grievances in order to win higher wages and benefits. But serious disputes were few. In the entire history of the Vollrath Company history there have been only three brief strikes: a seven week strike in 1946, a six week strike in the summer of 1968, and a six day strike in 1980. During the 1968 strike, led by the newly elected United Auto Workers union, the Vollrath Director of Industrial Relations issued a statement that said in part: "Reports issued by the United States Department of Industry, Labor and Human Relations show that The Vollrath Company average hourly earnings for the month of June 1968 are 53 cents per hour higher than our industry group and 64 cents per hour higher than the average for Sheboygan County."[13]

Vollrath employees usually referred to Walter as "the governor." Kessler and Gartman later remembered him as always impeccably dressed (Kessler said "He looked as though he was right out of a men's clothing store"), well-mannered, and kindly. The governor, they recall, never had a bad word to say about anyone, and would greet an employee in the plant or on the street even if he did not know his or her name.

There were (and are) seven single-car garages to the right of the plant gate, through which all workers passed. The first belonged to Kohler, whose black Cadillac bore a "1" on the license plate. Corresponding to the seven garages were seven large and handsome executive offices on the first floor of the red brick office building to the left of the factory gate. The offices were collectively referred to as "Mahogany Row."[14]

Wally Gartman recalled the time when a beautiful and buxom young woman, a new employee, walked down the hall in front of the executive offices. Walter emerged from his office and gave the girl a second, long look. "Then I knew he was really human," Gartman said.[15]

Walter made infrequent visits to the plant floor, and they were always announced well in advance. Bill Kessler would see to it that on those occasions the plant would be as clean as possible. (Walter once exploded at state employees for failing to clean the State capitol.) Bill Kessler saw Charlotte Kohler a couple of times, with her dogs, but she played no role in the company and remained aloof from all employees.[16]

Gartman recalled the time in the early 1960s when he was selected to ask the governor for $2,000 to send 15 plant softball players to a national tournament in Detroit. Walter asked if the men's wives were coming along. No, Gartman said, we are trying to cut expenses to the bones. Walter then said that he would give Gartman $4,000 to enable the wives to make the trip. "He knew that it was dangerous to send those young men to Detroit alone. It was a wise decision."[17]

Erna Schwartz, who had been with the Vollrath Company since 1938 and become Walter's personal secretary after the war, continued in his employ now that he was back at his position full time. She later remembered her boss as "good hearted," "compassionate," a man of strong integrity. Employee relations at Vollrath, she said, were excellent. Unlike his uncle at the Kohler Company, Walter did not want to be perceived as "the boss." Walter once asked Erna, "Do I look like a stuffed shirt?"

Employees, he complained, were passing his office without stopping to chat.

Kohler was not a particularly sociable man during this period, Erna recalled. He did not enjoy playing cards. A sister-in-law (probably Peggy, Bob's wife) would urge him to go to operas in Milwaukee, but at the close of the day he preferred to return to Windway and relax. He loved music but preferred to hear it at home. Erna appreciated the fact that her employer had a good sense of humor and was well educated. "He could quote Bible verses that put me to shame." She would continue to work for Walter for the rest of his life.[18]

Robert Selle was an investment counselor in the Milwaukee firm of Loomis-Sayles. His wife was related to Guido Rahr of Manitowoc, Walter's Yale roommate and long-time friend. Selle met Walter and Charlotte in the mid-1950s. In 1959, working on his own, he paid a call on Walter at the Vollrath Company. When Selle said that he was now self-employed, Kohler offered to give him some investments to manage. This led to a financial and personal relationship that lasted until Walter's death. Four times a year, Selle would travel to Vollrath to report on Kohler's investments. Each meeting was the same: Walter would walk down the hall to the reception desk to greet him and escort him to his office. After both men were comfortably seated, Walter would light up a big cigar and say, "Now, tell me," and Selle would go through the account in detail. Wealthy as he was, Walter was keenly interested in advancing his portfolio.

Selle also recalled that once, in a "flight of fancy," Walter purchased a couple of paintings by Corot. "He asked me to look at them. They were so expensive that the insurance was going to be high." Ever eager to save on expenses, Kohler donated the paintings to Yale University.

Selle remembered that on one occasion when Walter and Charlotte were scheduled to fly to New York, Charlotte took a long time packing. Finally she decided to bring an assortment of her jewelry with her, deciding what she would wear after they arrived at their Park Avenue hotel. When the Kohlers were out of the hotel room, thieves entered and took $40,000 worth of jewelry. Walter "was beside himself," said Selle. But the jewels were insured and no damage was done.[19]

Among his other responsibilities, Kohler was a director of the Security National Bank in Sheboygan, and a director of the E. J. McAleer Company in Philadelphia. He would later become a director of the Square

D company in Milwaukee. By the late 1950s, the governor had a wide reputation for being a knowledgeable and shrewd businessman.

Walter was especially influential at the Security National Bank. James Raffel, a young Security National Bank employee in the early 1960s, later recalled being assigned the task of making a presentation to the bank's Board of Directors. His boss, bank president Clarence Weber, advised him to be aware that Kohler was one of the greatest business executives ever, and that no matter where he sat around the table, he was the real Chairman of the Board. Be very, very careful, said Weber, for if you make a mistake, the governor will spot it. In a kindly way, Kohler did ask some questions. In the next few years, Raffel heard Kohler address meetings every month, often asking questions that were "very astute and penetrating." He firmly believed that Walter was "a great human being" and "highly impressive."[20]

Attorney Roland Neumann, a senior vice president at the same bank, remembered Walter as "very efficient," the only member of the Kohler family who was always on time for everything. He came to board meetings prepared and could run a meeting with the aid of a single 3x5 card. Neumann saw Kohler as a "soft-spoken gentleman" who could "make his point and then let it lie." He was conservative in fiscal matters but could also be generous. The governor ran a small foundation through which he did some good deeds.[21]

Neumann also emphasized Kohler's keen sense of propriety. When the bank directors once contemplated setting up a temporary trailer in which to do additional banking, Walter strongly objected, saying "you don't bank in a trailer." The proposal was dropped.[22]

By early 1958, the Vollrath Company could boast of having doubled sales in a decade. Its gross profit margin was 26.68%, and it had $837,688 cash on hand in addition to considerable investments. The company's advertising bill was a record $142,000.[23] Later that year, officials noted that sales to hotel and hospital supply jobbers accounted for more than 40% of the Company's business, and department store sales amounted to a little over one percent of sales.[24] This was to be the trend in Vollrath's future.

By September, 1960, sales surged beyond the $11 million mark, and profits set a record at $743,000.[25] Walter's Christmas bonus that year was $11,000, and Paul Rohling and two other executives received the same amount.[26] The Company soon invested in a subsidiary finance company.[27] In brief, under the governor's leadership, times were good at the Vollrath Company.

❧ ❧ ❧ ◉ ❧ ❧ ❧

On December 9, 1958, Walter sued his uncle and the Kohler Company in federal court for misrepresenting the value of the company when he sold his stock in 1953 for $2,462,725. Walter, the suit stated, was "induced" to sell his stock for "at least $214,156 less than the actual value." The charges cited the failure to disclose a federal tax refund of $885,355 and three internal accounting factors that increased the actual value of the company. This was a violation of the federal securities exchange act, the suit contended.

Herbert V. Kohler angrily replied that there was "no substance" to the charges and called them a "fantastic claim." Walter had approached the company offering to sell his stock, the senior Kohler said, and was not induced in any way to sell. "Kohler Company did not refuse any information it was asked for. In fact, it could not have refused since a stockholder has the right to inspect the company's books. If he had looked at the books or even asked about it [financial information], as any competent seller would have done, if he thought it important to the question of value, he would have received the information....He was familiar with how the books were kept and never raised any of the objections he is now making. His complaint sums up to a claim that he not only did not know the value of his stock but he also did not know what questions to ask or what investigation to make to determine it. We do not think that five years later he can renege on a deal on any such basis."

Walter replied, "It is my conviction that a court case should be tried in court and not through the issuing of self-serving statements. The fact is that if the auditors of the Kohler Company had given me both correct and complete information there would now be no suit....Any impressions that this is a personal and perhaps vindictive suit against Herbert Kohler are false and completely without basis. In any event, no amount of bluster or bombast by the defendants is going to dispose of the issues involved."[28]

In a 1960 stipulation, the defendants acknowledged that they had not told Walter Kohler that an audit of 1952 was available on February 14, 1953, a few days before he sold his stock.[29]

Walter's eagerness to increase his wealth was real enough, as was his sense of justice. But it is hard to rule out completely an element of revenge in the lawsuit. Herbert had treated the four Kohler brothers very badly since the death of their father, nearly two decades earlier. Moreover, he had responded rudely to Governor Kohler's offer, however politically inspired, to help end the Company strike. Still unsettled four years later, the strike had a negative impact on the Senate race. Of course, Walter had to deny publicly that the lawsuit was about getting even, for such an admission would have branded the effort as frivolous.[30] Still, his firm denial of such a motive must be taken seriously. No written evidence suggests anything other than a monetary pursuit.

At a hearing in January, 1959, Walter admitted that the threatened strike at the Kohler Company had been a factor in the sale of his stock. He said that he feared political embarrassment.[31] The trial began in Milwaukee on January 2, 1962. By now defendants included a national accounting firm and a partner who lived in Chicago and had been directly involved in the case.

The tone of the proceedings was bitter from the start. Company attorney Lyman C. Conger said that the lawsuit involved "a man who sold his stock in an arm's length deal, and five and a half years later feels he didn't get enough money for it and wants to renege on the deal." He also claimed that the Company representative in the agreement had not offered the specific price of $115 a share, as Walter alleged, but had given the governor a range of prices out of which came the agreement to sell for $115.

In his testimony, Walter said that as governor he was extremely busy and relied upon data provided him by the Company and a Chicago accounting firm. He did not become aware of the true value of the Company, he said, until 1958 when he found some Kohler stock in Terry's trust fund and wondered what it might be worth. He said that the source of his information was his brother Robert, who sent him balance sheets.[32]

The trial lasted a week. Lyman Conger showed that in 1959 both Robert and Terry had sold stock back to the Company at $115 a share, contending that if Walter had not sold for six years he would have received the same amount of money.[33] Accountants from both sides used clashing figures. When called to the stand, Herbert said that he alone set the $115 price. "I am the head of the company," he declared. He once referred to his nephew as "the man."[34]

During each day of the proceedings, Walter and Charlotte and a few interested friends and witnesses for the plaintiff sat on the right side of the courtroom's single aisle. Herbert Kohler and several officers and accountants of the Company sat on the left. Neither branch of the family acknowledged the other's existence. In answer to a blunt question from a reporter, Charlotte said, "Once in a while we meet at a funeral or some such event where it is unavoidable. We do not speak. Nobody would think of inviting us to the same party." Herbert replied to the same question with: "I got a Christmas card from his son. That ought to tell you what you want to know." A reporter observed that at times during the trial Walter appeared slightly nervous. His uncle, now 70, sat nearly motionless. "The picture was one of inflexibility."[35]

In September, 1962, Federal Judge Kenneth P. Grubb, who presided during the trial, dismissed the lawsuit. "This is a plaintiff who is a highly successful businessman and was familiar with financial statements and specifically with all the accounts about which he now claims were not explained to him. The defendants have violated no statutory or common law duties in the negotiation for the purchase of the plaintiff's stock and the plaintiff has suffered no damage. The value of his stock was $115 per share at the date of the sale. Plaintiff has not established a cause of action for fraud....His proof falls far short of establishing fraud by clear and satisfactory evidence." Herbert gleefully called the dismissal "a full vindication of the Kohler Company and its auditing firm."[36]

Walter then spent even more on legal fees, appealing the case to the 7th circuit court of appeals. But he got nowhere.[37] Perhaps he took some pleasure in confirming publicly once again that he and his uncle were very different people despite their common surname. But it was a financially expensive educational effort that also placed strains on relations within the large Kohler family that have remained to this day.

❖❖❖◈❖❖❖

After the senate race, Walter stayed completely out of politics for a time. He watched silently in 1958 as the State GOP convention endorsed a two percent sales tax and favored passage of a state right-to-work law, the latter being a direct assault upon the labor organizations that were major contributors to the Democratic party. These political stands were instrumental in Democrat Gaylord Nelson's defeat of Governor Vernon Thomson and Senator Proxmire's landslide victory over a sacrificial no-name candidate.

In 1958, Democrats also won election in the races for attorney general, lieutenant-governor, and state treasurer, and they took two congressional seats away from Republicans. Democrats replaced fifteen GOP incumbents in the Assembly and three in the Senate.[38] As the Wisconsin GOP grew more conservative, State Democrats seemed more liberal and responsive to the needs of most people. They appeared to be the heirs of the Progressives now that their opponents had wandered away from Eisenhower moderation into often cranky and narrow right-wing paths.

The following year, Walter again found his voice, publicly expressing his personal interest in helping Richard Nixon win the GOP presidential nomination in 1960. He attended some organizational meetings and said that he would be honored if the Vice President asked him to join a Nixon-pledged delegation to the national convention. The state party organization remained split. While Tom Coleman and other former Taft backers supported Nixon, Congressman O'Konski and Steve Miller, both former McCarthyites, favored the candidacy of Nelson Rockefeller.[39]

While Coleman and Kohler now backed the same candidate, the "boss" continued to harbor ill feelings about the former governor. He confided to Glenn Davis, "The simple fact is that I do not want to be associated with Walter Kohler in any political project....I consider that Kohler has done more to damage our party and to destroy the work that I did over twenty-five years than any one or group of persons. There was some measure of appreciation from Walter, Sr., but quite the reverse from junior."[40]

Walter was named a delegate to the 1960 Republican national convention.[41] He was undoubtedly elated when Richard Nixon won the presidential nomination and saddened by John F. Kennedy's narrow victory in November. (Wisconsin went for Nixon in 1960, 51.8% to 48.0%.) At any rate, Walter's already minimal participation in Republican politics, on the state and national level, ceased after 1960. When his son asked him why he hadn't run against Proxmire in 1958, he replied simply, "Because nobody asked me." That was Walter's way of saying, Terry thought, that he acknowledged his outsider status with the reigning Taft-McCarthy wing of the State GOP and no longer had a political future.[42]

✦✦✦◉✦✦✦

In early 1960, Walter and Charlotte began a cruise around the world on the Cunard luxury liner RMS Caronia. The 34,183 ton "Green Goddess" carried nearly 1,000 passengers (581 first class) and could boast an art déco interior, ten decks, and a wide assortment of restaurants and recreational facilities. The tour began on February 5 from New York and returned on May 10. The itinerary included stops at Trinidad, Rio De Janeiro, Cape Town, Durban, Zanzibar, Bombay, Colombo, Singapore, Bangkok, Manila, Hong Kong, Kobe, Yokohama, Honolulu, Long Beach, Acapulco, Balboa, and Cristobel before returning to New York.[43]

The couple filled three photograph albums with shots of their trip. One featured Walter in front of the Taj Mahal. Another showed him in a pool, floating with a cigar in his mouth. A photo aboard ship showed him playing the piano before several appreciative party goers.[44]

Robert Selle met the Kohlers at the dock when they returned to New York. Walter told Selle that he hated India, noting the cows loose on the street and dung everywhere. After clearing customs, Selle later recalled, the Kohlers went to the Waldorf Hotel where they took a "huge and lavish" suite.[45]

In this post-political phase of their lives, the Kohlers traveled often, enjoying the changes of scenery and luxuries that wealth brought them. Charlotte, as we have seen, made four trips to New York each year with her maid to buy the latest fashions. Walter and Charlotte spent several weeks in the winter at their cabana in Antigua. They were often in New York on pleasure and business; former Governor and GOP presidential candidate Thomas Dewey was a favorite friend and frequent host.[46] And there were many additional travels. A single letter to Terry in November 1960 revealed a Thanksgiving in Cuernavaca, Mexico and business trips to Houston and Los Angeles.[47] In 1966, Walter traveled alone to Ireland, Scotland, Iceland, Norway, and Sweden.[48] Bob's daughter Vicki was surprised one day to run into Walter and Charlotte in Venice, Italy. Walter's jocularity surprised her. "So he does have a sense of humor," she remembers saying to herself.[49]

Bernice Blanke, Charlotte's personal maid, recalled a trip the Kohlers made to Spain to attend a party for the King and Queen. Charlotte purchased expensive silk in New York and Bernice used a pattern to put together a splendid gown for the occasion. While the Kohlers were away, a hired couple at Windway borrowed one of the family Cadillacs for a couple of days of vacation. When Charlotte returned and learned of the lark, she fired the couple on the spot, giving them twenty minutes to clear out.[50]

❖❖❖◉❖❖❖

In 1960, Walter established trust funds for his two children. A year later he donated 10,000 shares of his Vollrath stock to each trust fund, and he continued to make additional contributions.[51] In 1961, Niki was in a facility called Little City, in Palatine, Illinois, outside Chicago. Celeste had moved into a new home at St. Thomas in 1958 and placed her daughter in the institution at Palatine to be near some relatives who lived in Winnetka.[52] (The closer proximity of his daughter did not alter Walter's firm belief, however, that Niki should remain at almost all times in the care of institutional professionals. Niki visited her father and step-mother only about twice a year and lived with her mother for brief periods of time. Celeste, who wanted Niki to spend summers with her, complained bitterly to Terry that Walter was being unreasonable in denying Niki more personal freedom.)[53]

Terry was now living in Massachusetts and was hard at work completing his education. In the spring of 1958, Air Force officials had told Terry that there were too many pilots and that missiles would be replacing his crew. He was about to be assigned to work underground in the Strategic Air Command, a position he did not relish. At the same time, Celeste was sending her son scores of college catalogues, urging him to go back to school and earn a degree. Terry was married, and the father of an infant daughter, Leslie. (A second daughter, Michelle, was born in 1960.)[54] He applied to the Massachusetts Institute of Technology and was accepted by the School of Industrial Management, created by the Sloane Foundation in 1952 with the charge of producing "the ideal manager."[55]

In 1959, Terry resigned from the Air Force, moved his family to Boston, and plunged into his new studies. Terry received a bachelor of science degree in 1962 in industrial management, and a Master's degree in the same field a year later.[56]

Even before Terry completed his bachelor's degree it was understood that he was to succeed his father at the Vollrath Company. In the fall of 1961, however, Terry thought he might try to learn the practical side of business management in a company other than Vollrath. It was perhaps a belated bit of emotional resistance to a strong-willed father. Walter considered this approach unwise and asked his son to spend the summer of 1962 at Vollrath, where he could begin to understand the company fully. After some correspondence between the two, and a frantic letter from Celeste to her son, warning him against pride and spite, Terry complied.[57] His first boss was Wally Gartman, and his more complete training came from Paul Rohling. Rohling was also selected to be a buffer between the two Kohlers, minimizing the mixed emotions that the two men often experienced in each other's company.[58]

Letters exchanged between Walter and Terry during this period reveal some of the tensions between the father and son that had existed at least since Terry's expulsion from Andover. In 1961, Terry communicated regularly with his father, confessing more than once that while his grades were not as high as they might be, he was working hard.[59] Telephone calls between the two left Terry feeling as though he once again was not living up to his father's high standards.[60] Still, Walter regularly sent encouragement, and Charlotte knitted Terry a vest and sent new clothes to Leslie.[61] That fall, after Terry and his family moved to Brookline, Walter bought a pony for Leslie.[62]

In a letter written in December, 1961 Walter gently derided the "science of management" and computers, both of which Terry had been studying exhaustively, in favor of more hands-on business experience.[63] Stunned by his father's apparent unwillingness to appreciate the knowledge he was acquiring, Terry wrote a heated and often sarcastic reply.[64] Walter responded, "I'm sorry if my letter gave the impression that my hackles were raised. Not so—I just wanted to warn you, when you come out here this summer, not to make the mistake of parading a lot of technical jargon which could so easily be interpreted as an attempt to show off your book larnin. I was trying to protect you—not belittle you."[65] The fuss soon blew over, and Terry's spirits were raised considerably in March, 1962 when he reported to his father that he had made the Dean's list.[66] Walter quickly expressed his delight.[67]

Terry and his family moved to Sheboygan in June, not long after Terry proudly reported that he had been accepted into MIT's graduate school and had secured a year-long teaching position in the School of Industrial Management.[68] The summer work at the Vollrath Company appeared to go smoothly for all concerned.

In November, 1962, however, Terry wrote a stinging letter to his father, who appeared to be resisting computer innovations at the plant that Terry had strongly recommended. He contended that ignorance prevailed at the plant, predicted the death of the Vollrath Company, and threatened to bolt.[69]

In a strong reply, Walter called Terry's letter "intemperate," and said that it contained "misinformation." There had been no decision to reject computers, Walter said; such an important innovation simply required time to study and digest. "Your disparaging and contemptuous references to the Vollrath Co. are not easy to understand—or to forgive. Organizations are composed of human beings, and human beings 'fear the unknown and direct threats to vested interest and power.'" He continued, "A threat is a threat, or an insult is an insult, whether you preface its delivery with a disavowal or not. True, your threat was petulant and childish and should be taken about as seriously as one of Leslie's tantrums. But it is ironic that you should characterize as 'a loser' a company which has seen many a competitor fold during its 88 years of existence and currently is having its biggest year in sales, in earnings, in dividends and has *never* been financially stronger."[70]

Terry, in a highly revealing response, was mildly apologetic, but he appealed to his father to better inform him about Vollrath, and he asked to be taken seriously. Above all, he wanted to communicate more effectively. "Now—I cannot do else but confess without shame, Dad, that my letter was deliberately 'intemperate.' If this sound impious, I can only shrug my shoulders in helplessness, but in the rapidly lengthening span of my memory I can only remember two occasions during which you and I were able to communicate—not just talk. Both were less than an hour in length. I do not remember you prior to 1948, although I was 14 then. Since, I have not known you. I was allowed to drink at your trough this Summer, Dad, and it was an extremely invigorating experience. I am no longer able to ignore the Vollrath Company as if it had no meaning to me." He continued, "You do not know me, Dad, and I do not know whether you want to—but I do want to know you, and I want to know the Vollrath Company, for I left some sweat and some emotions there..."[71]

Walter did his best to understand Terry's cry for understanding. He wrote, "I am sorry you feel so short changed. This probably is the disillusion I was sure you would feel in making the transition from the grove of Academe to the factory....I'm sure you want to communicate. So do I—and, I guess, every other human being. Another way of putting it is that you want to be understood (and conversely, not *mis*understood) and I certainly want to do more than my share of understanding. It's a little hard, however, to let you or anyone else know much about 'what the hand on the helm' is doing since so many of the decisions that are constantly being made are not of themselves staggeringly important but together add up to the direction an organization takes. More important than the decisions are the reasons behind them. So...it gets both voluminous and complicated." He then expressed the wish that Terry be in Sheboygan more often to help solve company problems.[72] The young man had made his case, however emotionally put, and the response was clearly affirmative.

After graduation, Terry and his family moved to Sheboygan in June, 1963.[73] He was soon busily planning and implementing business reforms at Vollrath, including computer systems. In 1964 the IBM 1440, the first of its kind in the Sheboygan area, was hoisted through a second story window at the plant.[74]

By now it was clear to all that the boss's son was in training to be the Company's future president. Terry and his trust fund quickly became major Company stockholders.[75] In March, 1967, Walter announced that Terry had been promoted from Assistant Secretary to Assistant Executive Vice President, working directly under Paul Rohling. He was also a member of the Company's Board of Directors.[76]

During the first six years of the decade, the Vollrath Company continued to expand and prosper. In 1966, sales leaped to a record $17,047,000 and profits surpassed the million dollar mark for the first time.[77] A year later sales had climbed to $19,132,662, and profits rose 7.6% to $1,077,757.[78]

In 1968, Paul Rohling became President of the Company, and Walter took the title Chairman of the Board. Terry rose to Executive Vice President. Generous executive bonuses were distributed, celebrating the success all had worked for and to commemorate Walter's semi-retirement. Walter turned 64 in 1968, and he thought it time to turn the day-to-day operations over to veteran Rohling in preparation for Terry's eventual presidency. Walter would hereafter serve as the Company's principal planning officer, but his authority remained equal, in financial matters, to Rohling's.[79] He continued to run board meetings and keep active in Company affairs.

Vollrath's prosperity continued. In 1968, a 96,000 square foot fabrication building was dedicated. A year later Vollrath began molding medical plastics in Sheboygan. Manufacturing plants in Tennessee were soon opened, and in 1974 Vollrath purchased assets of the Admiral

Craft Corporation of New York. Two years later Vollrath entered the food service plastic marketplace.[80]

Net sales by Vollrath and its subsidiaries in 1971 amounted to $23,947,000, and net profits were $1,173,000[81] The following year, Walter reported to the board, sales were $28,961,000, a jump of 17% in one year, and net profits were $1,331,000, 14% higher than in 1971.[82] By 1975, net revenue of Vollrath and its subsidiaries was $41,959,000, and net earnings were $2,141,000.[83] The numbers verified Walter's reputation as a businessman.

❧❧❧❀❧❧❧

In 1968, the *Milwaukee Sentinel* conducted interviews with Wisconsin's five living former governors. Walter told a reporter that he thought advances in higher education were the state's most outstanding achievement since he left office. Since 1965, he had been chairman of the State's coordinating committee for higher education (he would serve until 1970), and he spoke glowingly of the educational opportunities now offered. "One institution, Oshkosh State University, now has more students than the whole state university system had when I left. The character and quality of the state system are vastly improved."

Walter also had positive things to say about the current governor, his old friend Warren Knowles. Recent developments he singled out for praise were the institution of four-year terms of office, the sales tax, a sympathetic approach to industrial growth, and an improved highway system.

Several issues called the former governor concern, however. Walter decried the growth of urban problems, noting that the flight to the suburbs only increased the financial burdens of those left behind. And he deplored the fact that city leaders often ran to the federal government for help. "How you stop that I don't know. The federal government wants to make itself important at the expense of the states and municipalities and continue aggrandizing itself." The civil rights movement also earned negative marks by Kohler. "I don't think you can legislate human relations," he said. The solution begins with education, he contended, and "it may well be there has been a lack of educational opportunity in the core of the cities. If that has been so, it should be corrected immediately."

Walter was also critical of highway safety appropriations and called for the restructuring of local government. "I mean consolidation of counties and perhaps the elimination of town governments. That's going to be the most difficult reform of all."

The reporter, who interviewed Walter at his office in Windway, noted that the former governor was well-tanned and handsome, looking nearly as fit as the combat navy officer he once was.[84]

❧ ❧ ❧ ◉ ❧ ❧ ❧

In the late 1960s and early 1970s, Walter's physical health began to falter. In 1972, he underwent surgery at the Mayo Clinic for skin cancer.[85] About the same time, he suffered severely from shingles.[86] As the need to be near medical care increased, Walter and Charlotte sold their home in Antigua and rented a house on Jupiter Island, Florida, north of Miami. The Kohlers and the dogs flew to and from Florida in a private jet. They would stay for perhaps three months, and a caretaker would look after the home the rest of the year.[87]

By the early 1970s, Charlotte too was having physical problems, largely the result of her many years of drinking. At one point, inebriated, she fell down a flight of basement stairs, breaking a leg and suffering head wounds. When Walter returned home and learned what had happened, he began to cry. "How could anyone be so stupid?," he sobbed.[88] Still, the couple remained devoted to each other, and the consensus among relatives and friends was that the marriage was always unshakable.[89]

Walter's first wife, Celeste, died on August 2, 1974. She had suffered a stroke at her home in Pompano Beach, Florida in 1973. She died of lung cancer in a Chicago hospital. Celeste, like Walter and Charlotte, had smoked heavily all of her adult life. A granddaughter, Leslie Kohler Hawley, recalled that in her later years Celeste retained her vivacious personality to the point that that much younger men continued to find her interesting. The last time Tim and Barbara Gorham saw Celeste was at Pentwater. She had just returned from Europe and was accompanied by a young man who might have been a gigolo. During the summers at Pentwater, Leslie Kohler Hawley recalled, Celeste still rode a dune buggy on the sand, and drove her Mercedes everywhere "like a demon."[90]

At some point, probably in 1975, Walter had heart surgery at the Roosevelt Hospital in New York. Before leaving for New York, Walter asked Bernice Blanke, Charlotte's maid, to say a prayer for him. He explained that he hadn't gone to church in many years and thought that perhaps she was closer to God than he.[91] Despite the surgery, Walter continued to have heart troubles in October of that year that hospitalized him in Sheboygan and in Florida. It was clear to all, including Walter, that the end was nearing.

On December 10, Terry received an urgent call from Florida, reporting Walter's serious illness and asking him to fly the corporate plane down and bring his father home. On March 21, at Windway, Walter suffered a massive heart attack and died in Sheboygan Memorial Hospital that evening. He was 71.[92]

After a private service held at the Woodland Cemetery in Kohler, led by a Congregationalist minister, the cremated remains were buried in the family plot. There was much sorrow in Wisconsin and elsewhere at the passing of an exceptional, honorable, dignified, distinguished, and highly productive gentleman.

State newspaper reaction was strongly positive, citing Walter's educational attainments, his military service, his record as a three-time governor, his charitable work, and his success in business.[93] Achievements emphasized during his years as governor included the innovations in higher education, the commitment to public welfare, and the efforts to promote highway safety. Also mentioned were Kohler's successful promotion of revisions in state statutes, including the criminal code, children's code, and administrative code, and his creation of the Division of Industrial Development to promote business and industry in the State.

The *Milwaukee Journal* recalled the 1952 election, and Walter's role in helping Eisenhower placate McCarthyites during the candidate's swing through Wisconsin. Indeed, Walter's participation in that campaign as a whole was the episode that most clearly mars his historical reputation. Still, it must be said that Republicans all over the nation, and some Democrats as well, were swept up by the hysteria of the Second Red Scare. And in 1952, party loyalty virtually required obeisance by Republicans to at least the broad sweep of Joe McCarthy's charges, especially by Republicans living in Wisconsin. Kohler had serious doubts about McCarthy before and after the campaign that elected Eisenhower. But he was unable during the frenzy of 1952 to resist the temptations that were thought likely to win votes for GOP candidates. To do otherwise, in that historical setting, would have been highly irregular and meant political death.

Moreover, Walter believed at the time and later that McCarthy and his allies were not entirely wrong. In a 1971 interview, he mentioned Alger Hiss, John Abt, Nathan Witt, John Stewart Service, and Harry

Dexter White. "I don't know whether these men were Communists or not, but there was a lot of smoke at that time. And I was not all sure that McCarthy was entirely wrong by any means."[94] Not a major Republican in the 1950s, including President Eisenhower, would have disagreed, and not many in the Nixon White House would have taken exception either. (Recent evidence, from decoded Soviet communications, has confirmed earlier charges that Hiss, Abt, Witt, and White were Communist spies.)[95]

The *Milwaukee Journal* described Kohler as a member of the moderate, pragmatic wing of the GOP. That fact played an integral part in the political turmoil that surrounded Kohler's political efforts, for the centrist position was largely in disfavor among the most active State Republicans in the 1950s. A lesser man would have joined the far Right enthusiastically, embraced Tom Coleman, and insured his political future. That Kohler was able to overcome this ideological handicap and win three gubernatorial elections, is a tribute to his energy, integrity, and perseverance. That those three terms produced valuable reforms and innovations was in large part attributable to the governor who, while not a professional politician, was able to persuade and educate effectively.

The *Milwaukee Journal* concluded its laudatory editorial with: "After Kohler declined to seek a fourth term in 1956, The Journal rated him as 'one of Wisconsin's ablest governors—sincere, conscientious, intelligent, accomplishful [sic]'. Twenty years of hindsight have produced no reason to alter that assessment."[96] The *Milwaukee Sentinel* declared in a similar editorial that Walter J. Kohler, Jr. "should be remembered in history as an outstanding governor, and a dedicated public servant." Both evaluations, in retrospect, ring true.

The letters that poured into Windway after Walter's death talked far more about the man than the public servant or business executive. A telegram from a leading official at the Mill Reef Club stated, "His countless contributions, his wonderful character, and always courtly and dignified demeanor will be long cherished by all those privileged to know him."[97] The President of the Jewish Welfare Council of Sheboygan told Charlotte how her late husband had purposely hired and defended several refugees from German concentration camps. "Our relationship had nothing to do with our respective token political affiliations, because I respected him strongly as a complete, compassionate human being and had the utmost of confidence in him, and I believe it was mutual."[98]

Sally Bliss, the wife of New York attorney and patron of the arts Anthony Bliss wrote, "Tony and I had such a great respect for Walter. We loved being with him and enjoyed his quiet sense of humor."[99] The wife of painter and illustrator Boris Chaliapin (son of the famed Russian opera star Fedor Chaliapin) wrote, "We have the lovely memories of those pleasant hours spent with you and Walter when you were visiting in New York."[100] Gerry Deknatel, wife of the late Windway architect, said, "Walter was one of the dearest friends we ever had and Bill and I admired and loved him."[101]

GOP leader Philip G. Kuehn assured Charlotte, ""Without question he was one of the gentlest gentlemen I have ever known. Despite his gentleness he was a great leader and will go down [in] the annals of Wisconsin as one of its greatest governors."[102] Newspaperman John Wyngaard agreed, writing: "You will be comforted, I am sure, by the realization that the governor was one of the most respected men of his time, and a real ornament of the Wisconsin governmental process."[103]

Notes

[1] The original source was Julilly Kohler, John's wife, as recalled by her daughter in Julilly Kohler interview, October 7, 2003. See Julilly Kohler interview, October 7, 2003, and Melvin Laird interview.

[2] Vollrath Company Minutes, May 14, 1951. See also Roland Neumann interview, December 10, 2003.

[3] Vollrath Company Minutes, April 5, 1954.

[4] *Ibid.*, March 27, 1957.

[5] *Ibid.*, November 15, 1954.

[6] *Ibid.*, December 10, 1956.

[7] *Ibid.*, March 28, 1955.

[8] *Ibid.*, March 26, 1958. Robert took a seat on the Board following Minneline Detling's death in August, 1952. He rarely attended meetings but could be counted on to vote with his brother. In 1967, he held 116 shares of preferred stock. Vollrath Company minutes, March 21, 1968.

[9] See Vicki and Jill Kohler interview, December 19, 2003. Ever the admirer of his brother, Robert had a huge glass wall placed in the front room that featured a view to the south and Windway, which could be seen through the woods. The architect was William Deknatel, who had designed Windway twenty years earlier.

[10] "Rohling, Terry Kohler Promoted In Top Vollrath Executive Posts," *Sheboygan Press*, March 23, 1967.

[11] *The Vollrath Story, Celebrating 125 years*, 20.

[12] Bill Kessler and Wally Gartman interview. Gartman started in 1957 at $1.30 an hour, "better than most." In March, 1958, the average rate of pay for male employees was $2.11 an hour, the national average. Vollrath Company Minutes, March 26, 1958.

[13] Bill Kessler and Wally Gartman interview; copies of labor documents provided by Kessler in Vollrath file. The document quoted was from F. E. De Reus to Vollrath Bargaining Unit Employees, August 6, 1968, *ibid.*.

[14] Bill Kessler and Wally Gartman interview. All but one of the seven offices has since been altered. Room 114 marks the spot today where Walter's office was.

[15] *Ibid.*

[16] *Ibid.* On Walter and the state capitol, see "Keeping Capitol Clean Will Cost State $6,300," *Milwaukee Journal*, September 21, 1956.

[17] Bill Kessler and Wally Gartman interview.

[18] Erna Schwartz interview.

[19] Robert and Katharine Selle interview. Selle continued to manage some Kohler family investment accounts for decades after Walter's death.

[20] James Raffel interview. This interview is a good source of information about Clarence Weber, a long-time friend of Walter's. Raffel a trust investment

officer and Senior Vice President at the bank, worked closely with Weber for many years, calling him "the most impressive human being I have ever met."

[21] The Windway Foundation, created by Walter, was a non-profit Wisconsin corporation with exclusively charitable, scientific, religious, and educational purposes. Annual donations by the Vollrath Company were small and seem quite perfunctory. Lakeland College in Sheboygan was treated well, and Walter received an honorary doctorate from the institution in 1960. In 1966, Northland College, in Ashland, Wisconsin, bestowed an honorary Doctor of Laws degree upon Walter, at least in part as a response to his financial donations.

[22] Roland Neumann interview. Walter was also a stockholder in the bank and preferred to use it for Vollrath deposits and loans. Walter Kohler to Terry Kohler, June 13, 1961, Terry Kohler papers. Clarence Weber joined the Vollrath board in late 1964.

[23] Vollrath Company Minutes, March 26, 1958.

[24] *Ibid.*, September 2, 1958.

[25] *Ibid.*, September 9, 1960.

[26] *Ibid.*, December 3, 1960.

[27] *Ibid.*, April 1, 1961.

[28] "Kohler Sues His Uncle, Claims $214,156 Loss," *Milwaukee Journal*, December 10, 1958.

[29] "Set Jan. 2 Trial Date In Kohler Stock Suit," *Sheboygan Press*, December 27, 1961.

[30] Evidence that money was the dominant if not exclusive motive in the lawsuit included the wish, expressed by Walter to Terry, that the case be settled out of court. Walter Kohler to Terry Kohler, March 15, 1962, Leslie Kohler Hawley collection.

[31] "Sold Kohler Stock Because Of Strike: Walter Kohler," *Sheboygan Press*, January 4, 1962.

[32] "Trial Is Opened in Suit Over Kohler Co. Stock," *Milwaukee Journal*, January 2, 1962. Jill Kohler, Bob's daughter, denies that her father was a vengeful person and strongly doubts that he was involved in the case for any reason other than to right an injustice done to his brother. E-mail, Jill Kohler to the author, July 25, 2005, Robert Kohler file.

[33] "Kohler Price in 1959 Told," *Milwaukee Journal*, January 9, 1962.

[34] "Herbert V. Kohler Says Stock Price Was His Decision," *ibid*, January 5, 1962.

[35] "Harry S. Pease, "Kohlers' Quiet Hatred Fills Milwaukee Courtroom," *ibid.*, January 4, 1962.

[36] "Ex-Governor Loses Fight Over Stock," *ibid.*, September 7, 1962.

[37] "US Court Rejects Kohler's Appeal in Stock Price Case," *ibid.*, June 27, 1963. In recent years, several members of the Kohler family have sued Herbert V. Kohler, Jr., head of the Kohler Company, on the same ground of offering too little money for shares. See Vicki and Jill Kohler interview and Avrum D. Lank, "Kohler Estate Takes IRS to Court," *Milwaukee Journal Sentinel.*, May 4, 2003.

[38] Thompson, *The History Of Wisconsin, Volume VI*, 672-677.

[39] "State GOP Leaders Predict Nixon Will Enter Primary," *Wisconsin State Journal*, August 12, 1959; copy, Thomas E. Coleman to Glenn Lewis, October 14, 1959, Thomas E. Coleman papers.

[40] Thomas E. Coleman to Glenn Davis, October 14, 1959, box 6, *ibid.* A typed copy is in the Wayne Hood papers, indicating that the handwritten letter was typed and circulated among top State GOP leaders.

[41] See the list of GOP delegates in the Wayne Hood papers. Walter was a delegate-at-large, along with such prominent party members as Glenn Davis, Harvey Higley, Warren Knowles, Philip Kuehn, Melvin Laird, and Everett Yerly.

[42] Terry Kohler interview, March 25, 2004. In 1964, Wisconsin favored Lyndon Johnson over Barry Goldwater by the whopping margin of 62.1% to 37.7%. In 1968 and 1972, the State again went for Nixon.

[43] See www.caronia2.info/yr1960.htm.

[44] The three medium size photo albums from the world tour are in the Leslie Kohler Hawley collection.

[45] Robert and Katherine Selle interview.

[46] Terry Kohler interview, March 25, 2004. Dewey also had a villa near the Kohlers in Antigua. Roland Neumann interview.

[47] Walter Kohler to Terry Kohler, November 19, 1960, Leslie Kohler Hawley collection.

[48] Photographs from this trip are in *ibid.*

[49] Vicki and Jill Kohler interview, December 19, 2003.

[50] Bernice Blanke interview, August 25, 2004.

[51] Vollrath Company Minutes, April 7, 1961. Walter retained 82,854 shares and enjoyed voting rights on behalf of the two trusts. By the end of 1964, Terry's trust fund contained 18,941 shares and Niki's held 15,000 shares. Vollrath Company Minutes, March 25, 1965.

[52] Terry and Mary Kohler interview, May 7, 2004; Celeste MacFadden to Terry Kohler, undated but probably from 1959, Leslie Kohler Hawley collection. Tim Gorham, a cousin who lived in Winnetka, served on the board of the Little School at the time, and his wife, Barbara, was in very frequent touch with Niki. "I was her lifeline," she said later. Tim and Barbara Gorham interview, October 24, 2004.

[53] Terry and Niki Kohler interview, May 6, 2004; Celeste Macfadden to Terry Kohler, undated but probably from 1961, Leslie Kohler Hawley collection. Celeste admitted, however, that Niki was having "spells" that posed a problem when she was out of the institution. In the summer of 1961, Walter permitted Celeste to take Niki with her to Europe. See Celeste Macfadden to "My dears" [Terry and Danny], June 5 [1961], *ibid.*

[54] The couple eventually had three daughters: Leslie (June 4,1958), Michelle (October 9, 1960), and Danielle (July 20, 1964).

[55] See http://mitsloan.met.edu/about/b-main.php.

[56] Terry Kohler interviews, June 12, 2003 and March 25, 2004.

[57] See Celeste Macfadden to Terry Kohler, undated but with a 1961 Paris postmark, Leslie Kohler Hawley collection.

[58] Terry Kohler interviews, June 12, 2003 and March 24, 2004; copy, Walter Kohler to Terry Kohler, October 11, 1961, Terry Kohler papers; Terry Kohler to Walter Kohler, November 11, 1961, *ibid.*; copy, Walter Kohler to Terry Kohler, November 16, 1961, *ibid.* Gartman said later that at no time, however, did Terry work on the plant floor. Bill Kessler and Wally Gartman interview. Walter broke the family pattern in this regard, no doubt out of respect for his son's age, experience, and formal education.

[59] Terry Kohler to Walter Kohler, , February 25, March 17, October 8, 1961, Terry Kohler papers.

[60] Terry Kohler to Walter Kohler, April 19, 1961, *ibid.*

[61] Terry Kohler to Walter Kohler, May 17, 1961, *ibid.* Walter was upset by what he considered Terry's lavish spending. Terry owned a Mercedes 190 convertible at the time, for example, that took 20 gallons to fill. Robert and Katharine Selle interview; Roland Neumann interview. A trust fund established by Walter paid Terry's educational expenses. Terry Kohler interview, December 5, 2005.

[62] Terry Kohler to Walter Kohler, October 8, 1961, Terry Kohler papers.

[63] Copy, Walter Kohler to Terry Kohler, December 1, 1961, *ibid.*

[64] Terry Kohler to Walter Kohler, December 4, 1961, *ibid.*

[65] Copy, Walter Kohler to Terry Kohler, December 18, 1961, *ibid.*

[66] Terry Kohler to Walter Kohler, March 11, 1962, *ibid.*

[67] Copy, Walter Kohler to Terry Kohler, March 15, 1962, *ibid.*

[68] Terry Kohler to Walter Kohler, March 24, 1962 [misdated 1961], *ibid.* Celeste expressed great pride in her son's achievements. "I am sure that getting a teaching post is a great feather and as usual you make me proud to have mothered at least one of you." Celeste Macfadden to Terry Kohler, May 11, 1962, Leslie Kohler Hawley collection.

[69] Terry Kohler to Walter Kohler November 14, 1962, Terry Kohler papers.

[70] Copy, Walter Kohler to Terry Kohler, November 21, 1962, *ibid.*

[71] Terry Kohler to Walter Kohler, November 25, 1962, *ibid.*

[72] Copy, Walter Kohler to Terry Kohler, December 17, 1962, *ibid.*

[73] "Terry Kohler Receives MS; Will Live Here," *Sheboygan Press*, June 10, 1963.

[74] *The Vollrath Story, Celebrating 125 Years,* 19.

[75] Vollrath Company Minutes, March 24, 1965.

[76] "Rohling, Terry Kohler Promoted In Top Vollrath Executive Posts," *Sheboygan Press*, March 23, 1967.

[77] Vollrath Company Minutes, March 21, 1967.

[78] *Ibid.*, March 21, 1968.

[79] *Ibid.* By 1971, Vollrath shares were valued at $68 apiece. In 1962, the estimated price was $33.19. *Ibid.*, March 28, 1963 and January 4, 1971.

[80] *The Vollrath Story, Celebrating 125 Years,* 17-19.

[81] Vollrath Company Minutes, March 16, 1972.

[82] *Ibid.*, March 18, 1973.

[83] *Ibid.*, April 1, 1976.

[84] Gene Divine, "State's Progress Pleases Kohler," *Milwaukee Sentinel*, February 27, 1968.

[85] E-mail, Terry Kohler to the author, August 9, 2004, in Miscellaneous file.

[86] Bernice Blanke interview, August 25, 28, 2004.

[87] *Ibid.* The Cape Cod style house was between 1,600 and 1,800 square feet and sat on .7 of an acre. A lengthy golf course was close at hand. Actor Burt Reynolds had lived nearby, as had the first President Bush's mother. Charles Koehler interview.

[88] Bernice Blanke interview, August 25, 2004.

[89] Guido Rahr, Jr., the son of Walter's long-time college friend, has a different view. He often saw Walter and Charlotte over the years, especially at the Mill Reef Club in Antigua, and thought their marriage unhappy. Walter would visibly cringe when Charlotte would be talking to a group, Rahr said. "She was no intellectual." Guido R. Rahr, Jr. interview.

[90] Leslie Kohler Hawley interview; Tim and Barbara Gorham interview, October 24, 2004. Celeste's death certificate is in the Celeste Kohler file. She died in Rush Presbyterian-St. Luke hospital in Chicago.

[91] Bernice Blanke interview, August 25, 2004.

[92] "W. J. Kohler, Ex-Governor, Dies At 71," *Sheboygan Press*, March 22, 1976; Bernice Blanke interview, August 25, 2004; Terry Kohler, March 25, 2004. The death certificate is in the Terry Kohler papers. When Walter's desk was cleaned out, Erna Schwartz discovered his divorce papers. They were destroyed, along with some other personal documents. Erna Schwartz interview. Terry Kohler's daughter Leslie scooped up many of Walter and Charlotte's photographs and documents after their deaths, preserving them for the family. Other materials were later found at Windway and in Terry Kohler's Sheboygan office. See the Leslie Kohler Hawley interview.

93 Several newspapers also noted Walter's service on the Board of Directors of the National Boy Scout Council as well as his work for the American Cancer Society.

94 Walter J. Kohler, Jr. Oral History, Columbia University, 1971, 24. Interestingly, each of Walter's specific examples stemmed from the pre-McCarthy years. Major General Patrick J. Hurley had put Service's name in the headlines in 1945. Elizabeth Bentley named White in July, 1948. Whittaker Chambers fingered Abt, Witt, and Hiss a month later. These cases, often cited by McCarthy, did indeed produce evidence of "smoke." See Reeves, *The Life and Times of Joe McCarthy*, 205-222.

95 Hayes and Klehr, *Venona: Decoding Soviet Espionage in America*, 62-64, 90-91, 125-126, 139-143.

96 Editorial, "Walter J. Kohler Jr.," *Milwaukee Journal*, March 23, 1976.

97 March 23, 1971 telegram, Terry Kohler papers.

98 David Rabinowitz to Charlotte Kohler, April 5, 1971, *ibid.*

99 Sally Bliss to Charlotte Kohler, March 29, 1971, *ibid.*

100 Hecia Chaliapin to Charlotte Kohler, April 17, 1971, *ibid.*

101 Gerry Deknatel to Charlotte Kohler, April 19, 1971, *ibid.* William F. Deknatel died on March 15, 1973. He had been a long-time friend of both the Gorhams and Kohlers.

102 Philip G. Kuehn to Charlotte Kohler, March 25, 1971, *ibid.*

103 John Wyngaard to Charlotte Kohler, April 19, 1971, *ibid.*

Postscript

Charlotte lived another 19 years. They were increasingly difficult years, for her and everyone around her. She continued to live at Windway, where she hired, fired, and shouted at scores of low-paid servants and attendants and continued to growl about Wisconsin and the allegedly uncouth people who lived there. It was not long before she began to suffer an assortment of painful ailments. Even before Walter's death, macular degeneration had been diagnosed, and she was scheduled for eye surgery. By 1990, she was nearly blind, and her eyesight soon failed entirely. Charlotte also suffered from bleeding ulcers and had arthritis so severely that in her last few years she was in a wheelchair. Heavy drinking and chain smoking did not help either her increasingly negative attitude or her physical problems.

Charlotte complained incessantly about family members she claimed were denying her the amenities and nursing services commensurate with her considerable wealth.[1] She clashed strongly with Mary Kohler, Terry's second wife (see below), a person of equally strong will who would not be intimidated by the older woman.[2]

When certified nursing assistant Ann Kraft came to work for Charlotte in 1988, she was appalled at the condition of Windway and the life style of its mistress. Charlotte's three Yorkshire Terriers were out of control and had fouled every room with excrement. Charlotte was living on one egg and toast, and was always dressed in a nightgown and robe, even when visiting her physician. She lived in the master suite at Windway (now owned by the Vollrath Company) and was upset about renovations underway at the home.[3] Ann had the day shift and an assortment of girls worked at night. Charlotte knew the names of none of the help. Staff members hid and watered down their employer's liquor supply in the hope of softening her wrath. Still, Charlotte exhibited kindness at times, and staff members reciprocated by reading books aloud to her by the hour and doing their best to please her.[4]

Janet Raye, Ann Kraft's sister, became an employee in 1990. By this time, Charlotte had purchased Thornhill, the Robert Kohler home nearby. (Robert died that year). The move from Windway was in large part a product of the continuing battle between Charlotte and Mary Kohler. By this time, Charlotte was completely dependent and somewhat less difficult. Still, she often shouted for help, "Girls, girls, girls." A common expression among the girls was, "If you weren't fired at least once a week, you weren't loved." Janet often accompanied her employer to Florida on the corporate jet. Charlotte purchased the Florida home she and Walter had enjoyed together and was now spending six months a year there. In her last couple of years she was too infirm to make the journey.

At the end, when she could no longer remember Walter, Charlotte told Janet that her first husband was named Peter Marshall, and she often asked repeatedly about the whereabouts of her handsome, blond husband. "She was really hard on me," Janet later recalled. In fact, Peter Marshall was the host of the television program "Hollywood Squares," which Charlotte rarely missed. Mrs. Kohler died at Thornhill on July 2, 1995 at the age of 82.[5]

Not long after her death, most of the personal fortunes of both Charlotte and her late husband were combined in the Charlotte and Walter Kohler Charitable Trust. After probate, it was worth about $20 million.[6]

❧ ❧ ❧ ◆▆◆ ❧ ❧ ❧

Terry Kohler became Vollrath's president shortly after his father's death. Paul Rohling was elected chairman of the board and chief executive officer. Terry, now 42, had been with the Company full-time for 13 years and had long earned the complete trust of his father and the Board of Directors. In 1981, Rohling retired, and a year later Terry became the chairman of the board and chief executive officer.

Under Terry's capable leadership, the Vollrath Company expanded dramatically. In April of 1983, nine divisions of the Company were created: food service, management systems, refrigeration, information network, management services, management consulting and education, consumer products, health care, and international. Each division under the corporate umbrella had its own president. In 1989, Thomas G. Belot became Vollrath's president and chief executive, and the Vollrath Company became a separate corporation under the majority ownership of Windway Capital Corporation, a holding company. Other operating Vollrath divisions became separate corporations: the Vollrath Group, Inc., Gallaway, Tennessee; Vollrath of Canada Ltd., Mississauga Ontario; Medica International, Ltd., Chicago Illinois; North Sails Group, Inc., Milford, Connecticut; and North Surf Sails Antilles, N.V., Penzberg, Germany.

In 1992 Vollrath had $100 million in sales. In 2004 its net sales amounted to $158,951,000.[7] That same year, North Marine, which builds boats, provides marine parts and accessories, and is the world's largest manufacturer of high-tech racing sails, had net sales of $89,823,000.[8] It has plants in Nevada and Sri Lanka and will soon be expanding production facilities to Toronto, Canada and Newport, Rhode Island.[9]

In 2005, Terry is President and Chairman of the Board of Windway Capital Corporation, and Chairman of North Marine Group. He is also a board member at Vollrath.[10]

Terry and Diane divorced in 1976. Four years later, Terry ran unsuccessfully for the GOP nomination as United States Senator. In 1981, he married Mary Simpson, his highly intelligent campaign manager. Mary was born in 1929 into a wealthy family and was accustomed to the social and economic standards enjoyed by the Kohlers. A graduate of the University of Wisconsin, she had been married twice before and was the mother of four sons. With Mary's assistance, Terry ran for governor in 1982 but was defeated. Today Mary is the Executive Director of the Charlotte and Walter Kohler Charitable Trust.[11]

Terry and Mary Kohler are widely known today for their philanthropy, their efforts in environmental protection, and their generous contributions, in money and time, to the Republican Party. In 2002, Terry was elected to the GOP National Committee. In 2004, he was a member of the Bush/Cheney Campaign Steering Committee.[12] Both Kohlers have also been active in the traditionalist wing of the Episcopal Church, and Mary is a long-time board member and benefactor of Nashotah House seminary in Wisconsin.[13] The Kohlers continues to live at Windway part of the time, but their business interests and intellectual curiosity take them all over the globe each year.

In 1989, Niki Kohler left the facility in Illinois and returned to Windway for a couple of months before moving to a three condominium complex, which she owns, surrounded by relatives and friends. Mary Kohler was responsible for the move, having visited Niki and been disappointed with the quality of her environment. (Charlotte disliked Niki and opposed the move.) Niki expresses great appreciation for her return, after nearly four decades in institutions, and today lives happily in the friendly environment of her youth. She possesses a fine collection of Kohler photographs and is often on the telephone with relatives, chatting about family matters.[14]

❧ ❧ ❧ ❋ ❧ ❧ ❧

After being evicted from Windway and living four years with Tim and Barbara Gorham, Jackie Holden married a working class man, Tiny Thompson of Birmingham, Alabama. The couple lived in New Jersey. The marriage lasted only briefly, perhaps in part because of Jackie's heavy drinking and mercurial temperament. She traveled a bit, being in Spain in 1953. Family members saw her mainly at Pentwater during the summer. In 1964, Jackie purchased a 32-foot houseboat in Michigan and had it shipped to Fort Meyers, Florida. She would live there on the boat for the rest of her life.

In the late 1960s, Jackie married a retired Navy man, Louis M. Bender, Jr. Some family members were aghast at his alcoholism and plebian ways, no doubt causing Jackie considerable pleasure. Celeste, in her will, declared in no uncertain terms that her son-in-law was not to have a penny of her money. The marriage lasted until 1979, when the couple was divorced. Bender later died of cancer.

In her fifties, Jackie began to experience an assortment of physical problems. Both hips were replaced, and a knee was operated on. In 1976, she fell and broke a leg. Two years later she was mugged in Detroit, causing her to be hospitalized for five days. By now, her alcoholic condition was obvious to everyone. In 1981, living with a man on her houseboat, photographs were taken that revealed the sad state of her physical and mental health.

During the last forty years of her life, Jackie had rarely worked. Both Celeste and Walter left her with a small annual income, and she had some stocks that brought in dividends. At least twice she borrowed money from Terry.

On the evening of December 30, 1981, Jackie fell aboard her boat and broke a hip. She was hospitalized, went into convulsions, and died of a heart attack. She was 57.

After her second divorce, the judge in the case had granted permission for Jackie to use her "original" surname, Kohler. She used the name thereafter, and it appeared on her death certificate and in the obituary in the *Sheboygan Press*. Her cremated remains, however, were not permitted to enter the family ground at the Kohler cemetery. In death as in life, Jackie was rejected.[15]

❧❧❧◉❦❦❦

William Proxmire continued to campaign furiously and was reelected in 1958, 1964, 1970, 1976, and 1982, serving longer in the Senate than anyone else in Wisconsin history. Ever the maverick, he broke from many liberal Democratic principles, stressing doubts about certain New Frontier and Great Society programs, criticizing defense spending, and proposing a sort of neo-isolationism. He became famous throughout the country for his "Golden Fleece Awards," which identified what he said was wasteful federal spending. Proxmire flew to Wisconsin every weekend. He was also noted for his Spartan lifestyle and was often seen running five miles from his home to Capitol Hill and back in all sorts of weather. He went more than 20 years without missing a role-call vote.

In 1971, Bill and Ellen Proxmire separated. By this time, Proxmire had presidential aspirations, and there was evidence that Ellen had grown weary of what she called "a life of perpetual inconvenience…and substantial sacrifice." A man who had known the Senator for over 20 years said of him, "he was born to be alone…. He devoted his whole life to politics."[16] The couple reconciled, however, and Ellen returned to her often lonely duties as a Senatorial wife.

In 1987, Proxmire stunned everyone, including Ellen, by announcing that he would not seek reelection. Soon, Ellen and others began to notice unusual behavior. In 1994, Proxmire was diagnosed with Alzheimer's and faded from public view. For a few years, Ellen tried her best to provide home care for her husband, but he dropped to 129 pounds and grew increasingly difficult. After living several years in an Alzheimer's facility in Maryland, Proxmire died on December 15, 2005. Ellen told a reporter, "He had a fabulous career, and he loved every minute of it."[17]

Notes

[1] Ann Kraft interview; Janet Raye interview; Bernice Blanke interview, August 25, 2004; Leslie Kohler Hawley interview.

[2] Terry and Mary Kohler interview, May 7, 2004.

[3] Terry had long-time family friend Rosemary Miley supervise the restoration of Windway. It appears today very much as when Terry was growing up. See the Robert and Katharine Selle interview for more on Charlotte's physical and mental deterioration and the condition of Windway before its restoration.

[4] Ann Kraft interview.

[5] Janet Raye interview. For more on Charlotte at Thornhill, see Robert and Katharine Selle interview. See also "Charlotte McAleer Kohler," "Gov. Kohler's widow, Charlotte, dies at 82," *Sheboygan Press*, July 5, 1995.

[6] E-mail, Terry Kohler to the author, July 27, 2005, Terry Kohler file.

[7] *The Vollrath Story, Celebrating 125 Years*, 21, 23; Doris Hajewski, "Warming Up To Home Chefs," *Milwaukee Journal Sentinel*, April 4, 2004. In 2004, Vollrath employed 784 people at five plants in Wisconsin. The company is primarily known for its huge menu of commercial kitchen equipment.

[8] E-mail, Terry Kohler to the author, July 27, 2005, Terry Kohler file; copy, John McClary to Terry Kohler, July 28, 2005, *ibid*. On North Sales, see *www.northsailsod.com/index.html*. Terry himself is a world renowned sailor, having competed in racing for more than six decades.

[9] E-mail, Terry Kohler to the author, July 28, 2005, Terry Kohler file.

[10] E-mail, Terry Kohler to the author, July 27, 2005, *ibid*. While Walter owned about 62% of Vollrath, Terry now owns over 80% of both Vollrath and North Marine Group.

[11] *Ibid*.

[12] See *www.gop.com/States/StatesDetails.aspx?state=WI*.

[13] On Nashotah House, see *www.mediatransparency.org/recipientsoffunder.php?funderID=36*. See the interview with Mary at *www.heartland.org/Article.cfm?artId=9568*

[14] Terry Kohler interview, March 5, May 6, 2004; Terry and Mary Kohler interview, May 7, 2004.

[15] This account was taken from the small collection of Jackie Kohler materials found in the Terry Kohler papers. See also Tim and Barbara Gorham interview, October 24, 2004; Roland Neumann interview; e-mail letters from Terry Kohler to the author of October 26, 27, 2004, Celeste Kohler file. The ashes of both Celeste and Jackie were placed in Lake Michigan.

[16] Sykes, *Proxmire*, 244-245.

[17] See Ellen Proxmire's story in the *Madison Capital Times* at: http://www.madison.com/archives/read.php?ref=tct:2004:12:13:396978:FRONT. See also the obituary in the *Milwaukee Journal Sentinel*, December 16, 2005.

Acknowledgements

I am especially thankful to the members of the Kohler and Vollrath families, who have been of great assistance with their memories, documents, and photographs. Terry Kohler, Walter's son, and his daughter Leslie Kohler Hawley, a collector of family history, have been especially helpful. Mary Ten Haken, Terry Kohler's Executive Assistant since 1981, was an intrepid seeker of primary sources. Michael and Julilly Kohler, children of John Michael Kohler III, are perceptive and helpful students of their family's history. Michael read the entire manuscript, often providing valuable insights and corrections. Herbert V. Kohler, Jr., permitted me to be the first outsider to study materials from the extensive Kohler Company archives. His primary staff member in this regard was Lynn Kulow. Tim and Barbara Gorham, who are related to Celeste Kohler, were also extraordinarily cooperative.

I am deeply grateful to Helmut Knies and his colleagues in the archives of the Wisconsin Historical Society for their assistance. Tim Ericson, now at the School of Information Studies, and the entire archival staff at the University of Wisconsin-Milwaukee were also cooperative. Dr. S. M. Hutchens provided me with valuable historical information about the Schroeder family of Kenosha. I am also indebted to my research assistants Nick Katers and Johnny Burns. My research materials are on deposit at the Wisconsin Historical Society.

This book was funded by a grant from the Wisconsin Policy Research Institute.

Appendix A

Interviews and Conversations with the Author

Mary Kohler Ahern
Ken Benson
Bernice Blanke
Dorothy Engleman
Peter Fetterer
Ann Fichtner
Harry Franke
Wally Gartman
Tim and Barbara Gorham
Leslie Kohler Hawley
Arthur Hove
Bill Kessler
Charles Koehler
Herbert V. Kohler, Jr.
Jill Kohler
Julilly Kohler
Marie Kohler
Mary Kohler
Michael Kohler
Niki Kohler
Peter and Nancy Kohler
Robert E. Kohler
Terry Kohler
Vicki Kohler
Ann Kraft
Lynn Kulow
Bill Kurtz
Melvin Laird
Patrick Lucey
Gaylord Nelson
Roland Neumann
Dennis Ohl
Ellen Proxmire

James Raffel
Guido R. Rahr, Jr.
Janet Raye
Peter Reichelsdorfer
Donald Rowe
Erna Schwartz
Robert and Katharine Selle
Jean Dor Serabian
Margery Uihlein
Pat von Rautenkranz
Philip K. Vollrath
Walter Vollrath, Jr.
Mike Weber
Paul Weyrich
Frank Zeidler